Linguistic Archaeology

an introduction

with a foreword by
Dr. Ove Hinrichs

EDO NYLAND

Book design, typesetting:
VRG design & publishing services
www.inetex.com/vivencia
Cover: Roy Diment, VRG

National Library of Canada Cataloguing in Publication Data

Nyland, Edo, 1927-

  Linguistic archaeology

  Includes bibliographical references and index.

  ISBN 1-55212-668-4

  1. Language and languages--Etymology. 2. Onomastics. 3. Linguistic
paleontology. I. Title.
P321.N94 2001   417'.7   C2001-910425-1

TRAFFORD

This book was published *on-demand* in cooperation with Trafford Publishing.
On-demand publishing is a unique process and service of making a book available for retail sale to the public taking advantage of on-demand manufacturing and Internet marketing.
On-demand publishing includes promotions, retail sales, manufacturing, order fulfilment, accounting and collecting royalties on behalf of the author.

Suite 6E, 2333 Government St., Victoria, B.C. V8T 4P4, CANADA
Phone   250-383-6864   Toll-free   1-888-232-4444 (Canada & US)
Fax   250-383-6804   E-mail   sales@trafford.com
Web site   www.trafford.com   TRAFFORD PUBLISHING IS A DIVISION OF TRAFFORD HOLDINGS LTD.
Trafford Catalogue #01-0069   www.trafford.com/robots/01-0069.html

10   9   8   7   6   5   4   3   2

CONTENTS

ACKNOWLEDGMENTS

EDWARD FURLONG'S RADIO DOCUMENTARY

The writing of this book would not have been possible without a talk given on November 5 and 6, 1984 by historian Edward Furlong on the "Ideas" program of the Canadian Broadcasting Corporation. His two hour documentary was entitled "Where Did Odysseus Go?" and in it he pointed out various places and happenings described by Homer which did not fit at all in the Mediterranean, but obviously belonged in the North Atlantic. His radio documentary was the result of 15 years of research. He came to the conclusion that Odysseus had visited Ireland, Scotland and Norway.

I was intrigued by his reasoning and visited Ireland and Scotland on several occasions to see for myself the areas he suggested. I then visited some of Odysseus' suggested landing sites, placed them more accurately than Furlong had done and became convinced that he was right in almost all he had said on the radio. However, pointing to the likelihood that Odysseus had sailed the Atlantic was one thing; proving to the academic world that Odysseus was in Ireland, Scotland and Norway was a different matter entirely. It required some new developments in linguistics, which took me some years to come to grips with.

BOB QUINN'S VOYAGE OF DISCOVERY

A host of authors has tied Ireland's past to the European Continent, especially to the Keltic region, as a sort of quaint island fringe stitched onto the civilized centre. This was not what writer and film maker Bob Quinn found when he looked at the music, art, names, archaeology, mythology etc. of Ireland and found a much closer relationship between Ireland and North Africa, than between Ireland and the Continent, or even between Ireland and Britain. On his visits to Africa he filmed all that struck him as being related to Ireland and made a revealing and most instructive film about it. He then described his findings in a wonderful little paperback called "The Atlantean, Ireland's North African Heritage" (Quartet Books, New York, 1986). Many of my ideas in this book grew from seeds planted by Bob in his Atlantean. He also gave me permission to use anything written in his Atlantean for this book.

ANTHONY JACKSON'S SYMBOL STONES

I found Dr. Jackson's book: "The Symbol Stones of Scotland" in a bookstore in the Town of Stornoway in Scotland. It described many beautifully carved animal- and geometrical symbols, which had puzzled people for many centuries. Jackson offered a logical explanation for them, saying that the symbols represented totems and belonged to different Scottish tribes. He explained that the manner in which these symbols were shown on the stones had organized cooperation between these tribes in matters of marriages and other joint projects. He also wrote about the Ogam script, found carved on hundreds of pre-Christian stones, and illustrated his text with some 30 Ogam inscriptions found in Scotland. He further explained how the Scottish Ogams had never been translated but that the Irish ones were, which sounded strange to me. He also made deciphering a challenge which I took up. When I came to Barra I took three rainy days in my B&B to experiment with different solutions to the puzzle. To my great surprise I was successful in breaking the code and also discovered the language in which they were written, at least so I thought. I mailed my effort and translations to Jackson but he was not impressed and commented on it in his next little book: "Pictish Symbol Stones?" (1993) saying: *"There is a popular theory that they are Basque but this does not work either"* (p 118). This spurred me to greater efforts and the results are shown in the Ogam section of this book. It turned out that the Irish Ogam inscriptions had not been deciphered either, just guessed at. In spite of his negative reaction, I am much indebted to Dr. Jackson for having introduced the archaic Ogam script and symbol stones of Scotland to me and for the challenge he tossed to his readers.

Maurice Chazottes' Support

A man of many talents, mayor, councillor, chairman of the Victoria Library Board, public relations consultant etc. From the beginning of this effort Maurice has helped me by reading and discussing my drafts, he advised me how to organize my topics, corrected my spelling and sentence structure and gave general encouragement to this rather complicated and unusual research. When I sent him my final product, he wrote back: "One of the most interesting aspects of your research is the consistency of the translations. I find it hard to believe that even the most cynical scholar could dismiss your work as fantasy or fakery." Thank you Maurice for all your help and inspiration.

Gorka Aulestia's Dictionary

None of this linguistic work would have been possible without Gorka's invaluable Basque-English and English-Basque dictionaries. He had taught Basque language and literature courses at the University of Nevada since 1977 and was disappointed with the limited amount of educational material available. In August 1979 the head of the Basque Studies Program, Dr. William Douglass, suggested that he compile a good quality Basque-English dictionary as an instructional aid for students taking the courses. No one involved could expect that this project would take nine years of Gorka's life to complete. Compiling a dictionary is difficult and totally absorbing work. The lexicographer J.J. Scaliger wrote once: "The worst criminals should neither be executed nor sentenced to forced labour, but should be condemned to compile dictionaries, because all the tortures are included in this work" (page a13 in the Dictionary).

Gorka documented how amazingly logically the Basque language is organized, yet he told me that he did not understand how I decoded the agglutinated words belonging to many languages, including Basque, with the use of his dictionary. But that does not matter because we make our own contributions to the marvelous and ancient puzzle known as Basque. Thank you Gorka for the work you did; it has given me many years of pleasure.

CONSTRUCTIVE COMMENTS FROM EVERYWHERE

Hundreds of people from many countries have offered helpful suggestions, corrections, constructive criticism etc; they suggested pertinent literature, and many of these have linked my homepage to theirs. The number of supportive comments far outweighs the negative ones. I received the international 'Links2Go' internet award for the "The Origin of Yiddish" article was much appreciated and resulted in a great deal of contact with scholars studying the Semitic languages. The name translations using the Basque dictionary elicited many inquiries from Basque students in Euskadi and the U.S.A. One totally unexpected response from many people was the sending of books, copies of pertinent articles, references to items on the web and in literature, in several languages, all pertaining to the subjects discussed. I had not been aware of the existence of many of these books. Their help was much appreciated and the information is included in my writing. As a result, this book has become much bigger than anticipated and several interesting subjects had to be left out, however, there is a limit to what can be done by one person.

.

ROBIN DUNN'S TECHNICAL HELP

I thank Robin Dunn for his helpful technical computer advice, for upgrading my equipment when necessary and for his many bits of wisdom and unfailing support which kept me progressing on the straight and narrow.

EVEN NEGATIVE COMMENTS WERE OF HELP.

One university linguist made the following comment to me: "You are excavating recesses into which an academic, with the instincts of a gentleman, would never venture." I took this as an indication that I was on the right track and it energized me to continue "excavating."

FOREWORD

INTRODUCTION

Books, says the French poet Jean Paul, are more voluminous letters to friends. This is right, but only half of the truth. Those who prefer to look at both sides of the medal would say: Books, if they are important, are polarizing its readers into friends and enemies of the author and his ideas. Both, friends and enemies, are equally important for the author, especially for Edo Nyland, who is convinced that "controversy is the lifeblood of scholarship." And not the selling numbers, but the change of conciousness and the intensity of reaction of readers should in consequence be the measures for the importance of his new book "Linguistic Archaeology".

It is obvious how a writer of a foreword has to proceed in this case: He has to give the readers of the book some background information, necessary to evaluate the book's importance, thus enhancing the process of readers' reaction and polarization.

The starting point of Edo Nyland's book "Linguistic Archaeology" is the history reported in the Bible in the chapters of Genesis:

Genesis 11:1   "… now the whole earth had one language…"

Genesis 11:7   "… come, let us go down and there confuse their language, that they may not understand one another's speech."

Edo Nyland describes his own approach to the monogenetic hypothesis, which finally led him to start his research:

"In Genesis 11:1 we are told 'Now the whole world had one language' and the challenge for me became to discover if this was factual and if so, what language this was. Would it be possible to show that this language had indeed been spoken over the entire world?"

In solving the task defined above, he made many new discoveries, rather exiting for those who know the present state of linguistic knowledge; he writes in the introduction to his web site:

"Here is my first effort to form **hypotheses** (suppositions) which form the foundation for my **theory** (the basis for experimentation), which attempts to explain my linguistic findings.

Hypo 1: The Saharan language was the language of the peoples living in the Sahara during the last Ice Age, who had created the first true civilization on earth. As a result of deglaciation, starting in earnest ca 11,000 before present (B.P.), resulting in ever-expanding desertification, these tribes were forced to flee for their lives, creating an exodus culminating between 9,000 and 5,500 B.P. These refugees created four main secondary civilizations in Mesopotamia, Egypt, the Indus Valley and Anatolia.

Hypo 2: The Saharan language is still spoken as Dravidian in India (170 million speakers), as Ainu on the island of Hokkaido (18,000 speakers) and as Basque in Euskadi, Spain (800,000 speakers). Basque is likely the closest resembling the original language of the exodus.

Hypo 3: The people of the exodus from the Sahara brought with them a matrilineally organized society, the nature based Goddess religion and the first highly developed language, maintained by very strong oral traditions.

Hypo 4: As a result of several major advances in a number of fields such as agriculture, metallurgy, domestication of the horse and camel, astronomy etc. the female-based religion was weakened and male domination arrived ca 5,000 B.P. in Egypt, Mesopotamia and Anatolia, and about 3,500 B.P. in India. The newcomers brought along learned priesthoods who proceeded to invert all aspects of the old religion, society, language, legends etc. A new language was invented for each large area and placed under the control of a king, e.g. Sumerian and Akadian in Mesopotamia, Old Egyptian in Egypt, Samskrta and Hindi in India, Hebrew in Palestine, Hittite and Luvian in Anatolia etc. All these were the product of formulaic distortion and scholarly manipulation of the original Saharan language. The Bible repeats the command to distort the original language in Gen. 11:7.

Hypo 5: These newly created languages were then introduced to the local populations by taking young boys into residential schools and forcing the new order onto them, where they were often brutally treated. The purpose was to destroy the old religion and language and the traditional oral teaching of wisdom, religion and legends, replacing it with a patriarchal vision of the world and civilization. They almost succeeded.

Theory: All highly developed languages on earth (except possibly Chinese) can be shown to have been developed from the original Saharan language, which in itself was also scholarly enhanced from the neolithic substratum. There exists no "family" of Indo-European or Semitic languages. Indo-Europeans never existed and there was no proto-I-E. language; all these unstable languages are invented by scholars. Only Saharan has remained relatively unchanged and is now spoken as Basque."

Many of these results sound rather revolutionary. Therefore, in order to give his book a fair evaluation we have to consider the actual state of official scientific opinion and the known history of linguistic archaeology and then to compare Edo Nyland's ideas, methods and results with the official doctrines.

ESTABLISHING A REFERENCE FRAME

As a first reference we choose Richard Fester's popular book "Urwörter der Menschheit" [1] with the promising subtitle "Eine Archäologie der Sprache" (an archaeology of speech) and the appraisal "Der gemeinsame Ursprung aller Sprachen der Menschheit – hier endlich wird er schlüssig, einleuchtend und überzeugend nachgewiesen" (The common origin of all languages of mankind – here finally it is proved in deductive, comprehensible and convincing form).

These announcements are suggesting that Richard Fester already solved the task which Edo Nyland defined above; we will see later, whether this holds true.

Richard Fester contributes arguments supporting the thesis of a common origin of all languages of mankind. The kernel of his discoveries are six "Urworte," which he calls archetypes: BA, KALL, TAG, TAL, OS and ACQ. He distilled these archetypes from many different languages from all over the world (including the so called non-Indo-European languages) by analyzing words of the same meaning.

Richard Fester presents so called word equations (words from different languages with same meaning and similar sound) in large wordlists.

This form of presentation evokes associations to the books of his predecessors, for example Arnold Wadler [2], who too has been in search for the common mother language, which is said to have been in use before the babylonian speech confusion.

Arnold Wadler presented in 1935 similar lists of word equations from different languages and he developed a set of rules describing how language changed over the centuries. These rules of change helped him to discover many new word equations, which could not be recognized by simple comparison of sound or writing.

Arnold Wadler gives references to his predecessors, for example Friedrich Delitzsch, Leo Reinisch, Hermann Moeller and Alfredo Trombetti. But these names represent only the very ultimate part of the long history of linguistic archaeology.

The reader interested in the more remote history of linguistic archaeology and the many ideas and related methods of linguistic research developed up to now may read some chapters of Umberto Eco's book about the search for the perfect language [3]. Umberto Eco considers the perfect language to be a myth and a utopia. He states that the myth of a perfect language, having been used worldwide and having been confused intentionally, as well as the task of its reconstruction or the utopy of a reinvention, has been a common idea of all cultures of the world.

Umberto Eco starts his documentation of the search for the perfect language at the beginning of recorded history and ends up at our times, giving a long list of 266 references to literature (in contrast to Richard Fester, who (with few exceptions) is only willing to reveal the lexica of different languages which he scanned for the archtypes) and moreover Umberto Eco supplies us with an impressive name register with approx. 500 entries, showing how many famous persons have been occupied with the reconstruction or reinvention of the perfect language.

Basic ideas of current linguistics.

Our present sciences, linguistics included, may be characterized by materialism, rationalism and quantitative methods. The current mainstream linguistic theory is based on conflicting ideas.

One idea is the evolution of languages analog to the evolution of life species. This is early darwinism as described in Darwin's book of 1859 "On the origin of species by means of natural selection, or preservation of favoured races in the struggle of life."

Wadler is describing how darwinism influenced linguistics. The idea of evolution led Darwin to the assumption of a monogenesis of mankind; this should have led the linguists to the analog assumption of a monogenesis of languages. But the known linguist August Schleicher published in 1863 a book "Die Darwin'sche Theorie und die Sprachwissenschaft," where he acknowledged Darwin's idea of evolution, but postulated nevertheless the polygenesis of languages.

When Darwin developed his own theory about the genesis of languages (in his book "The descent of man..."), he consulted contemporary linguists in order to get a decision between the concurrent ideas of monogenesis and polygenesis of language. One of his consultants pleaded for the monogenesis, three others including Prof. August Schleicher (Jena) pleaded for polygenesis. Darwin decided to follow Schleicher and ended up with monogenesis for the human races but polygenesis for the human languages.

According to the polygenetic hypothesis linguists are defining genetically unrelated language families (like Indo-European, Semitic or Finno-ugric). Only members of the same family are assumed to be related. All languages are slowly changing due to evolution.

Now it becomes obvious what kind of exiting news is being communicated in Edo Nyland's book "Linguistic Archaeology": He gives strong proofs for the monogenesis of languages, contradicting the common opinion of polygenesis, and he gives proofs for his thesis that the languages spoken today have been constructed from the previously universal language by skilled linguists instead of having evolved from one ancestor language of their family, thus contradicting Darwin. Edo Nyland writes in the chapter Translating Ogam:

"It has long been known that languages were being invented, Wittgenstein wrote: "Man possesses the capacity of constructing languages, in which every sense can be expressed, without having an idea how and what each word means - just as one speaks without knowing how the single sounds are produced" (Tractatus 4.002).

That is exactly what was done by the Benedictines and their grammarians when they made up the western European languages. Even all the names of their saints and monasteries were constructed without the uninitiated having the slightest idea what each name meant. By the time Darwin wrote his "Descent of Man" the language invention efforts had been forgotten because he commented: "No philologist now supposes that any language has been deliberately invented: it has been slowly and unconsciously developed by many steps." How soon we forget! This will be elaborated upon when I discuss the linguistic activities of the Benedictines."

THE TROUBLESOME RELATION BETWEEN SCIENCE
AND ITS AMATEURS.

Edo Nyland describes his rather unusual life story in his website. After having retired from money making professions, he started his odyssey into the science of linguistic archaeology as an amateur.

In his chapter "How all this came to be" he asks: "Now why would someone with formal training in forest and land administration, surveying, aerial photo interpretation, aerial wildfire suppression, forest ecology, botany etc. venture into fields as remote as linguistics, Homeric studies, Irish Ogam inscription translation, pre-Christian religion and archaeology? Because here was obviously a wide-open and interesting field of study which, for centuries, had attracted many non-academic outsiders who made great contributions to the science they chose to work on."

These great contributions of the outsiders, blaming the scientific establishment, are the cause for the troublesome relations between interlopers and establishment. Those who are interested in this topic may read the book of Frederico Di Trocchio [4], who writes:

"Jeder kann einmal eine gute Idee haben. Das Schwierige ist nur, die anderen davon zu überzeugen. Denn da gibt es jene, die sie einfach nicht verstehen, und andere, die sie aus den unterschiedlichsten Gründen, von Neid bis Vorurteil, ablehnen. Wieder andere sind dagegen, weil sie die Idee stehlen oder eine ähnliche Idee selbst nutzen wollen. Schließlich sind da noch die Experten, die es mit Recht nicht gerne sehen, von Dilettanten und Außenseitern in den Schatten gestellt zu werden."

(Everybody may have a good idea. There is only the difficulty to convince the others. Because there are those, who simply do not understand it, and others who reject it due to different reasons from envy to prejudice. Others decline, because they want to steal the idea or want to use a similar idea for their own. Finally there are the experts, who have good reason to be in fear of being put into shadow by dilettantes and outsiders.)

These bad habits of the establishment evoke plain answers from the amateurs, see for example Edo Nyland's statements in the chapter Indo-European Linguistics.

But there seems to be yet another enigma, which has to be solved in order to fully understand the behaviour of scientific establishment. Edo Nyland writes in the Chapter Classifying the World's Languages, a possible new approach:

"Through the years, there have been a few courageous doubters among the linguists such as M. E. Landsberg (Columbia Univ. S.C.) who wrote: 'Indeed, courses in historical linguistics at Universities all over the world, in spite of much perplexing evidence to the contrary, mostly still persist in adhering to strict Indo-European theories.' Those who did not follow the Indo-European gospel and sounded the alarm bell risked their immaculate academic reputations by indulging in what was called "translinguistic investigations," resulting in being censored by the dogma-ridden majority which still rules the discipline. Students are forbidden to study the possible academic fraud behind the Indo-European theory and those who did look into it were stonewalled and ridiculed. Doubting the Indo-European theory became "taboo" and resulted in a quick forced exit from the profession. One professor to whom I explained my findings commented: *"You are excavating recesses into which an academic with the instincts of a gentleman, would never venture."*

In order to understand this dark professorial statement we are consulting our referees Richard Fester, Arnold Wadler and Umberto Eco. And indeed, all three of them are giving their contribution.

Richard Fester for example writes:

"… die Frage nach der Entstehung von Sprache (war) schon seit dem Altertum gestellt worden, einem Altertum übrigens, das sich in seinen Mythen und späteren naturphilosophischen Denkweisen den Menschen stets von Anbeginn an *sprechend* vorgestellt hatte. Oft recht phantasievolle Hypothesen führten schließlich in der Mitte des vorigen Jahrhunderts dazu, daß sich die internationale Vereinigung der Sprachwissenschaftler dazu verstand, keine weiteren Arbeiten über den gemeinsamen Ursprung von Sprache mehr zur Veröffentlichung oder Erörterung anzunehmen. Noch 100 Jahre später gehörte es zum guten Ton einer linguistischen Doktorarbeit, irgendwo zumindest in einem Nebensatz einen gemeinsamen Ursprung menschlicher Sprache als unbeweisbar oder gar als unmöglich abzuqualifizieren."

(…the question how speech arose had been asked since antiquity, an antiquity, by the way, which in its myths and later in its natural philosophy imagined mankind as having been spoken since the earliest beginning. Due to some rather fanciful hypotheses of speech origin, the international society of linguists decided to refuse publishing or discussion of further papers on the origin of speech. Yet 100 years later it was a common habit in a linguistic doctoral thesis, to disqualify a common origin of language, at least in a subordinate clause, as being not to be proved or even as being impossible.)

Richard Fester seems to speak of the french Société de Linguistique, Paris, and its decision of 1866 to reject any articles about universal languages and about the origin of language.

We may draw from this citation the conclusion that we are dealing here with an area of research, on which a prohibition of thinking has been decreed. Edo Nyland seems to be unconcerned enough to ignore this, using his imagination and good nose to work out research results, where official science has nothing to offer.

There are known and plausible reasons for other prohibitions of thinking and research, remember for example the various indices of forbidden books, edited by the Roman Catholic and other churches, the book burnings by Alexander the Great, the Roman Catholic church, the nazis or recently by the American Drug and Food Administration (burning in 1954 books and periodicals written or edited by Wilhelm Reich); the suppression of research on free energy devices by energy supply industries or the prohibition of unorthodox healing methods by institutions controlled by healthcare industries.

But which interest group would have a plausible reason to prevent research on the myth of a universal language, spoken worldwide before the babylonian speech confusion, or on how this language might be reconstructed from the confused remains or newly designed from scratch? You will find more than one answer in this book.

EVALUATING EDO NYLAND'S METHOD OF WORD DECONSTRUCTION AND BACK–TRANSLATION INTO HIDDEN MEANING.

In order to evaluate Edo Nyland's method of word deconstruction and backtranslation we have to compare it with the state of the art methods of modern linguists. Edo Nyland gives a short description of one such method in the chapter Comparing Basque and the Dravidian Languages:

"A group of comparative linguists in the U.S.A. developed a system which they called the '**lexico-statistical method**' and attempted to put a percentage figure on the degree in which languages are related (M.Swadesh, *Linguistics Today*, 1954). It is based on the percentage of resemblances between 200 words considered to be essential in a language:

1.   the oldest names for parts of the body and its functions

2.   pronouns and numerals

3.   names for dwellings, children and families

4.   domestic animals

The well-known Basque linguist A. Tovar followed this method to measure the degree of kinship of Basque with other languages of non-Indo-European origin. The closest relationship he found was with Berber (11%) followed by Circaskian/Kirrukaskan (7.5%), Coptic (6.5%), Arabic (3.25%)."

Our referee Richard Fester seems to have gone one step farther, defining the most prominent of these resemblances, found by lexico-statistical methods, as archetypes and having a closer look at words of different languages containing these archetypes.

Richard Fester defined the following archetypes: BA, KAL, TAG, TAL, OS and ACQ.

He asserts that these archetypes, embedded in words of all languages, are giving related meaning to these words. In the following we are using the archetype KAL as an example to describe Richard Fester's method.

The embedding of the archetype KAL is described by Richard Fester's structure formula shown below.

Table 1 (from Lit [1])

Das KALL-Schema

```
+ — W —   Q   \           N — Nk (Ng)
+ — H —  CH  >  ‾K‿★‿L‾  <   ★ — J
    J — SCH  /              ★ — V
                           R — +

                             SCH
           Lj — ‾L‿★‿K‾  <  CH — R
                             Nk — N   H

        oder           sowie
      ‾K‿L‿★‾         ‾★‿L‿K‾
      ‾K‿R‿★‾         ‾★‿R‿K‾
      ‾K‿N‿★‾         ‾★‿N‿K‾
```

★ bezeichnet jeden beliebigen Vokal, + den Verlust eines Konsonanten. Der Lautabtausch wie bei K★L und L★K ist auf jeder weiteren Stufe gleich gut möglich, etwa KAN/NAK, KOR/ROK, LIN/NIL, wobei das -L- am Ende wieder zu -N- werden kann, also zu NAN, NA und AN.

*(* is a wildcard for any vowel; + marks a missing consonant.)*

This structure allows many alternatives and variants of KAL, e.g. vowel replacement (K*L or KL*), inversion (L*K instead of K*L or *LK instead of KL*) and replacement of consonant L by R or N.

The structure formula is used as a search filter. Richard Fester is scanning the lexical contents of some 30 languages, searching for words containing variants of the archetype and testing these words for related meaning.

Because of the large amount of search hits, he is grouping his findings thematically into 11 tables. We are showing one half of one of these tables containing embedded variants of KAL related to human head and brain as an example:

Table 2 (from Lit [1])

Tafel 3: Kopf und HIRN

spanisch	laddinisch	australisch	batak
CAL'va	CAL'vari	po'GAL	ta'KAL
(BA) Kopf, head	(BA) Schädelstätte	(BA) Kopf, head	Kopf, head (TAG)
cabeza	CALvary, CALvario	CALva	CALva
laddinisch	thai	ilocan	schottisch
VAUL	KALOOG*	CALLO'GONG*	HARNS
HIRN, brain	Schädel, SKULL	Hut, hat	HIRN, SKULL
CERE'bro	CALva	sombrero	CAL'va
telugu	spanisch	spanisch	griechisch
ŠALA	CALA'morra	CALA'vera	KARA
Kopf, head	Schädel, SKULL	(BA) Totenschädel	HIRN, HARNS
cabeza	CAL'va	SKULL	CERE'bro
spanisch	finnisch	samojed	baskisch
CALANtica	KALLO	KALLO	KALOI
Kopfschmuck, head-	HIRNSCHALE	Stirn, forehead	Schädel, SKULL
Ornament	SKULL, Cerebro	frente	CAL'va
europäisch	finnisch	griechisch	maori
KAL'otte	pää'KALLO	KALY'mma	KARU
Schädeldecke	Schädel, SKULL	HIRNSCHALE	Kopf, head
CAL'otta	CALA'morra	SKULL, CAL'va	cabeza
baskisch	lateinisch	lateinisch	lateinisch
GARUN	GALEa	GALE'rum	CALI'ptra
HIRN, brain	HELm, HEL'met	HAU'be, hood	Mütze, cap
CERE-bro	YEL'mo	GORRA	GORRo
tibetisch	tibetisch	slowakisch	laddinisch
GLA'd	KLA'd	HLAVA	CHAV'azza
HIRN, brain	Kopf, head	Kopf, head	Schädel, SKULL
CERE'bro	CAL'va	cabeza	CAL'va
maori	thai	guarani	baskisch
KAWIU	KAN	A'CAN	KAN'KAR*
SKAL'p	Kopf, head	Kopf, head	HIRNSCHALE
es'CAL'po	CALA'morra	cabeza	SKULL, CALA'mor
quechua	arabisch	arhuaco	ph-subnun
I'NACA	NAcHA	tiu'KANE	GANGA'S
Kopftuch, head-	HIRN, HARNS	Stirn, forehead	Stirn, forehead
dress, pañuelo	CERE'bro	frente	frente
ph-bilaan	maori	maori	nheengatu
QANGA's	pa'ANGANGA	ANGA'ANGA*	A'CANGA
Stirn, forehead	Schädel, SKULL	Kopf, head	Kopf, head
frente	CAL'va (BA)	cabeza	cabeza

Each table entry has 4 lines.

1st line: Language
2nd line: Word from this language filtered out with KAL-filter.
3rd line: Meaning (in german and english translation.)
4th line: Reference to other findings

KAL-variants contained in lined 2 - 4 are printed in capital letters.

Table 2 shows many words from languages of different families, containing KAL variants and having similar meaning, which would support the monogenetic hypothesis. But if you look into tables of other word groups (not shown here), you will detect similar words with quite different meaning:

Table 3 (assembled from different tables of Lit [1])

Richard Fester builds his proof for monogenesis of languages on a significant number of words, searched from different language families, containing the same archetype, and having related meaning.

His opponents might use the same sample of outcomes to select a significant number of equally similar words with different meaning in order to declare all

quiché CALA'ba wegnehmen, take away, tomar	quechua CALL'pa Kraft, power fuerza (BA)	spanisch CAL'va (BA) Kopf, head cabeza	guarani CAN'ba schwarz, bLACK NEGre
spanisch GAL'farro Sperber, HAWK HALCON	arabisch KAL'b HUND, HOUND CAN	hindi KAL'basu Barbe, barbel barbo	griechisch KALLA'bis org. Tanz, dancing bailando orgiastic.
griechisch KAL'pis URNE, Vase, vessel URNA	quechua KALL'pa LÜCKE, HOLE LAGUNA	finnisch KAL'pa gr. Messer, big KNIfe, CUCHILLo	tibetisch m'GAL'-pa Hütte, hut choza, barRACa
quechua yana'KALL'wa SCHWALbe SWALLOW	griechisch KAL'pe GAUL, horse CAVALLO	phönizisch KAL'pe Meerenge, straits estrecho	finnisch KEL'po fähig, able apto

outcomes of this method as chance hits.

Now we will have a look at Edo Nyland's method of decomposition and backtranslation of words, which is described in great detail in this book (please read the tutorials in chapters "Are Words a Shorthand?" and "Translating Ogam").

The method has to be performed with the following steps:

"Step 1) Arrange the letters of the word to be analyzed as a sequence of vowels (V) and consonants (C), VCVCVCV, placing dots where vowels or an ‚h' were eliminated. Then replace C and Q with K, V with B or F, W is ignored and Y with I or J.

Step 2) Break up the sequence so obtained into VCV-VCV-VCV-VCV etc. in which the vowels of either side of the hyphen are the same.

1ˢᵗ example: energy,
ene - er. - .gi

Step 3) Using the VCV word list (or the dictionary), arrange the appropriate words under each VCV. (There is usually no need to list words which are obviously unrelated to the meaning at hand.) The result of this can be that a list of possible words for e.g. ENE, representing several different meanings, may be quite different from another list with the same VCV, depending on the words to be decoded. For name decoding all or most words supplied in the VCV word list are used, although character traits are often involved.

1ˢᵗ example continuation:

ene	try: **era**	try: **agi**
my	profit, available	I wish, I hope
attract me	method, sample	*powerful*
always	suffer, storm	to order
before	*to motivate*	promise
in me	attack, to scatter	threat
	try: **ere**	try: **egi**
	scatter, wasteland	to create, action
	occasion	possible, undone
	try: **eri**	try: **igi**
	sickness, recovery	harvest
	compare, fight	sickle
	strong, skillful	
	try: **ero**	try: **ogi**
	risky, transport	bread, crust, maid
	insanity, comfort	baker, easygoing
	try: **eru**	try: **ugi**
	mistake. producing	N.A.
	abundant	

Step 4) Select those words which make a sentence most closely describing the words to be decoded.

1ˢᵗ example continuation:

ene   ene   *-enetan*   always
er.   era   *eragin*   to motivate
.gi   agi   *aginbidedun*   powerfully
"Always powerfully motivated."

2nd example: …the name **"Vatican"** proves to be pure Basque when analyzed
with the VCV formula:

.ba - ati - ika - an.
aba - ati - ika - ana
abadeburu - atxiki - ikasgiro - anaiarte
head priest/pope - faithful - learning environment - brotherhood
"The faithful pope's learning environment for the brotherhood."

It is obvious that the VCV's used by Edo Nyland are smaller items than Fester's archetypes, e.g. the archetype KAL may be decomposed into two VCV's :

.ka-al.

This form has 25 alternatives of augmenting missing vowels (aka-ala, …aka-
alu, …uka-ala, …uka-alu). For each augmented VCV-pair there are many
alternatives for possible translations (see the VCV-dictionary in this book).

The language-inventing linguists could therefore have used embedded KAL-
forms like

aka-ale	to argue – carefully
eka-alu	contribution – stupid
ika-ale	to learn – effort
ika-alu	student – stupid

to construct words containing some meaning related with the human head or
brain (as assembled in Fester's table 2 above).

But KAL-forms could equally well be used to construct words containing very
different meanings like

aka-ala	the end – happy
aka-alo	perfect – wage
eka-ale	contribution – rejoicing
ika-ala	fright – outcry
oka-ala	bellyful – feeding
uka-ale	possession – grain abundance
uka-alu	hand – feeble

This was experienced by Fester, who assembled 11 tables with words having
embedded KAL with different meaning, some of which were shown in table 3
above.

This inquiry is revealing many advantages of Edo Nyland's method compared with one of the lexico-statistical methods:

1. Edo Nyland's method uncovers a reasonable meaning for each word.
    (the lexico-statistical method or the improved version used by Fester gives only word lists with vague and widespread relations of meanings)

2. The same VCV's may be backtranslated differently according to the word at hand and according to context with different other VCV's in this word. (Fester had no explanation for the fact that words containing his archetypes could have very different meaning).

3. All VCV's of a word are processed.
    (Fester did not process the leading and trailing parts of the words, into which the archetypes, e.g. KAL, were embedded).

4. Different type and position of vowels give different results of backtranslation.
    (Fester's filters worked with wildcards for vowels, e.g. K*L, and did not discriminate different vowel positions, e.g. K*L; KL*)

5. Mirrored VCV's (e.g. EDO; ODE) give different backtranslation.
    (Fester's filters did not discriminate between K*L and L*K or KL* and *LK)

6. Modern characters are replaced before backtranslation, e.g. replace C and Q with K, V with B or F, W is ignored and Y with I or J.
    (Fester did not pre-process the vocabulary before filtering).

In order to enhance controversy, we will finish this comparison of methods with some adequate citations from this book. Concerning the lexico-statistical method, Edo Nyland writes:

"This method is of no use with invented languages such as Latin, Greek, Sanskrit, Hebrew, English, German etc. because all of these are made up almost 100% by formulaic manipulation and mutilation of the Basque/Saharan language."

And he does not conceal the opinion of scholars of linguistics, communicating and commenting these in this book:

"Most of the linguists who have bothered to look at my research have suggested "more reasonable" possibilities to explain the observed inconsistencies in our present knowledge, pointed out by me. They then invariably decided to ignore the issue until a reason for a more thorough examination arose. In such cases the status quo has always ruled and the needed examination has been stonewalled until now. The burden of proof is the responsibility of those shaking the status quo. It is up to the shaker to provide evidence rather than for those simply suggesting that the evidence can be accounted for by existing paradigms. In this respect I have been told repeatedly by academics that nothing can be true outside of the status quo. Therefore nothing outside the status quo needs to be investigated, which is a sure prescription for continued ignorance and high intellect superstition. Science has thus been turned into dogma, and what can a non-academic scholar do about it? Work the internet and be patient!"

If it is up to the shaker to provide evidence, then we finally have to deal with the question, whether Edo Nyland's book will give enough evidence to exclude "more reasonable" possibilities to explain the observed inconsistencies in our present knowledge.

EVIDENCE

Edo Nyland's method of word deconstruction and backtranslation has to be handled with care, as he points out at different locations:

"IMPRECISION IN THE EXTRACTION OF MEANINGS."

Where the meaning of the word being translated from the VCV shorthand can be checked by context, it is important that it be checked again in completing the entire translation. Forced, unnatural or inappropriate results should be suspect. In this case, we may have a CV syllable which is never part of the VCV list and must be translated directly with the use of the dictionary. Where we have one word only, we face a problem which is common in handling language. Consider if one is given the task of finding a meaning for the letters D U C K. We could say the meaning was an aquatic bird, a quick downwards movement, a score at Cricket, an avoidance of an issue etc

The meaning of… **words** will usually help to guide the decoding process. However, most… **names** do not have an obvious meaning, which makes the decoding more time consuming.

Occasionally more than one possible meaning appears in which case both should be reported and/or earlier spellings researched.

In general, every consonant represents a full word, and the more consonants in a word or name, the longer the hidden sentence is and the more likely it is that it can be recovered."

The results are thus depending too on the skills of the user (a disadvantage in the eyes of scientists who prefer methods which yield results independent of user skills).

It seems to be difficult to evaluate the evidence of the method under these circumstances. But the evidence of the method is proved by important discoveries, which Edo Nyland achieved by applying his method on problems which had been unsolved before. His most important solutions are the decipherment of the OGAM script, as well as considerable improvements in translating the Auraicept of the Benedictines, the names of the pharaohs, and the Minoan Linear-B tablets.

When Edo Nyland started his OGAM research, the Ogam scripts had been transcribed to the alphabet, but not yet translated satisfactorily into English. By interpreting Ogam as a shorthand of the universal language, he was able to find convincing translations for many of the Ogam scripts documented in literature (see the OGAM chapters in this book).

His method worked equally well in translating the Auraicept, an amazing book of the Benedictines. Edo Nyland writes:

"The Auraicept na n'Eces is an astonishing book. The meaning of its name had been generally accepted as: "The Scholars' Primer." Calder calls it the "Handbook of the Learned," which is only a guess, but ever since it was printed in 1917 the book has been subjected to a variety of choice derogatory comments....

Irish scholars insisted that the book was written in "Celtic" but were unable to provide a single translation that made sense... I explain that the language of the Auraicept is Basque, more accurately: coded Basque, which can be decoded by using the VCV formula and a modern Basque dictionary, as shown. In the Auraicept it is described how the grammarians made up languages..."

"Some of the previously available 'translations' of the Auraicept from Calder and the new ones from Edo Nyland are both shown in the book for comparison.

A similar improvement was achieved with the translation of Minoan Linear-B-tablets. Examples of the original and the new translations of Linear B tablets, done by Michael Ventris and Edo Nyland, may too be compared in the book.

The deconstruction of words from invented languages into meaningful sentences of the universal mother language (Basque/Saharan) is working equally well for very different families of invented languages (Indo-European and non Indo-European), thus supporting the hypothesis of large scale, intentional language construction rather than natural polygenesis.

If Edo Nyland's research results were adopted by official science, then many textbooks of linguistics, and of history too, have to be rewritten. See for example the chapter Classifying the World's Languages or "Towards a New Etymological Dictionary for English."

Umberto Eco compiled in his book [3] a rather complete historical overview of the many methods which have been tried to reconstruct the universal language. None of these methods is comparable to Edo Nyland's. So a knowledgeable reader would have to admit that Edo Nyland found something new.

Edo Nyland himself is very moderate, writing "MANY HAVE SAID IT BEFORE I DID" and giving two of his early predecessors, Abbot Dominique Lahetjuzan (1766-1818) and the French Abbot Diharce de Bidassouet (1825) the honour of a citation. Many others, not having said it, must have known it, as Edo Nyland is showing by analysis of a word which had been constructed by Shakespeare:

"In *Love's Labour's Lost* Shakespeare presents us with a Latin sounding riddle: *honorificabilitudinitatibus* (Act V, i, 39). Up to now it has frustrated all efforts to decode it. This is supposed to be the longest "Latin" word in the dictionary, but where did this "Latin" word come from? Probably not from Latin! The fact that he used this word tells me that he knew about the Benedictines' operational manual, the "Auraicept" in which it is mentioned at least twice. It is likely that the "word" was made up in Ireland by one of the Benedictine grammarians. In line 1438 the word starts with *tinerifica* while the version in line 1741 is *tenerifica*. Let us first apply the VCV formula to Shakespeare's version and see what happens:

honorificabilitudinitatibus:

.ho	*ahogoza*	delicious
ono	*onon*	exquisite
ori	*orrits*	banquet
ifi	*ibili*	to go
ika	*ikaskai*	lesson
abi	*abiatu*	to begin
ili	*ilinti*	fiery preacher
itu	*itundu*	to be advised
udi	*udikan*	to get out, to go away
ini	*initz,ainitz*	many
ita	*itaun*	question
ati	*atxiki*	to retain
ibu	*aburu?*	opinion
us.	*usutu*	often expressed

"Going to the delicious and exquisite banquet was the lesson the fiery preacher began with. I was advised to go away with my many questions and retained my often expressed opinion."

LET IT BLEED

"Controversy is the lifeblood of scholarship," says Edo Nyland.

The writer of this foreword tried to get controversy started by crossing the borders between official and amateur science and commenting on serious scientific problems with a cunning smile.

Now the readers are invited to enjoy the book and to contribute to the controversy about it; the main goal being multiplicity of scientific ideas and methods and the only rule to be obeyed being fair play.

Dr. Ove Hinrichs

LITERATURE

[1] Richard Fester:
Urwörter der Menschheit.
Eine Archäologie der Sprache.
Kösel Verlag, München 1981.

[2] Arnold Wadler:
Der Turm von Babel.
Urgemeinschaft der Sprachen. 1935
Reprint by Fourier Verlag, Wiesbaden, ISBN 3-921695-38-4

[3] Umberto Eco:
La ricerca della lingua perfetta nella cultura europea.
Laterza, Roma-Bari, 1993
German edition (used for this foreword):
Die Suche nach der vollkommenen Sprache.
C.H.Beck, München 1994, ISBN 3-406-37888-9

[4] Frederico Di Trocchio:
Il genio incompresso.
Uomini e idee che la scienza non ha capito.
Arnoldo Mondadori Editore S.p.A., Milano 1997
German edition: Newton's Koffer:
Geniale Außenseiter, die die Wissenschaft blamierten.
Campus Verlag, Frankfurt/New York, 1998. ISBN 3-593-35976-6.

PREFACE

Language must have been around before light. If it hadn't, the
Lord couldn't have said in the beginning "Let there be light".

INTELLIGENT DESIGN?

 This book grew in bits and pieces, one brainwave after another. First there was
the chance-listening to a radio broadcast about the Odysseus epic, which Homer
sifted and mutilated and edited then dragged, piece by piece, into the Mediterranean. If he had not done this, we would never have known about his incredible
voyage and adventures. The talk resulted in my making three trips to Scotland
and Ireland to see the places where the old sailor was said to have been. This
was followed by an attempt to translate the names in the Odyssey and place
names in Ireland and the Hebrides. The only language that could make sense
out of the many names was Basque, so I bought a good Basque dictionary,
which got me involved in linguistics. The many early Christian inscriptions on
standing stones in Ireland and Scotland, called Ogam writing, were crying out
for someone to translate them and Dr. Anthony Jackson, an anthropologist in
Edinburgh, had challenged anyone to crack the code in which they were written. When I did just that, with the help of my Basque dictionary, he did not
agree with me and pushed my considerable effort aside and insisted that no
translation was possible. I then started to write my book "Where Did Odysseus
Go?" and included my Ogam research in it. One result of my Ogam translation
effort was another brainwave urging me to explore the Basque content of the
Indo-European (I-E) languages, which many linguists had detected. It did not
take long to realize that I was onto something big, so I pushed the Odysseus
chapters onto the back burner and concentrated on proving that the "family"
of Indo-European languages was no family at all, but instead was a group of

totally invented languages. I then explored as many different I-E vocabularies as possible.

The linguists I consulted were unanimous in their condemnation of my efforts, even after giving my work the merest of reluctant glances, which reinforced my belief that I was really onto something different. The linguists appeared to be very happy with their status quo, even though every European language I looked at seemed to have a huge sign attached: "I am the product of intelligent design." Even Homer's Odyssey had the same label attached. But the academics could not see it, as one said: "The time for a layman to make significant academic contributions is past. Please shut the door behind you." What was going on here?

WHAT THIS BOOK IS NOT

I am no linguist and therefore not bound to linguistic conventions. This book is not written for experts, the writing is simple and often speculative, yet academics may well be interested in my findings. This book is not easy bedtime reading, instead it is more like a cross between a textbook and a reference work. To my knowledge, no one has done this before; there is no other book like it in existence, unless it is the Auraicept na'n Ecez, the eighth century A.D. operational handbook of the Benedictine monk-linguists. However, the Auraicept has not yet been decoded and translated, in spite of persistent efforts by several Gaelic scholars, who used the wrong language.

As historical linguistics refuses to recognize that many of our major languages were invented several millennia ago, this book cannot be about historical linguistics. Archaeology is the searching out and interpretation of the remains of humans and their activities. Archaeo-linguistics studies the manner in which humans have influenced the evolution and creation of languages and have left evidence of their linguistic activities in various places. To me the discipline of linguistics should not be a stand-alone fortress, protected by dogmatic acceptance of old theories and obscured by incomprehensible jargon. Linguists will never lift their discipline out of the backwater of academia until the gates are opened wide and their field of study becomes interdisciplinary.

WHAT THIS BOOK IS ABOUT

How did historical names originate? Who made up the spoken words? This book is about the invention of words and names in European and other languages and about descriptive sentences and early history hidden in these words and names. It recognizes that most, if not all, major languages on earth are the product of intelligent design or invention. Some retain part of their original un-manipulated vocabulary, like Basque, others are totally invented by highly skilled monk-linguists such as Latin, Sanskrit, English, German.

Many names are formulaically composed, such as in Sumerian, English, Sanskrit, Ancient Egyptian, while others just agglutinate the first letters of applicable Basque words such as in some of the Germanic languages. Those languages that stick faithfully to one formal system of encoding or the other are the easiest ones to show the inherent artificiality of, such as Latin, Sanskrit, Greek, Hebrew and English. It was a fair comment when someone said that I was breaking down language into "bit management" as we would in a complex computer program. The one language that uses the biggest variety of agglutinating systems and linguistic creativity using such bits is Basque itself, the oldest of all invented languages. The study of Basque must have been an almost magic source of wisdom to the ancient linguists.

My system of decoding shows the way in which to recover the hidden sentences in words and names. Almost every one of the words in some languages can be readily decoded, such as in English, Hebrew and Yiddish. The instructions and examples given should be clear enough for other students of the subject to do their own decoding, but don't expect immediate success because it takes considerable practice. Follow the instructions in a systematic way and remember that five steps are involved in revealing the hidden sentences. These five stages must be shown by decoders and also by those criticizing their work. The encoded words of some other languages are much more difficult to show, such as in Slavic, Scandinavian and Hungarian, the most recent of the many language inventions. In their efforts to create languages, which turned out quite different from the ones already invented, the monk-grammarians did some amazing mental gymnastics. Their twisting and turning created problems for this technician trying to uncover the hidden sentence, if such a sentence was buried. The more difficult ones I leave for scholars to try their skill on. In the meantime there is no doubt in my mind that the languages were all invented.

There are translations which may be objectionable to some people, especially the meanings of some religious names and words which contradict words in the Bible. The names of the pharaohs contain some new historical information, some of which contradict classical writings, a problem which cannot be avoided.

I didn't make up the names or the words, I just interpreted them. I have no axe to grind, no dogma to defend, just a wish to expose what I see as the truth, no matter what long toes I may happen to step on in the process. There is no malice intended. Also, a certain amount of duplication could not be avoided.

I am a retired professional forester with a degree from the University of British Columbia, Canada (1957). Before that I also studied botany at the University of Amsterdam. Forestry is a good discipline to train in because it must be the most interdisciplinary university study of any, more so than geography and archaeology, which helped me to see through the legion of problems which are encountered in modern Indo-European linguistics. Even though the amazing Basque language plays an important role in my writing, this book is not mainly about Basque, or even a guide to it. Although I touch here and there on grammar, the comments are overwhelmingly about the invention of vocabulary and names. I hardly use linguistic jargon, mainly because I have no academic grounding in it, but also because I want the layman to know what I am talking about. I decode and translate many hundreds of names and words, yet this book is no etymological dictionary. What I discovered appeared to have a bearing on the teaching of linguistics at all our universities. The present "science" of Indo-European linguistics starts to look like it has insurmountable problems. The entire "family" appears to be a product of intelligent design, an invented science and thus no true science at all. If this sounds preposterous, that's what was staring me in the face. I wish that, after all this, I would be able to speak some Basque sentences, but to my regret such is not the case. My brain is just no longer spongy enough for these unfamiliar words to stick.

THE GRAMMARIANS' SKILLS STILL EXIST

The basic structure of this group of formulaically invented languages was the VCV (vowel-consonant-vowel) arrangement of three letters which were then agglutinated into words. The skills necessary to do the encoding of Saharan-Basque VCV's into new words and names, still exist in several places. The name Windsor shows that this skill is still maintained in England, probably by members of the Inner Circle of the Masonic Lodge. During, and for some years after, the reign of Queen Victoria this secret organization maintained and trained a core of skilled linguists in the Basque city of Biarritz. Their buildings (e.g. their former Anglican church, now city museum) and many graves (in St. Martin's grave yard) are still clearly marked but the cemetery is now dreadfully neglected. The Roman Catholic church still possesses this capability at the Vatican (but no one would or could talk about it) and likely also at the thousand-year-old monasteries of Pannonhalma (Hungary), Cluny (France) and

Tiniecz (Poland). In Eastern Europe this knowledge is still stored at Kiev's Prezelska Lavra, as the meaning of the name "Stalin" shows. Over the millennia the Jews have been very active in making up and introducing new languages such as Hebrew, Arab, Ge'ez etc. and it is most likely that, even today, they still have the skills necessary to do so again. This secrecy in protecting the technique of encoding agglutinated words and using a carefully designed word list, means that we are dealing with a secret, even holy or magical, language. The names of the oldest pharaohs and their gods show that the technique of encoding and the vocabulary they used to do this, has changed very little for over 5200 years.

It is interesting to see that most names have their occluded built-in sentence which tells one story, often kept secret, but then the name itself was later given a fictitious meaning which was popularly accepted. Many people for whom names were designed did not know the hidden meaning of it, some of the pharaohs included. For instance, when the Persian king Cambyses conquered Egypt and wanted to be known as a pharaoh, he asked the priest Wedjahorresnet to make him up a proper pharaoh's name. He would have killed him had he known the real hidden meaning of the name Mesutira, which the priest made up for him. Cambyses was told it meant "Conqueror of Two Lands" (i.e. Upper and Lower Egypt") but what the hidden sentence said was "You skinny dreamer, get out of here and suffer." Wedjahorresnet boasted about his linguistic skills on a beautiful statue which was carved for him, now in the Vatican Museum. He is the only named person I have so far been able to find, who admitted to knowing the formulaic secret of name invention. That this type of revenge has been with us from ancient until modern times is shown by the name Stalin, which for public, and his own, consumption meant: "Man of Steel", but in fact means "In a brutish way he kills people any way possible." (See Slavic names).

Common people did not escape the priests' wrath either, as the Ukrainian name "Zadaprushki" shows. The hidden sentence in this name says: "You are insincere and deceiving and have a tendency to be cruel; Get lost!" These last two names made me realize that the monks of the almost 1000 year old monastery at Kiev are among the few who had preserved this ancient agglutinating skill, and no doubt still possess it.

I

HOW THIS all BEGAN

A Seemingly Aimless Journey

It Started With A Radio Talk

At first there was no thought of a research project, no theory to contemplate, no probability to examine, nothing particularly in mind. There was, however, a lifelong interest in the activities which had taken place in the Bronze Age, as supposedly described in the writings of Homer and Apollonius of Rhodes and as carved on some of the Egyptian temples. Then I heard a radio talk by a historian who was musing about the whereabouts of Odysseus. It was the start of a busy retirement.

On November 5, 1984, while driving home, I listened on the car radio to historian Edward Furlong speaking on the Ideas Program of the Canadian Broadcasting Corporation. He was talking about the Odyssey, an epic sea voyage which happened circa 1186 B.C. He thought it had taken place mostly in the North Atlantic, not the Mediterranean as the majority of the writers had said. For a variety of quite obvious reasons he concluded in his documentary that the Odyssey was tailor-made for the north Atlantic. During his radio presentation he interviewed several specialists who contributed their knowledge and opinions about a number of points raised in the Odyssey, from astronomy to ship building to Greek translation etc. I was fascinated by what they had to say, because it made so much sense and created a whole new way of looking at Homer's writing. Furlong finished his informative discussion the next night. For the following four years I was busy with more practical things, but then I was given a transcript of Furlong's talk by a friend. Both of us were interested in Bronze Age history and we brought out the necessary maps to see the areas mentioned by Furlong. We then discussed and researched in detail several of the statements made by this historian. His conclusions sounded reasonable so I decided to visit the Irish and Scottish locations which had been identified by Furlong.

EDWARD FURLONGS'S DOCUMENTARY

Edward Furlong, who had studied to be a historian, later became a chartered accountant in Toronto. He was one of the latest in a long line of students of Homer who realized that the geographical and environmental descriptions in the Odyssey did not fit well within the confines of the Mediterranean and in several cases could definitely not have happened there. In his two, one hour presentations on the C.B.C. he suggested that Odysseus had visited Ireland and Scotland. Furlong then selected four exact locations he thought were described in the epic: The isle of Barra in the Outer Hebrides (north of Ireland), the north tip of the Isle of Jura in the Inner Hebrides (70 km west of Glasgow), Lough Swilly in County Donegal, northern Ireland, and the Isle of Stroma at the far NE tip of Scotland. He also concluded that Odysseus had been in Norway where the Phaiakians lived.

During the Second World War, Furlong had been a navigating officer on a Canadian warship in the Atlantic and the Mediterranean and saw many of the places where Odysseus could have visited. After spending a fair amount of time researching the epic, he had come to the conclusion that it had a core of true history. In his radio talk he pointed out that Homer was talking about an endless gray sea, terrible storms and tides, a ship-swallowing whirlpool, hoarfrost at sea level in mid-summer, a town covered in fog and clouds for long periods, a gannet which is a sea bird of the North Atlantic, a day so long that a person could do two days of work in the span of one day because of the very short night. None of these occurrences fitted in the Mediterranean but all were part of the North Atlantic. Then there was the star bearing which Odysseus used to sail away from Kalypso, which according to traditional thinking was supposed to have been from southern Italy or Malta to the Island of Corfu.

THE STAR BEARING (BOOK V: 269)

Furlong took the star bearing to the planetarium in Toronto and asked the astronomer, Dr. Clark, to test this bearing in two locations, first the traditionally accepted route to Corfu and second on the course which Furlong thought that Odysseus had taken to Norway.

"Glorious Odysseus, happy with the wind, spread sails and taking his seat artfully with the steering oar he held her on her course, as he kept his eye on the Pleiades and late-setting Boötes and the Bear to whom men give also the name of the Wagon. For so Kalypso, bright among Goddesses, had told to make his way over the sea, keeping the Bear on his left hand. Seventeen days he sailed and on the eighteenth day there showed the shadowy mountains of the Phaiakian land... "

(V: 269-280)

As Edward Furlong explained in his radio talk, Dr. Clark first examined the star bearing in the Mediterranean setting, the traditionally accepted location of the voyage:

"By precessing the planetarium backwards we place the point directly over the earth's North Pole in its correct position among the stars, and so the constellations appear as they would be seen in 1200 B.C. Considerable expense has gone into the design of these machines to make them quiet, but at high speed you can perhaps hear the equipment as the polar attitude is changed and we bring it into position for latitude 37 5 degrees."

Furlong then explained how after some time this bearing turned 30 to 40 degrees south of east and the sailors are going much too far south to come close to Corfu. The conclusion was that **Odysseus' bearing did not belong in the Eastern Mediterranean**.

The planetarium was then arranged to represent the northern sky at 58 degrees north, which produced an entirely different configuration of the constellations; the sun, which before was on the horizon, is now well above it because in the North the nights are much shorter. So the sun was put back on the horizon and Boötes is now almost due west. A little later, Dubhe, the first star of the Great Bear, is almost true north and the Pleiades have not come up yet. At midnight the Bear is just crossing the pole, it's halfway through true north, and there are the Pleiades coming up, so now there is an easterly line for Pleiades; the sun has just come up. The Great Bear is still exactly right for giving us the bearing due east. The bearing which Odysseus had been following lead him directly to southern Norway. The conclusion was that **Odysseus' star bearing fits perfectly in the North Atlantic**. Also the 17 days sailing with a small home-made boat was reasonable.

However, as convincing as this planetarium test was, it was only part of the true story and much more proof was needed to convince the skeptics that the old sailor was indeed in Ireland, Scotland and Norway. Furlong then went on to discuss the Aeolian island where Odysseus obtained the bag with all the courses of the winds from King Aiolos, which Furlong interpreted as a waterproof leather bag with navigational charts. He theorized about the giant Laistrygonians who sank all but one of Odysseus' ships and then killed and ate all the men of the eleven crews. He tried to pinpoint the sky-towering cliffs which he felt could be the Cliffs of Mohar, south of the city of Galway on the west coast of Ireland. The town hidden in fog and cloud he placed correctly in Loch Swilly and he located the Goddess Kirke, whom Odysseus encountered and loved, on Barra, also right on the mark. The dreaded whirlpool of Charybdis he placed at the north tip of the Isle of Jura, the sacred island of Helios, and mentioned many other of Homer's remarks which indicated that the place of the Wanderings had finally been accurately pinpointed. As you will see later, he was right in most of his assumptions, but the story turned out to be much bigger than Edward Furlong could have anticipated. Odysseus had been on a very special mission in the Mediterranean, a mission which some day must become part of Ireland's and Scotland's pre-Christian history, because Odysseus was no Greek or Mycenian. Instead it is likely that he was born on Barra, Scotland. What then had he been doing for so many years in the eastern Mediterranean and why? And why did Homer make a Greek king out of this Atlantic sailor? Why did Homer go to all that trouble to make it look as if the entire epic voyage had been in the Mediterranean?

THE BEGINNING OF MY LINGUISTIC ODYSSEY

After having read the Odyssey at least three times and reviewing what many others had said about the voyage, it was clear to me that new information about the epic would be required to prove that Furlong had been right in locating Odysseus in Ireland and the Hebrides. Was there such information, that no one had paid attention to, hidden somewhere in Homer's writing? After much soul searching it appeared that the only place such information could be hidden was in the names given by Homer. The many names supplied by him were very different from each other and some were quite long, almost as if they told a story. I decided to look for a name which appeared to tell such a story and chose the name "Laistrygonians" (X:106), the giant cannibals of the "beautiful harbour," and spent some time searching for a clue to the meaning using the Latin, Greek and Celtic dictionaries, which were, I thought, the only languages which could have been used. Nothing of interest appeared from this effort so I put that possibility on the back burner and continued to read everything I could lay hands on about the history of the Bronze Age, in which Odysseus had lived.

The questions which had forced themselves upon me could be worded something like this:

1) Would it be possible that some or all of the names of the Odyssey could have been assembled out of agglutinated words, or parts of words, containing meaningful information?

2) If the names contained such information in the form of, for instance, a sentence in shorthand, how was the agglutination done? What language was used? Was there more than one method of agglutination?

3) Would it be possible to recover the hidden meaning in some or most of them?

These questions I asked myself at every topic I researched, always alert for surprises, and indeed, this search produced a long series of surprises. My first big break came at the end of 1991. It was December 1991 when I noticed an article written by Dr. Luigi Cavalli-Sforza in Scientific American (November 1991 issue) entitled "Genes, Peoples and Languages." He mapped and described the high Rh-negative frequency among the people of the Atlantic coast of Europe. The highest frequencies were found among the Basques, who had concentrations of up to 32%, the Northern Irish and Scots with 25 %, and people on the Atlantic islands of Norway and the City of Bergen had ca. 17%. Other information showed that some of the Berber tribes living in the Atlas mountains of Morocco were as high as 40% Rh-negative.

I knew that the Berbers and Basques were dark-featured people, many with wedge-shaped faces and prominent pointed chins. Was there such a population in Ireland? There was indeed and they were known jokingly as the Black Irish. It was known that these people were often more superstitious than others and several still had stories to tell about leprechauns who helped farm women do work for them during the night, but only if they were treated with respect and given a dish of milk at dusk. The little people had not been seen as long as anyone living could remember, but their tiny cups and saucers were sometime found when a tree, under which they had been living, died and blew over, exposing their former dwelling place. Similar stories had been told in Euskadi, the Basque country. In Scotland the dark featured people were also found, but were not called Black Scots, instead they were just Highlanders or Picts, as the Romans had called them. But these Scottish people possessed something very special, their symbol stones, expertly carved with animal and geometrical totems, which organized inter-tribal cooperation and marriages in a matrilineal society, just like the Basques had until recently. Cavalli-Sforza had suggested that the presence of these people represented an early ocean-born migration which had taken place in the distant past. The Basques were the only tribe of all these Rh-negative Atlantic coast peoples who still spoke their pre-Christian or neolithic language. It was logical to suggest that all these dark featured Berber types, up and down the Atlantic coast, had spoken the same language at the time of their migration. It was worth a try. To do this I needed a Basque dictionary. The University of Victoria had a Basque-German etymological dictionary which was of little help, so I phoned a Basque speaking person I had heard of in Vancouver and asked him if a Basque-English dictionary was available somewhere. He told me that the University of Nevada had recently published an excellent one, written by Gorka Aulestia, professor of Basque literature at DEUSTO, the Jesuit university in Donostia (San Sebastian), Euskadi. I ordered it and its companion volume English-Basque and tried my luck using this language on **Laistrygonian**. Almost instantly there appeared the first letters *lai*, complete Basque word: *laino* meaning fog, which was right on for foggy old Ireland, and things started to look up instantly. In short order there appeared

lai – istri – goni – an
laino – istripu – gonbidatu – aniztasun
fog – accident – to invite – many
"Fog invites many accidents"

which was Ireland all right! The four word sentence had been glued together in one shorthand word. The 'name' of the feared cannibals turned out to be a weather warning for mariners entering the 'beautiful harbour.' After decoding several more Homeric names in the same manner, I knew I had found the key to translating the names of the Odyssey. Greek, Latin or Celtic had nothing to do with the Odyssey, mainly as I learned later, because none of these languages had existed at the time of Odysseus, but Basque from the Atlantic shore turned out to be the right language. Ever since, Aulestia's marvelous dictionary has been my constant companion and it still is, as tattered, grubby and worn as it has become. When I met the great Dr. Aulestia-Txakartegi later, he autographed my well-worn book with the words:

Edo Nyland, neure lagun eta euskaltzale sutsuari
(Edo Nyland, my friend and bascophile enthusiastic.)

However, my discovery posed many new questions for which no answers appeared to be available in literature, such as "What were these Basque speaking people doing in the Hebrides and Ireland, even as far north as Arctic Norway?" Where did they come from? Were they Basques or Picts or Berbers or what? I decided to somehow find answers to all of them. This is how my retirement hobby in archaeological linguistics and its place in Late Bronze Age history started, a field of study about which I knew next to nothing, in fact no one did. But one thing appeared very clear, Bronze Age history, Bronze Age religion and the Basque language all were intimately connected, even though I did not have the slightest idea how this could be shown in a scientifically acceptable way.

Testing Atlantic Coast Names For Basque Content

Orthodox Christian missionaries, coming to Ireland from the continent in the seventh and eighth century, could not communicate with the people and they had called the language spoken by the people the 'Iron Language.' The missionaries spoke in a derogatory manner about the language and always indicated that it was something to be gotten rid of quickly. Could it be that the people had spoken Basque? My first step was to obtain detailed maps of the west coast of Ireland and the Hebrides to see if Basque was recognizable in the geographical names, similar to 'Laistrygonian' which was located in Conamara, Ireland. Just north of the entrance to the 'beautiful harbour' (Killari harbour) is found a jagged point of rock sticking into the ocean; it is called Tonakira Point. The nearest Basque word is *tontakeria* which means 'stupidity'; someone had made a bad mistake there and possibly paid for it with his life. It turned out that many names on the Irish west coast were definitely Basque related, so next I tried the Hebrides. One of the first tested was a small round rocky island named 'Biruasium.' At high tide it was attached by only a narrow sliver of rock to the isle of Vatersay in the southern Outer Hebrides. The name simply breaks up into: biru – asi – um; in Basque *biru* means 'fibre' or 'cord,' *asieran* means 'initially' and *ume* means 'child,' "a child initially attached by the cord." And that's exactly what this lumpy little island looks like on the map.

The next island to the north was Barra, which is a Basque word meaning 'pier' or 'dock,' and therefore makes sense for an island with an excellent harbour and a stable population. An interesting bit of information was that a fishing harbour exists on the coast of Senegal, which is also called Barra and also has the same high Rh-negative blood occurrence among its white population. This would appear to expand the area of study to the Atlantic coast of the Sahara. In the middle of the Isle of Barra are the ruins of a major archaeological complex called 'Talamhanta' or more accurately 'Talamhantu,' which is almost pure Basque:

tala – ama – hantu
vantage point – mother/priestess – tall
"The vantage point of the tall priestess."

Indeed it is a wonderful vantage point because from there even the far-away St. Kilda islands can be seen on a clear day. Homer had written about a woman-led (gylanic) society, like the Basque country used to have, because in pre-Christian days our ancestors had a Goddess, not a God, and her representative on earth was the priestess. Didn't Apollonius of Rhodes tell about a tall, blond Georgian princes by the name of Circe from the east coast of the Black Sea who became the priestess on an island, far, far away? She received a visit from Medea and Jason seeking absolution for their murder of Medea's half brother Apsyrtus. Shortly after that visit Odysseus visited Circe on her island and according to Homer had a love affair with her. The plot was starting to thicken. The word 'far' or 'afar' both come from Basque *ifar* meaning north, which Barra is. Barra was indeed far away from, and north of, the Mediterranean (compare the Faroe islands far north of Scotland).

Another strong indication that Basque at one time was spoken in Scotland is the family names of the clans. Some were not very flattering and obviously were coined by people who didn't like them, such as MacKenzie; in Basque *kentze* is the act of depriving, of taking away, so could this clan have been "the clan of thieves"? The MacUsker family name is a nasty one, because an *uzker* is a fart "The clan of the farters." A name which tells us something about the region the tribes lived in is Donald, again pure Basque, from done-alde, *donetsi – alde*, to sanctify – region: "The Sanctified Region" or "Holy Land." Had their region been the original Holy Land, as Claudius Claudianus hinted in "The First Book Against Rufinus" (p.35) before Homer moved it into Palestine, just like all other parts of the Odyssey had been shoved into the Mediterranean? Also Douglas, from dug-las, *dugu – lasai*, we have it – comfortable: "We have a good life." The MacNeal name is sometimes still spelled MacNial and MacNiald, from *ni – alde*, "my – region/land." MacEwen is spelled *uhin* in Basque and means wave, "the Clan of the Waves," the navigators.

Going north from there, along the coast of Norway, as far north as Finnmark in the Arctic, the same was found. Many names, in fact most, could be translated with Aulestia's dictionary and provided meaningful information. Again, some of the Lapp families of the area have a slightly higher Rh-negative blood frequency among their members than the non-Lapp population in the north. What on earth could it have been that the Berbers and Basques were doing way up in the Arctic? After having translated hundreds of names all along the west coast it became a certainty that Basque had been spoken there at some very early time and that they had been involved in a large scale hunt of reindeer. I remembered I had read somewhere that some linguists had theorized that all of Europe at one time was unilingual, in other words, everybody had spoken the same language. The plot was thickening all the time, or was it becoming a stew? Not only could all the names in the Odyssey be translated with the Basque dictionary, so could many of the geographical names along the west coasts of Ireland, Scotland and Norway.

How could I make sense out of all the apparently unrelated and diverse bits of information which were coming together? There had to be a way to make sense out of all of it. This problem would be getting much worse before it got better. Some other information would be needed but I had no idea where it would come from. The search for such information provided so many data that a second book was necessary to tell about the results. It will be published as the sequel to this book and describes historical and religious activities in the Bronze Age.

Discovering Ogam

My first trip to Ireland and the Hebrides was an exploratory one; its purpose was to try to get the 'feel' of the country and the people, to visit the Bronze Age monuments and ruins, and to see what items from the time of Odysseus were displayed in the museums. As the Odyssey appeared to give a great deal of information about the Outer Hebrides, I decided to travel the full length of this long string of islands starting in the north. To get there I took the bus from Glasgow to the harbour of Ullapool in NW Scotland and from there with the ferry across the Minch to Stornoway on Lewis. Stornoway is the largest town on the Outer Hebrides and is situated on Lewis and Harris, the largest island. The town lies sheltered from the Atlantic gales on the east side of the island and has a pleasant and inviting appearance with its many trees, well-tended gardens and diverse architecture. However, the island itself is almost totally treeless and looks very stark and barren. The island name, Harris, may well be Basque because it appears agglutinated from harri-is, *harri – istinga*, rock – bog, which is a good description of this "rock and bog" island.

During a day spent touring the island, I visited a broch and the standing stones of Callanish, which is an imposing Bronze Age monument, and obviously of great significance to our pre-Christian ancestors. There are several more-or-less complete stone circles and standing stones in the vicinity of Callanish but we know next to nothing about the function of any of them. Some young men were busy at work with large crystals dangling from strings, testing the stones and the soil on a grid system all over the area of the ancient monument, claiming to measure "the earth radiation" in different spots, and recording the signals they received. I have to admit total ignorance of what it was they were doing. However, one never knows what comes out of such studies, so I will keep an open mind. The funny thing was that these people seemed to feel the same way about what I was doing there. Every little creature has its pleasure here on earth.

Back in Stornoway I meandered through the pleasant and very clean town centre and found a little bookshop tucked away in a corner where I explained the reason for my visit to the store keeper, who recommended that I buy Anthony Jackson's book "The Symbol Stones of Scotland." After Aulestia's Basque dictionary, this became the second most important book in my quest for the pre-Christian language of Scotland, and contributed a great deal to the content of my own articles and subsequent discoveries in archaeo-linguistics. In '*Symbol Stones*' Jackson devoted a chapter to the Pictish Ogam inscriptions which he said "are quite meaningless and have given rise to the belief that the Picts spoke some unknown tongue." Some linguists had even suggested that this tongue was Basque, and I had the Basque dictionary with me, so I took Jackson's comments as a challenge and decided to see if I could make sense out of this fascinating and often very carefully carved script called Ogam, which had been entirely new to me. It was my study of the Ogam script which eventually led to the discovery that all highly evolved languages on earth, with the possible exception of Chinese, had been invented by scholarly priest/linguists, living centuries, even thousands of years ago.

The Trip To Barra

Having done a typical tourist sweep of the Isle of Lewis, I was ready to start walking south. There was no possibility of getting lost because there was only one main road down the isles, and well-signed, even if it was very narrow in places. A short distance west of the downtown area of Stornoway, the main road divides, one going west to Callanish and the other south to the Isle of Uist (pronounced: you-ist) and on. After walking for over an hour along that quite straight and level road skirting many lakes, the barren scenery became quite boring with little to be gained for the time spent. The country looked so dreary and unproductive, yet at the same time had obviously been populated for such an incredibly long time, that it made me wonder what the attraction had been for the early settlers, who had had the pick of the best soils in all of western Europe, waiting to be occupied, yet had chosen this gloomy wind-swept chunk of rock. There had to be a reason for this.

Walking was not getting me anywhere fast so I decided to do some hitch-hiking, then at least I had someone to talk to. It seemed like almost everyone was interested in picking up a lone stranger, because they wanted to know what on earth that old fellow with his big back pack was doing walking along the empty road. A car took me to a small but very pleasant little place called Tarbert. It is not located at the south end of the island but it is the main ferry harbour for traveling south. After I spent a few hours looking around, the ferry came and took me through a maze of small islands to Loch Maddy on North Uist. Overnight in a very nice B&B (bed and breakfast) and the next day walking again until a Royal Air Force technician gave me a ride to the Isle of Benbecula. Before getting there I had expected to have to take another ferry to get to the Isle of Benbecula but instead a long causeway had been built between the islands. Several military jets screaming low overhead told me that I was near the large air force base. The island has some Bronze Age standing stones and other monuments, which seem totally out of place in this incredibly noisy jet-age environment. The name **Benbecula** may be broken down into:

ben – be – eku – ula
benta – begirune – ekuru – ulatu
inn – courteous – peaceful – to welcome
"Courteous, peaceful and welcoming inn."

Where this inn would have been located I have no idea. Leaving the Isle of Benbecula there was another long causeway through large mud-flats and the driver took me onto the Isle of South Uist. Then followed a long road to the harbour at Loch Boisdale. I had been told that the ferry was to leave at 4 PM, but that turned out to be the next day. However there was a small, private, somewhat cheaper, passenger ferry from the Isle of Eriskay which left the same day from nearby Ludag for my final destination, the Isle of Barra, which loomed very high in the distance. We left at 4:30 P.M. to go to the north tip of the Isle of Barra, a boat landing called Eoligarri. I had finally arrived at the island of Odysseus and Kirke and what a very different impression it presented from the other stark Hebridean islands to the north.

THE BARRA OF MY DREAMS

Here was the island I had longed so much to see ever since I had heard Furlong's talk. The island where Odysseus and the priestess Kirke had met and had loved each other. The moment I stepped ashore it felt to me like holy ground. Close to the small ferry dock was the very ancient Kille Barra cemetery which used to have a tall stone with a long Ogam inscription, now in the museum in Edinburgh. Just to the north were the ruins of the large corpse-exposure facility of Ben Scurrival, used in pre-Christian days for primary burial. Compared to the islands to the north, Barra was definitely mountainous. It appeared quite prosperous, and was more densely populated with a busy road. There was no desolate feeling here, or wondering what on earth people were doing in this place.

No bus met the little ferry, but even though I started out walking without thumbing, a car soon stopped to offer me a ride, which I gladly accepted. The driver was most accommodating and told me about some of the sights, among others about the large tidal flat east of the road which doubled as the airport for Barra. It is used by the only scheduled airline in Europe which flies according to tidal tables. I asked my host about the early history of the island and was told that nothing was known before the coming of Christian missionaries, in spite of the many large stone monuments. My first impression of this incredible island was astonishment. This place had had a long and interesting history for many thousands of years associated with the ocean, and the people didn't know about it. The ones I talked to didn't even want to know because to them history started with the coming of Christianity and later the Vikings. Everything before that was pagan, and apparently not worth knowing. Even the executive of the historical society which I met later, thought that way. The short trip to the main town Castlebay took four different rides. It is a marvelous little town looking south over a large and deep harbour, which has an ancient castle apparently floating in the middle, hence the name of the town. Exploring this most interesting place had to wait. My driver dropped me off at an old couple's house which they operated as a bed-and-breakfast place and I was lucky to arrive in time for supper. I had arrived on the isle of my dreams and my first impressions had been most encouraging. My visit to this island will remain with me for the rest of my days. It was here in the bed-and-breakfast home of Theresa McCormick that I laid the foundation for the writing and research which would keep me occupied for many years to come and result in the production of two books.

Contemplating The Ogam Script

The next day my first trip was up the mountain behind Castlebay, which Homer had called Mount Neritos, from *neri* (to me) *tosta* (rowers bench), "to me it is a rowers bench." It was a stiff hike, and indeed, when I reached the top, I saw that there were two tops which had a smoothly shaped saddle in between, slightly oversized for a person. As Homer had written, the sea was all around and I took the necessary pictures to prove it. With my back against a rock and looking out over Castlebay I re-read the passage in the Odyssey which applied to Barra. Before I walked back down, I followed a trail into the steep hills to the north, but then clouds moved in and rain was threatening, so I fled back to the safety of my cozy B&B. Had a meal at the hotel in Castlebay and walked home in the rain. The travelling of the last days and the hike up the mountain had tired me out, so when I came home at 4 PM I fell sound asleep on Mrs. McCormick's couch. When I woke up, the rain was coming down in buckets and it was a good time to start reading my newly acquired book about the Symbol Stones of Scotland and the Ogam script (p.174-182).

Looking at those simple chicken scratches, arranged along a centre line, the Ogam script looked like nothing could be done with them, just like Dr. Anthony Jackson had said. However, he had been able to transliterate them because the letters of the Ogam script were known, but the result was just as unintelligible.

Remembering how I had decoded the word Laistrygonian, I tried the same thing here and looked for an inscription which was undamaged and well legible, and settled on Jackson's #19, called the Lunasting stone, located in the northern Shetlands islands The script was divided by three colons into four parts, which I presumed were four sentences. Jackson transliterated:

ETTECUHETTS : AHEHHTTANNN : HCCVVEVV : NEHHTONN

Now what was anybody going to make out of this jumble of consonants with a few vowels scattered in between? Yet, there had to be a meaning because the inscription had been carefully engraved and had remained legible for some 1500 years, exposed to the extreme vagaries of the Shetland weather. That kind of care and durability had to convey some sort of meaning. Jackson gave the letters numerical values and had detected some interesting mathematics in the totals, based on prime numbers, which could not have happened at random. The failure of linguists to make sense out of the 'writing,' had made him decide that there was no meaning to the writing, just a cabalistic text of numbers intended to overcome the powerful pre-Christian magic of the priestess. I could not accept this because I had the feeling that 1) there was an encoding formula hidden in the four 'sentences' and 2) the linguists had used Celtic which was the wrong language. It became my challenge to prove that this language was Basque.

There are indeed some languages which are written entirely without vowels, such as Hebrew and old Egyptian. However, it had not been difficult to find the missing vowels in Hebrew writing, because the oral law, called Talmud, had been codified and memorized for millennia and this oral record had provided the missing vowels for most Hebrew words. But the Ogam script was different; I had never seen a language which had removed most of the vowels in such a strangely haphazard manner resulting in many paired consonants. There had to be a trick to the Ogam puzzle. Could it be that a system of encoding was involved which had left only the most essential vowels to allow decoding of the text? If this were true all consonants were needed, but only a limited number of vowels was required and a formula to tie it all together. The hidden text would have been intended for some educated initiates only, probably Christian monks.

Many linguists had tried to make sense of the letters, but all had given up, except one or two who had detected Basque in the jumble, such as Henry Guiter, a Basque scholar from France. His translations had not impressed anyone and Guiter became the laughing stock of those who had failed. But I had already determined that Basque had to be the pre-Christian language of Scotland although this did not necessarily mean that Ogam was written in Basque. But I had at my disposal the best Basque dictionary ever written, which was reassuring. So I started filling in vowels experimentally between the consonants. As I had been unable to conceive of a system in which only one consonant could express a whole word, I assumed at first that two consonants were required and I tried to make up different words by filling in the spaces, between the known consonants, with the five vowels. My new dictionary had a great work-out, but it led nowhere. I worked on this till after midnight, had wasted a lot of paper and wore out two pens, then fell into bed exhausted from concentration. My first effort was a total failure, or so I thought, but I was not ready to give up. One hasn't failed until one quits trying.

Undaunted Onward

The next day was May 30, 1992. The morning sky was brilliantly blue and the islands in the distance were unusually clear and calling me, but the Ogam puzzle had taken a solid grip on my soul. Back to my little B&B table to contemplate the stubborn double consonants and their frustrating missing vowels. Again I filled in vowels between the consonants, then took the Basque dictionary to see if some of it made sense. This day I decided to see what would show up if I assumed that one consonant with its flanking vowels could represent one full word. Again back and forth, back and forth from brain wave to dictionary, systematically exploring all possibilities. Another day of fruitlessly searching possible Basque letter combinations, this time till 2 in the morning. I was just about to give up when I thought of attempting to decode the name of the place where the stone was found: Lunasting. If Homer's Laistrygonian could be decoded, why not Lunasting? The name could be separated into a number of different syllable combinations but, having attained more experience with Basque, I tried the most logical sounding combination first:

.lu – una – asti – ing.
alu – una – asti – ingu
alu – unagarri – aztiatu – inguraldi
stupid – boring – superstitious – place
"A stupid boring superstitious place."

Now that sounded encouraging. The monk who had been there and called it a stupid boring superstitious place could not have been made very welcome, probably because the old religion was still alive and well in that part of the world when he visited there. But take a good look at the way the VCVs in the second line are connected! The vowels on either side of the hyphens are the same. Could that be the feature of the formula which tied the apparently scattered or unconnected character of the letters together? A descriptive term 'vowel-interlocking' came to mind, which I have used ever since. The names of the Odyssey and the geographical names of the west coast had not been so carefully agglutinated in this manner, therefore the consistent, formulaic vowel interlocking could have been a characteristic of the missionaries who brought Christianity to Ireland, probably from North Africa. My second day of searching ended on the same note as the first one: mentally exhausted but a bit happier.

Light At The End Of The Tunnel

Sunday May 31, 1992. After a good sleep and hearty breakfast I went back to the grindstone at the little table for the third day and somehow, quite unexpected, results started to come. I had decided to switch tactics and to examine an inscription which contained more vowels than the others and selected the **Burrian** stone:

IDBMIRRHANNURRACTEEVVCERROCCS.

If Lunasting followed a vowel-interlocking rule, maybe the inscription designer had used the same system. But Basque has no C or V, so first these had to be replaced with K and B respectively:

IDBMIRRHANNURRAKTEEBBKERROKKS

First I filled in the vowel 'A' between D, B and M and obtained IDABAM which didn't make any sense, but then I tried IDEBAM and suddenly a light appeared: 'ide' are the first letters of *ideki* (to open) and 'eba' *Ebanjelio* (Gospel); in other words I had obtained: **"Open the Gospel."** That was a logical thing to say and something every missionary would do. He was bringing a new religion to a long established population and I felt my first apparent success could be a promising start. But what then? It took several hours to make some sense out of the entire inscription using trial and error and the vowel-interlocking rule throughout, but then I felt I had obtained something that made good sense. No two consonants apparently were allowed together, a missing vowel had to be recovered between every two consonants. Only Basque words starting with VCV had been used. In the spot of every missing vowel I placed a dot as follows:

ID.B.MIR.R.HAN.NUR.RAK.TEEB.B.KER.ROK.K.S

then parted into VCVs:

ID. – .B. – .MI – IR. – .R. – .HA – AN. – .NU – UR. – .RA – AK. – .TE – EE – EB. – .B. – .KE – ER. – .RO – OK. – .K. – .S.

id.	ide	*ideki*	to open
.b.	eba	*ebanjelio*	Gospel
.mi	ami	*amildu*	to oust
ir.	iru	*iruzurkeria*	false belief
.r.	ure	*urreraketa*	drawing closer
.ha	eha	*eha*	(emphasis) wonderful
an.	ano	*ano*	nourishment
.nu	onu	*onuste*	good faith
ur.	uri	*urrikalmendu*	mercy
.ra	ira	*irakatzi*	sermon
ak.	aka	*akatsbako*	perfect/pure
.te	ate	*aterpe*	refuge
ee	ee	*ee*	to call, to pay attention
eb.	eba	*ebanjelari*	evangelist
.b.	abi	*abiatu*	to begin
.ke	ike	*ikertaldi*	visit
er.	ere	*errezibimendu*	welcome
.ro	ero	*eroan*	to suffer
ok.	oke	*okerbidetu*	gone astray
.k.	eka	*ekarri*	to bring
as.	aska	*askamen*	freedom

My first translation therefore read:

Open the Gospel book to oust false beliefs and get closer to the wonderful nourishment of good faith and mercy. Hear the perfect sermon in our refuge and pay attention to the evangelist who begins his welcome visit. He will bring freedom to those who are suffering and gone astray.

Life in the strictly controlled community structure of the pre-Christian religion wasn't all happiness, as few tightly disciplined families are, and the evangelist had exploited the feelings of the disgruntled, promising the considerable personal freedom which the early Irish church promoted. It looked like success was smiling on me, but I still had the lumpy cobwebs of many hours of trial and error on my brain so I decided I deserved a long hike the next day. I went to bed very pleased with myself.

Doubts Appear

The next morning I looked over what I had concocted the previous day, but now I was not nearly as happy with the results as before. Would it really be possible to extract whole sentences from a few scattered letters carved 1500 years ago on rock? The system I had developed looked frail and it seemed to me that it could well be shot full of holes by anyone who took the time to try his own luck with it. The possibilities appeared to be so numerous that surely I could make the inscription say just about anything I put my mind to, or could I? The process would need many more successful translations to get experience, followed by a total review, looking for ways to tighten up and explain the decoding and translation system. I decided to get a good day of fresh air before testing the system I had stumbled onto. In the following chapters I'll show that my – at first aimless – journey was no longer aimless. But the fascinating consequences of what I was finding had not penetrated yet. That was to come slowly from studying the origins of many different languages. After I returned home to Canada the real work started and the results are shown in the following pages.

II

THE EARLY CHRISTIAN OGAM SCRIPT

WHAT IS OGAM?

INTRODUCTION

Ogam is the oldest form of writing in Ireland. It can still be seen inscribed on hundreds of large and small stones, on the walls of some caves, but also on bone, ivory, bronze and silver objects. The Ogam script was especially well adapted for use on sticks which were used to be carved with messages written in Ogam. Sticks are part of the Basque word for "alphabet": *agaka*, agglutinated from *aga-aka*, *aga* (stick or pole) and *akats* (notch). The meaning of the word *agaka* therefore isn't so much "alphabet" as "writing," a stick with Ogam notches conveying a message. The name Ogam likely comes from *oga-ama*, *ogasun* (property, wealth) *ama* (Priestess, mother), "property of the Priestess," which indicates that the script may originally have been designed for use by the clergy of the pre-Christian religion.

Ogam is likely to have originated in Libya, whence the first Gnostic missionaries are thought to have come. It was adopted and further developed by the first (Gnostic) monks in Ireland around 350 A.D. Our earliest written information indicates that they were not sure as to where Ogam came from. According to the Benedictines' "Auraicept" the origin of Irish and Ogam must be sought in the Near East: "In Dacia it was invented, though others say it was in the Plain of Shinar" (line 1105-06). A "made in Ireland" version is recorded in "In Lebor Ogaim" in which the inventor is "Ogma mac Elathan who is said to have been skilled in speech and poetry and to have created the system as proof of his intellectual ability and with the intention that it should be the preserve of the learned, to the exclusion of rustics and fools" (McManus 8.4). The script was used by the Gnostic monks as a monument script between 400 and 800 A.D. and the succeeding Roman Catholic Benedictines used it for literary purposes between ca 700 and 900 A.D. on paper and vellum. For every time the script was inscribed in stone it must have been used thousands of times on sticks, the medium for which the script was obviously designed. Over 600 Ogam inscriptions are known from Ireland (collected by R.A.S. Macalister), some 30 from Scotland (A. Jackson) and a growing number from the east coast of North America. The fact that not a single one had been successfully translated was not so much the fault of the monks who wrote the texts, as of our linguists, all of whom assumed that the language of the script was Gaelic. However, this assumption was totally without foundation, because the syntax of the Gaelic language in no way lends itself to be written in traditional Ogam. In fact, the Gaelic language did not exist when the first inscriptions were made.

Prof. Damien McManus, at Trinity College, Dublin, suggested that the Ogam script had its origin in the scoring of the tally stick, a knife cut for each count, a V for five scores, etc. From this simple beginning the system was only an inventor's step away from writing. However, Carney guessed that it was likely developed "in an area where Romans, Celts and Germans were in contact and was brought into being by political or military necessity. Its purpose could be to send messages, probably on sticks, which, if intercepted could not be read or interpreted." That begs the question: Why did the evangelists in Ireland and Scotland go to all that trouble to inscribe so many hundreds of stones with religious texts and other information, if only a few literate monks could read them? Were the inhabitants really as illiterate as we have been told over and over? Or could it be that it was the magic, built into the inscription, which was the most important feature?

It would appear that the true origin of Ogam must be sought much earlier than 400 A.D. In her monumental book, "The Language of the Goddess," Marija Gimbutas describes the Ogam-like "Old European Script" the earliest evidence of which she dates at 5300 B.C. (p.308). It appears therefore that the Ogam script has gone through a very long period of evolution. It may well be that all the authors who suggested origins for Ogam were right, that all the places mentioned and all the different uses over the ages played a role in the development of the script. Whatever its early history, the form of the Ogam script we know today is certainly of Irish origin.

The Ogam pages which make up this chapter include a large inscription found in West Virginia U.S.A., as well as a growing number from Ireland and Scotland. The variety of topics inscribed on the Irish stones is quite astonishing and a sampling is provided. Most of the Scottish inscriptions are made by Christian missionaries using the ancient script to convert the worshipers of the ancient Goddess religion to Christianity. There are indeed Ogam grave stone inscriptions in Ireland but they appear to be in the minority. Most relate to the evangelical efforts by the monks and none display names.

To recap, it is my opinion that the Ogam script originated in Libya or Egypt, was then taken by the monks to Ireland where it was given the form we know today. The only language capable of being written in the Ogam script is Basque, because it requires words which start with VCV (vowel-consonant-vowel) which only Basque possesses; otherwise the required vowel interlocking rule could not be satisfied. The Ogam writing found in the eastern United States appears to be of the Libyan type. At the same time that these inscriptions were made, Libya was conquered by the army of the Four Khalifs who brought Islam to this formerly Christian country. Many occupants fled to Ireland where they may have been shown the way to North America.

Translating Ogam

The Ogam Alphabet

There is a tradition in North Africa that St. Patrick was dispatched from Libya to Ireland to evangelize. Our traditional knowledge tells us that Patrick came from England, but this information came via the Benedictines whose task it was to distort and re-write as much as possible of the pre-R.C. Irish legends. As most of the Ogam writings are Gnostic-Christian in nature, it very likely that Gnostic missionaries came from Libya, not the continent of Europe, and preached the early Irish Christianity which was very different from the Judeo-Christianity of the Benedictines. These Irish monks believed in magic, just as the pre-Christian inhabitants of Ireland did. Anthony Jackson (1993) discovered that their magic took the shape of numerical wizardry with letters. The Gnostic missionaries used the script to spread the Gospel by carving Biblical phrases on standing stones, erected during the Neolithic or earlier, to convert the people from their ancient Goddess religion to Christianity. Around 650 A.D. Benedictine monks and their grammarians came to Ireland with biblical instructions (Genesis 11:7) to create a distinct language to replace the highly developed "iron" language of the Irish, which they called Cruithin. They adopted Ogam but found it necessary to augment the early alphabetic script with some diphthong characters, called Forfeda (see below) and further develop it to accommodate the linguistic and literary activities they had in mind. There is no doubt that these Benedictines and their grammarians were linguistic professionals in the very best tradition.

The Ogam alphabet, as it is known to us today, is composed of 15 consonants followed by five vowels. This is the only alphabet known which organizes consonants and vowels in this manner. The Benedictines' operation manual, the "Auraicept," parts of which appear to have been written as early as 700 A.D., in the very early years of Irish Judeo-Christianity, described the Ogam alphabet as follows (translation by Calder).

> *This is their number: five Ogmic groups, i.e., five men for each group, and one up to five for each of them, that their signs may be distinguished. These are their signs: right of stem, left of stem, athwart of stem, through stem, about stem. Thus is a tree climbed, to wit, treading on the root of the tree first with thy right hand first and thy left hand after. Then with the stem, and against it and through it and about it.* (Lines 947-951).

Prof. Damien McManus clarified this:

> *"This is their number: there are five groups of Ogam and each group has five letters and each of them has from one to five scores and their orientations distinguish them. Their orientations are: right of the stemline, left of the stemline, across the stemline, through the stemline, around the stemline. Ogam is climbed as a tree is climbed..."* (McManus 1.5).

By the time the fifth column of Forfeda symbols had been added, the script was written horizontally, from left to right but the above quote still appears to record the original way of vertical writing, read from the bottom up. I am showing the original 20 symbols in both the original vertical as well as the later horizontal way of writing. Most of the early inscriptions on stone in Scotland and Ireland are written in the vertical form. The Ogam texts in books such as the Auraicept and on the petroglyphs in West Virginia are written in the horizontal literary tradition. At first sight the peculiar arrangement of the letters in the Ogam alphabet appears to be completely unrelated to the pre-existing Greek and Latin alphabets. McManus searched elsewhere for the origin and found that "there is a clear connection with the North Etruscan alphabets." Anthropologist Anthony Jackson from Edinburgh University, however, discovered that the arrangement was directly related to the ordinal numbers of the letters in the Latin alphabet:

1	2	3	4	5	6	7	8	9	10	11	12	13	14	15	16	17	18	19	20
A	B	C	D	E	V	G	H	I	Z	L	M	N	O	NG	Q	R	S	T	U

The total of the ordinal numbers in the Latin alphabet is 210. The 20 original Ogam characters were divided into four columns, which, arranged according to a cabalistic system of calculation, totaled 50, 50, 61 and 49 respectively:

```
N   13  +  Q   16  =  (1x29)          R   17  +  I    9   =  (2x13)      5x11
S   18  +  C    3  =  (3x7)           Z   10  +  E    5   =  (3x5)       3x3x4
V    6  +  T   19  =  (5x5)           NG  15  +  U   20   =  (5x7)       3x4x5
L   11  +  D    4  =  (3x5)           G    7  +  O   14   =  (3x7)       3x3x4
B    2  +  H    8  =  (2x5)           M   12  +  A    1   =  (1x13)      1x23
    ___        ___      ___               ___        ___       ___        ___

    50  +      50  =  100                 61  +      49   =  110        210
  10x5        10x5   (10x10)            1x61        7x7     (10x11)    2x3x5x7
```

BLVSN / HDTCQ / MGNGZR / AOUEI.

The sequence of the letters within each column appears to be in relation to the primary numbers, however, the calculations go beyond the scope of this article. The interested reader is referred to Jackson's monograph, chapter 7.

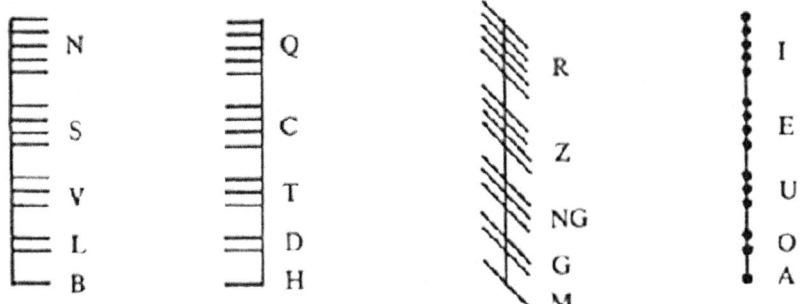

As you will have noticed, there are several letters missing from the Latin alphabet shown above: F, J, K, P, X and Y. The same letters are missing from the newly re-arranged Ogam alphabet. This probably means that the linguist who designed the Ogam alphabet was selective in choosing only those Latin letters which made the cabalistic calculations and arrangement possible. The V had replaced the B and the F; the I replaced the J and Y; the C and Q replaced the K; the B, a labial, took the place of P (also a labial), the character X was used for the Ogam diphthong EA, but in the Ogam script sometimes is written as KS. It is interesting to note that Q-Celtic has no F, J or P. Neither is there a P in Arabic. Only a few words in Basque start with F, which letter may be a quite recent addition to this language; the V, C, Y and Q still do not exist in Basque, and the Basque X represents "sh."

Written horizontally:

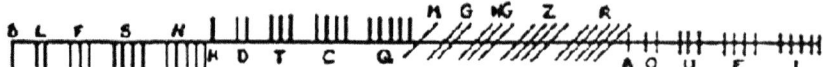

Note that the "f" in the horizontal script should be a "v," the same as it is in the vertical script.

The reason why all 15 consonants are listed first in the alphabet and the 5 vowels following, has to do with the special arrangement of the words in the monks' dictionary. The primary organization of their dictionary is according to the consonants. Half of the Basque language is made up of words starting with vowel-consonant-vowel (VCV, called a morpheme) and it is mainly this half of the language which the monks used in the construction of the Romance languages and English. These words were then arranged according to the consonants in the words, each consonant was then subdivided again into 25 VCV combinations such as under D: ada, ade, adi, ado, adu; eda, ede, edi, edo, edu; ida, ide... etc. Under each such VCV were then listed all those words with their translations which started with these three letters. This arrangement is still the best way for us to decode Ogam writing.

From this it must be obvious that such a special arrangement applies only to a language which is organized in the VCV manner and Basque is the only language which fits the mold. **The syntax of modern Irish (i.e. Gaelic or Celtic) is totally unsuited to this VCV system and consequently this language cannot be written in traditional Irish Ogam.** All Ogam writing anywhere must have been in the Basque language, which means that the "iron" language of pre-Roman-Catholic Ireland was the universal language we call Saharan or Basque today. This explains why "Celtic" scholars have been unable to translate even one single Ogam inscription correctly.

FORFEDA

The Forfeda revision made by the Benedictines, the addition of the five extra diphthong characters, was almost certainly accomplished in Ireland. Ogam was originally designed for record keeping and the sending of short messages, not for literary expression. However, this is what the Benedictine monks of Ireland were using it for. One of the main "reasons for being" of the Benedictine Order was the replacement of the ancient pre-Christian, gylanic oriented, language with a church-approved one. The syntax of the Basque language was ideally suited – and indeed designed – for the agglutination of new words, which then appeared to have no relationship to the original language. The VCV formula made this possible. However, traditions governing this ancient formula did not allow two vowels to be written side-by side without a space separation, which demanded separate words. This rule created problems and restrictions for those writing in the script. As the monks wished to simplify the rules of writing, they created words and names with diphthongs in them, by the invention of five new "Forfeda" characters permitting the combination of: ea, oi, ui, io and ae, the use of which then also allowed these to be part of the creation of new words starting with eha, ohi, uhi, iho and ahe. The design of the characters they created was totally out of style with the original script. McManus observed that they "missed the opportunity of completing the symmetry of the system by having the fifth series mirror the third in the way that the second mirrors the first" (McManus 1.2).

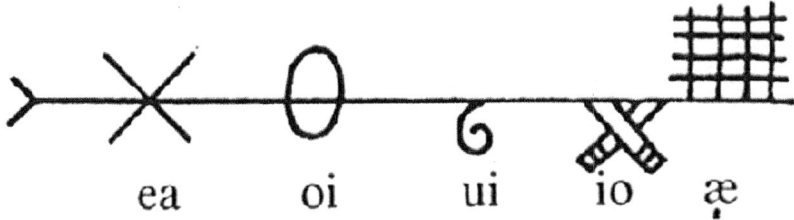

Now let us look at what the name "forfeda" really means. The monks obviously were not very happy to be forced to use the "heretical" Ogam script, but had nothing quite as ingenious, concise and useful to replace it with, until they had invented their new Irish language. In the following analysis of "Forfeda," the first "f" has to be a "b," a common letter shift; (the second "f" is correct).

It seems that the X character for 'ea,' was already in existence before the Benedictines reached Ireland, because this symbol is found in the Ogam inscriptions in the eastern U.S.A., e.g., the Horse Creek petroglyph. These inscriptions are thought to have been made around 600 A.D. How the words were selected from the choice available is explained below.

FORFEDA,.bo-or.-.fe-eda;

.bo	ebo	*eboluzionatu*	to develop, evolve, expand
or.	ori	*ori*	that
.fe	ife	*ifernuko*	damned, infernal
eda	eda	*edabe*	potion, fabrication

Develop that infernal fabrication!

Notice how the word "forfeda" breaks up into four three-letter VCV roots, ebo-ori-ife-eda, each composed of vowel-consonant-vowel (VCV), with the vowels interlocking to form a chain of interdependent roots. This interlocking is the main characteristic of Ogam writing, is basic to all Ogam inscriptions and is indispensable in deciphering. Any missing (purposely removed) vowels in the words analyzed, are represented by a dot until identified. Forfeda symbols are never eliminated. The monks later embellished this word to "Foirfeadha," to make it look as if the word had originated with the awkward "Celtic" language, which is characterized by an excess of unnecessary vowels and h's. Some remarks in the Auraicept pertain to the creation of Forfeda characters such as:

IN LEBOR OGAIM. in.-.le-ebo-oro-oga-ahi-im.; (5465 etc)

in.	ina	*inauguratu*	to innovate
.le	ale	*aleǵiñez*	carefully
ebo	ebo	*eboluzionatu*	to develop
oro	oro	*orobateko*	similar
oga	oga	*oǵasun*	wealth
a.i	ahi	*ahituezin*	timeless
im.	imi	*imitazio*	character

Innovate by carefully developing a similar wealth of timeless characters.

(Note: there is no break in the interlocking vowels, even though the text is broken into three "words."

STEPS IN TRANSLATION

Ogam decoding requires the following steps:

Step 1. Transliterate the Ogam characters into our Latin letters,

Step 2. Replace the letters c, q, v, w, y with equivalent Basque letters, c and q become k, v becomes b, the y becomes i.

Step 3. Arrange these corrected letters into the VCVCV format, placing dots where vowels are missing,

Step 4. Fit these letters into the VCV formula,

Step 5. List the various meanings underneath each VCV,

Step 6. Arrange the hidden sentence.

The best way to explain the process is with a few examples of real Ogam inscriptions, starting with an inscription which has only one vowel missing:

"cunovato"

(Macalister #11.)

Step 1. The middle part of the inscription was damaged, but after careful study Dr. Jost Gippert at Frankfurt University decided that it should read:

"cunavato"

Step 2. All Ogams in Ireland are based on the Basque language, however, Basque does not have a "C" or a "V," so the inscription will now read

"kunabato"

Step 3. When fitting the letters in the VCVCVCVCV format, it appears that only one, the first vowel, is missing, which must therefore be represented by a dot. The inscription to be translated now reads:

".kunabato"

Step 4. There are four consonants so this VCVCVCVCV line is then broken up by hyphens into four three-letter VCV's in which the V's on either side of the hyphens are the same (called interlocking): VCV_1-V_1CV_2-V_2CV_3-V_3CV, which therefore represents four words:

.ku-una-aba-ato

Step 5. With the preliminaries out of the way, the next step in decoding an Ogam inscription is to list the possible meanings underneath each VCV. In the case of the one missing vowel, all five possibilities must be tried (aku, eku, iku, oku, uku) as follows:

(aku)	una	aba	ato
to incite	boredom	priest	tow
to stimulate	annoyance	occasion	tug boat
to rent, lease	cowherd	slingshot	to arrange
acoustics	fatigue	advantage	to seize
(eku)	dull	rower	embellish
equator, worried		almost	to solve
peace of mind		shade	come!
(iku)		branches	
shirt			
to touch, to visit			
flag, motto, watchful			
(oku)			
fertile field			
(uku)			
stable, falsify			
go bad, smelly			

Step 6. To discover the hidden or occluded sentence we must match up the words which obviously belong together, starting with the complete VCV's. For instance take the pair **aba** and **ato** and immediately out pops **priest** and **come!**, "the priest says: Come!" Why would he say come!? "To stimulate" (**aku**) your "boredom" (**una**). The translation of CUNAVATO therefore is:

"The priest will stimulate your boredom; come!" The completed words are: *akuilatu* (to stimulate) *unadora* (boredom) *abade* (priest) *ator!* (Come!) That is exactly what one would expect a missionary to say, it's his job.

Occasionally more than one reasonable meaning appears in which case we have a problem. Lay this work aside and return to it later; often new insight will be obtained and the proper translation decided upon. In the following pages you will see hundreds of decodings, and will learn that applying the VCV formula is not an exact science. But guessing the mood of the monk, who made up the word, can be fun because some of the grammarians had a sense of humour. Decoding Ogam may not be an exact science, but it works in most cases.

A second example.

Now I will decode an Ogam inscription which has two vowels missing (Macalister # 364):

Step 1. barcuni

Step 2. barkuni

Step 3. .bar.kuni

Step 4. .ba-ar.-.ku-uni

Step 5. Three VCV's have a vowel missing. Each of those represents five VCV's e.g. **.ba** can be **aba, eba, iba, oba** or **uba**.

Go to the VCV dictionary and list the possible meanings under each of these five VCV's. Do the same with **.ar** and **.ku**

The last one, uni, is complete and only has a few possible meanings.

Step 6. When assembling the sentence built into the inscription, keep in mind who the people were that carved it. The words that pop out immediately are "evangelist" and "priest" under **eba**, which goes together with "prayer" under **are**: "the evangelist's prayers." What do they do? They give peace of mind, under **eku**. The sentence therefore reads: **"The evangelist's prayers (give you) general peace of mind."** The four words completed are then: *ebanjelari* (evangelist) *arren* (prayer) *ekurutasun* (peace of mind) *unibertsal* (general).

A third example.

My third example is considerably larger and will therefore be presented in a different manner, which has the disadvantage of not being able to show how the missing vowel is recovered, but this is difficult to avoid.

Step 1.

Bladnach cogradedena
and
Bladnach cuilen

(McManus, p. 132). Macalister #1086, 1949, shows the second word as Cogracetena, which is incorrect. Both inscriptions are found on a bronze hanging bowl, likely an incense burner, dug up from a swamp in County Kerry. "They are inscribed along the upper surface of the rim and on one of the escutcheons." (McManus 7.6)

Step 2. Bladnak kogradedena and **Bladnak kuilen.**

Step 3. .B.lad.nak. .kog.radedena and **.B.lad.nak. .kuilen**

Step 4. .B.-.la-ad.-.na-ak. .ko-og.-.ra-ade-ede-ena, and
.B.-.la-ad.-.na-ak. .ku-ile-en.

Step 5. This time I place the given VCV's along the left border:

Bladnak:

.B.	abe	*abe*	cross
.la	ela	*ela*	story
ad.	ade	*adelatu*	to prepare
.na	ena	*ena*	that
ak.	aka	*akabu*	ultimate, superior

kogradedena:

.ko	ako	*akorduan euki*	to remember
og.	ogi	*ogizatitze*	breaking of the bread
.ra	ira	*iragan*	to suffer
ade	ade	*adelatu*	to prepare
ede	ede	*edergi*	to confide in
dena	dena	*Deuna*	Lord

Step 6. The story of the Cross prepares us for that ultimate remembrance while preparing for the breaking of the bread (for His) suffering (while we) confide in the Lord.

kuilen:

.ku	eku	*ekurutasun*	peace of mind
ile	ile	*ilezin*	everlasting
en.	ene	*eneganatu*	to come over me

The story of the cross prepares me for that ultimate everlasting peace of mind (which will) come over me.

Some Additional Remarks

All words and many names in any invented language have known meanings. This is not the case with the words written in Ogam script and this fact does not make the job of decoding any easier. Also, no effort was made to allow easy pronounciation. On the contrary, all ingenuity was aimed at insuring that the writing looked as awkward as possible so that only specialists would be able to interpret it. This disguising was done mostly by applying the VCV Code and the removal of vowels, as many as possible, following the example of Hebrew where often no vowels are left at all; such as the name Talmud (Oral Law) being written as "lmd," originally from Saharan/Basque "tala-muda," *tala* (watch out) *mudatu* (to alter): "watch out for alteration," or freely translated: "pass on unaltered," which is what an oral law is all about. The meaning of the word Talmud today has been accepted as something like "instruction."

In Scotland several of the Christian Ogams were inscribed aggressively over pre-existing animal- and geometrical symbols/totems which had been carved in the 7th century. These symbols organized marriages and other co-operative arrangements between groups of (usually) four tribes (Jackson) and ever since had been regarded with great respect by the population. The over-writing was probably done to destroy the "magical powers" of the "heathen" symbols. Deciphering the Ogams usually poses no real problem as long as the inscription is complete and legible.

Rating The Consonants

In analyzing Ogam inscriptions and names or words, especially those from which too many vowels have been removed, it may be helpful to know which consonants are easier to decode than others. I devised a rating system which I found helpful, but keep in mind that the Basque language uses some consonants that are different from the Ogam alphabet which has 15 in total. It involves writing down all the possible VCV combinations and then counting only those which are found in Aulestia's dictionary. For instance take "F":

afa	efa	*ifa*	ofa	*ufa*
afe	efe	*ife*	ofe	ufe
afi	efi	*ifi*	*ofi*	ufi
afo	efo	ifo	ofo	ufo
afu	efu	ifu	ofu	ufu

Out of the 25 VCV possibilities of "F," only the six italicized VCV's are the first letters of existing Basque words: afa (pleasing, supper), ifa (north), ife (infernal, hell), ifi (from ibi, to be, to go), ofi (craftsman, official), ufa (panting, blowing, scornful). The rating of the consonant "F" is therefore 6, making it the easiest of all letters to find meanings for. The ratings of all the consonants used in the Basque language are as follows:

F-6, J-9, X-10, Z-18, B-18, M-18, D-21, G-20, S-21,
K-22, L-23, N-23, P-22, T-22, H-24, R-24, RR-22.

The use of the letter "R" in the inscriptions poses somewhat of a problem because no distinction is made between "R" and "RR," each having its own set of 24 and 22 VCV combinations respectively. Also the large number of words associated with each combination of this letter make it sometimes difficult to select the appropriate word. The analysis of the "R" or "RR" is therefore usually kept to the last.

Inventing Languages is Old Hat

It has long been known that languages were being invented, Wittgenstein wrote: "Man possesses the capacity of constructing languages, in which every sense can be expressed, without having an idea how and what each word means – just as one speaks without knowing how the single sounds are produced" (Tractatus 4.002). And that is exactly what was done by the Benedictines and their grammarians when they made up the western European languages. Even all the names of their saints, clergy and monasteries were constructed without the uninitiated having the slightest idea what each name meant. By the time Darwin wrote his "Descent of Man" the language invention efforts had been forgotten because he commented: "No philologist now supposes that any language has been deliberately invented: it has been slowly and unconsciously developed by many steps." How soon we forget! This will be elaborated upon when I discuss the linguistic activities of the Benedictines in England.

Ogam Inscriptions
In Scotland

You Have Four Choices, Take Your Pick

From the following it becomes clear that academia is groping.

1) OGAM IS NUMERICAL, NOT LINGUISTIC.

In his book "The Symbol Stones of Scotland" (1984), Dr. Anthony Jackson, anthropologist at the University of Edinburgh, illustrated and transliterated more than thirty Ogam inscriptions found in Scotland and remarked that the best of efforts by linguists and others had not resulted in even one translation. There had been few problems transliterating them, but no one had been able to do anything with the "meaningless" series of letters obtained. In October of 1993, Jackson then followed this work up with a small edition monograph called "Pictish Symbol Stones?" in which he updated his earlier Ogam research. Probably referring to efforts like Henri Guiter's (see below), Jackson stated: **"There is a popular theory that they are Basque but this does not work either."** (p.118) Jackson also commented:

> *"It is curious that this small number of Ogam inscriptions has caused more headaches than all the other problems of the Picts put together. As one leading archaeologist put it: it is not really the fault of the Picts but the interpreters of the Picts that are to blame!* (p. 117)

This remark was so true, but Jackson decided to give up entirely on translating the puzzling writings and wrote:

> *"All research along linguistic lines has ground to a halt, unsurprisingly"* *(p.135) and: "It is clear that the Ogam inscriptions are numerically based and not linguistic"* (p.153)

in other words, he thought they were numerical magic, possibly a form of numerology, inscribed on the ancient standing stones to overcome the pre-Christian magic: **"thus we seem to have a battle between rival magics"** (p. 154). I agree with his suggestion that magic is involved, because the inscriptions are so complicated in design that it is hard to believe that they were intended to be read by the common people or even by most of the clergy. They belonged to a very different level of theology.

2) OGAM IS BASQUE WRITING

In 1968 a Basque scholar from France, **Henri Guiter**, thought he could see Basque words in the transliterated inscriptions and tried to make sense of some of them. He published two papers in French, which received mixed reviews such as from **Oliver Padel** who could not find the first paper, but **"if one is to judge by the information supplied in the second, this is no great loss."** Another person who criticized Guiter was Douglas Gifford, Dept. of Spanish of St. Andrew's University in Scotland. In a radio talk he said that Guiter had twisted the evidence, but also suggested that the Basque connection was worth a further look. I have now taken this 'further look' and decided to include Guiter's work in this article because his approach was so very different from anyone else's. The reader will see that his translations appear to make little sense. The people who composed the inscriptions were a great deal more sophisticated linguistically and mathematically than our modern scholars have ever given them credit for. Guiter's effort had also been published in Spanish in a book called "Garaldea" (Basque for 'the high country') by Federico Krutwig and the Spanish translations of Guiter's effort are shown in this chapter.

3) OGAM IS WRITTEN IN OLD NORSE

Another approach was taken by Richard A.V. Cox, lecturer at Aberdeen University in the Department of Celtic. He decided that 17 of the Scottish Ogam inscriptions were written in Old West Scandinavian, commonly known as Old Norse (1050 – 1350).

> *"The use of the Norse language in these inscriptions suggests that the language of their composers was Old Norse. Accepting that they were indeed Norse speakers, it seems likely that the impetus for carving inscriptions in this way would have derived from Scandinavian, rather than any indigenous traditions, otherwise we might expect to find evidence of the practice elsewhere in Scotland."* (page 166)

The problem with this reasoning is that by 800 A.D. the carving of Ogam inscriptions had long stopped. The invention of the Old Norse language had not started until the Benedictine monastery had been built in Nidaros (Trondheim), shortly after 1000 A.D. This language could not have been used because it didn't exist yet at that time. Cox's approach and results make about as much sense as Guiter's.

4) OGAM IS WRITTEN IN GAELIC

The traditional view of the Ogam script is that it is written in Gaelic or Irish. Dr. Damien McManus, professor of Celtic at Trinity College in Dublin, Ireland, wrote:

> *"... it can be shown without reasonable doubt that the Ogam alphabet was designed for the Irish language. It is likely that its framers were Irish and probably that they resided in the south of the country, possibly in the fourth century."* (page 1)

He also wrote:

> *"The evidence suggests that they had a language with a phonemic inventory of its own in mind, that the creation was accompanied by a careful analysis of the sounds of that language, and that the alphabet was designed as a vehicle for them."* (p.31)

It thus depends on who was interpreting the "evidence" which Dr. McManus is referring to. When I talked to him he rejected my findings out of hand, without even looking at my research, just as Anthony Jackson had done. This convinced me that publishing my research was the only way to get a larger number of interested people to take a good look at my findings.

THE BASQUE CONNECTION

Dr. Gifford's suggestion that Basque could well be the language of the Ogam inscriptions was supported by genetic and linguistic evidence in Ireland and Scotland. Geneticist Dr. Cavalli-Sforza from Stanford University had published a world map in Scientific American (Nov. 1991), showing the distribution of the Rh-negative people. The populations with the highest proportion of their members with Rh-negative blood were found among the Berbers in Morocco, the Basques in Euskadi, and the dark featured peoples of Northern Ireland and Scotland, all with over 25% of the people with this blood peculiarity. Dr.Cavalli-Sforza commented **"... the resulting pattern roughly coincides with anthropological reconstructions of ancient migrations."** Of these four groups, only the Basques still spoke their pre-Christian language. It was therefore reasonable to suggest that the entire migration had spoken this language. But that was not all, the migration had definitely reached farther north because the people of the Norwegian islands and the City of Bergen on the mainland had 17% Rh-negative blood. This meant that the Scandinavians could also have spoken Basque before Christianity arrived. This possibility was crying out for proof. Fortunately a very large number of early inscriptions on stone, silver, brass, bone etc. were available; over 600 in Ireland and some 30 in Scotland. None of these inscriptions had ever been translated with certainty. The fact that none had been found in Norway shows that the Ogam script was not at home there. Transliteration from the Ogam script had not been a problem, but only apparently meaningless series of letters, mostly consonants, had been obtained. However, as considerable time and effort must have gone into carving these inscriptions, I assumed that some system of decoding had to exist.

From the moment I tackled the problem, it appeared likely that most of the vowels had been removed for some good reason, based on a certain pattern. After a great deal of experimentation, I found that the basic pattern had to have been VCVCV etc. This letter-pattern looked strikingly like that of thousands of Basque words such as: *"ohitura"* (custom). But, Basque being an agglutinated language, this word in itself was composed of three other roots, ohi-itu-ura: *ohi* (habit) *itungaitz* (disagreeable) *urratu* (to break), meaning: "Break that disagreeable habit," creating a VCV-VCV-VCV pattern. The word ohitura had a built-in hidden sentence and my hope was that the Ogam inscriptions had the same. In addition, the vowels on either side of the hyphens were always the same, completing the formula: $VCV_1-V_1CV_2-V_2CV_3$. I called this the "vowel-interlocking" or "VCV formula." Trial and error proved that this was indeed the formula used in every Ogam inscription examined to date, without exception. For more examples see "The Saharan-Basque Language."

I then looked for linguistic evidence of Basque in the family and geographical names of these countries. In Scotland many family names immediately stood out, e.g:

MacKenzie, *kentze* is the act of depriving, of taking away, to steal from, probably referring to territory. The MacKenzie tribe was therefore known by their neighbours as the people who had conquered or taken something that didn't belong to them.
MacArthur, *arturen* means assets, possessions, and the tribe was therefore known as 'well off.'
MacUen or **MacEwen**, from *uhin* (wave), was the tribe of the navigators.
Stuart/Steward, a name of royalty, clearly came from stu-art, astu-arti, *asturu* (luck, fortune) *arti/ardi* (sheep): "A fortune in sheep."
Campbell, from kam-bel, *kamaina* (improvised bed) *bela* (sails); they were sailors and fishermen and slept on stored sails.

Douglas, from dug-las, *dugu* (we have it) *lasai* (comfortable): "We have it comfortable, we have it easy."

 With these and many more examples of names, my search for the needed proof looked more promising . But indisputable proof could only come from many successful translations.

THE SYSTEM OF ENCODING AN OGAM INSCRIPTION

1) In the sentence to be inscribed, use only those Basque words which start with vowel-consonant-vowel (VCV).

2) Select only those VCV's which have the vowels interlocking, as shown in the VCV formula: $VCV_1\text{-}V_1CV_2\text{-}V_2CV_3\text{-}$etc.

3) Agglutinate all these VCV's into one line-up of letters: $VCV_1CV_2CV_3C$ etc

4) Remove those vowels and H's which do not contribute to the strokes and values of the magical system of prime numbers. (see Jackson '93, pages 117-152).

5) Replace all B's by V, the K's by C or Q as dictated by numerology. Inscribe the results.

THE SYSTEM OF DECODING

1) Restore the original letters: V becomes B, C and Q become K.

2) Restore the original position of the letters by inserting them in the vowel-interlocking formula, placing dots where vowels were removed. In case of double vowels, an H has usually been removed. Keep in mind that every consonant represents a word.

3) Occasionally the first vowel of the first syllable is not used (e.g. in Birsay 1) and the first word therefore starts with CV.

4) Systematically list all likely meanings under each VCV and select the words that form the appropriate sentence.

ABOUT THE TRANSLATIONS

In this chapter I will compare all four interpretations by Guiter, Jackson, Fox, McManus and my own together for each of the inscriptions and let the reader be the judge. The order in which the inscriptions are presented is taken from Jackson's 1993 publication "Pictish Symbol Stones?." The transliteration used is also taken from Jackson because I consider his interpretation superior to any other efforts. Translating Ogam is certainly no exact science, it is only the best currently available approximation. It may well be that some of the inscriptions were designed to be magical, yet when they were finally translated, most made good sense from the standpoint of evangelizing a "heathen" country. Two of the larger inscriptions, Brodie B and Golspie, in spite of several hours of work, have so far resisted the decoding process. Some like Altyre and Cille Barra describe natural disasters which make no reference to evangelism. Aboyne B and Altyre are grave markers. Some of the following translations may need revisiting to see if a better translation can be found. **Strictly adhering to the vowel-interlocking between the VCV roots is the key to decoding the inscriptions.**

Map showing the location of the following inscriptions.

Lunnasting
Whiteness
Bressay
St. Ninian's Isle
Lerwick
Cunningsburgh
Gurness
Birsay
Burrian
Buckquoy
Pool
SCOTLAND
Keiss Bay
Latheron
North Atlantic Ocean
Golspie
Brodie
Altyre
Inverness
Spey
Peterhead
Newton
Loch Ness
Aberdeen
Logie
Cille Barra
Dee
Brandsbutt
Aboyne
Dunadd
Dundee
Auquhollie
Lock Lomond
Tay
St. Andrews
Inchyra
Forth
Abernethy
Scoonie
North Sea
Glasgow
EDINBURGH

BRESSAY. A) CRROSCC- B) NAHHTVVDDADD – C) DATTRR –
D) ANNBENNISES – E) MEOODDRROANN. (page 66.)

Guiter: **Basque reading:** Berriz Enekoaren Kroska naiz Udak daragina.
Spanish translation: De nuevo estoy en la Cruz de Eneko. La
que el verano obliga a hacer.
In English: Again I am in the cross of Eneko. The one that the
summer obliged to do.

Jackson:				
A)	28	7x4	75	5x5x3
B)	30	5x6	96	12x8
C)	19	prime	77	7x11
D)	43	prime	110	11x5x2
E)	42	7x6	132	11x6x2
Total	162	9x9x2	490	7x7x5x2

Cox: **Norse reading:** krosk en eft Ottars dottur, Ornu, Bjarni setti mik
– Drottinn [hjalpi] ondu [hennar]
English translation: cross and in memory of Ottarr's daughter,
Arna, Bjarni erected me – may the Lord save her soul.

Nyland:

A: KRROSKK

.k.	eka	*ekarri*	I bring
.r.	ero	*erospen*	redemption
os.	osa	*osasun*	health
.k.	aka	*akatsbako*	perfect
.k.	aku	*akuilaketa*	motivation

"I bring welcome redemption, health and perfect motivation."

B: NAHHTBBDDADDS

.na	ana	*anaiak*	religious brothers, wise men
ah.	aho	*ahozuriketa*	adulation
.h.	oha	*ohartu*	to observe
.t.	ata	*atadi*	entrance
.b.	abe	*aberetegi*	stable
.b.	ebe	*ebertar*	Jew, Jesus
.d.	ede	*eder izan*	to esteem, to revere
.da	eda	*edangura*	thirsting for
ad.	ado	*adoratu*	to worship
.d.	odo	*odolgarbiko*	noble
.s.	ospe	*ospetasun*	majesty, king

**"The wise men, in adulation, observed from the entrance of revered
Jesus' stable, thirsting to worship the noble King."**

C: DATTRR

.da	ida	*idazti*	scripture
at.	ate	*aterapen*	outcome
.t.	eto	*etorri*	inspiration
.r.	orai	*oraingoz*	on that moment
.r.	aire	*airegabeki*	awkward

"The scripture's outcome gave inspiration on that awkward moment."

D: ANNBENNISES

an.	anai	*anaideak*	disciples
.n.	aina	*aina*	as much as, as well as
.be	abe	*abeltalde*	flock
en.	enu	*enulkeria*	weakness
.ni	uni	*unibertsal*	general
ise	ise	*isekatu*	to ridicule, to mock
es.	estu	*estuasun*	moment of tribulation

"The disciples, as well as the flock, (Mark 14:50) **in general weakness were mocking during that moment of tribulation."** (Mark 15:17-20)

E: MEOODDRROANN

.me	eme	*emeki*	quietly
e.o	eho	*ehorzleku*	tomb
o.o	oho	*ohorarazi*	to praise, to honor
od.	odi	*odieria*	round opening
.d.	ido	*idoropen*	discovery
.r.	orai	*orain*	presently, right then
.ro	airo	*airos*	graceful
o.a	oha	*oharkuntza*	vigil
an.	anai	*anaiarte*	gathering
.n.	ain	*aingeru*	angels

"Quietly at the tomb to praise by the round opening, (they made) the discovery and right then saw the graceful vigil of the gathering of angels."

BURRIAN. IDBMIRRHANNURRAC TEEVVCERROCCS

Guiter: **Basque reading:** Don kuorari añu(ti)ra dan kerroke.
Spanish translation: Duan koorariannu Iraktaen kerroke.
In English: The dog that goes to the shadow of this cross.

Jackson: 95 19x5 284 71x4

Cox: **Norse reading:** etter Arna er reistr thenna kroks
English translation: This cross is raised in memory of Arni.

Nyland: IDBMIRRHANNURRAKTEEBBKERROKKS

id.	ide	*ideki*	to open
.b.	eba	*Ebanjelio*	Gospel
.mi	ami	*amildu*	to oust
ir.	iru	*iruzurkeria*	false belief
.r.	ure	*urreraketa*	drawing closer
.ha	eha	*ea*	(emphasis), wonderful
an.	ano	*ano*	nourishment
.nu	onu	*onuste*	good faith
ur.	uri	*urrikalmendu*	mercy
.ra	ira	*irakatzi*	sermon
ak.	aka	*akatsbako*	perfect
.te	ate	*aterpe*	refuge
ee	ee	*ee*	to call, pay attention
eb.	eba	*ebanjelari*	evangelist
.b.	abi	*abiatu*	to begin
.ke	ike	*ikertaldi*	to visit
er.	ere	*errezibimendu*	welcome
.ro	ero	*eroan*	to suffer
ok.	oke	*okerbidetu*	gone astray
.k.	eka	*ekarri*	to bring
as	aska	*askamen*	freedom

"Open your Gospel to oust false beliefs and get closer to the wonderful nourishment of good faith and mercy. Hear a sermon in our perfect refuge by paying attention to the evangelist who begins his welcome visit; he will bring freedom to (those) suffering and gone astray."

WHITENESS. VNDAR (page 166)

Guiter: No reading.
Jackson: 16 4x4 41 prime
Cox: No reading.

Nyland: BNDAR.

.b.	ebe	*ebertar*	Jew, Jesus
.n.	ene	*eneganatu*	to come to me
.da	eda	*edan*	to thirst for
ar.	ara	*arraitasun*	happiness

"Jesus (says) come to me (those) who thirst for happiness."

LUNASTING. A) ETTECUHETTS – B) AHEHHTTANNN –

(page 166)   C) HCCVVEVV – D) NEHHTONN

Guiter: **Basque reading:** Etxekoez aiekoan nahigabe ba nengoen.
Spanish translation: El de la casa me encontraba sin voluntad en el dolor.
In English: The one of the house found me without will in the pain.

Jackson:

A	36	6x6	140	7x5x2
B	30	6x5	108	6x6x3
C	25	5x5	43	43x1
D	26	2x13	93	3x31
Total :	117	3x9 3	84	6x4x4x4

Cox: Shows the location on his map but gave up.

Nyland: A: ETTEKUHETTS

et.	eta	*etariko*	one of our group
.te	ate	*atera*	to get away
eku	eku	*ekurugaitz*	anxiously
uhe	uhe	*uherdura*	confusion
et.	etai	*etaipa*	period
.t.	aita	*aita*	Father
.s.	aska	*askamen*	freedom

"With the help of the Father, one of our group anxiously got away to freedom during the period of confusion."

B: AHEHHTTANNN

ahe	aihe	*aiher*	full of anger
eh.	ehu	*ehun*	hundreds
.h.	uhe	*uherdura*	in uproar, confusion
.t.	eta	*-eta*	(emphasis of previous word)
.ta	ata	*atako*	outside
an.	anai	*anaitu*	to gather
.n.	aina	*aina*	as well as
.n	an	*-an*	inside

"Hundreds, full of anger, were in uproar and gathered outside as well as inside."

C: HKKBBEBB

.h.	aha	*ahal*	I wish
.k.	ako	*akorduan euki*	to remember
.k.	oka	*oka*	fullness
.b.	abo	*abots*	voice
.be	obe	*obeditze*	obedient
eb.	eba	*ebanjelari*	evangelist

| .b. | abe | *abe* | cross |

"I wish to remember the fullness of the voice of our obedient evangelist of the Cross."

D: NEHHTONN.

ne	ne	*nebarrebak*	brothers and sisters
eh.	eha	*ea*	do everything
.h.	aha	*ahalgarri*	possible
.to	ato	*atonketa*	preparation
on.	ona	*onarpen*	admission, salvation
.n.	anai	*anaide*	brother in Christ

"Brothers and sisters do everything possible to prepare for the salvation of our brother in Christ."

The place name **Lunasting** itself is interesting:

.lu-una-asti-ing

.lu	alu	*alu*	stupid
una	una	*unagarri*	boring
asti	azti	*aztiatu*	superstitious
ingu	ingu	*inguraldi*	place

"A stupid, boring, superstitious place."

ST. NINIANS. BESMEQQNANAMMOVVVEZ (page 66)

Guiter: **Basque reading:** Eneko ba nago bez.
Spanish translation: Yo Eneko me encuentro debajo.
In English: I Eneko I find myself under/underneath.

Jackson: 54 6x9 172 43x4

Cox: Has it on his map but gave up.

Nyland: BESMEKKNANAMMOBBEZ

.be	be	*bedeinkagarri*	blessed one
es.	ese	*eseri*	to sit
.me	eme	*ementxe*	right here
ek.	eka	*ekarri*	to bring about
.k.	ako	*akordio*	agreement
.na	ona	*onarpen*	acceptance
ana	ana	*anaitu*	to unify
am.	ama	*ama*	priestess
.mo	amo	*amodiotsu*	blessing
ob.	obe	*obeditu*	to obey, to follow
.be	ebe	*ebertar*	Hebrew, Christ
ez.	ez	*ezikuntza*	education, teachings

"The blessed one (St. Ninian?) sat right on this spot to bring about acceptance of the unifying agreement, with the Priestess' blessing, to follow Jesus' teachings."

BIRSAY. 1) MBOLMVNORRALVRR – 2) BQIAB (page 67)

Guiter: Basque reading: None.
Jackson: 43 prime 170 5x2x17
Cox: Has it on his map but gave up.

Nyland: 1) MBOLMVNORRALBRR

m.	ma	*maisu*	teacher
.bo	abo	*abots*	voice
ol.	ole	*oles egin*	to call upon
.m.	ema	*eman*	to celebrate
.b.	abo	*aboskatu*	to proclaim
.no	ono	*onon*	(superlative)
or.	ora	*oraindanik*	from now on
.ra	ara	*aratz*	pure
al.	ala	*alatz*	miracle
.b.	abe	*abe*	cross
.r.	eru	*errukigabe*	cruel
.r.	uru	*urruingarri*	to despise

"The teacher's voice called upon (all) to celebrate and clearly proclaim the pure miracle on the cruel and despised cross."

Birsay 2) BKIAB

.b.	be	*bedeinkagarri*	the blessed one
.k.	eki	*ekin*	to continue
ia	ia	*iaio*	cheerful
ab.	abo	*abots*	voice

"The blessed one continued in a cheerful voice."

BUCKQUOY. ETMIQMSSALLC (page 67)

Guiter: Basque reading: None.
Jackson: 36 6x6 135 5x3x3x3
Cox: Norse reading: Asa lagade mik
           English translation: Asa made me.

Nyland: ETMIKMSSALLIK

et.	eti	*etika*	ethics
.mi	imi	*imitagarri*	exemplary
ik.	ika	*ikasbide*	teachings

.m.	amo	*amodio*	love
.s.	oso	*oso*	sincere
.sa	osa	*osatu*	to heal
al.	ala	*alaitu*	to fill with happiness
.l.	ale	*alen*	total
.k.	eku	*ekurutasun*	peace of mind

"Exemplary teachings of ethics and sincere love will heal, fill with total happiness and peace of mind."

CUNNINGSBURGH. 1) IRO–2a) EHTECONMORS– (page 67)
2b) DOVHDDRS –3a) ETTECA –3b) VDATTVB 3c) RTT

Guiter: Basque reading: A few individual words only.

Jackson:

(1	12	3x4	40	5x2x4
(2a):	35	7x5	134	2x67
(2b):	21	7x3	75	5x5x3
Total	56	7x8	209	11x19
(3a):	19	prime	52	4x13
(3b)	16	4x4	57	3x19
Total	35	5x7	109	prime
(3c)	11	prime	55	5x11

Total C:46 23x2 164 4x41

Cox: Norse reading: No try.

Nyland: 1: IRO (on stone slab)

| iro | iro | *irol* | privy, outhouse |

"Outhouse." (It is gone, but the stone sign survives)

2a: EHTEKONMORS

eh.	ehu	*ehun*	hundreds
.te	ute	*uste*	faith
eko	eko	*ekoitzi*	to be fruitful, to be exuberant
on.	one	*onespen*	blessings
.mo	emo	*emon*	celebrate
or.	orai	*oraintxe*	right now
.s	ais	*aiskide*	friends

"Hundreds who have faith will be exuberant and celebrate the blessings right now with friends."

2b: DOBHDDRS

do	do	*doatsutasun*	happiness
ob.	oba	*obakuntza*	improvement
.h.	aha	*ahalguzti*	almighty

.d.	ado	*adoratu*	to worship
.d.	odo	*odolkidetasun*	relative
.r.	oro	*orobatu*	to come together
.s.	os.	*ospatu*	to celebrate

"Improve your happiness by worshiping the Almighty. All relatives come together to celebrate."

3a: ETTEKA

et.	eti	*etikoa*	ethical
.te	ite	*itegun*	work performed, hard work
eka	eka	*ekandu*	make it a habit

"Make ethical behaviour and hard work a habit."

3b: BDATTBB

.b.	abe	*abegitasun*	fondness of
.da	eda	*edan*	to drink
at.	ata	*atalbako*	simple
.t.	ate	*aterapen*	outcome, consequence
.b.	ebo	*eboluzio*	development
.b.	obe	*oben*	sin

"The consequence of a fondness for simple drinking is the development of a sin."

3c: RTT

This last inscription has no identifiable vowel and therefore is not translatable with the vowel-interlocking method.

POOL. RVMVORC (page 67)

Guiter: **Basque reading:** None.
Jackson: 23 prime 75 5x5x3
Cox: **Norse reading:** Hrolfr af Orkneyjum
             English translation: Hrolfr from (the) Orkneys.

Nyland: **Pool: RBMBORK**

.r.	ara	*arraro*	strange, odd
.b.	aba	*abaildura*	weariness
.m.	ama	*ama*	priestess
.bo	abo	*abots*	voice
or.	oro	*oroz*	completely
.k.	oka	*okaztatu*	disgusting

"The strange weariness in the Priestess' voice was completely disgusting."

GURNESS. NEITTEMTOS M0CS (page 67)

Guiter: **Basque reading**: None.

Jackson: 50 5x10 189 7x3x3x3

Cox: **Norse reading:** innan ettermun Mats innan ettermun Kvamms
English translation: "in memory of Matts" or "in memory of Kvammr"

Nyland: NEITTEMTOSMOKS.

.ne	ene	*enekin*	with me
e.i	eja	*eia*	come along, let's go
it.	ita	*itaun egin*	to ask questions
.te	ate	*aterpe*	refuge
em.	eme	*emekiro*	peaceful, gently
.to	eto	*etor*	come!
os.	osa	*osatu*	to perfect
.mo	amo	*amodio*	love
.k.	oki	*okitu*	total
.s.	isu	*isurialdi*	inspiration

"Come along with me to our peaceful refuge and ask questions. Come to perfect love and total inspiration."

NORTH UIST. H QUNCENTC T (page 68)

Guiter: **Basque reading:** Belaskuanuk... ta
Spanish translation: Parece que se encuentra el nombre antiguo vasco Belasko, es decir, cuervo.
In English: It seems that one finds the old name Belasko, is to say, crow.

Jackson: 37 prime 119 7x17

Cox: **Norse reading**: He gave up.

Nyland: HKUNKENTKT

.h.	ohi	*ohitu*	to get used to
.ku	iku	*ikurton*	sacrament
un.	uni	*unibersal*	universal
.ke	ike	*ikertu*	to study
en.	ena	*ena*	that
.t.	ate	*aterapen*	result
.k.	eku	*ekurutasun*	peace of mind
.t	ut	*uts*	pure

"Get used to studying the universal sacraments that result in pure peace of mind."

WEETING. 1) VLVEVVUTE – 2) GEDEVIM DOS Page 68)

Guiter: **Basque reading:** None.
Jackson: 1) 28 7x4 84 7x3x2x2
              2) 29 prime 84 7x3x2x2
Cox: **Norse reading:** No dice.

Nyland: Weeting 1: Jackson: BLBEBBUTE, Nyland: BLBEBBETE

.b.	aba	*abagadune*	occasion
.l.	ala	*alai*	joyful
.be	abe	*aberastu*	to enrich
eb.	eba	*ebanjelio*	gospel
.be	abe	*abestu*	to sing
ete	ete	*etengabe*	uninterrupted

"Joyful occasion to enrich everyone with uninterrupted gospel singing."

Weeting 2: GEDEBIMDOS

.ge	age	*agerpen*	revelation
ede	ede	*eder*	beautiful
ebi	ebi	*ebide/elebide*	theme of conversation
im.	ima	*imatz*	house with wicker walls
.do	ado	*adoratu*	to worship
os.	oso	*oso*	sincere

"The beautiful revelation was the theme of the conversation in the house of sincere worship."
(There exists no VCV: "ebi" in Basque. Elebide is the closest word that applies.)

BRANDSBUTT 8/45. IRATADDOARENS (page 68)

Guiter: **Basque reading:** Iratakoaren.
              Spanish translation: De Iratako
              In English: From/of Iratako.
Jackson: 40 5x8 123 3x41
Cox: **Norse reading:** gerthi Olafr I
              English translation: Olafr I[varsson] (or similar) made this.

Nyland: IRATADDOARENS (two possible translations)

ira	ira	*irakatsi*	to preach a sermon
ata	ata	*atalbako*	simple
ad.	ada	*adarkadura*	consequence
.do	ado	*adoratu*	to worship
o.a	oha	*oharkuntza*	pay attention

are	are	*arrerosle*	Redeemer
en.	ena	*-ena*	(superlative) wonderful
.s.	asa	*azalpen*	manifestation

"Preach a simple sermon about the glory of worshiping and pay attention to the Redeemer's wonderful manifestation."

Nyland: IRATADDOARENS

ira	ira	*irabazi*	to earn, to deserve
ata	ata	*atano*	better world
ad.	ade	*adeitsu*	gentle
.do	edo	*edonoizko*	for ever, from now on
are	are	*aren*	please
en.	ene	*eneganatu*	come to me
.s.	esa	*esan*	advice

"You deserve a better, more gentle world so from now on, please come to me for advice."

INCHYRA – A1: OOTTLIETRENOIDDORS (page 68)
INCHYRA – A2: UHTUOAGED
INCHYRA – B1: INEHHETESTIE
INCHYRA – B2: INNE
INCHYRA – C 41/44: SETU

Guiter:	**Basque reading:** Etorkoaren …holoi…ina otsa utz diet dinua?
	Spanish translation: Muy poco segura.
	In English: Very little sure. (segura is feminine).
Cox:	**Norse reading:** Has it on his map but gave up.
Jackson:	A1) 60 5x12 225 5x5x5x3
	A2) 22 2x11 98 7x7x2
	TotalA: 82 2x41 323 17x19
	B1) 43 prime 123 41x3
	B2) 19 prime 40 5x8
	Total B 62 2x31 163 prime
	A+B 144 12x12 486 6x9x9
	C) 14' 7x2 62 31x2
	A+B+C 158 79x2 548 137x4

Nyland: A1: OOTTLIETRENOIDDORS (this is a very strange one.)

o.o	oho	*ohoregabe*	dishonored
ot.	otoi	*otoikatu*	begging
.t.	oitu	*oiturazko*	common
.li	uli	*uli*	coward
i.e	ihe	*ihesarazi*	to escape

et.	eto	*etorki*	lineage, tribe
.re	ore	*orrenbesteko*	just like the other one
eno	eno	*enora*	warts
o.i	ohi	*ohinazedun*	afflicted with
id.	ido	*idor*	dry
.do	odo	*odoldu*	to bleed
or.	oro	*oro*	all over
.s.	osa	*osaezin*	incurable

"Dishonored and begging like a common coward who is escaping from the tribe, just like the others suffering from incurable bleeding dry warts all over."

A2: UHTUOAGED

uh.	uhe	*uherdura*	confusion
.tu	etu	*etsitu*	to despair
u.o	uho	*uholde*	flooding
o.a	oha	*ohartu*	to become aware of, to be warned
age	age	*ageriz*	obviously
ed.	ede	*eduki*	to hold onto, to heed

"The confusion and despair during the flooding is obviously a warning to heed."

B1: INEHHETESTIE.

ine	ine	*inertzia*	passive, downtrodden
eh.	ehi	*ei*	they say
.he	ihe	*ihesari eman*	to escape
ete	ete	*eten*	to break
es.	esi	*esibarruti*	fenced in area, bonds
.ti	iti	*itxiki*	faithfulness
i.e	ihe	*ihes egin*	to escape, to run away

"To the downtrodden they say to break the bonds and run away to faithfulness."

B2: INNE –

in.	ine	*inertzia*	passive, downtrodden
.ne	ene	*eneganatu*	to come to me

Downtrodden? Come to me!

C: SETU

.se	ase	*asetu*	to be filled with
etu	etu	*etu/etsitu*	to despair

It could be that B and C belong together, first C then B2, but the style of writing is quite different.
"Filled with despair and downtrodden? Come to me."

KEISS 41/7: NEHTETRI (page 68)

Guiter: **Basque reading:** Nauke tagona.
            Spanish translation: Me tiene el que esta aqui.
            In English: The one who is here has me.
Jackson: 30 5x6 95 5x19
Cox: **Norse reading:** Doesn't mention it..

Nyland: NEHTETRI

ne	ne	*negarreztatu*	grieving
eh.	eho	*ehortze*	funeral
.te	ote	*ote*	might, may
et.	ete	*eten*	to interrupt, to stop
.ri	eri	*errieta*	fighting

"Grieving at the funeral may stop the fighting."

LOGIE 8/5: CALTQU (page 68)

Guiter: **Basque reading:**   Kalkakoa
            Spanish translation: Seguramente un nombre proprio.
            In English: Obviously a proper name.

Jackson: 18 6x3 70 5x2x7

Cox: **Norse reading:** He doesn't show this one.

Nyland: KALTKU

.ka	aka	*akabu*	death
al.	ala	*alabeharreko*	unavoidable
.t.	aita	*aita*	father, Jesus
.ku	aku	*akuilatu*	to spur on

"Jesus' unavoidable death spurs us on."

ABOYNE A: NEHHTVROBBACC – ENNEVV (page 69)

ABOYNE B: MAQQOTALLUORR

Guiter: **Basque reading:** Lemako da lurrpe. Dator doaken enea.
            Spanish translation: Lemako esta debajo de la tierra. Viene el mio que sa va.
            In English: Lemako is under the earth/soil. Come my that goes away.

Jackson:	A)	59	prime	149	prime
	B)	37	prime	169	13x13

Total: 96 16x6 318 53x6

Cox: He does not mention this inscription.

Nyland: A) NEHHTBROBBAKK – ENNEBB

.ne	ene	*enetan*	always
eh.	eha	*ea* place	emphasis, spotlight
.h.	aha	*ahalguzti*	Almighty
.t.	ata	*atalgabeko*	simple
.b.	abo	*aboskatu*	to proclaim
.ro	oro	*oroegile*	Creator
ob.	obe	*obeto*	perfect
.ba	eba	*ebanjelari*	evangelist
ak.	aki	*akigarri*	aging
.k.	ike	*ikertu*	to visit

"Always place emphasis on the Almighty by simply proclaiming the perfect Creator, (said) the aging visiting evangelist."

en.	ene	*enetan*	always
.ne	ene	*eneganatu*	to come to me
eb.	eba	*ebanjelari*	evangelist
.be	abe	*abe*	Cross.

"Always come to me, the evangelist of the Cross."

B: MAKKOTALLUORR.

.ma	ama	*ama*	mother
ak.	aka	*akabu*	death
.ko	ako	*akorduan euki*	to remember
ota	ota	*otalurmendiak*	wild mountains
al.	ali	*alienatu*	to kill a person
.lu	ilu	*ilunbera*	sad, tragic
u.o	uho	*uholde*	flood, torrential rain
or.	ora	*orain*	always
.r.	aro	*arroztiar*	hospitable

"We remember mother's death in the wild mountains where she was tragically killed by the torrential rains; she was always hospitable."

BRODIE BRODIE A 31/5:   VONECCO (page 69)

BRODIE B 31/5:   RAMINNGCHQODTOSLMBS

BRODIE C 31/5:   EDDARRNONR TTI

Guiter: **Basque reading:** Idarreko noa doa mokorra erala behar aikaz bedi.   Du sutu ocean iasoa lurreko karrak. Ba lo elhurra-be dago, haike,   aikako ibaia du.

Spanish translation: Idarreko me voy, llega malhadada. De esta forma la necesidad esta llena de lamentos. Ha dao fuego a la cama la llama. Esta durmiendo bajo la nieve. Levantate. Tiene un rio de lamentos.

In English: Arise ill-starred. In that way the need is full of lamentation. The flame has given fire to the bed. He/she is sleeping under the snow. Get up. He/she has river of lamentation.

Jackson:

A)	24	8x3	58	29x2
B)	51	prime	194	97x2
C)	53	prime	169	13x13
Total:	128	8x8x2	421	prime

Cox: **Norse reading:** The only reading is 'C' guessed to be "in memory of"

Nyland: A: **BONEKKO.**

.bo	abo	*aboskatu*	to express
one	one	*oneraspen*	devotion
ek.	eku	*ekurugaiztasun*	worry
.ko	uko	*uko egin*	to renounce

"Express your devotion and renounce your worries."

B: RAMINNGKHKODTOSLMBS.

This fairly long inscription is a complicated puzzle, which has not yet yielded its secret, probably because of the difficulties with reading the badly eroded inscription.

C: EDDARRNONR TTI

ed.	eda	*edan*	to drink
.da	ada	*adarkadura*	ramification
ar.	arau	*araugabeko*	irregular
.r.	aura	*aurantzeko*	childish
.no	ano	*anormal*	abnormal
on.	ona	*onartezin*	unacceptable
.r.	ara	*aratusteldu*	to corrupt
.ta	ate	*atxekimendu*	loyalty, adherence
.ti	eti	*etika*	ethics, ethical standards

"The ramifications of getting drunk are irregular, childish and abnormal behaviour, which corrupt loyalty and ethical standards."

GOLSPIE 17/31: ALLHHALLORREDDMEOO – NUUVALHNRERR (page 69)

Guiter: **Basque reading:** Aldalurrekoak hartza lotu zuan.
Spanish translation: El de la tierre del lado ha atacado el oso.
In English: The one from the land of the side has attacked the bear.

Jackson: 88 8x11 320 5x8x8

Cox: **Norse reading:** Hallgeir la rett mik en Ivarr gerthi
English translation: Hallgeirr set me up and Ivarr made me.

Nyland: This large inscription looks authentic and should have given up its secrets, but I didn't succeed yet in decoding it. Give me time.

LATHERON 40E/41: DUVNODNNATMAOONAHATO (page 69)

Guiter: **Basque reading:** Doana da Eneko t'ekaitsua
Spanish translation: El que se va es Eneko y la preocupacion.
In English: The one that goes is Eneko and the pre-occupation.

Jackson: 56 8x7 208 13x4x4

Cox: **Norse reading:** Has it on his map but then gave up.

Nyland: **DUBNODNNATMAOONAHATO**

.du	edu	*eduki*	to have
ub.	ube	*ubelilun*	bruised
.no	eno	*enora*	wart
od.	odo	*odolusketa*	bleeding
.n.	one	*oneik*	these
.na	ena	*-ena*	(superlative suffix)
at.	ate	*ateots*	knock on the door
.ma	ema	*emanaldi*	sermon
a.o	aho	*ahogarbi*	eloquent
o.o	oho	*ohore*	to worship
ona	ona	*onartu*	to accept
aha	aha	*ahalguztidun*	Almighty
ato	ato	*ator!*	come!

"If you have these bruised and bleeding warts then knock on the door, (hear) the eloquent sermon to worship and accept the Almighty. Come!"

SCOONIE -/31: EDDARRNOSN (page 69)

Guiter: **Basque reading:** udara zan onsa.
Spanish translation: La recolecta fue buena.
In English: The crop was good.

Jackson: 35 5x7 106 53x2
Cox: **Norse reading:** Cox gave up.

Nyland: EDDARRNOSN

ed.	ede	*eder egin*	to give pleasure
.da	eda	*edan*	to drink
ar.	ara	*arraitasun*	happiness
.r.	ara	*aratz*	pure
.no	ano	*ano*	wine
os.	osa	*osatasun*	unification
.n.	ana	*anaigo*	congregation

"It gives pleasure to drink happiness with pure wine to (celebrate) unification of our congregations."

ALTYRE: AMMAQQHTALLMVBVMAA-HHRRASSUDDS

Guiter: **Basque reading:** None.
Jackson: 66 11x6 281 prime
Cox: **Norse reading:** [reist] I mik, Kalum vas magr Asmunds
English translation: (X raised) me (in memory of K), K was A.'s in-law.

Nyland: AMMAKKHTALLMBBBMAAHHRRASSUDDS

am.	ama	*ama*	mother
.ma	ama	*amaitu*	to end
ak.	aka	*akabu*	death
.k.	aki	*akipen*	exhaustion
.h.	ihe	*ihes egin*	to escape
.ta	eta	*eta*	and
al.	alo	*alor*	farmer
.l.	ola	*ola*	cabin
.m.	ama	*ama*	mother
.b.	abi	*abilgabetasun*	inability
.b.	ibi	*ibitu*	to cross, to ford
.b.	iba	*ibai*	river
.ma	ama	*amaika*	many
a.a	aha	*ahaleginaz*	anxiously
ah.	ahu	*ahurrea eman*	to confront, face
.h.	uho	*uholde*	flood
.r.	oru	*orru*	roar
.ra	ura	*uramil*	rising waters
as.	asi	*asi*	to begin
.su	isu	*isurle*	to overflow, to rise

ud.	udi	*udikan*	get out!
.d.	ido	*idola*	flood waters
.s.	osi	*osintsu*	very/too deep

"Mother's (life) ended in death from exhaustion, while escaping from her farm cabin. Mother was unable to cross the river where many anxiously faced the roaring flood which had begun to rise. She (tried) to get out when the flood waters were too deep."

ABERNETHY: QMI. (page 70)

Guiter: **Basque reading:** None.
Jackson: 11 prime 37 prime
Cox: Has it on his map but made no effort.

Nyland: **KMI**

| .k. | ika | ikara | fears |
| .mi | ami | amildu | to oust, to throw off |

"Throw off your fears."

This is the first translation that appeared. KMI is very short, doesn't leave much to work with, and cannot be translated with certainty.

AUQUHOLLIE: VUUNON – TEDOV – BB (page 70)

Guiter: **Basque reading:** Hila du ileko obiak.
             Spanish translation: El muerto lo tiene la cueva de la colina.
             In English: The cave of the hill has the dead.
Jackson: 37 prime 138 6x23
Cox: **Norse reading:** Ingjaldr Oleifs(son) ek hjogga ut.
             English translation: Ingjardr, the son of Oleifr, I inscribed (this).

Nyland: VUUNON. The transliteration of this inscription is a problem. Only part makes sense, the VCV "uno" does not exist and **"BB"** has no vowel.

(TEDOV) should read: **TSOLV**

.te	ate	*atedanbada*	knock on the door
.so	eso	*esonde*	advice
ol.	ole	*oles egin*	to call upon
.b.	eba	*ebanjelari*	evangelist.

"Knock on the door and call upon the evangelist for advice."

NEWTON: Jackson: **A:** IDDARQNNNVORRENNIEUA **B:** IOSRE
             Nyland: **A:** IEARKNNNVDRRENNIEUA **B:** IOSRZ

(page 70)

Guiter: **Basque reading:** Idarkoari hor Eneko dio zagor.
Spanish translation: A Idarko Eneko le dice "Zagor."
In English: To Idarko Eneko he/she says "Zagor."

Jackson: **A)**   77 7x11   210   7x3x10
B)   20 5X4 100   5x5x4

Cox: **Norse reading:** **A:** etter Gunnvoru en Ingjaldr (gerthi) krosk
B: guess: may be 'monument.'
English translation: A: In memory of Gunnvor, and Ingjaldr
(made this)_monument.

Nyland: A:
IEARKNNNBDRRENNIEUA

i.e	ihe	*ihesleku*	find shelter
e.a	eha	*ea*	come on
ar.	aro	*aro*	weather
.k.	oka	*okaztagarri*	disgusting
.n.	ana	*ana*	over there
.n.	anai	*anaiak*	brothers
.n.	aina	*aina*	as many as possible
.b.	abe	*aberrietsai*	enemy of the homeland
.d.	edo	*edo*	or
.r.	ora	*oratu*	to grab
.re	are	*arretatu*	to prevent
en.	ena	*ena*	that
.ni	ani	*aniztasun*	majority
i.e	ihe	*ihesgile*	to escape
e.u	ehu	*ehun*	one hundred
u.a	uha	*uharte*	island

"Come on and find shelter from this disgusting weather with our brothers over there. (Then we will grab) as many as possible of the enemies of our land to prevent that the majority escapes to the hundred isles." (The Shetland islands number 100).

NEWTON B: IOSRZ

i.o	iho	*ihortziri*	thunder
os.	oso	*osoro*	completely
.r.	oro	*orroaldi*	continual roar
.z	ozto	*oztope*	impediment

"The completely continual roar of the thunder is an impediment."

DUNADD A: AESD – T – V – LVA – TV (page 70)

DUNADD B: L – VIRRAMDNA

Guiter: **Basque reading:** None.

Jackson: A) 29 prime 96 4x4x6
B) 35 7x5 100 5x5x4

Cox: **Norse reading:** The place is on his map but that's all.

Nyland: **A: AESD – T – B – TB.**

This inscription is too fractured to do anything with it.

B: L — BIRRAMDNAI

L ?		*lagun?*	friends?
.bi	abi	*abiatu*	to start walking
ir.	ira	*iradoki*	get away
.ra	ara	*arakintza*	massacre
am.	ami	*amilkatu*	to fall down
.d.	ido	*idortasun*	thirst, dryness
.na	ona	*ona*	here
a.i	ahi	*ahipen*	fatigue

"(Friends?) I started walking to get away from the massacre and fell down here from thirst and fatigue."

CILLE BARRA STONE. (not shown)
TIRTHURKIRTHUS;INRRISKURSSIARISTA:A

  This stone was removed in 1865 from the Cille Barra cemetary (Isle of Barra) and taken to the Museum of Antiquities in Edinburgh. It was always thought to be a gravestone, which it obviously is not. The transliteration was copied from a local tourist pamphlet. The twin islands Barra-Vatersay are the most southerly populated islands in the Outer Hebrides of Scotland. The inscription is found in neither Jackson's, Cox's nor Guiter's writings. Somehow this translation sounds to me more like a weather report than something that should be carved in stone. Other efforts are invited.

TIRTHURKIRTHUS

.ti	uti	*utikan!*	get away from here!
Ir.	iro	*irol*	run-off
.t.	ota	*otamendi*	brush covered mountain
.hu	ahu	*ahundiarazi*	to enlarge, to get worse
ur.	ure	*ure*	water
.ki	eki	*ekin*	to continue

ir.	iru	*irudi*	to look like
.t.	utsi	*utsitu*	to empty, to surge
.hu	ihu	*ihurtzuri*	thunder
us.	usta	*ustakatu*	to scourge

"Get away from here! The run-off from the brush-covered mountain is getting worse and it looks like (the flood) will continue to surge and the thunder to scourge."

INRRISKURSSIARISTA:A

in.	ino	*inor*	everyone
.r.	ora	*orratio*	dismayed
.ri	ari	*arritu*	petrified
is.	isi	*isiltze*	overwhelmed
.ku	iku	*ikustaile*	eye-witness
ur.	ura	*uraldi*	flood
.s.	asa	*asaldagarri*	shocking
.si	asi	*asialdi*	beginning
i.a	iha	*ihartu*	to dry up
ari	ari	*arinari*	to escape
is.	isi	*isiltoke*	shelter
.ta	ita	*itaizur*	leaky
a	?	?	

Everyone is dismayed, petrified and overwhelmed to be eye-witness to this shocking flood from the beginning; to dry up we escaped to this leaky shelter.

CONCLUSION

It must be pointed out that these are not Pictish Ogams; instead they are Irish Ogams in Pictland because they were written by early Irish evangelists who came to Scotland to convert the Pictish "heathens" to the Irish form of Christianity. All of the Irish and Scottish Ogam inscriptions that I have translated, and I have done close to one hundred, are written in the Basque language, without exception. Many, if not most, geographical and family names of Ireland and Scotland can also be translated with the Basque dictionary using the technique demonstrated above. Considering the evidence, it appears certain that prior to the coming of Roman Catholicism in about 650 A.D., **the Basque language, or an earlier form of it, was spoken as the popular language of**

the islands. This language was generally referred to by continental evangelists as the "Iron Language," also called **Pictish** in Scotland and **Cruithin** in Ireland. It seems to indicate that the Basque language hasn't changed much over the past 1500 years.

Figure 1

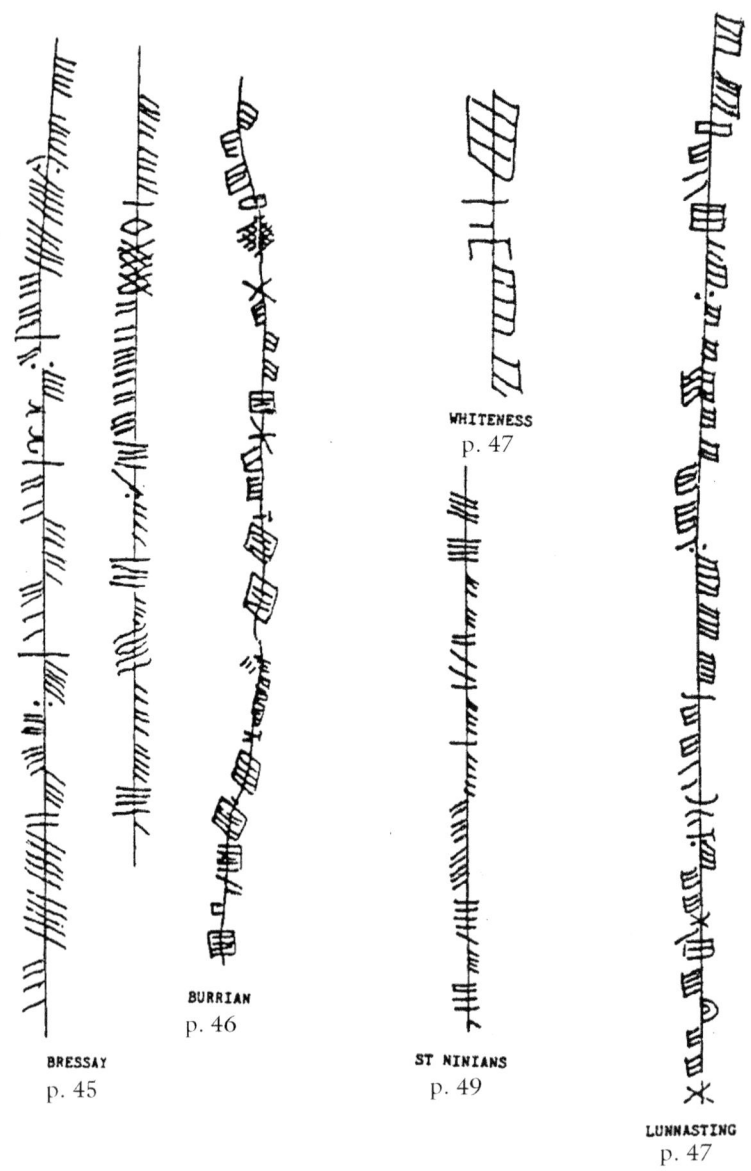

WHITENESS
p. 47

BURRIAN
p. 46

BRESSAY
p. 45

ST NINIANS
p. 49

LUNNASTING
p. 47

Reprinted by permission from Anthony Jackson, 'Pictish Symbol Stones?,' 1993

Figure 2

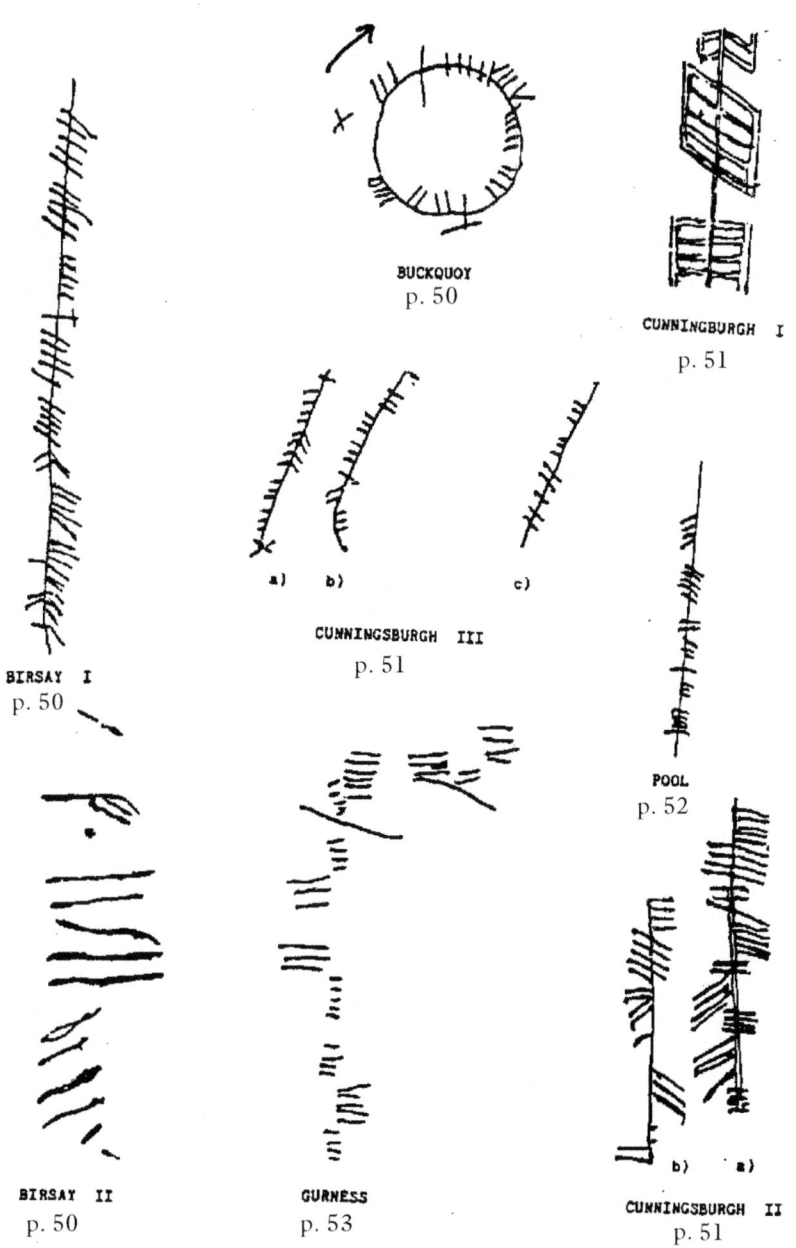

BUCKQUOY
p. 50

CUNNINGBURGH I
p. 51

BIRSAY I
p. 50

a) b) c)

CUNNINGSBURGH III
p. 51

POOL
p. 52

BIRSAY II
p. 50

GURNESS
p. 53

b) a)

CUNNINGSBURGH II
p. 51

Reprinted by permission from Anthony Jackson, 'Pictish Symbol Stones?'

Figure 3

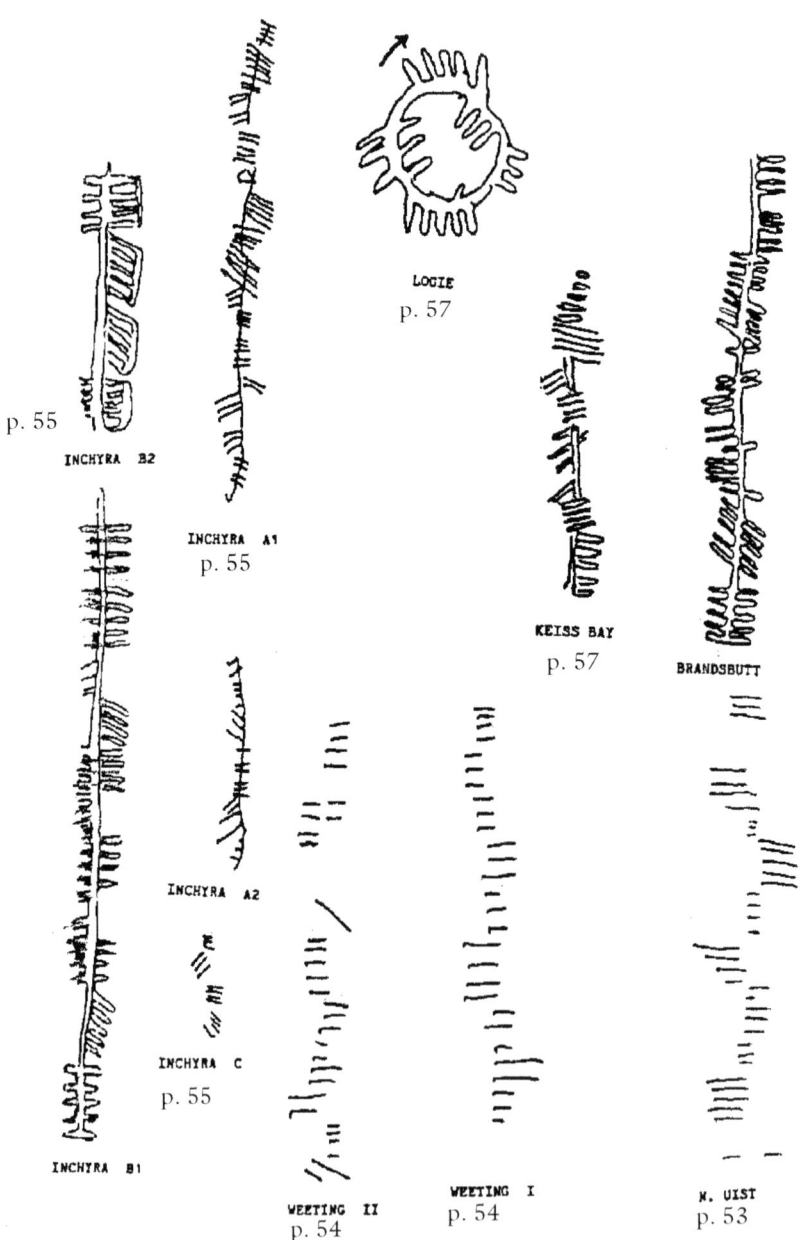

Reprinted by permission from Anthony Jackson, 'Pictish Symbol Stones?' 1993

Figure 4

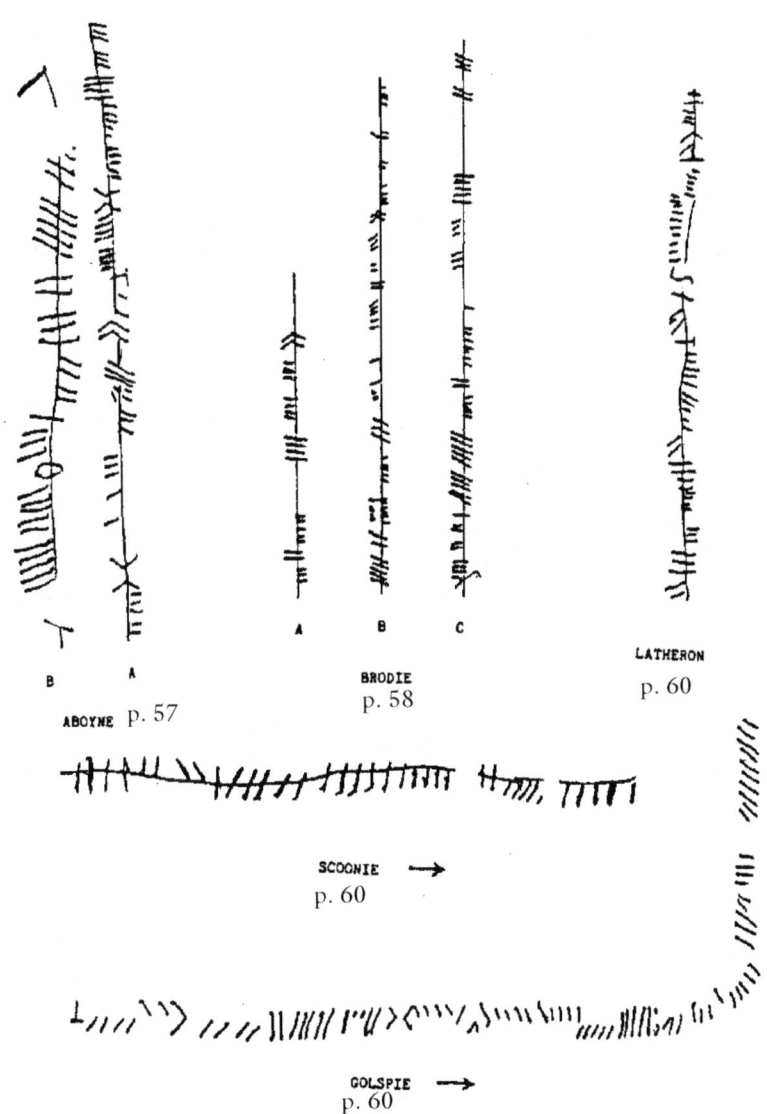

ABOYNE   p. 57

BRODIE
p. 58

LATHERON
p. 60

SCOONIE →
p. 60

GOLSPIE →
p. 60

Reprinted by permission from Anthony Jackson, 'Pictish Symbol Stones?' 1993

Figure 5

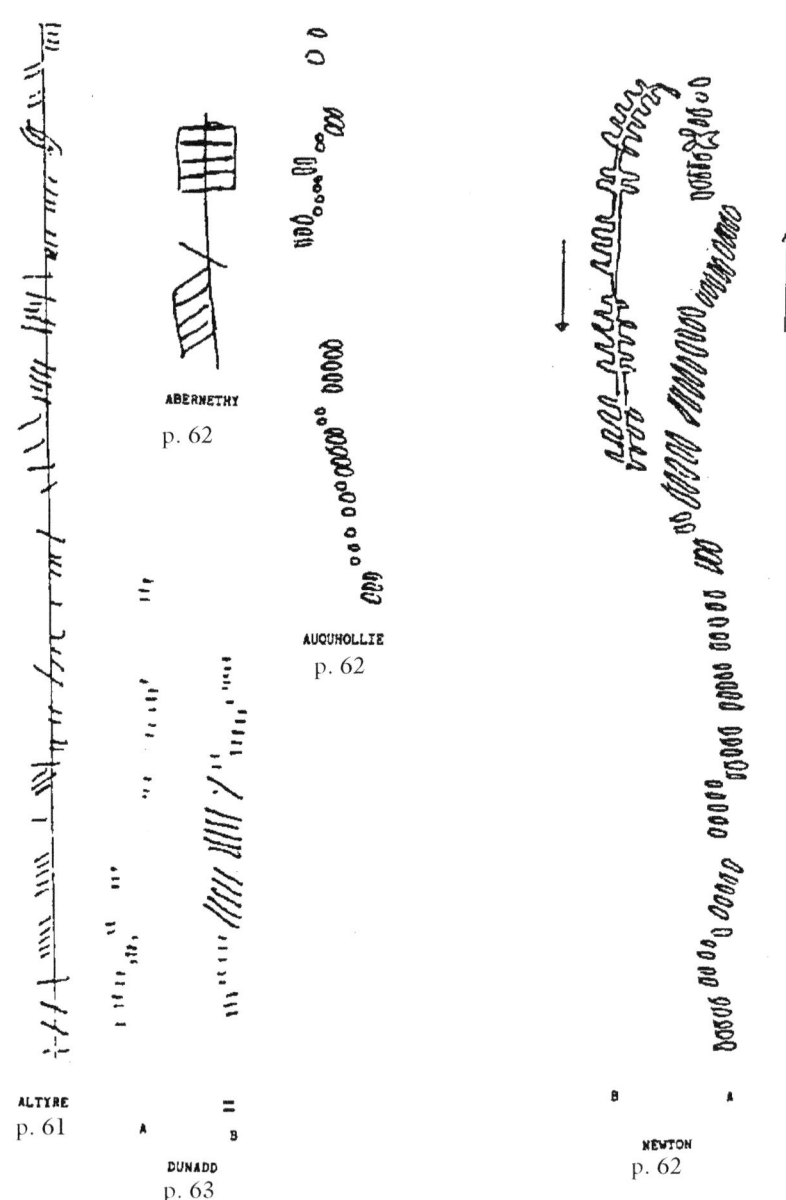

Reprinted by permission from Anthony Jackson, 'Pictish Symbol Stones?' 1993

Irish Ogam Inscriptions

Introduction

Both the early Irish clergy and the succeeding Roman Catholic monks used the Ogam script. As the following examples show, long sentences were condensed into very short Ogam inscriptions by compiling the first consonants of words of the indigenous language of Ireland (Basque) into one "word" with a few vowels thrown in between. The word so acquired usually made no apparent sense at all and wasn't supposed to. The amazing thing about this Ogam script is that it was designed for – and could be used with – one language only. The encoded sentence could be decoded and read with considerable confidence, on condition that the inscription should be clearly legible. The language used was the universal Saharan language, which is still spoken in western Europe as Basque. Many people have tried to translate the inscriptions using the Celtic language, but without any success. **Not a single genuine Ogam inscription is written in Celtic, and so far I have not found a single name in any of them.** The Celtic language did not yet exist at the time these petroglyphs were made, as explained in the Benedictines' own operations manual the "Auraicept." Only the Basque language possesses a complete set of words starting with the vowel-consonant-vowel (VCV) structure of the morphemes, which allows the encoding of almost any sentence into the Ogam script. The modern Basque-English dictionary by Gorka Aulestia is eminently suited to decode and translate many of these very old inscriptions, in combination with my VCV dictionary, as the many examples below show. About half of the words in the Basque vocabulary start with VCV, and it was this VCV half which was used exclusively in the Ogam inscriptions. See also the "Saharan-Basque Language." One very special characteristic of both the Ogam script and the language is that numerical – and letter – magic is built into the structure of the inscription, which early Christian magic was intended to overpower the magic of the pre-Christian religion (see Jackson 1993, chapters 7 and 8). For instance both Q and K are used in the inscriptions and both represent a K, however, the number of strokes in the inscription and the total value of the letters is different, which has to do with the numerical magic of the inscription. The numbers behind the inscription names refer to the "Corpus Inscriptionum Insularum Celticarum" by R.A.S. Macalister, Dublin, Government Printer 1945.

THE BALLISPELLAN BROCHE #27

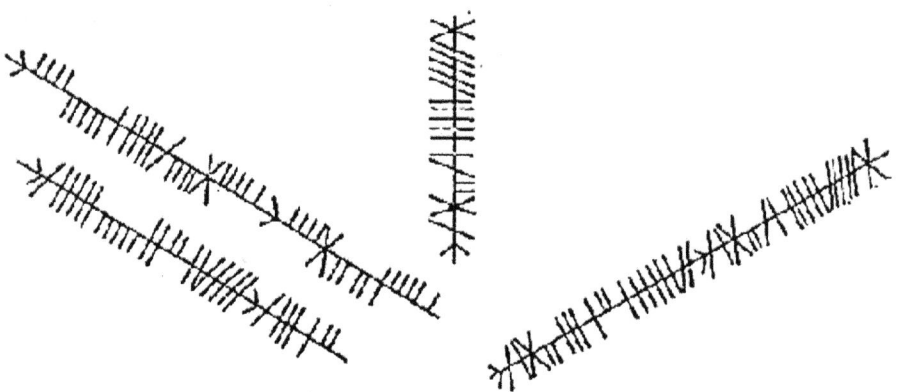

The silver Ballispellan broche is located in the Treasury of the National Museum of Ireland, Dublin. Beside the broche was a description saying that the Ogam engraving on the back side had not yet been translated but that it was expected to give the name of the artist who made the broche. Two years later this card was replaced with the suggestion that the inscription represented the names of four successive owners, even though the lettering was done in exactly the same hand. These remarks were obviously guesswork and became a challenge for me because the Ogam inscription is one of the longer known and has far too many letters to be merely an artist's name or even four names. In fact, the four carefully inscribed lines are one tragic story and there is no break in the interlocking between them. This inscription is #27 in the Irish National Register compiled by R.A.S. Macalister.

CNAEMSECHCELLACH MINODORMUAD MAELMAIRE
MAELUADAIG

As the "C" is not part of the original Ogam alphabet, this letter had to be written as "K." The complete coding would show alternating vowels and consonants: VCVCVCV etc. However, many vowels and some h's were removed so that only people (mostly monks) knowledgeable of the system could read it.

The removed vowels and H's are represented here by dots. The three spaces indicate the places where the vowel-interlocking is interrupted.

.K.NA.EM.SEK.H.KEL.LAK.H. .MINODOR.MU.AD.
.MA.EL.MA.IRE .MA.ELU.ADA.IG.

.k.	aka	*akabu*	death
.na	ana	*anai*	brother
a.e	ahe	*aihezka*	grieving
em.	ema	*emazte*	wife
.se	ase	*aserregorri*	fury
ek.	eka	*ekaizte*	storm
.h.	ahi	*ahituezin*	endless
.ke	ike	*ikertu*	to explore, search
el.	ele	*ele*	story
.la	ela	*elaberriti*	talker, story teller
ak.	aka	*akabu*	dead
.h.	aha	*ahaideko*	relative
.mi	ami	*amilketa*	fell down cliff
ino	ino	*inolaz*	somehow
odo	odo	*odolgaizto*	violently
or.	ora	*oratu*	seized
.mu	amu	*amultsuki*	affectionately, gently
u.a	uha	*uharka*	water body
ad.	ada	*-ada*	roaring
.ma	amai	*amaitu*	endlessly
a.e	aihe	*aihenatu*	to disappear
el.	ele	*elegile*	storyteller
.ma	ama	*emakumezko*	woman
a.i	ahi	*ahitortu*	to witness
ire	ire	*irensle*	swallowing by the sea
ema	emai	*emaitza*	ending
a.e	aihe	*aihenegarri*	lamentable
elu	elu	*elurtu*	to freeze
u.a	uha	*uhalde*	coast
ada	ada	*adarreztatu*	to cover with branches
a.i	ahi	*ahizpa*	woman
ig.	iga	*igar*	dead

"My dead brother's grieving wife searched endlessly in the fury of the storm. The story teller's dead relative had somehow fallen violently down a cliff, was seized gently by the endlessly roaring water and then disappeared. The story teller witnessed the woman being swallowed by the sea. The lamentable ending on that frozen coast was the covering of the dead woman with branches."

Note: The word *irensle* (swallowing) comes from the verb *irentsi* (to swallow). In the context it is a shortening of *itzasoak irentsi hura* (the sea swallowed her). I estimate the inscription on the Ballispellan broche to have been made between 600 and 700 A.D.

DRUMMIN #11

CUNAVATO corrected to: KUNABATO
(also used as an example in "Translating Ogam")

.ku-una-aba-ato

.ku	aku	*akuilatu*	to stimulate
una	una	*unadora*	boredom
aba	aba	*abade*	priest
ato	ato	*ator*	Come!

"The priest will stimulate your boredom; come!"

AHALISKY #70

CUNAGUSOS MAQI MUCOI VIRAGNI
corrected to:
KUNAGUSOS MAKI MUKOI BIRAGNI.

.ku-una-agu-uso-os.   .ma-aki   .mu-uko-oi   .bi-ira-ag.-.ni

.ku	iku	*ikuste*	the act of seeing
una	una	*unatu*	to tire
agu	agu	*agur egin*	to worship
uso	uso	*uso*	dove, holy man
os.	oso	*oso*	sincere
.ma	ama	*ama*	mother
aki	aki	*akiarazi*	to tire, to age
.mu	amu	*amultsu*	affectionate
uko	uko	*uko egin*	to renounce
oi	oi	*oiheskeria*	vulgarity
.bi	ubi	*ubil*	whirlpool
ira	ira	*irauti*	patient
ag.	agu	*agur egin*	to worship
.ni	uni	*unibertsal*	general

"After seeing the tired and sincere holy man in worship, our aged and affectionate mother renounced the vulgarity of the whirlpool by patient general worshiping." (The 'vulgarity of the whirlpool' refers to the human sacrifice, repeated every eight years.)

CARHOOVAULER #73

DOMNGEN

.do-om.-.n.-.ge-en.

.do	ado	*adoratu*	to worship
om.	oma	*oma*	grandmother
.n.	ana	*anaia*	religious brother
.ge	age	*agerian*	openly
en.	ene	*enetan*	always

"Grandmother's religious brother always worshiped openly."

BALLYKNOCK #89

BOGAI MAQI BIRACO
corrected to:
BOGAI MAKI   BIRAKO

.bo-oga-ai   .ma-aki   .bi-ira-ako

.bo	abo	*abonau*	to approve of, to voice
oga	oga	*ogasun*	wealth
ai	ai	*aiene*	lament
.ma	ama	*ama*	mother
aki	aki	*akiarazi*	to tire, to age
.bi	obi	*obi*	grave
ira	ira	*iraunkor*	suffering
ako	ako	*akorduan euki*	to remember

"Voicing a wealth of lament, we remembered our aged mother's suffering by her grave."

BALLINOCK #93

ERCAIDANA corrected to: ERKAIDANA

er.-.ka-ai-ida-ana

er.	eri	*erri*	common people
.ka	ika	*ikaserazi*	to teach
ai	ai	*ai*	strong desire
ida	ida	*idatzi*	to write
ana	ana	*anaia*	religious brother

"While teaching the common people, the religious brother had a strong desire to write."

BALLYKNOCK #94

DEGO MACI VEDUKURI
corrected to:
DEGO MAKI BEDUKURI.

Macalister, because of lack of clarity, had to decide between DOMMO MACI and DEGO MACI and he picked the first one which was impossible to translate. He also rejected someone else's transliteration VEDUCURI in favour of his own VEDUCERI. Again his chosen interpretation was impossible to translate because there exists no such letter combination in Basque as UCE (UKE).

.de-ego	.ma-aki	.be-edu-uku-uri	
.de	ede	*eder egin*	to be pleased
ego	ego	*egon*	to stay
.ma	ama	*ama*	mother
aki	aki	*akitu*	to be exhausted
.be	abe	*abelgorri*	cattle
edu	edu	*eduki*	to keep
uku	uku	*ukuilu*	stable
uri	uri	*urrindu*	to smell

"The exhausted mother was pleased to stay with the cattle, kept in the smelly stable."
Could this refer to Maria giving birth between the cattle in the barn?

BALLYKNOCK #95

ANM MEDDOGENI.

an.-.m. / .me-ed.-.do-oge-eni			
an.	ana	*anaia*	religious brother
.me	ame	*amestu*	to imagine, to wonder
.me	eme	*emen*	here
ed.	edi	*ediren*	to find
.do	ido	*idor*	dry
oge	oge	*oge*	bed
eni	eni	*enitzat*	for me

"The religious brother wondered: 'How do I find a dry bed out here for me?'"

This hardly sounds like an immortal phrase to me. Someone else please give it a try.

BALLYKNOCK #96

COVALOTI corrected to: KOBALOTI.

.ko – oba – alo – oti

.ko	oko	*okolu*	stable
oba	oba	*oba*	better
alo	alo	*alorgizon*	farmer
oti	oti	*otzikaratu*	to shiver

"The shivering farmer (felt) better in the stable."
(another phrase which is hardly immortal)

BALLYHANK #100

AB ULCCAGNI corrected to AB. ULKKAGNI

ab. ul.-.k.-.ka-ag.-.ni

ab./	aba	*abade*	priest
ul.	ula	*ulatu*	to welcome
.k.	aki	*akigabe*	tirelessly
.ka	ika	*ikaserazi*	to teach
ag.	agu	*agur egin*	to worship
.ni	uni	*unibertsal*	general

"The welcome priest tirelessly teaches general worship."

KILMARTIN LOWER #109

UDDMENSA CELI NETTASLOGI

ud.-.d.-.me-en.-.sa / seli-.ne-et.-ta-.as.-.lo-ogi

ud.	uda	*udazken*	autumn
.d.	ade	*adelatu*	to prepare
.me	eme	*emen*	here
en.	ena	*-ena*	(superlative) great
.sa	asa	*asaldaketa*	excitement
.se	ase	*asete*	period of abundance
eli	eli	*elikatura*	food
.ne	ane	*anega*	grain measure/supply
et.	ete	*etenkatu*	to interrupt
et.	eta	*-eta*	action/work
as.	ase	*asegaitz*	craving
.lo	alo	*alorgizon*	farmer
ogi	ogi	*ogi*	bread

"In the autumn we prepare here for the great excitement of the period of abundant food of the grain supply, the work only interrupted by our craving for farmer's bread."

KNOCKSHANAWEE #112

MICANAVVI MAQ LUGUNI
corrected to:
MIKANABBI MAK LEGUNI

Macalister comments that the two U's are very faint, and indeed the first U is incorrect because there is no morpheme UGU in the Basque language. The following translation will show why it should have been EGU.

.mi-ika-ana-ab.-.bi .ma-ak.   .le-egu-uni

.mi	umi	*umil*	humble
ika	ika	*ikasi*	to learn
ana	ana	*anaia*	religious brother
.ba	aba	*abantailadun*	privileged
ab.	abi	*abilitate*	talented
.ma	ema	*eman*	to teach
ak.	aki	*akigabe*	tirelessly
.le	ele	*ele*	story
egu	egu	*egundainoko*	eternal
uni	uni	*unibertsal*	universal

"Humbly learn from the talented and privileged religious brother who is tirelessly teaching the eternal story of the universal God."

KNOCKSHANAWEE #113

VEQIKAMI MAQI LUGUNI
corrected to:
BEKIKAMO MAKI LEGUNI

.be-eki- ika-ami   .ma-aki .le-egu-uni

.be	ebe	*ebertar*	Hebrew, Jesus
eki	eki	*ekinalean*	as much as possible
ika	ika	*ikasi*	to learn
ami	amo	*amodio*	love
.ma	ema	*eman*	to teach
aki	aki	*akigabe*	tirelessly

.le	ele	*ele*	story
egu	egu	*egundainoko*	eternal
uni	uni	*unibertsal*	universal

"Learn as much as possible about Jesus' love, then tirelessly teach the eternal story of the universal God."

MONATAGGERT #118

VEQREQ MUCOI GLUNLEGGET
corrected to:
BEKREK MOSOI GLUNLEGGET

In the entrance hall of the National Museum of Ireland in Dublin stands a tall slim stone, one of the thousands of megalithic stones which were placed upright by the pre-Christian Irish. It was found in 1872 and had been used as building material in an underground chamber in Monataggert, County Cork. On this stone (#118 in Macalister's National Register) an Ogam inscription was carved which to this day is regarded as the grave-marker of Mr. Glun Legget, whoever he may have been. They say this only because the last letters of the inscription read GLUNLEGGET. The fact that this "name" is written in one word, is explained as a "typo" made by the inscriber, who "forgot" to leave a space after GLUN (McManus 5.29). The binomial system of naming was not introduced until several centuries later. But so ingrained is the belief that all Irish Ogam stones are grave markers and that the inscriptions say something like: "here lies Johnny mourned by Mary," that any suggestion a quite different explanation could exist was rejected right out of hand by museum staff. The letters "Legget" were adopted by an Irish family as their tribal name.

.be-ek.-.re-ek. .mo-oso-oi .g.-.lu-un.-.le-.eg.-.ge-et.

.be	abe	*abe*	cross
ek.	eku	*ekurutasun*	peace of mind
.re	ure	*urentasun*	nobility
ek.	eka	*ekarri*	to bring
.mo	amo	*amodio*	love
oso	oso	*osoro*	totally
o.i	ohi	*ohilkor*	oppressed
.g.	agi	*aginbide*	authority
.lu	ilu	*ilun*	dull
un.	una	*unagarri*	darkness
.le	ale	*alegera*	rejoicing
eg.	egi	*egiazki*	true
.ge	ige	*iges*	escaping
et.	eto	*etorki*	caste, clan

"The peace of mind of the noble Cross brings love to the totally oppressed. It has the authority (to change) dull darkness into true rejoicing when escaping from the clan."

GLEBE #131.

LITUBIRI MAQI QESIA
corrected to
LITUBIRI MAKI KESIA

.li	ali	*alienatu*	to kill a person
itu	itxu	*itxurigabe*	senseless
ubi	ubi	*ubil*	whirlpool
iri	iri	*iritzezin*	inconceivable
.ma	ima	*imajina*	statue, idol
aki	aki	*akiakula*	excuse
ake	ake	*akela*	Goddess, priestess
esi	ezi	*ezigabe*	savage
i.a	iha	*ihabali*	frightening

"The senseless killing of a person in the whirlpool as an idol is an inconceivable excuse by the savage priestess and is frightening."

COOLMAGORT #197.

DEGOS MAQI MOCOI TOICAKI
corrected to
DEGOS MAKI MOSOI TOIKAKI

.de-ego-os.	.ma-aki	.mo-oso-oi	.to-o.i-ika-aki
de	de	*deboziotu*	to be devoted
ego	ego	*egoki*	to be concerned
os .	oso	*oso*	sincere
.ma	ama	*ama*	mother
aki	aki	*akigarri*	aging
.mo	emo	*emonkor*	generous
oso	oso	*oso*	sincere
oi	oi	*oialgin*	weaver
.to	eto	*etorri*	inspiration
oi	oi	*oituraz*	always

| ika | ika | *ikaserazi* | teaching |
| aki | aki | *akigabe* | tireless |

"Devoted, concerned and sincere, our aging mother was an inspiring weaver, always teaching tirelessly."

COOLMAGORT #199.

CUNACENA corrected to: KUNAKENA.

Seven stones found in a souterrain in 1838 were presented by the owner to the Irish people and were brought to the surface and protected from the elements. This is stone #3.

.ku-una-ake-ena

.ku	uku	*ukur*	evil
una	una	*unagarri*	annoying
ake	ake	*akela*	priestess
ena	ena	*ena*	(superlative) extremely

"The priestess is extremely evil and annoying."

KILCOOLAGHT #211.

RITTUVVECC MAQI VEDDONOS.
corrected to:
RITTUBBEKK MAKI BEDDONOS.

.ri	eri	*erio*	death
it.	iti	*iti*	to denounce
.tu	itu	*ituragabe*	senseless
ub.	ubi	*ubil*	whirlpool
.be	ibe	*ibeni*	to bring about
ek.	eko	*ekoizpen*	fertility
.k.	oka	*okaztagarri*	disgusting
.ma	ama	*ama*	mother
aki	aki	*akiarazi*	aged
.be	ebe	*ebertar*	Jew, Jesus
ed.	eda	*edangura*	thirsting for
.do	ado	*adoratu*	to worship
ono	ono	*onon*	wonderful
os.	oso	*oso*	sincere

"(Mother) denounced the senseless death in the whirlpool to bring about disgusting fertility. Our aged mother thirsted for Christ's wonderfully sincere worship."

WHITEFIELD #215.

ALATTO CELI BATTIGNI
corrected to:
ALATTO KELI BATTIGNI.

ala	ala	*alabeharreko*	necessary
at.	ate	*ateratu*	to leave
.to	eto	*etorri*	come!
.ke	ike	*ikertu*	to visit, to go to
eli	eli	*eliza*	church
.ba	aba	*oba*	better
ati	ati	*atiki*	to gather
ig.	iga	*igar*	dead, body
.ni	ani	*ani*	anitz

"It is necessary to leave. Come, let's go to the church. It is better to gather the many bodies at the refuge."

WHITEFIELD #216.

GOSOCTEAS MOSAC MAKINI.

.go	ago	*agortu*	to dry up
oso	oso	*oso*	perfect
ok.	oka	*okaldi*	bellyful
.te	ate	*atera*	to get
as.	ase	*asearazi*	to stuff
.mo	umo	*umo*	sensible
osa	osa	*osaketa*	healing
ak.	ako	*akorduan euki*	to remember
.ma	ama	*ama*	mother
aki	aki	*akiarazi*	aged
ini	ini	*ini*	my

"It is perfect to dry up and get your belly stuffed full. We remembered the sensible healing by our aged mother."

KINGULBIN EAST #1086

BLADNACH COGRADEDENA and BLADNACH CUILEN
BLADNAK KOGRADEDENA and BLADNAK KUILEN.

These inscriptions are found on a bronze hanging bowl, probably an incense burner, dug up from a swamp in County Kerry. McManus (7.6) writes: "They are inscribed along the upper surface of the rim and on one of the escutcheons." This bowl may be seen in the National Museum in Dublin.

Bladnak:

.b.-la-ad.-.na-ak

.b.	abe	*abe*	cross
.la	ela	*ela*	story
ad.	ade	*adelatu*	to prepare
.na	ena	*ena*	that
ak.	aka	*akabu*	ultimate, superior

kogradedena:

.ko-og.-.ra-ade-ede-ena

.ko	ako	*akorduan euki*	to remember
og.	ogi	*ogizatitze*	breaking of the bread
.ra	ira	*iragan*	to suffer
ade	ade	*adelatu*	to prepare
ede	ede	*edergi*	to confide in
dena	dena	*Deuna*	Lord

"The story of the Cross prepares us for that ultimate remembrance while preparing for the breaking of the bread (for His) suffering (while we) confide in the Lord."

kuilen:

.ku	eku	*ekurutasun*	peace of mind
ile	ile	*ilezin*	everlasting
en.	ene	*eneganatu*	to come over me/us

"The story of the cross prepares us for that ultimate everlasting peace of mind (which will) come over us."

THE BALLINTAGGERT STONE

Transliteration:
B.Fell: **Ma-q -q -i -i -a -r -i y i m a**
E.Nyland: **.MAK.KI.IARI.E.A.IMA**

This rather startling Ogam inscription is included here to give an impression of the great variety of topics written on stone in Ireland. The Ballintaggert text is inscribed on a phallic stone from County Kerry, Ireland (James P. Whittall II). The transliteration was published in Barry Fell's book *America B.C.* (p.22) and corrected by me. I inserted dots to show where the author of the inscription had eliminated vowels. Fell's "y" in the transliteration could not be used as this letter is not part of the Ogam alphabet. Also, the "X" shown in the inscription is the standard forfeda character for "EA." More about the five forfeda characters in the article on translating Ogam.

.ma–ak–.ki–i.i–i.a–ari–i.e–e.a–ima

.ma	ema	*emagose*	sexual desire
ak.	aku	*akuilatu*	stimulate
.ki	uki	*ukitu*	to touch
i.i	ihi	*ihizitegi*	secret place
i.a	iha	*ihardun*	to spend time
ari	ari	*arrigarri*	marvelous
i.e	ihe	*ihesaldi*	escape
e.a	eha	*ea*	emphasis
a.i	ahi	*ahigarri*	exhausting
ima	ima	*imatz*	wattle shelter

"Stimulate your sexual desire by touching your secret place and spend a marvelous time in exhausting escape in the wattle shelter."

THE HORSE CREEK PETROGLYPH OF WEST VIRGINIA

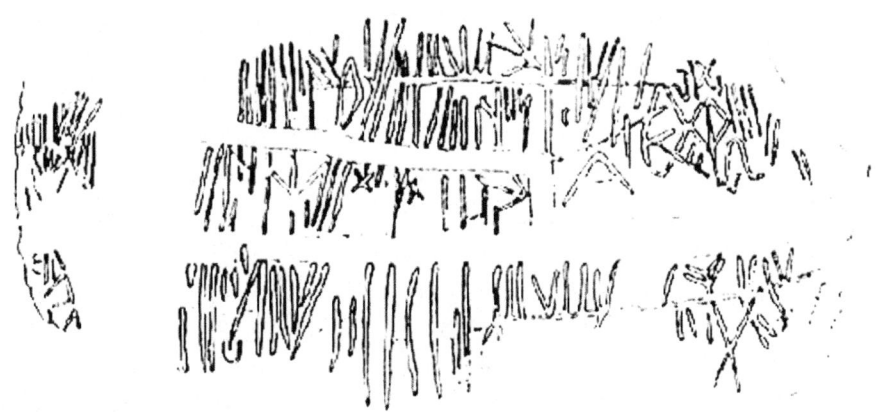

The Horse Creek Ogam inscription was first published in the March 1983 issue of *Wonderful West Virginia*. The transliteration from the Ogam script to our characters was done by Dr. Barry Fell, professor emeritus from Harvard University, a difficult job well done. He also made an attempt at translation, assuming that the writing was in the Gaelic language, which it was not. The result of this effort was published in the same article but was severely criticized by a number of academics.

The letter sequence, as transliterated by Dr. Fell, is as follows (his c's are shown here as k's):

Top line: **RGHMKUIHMNMKSBDLKSTUIGNMO*IDI*AAIOSAMFLL**

Middle line: **MGNTLGMIATGEANBT**

Bottom line: **BHGTOIRGLGGBMOITKDIAHFKIOND**

The eye: **TLMDSDIADIONL**

This petroglyph may well be the longest known Ogam inscription in the world. Ogam writing is always done in a severely abbreviated manner, in which each consonant of the inscription represents a full word. Except for the first word of each line, the author of the inscription used words which began with vowel-consonant-vowel (VCV, occasionally VCCV). The drafting of an Ogam inscription is an exacting and time consuming task; first the words are selected and abbreviated to their first three letters and arranged as: VCV_1-V_1CV_2-V_2CV_3-V_3CV_4-V_4CV etc. The words are so chosen that the vowels on either side of the hyphens are identical, indicated by the numbering. I called this the "VCV vowel interlocking formula" and is used in all Ogam inscriptions without exception. It is this vowel-interlocking feature of the formula which allows the restoration of the missing vowels. When the design was completed, all but a few of the vowels and h's were carefully selected and eliminated by the writer, creating an apparently unintelligible jumble of consonants with a few vowels sprinkled here and there. The main body of the Horse Creek petroglyph has only two breaks in the interlocking, which were used by the author to create three lines, top, middle and bottom.

Carefully designed Ogam inscriptions, especially those from which the majority of the vowels have been purged, contain a "translation key." This is intended as the place to begin deciphering, often in the form of a complete VCV, which expresses a key word in the inscription. This is the case here in the VCV: *idi*, located in the top line, which means "ox or bison." It was not until a full year after having translated the inscription that I noticed the entire petroglyph was also arranged in the shape of a bison, complete with the characteristic hump formed by the top line, with the eyes and mouth outlined by smaller characters, all artistically arranged. See the issue of *Wonderful West Virginia*.

In the following translation the letters provided in the inscription have been inserted in the VCV vowel-interlocking formula. In most cases the consonants stand alone, but flanked by dots which represent the missing vowels. As the key word *idi* suggested, the language of the inscription is **Basque**. Working systematically with a good quality Basque dictionary such as Aulestia's, the words can be restored and translated with considerable confidence. All Basque words are shown in italics. Basque has no "c" and our "sh" is written as "x."

Top Line: RGHMKUIHMNMKSBDLKSTUIGNMO*IDI*AAIOSAMFLL

All the Ogam letters up to and including **IDI** are analyzed to provide a quite elaborate example of the decoding process used. Even though the letters are recorded here in the normal given order, we have to work backward from **IDI** to restore the VCV's used by the designer of the inscription. This means, of course, that we read the tables from right to left starting from **IDI**.

.R.G.H.M.

.Ri			**.Ga**	**.Ha**		**.Me**
ari	**iri**	**uri**	**aga**	**aha**	**oha**	**ame**
mission	town, city	city	long pole	I hope	bed, warning	makefortune
to him/her	to open	city forest	abundance	perhaps	concubine	dream
active, race	pulverize	low tide	hitting	anger, trial	comment	unreal
wound, soul	wasteful	butter	to lash	argument	thoughtful	nightmare
ruthless	achievement	urban	to whip	capable	spontaneous	*mirage*
escape, light	judge	grease	**ega**	attempt	distracted	fancy
thoughtless	arrive, to get	escape	possible	possible	attraction	idealize
pertinent	agreement	scarce	flying	*powerful*	lookout	**eme**
arri	moderator	defective	edge, wing	shame, bold	counselor	female
rock, stone	**irri**	miserable	protection	mouthful	**uha**	smooth
surprise	malignant	to decrease	thirsty	to forget	belt, coast	shy, here
amazing	smile	be merciful	anxiety	injury	pebble	enlarge
awful	laughable	reduction	to favour	ram, dirt	flood	native
landmark	jovial	repentant	**iga**	duck, bark	deluge	peaceful
to risk, pave	ridicule	aroma	fruit	**eha**	to fasten	**ime**
eri	ambition	fem. animal	to rise	emphasis	watertower	N.A.
sickness	anxious	hazel trees	to dress up	indirect	riverbed	**ome**
finger	risk, sliding		wilted	question	turbidity	honor, fame
noxious	skate, sled		prophet	**iha**	island	tribute
death	yearn for		to guess	jovial	turn yellow	according to
agony	sarcastic		to travel	expertise	floodgate	**ume**
opinion	**ori**		tolerant	dry, wallow	lettuce	child
to compare	that, yellow		last year	answer		young
to think	gold colored		unpredictable	argue		give birth
erri	except		*to pass by*	spend time		prolific
town, public	to paint		dead	carnival		overripe
region,native	freckle		bearable	to scatter		nursery
migration	**orri**			to discuss		womb
to fight	sheet			almost		to adopt
strong	foliage					orphan
skillful	banquet					
common people	covered with leaves					

.KU.IH.M.N.M.K.S.

.KU	UhI	Iha	.Mu	.Ne	.Me	.Ka
aku	**uhi**	**iha**	**amu**	**ane**	**ame**	**aka**
stimulate	*undulate*	expertise	fishhook	measure	fortune	death
to incite	wave	jovial	*unsuspecting*	**ene**	dream	ultimate
to lease		dry, argue	tender	my, always	unreal	to argue
acoustic		answer	affectionate	exclamation	nightmare	perfect
eku		frightened	distrust	property	fantasy	superior
equator		spend time	bait	attract me	idealize	**eka**
worry		to scatter	**emu**	when	**eme**	substance
peace of mind		to move	N.A.	my dear	female, shy	solstice
quiet		discuss	**imu**	**ine**	here	storm
to touch		cheerful	to pinch	inertia	native	used to
mention		almost	**omu**	do nothing	*peaceful*	contribute
flag, gift			N.A.	downtroddn	**ime**	*bringabout*
curiosity			**umu**	**one**	N.A.	habit
visible			N.A.	good, kind	**ome**	**ika**
to look				benefit	honor, fame	familiar
inspection				patience	tribute	fright
to visit				exemplary	according to	to terrorize
to wash				advantage	**ume**	to learn
hostility				come here	child	to come
oku				praise, best	give birth	**oka**
stable				tolerant	litter	nausia
chin				honesty	prolific	disgust
uku				conciliate	over ripe	occasional
to go bad				right now	nursery	**uka**
stable				**une**	womb	hand, arm
falsify				moment	to adopt	to have
smelly				place	orphan	possession
				spot, instant		to deny
				short distance		elbow

.S.B.D.L.K.S.TU

.Sa	.Ba	.Da	.La	.Ko	.So	.TU
asa	**aba**	**ada**	**ala**	**ako**	**aso**	**atu**
ancestor	priest	noise	in that way	agreement	N.A.	tuna
go away	rectory	to mend	necessary	*to remember*	**eso**	stoney place
shocking	occasion	horn	daughter	traditional	advice	oak forest
agitation	opportunity	*branches*	*shouting*	accordion	**iso**	better world
disturb	slingshot	tease, gore	indeed	**eko**	torrential rain	**etu**
to annoy	surpass		however	to produce	isolation	brambles
esa	rower		fate, amen	fertile	**oso**	resigned to
to say	*to advance*		casual	fruitful	total	**itu**
expression	almost		fatal	administrate	*whole*	leakage
speaker	branch,shade		I swear to	**iko**	global	agreement
meaning	**eba**		happy,widow	that	sincere	testament
moral	slice, thief		similar	swelling	simple	treaty
isa	harvest		miracle	hammer	absolutely	melancholic
broom, tail	remnant		feeding	lump	thorough	to agree
furze	evaluation		fill with joy	**oko**	**uso**	be advised
osa	evangelist		**ela**	stable	dove	fountain
to get well	gospel		word, story	chin	holy man	origin
uncle	to plunder		talkative	**uko**		frontal
therapy	to decide		swallow	refusal		**otu**
composition	**iba**		elastic	elbow		savage
incurable	river		**ila**	negative		to happen
doctor	lowland		dead, hair			meal
usa	shore, ferry		pea, moon			**utu**
dove, to use	valley		in a row			cloth
usage	**oba**		to murder			sailboat
stink	better		lunatic			
small, habit	naturally		tombstone			
aroma	improvement		lifetime			
holy man	**oba**		to destroy			
	cormorant		**ola**			
			factory, cabin			
			sledge, wave			
			ula			
			N.A.			

U.IG.N.MO.IDI.A

U.I	IG.	.N.	.MO	O.I	IDI	I.A
uhi	**iga**	**anu**	**amo**	**ohi**	**idi**	**iha**
wave	fruit, rise	fainting		custom	ox	almost
ripple	to wither	*fall back*	affectionate	adjust	*bison*	jovial
undulate	sign	*in fear*	grandmother	savage	crib	expertise
	prophet,travel	**enu**	mistress	stampede	to open	dry,answer
	tolerant	useless	gallantry	suffering		to wallow
	dead	weakness	to oblige	get used to		frightened
	to pass by	**inu**	fury, refund	forest		spend time
	unpredictable	to nurse	tolerant	cloth		to scatter
		evening,ant	**emo**	sailboat		to discuss
		heath	give, present			almost
		prickly	future			cheerful
		thunder	to transmit			hardly
		inspiring	**imo**			
		onu	N.A.			
		profit,earning	**omo**			
		perfect	N.A.			
		beneficial	**umo**			
		good faith	ripe, mature			
		unu	sensibly			
		N.A.	uterus, joke			
			funny,mood			
			bad tempered			

Fell's reading:

RGHMKUIHMNMKSBDLKSTUIGNMOIDIAAIOSAMFLL

Nyland's reading:

RGHMKUIHMNMKSBDLKSTUIGNMOIDIAOOSIEAMFLL

.r.	eri	*errialdaketa*	migration
.g.	iga	*igaro*	to pass by
.h.	aha	*ahaldun*	powerful
.m.	ame	*ameslilura*	mirage
.ku	eku	*ekuru*	quietly
u.i	uhi	*uhindu*	undulating
ih.	iha	*iharrosi*	to move
.m.	amu	*amultsuki*	unsuspectingly
.n.	une	*unetxo*	short distance
.m.	eme	*emeki*	peacefully
.k.	eka	*ekarraraki*	o bring about
.s.	asa	*asaldu*	disturbance
.b.	aba	*abantailatu*	to advance
.d.	ada	*adarrots*	rattling branches
.l.	ala	*alarao*	shouting
.k.	ako	*akorduaneuki*	to remember
.s.	oso	*oso*	whole
.tu	otu	*uhin*	wave
ig.	iga	*igaro*	to pass by
.n.	anu	*anu-egin*	fall back in fear
.mo	umo	*umoretxar*	bad tempered
o.i	ohi	*ohildu*	stampede
idi	idi	*iditalde*	herd of bison
i.a	iha	*ihabali*	frightened
aho	aho	*ahoketa*	entrance to narrow passage
oho	oho	*oholesi*	wooden fence
osi	osi	*osintsu*	abyss
i.e	ihe	*ihesean*	in flight
e.a	eha	*ea*	come and help!
am.	ama	*ama*	clan-mother
.f.	afa	*afa*	pleased
.l.	ale	*alegin*	effort
.l.	el	*elkarrune*	co-operative

"The migration passed by like a powerful mirage, quietly undulating and moving unsuspectingly a short distance, peacefully. To bring about a disturbance we advanced rattling branches and shouting."

"I remember that a whole wave happened to pass by and we fell back in fear (to avoid) the bad-tempered stampede of the frightened herd of bison (moving into) the entrance of the narrow wooden-fenced passage and into the abyss in flight. Come and help! The clan-mother was pleased with our co-operative effort."

Middle Line: **MGNTLGMIATGEANBT**

.m.	ma	*makila*	club
.g.	aga	*agakada*	blows
.n.	ane	*anega*	measure
.t.	eta	*-eta*	abundant
.l.	ala	*alako*	because
.g.	aga	*-aga*	many
.mi	ami	*amildu*	to fall into ravine
i.a	iha	*ihardukitze*	to resist
at.	ata	*atalkatu*	broken legs
.ge	age	*ageriz*	obviously
e.a	eha	*ea*	come and help
an.	ana	*anaiak*	brothers
.b.	abe	*aberehiltzaile*	slaughterer
.t.	ete	*etentze*	finished off

"Club blows in abundant measure (were needed) because many which had fallen into the ravine resisted with obviously broken legs. Brothers, come and help the slaughterer to finish them off."

Bottom Line: **BHGTOIRGLGGBMOITKDIAHFKIOND**

.b.	ibi	*ibilgetu*	to hold still, to prevent
.h.	ihe	*ihespide*	escape
.g.	ega	*egan egin*	to run away
.to	ato	*atonketa*	preparations
o.i	ohi	*ohituzko*	usual
ir.	iru	*irunakatu*	to divide in three parts
.g.	uga	*ugalde*	edge of the stream
.l.	ale	*alegeratu*	to rejoice
.g.	ego	*egoki*	convenient, welcome
.g.	oga	*ogasun*	riches
.b.	abe	*aberehiltze*	to butcher
.mo	emo	*emonkor*	plentiful

o.i	ohi	*ohigabe*	unaccustomed
it.	itu	*iturri*	origin, at first
.k.	uka	*ukagaitz*	undeniably
.di	adi	*adi-egon*	to pay attention
i.a	iha	*iharduki*	to be busy with
ah.	aha	*ahalik*	as ... as possible
.f.	afa	*afa*	happy
.ki	aki	*akipen*	exhausted
i.o	ho	*ihortziri*	thunder
on.	ona	*ona*	in this direction
.d.	ada	*-ada*	noise of the action

"Having prevented escape by running away, we made the usual preparations by the edge of the stream and happily rejoiced in dividing the welcome riches into three parts by plentiful butchering. At first unaccustomed (to the task) we undeniably had to pay attention. We were as busy as possible and so happily exhausted that (we didn't notice) the noise of the thunder coming in our direction."

The next line of the inscription (TLMDSDIADIONL), in smaller Ogam characters, is located just left of the top line and forms the eye and forehead of the bison. The translation indicates that it belongs after the three lines of the main inscription. Another small petroglyph, identified by Dr. Fell as written in Libyan Ogam, forms the nostrils and mouth, but these have not yet been transliterated, to my knowledge. Actually it is highly likely that the entire inscription was written in Libyan Ogam.

TLMDSDIADIONL

.t.	eta	*etapa*	some distance away
.l.	ala	*alabe*	in spite of
.m.	ama	*ama*	clan mother
.d.	adi	*adionez*	just in time
.s.	isi	*isilaldi*	period of silence
.di	idi	*idikorta*	cattle shelter
i.a	iha	*ihardun*	to wait out
adi	adi	*adindun*	sensibly
i.o	iho	*ihortziri*	thunder
on.	on	*ondo*	approaching
.l.	l?	*laguntxo?*	your dear friend?

"In spite of (being) some distance away, the clan mother, just in time, reached the cattle shelter during a period of silence, to sensibly wait out the approaching thunder. Your dear Friend (?)"

This long inscription was signed with "L" which could be an abbreviation for *laguntxo* (your dear friend), *lagun* (comrade), *lagunarte* (group of friends) etc. and was used to end a letter. The word "ama" is mentioned twice in the text, which may mean: mother, priestess or clan mother. It is suggested that the author of this inscription was a Gnostic Christian monk, who was trained in Ogam writing in Irish tradition, and that the ama mentioned referred to the head of the matrilineally organized clan. The symbol which Dr. Fell interprets as the Greek letter "omega" is probably a sketch of the ground plan of the wooden fence, while his "alpha" character may illustrate the A-frame type of construction used to build the bison fence. Concrete evidence of these people has been found in ancient graves which contained crucifixes and pendants with crosses, discussed by archaeologist R.L.Pyle in his book: *All That Remains* (p53-57). Based on archaeological information and the type of Ogam used, I estimate the date of the inscription to be between 600 and 700 A.D.

It appears from the description of St. Brendan's travels in the Navigatio that the early Irish evangelists, who were Gnostic Christians (centred in Alexandria), were experienced ocean sailors and had no problems maintaining contact with their brethren across the Atlantic. This changed when Roman Catholic Christians (based in Rome), being the landlubber variety, took control in Ireland and left the colonies in America to fend for themselves. Judging by the many megalithic stone structures left by these people in New Hampshire, Pennsylvania, Vermont, New York, Massachusetts, Virginia etc. (Boland and Fell) it is well possible that this colonization effort started centuries earlier. Robert Pyle mentions that in the *Saga of Eric the Red* the Norsemen saw men dressed in white robes in what appeared to be an Irish ecclesiastical procession. Several centuries later, early American settlers were astonished to see many native Indians with fair skin and blue eyes (Pyle p66). These people were quickly absorbed by the new wave of immigrants and are even today proudly remembered as ancestors of some of the "earliest" American families.

The name "Brendan" is of interest. It derives from "brenda-an": *barrenda* (to spy, to explore) and *anai* (religious brother, monk) i.e. exploring monk. It is now desirable that the other East Coast Ogam inscriptions are deciphered. I have no doubt that they are all written in the same language. Some will be difficult because too many vowels were removed from them, which makes accurate translation a real challenge but none are impossible. The Basque language is very logically, almost mathematically, arranged and these problematical Ogam inscriptions may lend themselves to computer decoding. A whole new chapter in the history of North America waits to be written.

THE AURAICEPT NA N'ECES

THE BENEDICTINES ARRIVE IN IRELAND

When the Benedictine monks arrived from the continent, they entered the thriving country of Ireland with its ancient civilization. They also found the Gnostic Christian church already firmly established and actively spreading its own Gospel. The level of education, the quality of the arts and the vibrant energy of life was at a far higher level in Ireland than anything the orthodox Christian monks had experienced on the continent. It was into this happy and caring civilization that they had been ordered to introduce their own more primitive brand of civilization and learning. This was an embarrassing situation because the Benedictine monks at first had far more to learn than to contribute. They started by establishing themselves in monasteries such as the ones in Bangor (County Down) and Clonmacnoise (County Offaly).

The North African connection with Ireland could not be tolerated by these continentals, so slowly they introduced the fictitious idea that this creative and energetic civilization had been brought to Ireland by "Celtic immigrants" from the European mainland, some 450 years before Christ. It didn't matter that these Celts had only migrated as far as southern England and had never set foot in Ireland, or that the true Celtic culture on the continent was in fact quite primitive compared to that of the Irish. Herodotus, who had given the Celts their name "Keltoi," didn't speak highly of them because the name translates to: "Worrisome, meat-eating savages" from: *.ke-el.-.to-o.i*, oke-eli-ito-ohi: *okela* (meat) *elikatu* (to nourish) *itoaldi* (worrisome) *ohil* (savage). Julius Caesar, who was in close contact with the real Keltoi, supplied us with many Keltic names in his book "Conquest of Gaul" and not a single one of them can even remotely be considered related to the Celtic language; they are all made up with the use of the vowel-interlocking formula and all can be translated with the Basque dictionary. In order to develop the respect they traditionally demanded, the monks somehow had to convince the Irish people that their North African based culture had originally been inferior to what the Keltoi had brought from the European continent. In that untruth they succeeded beyond expectation because even today many Irish proudly call themselves Celts, even though there is not one shred of evidence anywhere that the Keltoi ever reached Ireland, except for what the Benedictine monks themselves had written about it.

THE CREATION OF THE IRISH LANGUAGE

The Auraicept tells us about the origin of Irish:

> *Fenius Farsaid, a learned man in the three principal languages (**Latin, Greek, Hebrew**) journeyed together with Goidle mac Etheoir, Iar mac Nema and a retinue of 72 scholars from Scythia to the Plain of Shinar with the intention of studying the languages confused at Nimrod's Tower. Finding that these had been dispersed throughout the world he sent forth his scholars to study them, staying on at the tower himself co-ordinating the enterprise and supporting his scholars with food and clothing. Having completed their investigations the scholars returned after ten years and requested that Fenius select for them from all the languages of the world one which no-one else would know about but they alone. Fenius agreed and created "in Berla tobaide," meaning "the selected language," which he called Goidelc 'Gaelic' after Goidel mac Etheoir. And what was best of every language and what was widest and finest was cut into Irish and every sound for which a sign had not been found in other alphabets, signs were found for them in the "Beithe-luis-nin" (1053ff/4010ff). And there were 25 scholars of the school who were most noble and their names were given to the vowels and consonants of Ogam (1135ff/4236ff).* (McManus 8.3, p.148-49)

This tale has been dismissed by Bergin as 'fabulous' and by Graves as 'clumsy fiction'… embodying no authentic information with respect to the history of Irish letters, or as an 'absurd legend' containing no single element of truth. Nevertheless, the main theme is abundantly clear; Irish is a totally invented language. One relationship that deserves to be investigated is the eerie similarity I noticed between the writings in the Auraicept and those in the Ge'ez liturgical literature of the Ethiopian Jews. This seems to indicate to me that a group of monks indeed went east to study language invention and at least some of them ended up with the scholars inventing Ge'ez, which Gaelic resembles. When Fenius had created the new language and called it **"in Berla tobaide"** meaning 'the selected language,' he had condensed a Basque sentence:

in.	ino	*inola*	somehow
.be	obe	*obetoezin*	perfectly

er.	ere	*errezetatu*	to prescribe
.la	ela	*ela*	word
ato	ato	*atondu*	to arrange
oba	oba	*oba*	better
ide	ide	*idekotasun*	homogeneity

"Somehow perfectly arrange the prescribed words for better homogeneity."

COLLECTING IRISH LEGENDS

The forfeda additions to the original Ogam alphabet had helped to open the way to the creation of the new "Celtic" language as described in the Auraicept. The formerly sacred and magic Ogam writing had already been introduced to the Irish people by the Gnostic missionaries, some 300 years earlier, as a monument script. Even though only a few monk/missionaries were able to read the inscriptions and none of the people, the missionaries counted on its built-in magic to spread the words of the Gospel. The later arriving monks from Rome used the script at first for carving religious sayings but quickly started work to replace the "iron" language with a new language. When after several years of linguistic work the newly invented "Celtic" language was far enough developed to be introduced to the people and used for literary purposes, some Benedictine monks started to record the very large store of Irish legends and popular wisdom, which had up to then been orally passed from generation to generation. Any knowledge about the elaborate traditions and festivities of the previous Ashera religion and culture, as well as memories of the outstanding women who had guided this civilization, the fact that this had been a peaceful, egalitarian and self sufficient society of communal solidarity – all this was eliminated, to be lost forever. What remained of the ancient Irish treasure trove of memorized myths and legends, practical knowledge and religious wisdom was sifted, scrubbed, mutilated, rewritten and finally translated into the newly concocted "Celtic" language and the final product was then collectively named "Celtic legends." Conflict and glorification of war was introduced (on paper) as part of the Irish heritage, a civilization which had neither weapons of destruction nor defensive structures. A few names of remarkable women survived, such as Queen Medb and Derdriu, but they became portrayed in a negative and abusive light. Male prowess in contest, defending helpless maidens in distress, disciplining "unfaithful" wives, tales about ugly witches, anything that helped to put women in dependent or despicable positions, all made good grist for the monks' literary mill. Irish mythology had become patterned by Roman Catholic church authority and therefore no longer emerged from that once glorious Irish civilization.

However, memorized traditions are far more durable than parchment and vellum, and some Irish bards continued to tell the ancestral legends to their children, the way they had been told before the coming of Christianity. A few years ago in Conamara one of these men, with a treasure of such legends in his head, was telling them to his cows as he lovingly brushed them at night in the barn. His cows were the only audience he had until some knowledgeable person heard about him and captured on his tape recorder the treasures the bard had to offer. In this way some original legends and songs have survived the well-meaning but hopelessly misguided censors.

Some Comments Concerning The Auraicept

The Auraicept na n'Eces is an astonishing book. The meaning of its name has been generally accepted as: "The Scholars' Primer." Calder, who tried to translate it, calls it the "Handbook of the Learned," but ever since it was printed in 1917 the book has been subjected to a variety of choice derogatory comments. Very few modern academics had anything good to say about its contents. This was in stark contrast to the Middle Ages when the book was held in very high regard as a study book for monks, it being required reading. Why the switch from being regaled to reviled? Did the early teachers know something about the Auraicept that our modern linguists didn't, or didn't want to, know? It certainly looked like it because, just as they did with the Ogam inscriptions on stone, our university linguists had somehow decided among themselves that the Auraicept was written in Celtic, which it couldn't be because the Auraicept already existed before Celtic was invented. Instead, the Auraicept is written in coded Basque, which may make it the oldest Basque-language book known. Note that the writing in the Auraicept, in transliterated form, is almost identical to the Ogam writing on stone. To substantiate this statement here follow some translations from the Auraicept na n'Eces, using the Basque dictionary, starting with the name itself:

AURAICEPT NA N'ECES, Aura-ike-ep.-.t.-.na-ane-ese-ez:

Aura/	aura/	*aurrea artu*	take the initiative!
ike	ike	*ikerpen*	research
ep.	epai	*epaiaulki*	tribunal
.t.	aito	*aitortu*	to declare
.na	ona	*anargarri*	acceptable
ane	ane	*anega*	measure
ese	ese	*esetsi*	to attack
ez.	ez	*ezjakintasun*	illiteracy

"Take the initiative! The research tribunal has declared that the (proposed) measures to attack illiteracy are acceptable."

A Serious Problem With Translation

There are two versions of the Auraicept, the first one, starting with line 1 in Calder's compilation, came from the Book of Ballymote. The second version, starting at line 2260, was copied from the Yellow Book of Lecan. Both originals are located at Trinity College in Dublin. Version 1 starts with:

(line 1) **Incipit Auraicept na nEges .i. eraicept, ar er gach (2) toiseach. Cid dianad toisseach seo? Ni ansa. Don tebi (3) rotebed isin Gardilg, uair is ed toisseach arricht la Fenius (4) iar tiachtain din scoil...**

This was translated by Calder as:

"Incipit Primer of the Poets, that is, eraicept, beginning of lessons, for every beginning is er. To what is this a beginning? Not hard. To the selection that was selected in Gaelic since this is the beginning which was invented by Fenius after the coming of the school with the languages from abroad..."

Version 2 starts with:

(line 2260) **Incipit eraicept na n-Eiges .i. eraicept, uair er gach (2261) taoiseach: aicicht dono .i. icht aici, ar is i n-aici bios in (2262) deisgiopul agin maigister; no dono aicept, id est acceptus, (2263) airiti cugad...**

Calder provided no translation for the second version. I tried both and found that the second version makes good sense when translated with the Basque dictionary. I had trouble with version one which may have been written from memory. The "c" usually stands for "k," rarely for "s." A slash (/) is inserted where the vowel-linking is interrupted.

Version 2, line 2260: **Insipit eraikept**

in.	ina	*inauguratu*	to open, to start
.si	asi	*asipen*	basics
ipi	ipi	*ipini*	to supply, to give
it./	itu	*itundu*	to be advised
era	era	*eraz*	according to
ike	ike	*ikerpen*	research
ep.	epa	*epai*	decision
.t.	atu	*atutxa*	better world

"I start with giving you the basics. Be advised that according to the research this decision (will lead) to a better world."

na n-Eiges .i. eraikept,

.na	ona	*onartu*	to approve
.n.	ane	*anega*	measure
e.i	ehi	*ei*	certainly
ige	ige	*iges egin*	to flee
ez/	ez	*ezjakintasun*	illiteracy
.i.	aie	*aienatu*	to disappear
era	era	*eraz*	according to
ike	ike	*ikerpen*	research
ep.	epa	*epai*	decision
.t.	atu	*atutxa*	better world

"The approved measures (will) certainly (cause) illiteracy to flee and disappear. According to the research this decision will (create) a better world."

uair. er gakh

u.a	uha	*uhaska*	reservoir
a.i	ahi	*ahitugaitz*	untiring, enthusiastic
ir./	ira	*irakatsi*	to educate
er./	eri	*erri*	people
.ga	ega	*egarri*	strong desire
ak.	aka	*akabu*	superior
.h./	ahi	*ahitugarri*	ending, outcome

"with an enthusiastic reservoir of educated people who have a strong desire (to work towards) a superior outcome."

taoiseach: aicicht , line 2261.

.ta	ita	*itaundu*	to question
o.i	ohi	*ohi izan*	in the habit of
ise	ise	*isekatu*	to criticize
ak.	aka	*akastun*	faulty
.h.	aha	*ahalegin*	attempt
a.i	ahi	*ahituezin*	constant
isi	isi	*isil*	quiet
ik.	ika	*ikasketa*	study
.h.	aha	*ahalguzti*	Almighty
.t./	ate	*aterbe*	protection

"By being in the habit of questioning, by criticizing faulty attempts, by constant quiet study under the protection of the Almighty,"

dono .i. icht aici, ar is

.do	ido	*idoro*	to discover
ono	ono	*onon*	exquisite, superior
.i./	oia	*oialdu*	to weave, to assemble

ik.	ika	*ikaskera*	learning method
.h.	aha	*ahalegina*	to attempt
.t.	ata	*ataurre*	introduction
a.i	ahi	*ai*	I hope, I have a strong desire
isi/	isi	*isilik*	quiet
ar./	are	*arrera*	acceptance
is.	isu	*isurgarri*	fluid, smooth

"by discovering exquisitely assembled learning methods (with which) to attempt the introduction, I have a strong desire for quiet and smooth acceptance."

The difference between Calder's and my translation is rather startling. There is not a single word of agreement, except that both are talking about language. I have found no indication that the introduction of the new Celtic language was accepted smoothly. The fact that the original Basque tongue was still understood around 1800 A.D. (to be discussed later) probably means that there was substantial and long-lasting resistance. However, there was no such doubt about acceptance in the mind of the monk who wrote:

Beithe-luis nin (lines 1057, 1134, 4013):

.be	obe	*obetoezin*	perfectly
ite/	ite	*itegun*	work performed
lu	ludi	*ludi*	world
is./	isi	*isilean*	hidden from
ni	ni	*ninikatu*	to take root
in/	in	*inguru*	vicinity

"Work perfectly performed, hidden from the world, will take root in the vicinity."

The Auraicept probably started as an operations manual for the Benedictines, written in the pre-Chistian language of the Irish people, which closely resembled the Basque of today. It was also the same language which the Benedictines had used to create the Latin language. When the monks began work on the creation of the new language, they abbreviated words belonging to the indigenous language, following the example in the Auraicept. The letter combinations thus obtained were agglutinated into words, many vowels were eliminated and then, to confuse things even more, unrelated vowels and some consonants, mostly h's, were thrown in to make the new words pronounceable and new meanings were invented for the product. When this language had been far enough developed, it was given the name "Celtic." No other language has been manipulated so effectively to hide its Basque heritage as has Celtic. The Auraicept was retained in the simple abbreviated and agglutinated condition, without the extra embellishments which would have made it look and sound like "Celtic." Thus the ancient book was turned into a challenge for the testing of linguistic scholars and must have given Calder some sleepless nights.

Many of the Basque sentences in the original manual were condensed with the Ogam formula and retained as names. Even the best Celtic scholars, like E.C.Quiggin and Malcolm MacFarlane, assisting George Calder in this diffi-cult task, were often at a loss as to the meaning of these names, many words, whole sentences and even pages. Yet they somehow managed to translate some of the writings but their work will need a thorough review, as these examples show. The care with which Calder ensured the accurate reproduction of the original document, in spite of his doubts about its accuracy, is applauded. It gave others a chance to do their share in unraveling the puzzle he made avail-able to us. Here are some sentences which were agglutinated into names:

Briartharogam. .b.-.ri-ar.-.ta-aro-ogam (lines 47, 50, 5528 etc).(BR)

.b.	abo	*abonau*	approve of
.ri	ori	*oritzi*	give advice
ar.	ara	*arrazoiak*	to explain
.ta	ata	*atalbako*	in simple manner
aro	aro	*arro*	proud
ogam	ogam	*Ogam*	Ogam script

"I approve of, give advice and explain in simple manner the proud Ogam script."

Goidelic. (2282 etc.)

According to Webster the word "goidelic" means: "the division of the Celtic languages which includes Irish and Scottish Gaelic and Manx." The translation of the word tells a very different story:

.go	ego	*egokialdi*	good opportunity
ide	ide	*ideiatu*	to invent
eli	eli	*elizako*	church
ik.	ika	*ikasgo*	teachings

"Good opportunity to invent church teachings."

Berla Fene(1302).

.be	obe	*obetoezin*	perfectly
er.	ere	*ereduztatu*	to adapt
.la	ela	*ela*	word
af.	afa	*afa*	happy
ene	ene	*enetan*	every time

"A perfectly adapted word (makes me) happy every time."

Iarmberla (1304).

i.a	iha	*ihardun*	to keep busy
ar.	ara	*arazo*	task
.m.	amo	*amodiozko*	loving
.be	obe	*obetu*	to perfect
er.	ere	*ereduztatu*	to adapt
.la	ela	*ela*	word

"We keep busy with the loving task of perfecting adapted words."

Berla na filed. (McManus 8.3).

.be	obe	*obetuezin*	perfectly
er.	ere	*ereduztatu*	to adapt
.la	ela	*ela*	word
ana	ana	*anaidi*	religious order
af.	afa	*afa*	joy
ile	ile	*ilezin*	everlasting
ed.	ede	*eder*	satisfaction

"Perfectly adapted words are the religious order's joy and everlasting satisfaction."

These remarks clearly indicate the concentrated effort that went into the creation of the new language. As long as Celtic was still in the developmental stage, the Benedictine linguists made good use of the writing system of the pre-Christian clergy.

THE VIKINGS ATTACK A MONASTERY

The monks doing this unwanted work were often living and working among an uncooperative, even hostile population which did not hesitate to call upon relations and friends for help. That help eventually came in the form of highly destructive Viking raids which devastated the monasteries time and again. The aggressively advancing monk/missionaries, with their religion-, culture- and language-destroying activities, were a death threat to the ancient civilization and this trend had to be stopped at all cost. With the help of the Vikings this resistance soon became a full-scale religious war which lasted for centuries. The Vikings, themselves belonging to a caring and civilized society, never attacked the common people but these didn't write the history. The monks, however, did and in writing their own version gave themselves a holier-than-thou image while making the Vikings the epitome of brutality and savagery. The following is an example of the monks' style of history writing in the Auraicept:

og-uaim do-berait na filid forsin filideacht trid, ar is fri fedaib toimsither Gaedelg icna filedaib (5479-5481, p272).

which Calder translates as:

"oguaim, perfect alliteration which the poets applied to poetry by means of it, for by letters Gaelic is measured by the poets."

  How Calder came to translate the sentence in this manner is not explained, however, it doesn't appear to make sense at all. A totally different translation is obtained by using the vowel-interlocking formula. The event described in such spiteful language probably took place in the 9th century but which monastery was involved is not explained; it may have been Bangor, located near the ocean, which we know was targeted several times. The translation also indicates that this was a repeat attack.

og.	ogu	*oguzi*	yell out loud
u.a	uha	*uhalde*	deluge
a.i	ahi	*ai*	grief
im./	imi	*imitazio*	reproduction/repeat
.do/	odo	*odolkeria*	butchery
.be	abe	*aberezko*	brutal
era	era	*eraso*	attack
it./	ito	*itotzaile*	murderous

"With loud yells, the deluge of grief was repeated with brutal butchery and murderous attack"

.na/	ana	*anaidi*	religious brothers
.fi	ibi	*ibili*	to be
ili	ili	*ilintitu*	set on fire
ide/	ide	*-ide*	companions
fo	fo	*formal*	good
or.	oro	*orrolari*	scream
.si	osi	*osintsu*	piercing
in./	ino	*inon*	any place, everywhere

"on the brothers who were set on fire with their good companions amid piercing screams everywhere."

fi	fi	*fite*	quickly
ili	ili	*ilinti*	firebrands
ide	ide	*idekidura*	opening
ak.	aka	*akabu*	death
.h.	aha	*ahapaldi*	injury
.t.	ato	*ator*	come!
.t.	oto	*otoikatu*	to pray
.ri	ori	*oriska*	yellow
id./	ido	*idor*	cruel

ar.	ari	*arimagalduko*	ruthless
is.	isi	*isilume*	bastard
.f.	ifa	*ifar*	northern
.ri	ari	*arima*	soul
.fe	ife	*ifernu*	hell
eda	eda	*edaritxar*	poison
ibi	ibi	*ibili*	to be

"Fire brands were quickly (thrown into) the openings to cause death and injury; Come! We prayed that the souls of the yellow, cruel, ruthless northern bastards be poisoned in hell."

.to	ito	*itomen*	anguish
imi	imi	*imintzio*	gesture
.si	isi	*isilean*	silently
it.	iti	*itxi*	to abandon
ihe	ihe	*ihesleku*	shelter
er.	ere	*erre*	to burn
.Ga	ega	*egan egin*	to escape
ede	ede	*edegidura*	opening
elg./	elga	*elgarrekin*	together
ik.	ika	*ikara izan*	to tremble
.na/	ana	*anaidi*	brothers
fi	fi	*fidatu*	to trust
ile	ile	*ilezin*	forever
eda	eda	*edade*	judgment
ib.	ibe	*ibeni*	to place

"With anguished gestures the trembling brothers silently abandoned the burning shelter to escape together through an opening, placing trust in (His) judgment forever."

THE AURAICEPT MUST BE TRANSLATED

From the above bits and pieces selected out of the Auraicept we can deduce that this book contains a great deal of interesting historical material. I have shown how to translate the encoded text but have no time to do much more. I have waited too long already with the publishing of this book. The Auraicept is certainly worthy of at least one book of its own, probably several. It promises to be a best-seller, depending on how it is presented. Several efforts to use computer decoding have failed to my knowledge, therefore time consuming, long-hand decoding appears to be the only way.

III

Indo-European Languages and The Benedictines

ARE WORDS A SHORTHAND?

INTRODUCTION

Almost from the inception of linguistics as a field of study, the possibility of a common source language has been mooted. Recently, for example, Ruhlen and Bengston [1] have proposed 27 global roots.

I have empirically developed a standardized set of procedures which, when applied to words of a wide range of languages, consistently produces from each word a phrase descriptively relevant to the present meaning of that word. For example, the word "*adore*" produces "The hour of worship" while "*obese*" produces "He/She prefers to sit."

These procedures, of which examples are given in following text, use the modified 'Roman' alphabet of strict Basque (Euskera). Interestingly, the process can be applied, with similar results, to words transliterated from non-'Roman' languages. A tentative hypothesis might be that I am expanding a shorthand which arose when written language was developed from the spoken, original form; and that the seeming universality of the process is due the various languages of today having been derived/developed from a common ancestor tongue. The words of written language – regardless of the form of representation be it Roman alphabet, cuneiform or hieroglyphic – are shorthand representations of a single, ancient spoken language. I refer throughout this chapter to words having a hidden or occluded meaning; the occluded meaning is that which is elicited by the procedures I developed. Analogous to the process I seem to be reversing is the creation of acronyms; with subsequent incorporation into the language as a new word. The word 'laser' (**l**ight **a**mplification by **s**timulated **e**mission of **r**adiation) being a recent example of this.

Empirically developed, the technique presented is an academic orphan; I know of no precursor work, nor of pointers to it in other writings. Its performance and consistency have been tested against a large number of Indo-European languages from Sanskrit to Greek, Latin and Spanish, and Germanic languages such as Dutch, German, and Yiddish. In the majority of English words the first vowel seems to have been removed. This contrasts to Basque, which still has half of its vocabulary starting with a vowel.

PROCEDURES

Some background comments:

The occluded meaning in written words is hypothesised to be from a spoken precursor language similar to Basque. This shorthand for the occluded meanings is structured a vowel-interlocking formula:

$$(V_x)CV_1\text{-}V_1CV_2\text{-}V_2CV_3\text{-}V_3CV_4\text{-}V_4C... \text{ etc.}$$

Note that each vowel after the first, optional vowel, 'V_x,' is repeated. That is to say that, if the two 'Basque' roots/morphemes – '*ore*' and '*eto*' – were combined by this system one of the *e*'s would be dropped and they would appear in the interlocked form '*oreto*' (*equals* $V_1CV_2\text{-}V_2CV$). Since '*ore*' means balance, hour or mole, and '*eto*' means to come, origin or inborn, we might assign a tentative meaning to the word '*oreto*' of 'inborn balance' or 'the hour has come.'

This vowel-interlocking structure applies to Sanskrit vocabulary as well as all the Romance languages, including Latin, but there are differences in detail. In Latin words the vowels are persistent, most words generally adhering to the VCVCV structure. However, in English, many more of the vowels have disappeared leaving the CVC structure as shown in names (Bonner, Duncan, Hudson, Robson, Somner etc.) and, also in words (cellar, doctor, hawser, master, pillow, tartan etc.).

The fewer the vowels, the greater the number of possibilities in expanding the 'shorthand' to discover the occluded meaning of the word. However, at least one vowel must accompany the consonants for decoding to be practical.

The examples which follow illustrate the process, starting with the simplest situation, that in which no vowels were discarded. If the spelling of name or word was changed over time, it becomes more difficult, or it may not be possible to recover the hidden meaning. However, quite often the change in the word's spelling becomes very obvious when decoding (e.g. 'recidivist' from 'recitivist' below). Occasionally more than one possible meaning appears in which case both should be reported and/or earlier spellings researched. In general, every consonant can elicit a full word (except 'w'), and the more consonants in a word or name, the longer the occluded phrase and the more likely it is that it can be recovered with confidence. The accepted meanings of words will usually help guide the process.

Imprecision in the Extraction of Meaning

When dealing with one word only, we face a problem which is common in handling language – lack of context. Consider if one is given the task of finding a meaning for the English word "*duck*." We could say quite validly that it referred to an aquatic bird, a quick downwards movement, a score at cricket or the avoidance of an issue. Where the meaning elicited from the VCV shorthand can be checked by context, it is important that it be checked again upon completion. Forced, unnatural or inappropriate results should be suspect and rejected.

It is well accepted that in the Indo-European languages vowels are generally unstable i.e. they change frequently within the root (e.g. sing, sang, sung). In the Basque language on the other hand, the vowels seem extremely stable with only few, mostly purposely changed, exceptions (e.g. *Euskera* to *Euskara*, *Kriatzaile* to *Kreatzaile*) but the consonants are sometimes quite changeable: $F = B$, Y and $J = I$, Q and $C = K$. The letter H is often omitted, D sometimes becomes T (e.g. in *idi* to *iti*, *udikan* to *utikan*). In languages other than Basque, S, Z and X (pronounced '*sh*') are often interchanged during word development.

Basque has no 'C,' 'Q,' 'V,' 'W' and 'Y,' although some have sneaked into the names and some words e.g. the word *Basque* should itself be spelled *Bask*. The letter 'X' as used in English is spelled 'KS' in Basque.

When seeking the hidden meaning, I have observed what seems to be a basic rule; where most English words are concerned, the first syllable represents a Basque-like VCV with the first vowel removed. If an appropriate VCV was not available, then a 'Basque' word starting with CV was recruited. Using a CV root for the first syllable is common in Greek and the Germanic languages, but uncommon in English and unheard of in Old Egyptian names.

In the creation of English words it is fortunately infrequent to find many consonants clustered together, such as appears in the name Sanskrit ("samskrta," with five contiguous consonants) or Dutch ("angstschreeuw," with its eight contiguous consonants). In English three consonants together are common e.g., conclude, country, destroy, irksome, naughty, puzzle etc. but four is rarer e.g., instruct, minstrel etc. In decoding such words, the vowel-interlocking rule can be applied as usual, but the number of VCV combinations that need to be tried increases considerably and the reliability of decoding can diminish.

It is interesting to note that one quarter of all VCVs have no meanings attached and these 'unused' syllables are only rarely found in the English vocabulary – mostly in words misspelled or altered over time.

THE TOOLS

A: The vowel-interlocking formula.

This formula was worked out during research into the Ogam inscriptions of Scotland and Ireland. It may not be too surprising that there seems to be some linguistic relationship between Ogam and Basque. The Basques are a people genetically closely related to the Irish and Scots, especially as shown in their high frequency of Rh-negative blood, 25 – 32%. The Berbers and a small group of people in Chad are the only other peoples in the world with such high percentages.

B: The VCV word list.

See appendix 1. It was created by listing all 400 VCVs (ABA, ABE, ABI, ABO, ABU, EBA etc) and then listing the core meanings associated with these VCV's. Some 104 of these 400 VCV's have no meanings attached and merit particular study. Also, of the VCV's with recognizable meaning(s), many fall into related groups. For instance ABA which is used for words connected to the Christian 'manger scene.' Some VCVs have only one meaning such as "*iho*" (thunder) but some, like "*r*" and "*rr*" collect a very large variety of meanings. The "*rr*" is treated as single "*r*" for the purpose of decoding, but not for translating. The VCV list is only an aid and Aulestia's Basque dictionary should be consulted for greater detail.

C: The Basque Dictionary.

I have used the Basque-English and English-Basque dictionary by Gorka Aulestia (University of Nevada Press) as our standard source.

The simplest way to set out the decoding process is as a list of steps illustrated by examples. The least complicated English words for decoding are the ones in which full VCVs exist, as in the first examples which follow. The examples become more complicated as more vowels are missing. Occasionally, non-interlocking roots are combined into one, e.g. '*inoculate*.' Decoding requires that matching words only are taken from interlocking pairs. In the case of a double vowel (diphthong), an '*h*' has often been eliminated. This is common in Basque e.g. the word '*custom*' is both '*oitura*' and '*ohitura*.'

DECODING – THE PROCESS

The steps are:

1) Arrange the letters of the word to be analyzed into the form $V_1CV_2CV_3CV_4$. (It may be helpful to place dots where vowels are missing or an 'h' has been lost). Then

2) replace 'C' and 'Q' with 'K,' 'V' with 'B' or 'F,' 'W' is sometimes replaced by 'U' otherwise ignored and 'Y' is replaced with 'I' or 'J';

3) Convert the sequence so obtained into VCV-VCV-VCV-VCV etc. in which the vowels of either side of the hyphen are the same;

4) Using the VCV list (or a Basque dictionary), list the appropriate words for each VCV. There is usually no need to list words which are obviously unrelated to the meaning at hand, a skill acquired with practice; and

5) Select those words which make a phrase or sentence most closely fitting the meaning of the word being decoded.

Note: As explained in more detail later, the Basque language is made up of two quite different parts, 1) the original Neolithic, unmanipulated language which was subject to the normal alteration over time, and 2) the invented Magical Language in which each word starts with VCV. This language has always been the preserve of priesthoods and was passed on in almost unaltered form since early Egyptian times. The two parts are about equally divided in the Basque dictionary.

DECODING – THE RESULTS

Although these procedures have been applied successfully to languages as variant as Old Egyptian and Yiddish, the few examples which follow are from English. In these I show a few only of the possible meanings of each VCV. (For a more complete list the VCV list or Basque dictionary should be consulted).

Words with no vowel loss.

adore, ado – ore

ado	ore
to dress, food, to cheer up, to worship, courage	to grab, always, dog, hour

ado	ado	*adoratu*	to worship
ore	ore	*oren*	hour

"hour of worship."

ebony, ebo – oni

ebo	oni
develop, create, evolution	acceptable, useful, luck, consent

ebo	ebo	*eboluzionatu*	to develop, create
oni	oni	*onizan*	something useful

"Create something useful."

evade, eba – ade

eba	ade
thief, fraud, swindler, hide-out, to cut, remnant	to prepare, rude, temple

eba	eba	*ebasle*	swindler
ade	ade	*adeigabeko*	rude

"Rude swindler."

enumerate, enu – ume – era – ate

enu	ume	era	ate
useless, sedentary, inertia, stay at home	child, give birth, offspring, to adopt	education, patience, to sample, exercise	protection, main entrance, door to door, member

enu	enu	*enulkeria*	sedentary/stay at home
ume	ume	*ume*	offspring/birth
era	era	*erakutsi*	to show, to sample
ate	ate	*atez-ate*	door to door

"Go door to door to sample the offspring at home"

obese, obe – ese

obe	ese
to improve, well-meaning, guilty, to prefer	to sit, chair, to object, to argue

obe	obe	*obetsi*	to prefer
ese	ese	*eseri*	to sit

"(he/she) prefers to sit"

Words with one vowel missing.

cupola, .ku – upo – ola, (the first vowel is missing.)

try: **aku**	**upo**	**ola**
to rent, acoustics	stave, barrel shaped	cabin, canopy
try: **eku**		plank
equator, worried		just like this
try: **iku**		
watchful, to visit ,scenic		
try: **oku**		
fertile field		
try: **uku**		
falsify, smelly		

.ku	iku	*ikusgarri*	scenic
upo	upo	*upohol*	barrel shaped
ola	ola	*olana*	canopy

"Scenic barrel-shaped canopy."

delegate, .de – ele – ega – ate (the first vowel is missing)

try: **ade**	**ele**	**ega**	**ate**
temple,announce, courteous, to prepare	story, gossip, flattering	escape, anxiety, to make thirsty, to favour	outside, knock at the door, remark, to get, consequence
try: **ede**			
esteem, history, mislead, to be pleased, exaggerate			
try: **ide**			
companion, to compare, to open, to swap			
try: **ode**			
cloud, horizon			
try: **ude**			
summerhouse			

.de	ide	*idetu*	to compare, to swap
ele	ele	*ele*	story
ega	ega	*egarritu*	to make someone thirsty
ate	ate	*aterapen*	consequence

"The consequence of swapping stories is that one gets thirsty."

energy, ene – er. – .gi (the third vowel is missing)

ene	try: **era**	try: **agi**
my, in me, before, attract me, always	profit, available, attack, to scatter, method, sample, to motivate, suffer, storm	I wish, I hope, to order, powerful, threat, promise
	try: **ere**	try: **egi**
	scatter, wasteland, occasion	to create, action, possible, undone
	try: **eri**	try: **igi**
	sickness, recovery, compare, fight, strong, skilful	harvest, sickle
	try: **ero**	try: **ogi**
	risky, transport, insanity, comfort	bread, crust, maid, baker, easygoing
	try: **eru**	try: **ugi**
	mistake, producing, abundant	N.A.

ene	ene	*-enetan*	always
er.	era	*eragin*	to motivate
.gi	agi	*aginbidedun*	powerfully

"Always powerfully motivated."

obdurate, (persisting obstinately in wrong-doing.)
ob.-.du-ura-ate (second vowel missing)

try: **oba**	try: **adu**	ura	ate
better, naturally, improvement	luck, fortunate, to rave, to slobber	he/she, him/her, to flood, ocean, to float, watered wine,	protection, refuge, continually, beggar to leave, knock at door, to get, abrupt
try: **obe**	try: **edu**	urra	
preferable, to improve, blame, to sin, obedient	to have, powerful, possession, to keep	to break a law	
try: **obi**	try: **idu**		
tomb, to bury, cemetery	to have, distrust resemblance to appear		
try: **obo**	try: **odu**		
N.A.	N.A.		
try: **obu,** N.A.	try: **udu,** N.A.		

ob.	obe	*oben egin*	to sin
.du	edu	*eduki*	to have
ura	urra	*urratu*	to break a law

ate   ate   *atergabeki*   continually
"He has sinned by breaking the law continually."

Words with two vowels missing.

begin, .be-egi-in. (first and last vowels missing)

try: **abe**	**egi**	try: **ina**
to cut, harvest, support, cross, to sing, patriotic	to do, to make, create, truth, action, convince, something	hail, agitate, to open, to trim
try: **ebe**		try: **ine**
Hebrew, patriarchy		passiveness, inertia
try: **ibe**		downtrodden
to place, to put on, to start, introduce		try: **ini**, N.A.
try: **obe**		try: **ino**
obedient, blame, improve, well meaning		time to time, ever, never, somebody, sometimes
try: **ube**		try: **inu**
purple, royal, cistern, bruise		sunset, evening, inspiring

.be   ibe   *ibeni*   to start
egi   egi   *egindura*   the action
in.   ino   *inor*   somebody
"Somebody start the action."

dog, .do-og. (first and last vowels missing)

try: **ado**	try: **oga**
courage, bravery, stimulate, worship	wealth, property
try: **edo**	try: **oge**
or, anytime, common, anywhere	bed, 20,30
try: **ido**	try: **ogi**
torrential rain, mud, idol, unfeeling	bread, crust, thresh, easygoing
try: **odo**	try: **ogo**
blood, relative, cowardice, cruel, impulsive	N.A.
try: **udo**	try: **ogu**
N.A.	to pronounce, to speak out loud

| .do | ado | *adoretsu* | brave |
| og. | ogu | *oguzihe* | speaks out loud |

"Brave and speaks out loud."

recidivist (repeated anti-social behaviour), .re –eki –idi –ibi -ist.

try: **are**	eki	idi	ibi	try: **ista**
enemy, beggar, welcome, approach, sociable	persistent, as much as possible, attempt, activist	ox, crib, to open, (none apply to word at hand)	vagabond, walk, to be, to behave, to run, to act	N.A.
try: **ere**		iti		try: **iste**
occasion, side, wilderness, to burn, irritable, care, claim		to abandon, to allow, to stop, to denounce		N.A.
try: **ire**				try: **isti**
destructive, devour, to spread, to open				riot, disorderly, respect, anxiety
try: **ore**				try: **isto**
hour, balance				story, history, narration
try: **ure**				try: **istu**
gold, jewelry, nobility, water				village in Navarra

.re	are	*arrenkari*	beggar
eki	eki	*ekinkor*	persistent
idi	iti	*itxi*	to denounce
ibi	ibi	*ibili*	to behave
ist.	isti	*istiluzale*	disorderly

"Denounce the persistent beggar who behaves so disorderly."

Words with three vowels missing:

doctor, .do-ok.-.to-or.

try: **ado**	try: **oka**	try: **ato**	try: **ora**
courage, bravery, stimulate, worship	nausea, disgust, occasional, despise	tow, drag, arrange, embellish, come	dog, filling, always right now, to grab
try: **edo**	try: **oke**	try: **eto**	try: **ore**

or, anytime, common, to suck	twisted, injury, perverted, bad	to come, origin, inborn, welcome, inspiration	balance, aerialist, hour, mole, dentist
try: **ido**	try: **oki**	try: **ito**	try: **ori**
torrential rain, mud, idol, discovery	frightened, bored, complete, baker	anguish, disgrace, drip, impure, drown	that, except, pale, yellow, freckle
try: **odo**	try: **oko**	try: **oto**	try: **oro**
blood, rage, apathy, cruel, martyr, angry	stable, chin, pasture	please, prayer, beg, devout, mealtime	all, every, total, buy, memory, ambitious
try: **udo**	try: **oku**	try: **uto**	try: **oru**
N.A.	fertile field	utopia	building site

.do	odo	*odoldun*	bloody
ok.	oke	*okerkeria*	injury
.to	eto	*etorri*	to come
or.	ora	*orain*	right now

"A bloody injury, come right now."

trust, .t. – .ru – ust. (The second and third syllables fall quickly into place, which means that the first '.t.' has to be '.ta' and only five possibilities need to be tried. Again the 'r' and 'rr' need to be tested. The word ends in a VCCV, a matter of experimenting).

try: **ata**	try: **aru**	try: **arru**	try: **usta**
door, divide, hereafter, to smash, benefit	to wander, farther, movement	vulgar, **simply**, common	whip, lash
try: **eta**	try: **eru**	try: **erru**	try: **uste**
abundance, era, stage	N.A.	mistake, blame, guilt, cruel, mercy, accuse	**to trust/ be trusted**, creative, belief
try: **ita**	try: **iru**	try: **irru**	try: **usti**
to harvest, **to ask**, leak, manger	image, to seem, simulate, to appear, weaver, fraud, trick	N.A.	N.A.
try: **ota**	try: **oru**	try: **orru**	try: **usto**
basket, lobster, bite,wild mountains	building site, lot, place	N.A.	field of gamma grass
try: **uta**	try: **uru**	try: **urru**	try: **ustu**
N.A.	flour, to dip in flour	scorn, despite, far, to leave, nostalgia	to empty, to deflate

.t.	ita	*itaundu*	to ask
.ru	aru	*arruntki*	simply
ust.	uste	*uste ukan*	to be trusted

"Ask simply to be trusted."

Words with four vowels missing.

summons, .su − um. − .mo − on. − .s.

try: **asu**	try: **uma**	try: **amo**	try: **ona**	try: **esa**
newborn lamb, nettle	child, pregnant, birth, procreation	love, to yield, annoy, fury, gallantry, blunt	here, prosperity, closer, welcome,	to say, witty, wise, speaker, meaning
try: **esu**	try: **ume**	try: **emo**	try: **one**	try: **ese**
N.A.	child, young, orphan, adopt, prolific	to present, giver, to transmit to/tell, future	kind, patience, praise the best, recover, these	to hang, suspend, to sit, attack, debate
try: **isu**	try: **umi**	try: **imo**	try: **oni**	try: **esi**
flowing, canal, to spill, to inspire, to run	humble, humility	N.A.	success, acceptable, consent, luck	blockade, surround, fence, round-up
try: **osu**	try: **umo**	try: **omo**	try: **ono**	try: **eso**
N.A.	humour, sensible, bad, mood, prudent	N.A.	exquisite, wonderful, very good	advice
try: **usu**	try: **umu**	try: **umo**	try: **onu**	try: **esu**
often, frequently	N.A.	nature, humour, mood, bad tempered	profit, perfect, very nice	N.A.

.su	isu	*isubera*	running
um.	ume	*ume*	child
.mo	emo	*emon*	to pass on, to tell
on.	one	*oneratu*	to come here
.s.	esa	*esana egin*	to obey

"Tell the running child to come here and obey."

malignant, .ma – ali – ig. – .na – an. – .t.

try: **ama**	try: **ali**	try: **iga**	try: **ana**	try: **ana**	try: **ota**
mother, many, to destroy, cunning	possible, to destroy a person	to rise, prophet, to wither, notice	brother, religious order, to unite, anatomy	brother, religious order, to unite	stubble, crumb, basket, lobster, wild mountains
try: **ema**		try: **ige**	try: **ena**	try: **ane**	try: **ote**
female, giving,,to hit, performance		evade , master, to float, escape, frog	that, superlative, swallow (bird)	grain measure, to curse	perhaps, furze field
try: **ima**		try: **igi**	try: **ina**	try: **ani**	try: **oti**
statue, sculptor, magnet, wicker		harvest, sickle	agitate, to open, to trim, hail	animal, many, often	grass hopper
try: **oma**		try: **igo**	try: **ona**	try: **ano**	try: **oto**
grandma		to raise, climb, sender, annoint	here, closer, to admit, welcome	food supply, wine, abnormal	prayer, devout, meal, chapel
try: **uma**		try: **igu**	try: **una**	try: **anu**	try: **otu**
child, pregnant, fertile, ripening		despise, to wait, tolerance, sun	dull, cowherd, fatigue, annoying	to faint, to fall back in fear	to occur to, meal

.ma	ama	*amaitu*	to destroy
ali	ali	*alienazio*	destruction of a personality
ig.	iga	*igartu*	withering
.na	ana	*anatomia*	anatomy
an.	ano	*anormal*	abnormal
.t.	ote	*ote*	perhaps

"Withering of the anatomy and destruction of the personality is perhaps abnormal."

Parliament: .pa – ar. – .li – i.a – ame – ent. (without detailed analysis of the morphemes)

apa – ari – ili – iha – ame – ent
aparteko – -ari – ilinti – ihardukitze – ameslari – entzungarri
special – cause – fiery – arguing/oratory – idealistic – worthy being heard
"Fiery and idealistic oratory for a special cause is worthy of being heard."

And a curious word:

existence, ek. − .si − iste − en. − .se

This word is interesting in that the creator of the word expresses his personal feelings.

try: **eka**	try: **asi**	iste	try: **ena**	try: **ase**
contribution, be used to, to bring, storm	to begin, origin, start, craving,	N.A.	swallow (bird), that, superlative	
try: **eke**	try: **esi**	**izte**	try: **ene**	try: **ese**
N.A.	surround, siege, fence, blockade	thigh, armour, vocabulary, unpleasant	in me, my, come to me, always, when	to sit, debate, argue, chair, essence,
try: **eki**	try: **isi**		try: **eni**	try: **ise**
perseverance, initiative, sun, attempt	quiet, secret, to hide, pause, in a low voice		to me	joke, make fun, derisive, satirizing
try: **eko**	try: **osi**		try: **eno**	try: **ose**
to produce, fertile, administrator	pit, abyss, very deep		wart, afflicted	N.A.
try: **eku**	try: **usi**		try: **enu**	try: **use**
peace of mind, worried, equator.	to sneeze		useless, inertia, weakness	to sneeze

ek.	eka	*ekarpen*	contribution
.si	asi	*asierako*	original
iste	izte	*iztegi*	vocabulary
en.	ene	*ene*	my
.se	ese	*esentia*	essence

"(It's) the essence of my original vocabulary contributions."

Words which do not fit the vowel-interlocking scheme.

(The application of this scheme to language varies somewhat from language to language and imported words create specific issues. Where, for example, English has imported French words these may sometimes display different characteristics from those we have been using for English).

Consider:

forest, f-orest, in French **forêt**

The word 'pleasing' is often abbreviated from *afa* to fa or just plain f. Using Basque, we could say 'forest' contains an occluded meaning of *afa* (pleasing, happy) – *orritza* (foliage). The circumflex is said to indicate a missing consonant, but the analysis does not bear this out (fa-orrit). Forest used to be spelled with two 'r's, which was the correct way of spelling.

"Pleasing foliage."

fond, f-ond
Similar to 'forest,' we get *afa* (happy) – *ondartu* (to be attached to, to be with)
"Happy to be with."

gourmet, .go ' ur. -.me – et.
Here we have a diphthong which must be split between first and second syllables. This means that vowel interlocking is not present, a liberty taken by both French and English.

.go	ego	*egosi*	to boil
ur.	uro	*uroilanda*	marsh hen
.me	ome	*omenka*	according to
et.	eti	*etiketa*	instructions

"Boil the marsh hen according to instructions."

DISCUSSION

These procedures may still seem a little forced or convenient – in spite of my introductory remarks about lack of context making the extraction of meaning less precise. The question is whether these procedures are just some sort of artificial, meaningless construct or a tool to unlock information?

I have looked at possible controls and offer two indicators: The first illustrates how small, deliberate changes in words can affect the results of the procedures. It is drawn from reflection upon the activities of Noah Webster – the creator of Webster's Dictionary;

The second considers created words in Lewis Carroll's 'Jabberwocky.'

To 'OU' or not to 'OU.' (Webster's English)

Dictionary maker Noah Webster's desire was to create a distinctive form of English for the U.S.A. and he proceeded to alter the spelling of many English words. Some words spelled with 'ou' and pronounced 'o' were the first ones to be "simplified." Vigour became vigor, humour became humor, ardour became ardor, harbour became harbor.

Let us see what resulted by testing four words.

Vigour, .bi – igo – ur. (both the single 'r' and the double 'rr' must be tried)

try: **abi**	**igo**	try: **ura**	try: **urra**
nest, speed, start, walk, **begin**	to rise up, send, **climb**, raise, to rub, to annoint	**he/she,** flood, ocean, float, to wash, bank of the river	footstep, to tear, touching, to move, rupture, track, violate
try: **ebi**		try: **ure**	try: **urre**
N.A.		water, nobility, by the sea, to launch, irrigation, dropsy	gold, tarnish, next, get closer, silver, approach
try: **ibi**		try: **uri**	try: **urri**
to run, to behave, to go, to act		city, low tide, butter, urban	rare, be merciful, miserable,
try: **obi**		try: **uro**	try: **urro**
tomb, to bury, cemetary		brick casing, waterpipe, cistern, marsh hen	hazeltree, grove of hazels
try: **ubi**		try: **uru**	try: **urru**
whirlpool, canal, pipe		flour, to dip in flour	reject, distant, to leave

.bi	abi	*abiatu*	to begin
igo	igo	*igoera*	climb
ur.	ura	*ura*	he/she

"He/she began the climb."

Vig<u>ou</u>r has a sensible occluded meaning. Now we try with Webster's 'vigor.'

Vigor, .bi – igo – or.

try: **abi**	try: **igo**	try: **ora**	try: **orra**
as above	as above	catch, now, dog, always, update, modern	there, surprise, anger, comb, sewing, strip, despoil
		try: **ore**	try: **orre**
		putty, deer, balance, hour, watch, dentist, aerialist	juniper, because of that, that one, as much as, like that

		try: **ori**	try: **orri**
		that, yellow, except, pale, to paint, freckle	leaf, sheet, that one, banquet, covered with leaves
		try: **oro**	try: **orro**
		all, every, also, similar, moss, to unify, to hoard, total	to roar, to moo, to shout, to scream
		try: **oru**	try: **orru**
		lot, site, place, low ground	N.A.

It is possible to force a sentence out of this e.g. "The aerialist began to climb" but it does not really fit with the common meaning as does "vigour."

Similarly:

Humour, .hu – umo – ur.

.hu	ahu	*ahurkitu*	to be
umo	umo	*umorezko*	funny
ur.	ura	*ura*	he/she

"He/she is funny."

The Webster spelling "humor" does not have he/she, or anything else that makes sense.

Also:

Ardour (warmth of affection) ar. – .do – ur.

ar.	ara	*aragiz*	sexually
ado	ado	*adoretu*	to stimulate
ura	ura	*urragarri*	touching

"Touching is sexually stimulating."

In "ardor" the Webster spelling decodes to an incomplete sentence: "Always sexually stimulating," which does not tell us what it is that is sexually stimulating. All three Webster changes above amount to an impoverishment of the language.

Harbour, .ha – ar. – .bo – ur.

.ha	aha	*ahalgabe*	helpless
ar.	ara	*arazio*	worried
.bo	abo	*abotz*	voice
ur.	uri	*urrigalpen*	cry mercy

"Helpless, a worried voice cries for mercy."

Harbor, .ha – ar. – .bo – .or.

.ha	aha	*ahalgabe*	helpless
ar.	ara	*arazio*	worried
.bo	abo	*abotz*	voice
or.	oro	*oroegile*	God

"Helpless and worried a voice (cries) God."

In the case of "harbor" a slightly different but well acceptable hidden sentence is found. Webster accidentally created a new word which has a good hidden sentence, even though he did not know he had done so.

"JABBERWOCKY" BY LEWIS CARROLL

Lewis Carroll, of 'Alice in Wonderland' fame, was interested in words. In 'Jabberwocky' he succeeded in creating text which conveyed a sense to the hearer that it was of English words and described a more or less commonly perceived scene. Yet many of the words were unknown or nonsense words. Do such words produce meaning when examined by me?

> *" Twas brillig, and the slithy <u>toves</u>*
>
> *Did <u>gyre</u> and gimble in the <u>wabe</u>;*
>
> *All <u>mimsy</u> were the borogoves,*
>
> *And the <u>mome</u> raths outgrabe."*

Lewis Carroll

I will decode five of these "words" (toves, gyre, wabe, mimsy, and mome). If all five of these words mean something sensible, then I must in all probability reject the above procedures as simply creating useless artifacts. If the words do not, however, show occluded meanings, we must look to other reasons for the sense of familiarity which English speakers feel upon hearing them.

Note also that context is not too helpful here.

Toves, .to – obe – es.

try: **ato**	try: **obe**	try: **esa**
tug, drag, arrange, solve, come!, to gather	obedient, to sin, improve, blame, to prefer	to say, speaker, wise, meaning, idiom
try: **eto**		try: **ese**
come!, origin, docile, arrival, welcome, inspiration		to attack, to battle, debate, essence, to sit
try: **ito**		try: **esi**
to drown, murderer, quickly, anguish, impure		surround, fence, blockade
try: **oto**		try: **eso**
prayer, please, beg, devout, oratory, meal		advice
try: **uto**		try: **ugi**
utopia		N.A.

Toves does not appear to contain a meaningful sentence.

Gyre, .gi – ire

try: **agi**	try: **ire**
maybe, I wish, dentist, promise, powerful, legacy, to order, chief	your, to open, to dig, devour, destructive, absorb, ruin, swallow
try: **egi**	try: **irre**
to do, to be, truth, duty, create, action, to verify, possible, bargain	N.A.
try: **igi**	
harvest, sickle	
try: **ogi**	
bread, baker, maid, weasel, to thresh, easygoing	
try: **ugi**	
N.A.	

Gyre is an existing word, meaning: circle, spiral and wheeling motion. Although none of the words in the table directly support any of these meanings, several sensible combinations can be made such as: "your dentist," "to be destructive," "possible ruin," "devour the bread," "open the bargain." Without context we cannot proceed further.

Wabe, uabe?-uha – abe

uha	abe
coast, deluge, to fasten, floodgate, turbidity	cross, manger, stable, cattle, choir, to receive, riches

Wabe does not appear to have any sensible occluded meaning.

Mimsy, .mi – im. – .si

try: **ami**	try: **ima**	try: **asi**
stork, falling down, administrator, to oust	statue, wicker, wattle, idol, sculpture	to begin, origin, elementary, bite
try: **emi**	try: **ime**	try: **esi**
N.A.	N.A.	fence, blockade, surround
try: **imi**	try: **imi**	try: **isi**
measure, gesture, imitation, to serve, offer	measure, gesture, imitation, reproduction	quiet, secret, to scheme, whisper, to hide
try: **omi**	try: **imo**	try: **osi**
Hallowmass, prophesy	N.A.	pit, abyss, very deep
try: **umi**	try: **imu**	try: **usi**
humble, humility	to pinch	to sneeze

Mimsy does not appear to have any sensible occluded meaning.

Mome, .mo – ome

try: **amo**	try: **ome**
love, kind, mother, to yield, strict, fury, to annoy, blunt	to honor, fame, tribute, according to
try: **emo**	
to present, giver, future	
try: **imo**	
N.A.	
try: **omo**	
N.A.	
try: **umo**	
ripe, mature, humour, wit, moody, prudent	

Some good combinations can be made e.g. "honor your mother," or "present a tribute," however this is only possible because "mome" is very close to "mom." **Mome** , pronounced as "moam" is nonsense. Not a single Basque word ends in 'm,' neither written nor spoken.

'Jabberwocky' raises some issues not directly related to the content of this chapter but deserving of some comment, I believe. Why do the 'words' sound 'right' but not behave like real words? There may be some support here for the theories that speech is facilitated by patterns set into the human brain. Further, it suggests ways for those studying this question to differentiate between genetic and phenotypic patterning. For example, if similar nonsense verse can be found in other languages, what sense do the sounds convey or elicit in native speakers, non-native speakers, non-speakers and so on.

CONCLUSIONS

The application of a standardized procedure to words elicits a set of possible meanings which usually include at least one meaning consistent with – and expansive of – the dictionary meaning of the word. I believe that this is not an artifact of the process but, rather, indicative of many words being, in effect, acronyms of an old, widely distributed, spoken language precursor to writing.

ACKNOWLEDGMENT

I must express my thanks to Geoffrey Cadogan-Cowper of Brisbane, Australia, for his rewording of whole paragraphs, the editing of this chapter and for contributing the Jabberwocky test.

---

[1] Merritt Ruhlen – personal communication of 24 Aug. 1999 with Geoffry Cadogan-Cowper. (See also Bengston & Ruhlen – *On the Origins of Language* 1994 Stanford University Press)

THE ORIGIN OF SOME ENGLISH NAMES

NAMES ASSOCIATED WITH ROYALTY

Having experienced success in the translation of English words, I decided to be adventurous and apply my newfound knowledge about the mysterious vowel-interlocking formula to some names associated with the British royal family. The choice of the name "Windsor" was straight luck; the result was startling. There appears to be no other reasonable interpretation.

WINDSOR, in. – .d. – .so – or. Note: the W is meaningless, i.e. it does not represent a Basque word.

try: **ina**	try: **ada**	try: **aso**	try: **ora**
to agitate, to open	noise, to gore, deceive	N.A.	dog, right now, to grab
to trim, hail	branching, long hair		always, to despoil
try: **ine**	try: **ede**	try: **eso**	try: **ore**
inertia, neutrality	beautiful, esteem	advice	deer, balance
passive, downtrodden	defeat, history, pleased		hour, dentist
try: **ini**	try: **idi**	try: **iso**	try: **ori**
many	ox, crib	torrential rain	yellow, that, pale
	to open, bison	isolation, whoa	foliage, banquet, feast
try: **ino**	try: **odo**	try: **oso**	try: **oro**
never, somehow, naive	blood, *relative*, rage	total, global, entire	all, *unify*, thorough
alienated, *to bequeath*	nervous, nobility	*thorough*, simple	Creator, memory, buy
try: **inu**	try: **udu**	try: **uso**	try: **oru**
to nurse, sunset, tingle	N.A.	dove, holy man	building site
stupid, heath			lower part

in	ino	*inorenganatu*	to bequeath
d.	odo	*odolgarbitasun*	nobility
.so	oso	*osoro*	thorough
or.	oro	*orotar*	united

"Bequeath a thoroughly united nobility."

The British royal family took on the name Windsor early in the 20th century. It is fair to say that they must have known exactly what they were doing. The family has long been involved with the pre-history and Ogam script of Scotland. Queen Victoria herself financed the publishing of a voluminous book on very early Scottish inscriptions, entitled "The Early Christian Monuments of Scotland" (J.R. Allen), many of which monuments were not Christian at all, but belonged to the pre-Christian (Asherah) religion of the Picts. I decided to probe a bit deeper by analyzing other names associated with British royalty:

Buckingham: .bu-uki-ing.-.ha-am.

.bu	abu	*aburukide*	agreement
uki	uki	*ukitu*	to touch, to affect
ing.	ingi	*ingira*	disposition, formation
.ha	iha	*ihardunak*	activities
am.	ami	*aministratu*	government

"The agreement affects the formation and activities of the government."
This "agreement" probably refers to the signing of Magna Carta.

Balmoral: .ba-al.-.mo-ora-al.

.ba	eba	*ebanjelari*	evangelist
al.	ala	*alai*	happiness
.mo	amo	*amodiotsu*	loving
ora	ora	*oraingoan*	occasion
al.	ala	*alaitsu*	joyous

"The evangelist's happiness made this a loving and joyous occasion."

Carnarvon: .ka-ar.-.na-ar.-.bo-on.

.ka	aka	*akabu*	end
ar.	ara	*aratustel*	corruption
.na	ana	*anaibateko*	unanimous
ar.	ara	*araberatasun*	agreement
.bo	abo	*abonau*	to approve of
on.	one	*onetsi*	to bless

"Corruption was ended when the unanimous approval of the agreement was blessed."
This is another sentence which refers to Magna Carta.

Kensington: .ke-en.-.si-ing.-.to-on.

.ke	ike	*ikertu*	to investigate, to re-visit
en.	ene	*-enetan*	each time
.si	esi	*esiketa*	siege
ing.	ingi	*ingiratu*	to be disgusted
.to	ito	*itotasun*	anguish
on.	ona	*onargaitz*	intolerable

"Each time they re-visit that repugnant siege (it causes) intolerable anguish." (I have no idea what that refers to.)

Some Common English Names

The above unexpected success in my search for the origin of English names was encouraging so I started to analyze other well known and true English names. The spelling of many English names has changed over the years which may have made it very difficult or impossible to recover the hidden sentence. The following names were fairly easy to do:

Bigelow: .bi-ige-elo

.bi	ibi	*ibili*	to run
ige	ige	*iges egin*	to escape
elo	elo	*elorza*	thorny bushes

"Run! Escape through the thorny bushes."

Buchanan: .bu-uka-ana-an.

.bu	abu	*aburu*	opinion
uka	uka	*ukatu*	to refuse
ana	ana	*anaikidetasun*	brotherhood
an	andi	*andikeria*	arrogance

"He refused to give an opinion about the arrogance of the brotherhood."

Collier, .ko-ol.-.li-i.e-er.

.ko	ako	*akorduan euki*	to remember
oli	oli	*olibolio*	olive oil
i.e	ihe	*ihesi*	to prevent
er.	eri	*eri*	illness

"Remember that olive oil prevents illness."

Compton, .ko-om.-.p.-.to-on.

.ko	ako	*akorduan euki*	to remember
om.	ome	*omendatu*	to honor

.p.	epe	*epemuga*	deadline
.to	eto	*etorkizuneko*	upcoming
on.	one	*ondar*	final

"Remember to honor the upcoming final deadline."

Fulton, .fu – ul. – .to – on.

.bu	abu	*aburu*	opinion
ul.	ule	*ulertu*	to understand
.to	eto	*etorki*	nature
on.	one	*onespen*	blessing

"In my opinion, to understand nature is a blessing."

Furlong, fu – ur. – .lo – on. – .g.

fu	fu	*fundatu*	to establish
ur.	ura	*urrats*	footsteps
.lo	alo	*alorgizon*	farmer
on.	ona	*onarketa*	to accept
.g.	aga	*agazneurri*	measurement/dimension

"(I) accept the dimensions which the farmer's footsteps established."

Gibson, .gi-ib.-.so-on.

.gi	agi	*agian*	I wish
ib.	ibe	*ibeni*	to introduce, to give
.so	eso	*esonde*	advice
on.	one	*oneratu*	beneficial

"I wish to give beneficial advice."

Hamilton, .ha-ami-il.-.to-on.

.ha	aha	*ahal*	I hope
ami	ami	*amildu*	to oust, to overcome
il.	ilo	*ilordu*	agony
.to	oto	*otoitz*	prayer
on.	one	*oneratsu*	pious

"I hope to overcome the agony through pious prayer."

Holmes, ho – ol. – .me – es.

ho	ho	*honera*in	this location
ol.	ola	*ola*	cabin
.me	ame	*amets*	dream
es.	esi	*esibarruti*	fence

"My dream is a cabin with a fence in this location."

One of the best known sea captains of the age of exploration was Henry Hudson. From the meaning of his name it appears that he acquired the name Hudson during or after one of his arctic voyages. Hudson's Bay and the Hudson River were named after him.

Hudson, .hu-ud.-.so-on.

.hu	uhu	*uhui*	cry of happiness, joy
ud.	udi	*udikan*	to get out
.so	iso	*isolamendu*	isolation
on.	ona	*onargaitz*	intolerable, hostile

"He cried for joy to get out of the hostile isolation."

Millar, .mi – il. – .la – ar.

The names Millar and Miller are usually thought to be closely related, which is not the case at all. The 'a' fundamentally affects two of the name's four VCV's: .la and ar., while the 'e' controls .le and er., as shown below. The analysis for both names is shown in tabular form. See what the difference of one vowel means to the decoding:

try: ami	try: ila	try: ala	try: ara
tumbling, waterfall	dead, murder, to destroy	destiny, widow, sudden	proportion, agreement
administrator	*lifetime*, monthly, hair	*filled with happiness*	happiness, plunder
try: emi	try: ile	try: ela	try: are
N.A.	immortal, tease	word, story	*kindness*, caring, beggar
	funeral, complaint	talkative	please, prayer
try: imi	try: ili	try: ila	try: ari
unit of measure, *exemplary*	firewood, to revive	to murder, to destroy	to him/her, to hasten

.mi	imi	*imitagarri*	exemplary
il.	ila	*ilarteko*	lifetime
.la	ala	*alaitzaile*	filled with happiness
ar.	are	*arreratasun*	kindness

"An exemplary life (filled with) happiness and kindness."

Miller, .mi – il. – .le – er.

try: **ami**	try: **ila**	try: **ale**	try: **era**
waterfall	lifetime, destroy	trial, rejoicing	to carry, convenient
tumbling,administrator	*monthly*, weaken	*abundance of grain*	to tell, patience
try: **emi**	try: **ile**	try: **ele**	try: **ere**
N.A.	immortal, complaint	story, word	to scatter, to claim
	funeral, tease	to deceive	gift, simple, law, prayer

try: **imi**	try: **ili**	try: **ile**	try: **eri**
exemplary, to serve	firewood, to revive	immortal, complaint	death, finger, opinion
unit of measure	fiery	funeral, tease	common, spill, flow
try: **omi**	try: **ilo**	try: **ole**	try: **ero**
prophesy	grave, agony	to call upon	*miller*, millstone, basic
All Saints	to bury, corpse	last rites	dispute, lay eggs
try: **umi**	try: **ilu**	try: **ule**	try: **eru**
humble	darkness, confused	hair, example	mistake, mercy, cruel
humbleness	angry, evening	understanding	to produce, beg

.mi	imi	*imilaun*	unit of measure
il.	ila	*ilabetero*	every month
.le	ale	*aleketa*	abundance of grain
er.	ero	*errotazai*	miller

"Every month (take) a measure of our abundance of grain to the miller."

Molson, .mo-ol.-.so-on.

.mo	amo	*amona*	grandmother
ol.	ole	*oles egin*	to call upon
so	eso	*esonde*	advice
on.	onu	*onuts*	very kind

"Call upon grandmother for very kind advice."

Murdock, .mu-ur.-.do-ok.

.mu	amu	*amure egon*	to be suspicious
ur.	ure	*urentasun*	nobility
.do	edo	*edonoiz*	any time, always
ok.	oki	*okitu*	totally

"Always totally suspicious of nobility."

Norton, .no-or.-.to-on.

no	no	*nortasun*	personality, person
or.	oro	*orozale*	ambitious
.to	eto	*etorrialdi*	time of inspiration
on.	ono	*onon*	wonderful

"Ambitious person who has times of wonderful inspiration."

Ogden, og.-.de-en.

og.	oga	*ogaki*	richly
.de	ade	*adelatu*	adorned
en.	ene	*-enetan*	always

"Always richly adorned."

Osborne: os.-.bo-or.-.ne

os.	osa	*osatasun*	integrity
.bo	abo	*abogado*	lawyer
or.	oro	*orokorki*	universally
.ne	one	*onetsi*	esteemed

"The integrity of a lawyer is universally esteemed."

Pertelote (name of a chicken) .pe – er. – .te – elo – ote

.pe	ape	*apetatu*	to fancy
er.	ero	*erroin*	to lay eggs
.te	ote	*ote*	maybe
elo	elo	*elorrizuri*	spiny bush
ote	ote	*ote*	perhaps

"She fancies maybe she will lay her eggs in a spiny bush perhaps."

Purvis, .pu-ur.-.bi-is.

.pu	ipu	*ipuin*	gospel
ur.	uri	*urrikaltasun*	mercy
.bi	ibi	*ibili*	to be
is.	isu	*isurika*	inspiration

"Let the Gospel's mercy be an inspiration."

Ramsey (also a Benedictine Monastery in West Midlands)

.ra	era	*eraspen*	devotion
am.	ame	*ametsetsi*	to idealize
.se	ese	*esetsi*	debate
ei	ei	*eia*	come and participate

"We are devoted to idealistic debate. Come and participate."

Rogers: .ro – oge – er. – .s.

.ro	aro	*arrotzari*	innkeeper
oge	oge	*oge*	bed
er.	eri	*erito*	to fall ill
.s.	isi	*isilki*	quietly

"He fell ill and was quietly put to bed by the innkeeper."

Sebastian: .se-eba-asti-an.

.se	ase	*aserre*	dispute
eba	eba	*ebazle*	judge
asti	azti	*aztiatu*	to anticipate
an.	ana	*anaitze*	reconciliation

"Dispute judge who anticipates reconciliation."

A geographical name which became a household name is **Trafalgar**, where Nelson fought the sea-battle of 1805 and defeated Napoleon's fleet. The name must have been made up specifically for this occasion by someone who was there and familiar with the name invention game.:

Trafalgar: .t.-.ra-afa-alga-ar.

.t.	ate	*atertu*	to stop
.ra	era	*erasan*	attack
afa	afa	*afa*	happy
alga	alga	*algara*	loud laughter
ar.	ari	*arinaldi*	fast run

"We stopped the attack (amid) happy and loud laughter when they ran away fast."

Trafford: .t. – .ra – af. – .fo – or. – .d.

.t.	eto	*etorri*	inspiring
.ra	era	*erraile*	speaker
af.	afa	*afa*	happy
.fo	abo	*aboskatu*	to proclaim/to speak about
or.	ori	*orrits*	banquet
.d.	ido	*idoropen*	discovery

"The inspiring speaker happily spoke about his discoveries at the banquet."

Washington: ash. – ing. – .to – on.

ash.	axo	*axolagabetsu*	carefree
ing.	Ingi	*ingira*	disposition
.to	ito	*ito*	to laugh a lot
on.	one	*on esan*	to speak well of

"Well spoken-of person with a carefree disposition who laughs a lot."

Wilson: il. – .so – on. (the 'W' is meaningless)

il.	ila	*ilarteko*	lifetime/life long
.so	aso	*azokalari*	merchant
on.	one	*oneste*	act of blessing, honesty

"Life long an honest merchant."

I can go on and on to show that most, if not all, British names are made up out of Basque, although not all were assembled with the Ogam formula, such as "Campbell," from *kam-bel*: *kamaina* (improvised bed) *bela* (sails): "They slept on sails"; or "Stewart," from *.stu-art.*: *asturu* (fortune) *arti* (sheep): "A fortune in sheep." The linguists who created most of these names were dedicated professionals of the highest calibre and they did a marvelous job. Who they were and where they worked will be discussed in "The Benedictines." For now it is more important to show how basic the Basque language is to all aspects of English; it may well be true that the English language is fully 100% manipulated Basque. By now the reader will have understood that there is nothing "genetic" about the English language. It didn't evolve naturally from any other language; it was almost totally home-invented and had absolutely nothing to do with the Anglo-Saxons, Friesians, Celts, Vikings or whatever migrants happened to drift in from the continent.

SHAKESPEARE KNEW THE VOWEL INTERLOCKING FORMULA

In "Love's Labour's Lost" Shakespeare presents us with a Latin-sounding riddle: *honorificabilitudinitatibus* (Act V, i, 39). Up to now it has frustrated all efforts to decode it. This is supposed to be the longest "Latin" word in the dictionary, but where did this "Latin" word come from? Probably not from Latin! The fact that he used this word tells me that he knew about the Benedictines' operational manual, the "Auraicept" in which it is mentioned at least twice. It is likely that the "word" was made up in Ireland by one of the Benedictine grammarians. In line 1438 the word starts with *tinerifica* while the version in line 1741 is *tenerifica*. Let us first apply the Ogam formula to Shakespeare's version and see what happens:

honorificabilitudinitatibus:

.ho	*ahogoza*	delicious
ono	*onon*	exquisite
ori	*orrits*	banquet
ifi	*ibili*	to go
ika	*ikaskai*	lesson
abi	*abiatu*	to begin
ili	*ilinti*	fiery preacher
itu	*itundu*	to be advised
udi	*udikan*	to get out, to go away
ini	*initz,ainitz*	many
ita	*itaun*	question
ati	*atxiki*	to retain
ibu	*aburu?*	opinion
us.	*usutu*	often expressed

"Going to the delicious and exquisite banquet was the lesson the fiery preacher began with. I was advised to go away with my many questions and retained my often expressed opinion."

The 800 or 900 year older version in the Auraicept na n'Eces has two slightly different spellings and translations for the first halves:

Line 1741, **Tenerificabilitudinitatibus**: *.te-ene-eri-ifi-ika*: *ateots* (knock on the door) *ene* (come to me) *eritasun* (heavily laden) which therefore reads: **"Knock on the door, come to me those who are heavily laden; this was the lesson... etc."**

Line 1438 , **Tinerificabilitudinitatibus**: *.ti-ine-eri-ifi-ika*: *atikitzaile* (faithful) *inertzia* (downtrodden) *eritasun* (heavily laden) and therefore reads: **"Faithful but downtrodden and heavily laden; this was the lesson... etc."**

This made me wonder if there was anything special hidden in Shakespeare's name, and there was:

Shakespeare, she-ek.-.spi-ir. (pron: shay-ayk-spee-eer)

she	xe	*xedatu*	to decide
ek.	eka	*ekandu*	to get used to
.spi	azpi	*azpiko*	protective cover, pseudonym
ir.	ira	*irakatsi*	to teach

I decided to get used to teaching under a pseudonym.

The reason why none of the six known signatures of the great man were spelled the same must be because the basic sounds of "she-ek-spi-ir" were more important than the accurate spelling of his English "name."

ENGLISH IS AN INVENTED LANGUAGE

It is clear that none of the English etymological dictionaries are doing justice to the tremendous language creation efforts of the Benedictine linguists, a task later continued by famous writers such as Chaucer, Shakespeare and Tyndale. In fact, most of the modern word etymologies in our dictionaries appear to be guesswork or wishful thinking. The English language was totally invented by early linguists and forced onto a reluctant public by a determined and occasionally cruel church leadership.

Toward a New
Etymological Dictionary
For English

In this proposed etymological dictionary I will show how a large number of English words were formulaically assembled by agglutinating the first syllables of Basque words, mostly with the use of the vowel-interlocking formula. The missing vowels, represented by dots, will be revealed in the original Basque words which follow. Hyphens separate the hidden Basque words. The results are very different from the traditional etymological origins. Someone please help and finish this job.

A

abbey: ab.-.bi, aba-abi, *abade* (priest) *abiadura* (starting point): "The priest's starting point."
abdicate: ab.-.di-ika-ate, aba-adi-ika-ate, *abaildu* (to be tired) *adixkideki* (in a civilized way) *ikasbidetu* (to set an example) *ateratu* (to leave): "I am tired and will leave in a civilized way to set an example."
ability: abi-ili-iti, *abil* (skillful) *ilinti* (fiery, eloquent) *itxi* (to repudiate, to deny): "Skillful and eloquent repudiation."
abject: ab.-.je-ek.-.t., aba-aje-eku-uti, *abade* (priest) *aje* (deterioration) *ekurugaitz* (worried) *utikan* (get out!): "The priest is worried about the deterioration; get out!."
abnormal: ab.-.no-orma-al., *abadune* (chance) *anormal* (abnormal, unseasonable) *orma* (ice, frost) *alba* (dawn, in the morning): "A chance of unseasonable frost in the morning."
aboard: abo-ard, *aboskatu* (to voice, to tell) *ardigaldu* (late comers): "Tell the late comers."
abolish: abo-oli-ix., abo-oli-ixi, *aboskatu* (to voice, to tell) *oliodun* (oil-vendor) *ixi* (be quiet): "Tell the oil vendor to be quiet."

aboriginal: abo-ori-igi-ina-ala, *aboskatu* (to shout out) *origorri* (gold colored) *igita* (harvest) *inarrosi* (to shake, to thresh) *alaiarazi* (to fill with joy): "Shout it out that the threshing of the golden harvest fills with joy."

abort: abo-or.-.t., abo-ora-ate, *aboskatu* (to shout out) *oratu* (to seize, grab) *ateratu* (to get out): "He shouted to grab and get out."

about: abo-ut., abo-uto, *abotz* (voice) *utopia* (paradize, good times): "Voice (speaking about) good times."

above, abo-obe, *abotz* (voice) *obeditu* (to obey): "Obey the voice."

abrade: ab-.-.ra-ade, abe-erra-ade, *abenda* (race) *erramulari* (rower) *adelatu* (to prepare): "Prepare (the boat) for the rowing race."

abreast: ab-.-.re-ast., abu-urre-asta, *aburukide* (person who agrees) *urreratu* (to draw closer) *asta* (donkey) *aztarnatu* (track): " I agree the donkeys are drawing closer on the track."

abridge: ab-.-.ri-id.-.ge, abo-orri-ida-age, *abonau* (to approve of) *orri* (sheet, page) *idatzi* (to write) *agerkari* (document): "I approve of a one page written document."

abroad: ab-.-.ro-ad., aba-aro-ade, *abots* (to voice, to tell) *orogailu* (reminder) *adelatu* (to prepare): "Speak a reminder to prepare well."

abrogate: ab-.-.ro-oga-ate, abe-ero-oga-ate, *aberats* (rich) *erromes* (pilgrim) *ogasun* (wealth) *ateratu* (to leave behind): "The rich pilgrim left his wealth behind."

abrupt: ab-.-.ru-upt, aba-aru-upt, *abarreztatu* (to cover with branches) *arrunki* (simply) *upatxo* (small barrel): "Simply cover the barrel with branches."

abscess: ab-.-.s.-.ke-es.-.s., abo-osi-ike-eso-osa, *abonau* (to approve of) *osin* (deep) *ikermen* (examination) *esonde* (advice) *osagile* (doctor): "I approve of a deep examination and advice by the doctor."

absent: ab-.-.se-ent, *abialdi* (departure) *isekatze* (to make fun of) *entzutegabe* (unknown): "We made fun of his departure for the unknown."

abstain: ab-.-.sta-in., *aboskatu* (to proclaim) *ostatari* (innkeeper) *inolaz* (absolutely no more): "The innkeeper proclaims: absolutely no more."

abstract: ab-.-.st-.-.ra-ak-.-.t., aba-azte-era-aka-ata, *abantzu* (almost) *azterkor* (inquisitive) *eragin* (to promote) *akabu* (ultimate) *ataltasun* (simplicity): "Almost inquisitively promote ultimate simplicity."

absurd: ab-.-.su-urd, abi-isu-urde, *abilezia* (talent) *isuri* (to inspire) *urde* (male pig): "To inspire talent in a male pig."

abulia: abu-uli-iha, *aburu* (opinion) *uli* (coward) *ihalozkatu* (to wallow): "the opinion is that he is a wallowing coward."

abundant: from French abondant, abo-on.-.da-an.-.t., abo-one-eda-ono-oto, *abonau* (to approve of) *onezia* (healthfulness) *edan* (drinking) *ano* (wine) *otordu* (mealtime): "I approve of the healthfulness of drinking wine at mealtime."

abuse, ab-.-.ju-use, abo-oju-us, *abots* Voice) *oiu egin* (to cry out, to scream) *uspeldura* (battering and bruising): "A voice cried out from a battering and bruising."

academy: aka-ade-ami, *akabu* (perfect) *adelu* (preparation) *aministratzaile* (administrator): "Perfect preparation for administrators."

ache: ak-.-.he, aki-ihe, *akialdi* (tiredness) *ihesezin* (unavoidable): "Unavoidable tiredness."

accent: ak-.-.ze-ent, *akasdun* (defective) *azentu* (accent, speech) *entzungaitz* (difficult to understand): "Defective speech is difficult to understand"

accept: ak-.-.se-ep.-.t., ako-oze-epa-ata, *akordio* (agreement) *ozendu* (to resound) *epai* (decision) *atalbako* (simple): "Resounding agreement for the simple decision."

accident: ak-.-.ki-ide-ent, aka-aki-ide-ent, *akabu* (death) *akitu* (to be tired, aged) *-ide* (companion) *entzuera* (famous): "The death of my famous aged companion."

acclaim: ak-.-.k.-.la-im., aka-asi-ila-ima, *akabu* (perfect) *asialdi* (beginning) *ilarri* (monument) *imaginakin* (sculptor): "Perfect beginning for the monument sculptor."

accommodate: ak.-.ko-ome-eda-ate, *akabu* (perfect) *akordu* (memory, tradition) *omenezko* (honorable) *edate* (to quench thirst) *aterperatu* (to seek shelter): "It is a perfect and honorable tradition to quench the thirst of the shelter seekers." (Should be spelled accomedate).

accord: ak.-.ko-ord., aka-ako-orda, *akabu* (perfect, best possible) *akordio* (agreement) *ordainbidezko* (satisfactory, acceptable): "The best possible agreement was acceptable."

account: ak.-.ko-unt, aka-ako-untzi, *akabu* (perfect) *akordio* (agreement) *untzidun* (ship owner): "Perfect agreement with the ship owner."

actual: ak.-.tu-al., ako-otu-alo, *akordiozko* (traditional) *oturuntza* (meal) *alordun* (farmer): "A traditional farmer's meal."

adage: ada-age, *adarjo* (to make fun of) *ageriko* (in public): "To make fun in public."

adamant: ada-ama-ant, *adarkadura* (ramification, consequence) *ama* (mother) *antolarazi* (to make the child clean up): "The outcome was that mother made the child clean up."

adapt: ada-ap.-.t., ada-apa-ato, *adarkadura* (consequence, outcome) *aparteko* (special) *atonketa* (arrangement): "The outcome was a special arrangement."

addition: ad.-.di-iti-on., adi-idi-iti-one, *adi* (be careful) *idiki* (to open) *iti* (bull) *onen* (the best): "Be careful when you open (the fence) for the bull to do his best."

additive: ad.-.di-iti-ibe, adi-idi-iti-ibe, *adi* (be careful) *idiki* (to open) *itxi* (to close) *ibeni* (to put on): "Be careful when you open, to close again by putting (the lid) on."

address: ad.-.re-es.-.s., ade-ere-eso-osa, *adelu* (to prepare) *errezibimendu* (welcome) *eso* (advice, announce) *osatu* (to get together): "Prepare a welcome and announce the get-to-gether."

adept: ade-ep.-.t., ade-epe-eto, *adelu* (preparations) *epemuga* (due date, big day) *etorkunde* (arrival): "Prepare for the arrival of the big day."

adequate: ade-eku-ate, *adelatu* (to prepare, get ready) *ekuru* (quiet) *aterpe* (shelter): "Get a quiet shelter ready."

adhere: ad.-.he-ere, adi-ihe-erre, *adibide* (advice) *ihesluku* (shelter) *erretiratu* (to retire to): "My advice is to retire to the shelter."

adhesion: ad.-.he-esi-on., adi-ihe-esi-ona, *adi* (be careful) *ihesibili* (to escape) *esinguratu* (to hem in, to keep together) *onago* (closer): "Be careful to keep closer together when escaping."

adjacent: ad.-.ja-ase-en.-.t., ado-oja-ase-ene-ete, *adoratu* (to worship) *ojanguren* (edge of the forest) *aseguratu* (to insure) *enetan* (always) *etenkatu* (to get away): "Always worship at the edge of the forest to insure getting away."

adjust: ad.-.ju-ust., adu-uju-uste, *adurra jausi* (to rave, to cheer) *uju* (shout of joy) *ustegabe* (unexpected): "unexpected cheering with shouts of joy."

administration: ad.-.mini-ist.-.ra-ati-on., adi-imini-izte-era-ati-one, *adierrez* (in orderly manner) *imini* (to arrange) *iztegi*(dictionary) *era* (entire) *atiki* (to find) *oneratu* (to im-prove): "Arrange the entire dictionary in an orderly manner to improve the finding."

admirable: ad.-.mi-ira-ab.-.le, adi-ini-ira-abe-ele, *adi* (careful) *imitazio* (imitation) *iradoki* (to make) *abelaska* (manger) *ele* (cattle): "He/she made a careful imitation of the manger and cattle."

admiral: ad.-.mi-ira-al., adi-imi-ira-al, *adi* (careful) *imitagarri* (exemplary) *iradoki* (to make, to create) *aldezpen* (defensive strategy): "Create a careful and exemplary defensive strategy."

admire: ad.-.mi-ire, adi-imi-ire, *adi* (careful) *imitazio* (imitation, likeness) *ire* (yours, of you): "A careful likeness of you."

admit: ad.-.mi-it., adi-imi-itu, *adiskidegarri* (friendly) *imintzio* (gesture) *itunketa* (agree-ment): "A friendly gesture of agreement."

adoption: ado-op.-.ti-on., ado-opa-ati-oni, *adore* (encouragement, assurance) *opari egin* (to give) *atxiki* (to keep) *onik* (unharmed): "Give assurance to keep from harm."

adult: adu-ul.-.t., adu-ule-eto, *adurrajausi* (to be charmed) *ulerketa* (understanding) *etorkizun* (future): "Charmed with understanding the future."

adultery: adu-ul.-.te-eri, adu-ule-ete-eri, *adurra jausi* (to slobber) *ule* (hair) *etenkatu* (to break in, to enter) *erion* (to spill): "Slobber the hair (then) enter to spill."

affirm: af.-.fi-ir.-.m., afa-abi-ira-ami, *afa* (happy event) *abian* (about to) *iragarri* (to announce) *amiamoko* (stork): "The stork is about to announce the happy event."

again: aga-in., aga-ina, *aga* (abundance) *inarroskata* (agitation): "An abundance of agitation."

agenda: age-en.-.da, age-eni-ida, *agerkai* (document) *eni* (to me) *idazpuru* (heading): "Heading of the document (sent) to me."

agreement: ag.-.re-eme-ent, age-ere-eme-entzu, *ageriko* (public) *erretolika* (discussion) *emekiro* (peacefully) *entzupen* (hearing): "Public discussion at a peaceful hearing."

alderman, alde-er.-man (irregular), alde-eri-man, *alde* (region) *erri* (common people) *manatu* (to decide): "The common people of the region decide."

alienated: ali-ena-ate-ed., *alienatu* (to destroy a personality) *−ena* (superlative) *ateratu* (to leave) *eduki* (to have): "It sadly destroys a personality to have to leave."

almanac: al.-.ma-ana-ak. ale-ema-ana-aku, *aleketa* (abundance) *eman* (to produce) *anaikidetasun* (brotherly cooperation) *akuilatu* (to stimulate): "Produce an abundance of grain and stimulate brotherly cooperation."

amatory: ama-ato-ori, *ama* (mother) *atondu* (to prepare) *orrits* (lovely meal): "Mother prepared a lovely meal."

amber: am.-.be-er., ama-abe-era, *ama* (mother) *aberaski* (elegant) *erakarkor* (attractive): "Mother looks elegant and attractive."

ambition: am.-.bi-iti-on, ama-abi-iti-on, *ama* (mother) *abiadan* (speedy) *iti* (ox) *onbide* (good example): "Mother's speedy ox is a good example."

amen: ame-en., ame-ene, *ametsetsi* (to idealize) *ene* (exclamation): "Exclamation of idealization."

anabaptist: ana-aba-ap.-.ti-ist., ana-aba-apa-ati-isti, *anaiarte* (congregation) *abade* (priest) *apal* (humble) *atxiki* (to remain loyal to) *istildu* (to submerge): "The humble priest of the congregation remains loyal to submerging in water."

analysis: ana-ali-isi-is., *anatomia* (composition) *alik* (possible) *izigarri* (scary) *isurgai* (liquid): "The composition of the possibly scary liquid."

annihilate: an.-.ni-ihi-ila-ate, ani-ini-ihi-ila-ate, *animalia* (animal) *initz/ainitz* (many) *ihiztatu* (to hunt down) *ilarazi* (to kill) *aterpe* (shelter, blind): "Hunt down and kill many animals from a shelter."

aphrodisiac: ap.-.h.-.ro-odi-isi-ak., apo-ohe-ero-odi-isi-aku, *apokeria* (filthy deed) *oheadar* (bedpost) *erotiko* (erotic) *odi* (knothole) *isilean* (in secret) *akuilatu* (to masturbate): "It is a filthy deed to masturbate in secret (using) the erotic knothole in the bedpost."

apocalypse: apo-oka-ali-ip.-.se, apo-oka-ali-ipu-usa, *apokeria* (filthy deed) *okastagarri* (disgusting) *alienazio* (death of a person) *ipuinezko* (legendary) *usario* (tradition): "The disgusting and filthy killing of a person in the legendary tradition." This refers to the voluntary sacrifice of a young man (Tammuz, Ezekiel 8:14).

apparent: ap.-.pa-are-ent., ape-epa-are-entzu, *apez* (priest) *epaikunde* (judgement) *areago* (more) *entzunkor* (attentive): "The priest's judgement is to be more attentive."

approach: ap.-.p.-.ro-atch., ape-epe-ero-atxi, *apez* (priest) *epeluzapen* (to allow more time) *eroste* (to redeem) *atxikitzaile* (the faithful): "The priest gave more time for the faithful to be redeemed."

armageddon: ar.-.ma-age-ed.-.do-on.; ara-ama-age-ede-edo-one, *aragikor* (lustful) *Ama* (Goddess) *ageriko* (notorious) *ederrak hartu* (to be defeated) *edonongo* (everywhere) *onezkero* (right now): "The lustful and notorious Goddess must be defeated, everywhere and right now"; (2Kings 23:13-14).

assassin: as.-.sa-as.-.si-in., ase-esa-asi-isi-ino, *aserre* (angry) *esale* (speaker) *asi* (to begin) *isileko* (covert) *inozotze* (intimidation): "The angry speaker begins with covert intimidation."

assembly: as.-.se-em.-.b.-.li, asa-ase-ema-abe-eli, *asaldaketa* (excitement) *ase* (full) *emankizun* (performance) *abesbatza* (choir) *eliza* (church): "Full of excitement for the performance of the church choir."

associate: as.-.so-oki-ate, ase-eso-oki-ate, *asegale* (craving for) *esonde* (advice) *okitu* (complete) *aterbe* (confidence): "Craving for advice in complete confidence."

assure: as.-.su-ure, asi-isu-ure, *asi* (to begin) *isuri* (to inspire, show good will) *urreratu* (to get closer):"Begin with showing goodwill while getting closer."

asterisk: aste-eri-isk., *astergai* (subject of examination) *erizkatu* (to compare) *izkutu* (hidden, elsewhere): "Compare the subject of examination elsewhere."

astonish: asto-oni-ish., *aztoratu* (to confuse) *onik* (safe and sound) *ixartu* (to wake up): "To wake up confused but safe and sound."

asunder: asu-un.-.de-er., asu-une-ede-era, *asu* (newborn lamb) *unetxo* (short distance) *ederrak hartu* (to snatch away) *erratu* (to wander): "The newborn lamb wandered a short distance and was snatched away."

atom: ato-om., *ator* (come!) *omentze* (act of celebrating): "Come! Let's celebrate!"

attrition: at.-.t.-.ri-iti-on., ati-ita-ari-iti-onu, *atxiki* (to be loyal to) *itaundu* (to ask) *arrisku* (danger) *itxi* (to abandon, to ignore) *onuste* (good faith): "Ask the loyal ones to ignore danger and to have good faith."

augment: au-uga-ame-ent., *aupoza* (what joy) *ugari* (abundant) *ameskeria* (fantasy) *entzungabe* (unheard of): What joy it is to have abundant fantasies unheard of."

augury: au-guri, *aupatu* (to glorify/deify) *guritu* (to indulge in): "Indulging in glorifying."

auspice: aus.-.pi-ike, *ausitu* (to calm down) *ipini* (to place, to find a place) *ikerlari* (visitor): "Calm the visitor down and find a place for him."

author: au-ut.-.ho-or., auke-uto-oho-oro, *aukera* (opportunity) *utopikera* (ideal) *ohore eman* (to honor) *oroegile* (Creator): "Ideal opportunity to honor the Creator."

authority: au-ut.-.ho-ori-iti, au-uto-oho-ori-iti, *aukera* (opportunity) *utopikera* (ideal) *ohointza* (thievery) *orrits* (that) *itxi* (to stop): "Ideal opportunity to stop that thievery."

B

baby: .ba-abi, aba-abi, *abarroskatu* (to make noise, to cry) *abiatu* (to begin): "To begin to cry," "First cry."

bachelor: .ba-atxe-elor, oba-atxe-elor, *obakuntza* (betterment) *atxeki* (to stick with, to put up with) *elorrio* (hardship): "He puts up with hardship for betterment."

bacillus: .ba-aki.il.-.lu-us., aba-aki-ila-alu-usi, *abagadune* (occasion) *akitu* (tired) *ilaundu* (to weaken) *alukeria* (bad action, feeling) *usin* (sneeze): "On occasion tired, weak and feeling bad with sneezing."

back: .ba-ak.-.k., eba-ake-eka, *ebatzi* (to decide) *aker* (male goat) *ekarri* (to bring back): "He decided to bring the male goat back."

bacon: .ba-ako-on., eba-ako-onu, *ebakune* (slice) *akordiozko* (traditional) *onuts* (very nice): "Very nice traditional slice."

bacteria: .ba-ak.-.te-eri-i.a, aba-aki-ite-eri-iha, *abagadune* (on occasion) *akitu* (to be tired) *itegun* (work performed) *eritsu* (sick) *ihardun* (to spend time): "On occasion too tired to perform work and spending time being sick."

bad: from *abade* (priest of the pre-Christian Goddess religion), just remove first and last vowel.

badger: .ba-ad.-.ge-er., aba-adi-ige-ero, *abagadune* (opportunity) *adimentsu* (intelligent, smart) *igestoki* (hiding place) *errotu* (to settle, to establish a home): "Smart opportunity to establish a home in the hiding place."

bag: .ba-ag., eba-age, *ebaki* (to cut, harvest) *agerkin* (sample): "Cut a sample."

baggage: .ba-ag.-.ga-age, aba-agi-iga-age, *abagadune* (some time, occasion) *agian* (I hope) *igaro* (to travel) *agertu* (to discover): "Sometime I'd like to travel and discover."

bait: .ba-it., aba-ito, *abagadune* (opportunity) *ito arazi* (to snare): "Opportunity to snare."

bakery: .ba-ake-eri, eba-ake-eri, *ebadura* (slice of bread) *akeita* (coffee) *erri* (village): "A slice of bread with coffee in the village."

bale: .ba-ale, eba-ale, *ebakin* (cut hay) *aletegi* (barn): "The cut hay in the barn."

baleen/balein: bale-ina, *bale* (whale) *inara* (swallowed by): "Swallowed by the whale."

balk: .ba-alk., aba-alka, *abantzu* (almost) *alkartuezineko* (incompatible): "Almost incompatible."

ball: bal.-.l., balo-ol, *baloi* (ball) *olgetan* (to play): "To play ball."

ballad: bal.-.la-ad., bala-ala-adu, *balada* (ballad) *alaitu* (to fill with joy) *adura jausi* (charming): "A charming ballad fills with joy."

ballast: bal.-.la-ast., balda-ala-astu, *baldarkiro* (sluggish) *alabearreko* (necessary) *astunketa* (weight): "Necessarily sluggish with weight."

ballet: bal-.le-et., bala-ale-eta, *balakaldi* (adulation) *alegia* (fable) *etapa* (stage): "Adulation for the fable on stage."

balm: contraction of Baque word *baltsamo* (lotion): "Lotion."

balmy: bal-mi, *baldintasun* (condition) *miragarri* (wonderful): "Wonderful conditions."

balustrade: balu-ustera-ade, *balu* (if he had...) *usteragileki* (persuasiveness) *adeitasun* (courtesy): "If only he had persuasiveness and courtesy."

bamboo, from *banbu*, ban-bu, *banderamakila* (flagpole) *burujabetasun* (independence): "Our flagpole of independence."

banana, bana-ana, *banakatu* (to divide) *anaitu* (to bunch): "Divide the bunch."

band (music): from *banda*: "Music band."

banish: .ba-ani-ix, eba-ani-ixi, *ebasle* (thief) *anitzetan* (often) *ixilpetu* (to hide): "Thieves often hide."

beaker: .be-ake-er., *uberka* (water container) *akeita* (coffee) *erion* (to spill, to pour): "Container to pour coffee from."

beggar: .be-eg.-.ga-ar.; abe-ega-aga-are, *abegi egin* (to receive) *egape* (shelter) *-aga* (abundance of, much) *arreratasun* (kindness): "He receives shelter with much kindness."

begin: .be-egi-in., ibe-egi-ino, *ibeni* (to start) *egindura* the action) *inor* (somebody): "Somebody start the action."

beneficial: be-eni-ife-esi-al., (note "efi" in beneficial was originally "ife" as shown here; *beargorri* (extreme poverty) *eni* (to me) *ifernu* (damned) *esibarruti* (obstruction) *alaitasun* (happiness): "Extreme poverty to me is a damned obstruction to happiness."

bill: from *bildu* (to gather, to collect): "to gather."

boy: bo – oi, bozkarioz – oiuka, happy – shouting: "Happily shouting."

bravo: bra-abo, *brastadako* (sudden, spontaneous) *abonau* (approval): "Spontaneous approval."

brash, bra-ax., bra-axo, *brastadakoan* (suddenly) *axolagabeko* (careless): "Suddenly careless."

breast: .b.-.re-ast., abu-ure-azte, *aburu agertu* (to express an opinion) *urreratu* (to get closer) *aztergai* (subject of examination): "To express an opinion you have to get closer to the subject of examination."

C

calendar: .ka-ale-en.-.da-ar., eka-ale-ene-eda-ara, *ekainaldi* (solsticial season) *alegera* (rejoicing) *-enetan* (always) *edale* (drunk) *arratsera* (every evening): "Rejoicing during the solsticial season always means getting drunk every evening."

caliber: ka-ali-ibe-er., *katigu* (prisoner) *alienatu* (to kill a person) *ibeni* (to commit) *erailketa* (murder): "To kill a prisoner is to commit murder."

canal: kana-al., kana-ala, *kanaleztatu* (to cut a channel) *alabearreko* (necessary): "Cut a channel if necessary."

capable: .ka-apa-ab.-.le, eka-apa-abe-elka, *ekarri* (to bring) *aparteko* (superior) *abe* (support) *elkardura* (meeting): "He/she brings superior support to the meeting."

capital, .ka-api-ita-al., aka-api-ita-ala, *akatu* (in the end) *apika* (may be) *itxaro* (to have trust in) *aldaratu* (to save money): "In the end maybe have trust in saving money."

caprice, .ka-ap.-.ri-ise, eka-apa-ari-ise, *ekarri* (to get) *apa* (kiss) *arritasun* (surprise) *iseka* (joke): "To get a surprise kiss as a joke."

capture: .ka-ap.-.tu-ure; aka-apo-otu-ure, *akatsbako* (perfect) *apodun* (hoofed animal, ungulate) *oturuntza* (meal) *urreraketa* (to draw closer, coming up): "A perfect meal of ungulate is coming up."

carat, .ka-ara-at., aka-ara-ato, *akatsgabeko* (flawlessly) *aratz* (pure) *atondu* (to polish): "Flawlessly pure and polished"

caravan, .ka-ara-aba-an., aka-ara-aba-ano, *akabu* (the end) *ara* (towards, at) *abaro* (shady place) *ano* (food): "At the end there is a shady place and food."

carnal: .ka-ar.-.na-al., aka-ara-ana-alu, *akatsbako* (perfect) *aragikeria* (fornication) *anaitu* (to unite, to get together) *alu* (vulva): "Perfect fornication with a vulva."

carpenter: .ka-arpe-en.-.te-er., ika-arpe-ena-ate-era, *ikaragarri* (large) *arpegi* (front of the building) *-ena* (superlative, beautiful) *atenagusi* (main entrance) *eraiki* (to build): "He built the (beautiful) main entrance in the large building front."

carry: *erakarri* (to carry): "To carry."

castle, .ka-as.-.t.-.le, aka-asa-ate-ele, *akabu* (superior) *azalpen* (manifestation, display) *eleienda* (legend) *aterpe* (protection): "Superior display of legendary protection."

catholic: .ka-ato-oli-ik., aka-ato-oli-ika, *akatsbako* (perfect) *atontzaile* (organization) *oliotu* (holy) *ikasbide* (teachings): "Perfect organization for holy teachings."

caucus: kau-auku-us., *kausituketa* (meeting) *aukuratu* (to elect) *usadio* (according to tradition): "Meeting to elect according to tradition."

celebrity: (was celebrety) .se-ele-eb.-.re-eti, ase-ele-eba-are-eti, *asekaitz* (craving) *eleiza* (Christian assembly) *ebanjelari* (evangelist) *arrera egin* (to welcome) *etiketa* (ethical, moralistic): "The Christian assembly is craving to welcome the moralistic evangelist."

cellar: ke-el.-.la-ar., ke-eli-ila-ari, *keriza* (refuge) *eliza* (church) *ilarazi* (to kill) *arinari eman* (to escape): "Church refuge to escape the killing."

cemetary:.se-eme-eta-ari, *aseg. uratu* (to insure) *emetasun* (pleasing environment) *ete* (forever after) *arima* (soul): "Insure a pleasing environment for ever after for the soul."

century, .se-en.-.tu-uri, ase-ena-atu-uri, *asezindaku* (craving, longing for) *atutxa* (better world) *urrikalkor* (merciful): "I am longing for a much better and more merciful world."

chapter: cha-ap.-.te-er., txa-apa-ate-era, *txairoki* (gracefully) *apailatu* (to organize) *aterapen* (composition) *erakarle* (attractive): "Gracefully organize the composition to make it look attractive."

cherry: txe-er.-.ri, txe-ero-ori, *txertatu* (to graft) *erromuskil* (twig) *orridun* (leafy): "Graft a leafy twig."

chimney, txi-im.-.ni, txi-ima-ani, *tximinia* (smokestack) *imatz* (wicker) *anizkoitz* (multiple layered): "Smokestack (made of) multiple layered wicker." (A tube was woven of wicker, then lined with clay, which baked in the heat of the fire into a pottery chimney).

Christ: kri-izt., *Kriatzaile* (God, Creator) *iztun* (speaker): "God's speaker" or: "He speaks for God."

circus, .si-ir.-.ku-us, esi-iri-iku-us, *esi* (fence) *iriki* (to open) *ikusbide* (to view) *ustekabe* (the unexpected): "Open the fence and view the unexpected."

cistern: .ki-isti-irra-an. (was cistirn), *ekinalean* (do as much as possible) *iztil* (pool, water supply) *iragangaitz* (long lasting, durable) *aniztu* (to increase): "Do as much as possible to increase the durable watersupply."

civilization: .ki-ibi-ili-iza-ati-on., *ekinalean* (do as much as possible) *ibili* (to behave) *ilintitu* (to stir up, to encourage) *izari* (moderation) *atiki* (loyalty) *onestasun* (decency): "Do as much as possible to behave and encourage moderation, loyalty and decency."

clean, k.-.le-an., iku-ule-ani, *ikusi* (the wash) *ule* (hair) *anitzetan* (often, frequently): "Wash your hair frequently."

climax: .k.-.li-ima-ak.-.s., eki-ili-ima-aka-asa, *ekin* (to continue) *ilintitu* (to stir up) *imajina* (idol) *akabu* (supreme) *asaldaketa* (excitement): "Continue to stir up (your) idol to supreme excitement."

clitoris: .k.-.li-ito-ori-is., ike-eli-ito-ori, *ikertu* (to explore) *elizlur* (sacred spot) *itoaldi* (embarrassment) *ori* (that) *isilkeriaz* (in secret): "Explore that sacred spot of embarrasment in secret."

colonize, .ko-olo-oni-ize, *ekoiztu* (to produce) *olo* (oats) *onibar* (real estate, land) *izendatu* (to claim ownership): "Produce **oats** to claim ownership to the land."

color, .ko-olo-or., eko-olo-ori, *ekoitzi* (to harvest) *olo* (oats) *oribizi* (goldcolored): "Harvest the gold-colored oats."

come, kome, *komeni* (be helpful): "Be helpful."

comedy, ko-ome-edi, *komiko* (comic) *omen* (fame) *ediren* (to find, to achieve): "The comic achieved fame."

comic, komi-ik., komi-iku, *komiki* (comic) *ikusgura* (costume): "Comic costume."

common, .ko-ome-emo-on., *akordiozko* (traditional) *omentsu* (celebrated) *emonkor* (generous) *onestasun* (decency): "Celebrated traditional generousness and decency."

communion: .ko-om.-.mu-uni-on., ako-oma-amu-uni-one, *akorduan euki* (to remember) *oma* (grandmother) *amuros* (loving) *unibertsal* (universal) *oneste* (act of blessing): "Remember our loving grandmother's universal blessing."

compare, .ko-om.-.pa-are, ako-oma-apa-are, akorduan euki (remember) oma (grandmother) apailatu (to cook) arretaz (carefully): "Remember how carefully grandmother cooked?"

compassion: ko-om.-.pa-asi-on., ko-ome-epa-asi-one, *komeni* (to be helpful) *omenezko* (honorable) *epai* (decision) *asi* (to start) *oneste* (act of blessing): "To be helpful is an honorable decision to begin an act of blessing."

conclude: .ko-on.-.k.-.lu-ude, ako-ona-aki-ilu-ude, *akorduan euki* (to remember) *onarketa* (welcome) *akitu* (to be tired) *ilunalde* (evening) *udetxe* (summerhouse): "Remember the welcome at the summer cottage when we were tired in the evening?"

conquer: ko-on.-.ku-er., ako-ona-aku-era, *akordiotu* (to consent, to grant) *onartze* (permission) *akuilatu* (to incite, to launch) *eraso* (attack): "Permission is granted to launch an attack."

consent: .ko-on.-.se-ent, ako-ona-ase-ent, *akordio* (agreement) *onarketa* (welcome) *asebete* (to satisfy hunger) *entzuleria* (audience): "Welcome agreement satisfies the audience."

Coptic: .ko-op.-.ti-ik., ako-opa-ati-ika, *akordiozko* (traditional) *opagai* (offering) *atxikigarri* (faithful) *ikasbide* (teachings): "Traditional offering of faithful teachings."

copulate: The word originally must have read: copjulete: .ko-op.-.ju-ule-ete, ako-opa-aju-ule-ete, *akorduan euki* (to remember) *opa izan* (longing for) *ajuria* (heather field) *uletsu* (hairy) *etendura* (split, crack): "Remember how I longed for your hairy crack in the heather field"?

copy, .ko-opi, uko-opi, *ukozko* (negative) *opildu* (to flatten out), "Flatten out the negative."

cordial, .ko-or.-.di-al., eko-ora-adi-ale, *ekonomo* (administrator) *orain* (always) *adiskidetsu* (friendly) *aleginez* (careful): "The administrator was always friendly and careful."

core, kor, *kortxo* (cork): "Cork."

cormorant: ko-ora-amo-ora-ant., *koska* (ledge) *orraztu* (to rob) *amorrotuz* (determinedly) *oratu* (to grab) *antolatu* (to prepare): "Determinedly on the ledge to rob (the eggs) he prepared to grab."

corporal, ko-or.-.po-ora-al., ko-ora-apo-ora-ali, *kopetadun* (brazen) *orain* (always) *apokeria* (insulting) *orratio* (angry) *alukeria* (repulsive): "Always brazen, insulting, angry and repulsive."

cosmos, kosmo-os., *kosmo* (universe) *osin* (depth): "The depth of the universe."

country: .ko-un.-.t.-.ri, ako-une-eto-ori, *akordiogarri* (agreeable) *une* (place, spot) *etorki* (family) *orrits* (feast): "Agreeable spot for a family feast."

craft, .k.-.ra-af.-.t., eki-ira-afa-ato, *ekin* (to persevere) *irabazbide* (professional) *afa* (happy) *atondu* (to solve problems): "Persevering professional is happy to solve problems."

creation: .k.-.re-ati-on., oke-ere-ati-one, *okergabe* (pristine) *erregali* (gift) *atxikitzaile* (faithful) *onetsi* (to bless): "Pristine gift to the blessed faithful."

cruel, .k.-ru-el., oke-erru-ele, *okerkeria* (injustice) *errukigabekeria* (mercilessness) *ele* (story): "Story of injustice and mercilessness."

cry: .k.-.ri, oke-eri, *okerkeria* (injury) *eriotzordu* (agony): "The agony of injury."

cult: .ku-ul.-.t., ku-ule-eti, *kutsugarri* (contagious) *ulerkaitz* (incomprehensibe) *etikoagaitz* (unethical): "Incomprehensibly contagious and unethical."

cupola, .ku-upo-ola, iku-upo-ola, *ikusgarri* (scenic) *upohol* (barrel-shaped) *olana* (canopy): "Scenic barrel-shaped canopy."

current: from French courant, kurant: kura-ant., *kuraia* (force) *antepara* (canal which brings water to the waterwheel): "The force of the water from the canal turns the waterwheel."

curt: .ku-urt., *akuilatu* (to urge) *urten* (to leave): "Urged to leave."

D

dead: .de-ad., ede-ade, *edendu* (to poison) *adeigabeki* (rudely): "Rudely poisoned."

debate: .de-eba-ate, ide-eba-ate: *idetu* (to compare) *ebatzi* (to decide) *ateriki* (calmly): "Compare and decide calmly."

decadent: .de-eka-ade-ent., ede-eka-ade-ent, *ederra sartu* (to lie) *ekarri* (to cause) *adeigabeko* (rude) *entzuera* (reputation): "Lieing causes a rude reputation."

decision: .de-esi-isi-on., *adelatu* (to prepare) *esinguratu* (to surround) *isilka* (secretly) *onezkero* (right now): "Right now prepare to secretly surround them."

defense: .di-ife-en.-.s; adi-ife-enu-us, *aditu* (watch out for) *ifernu* (damned) *enultasun* (weakness) *usnatu* (to suspect): "Watch out for any damned suspected weakness."

delegate: .de-ele-ega-ate, *idetu* (to compare, to swap) *ele* (story) *egarritu* (to make someone thirsty) *atera* (to get): "Swapping stories makes one get thirsty."

descendant: .de-eske-en.-.da-ant, ide-ezke-eni-ida-ant, *idetu* (to compare) *ezkel* (cross-eyed) *eni* (to me) *idazkitu* (to establish) *antz* (resemblance): "(They) compared the cross-eyed (person) with me to establish a resemblance."

desideratum: .de-esi-ide-era-atu-um., *adei* (gently) *esinguratu* (to surround) *ideialki* (ideal) *erakasketa* (education) *atutxi* (better world) *ume* (child): "Gently surround our children with an ideal education for a better world."

desire: de-esi-ire, *debekuz* (deceitful) *esitzaile* (besieger) *irentsi* (to destroy): Destroy the deceitful besieger."

desk: .de-esk., *ederki* (beautifully) *eskuzko* (handcrafted): "Beautifuly handcrafted."

desperate: de-espera-atu, *dei* (calling) *esperantzagabe* (hopeless) *atutxa* (better world): "Calling hopelessly for a better world."

destroy: .de-est.-.ro-oi, ede-esta-aro-oi, *ederrasartu* (to lie, to mislead) *estakuru* (pretext) *arrotz* (foreigner) *oiher* (evil): "Misleading pretext of the evil foreigner."

devastate: .de-eba-azta-ate, *edeki* (to remove) *ebasle* (plunderer) *aztarna* (footprint) *ate* (door): "The plunderer removed his footprints by the door."

devout: .de-ebo-ut., ide-ebo-uto, *ideologia* (ideology) *eboluzionatu* (to develop) *utopia* (better world): "Ideology which develops a better world."

diary: .di-ari, adi-ari, *adieragin* (to explain) *ariketa* (activity): "It explains the activities."

dictionary: .di-ik.-.ti-ona-ari, edi-ika-ati-ona-ari, *ediren* (to find) *ikasgai* (study material) *atxiki* (to memorize) *onaldi* (prosperity) *arinaldi* (improvement): "To find study material to memorize for improvement in prosperity."

didactic: .di-ida-ak.-.ti-ik., adi-ida-aka-ati-ika, *adimentsuki* (intelligently) *idatzi* (to write) *akatsgabeko* (perfect) *atxiki* (faithful) *ikaskai* (lessons): "To intelligently write perfectly faithful lessons."

dignity: .di-ig.-.ni-iti, adi-igu-uni-iti, *aditze* (understanding) *igurikitza* (tolerance) *unibersal* (general) *itikor* (permissive): "His understanding and tolerance (makes him) generally permissive."

disciple: .di-is.-.ki-ip.-.le, udi-iso-oki-ipu-ule, *udikan* (go away) *isolamendu* (isolation) *okitu* (total) *ipuin* (gospel) *ulertu* (to ponder): "Go away into total isolation to ponder the gospels."

discover: .de-es.-.ko-obe-er., (was: descover):ade-esi-iko-obe-ere, *adelatu* (to prepare) *esibarruti* (enclosure) *iko* (that) *obetu* (to improve, make liveable) *eremu* (wilderness): "Prepare an enclosure that makes the wilderness liveable."

disgust: .di-is.-.gu-ust., adi-isi-igu-uste, *adi* (watch out!) *isilume* (bastard) *iguindu* (to despise) *ustelkeria* (morally corrupt): "Watch out for that despised and morally corrupt bastard."

distance: .di-ista-an.-.ke, adi-izta-ani-ike, *aditze* (to understand) *iztar* (thighs) *aniztu* (to increase) *ikermen* (rest stop): "Understanding the thighs he increased the rest stops."

doctor: .do-ok.-.to-or., *odoldun* (bloody) *okerkeria* (injury) *etorri* (to come) *orain* (right now): "A bloody injury; come right now"!

document: .do-oko-oju-ume-ent., ado-oko-oju-ume-entzu, *adoratu* (to worship) *okolu* (stable) *ojualdi* (crying) *ume* (child) *entzutetsu* (celebrated): "They worshiped in the stable (when they heard) the crying of the celebrated child."

dog: .do-og., ado-ogu, *adoretsu* (brave) *oguzi* (to speak out loud): "Brave and loud."

dogma: .do-og.-.ma, odo-ogu-uma, *odolaitortza* (martyrdom) *oguzi* (speak clearly) *umatu* (to be fruitful): "Speak clearly about his martyrdom and be fruitful."

doll: .do-ol.-.l., ido-ole-ela: *idolo* (idol) *olgetan egin* (to play with) *elastiko* (springy, soft) "Soft idol to play with."

doom: .do-om., ido-ome, *idolo* (idol) *omendatu* (to pay tribute to): "Paying tribute to an idol."

drink: .d-.ri-in.-.k., eda-ari-ina-ake, *edan* (to drink) *arin-arin* (quickly) *inara* (swallow) *akeita* (coffee): "Quickly drink your swallow of coffee."

drop: .d-.ro-op., odo-oro-opi, *odolberoaldi* (fit of rage) *oroz* (totally) *opildu* (to flatten):

"Totally flattened in a fit of rage."

dynasty: .dina-asti, *adina* (so many) *astiz* (bright future): "So many bright futures."

E

eager, ea-age-er., *ea* (emphasis) *ageriko* (honest) *erreaksio* (reaction): "Very honest reaction."

eagle, ea-ag.-.le, ea-age-ele, *ea* (emphasis) *agerbide* (symbol) *eleiza* (church): "Special church symbol."

ear, ea-ar., ea-ara, *ea* (emphasis) *arramaka* (shouting): "Loud shouting."

early, ea-ar.-.li, ea-ari-ili, *ea* (emphasis) *arinarazi* (hasten) *ilintitu* (to stir up a fire): "Hurry up and stir up the fire."

earn, ea-ar.-.n., ea-aro-onu, *ea* (emphasis) *arotz* (carpenter) *onura* (earnings, wages): "Good carpenter's wages."

earnest, ea-ar.-.ne-est, ea-are-ene-esta, *ea* (emphasis) *arreratsu* (kind) *ene* (to me) *estalgabe* (sincere): "Very kind and sincere to me."

earth, ea-ar.-.t.-.h., ea-ari-itu-uhu, *ea* (emphasis) *arrigarri* (marvelous) *iturri* (source) *uhui* (happiness): "Marvelous source of happiness."

easy, ea-azi, *ea* (emphasis) *azi* (to grow up): "Growing up fast."

Easter, ea-aste-er., *ea* (emphasis, special) *aste* (week) *eraspen* (devotion): "Special week of devotion."

east, ea-ast., *ea* (emphasis) *astro* (star): "Special star."

eat, ea-at., ea-ato, *ea* (emphasis) *atondu* (to prepare): "Especially prepared."

eave, ea-abe, *ea* (emphasis) *abegi egin* (to receive): "Special receptacle (for rainwater)."

ebb, eb.-.b., eba-abi, *ebatzi* (to decide) *abialdi* (departure): "It decides the departure" (of the ship).

ebony, ebo-oni, *eboluzionatu* (To develop, to create) *onizan* (something useful): "Create something useful."

echo, ek.-.ho, eka-aho, *atzera ekarri* (to return) *ahoziritu* (to mislead): "The returning (sound) is misleading."

education: edu – uka – ati – on., *edukitsu* (powerful) *ukan* (possessions) *atxiki* (to acquire) *onaldi* (prosperity): "Powerful possession to acquire prosperity."

ejaculate: eja-aku-ule-ete (note the shift from a to e): *eia* (come on, keep on) *akuilatu* (to stimulate) *uletsu* (hairy) *etendura* (split, crack): "Keep on stimulating the hairy crack."

emergency: eme-erge-en.-.ki, eme-erge-ene-eki, *eme* (female) *ergel* (foolish) *enegana ator* (come to me) *ekin* (to try): "Foolish woman, try to come to me."

empty: em.-.p.-.ti, ema-apu-utzi, *eman* (to give) *apurtxo* (a little bit) *utzik* (merely, just): "Give just a little bit."

encyclopaedia: en.-.si-ik.-.lo-opa-edi-i.a, ena-asi-ika-alo-opa-edi-iha, *-ena* (possessive suffix) *asi* (to begin) *ikaste* (learning) *alogeratu* (to engage, acquire) *opa* (desire) *ediren* (to find) *ihardetsaldi* (answer): "To begin learning, you must acquire a desire to find answers."

energy: ene-er.-.gi, ene-era-agi, *-enetan* (always) *eragin* (to motivate) *aginbidedun* (powerfully): "Always powerfully motivated."

envelope, originally spelled envellope: en.-.be-el.-.lo-ope, eni-ibe-ela-alo-ope, *eni* (to me) *ibeni* (to send) *ela* (letter) *alogereko* (mercenary) *opetsi* (to devote oneself/to love someone): "The mercenary sent to me a letter of devotion/love."

envious: en.-.bi-us., eni-ibi-usa, *eni* (to me) *ibilkeria* (behaviour) *usainka* (suspicious): "(His) behaviour to me is suspicious."

erotic: ero-oti-ik., *erromantiku* (romantic) *otzikaratu* (to tremble) *ikusaldi* (time spent looking): "Trembling romantically (during) the time spent looking."

estate: es.-.ta-ate, ese-eta-ate, *esertze* (act of being situated) -*eta* (place of) *aterpe* (refuge, safe place): "To be situated in a place of refuge."

estrus: est.-.ru-us., esta-aru-usa, *estaldi* (to mate animals) *arrunki* (simply, commonly) *usaindu* (to smell): "Mating animals commonly smell."

executive: (eksekutive), .ek.-.se-eku-uti-ibe, eka-ase-eku-uti-ibe, *ekaitz* (storm) *aserre* (anger) *ekurugaitz* (worried) *utikan* (get out) *ibeni* (act of putting on): "His act of putting on a storm of anger has me worried that I have to get out."

existence: (eksiztense) ek.-.si-izte-en.-.se, eka-asi-izte-ene-ese, *ekarpen* (contribution) *asierako* (original) *iztegi* (vocabulary) *ene* (my) *esentzia* (essence): "The essence of my original vocabulary contributions."

exotic, ek.-.so-oti-ik., eka-aso-oti-iku, *ekarri* (to bring) *azokari* (merchant) *otzitu* (to chill) *ikusnahi* (curiosity): "The merchant brought a chilling curiosity."

expect: ek.-.spe-ek.-.t., eka-aspe-eki-ito, *ekantze* (to become accustomed) *asperti* (revenge) *ekinaldi* (attempt) *itotzaile* (murderer): "He became accustomed to the murderer's revenge attempts."

experiment: (eksperement) ek.-.s.-.pe-ere-eme-ent, eki-isu-upe-ere-eme-ent, *ekin* (attempt) *isurgai* (liquid) *upeleratu* (to store in vats) *eredu* (example) *emendatu* (to enlarge) *entsegu* (experiment): "Attempt to store the liquid in vats as an example of how to enlarge the experiment."

extasy, ek.-.s.-.ta-asi, eka-asa-ata-asi, *ekarpen* (contribution) *asaldaketa* (excitement) *atano* (better world) *asi* (to start): "Contribution to the excitement of starting a better world."

F

facility: .fa-aki-ili-iti, *afa* (happy) *akiarazi* (to be exhausted) *ilintitu* (to revive, to recover) *itxi* (to allow): "Happy (place) where the exhausted are allowed to recover."

family: from French: famille: .fa-ami-ile; *afa* (happy) *amiamoko* (stork) *ilehartze* (joking): "Happy joking about the stork."

fast: .fa-ast., *afa* (happy) *astajoko* (donkey race): "Happy donkey race."

female: .fe-ema-ale: abe-ema-ale, *abegikor* (hospitable) *emakume* (woman) *alegera* (happy): "A hospitable and happy woman."

fever: (German: Fieber): .fi-ibe-er., ifi-ibe-ere, *ibili* (to act) *ibeni* (to put on, to apply) *erremedio* (cure, remedy): "Act by putting on a remedy."

finance: .fi-ina-an.-.se, ofi-ina-ana-ase, *ofiziale* (official) *inauguratu* (to open) *anaia* (brother) *ase ase* (overful): "The official opened the overful (trunk) of the brother."

fire:.fi-ire, ifi-ire, *ibini/ipini* (to be) *irestzaile* (destructive): "It is destructive."

flood: originally spelled floud) f.-.lo-u.o-od., fa-alo-uho-ode, *fabore* (help) *alorgizon* (farmer) *uhol* (inundation) *odei* (cloud): "Help the farmer during the inundation from the clouds."

flour: .f.-.lo-ur., afa-alo-uru, *afa* (pleased with) *alor* (farmer) *urun* (flour): "Pleased with the farmer's flour.."

flower: .f.-.lo-er., afa-alo-era, *afa* (happy, pleasing) *alor* (field) *errainuketa* (sunshine): "A pleasing field in the sunshine."

fond (of):.f.-ond., afa-onda, *afa* (happy) *ondartu* (to get stuck, attached to): "Happy to get attached to."

fortune: .bo-or.-.tu-une, abo-ora-atu-une, *abogadu* (lawyer) *orratio* (expression of surprise) *atutxi* (better world) *uneko* (instantaneous): "The lawyer's surprise instantaneously (opened up) a better world."

fragile: .f.-.ra-agi-ile, ifa-ara-agi-ile, *ifernu* (damned) *arrazkeria* (negligence) *agirakatu* (to be blamed) *ilezin* (forever): "Damned negligence; I'll be blamed forever."

freedom: .f.-.re-edo-ome, afa-are-edo-ome, *afa* (pleasing) *arreman* (relationship) *edozelako* (common) *omen* (honor): "Pleasing common relationship of honor."

frighten: .f.-.ri-ig.-.te-en., afa-ari-ige-ete-ene, *afa* (happy) *arriskatu* (to risk) *iges egin* (to escape) *etenbehar* (tension) *enegana* (to come to me): "Happy you risked to escape the tension by coming to me."

frugal: .f.-.ru-uga-al., afa-aru-uga-alo, *afari* (meal) *arrunt* (simple) *ugari* (fruitful, productive) *alor* (small field, garden plot): "A simple meal from a productive garden plot."

furlong: fu-ur.-.lo-on.-.g, fu-ura-alo-ona-aga, *fundatu* (to establish) *urrats* (footsteps) *alorgizon* (farmer) *onarketa* (to accept) *agazneurri* (measurement, dimension: "I accept the dimensions which the farmer's footsteps/paces established."

G

garlic: .ga-ar.-.li-ik., ega-ara-ali-ika, *egakortasun* (smell) *arranguratu* (to complain) *alienatu* (to destroy a person's composure) *ikaragarri* (awful): "(People) complain that the smell destroys a person's composure; it's awful"!

general: .ge-ene-era-al., *ageri* (honesty) *-enetan* (always) *eragin* (to promote) *alaitasun* (happiness): "Honesty always promotes happiness."

Genesis: .ge-ene-esi-is., *ageri* (revelation) *ene* (my) *ezingehiagoko* (supreme) *izadi* (creation): "Supreme revelation of Creation."

global: .g.-.lo-oba-al., uga-alo-oba-ala, *ugalkor* (lush) *alor* (field) *oba* (genuinely) *alaitu* (to fill with joy): "Lush fields genuinely fill with joy."

globe: .g.-lo-obe, uga-alo-obe, *ugalkortasun* (productivity) *alor* (field) *obetu* (to improve): "Improve the productivity of the fields."

Gnostic: .g.-.no-os.-.ti-ik., igo-ono-osa-ati-ika, *igoarazi* (to lift up) *on on* (exquisite) *osatasun* (perfection) *atxikigarri* (faithfulness) *ikaskai* (teachings): "Lift up to exquisite perfection our teachings in faithfulness."

goal, .go-al., ego-ala, *egokitasun* (opportunity) *alai* (happy): "Happy opportunity."

gonad: .go-ona-ad., igo-ona-adi, *igortzi* (to rub) *onartu* (to approve of, to like) *adi* (careful): "(I) like careful rubbing."

gondola, .go-on.-.do-ola, ego-oni-ido-ola, *egon* (to stay) *onik* (safe and sound) *idor* (dry) *olana* (canopy): "Stay safe and dry under the canopy."

gospel, .go-os.-.pe-el., igo-osa-ape-ele, *igo arazi* (to lift up) *osatasun* (perfection) *apez* (priest) *ele* (story): "Lift the priest's story up to perfection."

gossip: .go-osi-ip, ego-osi-ipu, *egodun* (winged) *osintsu* (foundationless, meaningless) *ipuin* (talk): "Winged meaningless talk."

gourmet: .go-ur.-.me-et., ego-uro-ome-eti, *egosi* (to boil) *uroilanda* (marsh hen) *omenka* (according to) *etiketa* (instructions): "Boil the marsh hen according to instructions."

grammatica: .g.-.ra-ama-ati-ika, iga-ara-ama-ati-iki, *igar* (dry) *arra-* (repetition) *amaikatxo* (many) *atxiki* (to memorize) *ikaskai* (lesson): "Many dry repetitions will memorize the lesson."

gust: .gu-ust., egu-uste, *egualdi* (weather) *ustegabe* (unexpected): "Unexpected weather."

H

Hansard: .ha-an.-.sa-ard., aha-ane-esa-ardu, *ahalegin* (attempt) *anega* (measure) *esan* (to narrate) *arduratu* (to take responsibility for): "An attempt to take a measure of responsibility for the narration."

harass: .ha-ara-as.; aha-ara-asa, *ahakargarri* (upsetting, worrisome) *arao* (blasphemy) *asaldatu* (to be perturbed): "To be perturbed by the worrisome blasphemy."

harbour: .ha-ar.-.bo-ur., aha-ara-abo-uri, (The prayer of a person in desperate need); *ahalgabe* (impotent, helpless) *arazio* (worried) *abotz* (voice) *urrikalpen* (mercy): "Helpless (in his boat) a worried voice (cries) mercy"!

heart: .he-art., ihe-artu, *ihesleku* (refuge) *artuemon* (trust): "Trusted refuge."

hell: el.-.l., ela-ali, (the "h" has no meaning in the word): *ela* (story, legend) *alienatu* (a person's destruction): "The story of a person's destruction."

help: el.-.p., ela-apa, (the "h" has no meaning), *ela* (word) *apalaldi* (weakness): "Word (expressing) weakness."

heretic: he-ere-eti-ik., *helburu* (destination) *erretxindura* (exasperation) *etikaezin* unethical) *ikaraz* (frightfully): "Destined to be a frightfully unethical exasperation."

heron: .he-ero-on., ohe-ero-on, *ohe* (bed, nest) *erromuskil* (twigs) *-ondo* (pertaining to tree): "A nest of twigs in a tree."

honesty: one-esti, *onegite* (doing good) *estimagarri* (appreciated): "Doing good is appreciated."

hospital: os.-.pi-ita-al., osa-api-ita-ala, *osasunda* (to get well) *apika* (perhaps) *itaunka* (asking for) *alatz* (miracle): "To get well, perhaps, is asking for a miracle."

honorary: .ho-ono-ora-ari, *ahobatez* (unanimous) *onon* (the very best) *oraingoan* (on this occasion) *ari* (to him/her): "On this occasion we unanimously wish our very best to him/her."

humanity: .hu-uma-ani-iti, *ahurka* (in large numbers) *umaketa* (reproduction) *aniztu* (to increase) *itxi* (to allow): "Births in large numbers allowed the increase."

hymen: .hi-imi-in., ohi-imi-ine, (note: originally hymin), *ohitu* (to get used to) *imitatu* (to reproduce) *inertzia* (lie still, be passive): "To get used to reproducing, lie still."

hysterical: iste-eri-ika-al., *izterbegiko* (unpleasant) *eri* (affliction) *ikaragarri* (frightening) *alarao* (scream): "Unpleasant affliction with frightening screams."

I

identity: ide-en.-.ti-iti, ide-ene-eti-iti, *identifikatu* (to identify) *ene* (my) *etiketa* (label, name) *itxi* (to permit, to allow): "You are allowed to identify my name."

impotent: im.-.po-ote-ent., imi-ipo-ote-entzu, *imini* (size) *ipotu* (to grow small) *ote* (perhaps) *entzungura* (anxiety): "To grow smaller in size is perhaps anxiety."

improvement: im.-.pro-obe-eme-ent, *imaginatu* (to sculpt, to shape) *apropos* (purposely) *obetu* (to perfect) *emendatu* (to increase) *entsegutu* (experiment): "To purposely shape and perfect the experiment to increase (production)."

impulsive: im.-.pu-ul.-.si-ibe, imi-ipu-ule-ezi-ibe, *imintzio* (gesture) *ipurgarbiketa* (adulation) *ulerterazi* (to listen to) *ezigaitz* (indomitable, irresistable) *ibintze* (act of putting on)): "Gesture of adulation (after) listening to the irresistible act put on."

inaugurate: ina-au-gura-atu, *inaustu* (to cut) *au* (this one) *gura* (desire/hoping for) *atutxa* (better future): "I cut this (ribbon) hoping for a better future."

indicate: in.-.di-ika-ate, ina-adi-ika-ate, *inauguratu* (to open) *adierazpen* (explanation) *ikasbide* (example) *aterri* (clear): "Open the explanation with a clear example."

inherit: in.-.he-eri-it., ina-ahe-eri-itu, *inauguratu* (to open) *aherentzia* (inheritance) *erio* (death) *itun* (sad): Opening the inheritance after a sad death."

initiate: ini-iti-ate, *injineru* (engineer) *itxi* (to close) *ate* (door): "The engineer closed the doors." **innocence**: in.-.no-oke-en.-.ke, ino-ono-oke-eni-ike, *inozo* (naive) *onon* (wonderful) *okerraragabe* (uncorrupted) *eni* (to me) *ikertu* (to visit): "A wonderfully naive, uncorrupted (person) came to visit me."

inquirer: in.-.ki-ire-er., ine-eki-ire-era, *inertzia* (passive/neutral) *ekinaldi* (attempt) *ireki* (to open up) *erakutsi* (to expose): "A neutral attempt to open up and expose."

integrity: in.-.te-eg.-.ri-iti, ina-ate-egi-iri-iti, *inauguratu* (to open) *atertu* (to clear the air) *egi esan* (to be truthful) *irizpidetu* (to pass judgement) *itxi* (to permit): "Be truthful and clear the air by opening the doors to permit the passing of judgement."

intelligent: in.-.te-eli-ige-en.-.t., ino-ote-eli-ige-ene-ete, *inolaz* (somehow) *ote* (perhaps) *elizdiru* (obligation) *igesegin* (to evade) *ene* (before) *eten* (getting tired): "Somehow perhaps evade the obligation before getting tired."

interrupt: in.-.te-erru-up.-.t., ina-ate-eru-upa-ata, *inauguratu* (to open) *atera* (to remove) *errudun* (faulty) *upa* (barrel) *atal* (fragment): "Open up and remove the faulty barrel fragment."

intolerable, in.-.to-ole-era-ab.-.le, ina-ato-ole-era-abe-ele, *inarrospen* (agitation) *atondu* (to find a solution) *oles egin* (to call upon) *erakusten eman* (to explain) *aberekeria* (brutality) *ele* (story): "To find a solution to the agitation he was called upon to explain the story of the brutality."

irksome: ir.-.k.-.so-ome, iro-oko-oso-ome, *irol* (manure) *okolu* (stable) *osoro* (total) *omenaldi* (tribute): "Manure from the stable was his total tribute."

irrigate: ir.-.ri-iga-ate, ire-eri-iga-ate, *ireki* (to open) *eriontegi* (spillway) *igartu* (to wilt) *atertu* (to stop): "Open the spillway to stop the wilting."

itinerary: iti-ine-era-ari, *itxi* (stop) *inertzia* (rest) *erazko* (convenient) *arriskugabe* (safe): "Stop for a rest at a convenient safe place."

J

jeopardy (crisis, danger): .je-opa-ar.-.di, je-opa-ara-adi, *jelostu* (to distrust) *opari egin* (to give) *arartegabeko* (immediate) *adiarazi* (to warn): "Distrust them, give immediate warning."

L

lamb: .la-am.-.b., ala-ama-abe, *alaitsu* (joyful) *amaigabeki* (endlessly) *abereborda* (sheepfold): "Endlessly joyful in the sheepfold."

leather: (from German Leder), .le-ede-er.: *alegina egin* (to make an effort) *ederki* (to take from) *eremu* (wilderness): "Make an effort to take it from the wilderness."

legality: .le-ega-ali-iti, *alegiña* (do your best) *egape* (escape) *alik* (possible) *itxiki* (to stop):

"Do your best to stop any possible escape."

legislature: .le-egi-isla-atu-ure, *ele egin* (to talk about) *eginahalez* (conscientiously) *isladatu* (to reflect upon) *atutxa* (better world) *urreraketa* (drawing closer): "To conscientiously talk about and reflect upon drawing a better world closer."

lemon: .le-emo-on., *ale* (fruit) *emonkor* (prolific) *onuragarri* (beneficial): "Prolific and beneficial fruit."

lesbian: .le-esbi-an., *ileta jo* (to complain) *ezbide* (unreasonableness) *anatomia* (anatomy, biology): "(He is) complaining about the unreasonableness of (her) biology."

libido: .li-ibi-ido, *ilintitu* (to stir up) *ibili* (to act, to behave) *idolatratu* (to idolize): "All stirred up he behaved like he was idolizing."

library: .li-ib.-.ra-ari, eli-ibi-ira-ari, *elizdiru* (religious duty) *ibili* (to acquire) *irakaskuntza* (education) *arrigarri* (marvellous, admirable): "It is your religious duty to acquire a marvelous education."

lion: .li-on., ali-one, *alienatu* (to destroy a person) *onean* (instantly): "Kills a person instantly."

litter: .li-it.-.te-er., ali-ito-ote-era, *alienazio* (to destroy a person's moral) *itoi* (pigsty) *ote* (perhaps) *errazkeria* (negligence): "A pigsty destroys the moral; perhaps (it is) negligence."

liturgy: .li-itu-ur.-.gi, eli-itu-ure-egi, *eliza* (church) *iturri* (origin) *urreraketa* (to approach) *egia* (truth): "The church's original approach to truth."

lord: .lo-ord., alo-ordu, *alogeratu* (to engage, contact) *ordudun* (when needed): "To contact when in need."

love: .lo-obe, elo-obe, *elorritsu* (bed of thorns) *obe* (better than): "(Love is) better than a bed of thorns."

magic: .ma-agi-ik., ama-agi-ika, *ama* (Priestess) *agindu* (to command) *ikarakortu* (to be afraid of): "Be afraid of the Priestess' command."

malignant: .ma-ali-ig.-.na-an.-.t., ema-ali-iga-ana-ano-ote, *emanaldi* (performance) *alienazio* (destruction of a person) *igartu* (withering) *anatomia* (anatomy) *anormal* (abnormal) *ote* (perhaps): "The destruction of a person's performance by withering of the anatomy is perhaps abnormal."

manufacture: .ma-anu-ufa-ak.-.tu-ure, *eman* (to produce) *anu* (fainting) *ufaztu* (to stink) *akabu* (dead) *atun* (tuna fish) *uregosi* (boiling water): "Dead tuna fish in boiling water produces a fainting stink."

manure: .ma-anu-ure, *emanaldi* (emission) *anu* (fainting) *urreratu* (to draw near): "The emission causes fainting when you draw near."

marriage: .ma-ar.-.ri-age, *emazte* (wife, woman) *ari* (active, energetic) *iritsi* (to get) *ageriki* (honestly): "To get an energetic woman honestly."

masculine: .ma-as.-.ku-uli-in., ema-asa-aku-uli-ina, *emakume* (woman) *asaldakor* (exciting) *akuilatu* (to stimulate) *uli* (coward) *inarrosi* (shaking): "The exciting woman stimulated the shaking coward."

massacre: .ma-as.-.sa-ak.-.re, ama-asi-isa-aka-are: *amaitu* (to kill) *asiera* (to begin) *isaskada* (death blows) *arerio* (enemy): "The killing began with death blows by the enemy."

master: .ma-aste-er., *emanaldi* (performance) *astegun* (working day) *erabaki* (to decide): "He decides the performance during the working day."

mathematics: .ma-ate-ema-ati-ik.-.s., ema-ate-ema-ati-ika-ase, *eskola eman* (to teach) *atergabe* (constant) *eman* (to produce) *atiki* (to memorize) *ikaskai* (lesson) *asezintasun* (craving, desire): "Constant teaching produces a desire to memorize the lessons."

mature: .ma-atu-ure, *emantsu* (generous) *atutxa* (evergreen oak forest) *urentasun* (nobleness): "Generous like the nobleness of the evergreen oak forest."

meaning: me-ani-ing., *mende egon* (to depend on) *anik* (often) *inguruka* (round-about description): "It often depends on a roundabout description."

meeting: .me-eti-ing., *emeriko* (peacefully) *etiketa* (formality) *ingurukatu* (to gather in a circle): "The formality of peacefully gathering in a circle."

menstruation: .me-en.-.st.-.ru-ati-on., eme-ene-ezta-aru-ati-ona, *eme* (female) *enea* (privacy) *ezta* (no way) *arrunt* (vulgar) *atxiki* (to catch, to collect) *onartuezin* (unacceptable): "It's female privacy, no way, it's vulgar; to collect it is unacceptable." (This refers to the use of menstrual blood in the religious ceremonies of the Asherah religion and some Gnostic groups).

mercenary: .me-er.-.se-ena-ari; ame-era-ase-ena-ari, *ameriketakegin* (to make a fortune) *erakarri* (cause) *aserre egin* (to fight) *-ena* (superlative) *arriskutsu* (dangerous): "He makes a fortune fighting for a most dangerous cause."

militant: .mi-ili-ita-ant., *imitatu* (to repeat) *ilindi* (fiery, militant) *itaunka* (interrogating) *antolatzaile* (organizer): "Repeat the interrogation of the fiery organizer."

minstrel: min-.stra-al., (originally minstral), *minbera* (sentimental) *astrapalatsu* (loud) *alegia* (fable, ballad): "Sentimental loud ballad."

mission: .mi-isi-on.; (originally written with one "s"), *umiltasun* (humbleness) *isilka* (quietly) *onegite* (doing good): "Doing good in humbleness."

moisture: .mo-oi-istu-ure; *umotasun* (sensible) *oian* (wood) *iztupaltu* (to caulk) *uretaratu* (to launch): "It is sensible to caulk the wood before launching (the boat)."

moment: .mo-ome-ent, *umore* (humorist) *omendun* (famous) *entzunarazi* (to pay attention): "The famous humorist (made them) pay attention."

monastery: .mo-ona-aste-eri, *amodiotsu* (loving) *onarketa* (welcome) *azaleratu* (to show) *aterpe* (shelter) *erikor* (ailing): "A loving welcome is shown and shelter for the ailing."

money: .mo-oni, emo-oni, *emoi* (present) *on izan* (useful): "Useful present."

monk: mo-onk., *moralezko* (moral) *onkide* (companion doing good works): "Moral companion doing good works."

monstrocity: .mo-on.-.st.-.ro-osi-iti, umo-ona-asta-aro-osi-iti: *umoretxar* (bad tempered) *onartezin* (unacceptable) *astakaiku* (brutish) *arrotz* (stranger) *osin* (abyss) *itxi* (to abandon): "The bad-tempered and unacceptably brutish stranger was abandoned in the abyss."

moody: .mu-udi, *amure egon* (to be distrustful) *udikan/utikan* (go away): "Go away! I don't trust you."

motive: .mo-oti-ibe, *umore* (humor) *otoi* (request, please) *ibeni* (to introduce): "Please introduce (some) humor."

mutilate: .mu-uti-ila-ate, *amure egon* (the be distrustful) *utikan* (get out) *ilarazi* (to murder) *atera* (to get): "Don't trust; Get out! You will get murdered."

narrative: .na-arra-ati-ibe, *inausi* (to trim, to abridge) *arranguraz* (carefully) *atikitzaile* (faithful) *ibeni* (to place, put in order): "To carefully abridge and faithfully put in order."

nation: .na-ati-on., *anaia* (brothers) *atxiki* (be loyal to) *onibar* (land): "Brothers be loyal to the land."

nature: .na-atu-ure, ena-atu-ure, *-ena* (superlative) *atutxa* (better world) *urreraketa* (to draw closer): "A much better world is drawing closer."

naughty: na-auk.-.ti, *nagusitu* (to walk over) *aukerako* (proper) *etika* (ethics): "To walk over proper ethics."

navy: .na-abi, .na-abi, *onartu* (to authorize) *abialdi* (departure): "Departure is authorized."

necessary: .ne-ese-es.-.sa-ari, onezkero (right now) *esetsi* (to attack) *esiketa* (blockade) *izapide* (according to plan) *arritu* (to surprise): "Attack the blockade right now according to plan to surprise them."

net .ne-et., ene-eta, *enetan* (always) *-eta* (bountiful): "Always bountiful."

noble: no-ob.-.le; *norbere* (my own) *obetu* (to prefer, to favour) *ele* (story): "My own favourite story."

O

obdurate: ob.-.du-ura-ate, obe-edu-ura-ate, *oben egin* (to sin) *eduki* (to have) *urratu* (to break a law) *atergabeki* (continually): "He has sinned by breaking the law continuously."

obsession: ob.-.se-esi-on., obe-ese-esi-oni, *obe* (preferable) *esetsi* (to attack) *esitzaile* (besieger) *onikatera* (to escape unharmed): "It is preferable to attack the besieger and escape unharmed."

obstinate: ob.-.sti.-ina-ate, oba-azti-ina-ate, *oba* (better) *aztiatu* (to foresee) *inarrosketa* (agitation) *aterapen* (consequence): "It is better to foresee the consequences of the agitation."

octave: ok.-.ta-abe, ok'ata-abe, *-ok* (suffix used to express the idea of being part of a group) *atalbanatu* (to divide into parts) *abestu* (to sing): "A group divided into parts for singing."

offense: ofi-in.-.se, ofi-ina-ase, (originally "ofinse"), *ofiziale* (official) *inarrosi* (to agitate) *aserretsu* (furious): "Agitated and furious official."

offer, of.-.fe-er., ofi-ibe-era, *ofiziale* (craftsman) *ibenikunde* (introduction) *erakarle* (attractive): "The craftsman's attractive introduction."

ombudsman, om-bods-man (irregular), *omen* (honor) *abots* (voice) *manatu* (to decide): "The voice of honor decides."

onanism: ona-ani-is.-.m., ona-ani-isu-umo, *onargaitz* (unescapable) *anik* (often) *isuri* (to spill, to waste) *umontzi* (womb): "It is often unacceptable to spill (inside) the womb."

opera: ope-era, *opetsi* (to offer) *erakartasun* (attraction): "To offer an attraction."

oracle: ora-ak.-.le, ora-ake-ele, *oraindanik* (from now on, future) *akela* (priestess) *ele* (story): "The priestess' story about the future."

orchestra: or.-.ke-est.-.ra, ori-ike-este-era, *orrits* (feast) *ikertu* (to visit) *estekada* (fullness, glut) *errainutsu* (radiant): "Visit the feast of radiant fullness."

orgasm: or.-.ga-as.-.m., ora-aga-ase-ema, *oratu* (to grab) *aga* (long pole) *asegaitz* (craving) *emazte* (wife): "He grabbed his pole, craving for his wife."

orgy: or.-.gi, oro-ogi, *orrokatu* (to scream) *ogipeko* (maid): "The maids are screaming."

original: ori-igi-ina-al., *origorri* (golden yellow) *igita* (harvest) *inarroskatu* (to winnow) *aletu* (to thresh): "The golden-yellow harvest is threshed and winnowed."

ornament: or.-.na-ame-ent, ori-ina-ame-ent, *orri* (paper) *inauguratu* (to unwrap) *ameki* (carefully) *entzunahi* (curiosity): "Carefully unwrap the paper from the curiosity."

ovation: oba-ati-on., *oba* (better) *atiki* (to be loyal to) *oneskarri* (worthy of respect): "It is better to be loyal and worthy of respect."

P

pagan: .pa-aga-an., *opari* (sacrifice) *-aga* (with abundance of) *anaigo* (group of worshippers): "Group of worshippers with an abundance of sacrifice."

pain: .pa-in, *opaisan* (pray for) *indar* (strength): "Pray for strength."

park: .pa – ark., apa-arko, *apatx egin – arkonada*, to sit down – pasture: "Sit down in the pasture."

Parliament: .pa-ar.-.li-iha-ame-ent, apa-ari-ili-iha-ame-ent, *aparteko* (special) *-ari* (cause) *ilinti* (fiery) *ihardukitze* (arguing, oratory) *ameslari* (idealistic) *entzungarri* (worthy of being heard): "Fiery and idealistic oratory for a special cause is worthy of being heard."

parson: .pa-ar.-.so-on., apa-are-eso-ongi, *apaitz* (priest) *arrenseskatu* (to ask earnestly) *esonde* (advice) *ongietorri* (welcome): "Ask the priest earnestly (for his) welcome advice."

passion: .pa-asi-on, *opa* (desire) *asierako* (initial) *ondonahi* (to make love): "Initial desire to make love."

pastor: .pa-as.-.to-or., opa-ase-eto-oro, *opa izan* (to desire for) *asegaitz* (craving) *etortze* (act of coming) *oroegile* (Creator): "He has a desire and a craving for the coming of the Creator."

patrimony: .pa-at.-.re-emo-oni, opa-ata-are-emo-oni, (note the vowel switch, i to e), *oparo* (rich) *aita* (father) *arrera* (welcomes) *emon* (to give) *oniritzi* (consent): "The rich father welcomes the giving of consent."

pauper: pau-aupar., *pausagabe* (restless) *aupari* (bold): "Restless and bold person."

peasant: .pe-asa-ant., *epe galdu* (shortage of time) *azaro* (planting season) *antolakizun* (organization): "Shortage of time during the planting season (requires) organization."

penis: .pe-eni-is., *epe luzatu* (to prolong) *eni* (to me, in me) *isuri* (to spill): "Prolong to spill in me."

perverse: .pe-er.-.be-er.-.se, ipe-eri-ibe-era-ase, *iperdi* (buttocks) *errizinolio* (castor oil) *ibeni* (to introduce) *eragin* (to promote) *asezina* (craving): "Introducing castor oil (between) the buttocks to promote a craving."

phallus: .p.-.ha-al.-.lu-us., apo-oha0ala-alu-uste, *apokeria* (filthy deed, rape) *oha* (bed) *alabearreko* (unavoidable) *alu* (repulsive) *ustelkeria* (morally corrupting): "An unavoidable rape in bed is repulsive and morally corrupting."

pig: .pi-ig., *opiltxo* (roll, chubby) *iges egin* (to run away): "Chubby ran away."

pleasure: .p.-.le-asu-ure, apa-ale-asu-ure, *aparte* (special) *alegeratu* (to make happy) *asuri* (newborn lamb) *urreratu* (to come close to): "It makes me especially happy to come close to a newborn lamb."

plunder: .p.-.lu-un.-.de-er.; opa-alu-una-ade-era, *opaezin* (undesirable) *alukeria* (repulsive) *unagarri* (annoying) *adeigabeko* (rude) *eraso* (attack): "Undesirable, repulsive, annoying and rude attack."

politics: .po-ole-eti-ik.-.s., opo-ole-eti-ike-ese, (The original spelling was poletic.), *oposaketa* (opposition) *olesegin* (to call upon) *etikoa* (formal) *ikertzapen* (investigation) *esetsaldi* (attack): "Call upon the opposition for a formal investigation into the attack."

possession: .po-os.-.se-esi-on, opo-ose-ese-esi-ondo, (possesion), *oposaketa* (antagonism) *osezin* (which cannot be completed) *esetsi* (to argue) *esibarruti* (fence) *ondo* (one side): "Antagonism and arguing over a fence which cannot be completed on one side."

prayer: .p.-.rai-er., opa-arai-ere, *opa* (desire) *arraiegun* (abstinence) *errezu* (prayer): "Desire for abstinence and prayer."

precipitate: pre-eki-ipi-ita-ate, *premia* (necessity) *ekin* (to persist) *ipini* (to place, to put) *itaun* (question) *atertu* (to clear the air): "There is a necessity to persist placing questions to clear the air."

president: (anglecized from praecedentium): .p.-.ra-ese-ede-en.-.ti-um., apa-ara-ese-ede-enu-uti-umo, (see Auraicept line 5085, page 259): *aparteko* (special) *arazo* (task) *esetsi* (to attack) *ederrak hartu* (to defeat): *enulkeria* (slothfulness) *utikan* (to drive away) *umoretxar* (moodiness): "It is a special task to attack and defeat slothfulness and drive away moodiness."

priest: .p.-.ri-ist., apa-ari-iztu, *apaiz* (priest) *ariketa* (assignment) *iztun* (talker, communicator): "The priest's assignment is to be a communicator."

proclamation: .p.-.ro-ook.-.la-ama-ati-on.; opo-oro-oki-ila-ama-ati-onu, *opor* (time off) *oroitarazi* (to commemorate) *okitu* (entire) *ilarteko* (lifetime) *ama* (mother) *atxikimendu* (loyalty) *onuts* (wonderful): "Take time off to commemorate mother's entire lifetime of wonderful loyalty."

professional: .p.-.ro-ofi-isi-ona-al., apa-aro-ofi-isi-ona-alo, (note spelling change), *aparte* (especially) *arrotsu* (proud) *ofiziale* (craftsman) *isilmandatu* (secret) *onartu* (acceptable) *alokairu* (salary): "The (trade) secret of an especially proud craftsman (calls for) an acceptable salary."

prolific: .p.-.ro-oli-ife-ek., apu-uro-oli-ife-eku, (vowel switch from "e" to "i"), *apurtu* (to break) *urontzi* (container) *olio* (oil) *ifernu* (damned) *ekurugaitasun* (worry): "The broken oil container is a damned worry."

prophesy: .p.-.ro-op.-.he-esi, apo-oro-opi-ihe-ezi, *apokeria* (insult) *oroegile* (Creator) *opio* (opium) *iheska* (escaping) *ezinbeste* (fate): "It insults the Creator (to use) opium to escape from your fate."

protocol: .p.-.ro-oto-oko-ol., opa-aro-oto-oko-olo, *oparitu* (to give) *arrotzari* (innkeeper) *otoi* (request) *okolu* (stable) *oloztatu* (to feed oats): "Give the inkeeper the request to feed (the horse) oats in the stable."

province: .p.-.ro-obe-en.-.ke, apa-aro-obe-eni-ike, (from French: provence), *aparteko* (special) *arroztiar* (hospitable) *obegipeko* (favourite) *eni* (to me) *ikertu* (to visit): "This especially hospitable place is a favourite for me to visit."

prurient: .p.-.ru-uri-ent, epa-aru-uri-ent, *epaipetu* (to judge) *arrunt* (vulgar) *urrikalgarri* (to be pitied) *entzuera* (reputation): "Judged to be vulgar and of pitiable reputation."

pudendum: .pu-ude-endu-um., *ipurterre* (impatient) *udetxe* (summer cottage) *endurtu* (to damage, to rupture) *umontzi* (hymen): "Impatient in the summer cottage to rupture the hymen."

pure: .pu-ure, *ipu* (moral) *urentasun* (nobleness): "Moral nobleness."

puzzle: .pu-uz.-.le, apu-usa-ale, *apur* (a bit) *usainhartu* (to guess right) *alegera* (to be happy): "A bit of guessing-right makes me happy."

pyramid: .pi-ira-ami-id.; *epika* (epic) *iragartzapen* (to prophesy) *amildu* destruction) *ideiadura* (ideology): "The epic prophesied the destruction of our ideology."

R

realize: .re-ali-ize, *urreratu* (to come close to) *alik* (possible) *izenpetu* (to sign): "We come close to the possible signing (of the agreement)."

rebuttal: .re-ebu-ut.-.ta-al., ere-ebu-utzi-ita-ala, *erreakzio* (reaction) *(e)buruharro* (conceited) *utziketa* (omission) *itaundu* (to ask) *alatu* (to cause pain): "His conceited reaction was to question the omission just to cause pain."

recognition: .re-eko-og.-.ni-iti-on., are-eko-ogu-uni-ixi-one, *arrera* (reception) *ekonomo* (administrator) *oguzi* (to speak out loud) *unibertsal* (everyone) *ixilik* (be quiet) *on esan* (to praise someone): "At the reception the administrator loudly asked everyone to be quiet so he could give praise."

regular: .re-egu-ule er., (was reguler), *arrezkero* (from then on) *egunero* (every day) *ulerbide* (example) *erreztu* (to make easy): "Every day from then on give an easy example."

relation: .re-ela-ati-on, *errez* (simple) *ela* (word) *atxiki* (to be loyal to) *ondoretasun* (lineage, family): "Simple word to be loyal to the family."

reliable: .re-eli-i.a-ab.-.le, ere-eli-iha-aba-ale, *erregutzaile* (prayer) *elizkoitu* (to be pious) *iharrosi* (to move, to change) *abaildura* (weariness) *alegera* (rejoicing): "Pious prayer changes weariness into rejoicing."

religion: .re-eli-igi-on, *erein* (to sow) *eliza* (church) *igita* (to harvest) *ongietorri* (welcome): "Sowing the church's welcome harvest."

renovate: .re-eno-oba-ate, *erremindu* (to burn out) *enora* (wart) *oba* (better) *aterapen* (results): "Burning-out warts gives better results."

response: .re-espo-on.-.se; *errepika* (tolling of the bells) *esposaberri* (newlywed) *onarpen* (reception) *asetze* (satiating, memorable): "The tolling bells (will announce) a memorable reception for the newlyweds." (In Basque the tolling of the bells more completely is: *kanpaien* (bells) *errepika* (repetitive) *zaratatsua* (boisterous).

resurrection: .re-esu-urre-ek.-.ti-on., are-ezu-ure-eka-ati-one, *arrentza* (prayer) *ezurruts* (body, skeleton) *urreratu* (to approach) *ekarrarazi* (to cause to bring) *atiki* (faithful) *onespen* (blessings): "Approach the body with a prayer and bring faithful blessings."

revelation: .re-ebe-ela-ati-on.; *arrerosle* (Redeemer) *ebertar* (Hebrew) *ela* (story) *atxikimendu* (faithfulness) *oneste* (blessing): "The Hebrew Redeemer's (Jesus') story of faithfulness and blessing."

revolve: .re-ebo-ol.-.be, ere-ebo-olo-obe, *erreminta* (tool) *eboluzionatu* (to develop) *olo* (oats) *obetu* (to improve): "Develop a tool to improve the oats. (i.e. a rolled-oats mill)."

right: .ri-ig.-.t., eri-iga-ata, *eri* (finger) *sign* (igargarri) *atalgabeko* (simple): "Simple sign with the finger."

ritual: .ri-itxu-al., ori-itxu-ala, *orrits* (feast) *itxura* (appearance) *alatzritsu* (miraculous): "Feast of the miraculous appearance."

root: .ru-ut, aru-ut, *arrunki* (simple) *utzarazi* (to stay behind): "(The root) simply stays behind."

royal: .ro-oia-al, *aroitarazi* (to commemorate) *oian* (forest) *altxamendu* (insurrection): "Commemorate the forest insurrection." (This may be related to Robin Hood's activities in the Sherwood forest.)

rude: .ru-ude, *arrunt* (coarse, vulgar) *urde* (male pig): "Vulgar male pig."

ruminate: .ru-umi-ina-ate, iru-umi-ina-ate, *irusta* (clover) *umilki* (humbly) *inara* (to swallow, to chew) *ate* (outside): "Humbly chewing the clover outside."

S

sanctuary: .sa-an.-.k.-.tu-ari, asa-ani-ike-etsitu-ari (irregular), *asagotu* (to go far away) *anitz* (many) *ikertu* (to visit) *etsitu* (to despair) *arinari eman* (to escape): "Many come from far away to stay here, desperate to escape."

scandal: .s.-.ka-an.-.da-al., usu-uka-ana-ada-alu, *usu* (frequent) *ukan* (to have) *anaitasun* (brotherhood) *adarra sartu* (to deceive) *alukeria* (repulsive action): "He has frequently deceived the brotherhood with his repulsive actions."

semen: .se-eme-en., *asetu* (to fill) *emeriko* (smoothly) *eni* (me): "Fill me smoothly."

senate: .se-ena-ate, *esetsi* (to argue) *-ena* (verbal suffix expressing future) *atergabeki* (incessantly): "(They) will argue incessantly."

sensual: .se-en.-.su-al., ase-eni-isu-alu, *asegaitz* (craving) *eni* (to me, in me) *isuri* (to spill) *alu* (vulva): "(I have a) craving in me to spill in a vulva."

service: .se-er.-.bi-ike; ese-era-abi-ike, *esetsi* (to attack) *eragozkarri* (problem) *abiatu* (to begin) *ikertu* (to investigate): "Attack the problem by beginning the investigation."

severe: .se-ebe-ere, *aserre* (angry) *ebertar* (Hebrew, Jew) *erreakzio* (reaction): "Angry reaction from the Jew."

sex: (seks), .se-ek.-.s., ase-eko-oso, *asezin* (craving) *ekoizpen* (fruitfulness) *oso* (simple): "A craving for simple fruitfulness."

shame: xa-ame, *xahutu* (to destroy) *amestoki* (wonderful place): It's a shame "to destroy a wonderful place."

shark: .xa-ark., *uxaketa* (shooing away) *arkitu* (to encounter): "Shooing away the encounter."

shelf: xe-el.-.f., xe-ela-afa, *xedatu* (to select) *ela* (story) *afa* (happy): "Select a happy story."

silk: .si-il.-.k., esi-ile-eko *esibarruti* (cocoon) *ilebigun* (silky) *ekoiztu* (to produce): "It produces a silky cocoon."

sinecure: .si-ine-eku-ure; (provides revenue without having to work for it); *isil* (reserved) *inertzia* (passiveness) *ekurutasun* (peace of mind) *urentasun* (nobility): "Reserved passiveness gives peace of mind to the nobility."

skeptic: .s.-.ke-ep.-.ti-ik., asi-ike-epa-ati-ika, *asi* (to begin) *ikertu* (to scrutinize) *epaipetu* (to pass judgement) *atxiki* (to accept) *ikaserazi* (to teach): "Begin with scrutinizing, then pass judgement before you accept and teach."

soak: .so-ak., is-aka, *isolamendu* (isolation) *akatsbako* (perfect): "Perfect isolation."

society: .so-oki-eti, *oso* (sincere) *okitu* (complete) *etikoa* (ethical): "Completely sincere and ethical."

sofa: .so-ofa, *osoro* (completely) *oba* (comfortable, natural): "Completely comfortable."

solution: (pronounced soljution) .so-ola-aju-uti-on., *isolamendu* (isolation) *ola* (cabin) *ajuria* (heatherfield) *utikan* (get away) *onespen* (blessing): "Getting away to the isolation of a cabin in the heather field is a blessing."

son: .so-on., eso-one, *esonde* (advice) *onezko* (beneficial): "Beneficial advice."

sorrow: so-oro, *so'il* (alone) *oro* (all): "All alone."

specialization: .s.-.pe-esi-iha-ali-iza-ati-on., ase-epe-esi-iha-ali-iza-ati-one, *aserrarazi* (to fight) *epemuga* (decisive) *esiketa* (blockade) *ihardun* (to keep busy) *alienazio* (to destroy the moral) *izapide* (tactics) *atiki* (to adhere to) *onen* (very best): "To fight a decisive blockade we must keep busy destroying their moral and adhere to the very best tactics."

spin: .spi-in., *azpitabestu* (to entwine) *ingiratu* (to prepare for): "To entwine in preparation for."

steam: .ste-am., *ustekabe* (accident) *ama* (mother's): "Mother's accident."

sterile: .s.-.te-eri-ile, osa-ate-eri-ile, *osagaitz* (incurable) *ateka* (situation) *erion* (flowing from, resulting from) *ilegabezia* (baldness): "Incurable situation resulting from baldness."

stop: .s.-.to-op., esa-ato-opo, *esau* (saying) *atondu* (to be prepared) *oposatu* (opposition): "It says to be prepared for opposition." Incidentally: **halt**: .ha-al.-.t., (German equivalent of "stop"), oha-ala-ate: *ohar* (warning) *alabeharreko* (unavoidable) *aterakeria* (abrupt command): "Warning! Unavoidable abrupt command!"

stork: .s.-.to-or.-.k., se-eto-ori-ike, *sein* (baby) *etorki* (family) *ori* (that) *ikertu* (to visit): "A baby will visit that family."

storm: .sto-orm., ozto-orma, *oztopo* (impediment, problem) *ormazulo* (hole in the wall): "The hole in the wall is a problem."

strength:.ster-eng-tz, *izterbegi* (enemy) *engainakor* (false) *aitzakitu* (promises): "The enemy's false promises."

sublime: .su-ub.-.li-ime, isu-ubi-ili-ime, *isuri* (to flow, to spill) *ubide* (waterpipe, canal) *ilintitu* (to revive, to restore) *imilaun* (measure, volume): "The flow (through) the waterpipe is restored in volume."

suffer: .su-ufa-ar, (vowel change from a to e): *isurbera* (running) *ufaldi* (panting) *arramaka* (crying): "Running, panting and crying."

sugar: .su-uga-ar., *isuri* (flowing) *ugari* (abundant) *aratz* (pure): "Flowing abundant and pure." (This sounds like maple syrup: *zugar* = elm, rowan).

summons: .su-um-.-mo-on.-.s., isu-ume-emo-one-esa, *isurbera* (running) *ume* (child) *emon* (to give an order) *oneratu* (to come here) *esana egin* (to obey): "Give the running child the order to come here and obey."

supervision: .su-upa-ar.-.bi-isi-on, isu-upa-ara-abi-isi-ondu, (note vowel change), *isurgai* (liquid) *upara* (store in vats) *arrataz* (carefully) *abiatu* (beginning) *isil* (slow) *ondu* (maturing): "Carefully storing the liquid in vats is only the beginning of the slow maturing process."

swelling: .se-el.-.li-ing., ise-ela-ali-ingu, *iseka egin* (to make fun of) *elastiko* (swelling, bump) *alizan* (noticeable) *ingurualdi* (round): "Making fun of a noticeable round bump."

symphony: .si-im.-.p.-.ho-oni, isi-ima-apa-aho-oni, *isiltarte* (a moment of silence) *imajina* (idol, celebrity) *apal* (humble) *ahozuriketa* (adulation, ovation) *oniritzi* (acceptance, approval): "(After) a moment of silence the humble celebrity accepted the ovation."

system: .si-iste-em., *esinguratu* (to surround) *izterbegi* (enemy) *eman* (to beat): "Surround the enemy to beat him."

T

talkative: .ta-al.-eka-ati-ib., ata-ale-eka-ati-ibi, *atalgabeko* (simple) *alegera* (joy) *ekarri* (to bring) *atiki* (to catch) *ibilkera* (the spirit): "Simple joy is brought by catching the spirit."

taxation: (taksation) .ta-ak.-.sa-ati-on, ita-aka-aza-ati-onda, *itaundu* (to demand) *akabu* (ultimate) *azartu* (to dare) *atxiki* (to seize) *ondasun* (assets): "Demand the ultimate and dare to seize the assets."

testament: .te-esta-ame-ent; *etekin* (profitable) *eztabaida* (discussion) *ames* (hopeful anticipation) *entzunmin* (anxious to hear): "Anxious to hear the profitable discussion with hopeful anticipation."

testicle: .te-esti-ik.-.le, ate-esti-iko-ole, *aterpetu* (to protect) *estimagarri* (valuable) *iko* (lump, ball) *oles egin* (to call upon, for future use): "Protect the balls for future use."

theatre: .te-at.-.re, ote-ato-ore, *ote* (perhaps) *ator* (to come) *orekari* (tightrope walker): "Perhaps come to (see) the tightrope walker."

tide: ti-ide, *tinkatze* (to push in) *idekotsu* (same, as ever): "It pushes in as ever."

totem: .to-otu-ume (from totum), *etorki* (lineage, clan) *otu* (to come to mind) ume (child): "The lineage of the children comes to mind."

tree: .t.-.ri, eto-ori, *ongi-etorri* (welcome) *orritsa* (foliage): "Welcome foliage."

tribe: .t.-.ri-ibe, ata-ari-ibe, *atalbako* (entire) *ariasendi* (family group) *ibeni* (to introduce): "I introduce the entire family group."

tribute: t.-.ri-ib.-.ju-ute, ta-ari-ibi-uju-ut, *taldeburu* (group leader) *arrigarrizko* (amazing) *ibitu* (to ford a river) *uju* (shout of joy) *utsitu* (to let out, bring out): "The group-leader's amazing crossing of the river brought out shouts of joy."

trust: .t.-.ru-ust.; ita-aru-ust, *itaundu* (to ask) *arrunt* (simple) *uste ukan* (to have faith): "Ask simply to have faith."

u

ubiquitous, ubi-iku-ito-us. (meaning periodic, recurring): *ubil* (whirlpool) *ikustatu* (act of watching) *itoarazi* (to drown) *usa* (dove/holy man): "Watching the drowning of the holy man in the whirlpool."

ugly: ug.-.li, uge-eli, *ugerdo* (dirty) *elikatura* (food): "Dirty food."

ukulele: uku-ule-ele, *ukurtu* (to go bad) *ulerbide* (example) *eleiza* (church): "A bad example in the church."

ulcer: ul.-.ke-er., uli-ike-eri, *uli* (coward) *ikertu* (to examine) *eri* (illness): "Examine the coward's illness."

ulterior: ul.-.te-eri-or., ule-ete-eri-oro, *ulertu* (to understand) *etekin* (benefit) *eri* (illness) *orobateko* (similar): "Understanding it would benefit other illnesses."

umbrage: um.-.b.-.ra-age, ume-eba-ara-age, *ume* (young) *ebasle* (thief) *arauhausle* (violator) *ager* (notorious): "The young thief is a notorious violator."

unabashed: una-aba-ase-ed., *unadura* (boredom) *abade* (priest) *asegaitz* (craving) *edan* (to drink): "When bored the priest had a craving to drink."

unabated: una-aba-ate-ed., *unadura* (boredom) *abade* (priest) *atera* (to get) *edanda* (drunk): "The bored priest got drunk."

unable: una-ab.-.le, una-aba-ale, *unatu* (to get tired) *abantari* (rower) *alegiña* (to make an effort): "The tired rower made an effort."

unacceptable: una-ak.-.se-ep.-.ta-ab.-.le, una-ake-ese-epa-ata-aba-ale, *unagarri* (annoying) *akela* (witch) *esetsaldi* (attack) *epaile* (judge) *atadi* (main entrance) *abadune* (opportunity) *alegin* (to attempt): "The annoying witch had the opportunity to attempt an attack on the judge by the main entrance."

unaccompanied: una-ak.-.ko-om.-.pa-ani-ed., una-aka-ako-ome-epa-ani-eda, *unagarri* (annoying) *akabu* (death) *akordiotu* (to cause) *omenka* (according to) *epaile* (judge) *anik* (many) *edabe* (drinks): "The annoying death was caused, according to the judge, by many drinks."

unaccountable: una-ak.-.ko-un.-.ta-ab.-.le, una-aka-ako-uni-ita-abu-ule, *unagarri* (annoying) *akabu* (death) *akordiotu* (to cause) *unibersal* (general) *itaunketa* (interrogation) *aburu* (opinion) *ulertu* (to ponder): "The pondered opinion was that the annoying death was caused during the general interrogation."

unaccustomed: una-ak.-.ku-us.-.to-ome-ed., una-aka-aku-usa-ato-ome-eda, *unagarri* (annoying) *akabu* (death) *akuilatu* (to motivate) *usadio* (custom, habit) *atondu* (to arrange) *omendatu* (to pay tribute) *edan* (drink): "The annoying death was motivated by the habit to arrange the paying of tribute with drinks."

unacknowledged: una-ak.-.k.-.no-ole-ed.-.ge-ed., una-aka-aki-ino-ole-edi-ige-ede, *unagarri* (annoying) akabu (death) *akiakula* (excuse) *inolaz* (somehow) *oles egin* (to call upon) *ediren* (evidence) *iges egin* (to evade) *ederra sartu* (to mislead): "The annoying death was somehow excused by calling upon evasive and misleading evidence."

unacquainted: una-aku-ai-in.-.te-ed., una-aku-ai-ina-ate-edi, *unatu* (to get tired) *akuilatu* (to urge) *aipatu* (to refer to) *inauguratu* (to open) *aterpe* (shelter) *ediren* (to find): "I am tired and urge you to refer me to find an open shelter."

unadorned: una-ado-or.-.ne-ed., una-ado-oro-one-eda, *unagarri* (annoying) *adoratu* (to worship) *oroegile* (Creator) *oneratu* (to come here) *edanda* (drunk): "It is annoying to worship the Creator when coming here drunk."

unalterable: una-al.-.te-era-ab.-.le, una-ala-ate-era-abo-ole, *unagarri* (annoying) *alabehar* (fate) *ateratu* (to leave) *eraile* (murderer) *aboskatu* (to proclaim) *oleazio* (last rites): "It is annoying to have to leave the murderer to his fate while proclaiming the last rites."

unarmed: una-ar.-.me-ed., una-are-eme-eda, *unatu* (to get tired) *arrera egin* (to receive) *emeriko* (peacefully) *edan* (drink): "Tired, he was received peacefully for a drink."

urge: ur.-.ge, ura-age, *urrago* (closer) *agerbide* (signal, sign): "Signal (to come) closer."

usury: usu – uri, *usu* (habitually) *urrindu* (to give off an offensive smell): "He usually gives off an offensive smell."

uterus: ute-eru-us., *uts-egin* (to be absent, to miss) *errutar* (season, period) *usu* (often): "(She) often misses her period."

V

vacation: .ba-aka-ati-on, *ebaskindegi* (hide-out) *akabu* (special) *atxikidura* (family ties) *onegin* (to benefit): "Special hide-out to benefit family ties."

vagina: .ba-agi-ina, *abadune* (opportunity) *agian* (I hope) *inauguratu* (to open): "I hope to open an opportunity."

validate: .ba-al-ida-ate, *ebaluatu* (to appreciate) *al izan* (capable) *idazkari* (secretary) *aterpe* (protection): "Have it appraised by a capable secretary for your protection."

venereal: .be-ene-ere-al., *abegi egin* (to welcome) *eneño* (my dear) *eregu* indulging) *alu* (vulva): "My dear is welcome to indulge in my vulva."

vicar: .bi-ika-ar., *abiatu* (to begin) *ikaserazi* (to teach) *araubide* (discipline): "He begins with teaching discipline."

violate: .bi-i.o-ola-ate, abi-iho-ola-ate, *abiratu* (to run towards) *ihortziri* (thunder) *olano* (small hut) *aterpe* (shelter): "The thunder (made us) run towards a small hut for shelter."

visit: .bi-isi-it, *ibili* (to behave) *isil* (quietly) *itzalgarri* (respectful): "Behave quietly and respectful."

voluptious: bolu-uptxo-us., (irregular construction), *boludun* (miller) *upeltxo* (barrel) *usantza* (habit, shape): "The miller's barrel shape."

W

walk: al.-.k., ali-ike, *al izan* (capable) *ikertu* (to visit): "(He is) capable to visit."

wash: ash, ax, *axola* (caring): "Caring."

water: ater, *atera* (to go out, to go get): "Go and get it"

window: in.-.do, ina-ado, (the "w's" are meaningless), *inauguratu* (to open up) *adoretu* (to encourage, please): "Please open up."

witch: itch, *itxuraldatu* (to change shape): "(She) changes shape."

witty: used to be wittoy: it.-.toi, ito-otoi, *ito* (to laugh a lot) *otoiztegi* (oratory, speech): "The speech made me laugh a lot."

word: ord, *ordainbide* (promise): "Promise."

worship: or.-.shi-ip.; ori-ixi-ipu, *orrits* (feast) *ixil* (quiet) *ipurgarbiketa* (adulation): "Feast of quiet adulation."

Y

yacht: .ia-ak.-.t., eia-aka-ate, *eia* (let's go, come on!) *akabu* (perfect) *aterrune* (the weather is clearing): "Let's go, it's perfect, the weather is clearing."

year: .ie-ar., aie-ari, *aienatu* (to slip away) *ariñeketan* (very fast): "Slips away very fast."

yearn: .ie-ar.-.n., aie-aru-une, *aienatu* (to disappear) *aruntz-onuntz ibili* (to wander, to rove) *unetxo* (short distance): "(He/she) disappeared after wandering a short distance."

yeast: .ie-ast., aie-asti, *aier izan* (to have a tendency to) *astintasun* (fluffiness): "It has a tendency to fluffiness."

yeoman:.ie-e.o-oma-an., aie-eho-oma-ani, *aiene egin* (to grieve) *ehortze* (funeral) *oma* (grandmother) *ani* (many): "Many grieved at grandmother's funeral."

yellow: .ie-el.-.lo, aie-ela-alo, *aierutsu* (suspicious) *ela* (story, tale) *alogereko* (mercenary): "Suspicious mercenary tale."

yes: .ie-es., aie-eze, *aiertu* (to tend to) *ezergabe* (the needy): "Tend to the needy."

yesterday: .ie-este-er.-.da-a.i, aie-este-ere-eda-ahi, *aieneka* (grieving) *estemin* (intestinal pain) *eregu* (indulging) *edate* (drinking) *ahituezin* (endless): "Grieving from intestinal pain after indulging in endless drinking."

yonder: .jo-ondar (note the vowel shift), *ajola izan* (to take care) *ondarreratu* (to go to the beach): "Take care when you go to the beach."

youth: .jo-ut.-.h., ajo-uti-iha, *ajola izan* (to take care) *utikan* (to go away) *ihaute* (carnival): "Take care when you go to the carnival."

Z

zealot: .ze-alo-ot., eze-alo-oto, *ezetza eman* (give a negative response, say no) *alogereko* (mercenary) *otoizbera* (devout): "Say no to the devout mercenary."

zebra: ze-eb.-.ra, ze-ebo-ora, *zerrendak* (stripes) *eboluzionatu* (to evolve) *orratio* (being surprised): *It's surprising that it evolved stripes.*

zenith: .ze-eni-it.-.h., eze-eni-iti-ihe, *ezelan* (somehow) *eni* (to me) *itxi* (to be thrown) *ihesindar* (centrifical force): "Somehow it looks to me as if (the stars) were thrown by centrifugal force."

zero: .ze-ero, eze-ero, *ezerez* (nothing at all) *erori* (to fall to, to drop to): "Dropped to nothing at all."

zest: .ze-est., oze-esti, *ozendu* (to make one's voice resound) *estima* (appreciation): "To make one's voice resound with appreciation."

zinc: .zi-in.-.k., azi-inu-uki, *azido* (acid) *inurritu* (to feel prickly) *ukitu* (to touch): "With acid it feels prickly to the touch."

zodiak: .zo-odi-ak., -*azo* (to make) *odi* (tube, round hole) *akabu* (perfect): "Make a perfectly round circle."

zulu: .zu-ulu, izu-ulu,*izuarazi* (to intimidate) *uluka egon* (to howl): "To intimidate they howl."

INDO–EUROPEAN LINGUISTICS, THE INVENTED SCIENCE

THE PHANTOM LANGUAGE

Every schoolchild in England and the U.S.A. has been told the same story. In early times a variety of peoples came to British shores from the continent of Europe. These peoples had names such as Angles, Saxons, Friesians, Vikings, Kelts, Normans, you name them, and they all brought their own peculiar and primitive little languages along with them. These languages then somehow magically blended into the beautiful, rich and practical language we speak today. History, on the other hand, tells us that small groups of people arriving in a new country almost always accept the language of their new environment, usually within two or three generations and surely this happened in Britain. But what happened to the highly developed language which was spoken by the inhabitants of Britain? That this language existed we know from the writings of several early missionaries. They even used it in their Ogam script on stone and in the Auraicept na n'Ecez, the early medieval operations manual of the Benedictine monks. In Scotland the original language was called Pictish, in Ireland Cruithin, and missionaries from elsewhere referred to it as the "Iron Language." Prof. Colin Renfrew writes in "The Human Inheritance":

> "... the Basque language may be regarded as the only early and indigenous language of Europe. It is very possible that the Basque language was spoken in Europe by our early ancestors." (p.27)

That was exactly my conclusion in 1993. Several linguists in this century had decided that the early language of Britain had been non-Indo-European and many of them agreed that all of Europe at one time had been unilingual, i.e. all people everywhere spoke the same language. This begs the question: If everyone spoke the same non-Indo-European language, what happened to change this into a plethora of unstable Indo-European and other languages? Could it be that the Basque language, still spoken in the western Pyrenees, is the last remnant in Europe of this phantom neolithic language? But how did it disappear everywhere else without a trace, where did it originally come from and was that early language very different from modern Basque? Surely there must be a very compelling reason for such an ancient and widespread language to vanish without a trace from such a huge area, to be maintained only in a corner of the remote mountain valleys of the Pyrenees? Or did it really disappear so completely?

One answer is suggested in Genesis 11:7 which tells us: "Come let us go down, and there confuse their language so they may no longer understand one another's speech." Could it be that the switch from the Universal language to the confusion of new and unstable Indo-European and Semitic languages was brought about through religious action? Did the religious leaders take this sentence to be a biblical command, demanding action? Could all the Indo-European languages have been invented by highly skilled religious linguists? It may be hard to believe but that is exactly what happened, as I shall show in this book.

A FAULTY THEORY AND A BAND–WAGON

In 1783 Sir William Jones was dispatched to India as a judge. Being an amateur linguist, he spent his evenings teaching himself Sanskrit, a dead language which was being maintained by priests who memorized its sacred hymns. In 1786 he told a gathering of the Asiatick Society in Calcutta that many of the classical languages, such as Sanskrit, Greek, Latin, Gothic, Celtic and Persian must come from the same source:

> *"a stronger affinity, both in the roots of verbs and in the forms of grammar, than could possibly have been produced by accident; so strong, indeed, that no philologer could examine them all without believing them to have sprung from some common source, which, perhaps, no longer exists."*

The "perfect" phonological relationships between the examples he gave was there for everyone to see and Bingo!, the genetic family of Indo-European languages was born, in time to be joined by a baffling assortment of laws of phonological correspondence and an Ur-mother-language which had supposedly given birth to the whole mess. The academic world built a big bandwagon and all jumped on, linguists, archeologists, anthropologists, geographers, everybody. All are now using the classification "Indo-European" as if it were a reality. All linguists agree that Indo-European is fundamentally a linguistic construct. Not one single gene has ever been found which would tie the I-E speakers together into a genetically related group. All agree that the term has no racial or cultural implications, yet, they all proceed then to talk about the Indo-Europeans, their homeland, their pastoral way of life and their proto language. Over the past two centuries thousands of highly paid linguists around the world have conducted their endless and fruitless research into the perceived genetic relationships. All they ask for now is a few more years of study to solve all the problems still remaining…

While studying the language "family" some of the smarter linguists realized there was something fishy. So they decided that the truth could be established by using classical comparative methodology. To accomplish this they proposed four criteria, supposed to be diagnostic:

1) phonological correspondence,
2) shared vocabularies,
3) common grammatical features,
4) identical constructive particles.

However, the ancient grammarians, active over the last five millennia, were well ahead of them. They had, very early on, recognized that spoken languages do change into dialects and independent languages and thus they had long ago built these same four criteria into the various languages they created, purposely giving it the impression of a genetic relationship. When the 18th and 19th century linguists jumped on the I.-E. band-wagon they had reasoned that if the observed relationship was not accidental, it had to be genetic, thereby totally underestimating the skill and determination of the ancient grammarians. Through the years there have been a few courageous linguists who expressed doubts about the troublesome Indo-European theory. One of them, M.E. Landsberg of Columbia University S.C., wrote:

> "Indeed, courses in historical linguistics at Universities all over the world, in spite of much perplexing evidence to the contrary, mostly still persist in adhering to strict Indo-European theories."

In his chapter in "The Human Inheritance" professor Don Ringe repeatedly expresses amazement at the observed, and illogical, regularity of sound changes. He then lists many such changes and comments:

> "I have taken my examples of regular sound change from an outstandingly uncompromising source, in which substantial irregularity should be evident. In languages which have been less affected by dialectic interactions, the observed regularity is even greater; in some it is almost total." (p.52)

Wouldn't it be reasonable for some little voice to whisper in his ear, "Don, the startling and illogical regularity of sound changes you observe all have the earmark of intelligent design. Could there be something fundamentally wrong with your reasoning? Go back to the very basis of your science and carefully reexamine the foundations of the Indo-European theory."

In spite of all this, no-one thought to ask if there might be another explanation for the unnatural regularity, for instance an **invented relationship**. And to this day this question is not being asked. I am sorry to be a party-pooper and derail the cushioned wagon ride, but **there never were any Indo-Europeans, there was no proto-Indo-European language, or a homeland, or a culture, and the family of Indo-European languages is a long perpetuated academic hoax.**

The Best Kept Secret in Science

English is an invented language. So are German, Latin, Greek, Russian, Sanskrit, Hebrew, Hungarian, Japanese etc. etc. but I am not concerned with these right now. Our English etymological dictionaries do no justice to the tremendous language creation efforts of the only group of west European scholars capable of such activities, the Benedictine monks and their grammarians. Almost every English word existing at the time of Shakespeare, was invented by these marvelous linguists. Most of the words they created have proven remarkably stable. It happened in their scriptoria of Canterbury, Rochester, York etc. that the Benedictines created the practical and expressive language which is ours today. **The Kelts, Vikings, Saxons and whatever ruffians came drifting to the shores of Britain, had nothing to do with the creation of the English language.**

The language used in this enormous effort was Basque, once the universal language of continental Europe and Britain, but now best represented only by the modern Basque language. The grammarians, who were professional linguists, worked for almost one millennium with the Benedictines. These professional linguists came mostly from Liguria, located in Northern Italy and the Alps. Their Ligurian language was, as far as I can determine, identical to the Basque spoken today in Euskadi. The method of new word construction used by them was generally done with the vowel-interlocking formula, which utilized the first three letters (VCV) of each Basque word in the description. The VCV's, which were then agglutinated, always had to have their vowels interlocked. To make the product pronounceable, several vowels were removed and also one or more h's, if present. The word decoding process is best illustrated with a few simple examples. Take the word "begin." For each vowel that had been removed, I place a dot, which needs to be replaced when the vowel is recovered with the use of my VCV dictionary. (Appendix 1)

begin:
.be-egi-in.
ibe – egi – ino
ibeni – egindura – inor
to start – the action – someone
"Someone start the action."

dog:
.do-og.
ado – ogu
adoretsu – oguzi
brave – speaks out loud
"Brave and speaks out loud."

doctor:
.do-ok.-.to-or.
odo – oke – eto – ora
odoldun – okerkeria – etorri – orain
bloody – injury – to come – quickly
"A bloody injury, come quickly."

The hidden sentences for each of these words make good sense. It is clear from these and hundreds of other examples in this book, that the English language is the formulaic product of intelligent design.

NAME INVENTION IS STILL VERY MUCH ALIVE

Most academics accept the Indo-European theory uncritically, teaching it to their students as proven science and using the term in a variety of ways and publications. In the 20th century many names have been attached to individuals in different parts of the world which clearly indicate that the secret of the vowel-interlocking formula and its associated language is still preserved and used.

The most prominent example is, no doubt, the name of the British royal family, **Windsor.**

Windsor (the 'w' is meaningless)
in. – .d. – so – or.
ino – odo – oso – oro
inorenganatu – odolgarbitasun – osoro – orotar
to bequeath – nobility – thorough – united
"Bequeath a thoroughly united nobility."

The British royal family adopted the name Windsor early in this century. It is fair to say that they must have known exactly what they were doing. They could not have picked a more appropriate name, but some linguist must have advised them. The name Windsor is of course a much older name, which was probably made up centuries ago by one of the many Benedictine linguists whose name has been long forgotten.

Another high profile name invented in this century is **Stalin**,

Stalin:
.sta – ali – in.
asta – ali – ino
astapotro – alienatu – inola
in a brutish way – to kill a person – in any way possible
"In a brutish way he kills people any way possible."

Now here is a fascinating name. Stalin was told by the linguist, who invented the name, that it came from the Russian word "stal" (steel), man of steel. What he didn't say was that it also was a word-play in the Basque language, the meaning of which told a very different, but more realistic, story.

A much more recent name is Habiari'mana, the Hutu president of Ruanda who, in 1994, organized and initiated the incredibly brutal genocide of the minority Tutsi people, long living in his country.

Habiari'mana:
.ha – abi – ari ' ma – ana.
aha – abi – ari ' ma – ana
ahalguzti – abiatsu – arimagalduku ' manatu – anaihilketa
almighty – impulsive – ruthless ' to demand – fratricide
"God, impulsive and ruthless, demands fratricide."

It is not known who made up this name, but it is a frightening thought that this mentality still exists in our world. It is a good possibility that the scholar who made up this name is still alive. Habiari'mana died when his plane was shot down shortly after the massacre started.

SOME EXAMPLES OF THE "GENETIC" RELATIONSHIP

If the languages are not genetically related, the Indo-European group cannot be a family. The Indo-European confusion started more than 200 years ago when Sir William Jones discovered the relationship between Sanskrit, Greek, Latin, Germanic etc. It looked so obvious, the "perfect" relationship between these words was there for everyone to see and, bingo!, the genetic family of Indo-European languages was born, complete with assorted laws of phonological correspondence and an Ur-mother language which gave birth to all. Even though controversy is the lifeblood of scholarship, all our academics happily climbed on the band wagon and the common people swallowed it, but where did this wagon take them? Here are two words to which the VCV formula has been applied. The first example is **father:**

SANSKRIT
Pitar:
pi-ita-ar.
pi – ita – ara
pindartu – itaun egin – arau
to get angry – to demand – descipline
"When angered he demands discipline."

LATIN
Pater:
.pa-ater
opa – ater
opa izan – aterpe
longing for – refuge
"Longing for my refuge."

FRENCH
père
pe-ere
pertsonaltasun – eredugarri
personality – exemplary
"Exemplary person."

GERMAN
Vater:
.fa-ater
afa – aterpe
happy – refuge
"Happy refuge."

Another example is **"field"**

SANSKRIT
ajras
aj.-.ra-as.
ajo – ora – ase
ajola izan – oraintxe – asetasun
to take care – right now – abundance
"Right now take care of the abundance."

GREEK
agros
ag.-.ro-os.
aga – aro – osa
aga – aroki – osatu
abundance – boasting – perfect
"Boasting (about) perfect abundance."

LATIN
ager
age-er.
age – ero
agerrune – errokatu
clearing – to settle
"A (forest) clearing to settle in."

DUTCH
akker
ak.-.ke-er.
aki – ike – ere
akitu – iketa – ereinlur
to get tired – you – land prepared for sowing
"You get tired preparing the land for sowing."

ENGLISH.
acre
ak. – .re
aki – ire
akiarazi – ireki
to tire – to dig
"Digging is tiring."

GOTHIC.
akrs
ak. – .r. – .s.
aki – ire – esa
akiarazi – ireki – esan
to tire – to dig – to say
"They say digging is tiring"

As you can see, the perceived relationship between these words is not genetic, such as naturally derived from some imagined proto-language, but instead they are contrived formulaic creations by highly skilled linguists using the Basque-Saharan language. The fact that most of these words appear to be related is not due to a genetic relationship, but because of skillful manipulation by the grammarians using the VCV system of agglutination. A totally new system of organizing the world's languages is urgently needed to accommodate the many invented languages, as well as a different approach to the teaching of linguistics.

EUROPE WAS INDEED UNILINGUAL

Wherever the Saharan refugees settled, the Saharan language was introduced. It couldn't have been any different because there was no other highly developed language anywhere else in Europe, the Near East, even India, Japan, Polynesia, the entire world. It appears that around 1,100 B.C. the decision was made in Kizzuwadna, the Anatolian province of Luvian male-domination, that the language, the religion and the tribal structure of the people from the Sahara was to be totally eradicated, to be replaced with invented languages, male gods, nationalism and private land-ownership. When this order was repeated in the Old Testament Bible it became a command for Judaists, Christians and Moslems alike. The Benedictine monks took this biblical command to heart when they built their monasteries in Britain and elsewhere. **The people who immigrated to Britain over the centuries, all spoke dialects of exactly the same language, the Saharan Basque language,** which can still be detected as a substratum in all European languages and is still spoken in Euskadi, the Basque country. Using acrostic manipulation and the vowel-interlocking formula, the versatile Basque language was professionally mutilated to the point where recognizing it was almost impossible. I show how this was done in many of the chapters. The fact that the names of the oldest Egyptian pharaohs can still be translated with the use of the modern Basque dictionary proves that the original language, carefully preserved by the ancient clergy over the millennia, changed very little. Gorka Aulestia's excellent Basque-English dictionary (published by University of Nevada) is used in my translations.

THE UNIFORMITARIAN PRINCIPLE

This principle states:

> *"Unless we can demonstrate that conditions of language use have been altered in such a way as to affect language structure and change, we must posit for unobservable language communities the same types of structures and changes that we observe in the historical record and at the present time."*
> (Human Inheritance p.47)

The task of demonstrating that conditions of Indo-European language use have indeed been altered to affect language structure and change, has fallen by default onto the shoulders of this retired forester. The burden of proof is the responsibility of those shaking the status quo. It is up to the shaker to provide evidence rather than for those simply defending that the evidence can be accounted for by existing paradigms. In this respect I have been told repeatedly by linguists that nothing can be true outside of the status quo. Therefore nothing outside the status quo needs to be investigated, which to me appears a sure prescription for continued ignorance and high intellect superstition. The well-known linguist Don Ringe from the University of Pennsylvania apparently believes that it is up to the academics to vote on which changes proposed are acceptable and which must be rejected, because he writes in "The Human Inheritance":

> *"... everything in linguistics is relevant to our hypotheses about prehistory. A hypothesis that is clearly incompatible with anything that is already certainly known, must be rejected. That is one of the major reasons why proposals about linguistic prehistory from outside the field have been received with so little enthusiasm by linguists: whatever the individual arguments may sound like, it always comes down to* a clear judgment by a large majority of linguists *that the hypothesis is seriously incompatible with something that is certainly known, and thus violates the uniformitarian principle. Such judgments are necessary to preserve the integrity of the field, because if we abandon the uniformitarian principle, we have no basis at all for scientific historical linguistics."* (p.47-48)

By saying that in present day linguistics some seriously disputed statements are known with certainty, professor Ringe's historical linguistics has been turned into dogma and thus his discipline has no place in serious science.

However, in spite of all this, I feel that linguistics can be a science again and does have a great future, but only if it ceases to be an academic fortress and becomes an openly discussed inter-disciplinary science, like geography, archaeology and forestry. In the future the discipline must demand from its students, as basic requirement, a detailed knowledge of the Basque language, which is the foundation of almost all advanced languages on earth. They also must study the evolution of religion and Bronze Age society and history, which so strongly influenced the formation of the Saharan/Basque language.

LATIN

LATIN IS MANIPULATED BASQUE

Students have long been taught that Basque is mostly borrowed and distorted Latin. The following examination of the words does not bear this out. Instead, it is clear from the following decodings of Latin words that this language is almost totally composed of formulaically manipulated Basque, which makes sense because Basque is a far older language than Latin.

Latin endings (e.g. -us, -a, -um) are usually not part of the occluded sentence, even though for some a suitable meaning may be found. Where the desired VCV word was not available, a CV word was used for the first letters of the word e.g. contra, familia, pendeo. The first vowel of the words is in most cases purposely eliminated in the word construction process and here represented by a dot. There appears to be no rule to guide the use of 'h' between double vowels. If the 'h' could be used, it was (e.g. the i.a in enuntiatio, quantum); if the 'h' could not be used, it was ignored (e.g. distoare, familia).

The meaning of the name "Latin" is interesting because it tells us that everybody had to memorize the invented words, whether they liked it or not:

Latin, .la-ati-in.

.la – ati – in.
ela – ati – ino
ela – atxiki gogoz – inornahi
word – to memorize – everybody
"Everybody memorize the words."

Some Examples Of How Latin Words Were Assembled

amoenus (charming)

amo – ohe – enu – us.
amodiozko – ohe – enulkeria – usain hartu
loving/affectionate – bed – weakness – to suspect
"Loving in bed is her weakness I suspect."

attingo (to touch) at. – .ti – in. – .go

ate – eti – ine – ego
atezatu – etikoa – inertzia – egoski
to stretch out – ethical – relaxing – to nurse
"Stretch out for ethical and relaxing nursing."

barbaricus (foreign, outlandish) .ba – ar. – .ba – ari – iku – us.

.ba – ar. – .ba – ari – iku – us.
eba – are – eba – ari – iku – us
ebatzi – arerio – ebatsi – arimagalduki – ikustari – us
to decide – enemy – to plunder – ruthlessly – explorer – Latin ending
"The enemy decided to ruthlessly plunder the explorers."

benevolens (kindhearted)

.be – ene – ebo – ole – en. – .s.
abe – ene – ebo – ole – ene – eso
abegikor – enetan – eboluzionatu – oles egin – eneganatu – esonde
hospitable – always – to evolve – upon – here – advise
"(We) evolved to be always hospitable, so come here and call upon us for advice."

cadaverosa (ghastly)

.ka – ada – abe – ero – osa
aka – ada – abe – ero – osa
akabatu – adarkatu – aberetsu – erro – osategi
to end a life – to gore – brutal – to suffer – hospital
"He suffered a brutal goring and ended his life in hospital."

contra (in opposition, in turn)

ko – on. – .tra
ko – ona – atra
kolpe egin – onargaitz – atrakatzaile
to grab – unacceptable/unwelcome – robber
"Grab the unwelcome robbers."

distoare (to separate, to be distant)

.di – is. – .to – are
edi – ise – eto – are
ediren – isekatu – etorrera – aren
to meet with – ridicule – arrival – his
"(Upon) his arrival he met with ridicule."

dogma (doctrine)

.do – og. – .ma
odo – ogu – uma
odolaitortza – ogusi – umatu
martyrdom – to articulate/speak clearly – to be fruitful
"Speak clearly about (His) martyrdom and be fruitful."

enuntiatio (proposition)

enu – un. – .ti – i.a – ati – o
enu – una – ati – iha – ati – o
enuldu – unagarri – atxiki – iharduki – atxikitasun
useless – boring – gathering – to discuss – faithfulness
"Useless, boring gathering discussing faithfulness."

errare (error, mistake)

er. – .ra – are
era – are – are
erratu – arek – arrezin
to make a mistake – he – unacceptable
"He made an unacceptable mistake."

familia (family)

fa-ami-ili-ia
fa – ami – ili – ia
farre egin – amiamoko – ilinti – iaio
to joke – stork – stirring up the fire – cheerful
"Joking about the stork while stirring up the cheerful fire."

filia (daughter)

.fi – ili – ia
ifi – ili – ia
ibili – ilinti – iaio
to be – fiery/energetic – cheerful
"She is energetic and cheerful."

fortuna (fortune)

.fo – or. – .tu-una
afo – ora – atu – una
abogado – orratio – atutxa – unai
lawyer – surprise – better world – cowherd
"The lawyer's surprise (opened up) a better world for the cowherd."

forum,

.f. – oru – um.
afa – oru – ume
afa – orrukatu – umekada
happy – to roar – childish
"Happy childish roaring."

galeritus (wearing a farmer's cap)

.ga – ale – eri – itu – us.
iga – ale – eri – itu – us
igandetu – alegeratu – errixee – iturritza – us
to dress up – to rejoice – common people – fountain/spring – (Latin ending)
"Dress up and rejoice with the common people around the fountain."

haruspa (sooth sayer)

.ha – aru – us. – .pa
ha – aru – usa – apa
haurresan – arrunki – usain hartu – apaindu
prediction – simply – to suspect – to make up
"Her prediction, I suspect, was simply made up."

inauguratu (to inaugurate)

ina – au – gura – atu
inaustu – au – gura – atutxa
to cut – this one – desire – better future
"I cut this one (ribbon?) in our desire for a better future."

inquisition (inquiry)

ink. – isi – ishi – on.
inke – izi – ixi – one
inkestatu – izigarrikeria – ixil – onegitasun
to make an investigation – atrocity – calmly – extreme patience
"Calmly and with extreme patience make an investigation of the atrocities."

justitia (justice)

.ju – ust. – .ti-iha
uju – uzti – iti – iha
uju – uzti – idiki – ihardukitze
to be pleased – omission – to expose – dispute
"(He/she) is pleased that the omission in the dispute was exposed."

koinonia (fellowship)

.ko – ino – oni – ia
akordiozko – inor – onirizte – iaio
traditional – anyone – acceptance – cheerful
"Traditional cheerful acceptance of anyone."

liquide (clearly, plainly)

.li – iku – ide
oli – iku – ide
olio – ikusi – idekotasun
oil – to look – clarity
"Look at the clarity of the oil."

locus (place, site)

.lo – oku – us.
alo – oku – usa
alorgizon – okuntza – usatu
farmer – field ready for sowing – to use
"The farmer uses the field ready for sowing."

lubrico (to oil)

.lu – ub. – .ri – iko
elu – ube – eri – iko
elur – ubeldu – erion – -iko
snow – to bruise – to slip/spill – that
"She/he slipped on the snow so that she/he bruised."

luxor (to live riotously, to have a ball)

lu – uk. – .so – or.
lu – uka – aso – ori
lupu egin – ukan – -azo – orritz
to procure – goods – to cause to happen – feast
"Procure the goods and we will have a feast."

maledicax (abusive)

.ma – ale – edi – ika – ak. – .s.
ama – ale – edi – ika – aka – asa
ama – alegia – ediren – ikaradura – akabu – asaldagarri
priestess – fake – to find – terror – death – shocking
"(Near) the fake priestess you find terror and shocking death."

natura (birth, nature, world)

.na – atu – ura
nabarmen – atutxa – urrats
showing – evergreen forest – footprint
"Footprints showing in the evergreen forest."

naufragium, (shipwreck)

.na – uf. – .ra – agi – um.
ina – ufa – ara – agi – umo
inauskatu – ufatu – arraio – agindun – umoretxar
to roll over – to blow – hell – commander – bad tempered
"Rolling in this blowing hell with a bad tempered commander."

opera (effort, pain, work)

ope – era
opetsi – erakarpen
to offer – attraction
"(We) offer an attraction."

orator (speaker)

ora – ato – or.
ora – ato – oro
orain – ator – orotara
now – to come – all together
"Now come all together."

pendeo (to hang, suspend)

pe – en. – .de – o
pe – ena – ede – o
pertxa – ena – edeki – o
coat hanger – that – to take – (Latin ending)
"Take that coat hanger."

perduco (to prolong)

.pe – er. – .du – uko
epe – eri – idu – uko

epe luzatu – errieta – iduko – uko egin
to postpone – fight – to have – to deny
"Postponing the fight has been denied."

posterior (later, next, after)

.po – oste – eri – or.
opo – oste – eri – ora
opor – -oste – eritasun – oraingoz
time off – after – sickness – for the time being
"For the time being take time off after sickness."

praecedentium (president),

.p. – .ra – ece – ede – en. – .ti – um
apa – ara – ese – ede – enu – uti – umo
aparteko – arazo – esetsi – derrak hartu – enulkeria – utikan – umoretxar
task – to attack – to defeat – slothfulness – to drive away – moodiness
"It is a special task to attack and defeat slothfulness and to drive away moodiness."
(Early spelling taken from the Auraicept na n'Ecez, line 5085, page 259).

quantum (as much as, how much)

.ku – an. – .tu – um.
iku – uha – ana – itu – um
ikuztontzi – uharka – anaitu – iturritza – um
bucket – cistern – to collect – spring – (Latin ending)
"(Take) the cistern bucket and collect from the spring."

ratio (calculation)

.ra – ati – o
ara – ati – o
arabera – atxiki – o
proportion – to memorize – (Latin ending)
"Memorize the proportion."

recido (to fall back, to sink)

.re – eki – ido
ire – eki – ido
irestzaile – ekinezko – idola
destructive – persistent – torrential rain
"Destructive and persistent torrential rain."

sata (daughter)

.sa – ata
asa – ata

asarrerazo – atalgabeko
to infuriate – simple
"Simply infuriating."
The monks made it a habit to give females names like that.

sperare (to hope for)

.spe – era – are
espe – era – are
espetxe – eramankizun – arrendu
prison – patience – to pray
"In prison pray for patience."

triste (sad, sorrowfully)

.t. – .ri – is. – .te
uti – iri – isi – ite
utikan – irrikatu – isilpetu – itegi
go away! – to desire/want – to hide – oxen's stable
"Go away! I want to hide myself in this oxen's stable."

turilega (incense gathering)

.tu – uri – ile – ega
atu – uri – ile – ega
atutxa – urrin – iletari – egapetu
evergreen forest – scent – mourner – to favour
"The mourners favour the scent of the evergreen forest."

ultra (farther, beyond)

ul. – .tra
ula – atra
ulatu – atrakaleku
to welcome – pier/dock
"Welcome (them) at the dock."

valetudinarium (hospital)

.ba-ale-etu-udi-ina-ari-um.
aba – ale – etu – udi – ina – ari – ume
abantzu – alen – etsitu – udikan hemendik – inarrosi – ariñeketan – ume
almost – total – despair – get out of there – to shake – very fast – child
"In almost total despair he got the shaking child out of there very fast."

vindicatio (punishment, avenging)

.bi – in. – .di – ika – ati – o
ibi – inu – udi – ika – o
ibili – inuzente – udikan – ikasi – atxiki – o
to behave – stupid – get out – to learn – to control yourself – (Latin ending)

"You behave stupidly; get out and learn to control yourself."

uxor (wife)

> uk. – .so – or.
> uko – oso – ora
> *uko egin – oso – orain*
> to refuse – simple – always
> **"(She) always simply refuses."** (other men)

zona (belt, sash)

> .zo – ona
> azo – ona
> *-azo – onarketa*
> to bring about – approval
> **"To bring about approval."** (i.e. "well dressed.")

SOME LATIN NAMES

(The supply is endless. Most Latin names can be decoded in this manner.)

Cronus

> .k. – .ro – onu – us.
> aka – aro – onu – uso
> *akabatu – arroztu – onuragabeko – uso*
> to end – exile – useless – holy man
> **"It ended in a useless exile for the holy man."**

Italia

> ita-ali-ia
> *itaitu – alik arinen – iaioki*
> to harvest – as fast as possible – cheerfully
> **"They cheerfully harvest as fast as possible."**

Nero

> .ne-ero
> ene – ero
> *enetan – ero*
> always – crazy
> **"Always crazy."**

Peter

.pe – ete – er.
ape – ete – era
apez – etengabe – eraspen
priest – constant – devotion
"Priest of constant devotion."

Ulysses

uli – is. – .se – es.
uli – isi – ise – esi
uli – isilkari – izentxarreko – ezigabe
coward – sneaky – infamous – savage
"Sneaky, infamous and savage coward."

The Romans made up this derogatory name for Odysseus (see Greek chapter) possibly because of his supposedly killing of the many suitors of his wife, however, the story is false and was added onto the Odyssey to make him look bad. He had been the leader of the attack by the Sea Peoples from the Great Green ocean and probably had devastated the Etruscans on his way to the battle in the eastern Mediterranean. This name was their revenge.

For a Canadian the most accessible Latin phrase is on the Canadian Coat-of-Arms. It reads:

Desiderantes meliorem patriam.

Desiderantes (desiring) .de – esi – ide – era – ante – es.

.de	ede	*eder izan*	to be pleased
esi	ezi	*ezi*	to control
ide	ide	*ideiatu*	to invent
era	era	*erabide*	method
ante	ante	*antepara*	bringing water to the waterwheel
es.	ezu	*ezusteki*	spontaneously

"Pleased to have invented a method to control the bringing of water to the waterwheel spontaneously."

meliorem (better) .me – eli – ore – em.

.me	ome	*menka*	according to
eli	eli	*elizaren hamar aginduak*	ten commandments of the church
ore	ore	*oreka*	balance, stability
em	ema	*eman*	to teach

"Teach stability according to the ten commandments of the church."

patriam (homeland) .pa – at. – .ri – am.

.pa	opa	*opa izan*	longing for
at.	ate	*aterpe*	shelter, protection
.ri	eri	*errialde*	region, homeland

| am. | amo | *amoltsu* | beloved |

"Longing for the protection of our beloved homeland."

The present meaning of the three words, "We desire a better homeland," makes sense for a country of immigrants, but the occluded meaning of the three individual words does not make a sentence.

Deciphia Arcani (secret mystery).

.de	ede	*ederretsi*	to be pleased
eki	eki	*ekin*	to persevere
ip.	ipi	*ipini*	to place, to build
.hi	ihi	*ihizitegi*	shelter, hide-out
i.a	iha	*ihardun*	to spend time
ar.	ara	*arakintza*	massacre
.ka	aka	*akabu*	death
ani	ani	*anitz*	many

"I am pleased to have persevered in building a hide-out in which to spend the time of the massacre with many deaths."

THE ORIGIN OF SPANISH

After finding that the hidden sentences in English words could easily be found, I applied this new knowledge to the vocabulary and names of other European languages. The Spanish language proved to be as straight-forward as English in the application of the word-agglutinating VCV formula, as shown in the well-known word **"amigo"** (friend): *ami-igo*, from the first letters of the Basque verbs *amilkatu* (to fall down) and *igoarazi* (to help up). This most appropriate description of a true friend therefore reads: **"When I fall down he helps me up."** Note how the middle vowel "i" is part of both roots, which is called "vowel-interlocking." This is a characteristic of the word-construction process for all Romance languages and English. It was obvious from this that the Spanish language was an invented language like Latin and English, and was not developed over time from a proto-language. The church linguists who invented the Spanish vocabulary often used Chistian teaching in their word-creation, such as in: "Español" which they spelled originally as "Espanjol" and also in "zurumbatico" (see below). To better illustrate the word-invention system which the church linguists used, here follow some more examples. In Basque, the Spanish "c" is usually a "k" (sometimes an "s"), the "v" is an "f" or a "b," and "sh" is written as "x."

analisis (analysis), ana-ali-isi-is.,

ana	ana	*anatomia*	anatomy, composition
ali	ali	*alik*	possible
isi	isi	*izigarri*	frightening
is.	isu	*isurgai*	liquid

"The composition of the possibly frightening liquid."

arbol (tree), ar.-.bo-ol.,

ar.	are	*arrendu*	to ask permission
.bo	ebo	*eboluzionatu*	to develop, to make into

ol.	ola	*ola*	wooden plank

"Ask permission to make (the tree) into planks."

brujeria (witchcraft), .b.-.ru-uje-eri-a,

.b.	obi	*obieta*	cemetary
.ru	iru	*irudikurtza*	idol worship
uje	uhe	*uhertasun*	maliciousness
eri	eri	*erigarri*	noxious
a	a	*a*	the

"The worshipping of idols in the cemetary is noxious maliciousness."

calendario (calendar), .ka-ale-en.-.da-ari-o,

.ka	eka	*ekainaldi*	solsticial season
ale	ale	*alegera*	rejoicing
en.	ene	*-enetan*	always
.da	eda	*edandatu*	to get drunk
ari	ari	*arrigarrizko*	awful

(the suffix -o gives the word a "typically Spanish" flavour.
"Rejoicing during the solsticial season always (results in) getting awfully drunk."

celebre (celebrated), .se-ele-eb.-.re,

.se	ase	*asekatu*	to have a craving, longing
ele	ele	*eleiza*	Christian assembly
eb.	eba	*ebanjelari*	evangelist
.re	are	*arreraegin*	to welcome

"The Christian assembly longs to welcome the evangelist."

civilizacion (civilization), .ki-ibi-ili-iza-asi-on.,

.ki	eki	*ekinalean*	do as much as possible
ibi	ibi	*ibili*	to behave
ili	ili	*ilintitu*	to encourage
iza	iza	*izari*	moderation
asi	atxi	*atxiki*	loyalty
on.	one	*onestasun*	decency

"Do as much as possible to behave and encourage moderation, loyalty and decency."

compasion (compassion), ko-om.-.pa-asi-on.,

ko	ko	*komeni*	to be helpful
om.	ome	*omenezko*	honorable
.pa	epa	*epai*	decision
asi	asi	*asi*	to start
on.	one	*oneste*	act of blessing

"To be helpful is an honorable decision to begin an act of blessing."

condor (condor), .ko-ondo-or.,

.ko	iko	*iko*	that
on do	ondo	*ondoratu*	to draw near, come closer
or.	ore	*orekari*	aerialist, high flyer

"That high-flyer is coming closer."

dilatar (to expand), .di-ila-ata-ar.,

.di	adi	*adi*	be careful
ila	ila	*ilarteko*	to make it last some time
ata	ata	*ataldu*	to divide,
ar.	ara	*aragi*	meat

"To make it last some time, be careful to divide the meat."

elegir (to elect, to choose), ele-egi-ir.,

ele	ele	*ele*	word
egi	egi	*egin*	to create, to choose
ir.	iru	*irudikari*	representative

"Word (used) to choose a representative."

español (Spaniard), es.-.pa-an.-.jo-ol.,

es.	esa	*esanahi*	significance
.pa	apa	*aparteko*	special
an.	ana	*anaitu*	to unite
.jo	ajo	*ajola izan*	to take care, to serve
ol.	ole	*oles egin*	to call upon

"It is of special significance that we unite and serve when called upon."

estatus (status), esta-atu-us.,

esta	ezta	*eztai*	celebration
atu	atu	*atutxa*	better world
us.	uste	*uste*	trust

"Celebrating our trust in a better world."

estragon (tarragon), est.-.ra-ago-on.,

est.	esta	*estali*	to cover
.ra	ara	*arrabeteko*	handful
ago	ago	*-agotu*	to add
on.	onu	*onuts*	very nice

"Add a handful and cover it very nicely."

fardel (knapsack), .fa-ar.-.de-el.,

.fa	afa	*afa*	happy
ar.	are	*arremankor*	together
.de	ede	*ederizan*	pleasing

el.   eli   *elikadura*   food

"Happy together with pleasing food."

fragil (fragile), .f.-.ra-agi-il.,

.f.   ife   *ifernu*   damned
.ra   era   *errazkeria*   negligence
agi   agi   *agirakatu*   to be blamed
il.   ile   *ilezin*   forever

"Damned negligence, I'll be blamed forever."

gramatica (grammar), .g.-.ra-ama-ati-ika,

.g.   iga   *igar*   dry
.ra   ara   *arra*   repetition
ama   ama   *amaikatxo*   many
ati   ati   *atxiki*   to memorize
ika   ika   *ikaskai*   lesson

"Many dry repetitions (will) memorize the lesson."

gratamente (pleasingly), .g.-.ra-ata-ame-ente,

.g.   agu   *agurtu*   to greet
.ra   ura   *ura*   her
ata   ata   *atadi*   main entrance
ame   ame   *amestu*   to dream about
ente   ent   *entzat*   destination

"She was greeted at the main entrance of the dreamed-about destination."

hechiceria (sorcery), .he-echi-ike-eri-a,

.he   ihe   *ihesari eman*   to escape
echi   etxi   *etxi*   house
ike   ike   *ikertu*   to investigate
eri   eri   *eriozkortasun*   noxiousness, maliciousness
a   a   *a*   the

"Escape from the house so the noxiousness can be investigated."

huerfano (orphan), .hu-er.-.fa-ano,

.hu   uhu   *uhui*   cry of happiness
er.   era   *erabideko*   polite
.fa   afa   *afa*   pleasing
ano   ano   *ano*   portion, hand-out

"A polite cry of happiness for the pleasing hand-out."

matutino (morning), .ma-atu-uti-ino,

.ma   ema   *eman*   to celebrate
at.   atu   *atutxa*   beautiful world

uti	uti	*utikan*	get out
ino	ino	*inoiz*	sometime

"Sometime get out (of bed) and celebrate this beautiful world."

notorio (well-known), .no-oto-ori-o,

.no	ano	*ano*	food
oto	oto	*otoikatu*	to beg
ori	ori	*orrits*	banquet
o	o	*-o*	suffix which gives the word a "typically Spanish" flavour.

"To beg for food at the banquet."

orador (orator), ora-ado-or.,

ora	ora	*oratu*	to grab, to engross
ado	ado	*adoretu*	to stimulate
or.	oro	*oroz*	completely

"To engross and stimulate completely."

pecadillo (sin), .pe-eka-adi-ilo,

.pe	ape	*apeta*	tendency
eka	eka	*ekarri*	to cause
adi	adi	*adikaitz*	incomprehensible
ilo	ilo	*ilordu*	agony

"(It has) a tendency to cause incomprehensible agony."

perentorio (urgent), .pe-ere-en.-.to-ori-o,

.pe	ope	*opetsi*	to offer
ere	ere	*ere*	also
en.	ene	*ene*	me
.to	eto	*etorri*	to come
ori	ori	*orrits*	banquet
o	o	*-o*	suffix which gives the word a "Spanish" flavour.

"He also offered me to come to the banquet."

pitonisa (fortune teller), .pi-ito-oni-isa,

.pi	ipi	*ipuin*	story
ito	ito	*ito*	to laugh a lot, laughter
oni	oni	*onibilera*	good fortune
isa	isa	*iseka*	to joke

"Story of laughter, good fortune and joking."

posada (guesthouse, lodging), .po-osa-ada,

.po	opo	*oporraldi*	time-off

| osa | osa | *osatu* | to unify, to get together |
| ada | ada | *-ada* | noise of the last word |

"Time-off for a noisy get-together."

senado (senate), .se-ena-ado,

.se	ese	*esetsi*	to argue
ena	ena	*-ena*	verbal suffix expressing the future
ado	ado	*adorez*	courageously

"They will argue courageously."

sofa (couch), .so-ofa,

| .so | oso | *osoro* | completely |
| ofa | oba | *oba* | natural, comfortable |

"Completely comfortable."

super (super), .su-upe-er.,

.su	isu	*isurgai*	liquid
upe	upe	*upel*	cask, vat
era	era	*erakuskariketa*	sampling

"Sampling the liquid in the cask."

tarantula (large spider), .ta-ara-an-.tu-ula,

.ta	ata	*atalgabeko*	simple
ara	ara	*aramu*	spider
an.	ane	*añendu*	to curse
.tu	etu	*etsitu*	despair
ula	uli	*uli*	coward

"A simple spider (causes) cursing and despair in a coward."

torrente (torrent), .to-orre-en.-.te,

.to	eto	*etorri*	come
orre	orre	*orrela*	that way
en.	ena	*-ena*	(superlative)
.te	ate	*aterpe*	safe haven

"Come that way to a safe haven."

veloz (quickly), .be-elo-oz.,

.be	ibe	*ibeni*	to sit
elo	elo	*elorri*	thorn
oz.	oze	*oze*	sharp

"To sit on a sharp thorn."

visitar (to call on), .bi-isi-ita-ar.,

| .bi | ibi | *ibili* | to go |
| isi | isi | *isilki* | quietly |

ita	ita	*itaundu*	to ask
ar.	aro	*arrotzari*	inn-keeper

"Go quietly and ask the inn-keeper."

zurumbatico (stunned), .zu-uru-um.-.ba-ati-iko,

.zu	izu	*izuizan*	to be terrified
uru	uru	*urruindu*	to be scorned, despised
um.	uma	*umadun*	pregnant
.ba	aba	*abade*	priest
ati	ati	*atxiki*	to find out
iko	iko	*iko*	swelling

"I am terrified to be scorned for being pregnant when the priest finds out about the swelling."

zurumbo (stupid with alcohol), .zu-uru-um.-.bo,

.zu	izu	*izuizan*	to be terrified
uru	uru	*urruindu*	to be scorned
um.	umi	*umildu*	to humiliate
.bo	ibo	*ibolada*	group of people

"I am terrified to be scorned and humiliated by the people."

Do I really need to decode more Spanish words to prove to the world that Spanish is an invented language, the same as all the other Romance languages, and that this language was made up by church linguists out of Basque?

THE ORIGIN OF DUTCH

In my writing about the English language, the Ogam script and the Benedictines, I showed how the Benedictine monks and their grammarians, working
in their scriptoria, invented thousands of words by manipulating the universal
language, the Saharan/Basque language, with the use of the vowel-interlocking VCV formula. The same was done when they created the Dutch and
German languages but with an important difference: for English they followed the strict example of Latin and Sanskrit, and used primarily that half of
the Basque vocabulary which started with vowel-consonant (VC). To invent
Dutch and German, both halves of the Basque language, VC and CV words
were used and the originally strict VCV rules of word agglutination were
relaxed, which were two reasons why their work resulted in quite different
languages.

THE EGMOND BENEDICTINE ABBEY

Although the two languages are not mutually understandable, it is relatively
easy for a Dutchman to learn both German and English because his language is
almost like a bridge between the two. The reason for this appears to be that all
three languages were made up during the same era by the same brotherhood of
Benedictine monks and grammarians who worked closely together and borrowed newly created words regularly from each other, then applied and shaped
the words according to predetermined sets of character rules. The Egmond
Abbey, which was built in 922 A.D. near the North Sea coast, west of the City
of Alkmaar in North Holland, appears to have been the central clearing house
for the exchange and distribution of words and literature. Contact between this
abbey and the other scriptoria was frequent, it being accessible by boat both
from the sea to the west, and from the Rhine hinterland to the east. The name

"Egmond" relates to the linguistic activities going on at the abbey: *eg.-mo-ond*.

eg. ' mo – ondo
egin ' moldez – ondorekidego
to create ' skillfully – common inheritance
"(We) skillfully create a common inheritance."

Documents available from Alcuin's time (see Shipley-Duckett) and later, tell us that the monks from England regularly sailed to the mainland, while the monks from Germany and Austria would go overland and by boat down the Rhine. These monks were highly mobile in their small boats and this may well have been the origin of the name

"Holland," *ol.-.la-and.*,

ola – ala – anda
olatu – alaitu – andar
waves – to fill with joy – speeding
"Speeding the waves fills us with joy."
(the "h" is meaningless).

The main linguistic centre of the French language, located in the large Benedictine Abbey of Cluny, appears to have had little direct contact with Egmond Abbey, reporting directly to the Vatican instead.

Cluny:

.k. – .lu – uni
eki – ilu – uni
ekinaldi – ilun – unibertsal
perseverance – darkness – general
"Perseverance (amid) general darkness."

The Scandinavian, Hungarian and East European linguistic efforts were still many years in the future. Over the centuries the Benedictine grammarians created tens of thousands of new words out of the universal language, many of which did not fit in the design plan for the home languages. Rejected words were taken in context to Egmond Abbey where they were evaluated by local Benedictine linguists and others visiting from other countries and then exchanged. Unwanted words passed into oblivion, which may have been the fate of a large number of the grammarians' creations.

CONTRIBUTIONS CAME FROM FAR AWAY

It was in about 1060 A.D. that the Abbot Willeram, of Ebersberg Benedictine Abbey in Bavaria (east of München) wrote a commentary on Solomon's Song of Songs, the Bible's wedding song. In it, love is explained in an allegorical sense as a dialog between Christ and His Church. The love bed is conceived as evangelism and lovely breasts as mercy. It is not likely that Willeram was the writer's real name because the meaning tells us that it was the title of his work:

Willeram: *il.-.le-era-am.* (the "w" has no meaning)

ile – ele – era – amo
ilezin – ele – erran – amodio
everlasting – story – to tell – love
I tell the everlasting story of love.

As was normal practice, shortly after completion, the manuscript was taken to Egmond Abbey and made available for study by the visiting monks/grammarians. Willeram's work had a profound influence upon the early development of both Dutch and German. The document is now located in the library of the University of Leiden, Holland. Similarly, at about the same time, the four lines of "Olla Vogala," written in the Rochester Benedictine Abbey near Chatham, England, were taken to Egmond after some of its new words were accepted into the English language (olla became "all," nestas became "nests" etc). All four lines were published in context which made it possible for me to bring out the hidden Basque sentences. In Egmond several of the newly created words were quickly picked up by the monks working on the Dutch and German languages e.g. 'hebban' became "hebben" in Dutch, "haben" in German, "have" in English, while vogala became "vogels" (birds) in Dutch and "Vögel" in German. First let us look in detail at "Olla Vogala" (van Oostrom).

OLLA VOGALA

The following lines were written on the back page of a prayer book dating from the 11th century, originating in the Benedictine scriptorium of Rochester, England. The third and fourth lines are considered by linguists to be the oldest known prose in the Dutch language, shown here in context:

> **quid expectamus nunc**
> **abent omnes volucres nidos inceptos nisi ego et tu**
> **hebban olla vogala nestas hagunnan hinase hic**
> **enda thu wat unbidan we nu.**

Lines 1 and 2 contain recognizable Latin words, be it a kind of dog-Latin.

Literally, in the order given they read: *"What do we expect now gone away all birds' nests begun except I and you"* (Furlong). Lines 3 and 4 are thought to say in Dutch: *Hebben alle vogelen nesten begonnen behalve ik en jij; wat verwachten we nu* ("All birds have started nest building except you and I; what can we expect now?"). Lines 1 and 2 therefore say roughly the same in Latin what lines 3 and 4 say in archaic Dutch. These words, supposedly coming from the pen of a Benedictine monk, were received with chuckles and wondering. It better applied to a lover telling his beloved to mirror herself on the behaviour of the birds. But is this really what the monk wrote? Again apply the VCV formula and see what happens; (the "/" indicates a break in the vowel-linking; "c" and "q" must be read as "k," "v" as "b."

kuid expektamus nunk : *.ku-id./ek.-.s.-.pe-ek.-.ta-amu-us./.nu-un.-.k./*

.ku	iku	*ikuskari*	visitor
id./	idu	*idurikortsu*	very distrustful
ek.	eka	*ekaitz*	storm
.s.	ase	*asetu*	to get tired
.pe	epe	*epel*	weak
ek.	eko	*ekoitzi*	to supply
.to	ota	*otapur*	crumb
amu	amu	*amultsu*	trusting
us./	usu	*usu*	usually
.nu	inu	*inular*	evening
un.	una	*una*	dull
.k.	aka	*akatsun*	miserable

"The visitors were very distrustful. Tired and weak from the storm, I gave crumbs to the usually trusting (birds) on that dull, miserable evening."

abent omnes volukres: *abe.ent./om.-.ne-es./.bo-ol.-.ju-uk.-.re-es./*

abe	abe	*abestu*	to sing
ent./	entz	*entzungale*	longing to hear
om.	ome	*omendatu*	to pay tribute, to thank
.ne	ene	*enegana*	to me
es.	esa	*esan*	to express
.bo	abo	*abots*	voice
ol.	ola	*ola*	cabin
.ju	aju	*ajuria*	field of heather
uk.	uka	*ukan*	to have
.re	are	*arremankor*	sociable
es./	esa	*esamesaka*	gossiping

"I longed to hear them sing, expressing thanks to me. Their voices (could be heard) from the cabin in the field of heather where they had their sociable gossiping time."

nidos inkeptos nisi ego: *.ni-ido-os./in.-.ke-ep.-.to-os./.ni-isi/ego/*

.ni	eni	*eni*	to me
ido	ido	*idoroketa*	discovery, revelation
os./	oso	*oso*	complete
in.	ino	*inoizka*	occasionally
.ke	oke	*okerbidetu*	to go astray
ep.	epe	*epel*	timid
.to	eto	*etorle*	arrival
os.	osa	*osatu*	to unify (with family)
.ni	ani	*anitzetan*	often
isi/	isi	*isilbidez*	quietly
ego/	ego	*egon*	to stay

"(It was) a complete revelation to me. Occasionally, when a timid arrival had gone astray, looking for its family, it often quietly stayed."

et tu hebban olla vogala: *et./.tu/.he-eb.-.ba-an./ol.-.la/.bo-oga-ala/*

et./	eto	*etor*	to come
.tu/	atu	*atutxa*	oak forest
.he	ihe	*ihesleku*	to shelter
eb.	eba	*ebatzi*	to decide
.ba	aba	*abarratsu*	many branched
an./	ana	*anaitu*	together
ol.	ole	*oles egin*	to call upon
.la	ela	*elaberritsu*	talkative, chattering
.bo	abo	*aboskatu*	to voice
oga	oga	*ogasun*	wealth
ala/	ala	*alaitasun*	happiness

"They came to the oak forest and decided to shelter together among the many branches and called upon (all) by chattering and voicing a wealth of happiness… "

nestas hagunnan hinase: *.ne-esta-as./.ha-agu-un.-.na-an./.hi-ina-ase/*

.ne	ene	*enean*	at the time
esta	esta	*estaldu*	to pair off
as./	ase	*asegaitz*	urge
.ha	oha	*oharatu*	to become receptive to mating
agu	agu	*agudotu*	to get active
un.	uni	*unibertsalki*	generally
.na	ina	*inarrosi*	to agitate
an./	ano	*ano*	foodsupply
.hi	ehi	*ehizaldi*	to hunt
ina	ina	*inarroskatu*	excitedly
ase/	ase	*asegabi*	greedily

"At the time that they got the urge to pair off. Becoming receptive to mating, they got generally active and agitated over their food supply. They hunted excitedly and greedily,"

hik enda thu wat unbidan we nu: *.hi-ik./en.-.da/.t.-.hu/at./un.-.bi-ida-an./eu/.nu*

.hi	ahi	*ahitugaitz*	inexhaustibly
ik.	ike	*ikerraldi*	exploring
en.	ena	*-ena*	superlative
.da	ada	*ada*	noise
.t.	ate	*ateratu*	to depart
.hu/	ehu	*ehundaka*	by the hundreds
at./	ata	*atano*	evergreen oak forest
un.	una	*unatasun*	fatigue
.bi	abi	*abiatu*	to leave behind
ida	ida	*idazlan*	writing
an./	ana	*anaia*	monk
eu	eu	*eu*	you
.nu/	inu	*inurritu*	to inspire

exploring inexhaustibly. Noisily they departed by the hundreds from the oak forest, leaving your exhausted monk behind to write and inspire you.

This is a masterful piece of "double speak" in three languages, Latin, Basque and Dutch. The unique creativity lies in the linguist's ability to write one sentence in Latin, translate this into archaic Dutch and still hide a quite different story in both sentences to be decoded with the use of Basque. This hidden story makes clear that the birds arrived at their wintering grounds in south-east England where they were fed and observed by the monk. In spring the birds paired off and departed to nest somewhere in the north. The monk's word "nestas" has therefore nothing to do with nest building; it simply means: "at the time they had the urge to pair off." The new word "vogala" certainly described the small song birds beautifully, they really do "voice a wealth of happiness." There are quite a number of song bird species overwintering in southern England such as blue and grey tits, which may have been the "vogala."

SOME WORDS LEFT OVER FROM PRE–CHRISTIAN DAYS

Dutch has many words and names which are unique to the language but most of these are also found in Basque, often meaning something closely related. Several of these words have been declared "slang" by linguists in an effort to rid the new language of pre-Christian vocabulary. About some of the words it is hinted that they were borrowed from Yiddish and therefore are supposedly not Dutch at all; don't believe it. The origin of Yiddish is discussed elsewhere.

DUTCH

afval (leftovers)
Assepoester (Cinderella)
atje (child's bottom)
bajes (quod, lock-up)
bedaard (calm, relaxed)
bezem (broom)
blaauw (blue)
boer (farmer)
botter (fishing boat)
elkaar (each other)
ergernis (annoyance)

foetsie (poof, gone)
frok (outer garment)
gaan (to go)
gajes (rabble)
gannif (swindler, thief)

geel (yellow)
geit (goat)
geus (freedom fighter)
gezeur (lamentive)
graan (grain)
hondeweer (disastrous weather)
jatten (to pilfer food)
jota (small amount)
kak (excrement)
kar (cart)
kenau (female leader)

kerel (fellow, chap)
kolder (giddy nonsense)
koop (purchase)
koorts (fever)

kop (cup)
kou (miserable cold)
labaaz (stinker, sneak)
laster (slander, smear)
leger (army)
maar (but)

mak (tame)

BASQUE

afal (dinner, supper)
astaputz (vulgar, coarse)
atze (backside, consequence)
baieztakor (assertive, firm)
bedardun (lawn, pasture)
besomotz (short arms)
blaust (blow on the eye) i.e. a black eye
buru (people)
botari (net caster)
elkar (mutual)
erge-era-aniz:
> *ergel* (foolish)
> *-era* (behaviour)
> *anitz* (frequent)

futz (puff of air)
fraka (trousers)
gana (movement towards a goal)
gaiez (undeserving)
ganibetada (knifing)
(f and b are interchangeable)

gelbera (fearful, afraid)
gaitzarin (damage)
geurez,ge'uz (our own initiative)
gezur (evade the truth)
garaun (seed, grain)
honda (disastrous)
jatun (having a good appetite)
jota (broke)
kaka (excrement)
erakarri (to carry)
ken-nau:
> *kenarazi* (revolt)
> *nausi* (leader)

ikerle (visitor)
koldar (cowardly)
kopuru (quantity)
ko-ortz:
> *kordokarazi* (to clatter)
> *ortz* (tooth): clattering teeth

kopau (mouthful)
kaukezia (misery)
labazomorro (cockroach), used in Friesland.
laster (to press, to push)
legeria (code of laws)
ma-ar:
> *ama* (mother's)
> *arrazoinbide* (reasoning)

ma-aker:

	ama (mother's)
	aker (goat)
mal (mold, form)	*malgy* (flexible)
malie (coat of mail)	*maila* (wire mesh)
matig (frugal, moderate)	*ma-ategain*:
	ama (mother's)
	ategain (lintels): mother's lintels
mazzel (good luck)	*mazal* (good, decent)
meer (lake)	*meru* (bass, a freshwater fish)
minne (heartache)	*min* (pain)
mug (mosquito)	*mugagabe* (without number)
moker (sledgehammer)	*mokor* (ferocious)
olijk (rogisch)	*olerk* (poetry)
onzeker (insecure, worried)	*onzi-ikar*:
	ontzi (ship)
	ikara (anxiety): worried about the ship.
oogst (harvest)	*ogits* (abundant in wheat)
risico (risk)	*arrisk, arriskatu* (to risk)
rood (red)	*rotu, arrotu* (flushed, blushing)
stad (town)	*statu, ostatu* (hotel, inn)
terp (safe mound)	*terpe, aterpe* (refuge, safe haven)
toeter (hooter)	*tutu* (horn)
varanda (porch with railing)	*baranda* (railing)
vee (cattle)	*bei, vei* (cow)
werp (throw)	*erpintsu* (pointed) possibly a spear.
zeil (sail)	*zail* (difficult)

INGVAEOONS

The Dutch use some rather strange sounding words without knowing the meaning of them; *Ingvaeoon* is possibly the most outlandish. The pre-Christian inhabitants of Holland were called *ingvaeoon* by Tacitus, a word which Dutch linguists say means: "living along the ocean, a Saxon word...." Where that wisdom came from is not known. To find out the original meaning, again apply the VCV vowel interlocking formula:

Ingvaeoon: *ing.-.ba-a.e-e.o-on*.

ing.	ingi	*ingira*	disgusting
.ba	iba	*ibarjende*	lowland people
a.e	aie	*aienekatu*	to grieve
e.o	eho	*ehorzkabe*	unburied
on.	ona	*onartezintasun*	unacceptably

"The disgusting people of the lowlands grieve (their dead) while unacceptably unburied."

Corpse-exposure was, of course, common practice among all peoples worshiping the supreme Goddess of the Asherah religion. Exposure to the elements was done in special protected facilities or on islands to properly release the soul of the deceased from the body for speedy re-incarnation into a newborn child. Dutch linguists use the word *Ingvaeoons* as the name of the language spoken by the pre-historic people of Holland, a use which the meaning of the word does not permit.

SOME DUTCH PLACENAMES

Most older Dutch place names can be decoded with the VCV formula and translated with the Basque dictionary. There is no doubt in my mind that the people spoke the pre-Christian language of all of Europe which was the universal language of the Neolithic, known today as Basque. Some of the sentences hidden in the following names must have histories of their own:

Amerongen: ame-ero-onge-en., *ameskor* (dreaming) *erosle* (Redeemer) *onginahi* (kindness) *enegana* (to me): "I am dreaming about the Redeemer's kindness to me."

Arnhem: ar.-.n.-.he-em., arro-oni-ihe-ema: *arrotz* (foreigner) *onik* (unharmed) *ihesaldi* (escape) *emarrapaketa* (abduction of a woman): "The foreign woman escaped unharmed from her abductors."

Assen: as.-.se-en., asa-ase-ene: *asaldaketa* (excitement) *asegaitz* (craving for) *ene* (come to me): "Craving for excitement? Come here!"

Barnegat: .ba-arnegat, *ebanjelari* (evangelist) *arnegatu* (to get angry): "The evangelist got angry."

Beveland: .be-ebe-ela-and., *ibeni* (to introduce, tell) *ebertar* (Hebrew) *ela* (story) *andi* (marvelous): "Tell the marvelous story of Jesus."

Blaricum: .b. – .la – ari – iku – um., abu – ula – ari – iku – umi, *aburukide* (person who agrees) *ulatu* (to welcome) *arritzeko* (fantastic) *ikusle* (visitor) *umildu* (to humble): "I agree, the fantastic welcome for the visitors was humbling."

Delden: .de-el.-.de-en., ade-ela-ade-ene, *adeitasun* (good manners) *ele* (conversation) *ederretsi* (pleasing) *adeitsu* (courteous) *-enetan* (always): "Good manners, pleasing conversation and always courteous." (compare this name with the neighboring town of "Hengelo"). (Delden is the author's family homestead).

Delft: .de-el-.f.-.t., ede-ela-afa-ati, *eder* (beautiful) *ela* (story) *afa* (happy) *atxikitzaile* (faithfulness): "Beautiful story of happy faithfulness."

Drachten, .d.-.ra-ak.-.te-.en, ada-ara-aka-ate-entz, *adarka* (by goring, stabbing) *arakintzo* (massacre) *akabatu* (to end a life) *atezatu* (to live on) *entzute* (fame): "The stabbing massacre ended his life, but his fame lives on." Was that about St. Boniface?

Drente, .d.-.re-en.-.te, *adei* (courteous) *errezibimendu* (welcome) *enetan* (always) *etenda* (tired): "Always a courteous welcome (for those who are) tired."

Ede: ede, *ederren* (the most beautiful): "The most beautiful."

Ellekom: el.-.le-eko-om., ela-ale-eko-ome, *ela* (story) *alegera* (happy) *ekonomo* (administrator) *omenezko* (honorable): "Happy story of the honourable administrator."

Enschede: en.-.ske-ede, *ena* (superlative) *aske* (free, independent) *eder* (beautiful): "Very independent and beautiful."

Goes: gus, *gustoko* (my favourite): "My favourite (town)."

Gouda: .go-uda, *egoitzar* (home) *uda* (summer): "Summer home."

Groningen: .gro-oni-inge-en., *aguro* (diligent) *onibilera* (prosperous) *ingiratu* (to get ready) *eneganatu* (to attract people): "Diligent, prosperous and getting ready to attract people."

Heilo: .he-ilo, ihe-ilo, *ihesari eman* (to escape) *ilordu* (agony): "(We) escaped the agony."

den Helder: .de-en./.he-el.-.de-er., ede-ene/ihe-ela-ade-ere: *ederren* (the most beautiful) *ene* (to attract, come to) *ihesleku* (shelter, harbour) *elaberritsu* (fond of the news) *adeitsu* (courteous) *errezibimendu* (welcome): "Come to the most beautiful harbour for the latest news and a courteous welcome."

Hengelo: .he-enge-elo, *uher* (malicious) *engera* (disgusting) *elorritsu* (crude): "Malicious, disgusting and crude." (Compare this name with neighboring "Delden").

Hilversum: .hi-il.-.be-er.-.su-um., *ahi* (I hope) *ilezin* (immortal) *ebertar* (Hebrew) *errixee* (common people) *isuri* (to inspire) *umiltasun* (humbleness): "I hope that the immortal story of Jesus will inspire the common people to humbleness."

de Koog: de/.ko-og., ede-ako-oga, *eder* (beautiful) *akorduan euki* (to remember) *ogasun* (estate): "Beautiful estate (worth) remembering."

Leerdam: .le-er.-.da-am., ale-ere-eda-am.: *alegera* (happily) *eregu* (indulging) *edan* (to drink) *ameskoikeria* (delirium): "Happily indulging in drinking (causes) delirium."

Medemblik: .me-ede-em.-.bli-ik., ome-ede-emo-obli-iku: *omenezko* (honorable) *edesti* (history) *emon* (to give) *obligazio* (obligation) *ikusbera* (vigilant): "Our honorable history obliges us to be vigilant."

Naarden: na-ar.-.de-en., *nabarmen* (obvious) *arazotu* (to be worried) *adelatu* (to prepare) *enetan* (always): "It is obvious that they are worried and always prepared."

Rekken: .re-ek.-.ke-en., *arrerakor* (kind) *ekarri* (to bring) *aker* (male goat) *eni* (to me): "Kind (of you) to bring the male goat to me."

Renkum: .re-en.-.ku-um., *arren* (please) *ene* (come to me) *ekurutasun* (peace of mind) *umiltasun* (humbleness): "Please come to me (to find) peace of mind and humbleness." Or:

Renkum: .re–en.-.ke–um., are-ene-iku-ume: *arrera egin* (to welcome) *enetan* (always) *ikustatu* (to visit) *umeak* (children: "You are always welcome to visit with children." (not preferred)

Staphorst: .sta-ap.-.ho-orst, esta-apa-aho-orrits: *estatuburu* (head of state) *apailatu* (to organize) *ahogozagarri* (delicious) *orrits* (banquet): "The head of state organized a delicious banquet."

Utrecht: ut.-.re-ek.-.t., uti-ire-eki-itu: *utzi* (to abandon, put a stop to) *iresle* (destruction) *ekinalean* (doing as much as possible) *itundu* (to make a treaty): "To put a stop to the destruction, do as much as possible to make a treaty."

Walcheren: adaption of: *alkarren* (together, mutual): "Togetherness."

Zwolle: .zu-ol.-.le, azu-ole-ele, *azurruts* (skeleton) *oleazio* (last rites) *eleizakoak* (Sacraments): "(He gave) the skeleton the last rites of the Sacraments."

WORDS INVENTED IN GROUPS

Certain letter combinations were used repeatedly by the Benedictines to make up a diversity of words, as can be seen in the following list — *gooien, hooien, looien, pooien, tooien, rooien* — which all use the Basque word *oian* meaning: forest or wood.

Some "oian" words

gooien (to throw) go-oien, ego-oian, *egotzi* (to throw) *oian* (wood):
Throwing wood.
hooien (to bring in the hay) .ho-oien, oho-oian, *oholtza* (high rack) *oian* (wood):
High wooden rack.
looien (to tan leather) lo-oien, lo-oian, *lortu* (to get, obtain) *oian* (forest):
Obtain (oak bark) from the forest.
pooien (to booze) po-oien, opo-oian, *oporrez* (lazily) *oian* (in the forest):
Lazy in the forest.
tooien (to decorate) to-oien, to-oian, *tontortu* (to decorate) *oian* (wood):
Decorate the wood.
rooien (to uproot, clear away) ro-oien, erro-oian, *errokatu* (to settle down) *oian* (forest):
Settling down in the forest.

Some "aue" words

The linguists took other Basque words with *"au"* such as *"auek"* (these) and used it to create a similar series of Dutch words out of the first three letters *"aue,"* written in Dutch as: **"ouwe"** or **"auwe,"** same pronounciation as in Basque.

bouwen (to build), .bau-auwe-en., abau-aue-ene, abaunza (branches to weave into wall) – auek (these) – ene (for me): "Weave these branches for me into a wall."
douwen (to push), from *daunba* (to punch, to push)
gouw (district, region) .ga – aue, oga – aue, *ogasun* (property) *auek* (these): "These properties."
houwen (to hack, to hew), from *hautsi* (to fracture)
jouw (your property) from *jaube* (owner) or *jauntzapen* (take possession)
kauwen (to chew, to munch) from kau-aue, *kausk* (sound of biting) – *auek* (these): "Bite these."
kouw (miserable cold), *kaukezia* (misery).
lauw (luke warm) from *lauki* (smoothly)?
louter (sheer, mere), from *lautasun* (simplicity)
mauwen (to mew), ma – aum mania (whimpering) autueta (talk): "Whimpering talk."
nauw (narrow, tight), from inaustu (to cut)?
pauw (peacock), from pausatuki (slow paced)
rauw (raw) from *arau* (discipline, corporal punishment)
touw (rope) from ato, *aurtiki* (to throw)
touwen (to dress leather) from *ito*, to dip into (tannic acid).
wauwelaar (twaddler, chatterbox), aue – ela – ar., *auek* (these) – *ela* (story) – *arri* (awful): "These awful stories."

Some "aik" words

Every newly invented language was given some "characteristic" peculiarities and Dutch was assigned (beside the gutteral scrape-throat "g") the "ij," pronounced something like "eye." Another letter combination, pronounced exactly the same way, is "ei," but Dutch shares this peculiarity with German. It is interesting to note that the "i" of "ij" is pronounced the English way instead of like in Latin, which may indicate that English grammarians had a hand in concocting this one. Here are a few Dutch words with "ij" or "ei" and their origin.

Dutch:	Origin:	Comment:

eik (oak)	*aika* (to grieve, moan):	Oaks moan in the wind.
dijk (dike)	*daik, daike* (he can have it):	He can have the land.
lijk (dead body)	*lai-ik, laiatu* (to spade) *ik* (you):	You do the spading.
rijk (rich)	*rai-ik, arrai* (kind) *ik* (you):	You are kind.
tijk (cloth, tick)	*tai-ik, taiaketa* (to fit) *ik* (you):	To fit you.
slijk (mire, mud)	*zla-aik., zula* (hole) *aiek* (this):	This (mud) hole.
gelijk (equal)	*gela-ik, gelakide* (roommate) *ik* (you):	Your roommate.
bereik (within)	*beraik, beraiek* (themselves)	Among themselves.
kijken (to look)	*kaik, kaiku* (freak)	Look at the freak.
sijk (filth, urine)	*saik, saikume* (vulture chick)	They are messy indeed.

Then there is the boy's name "Haiko or Heiko" which came from *aiko maikoka* (making excuses). *Maiko* (dinner guest) became the Dutch girl's name "Maaike" etc. One interesting bit about Prof. R. "de Rijk," the internationally known, Basque-speaking professor in Leiden, whose name is derived from: "de Rai-ik": *dei* (called) *arrai* (kind) ik (you): "called: you are kind." A good Basque name to have, even if he didn't know it. Many Dutch names start with "van" meaning "from." The origin of "van" is *ban* (b and v are interchangeable) which is an abbreviation of the Basque word banatu meaning "to disperse," "to separate from." Most Dutch names and words can be shown to have been wrought out of Basque; take my own "Nyland," ni-land.: *ni* (my) *landa* (field, region). An early branch of my family in Gescher (Westfalia), Germany, still spells the name as Niland. Many Dutch names have been distorted so much that it is nigh impossible to trace their origin with any certainty.

Some "aide" words.

beide (both)	bai-aide, *bai* (yes) *aide* (family):	**Say yes for a family.**
beiden (to linger)	bai-aide-en., *baizera* (hesitation) *aide* (family) *ene* (my):	**My family hesitates.**
heiden (heathen)	hai-aide-en, *haidur* (malicious) *aide* (family) *engainatu* (to deceive)	**maliciously deceiving family.**
lijden (to suffer)	lai-aide-en, *laida* (insulted) *aide* (family) *engainatu* (to deceive):	**Insulted and deceived family.**
mijden (to avoid)	mai-aide-en, *maiseatu* (to gossip, slander) *aide* (family) *endekatu* (degenerate):	**Gossiping and degenerate family.**
rijden (to ride)	rai-aide-en, *arraitu* (to be happy) *aide* (family) *endekoi* (sociable, together):	**Family happily together.**

Some "ust" words.

buste (bust)	*.bu-uste, aburu* (opinion) *uzte* (to leave out, to refuse):	**Refuse an opinion.**
gust (barren*)	*.gu-ust., igurtzi* (to rub) *ustu* (to empty):	**Rub to empty.**
justitia (justice)	*.ju-usti-iti-iha, uju* (shout of joy, pleased) *uzti* (omission) *itiki* (to discover, expose) *ihardukitze* (dispute):	**Pleased to expose the omission in the dispute.**

kust (coast) .*ku-ust., ekuru* (quietly) *uste* (hopeful):

Quietly hopeful.

lust (delight) *luzatu* (to make it last): **Make it last.**

rust (rest) .*ru-uste, arrunt* (simple) *uste* (trust):

Simple trust.

* not producing milk

Some "olde" words.

bolder (bitt) .*bo-olde.er., abonau* (to approve of) *oldez* (instantaneous) *erremolke* (towing):

Give the signal to start towing.

folder (brochure) .*fo-olde-er., ebo-olde-er.,eboluzionatu* (to develop, organize) *oldez* (instan taneous) *erabilgarbitasun* (availablility):

Organize instantaneous availability.

kolder (giddiness) *koldar* (cowardly): **Cowardly.**

polder (diked-in area) .*po-olde-er., oposatu* (to obstruct) *olde* (unrestricted, natural) *eraiketa* (movement):

Obstruct the natural movement (of the water).

soldeer (solder) .*so-olde-er., oso* (simple) *olde* (instantaneous) *erremedio* (to repair):

Simple instantaneous repair.

zolder (ceiling) *zo-olde-er., zohi* (sod) *oldei* (moss) *eraman* (to carry):

It carries the mossy sod.

CREATING A "GENETIC" RELATIONSHIP

We have no way to tell where the basic rules for the creation of the Germanic languages were first laid down. The original powerhouse of Germanic language-creation was apparently in York, England, where Alcuin had been the undisputed master of the grammarians and language teachers. In 782, after many years in York, England, Alcuin had joined Charlemagne at his Palace school in Aachen where he functioned as headmaster and motivator, as he had done before in York (see chapter on the Benedictines in Germany). It may have been Alcuin, the master organizer, who oversaw the development of the basic structure and grammar of Dutch and German. What is more important is to realize that all three languages had been totally invented, and were not evolved naturally. The rules laid down by the Benedictines were generally adhered to in the creation of the vocabulary, but exactly what these rules were, is still to be researched.

However it was done, the job was done so professionally that linguists at the University of Pennsylvania have been able to "prove without a doubt" the ex- istence of the "genetic" relationship, through "advanced computer analysis"

(Johnson).

This contrived relationship between English, Dutch and German is best shown by analyzing a number of words which display an "obvious genetic" relationship to each other. An attempt has been made to identify the word (shown in CAPITALS) which appears closest to the Basque language and it is assumed that this was the originally created word. The other two words were then supposedly touched up according to the rules laid down for each language. In case the words are all alike, no word was capitalized. As usual the "b" and "v or f" are interchangeable, so are "c" and "k"; the sharp "sch" is always written as "x" in Basque.

ENGLISH-DUTCH-GERMAN

BAKERY-bakkerij-Bäckerei: .ba-ake-eri, *ebadura* (slice of bread) *akeita* (coffee) *eri* (village): **"A slice of bread with coffee."**

BEAKER-beker-Becher: .be-ake-er., *uberka* (water container) *akeita* (coffee) *erion* (to pour from): **"Container to pour coffee from."**

BEAR-beer-BäR: ber, *berbizi* (to wake up): **"(Run, he is) waking up."**

bee-BIJ-Biene: *bai zera* (come away, come on). **"Get away!"**

BLOOD-bloed-Blut: .b.-.lo-od, eba-alo-odo, *ebakidura* (wound) *alor* (farmer) *odolisurle* (bloody): **"the farmer's bloody wound."**

blue-BLAAUW-BLAU: from *blaust* (blow on the eye), a "blue" eye, in English called a blackeye. **"A blue eye."**

Boer-BOER(farmer)-Bauer: *buru* (people); **"People."**

(on) board-AAN BOORD-AN BORD *borda* (ship's cabin); **"Ship's cabin."**

boat-boot-Boot: bota (to launch); To launch. or: bo-at, *bota* (to launch) *atoitu* (to drag): **"Dragging the boat (over the beach) to launch"**

bow(for arrows)-BOOG-BOGEN *boga* (to bend; **"To bend."**

BOOK-BOEK-Buch: buka, *bukatze* (finishing?); **"Are you finished?"**

boom (floating timber)-boom (tree)-BAUM: .bau-um, *abaunza* (mass of branches) *umo* (ripe, full grown): **"Mass of full-grown branches."**

break-BREEK-brechen: bre-ek, berre-eki, *berregin* (to re-do, to repair) *ekinaldi* (attempt): **"Attempt to repair."**

bread-brood-BROT: .bro-ot., *abaro* (shady place) *otarre* (basket): **"Put the basket in a shady place."**

bench-BANK-BANK: bank, *banku* (bench): **"Bench."**

BOSS-baas-böse (angry): *boz* (voice); **"Voice."**

butter-BOTER-Butter: .bo-ote-er., *eboluzionatu* (to produce) *ote* (perhaps) *eragin* (to churn): **"Perhaps produce it by churning."**

camp-kamp-Kamp: *kanpo* (outdoors); **"Outdoors."**

cantata-cantate-Kantate: .ka-an.-.ta-atu, *ekarpen* (contribution) *anaitu* (in unity) *atalkide* (member) *atutxa* (better world); **"In unity the members make a contribution toward a better world."**

card-kaart-KARTE *karta* (letter), **"Letter."**

cellar-KELDER-Keller: ke-eldar., *kentze* (to put away) *eldarniagarri* (delirious): **"Put him away, he is delirious."**

CHALICE-schaal-Schale: txali-is, *txalin* (wooden dish) *isurki* (liquid): **"Wooden dish for liquids."**

chamber-KAMER-KAMMER: kamar, *errekamara* (chamber):
"Chamber." (erre comes from *erretiroa*: to retire to).

cheese-KAAS-Käse: ka-as., *kario* (expensive) *asezin* (craving): **"Expensive craving."**

chest-KIST-KISTE ki-ist., *kinkila* (drygoods) *isterbabes* (protection):
"Protection for drygoods."

cloister-KLOOSTER-KLOSTER: .k.-.lo-oste-er, *akordio* (tradition) *ologi* (to feed oatbread) *oste* (large numbers of people) *erratu* (to wander, to travel):
"It is a tradition that oatbread is fed to large numbers of travellers."

coach-koets-KUTSCHE *kutsha*, kutxa (box, chest): **"(Large) box."**

coast-KUST-Küste: ku-ust, eku-uste, *ekuru* (quietly) *uste* (hopeful): **"Quietly hopeful."**

come-KOMEN-kommen: komen, *komeni* (to be helpful). **"Be helpful."**

cook-KOK-Koch: *kok* (bellyfull); **"Bellyfull."**

corn-KOREN-Korn: .ko-oren; eko-oren; *ekoitzi* (to produce) *orrenbeste* (same amount again):
"Produce the same amount again."

CRUST-korst-Kruste: currust, *kurrustu* (crust): **"Crust."**

DARK-DONKER-dunkel: donker, *donkeria* (evil, bad); "Evil," bad. or: **DARK:** da-ark., *dardara* (trembling) *arkaitzulo* (cave): **"Trembling in the cave."**

DAY-dag-Tag: dai, *daigun* (let's): **"Let's go."**

dead-DOOD-tot: .do-od., edo-odo, *edonon* (everywhere) *odol* (blood):
"Blood everywhere."

door-DEUR-Tür: deu-eur, *deuseztatu* (to shut out) *euriketa* (rain storm):
"Shut out the rainstorm."

double-dubbel-DOPPEL do-ope-el, *odolberoko* (spontaneous) *opetsi* (to offer) *elexurikeria* (adulation, applause): **"Spontaneously to offer applause, bis...bis!"**

DRAGON-DRAAK-Drache: .dra-ago-on., dura-ago-on., *adurra* (to drool) *ago* (mouth) *onargaitz* (intolerable) **"Drooling from the mouth is intolerable."**
or from:

DRAAK: dura-ak., adurra (to drool) *akarraldi* (in anger): **"He drools in anger."**

(A)DRIFT-(OP) DRIFT-(Ab)trift: dri-ifi-it, *iduri* (it appears) *ifili* (to be) *ito* (to drown, to go down): **"It appears to be going down."** (ifili is now spelled *ibili*).

drunk-BEDRONKEN-betrunken: .be-ed.-.ro-onki-in.; obe-eda-aro-onki-in; *obegipeko* (favourite) *edan* (drink) *arrotzetxe* (inn) *onkide* (round on the house) *inor* (everyone);
"His favourite drink in the inn is the round on the house for everyone."

dumb-dom-DUMM:du-um, idu-ume, *iduri* (to appear) *umekeria* (childish):
"Appears to be childish."

eat-ETEN-essen: *eten* (interruption). **"Interruption."**

evil-euvel-ÜBEL: *ubel* (purple), the favourite color of the Priestess. **"Evil."**

FAME-faam-famos: *fama* (fame); **"Fame."**

FAR-ver-fern: far, *ifar* (north): **"North."**

FAULT-fout-Fehler: *falta* (error); **"Error."**

feast-feest-FEST: fa-est., *afa* (happy) *este* (intestine): **"Happy intestine."**

fever-fieber-Fieber: .fi-ibe-er., *abiatu* (to begin) *ibeni* (to put on) *erremedio* (remedy);
"Begin with putting on a remedy."

fiddle-FIDEEL (jovial)-fidel (jolly): .fi-id.-.de-el., *ifili* (to be) *idekoki* (appropriately) *ederton* (appreciative) *elaberritsu* (jovial): **"Be appreciative and appropriately jovial."**

field-VELD-FELD: fa-eld., *afa* (happy) *eldu* (to ripen): **"Happy to (see it) ripen."**

FINGER-vinger-FINGER: .fi-ingir, .bi-ingir., *ibili* (to act) *ingiratu* (to be repugnant):
"To act repugnantly."

fiord-fjord-Fjord: fa-jor.-di, *afa* (happy) *jori* (abundance) *di* (place of),
"Place of happy abundance."

FLAG-vlag-Flagge: f.-.lag, afa-alaig, *afa* (happy) *alaigarri* (comforting).
"Happily comforting."

fleet-VLOOT-Flotte: *flota* (fleet);   "Fleet."

folk-volk-Volk: bolk, *boladak* (group of people).   "Group of people."

FRIEND-vriend-Freund: f.-.rend, *afa* (happy) *arrendu* (to call upon):
"Happy to call upon."

fusilier-FUSELIER-Füsilier: fa-uz.-elir, *afa* (happy) *uzkali* (to vanquish) *elikera* (food);
"Happily vanquishing food."

GARDEN-gaarde-Garten: *jardun* (to be busy with): (probably borrowed from France.)
"To be busy with."

good-goed-GUT: gut, *gutizia* (desire, longing).   "Desire."

gradual-GRADAAL (archaic)-graduell: .g.-.ra-ada-al; igo-ora-ada-al; *igon* (to grow tall) *oraindanik* (from now on) *ardaketa* (branching out) *aldaezinez* (constantly);
"From now on it will grow tall and branch out constantly."

grain-GRAAN-Grän: garan, *garaun* (grain);   "Grain."

grey-GRIJS-grau: *gris* (grey);   "Grey."

hand-hand-Hand: hand, *handiera* (extension).   "Extention."

honey-honing-HONIG: ho-oni-ig., *ahobeteko* (tasteful) *onizan* (useful) *igita* (harvest);
"Useful and tasty harvest."

house-huis-HAUS: hau-aus, *haundi* (large) *ausarki* (abundantly, more than enough):
"More than large enough."

HEATHER-heide-Heide: heder, *hederia* (bundled together, broom);
"Bundled together, broom."

king-KONING-König: kon-ing, *konde* (nobleman) *ingira* (disposition),
"Nobleman's disposition."

kitchen-KEUKEN-Küche: .ke-euki-in; *ikertu* (to examine) *eukitzaile* (contents) *inoizka* (from time to time);   "Examine the contents from time to time."

knee-knie-Knie: .k.-.ni, ika-ani, *ikaradun* (frightened) *anitzetan* (often).
"Frightened often (weak-kneed)."

lamb-lam-Lamm: la-am.-.b., ala-amai, *alai* (joyful) *amaigabeko* (endless) *abeltegi* (sheepfold):
"Endlessly joyful in the sheepfold."

lead-LOOD-Lot: *lodi* (overweight);   "Overweight."

lick-LIKKEN-lecken: *likin* (sticky);   "Sticky."

life-leven-LEBEN: .le-eban, *ele* (story) *ebanjelio* (gospels): "The story of the Gospels."

lust-lust-Lust: luzt, *luzatu* (to prolong, to stretch out):   "To prolong, make it last."

MAGIC-magie-Magie: ma-agi-ik, *ama* (mother, Priestess) *agindu* (command) *ikarakortu* (to be afraid of):   "Be afraid of the Priestess' command."

MAID-meid-Maid: ma-aid., *ama* (mother's) *aide* (relative); "Mother's relative."

MARKET-markt-Markt: me-erkat, *eme* (woman) *erkatu* (to compare):
"The women compare."

matey-MAAT-MAAT: ma-at, *ama* (mother's) *ateka* (bad moment);
"Mother's bad moment."

meager-MAGER-MAGER: ma-ager, *ama* (mother's) *ager* (appearance);
"Mother's appearance."

meal-MAAL-Mahl: ma-al, *ama* (mother's) *altzokada* (apron full); "Mother's apron full."

meteor-meteor-Meteor: me-ete-e.or, *mendi* (mountain) *ete* (perhaps) *ehortziri* (to bury):

"Perhaps to bury itself in the mountain."

metal-metaal-Metal: me-eta-al, *emendatu* (to increase) *eta* (amount) *al* (power, strength):
"To increase our strength."

midst-MIDDEN-Mitte: mi-iden, umi-iden, *umildu* (to be humble) *identifikatu* (to detect, identify)
"Too humble to be identified."

milk-melk-Milch: .me-elk., *emeta* (gently) *elki* (to empty); "Empty gently."

moon-MAAN-Mond: ma-an, ama-anu, *ama* (mother) *anu* (fainting);
"Mother's fainting."

mouse-muis-MAUSE: ma-aus, ama-auzo, *ama* (mother) *auzogabetu* (to move away):
"Mother runs away."

NAIL-nagel-Nagel: nai-il, *nai* (wish) *il* (death): "Deathwish."

needle-naald-NADEL: .na-ade-el, *anaia* (brother) *adelu* (finery) *elkarbatu* (to stitch together
"Stitch the brother's finery together."

neighbour-buur-NACHBAR: *nabari* (obvious, in sight): "In sight."

NIGHT-nacht-Nacht: nait, *naitaezko* (inevitable): "Inevitable."

nose-neus-NASE: nasa, *arnasa* (to breathe): "To breathe."

powder-POEDER-Puder: .po-ede-er, *opor* (time off) *ederreztatu* (to beautify) *ereti* (occasion):
"Take time off to beautify yourself for the occasion."

rest-RUST-Rast: ru-ust, arru-uste, *arrunt* (simple) *uste* (trust): "Simple trust."

red-rood-ROT: rot, arrot, *arrotu* (flushed): "Flushed face."

rider-ruiter-REITER: rai-tor, *arrai* (gentle) *aitor* (legendary patriarch), probably referring to St.Boniface. "Gentle legendary patriarch."

right-RECHT-RECHT: re-ekt, are-ekit, *arren* (please) *ekite* (to persevere):
"Please persevere."

rime (hoarfrost)-RIJP (pron: raip)-reif: .rai-aip., *arraitasun* (brightness) *aipa* (to mention);
"Mention the brightness."

SALMON-zalm-Salm: .za-al.-.mo-on, iza-ale-emo-on., *izate* (nature) *alegera* (rejoicing)
emonkortasun (generosity) *onarketa* (welcome): "We rejoice in nature's welcome generosity."

salt-zout-SALTZE: saltze, *gesaltze* (to melt).

scratch-KRAS-Kratzen: karras, *karrask* (scrape, scratch): "Scratch."

seldom-ZELDEN-selten: .zel-den, ezel-den; *ezelan* (somehow) *denbora ediren* (find time);
"Somehow find time."

send-ZENDEN-senden: .zen-den., izen-denok; *izeneztatu* ((signed by) *denok* (all of us);
"Signed by all of us."

ship-SCHIP-Schiff: .ski-ip, aski-ipu, *askitan* (many times, often) *ipurterre* (restless, sleepless):
"Many sleepless nights."

In Dutch the captain of the "schip" is called a "skipper" which therefore still retains the original "k."

shit-skyt/SKOIT: (Friesian)-Scheisse: .sho-it., exo-ito, *exorzizatu* (cast out, eliminate) *itoi* (filth):
"Eliminate filth."

short-kort-KURTZ: .ku-urtz, aku-urtz; *akuilatu* (to stimulate/bring about) *urtzintz* (sneeze);
"To stimulate a sneeze."

sing-zingen-singen: ing, *zingle* (delicate): "Delicate (voice)."

singe-verzengen-SENGEN: .zeng, *izengabetu* (to discredit): "Discredited (burned his
fingers)."

sink-ZINKEN-senken: .zin-ken; *ezindu* (incapacitated/unable) *kendu* (to avoid);
"Unable to avoid."

sister-ZUSTER-schwester: zuzter, *zuztertu* (growing up fast): "Growing up fast."

soldier-SOLDAAT-SOLDAT: .so-olda-at; *osoki* (totally) *oldar* (brave) *atxikimendu* (faithful/devoted);
"Totally brave and devoted."

soul-ZIEL-Seele: .zi-il, ezi-ilo; *ezik* (without) *ilordu* (hour of death); **"Deathless."**

stone-steen-STEIN: stai-in, *estai* (stay put) *indar* (strong, firm);

"Stays firmly in place."

storm-storm-STURM: stu-uri-im., *astundu* (to become heavy) *urizapparada* (downpour)
imitazio (repeat):   **"The downpour becomes heavy again."**

street-STRAAT-Strasse: sta-arrat, *asta* (donkey) *arrate* (narrow passage):

"Donkey's narrow passage."

SUGAR-suiker-Zucker: su-uga-ar, isu-uga-ara, *isuri* (to flow) *ugari* (abundant) *aratz*
(pure);   **"Flowing abundant and
pure."**
Probably from zugar (elm and rowan tree) tapped for sap in the spring.

supple-soepel-n.a.: su-upe-el, isu-upe-ela, *isuri* (to inspire, to cause) *upeohol* (stave) *elastiko*
(malleable):   **"To cause the stave to become malleable."**

sweat-zweet-SCHWITZE: xu-itze, *xukatu* (to mop up) *itzetik mustuka* (quickly with the
cloth).   **"Quickly mop up with the cloth."**

SWELLING-zwelling-Schwellung: .se-ela-ali-ing., *iseka egin* (to make fun of) *elastiko*
(bump/swelling) *alizan* (noticeable/capable) *ingurualdi* (round);

"Poking fun of a noticeable round bump."

thumb-duim-DAUME: dau-um., *daukat* (I have) *umoretsu* (fun).

"Thumb up, I have fun."

tobacco-TABAK-TABAK: ta-bake, *taldeko* (of the group, tribe) *bake* (peace); (Smoking the
peace pipe):   **"At peace with the tribe."**

true-trouw-TRAU: ta-arau, *ta* (slapping) *arau* (discipline): **"Slapping discipline."**

under-ONDER-unter: *ondar* (bottom):   **"Bottom."**

wall (wattle)-wal-Walle: wattle, *atela* (place of door opening): The "w" is usually meaningless.

"Place of the door opening."

warp-WERP-Wurf: erp, *erpintsu* (pointed):   **"Pointed."**

WATER-WATER-Wasser: ater, *atera* (to get).   **"Go get it."**

weather-weder-WETTER: etor, *etorki* (expecting). **"(What to) expect?"**

weave-weef-WEBE: ebe, eba, *ebaki* (making decisions). **"Making decisions."**

wife-wijf-WEIB: Weibe, ai-be, *ai* (strong desire) *be'ar* (necessity, indispensable):

"Strong desire for the indispensable."

wind-wind-Wind: ind, *indar* (strength, force).   **"Hard blow."**

wood-hout-HOLTZ: *oholtza* ("pile of lumber"). **Wood** could come from ud- *udare* (pear
wood).   **"Pear wood?"**

WORD-woord-Wort: ord, *ordainbide* (promisory note): **"Promise."**

work-WERK-WERK: erk, *erakarpen* (contribution).   **"Contribution."**

world-WERELD-Welt: ereld, *eraldatu* (to reform, to renew); the world was to be made
over.   **"To reform, to be renewed."**

yellow-geel-GELB: *gelbera* (hesitant, afraid):   **"Afraid."**

YESTERDAY-gisteren-gestern: .ie-este-er.-.da-a.i, aie-este-ere-eda-ahi: *aieneka* (grieving)
estemin (intestinal pain) *eregu* (indulging) *edate* (drinking) *ahituezin* (endless):

"Grieving with intestinal pain after indulging in endless drinking."

FRIESIAN PLACE NAMES

I will include here a list of the Friesian Islands, of which there are more than 50, now divided between the Netherlands, Germany and Denmark. With a bit of imagination and goodwill the names of these islands can be translated with the use of the Basque dictionary which confirms the same underlying language. Here are some:

Friesian islands belonging to the Netherlands.

Texel, the most westerly of all the islands: tek-sil, *tekadun* (having pods) *silo* (storage barn): "Storage barn for the pea and bean harvest." It must have been a high and prominent feature, clearly seen from the sea.

Vlieland, bili-landa, *bili* (to and fro) *landa* (region): "To and fro region?"

Terschelling, tera-schilin: *tera* (to, towards) *txilin* (tinkling bells, community pasture): "To the community pasture" where all the animals have bells to ward off bad spirits and dangers, and also to be heard and found.

Ameland, ame-landa, *amets* (strong desire, longing for) *landa* (country-side, region): "I long for my country-side"; it still is a wonderful place to be.

Schiermonnikoog, txir-mon-nik-oga, *txir* (oyster) *mondar* (beach) *nik* (my) *ogasun* (property): "My private oyster beach."

Rottum, rot-um, *arrotsu* (proud) *ume* (child): "Proud little island."

Urk, (island in the middle of the Zuider Zee); it may have had the Friesian corpse-exposure facility for the departed. If so, here the bodies were exposed to the air so the soul would be released from the body and proper re-incarnation could take place. The bones were later bundled together and placed in a tribal tomb. This practice was continued by the R.C. church which to this day displays the bones of many martyrs and Saints in glass show-cases. In early "Christian" times this holy site was desecrated by "*urka*" (gallows).

Some Friesian islands belonging to Germany

Borkum, bor-kum, *borda* (hut) *kuma* (cradle), "Hut with a cradle."

Juist, ju-ist, *jujatu* (to judge, evaluate) *istil* (mud): "Judge/evaluate the mud."

Baltrum, bal-trum, *bala* (profusion) *trumoi* (thunder clap): "A profusion of thunder claps."

Langeoog, langa-og, *langa* (barrier, fence) *ogasun* (property): "Fenced property."

Spiekeroog, sop-iker-og, *sopi* (soppy wet) *ikerketa* (to explore) *ogasun* (property): "Soaking wet I explored the property."

Minsener, min-senar, *min* (in pain) *senar* (husband): "My husband is in pain."

Oldoog, old-og, *oldar* (attack) *ogasun* (property): "Attack on the property."

Scharhorn, xar-horn, *xare* (small net) *horni* (supplying food): "Small net for supplying food."

Eiderstadt, ei-dor-suta-d., *ei* (they say) *dator* (he is coming) *sutargi* (home, homefire) *-da* (for/to me): "They say he is coming home to me."

Süderoog, sudur-og, *sudur* (sticking out, far out) *ogasun* (property): "Far out property."

Rantum, rant-um, *arrantzu* (large catch of fish) *ume* (child): "The child caught a lot of fish."

Some Friesian islands belonging to Denmark.

Jorsand, jor-sand, *joritsu* (rich) *santujale* (devout): "Rich and devout" (person).

Rømø, ro-mo, *arro* (proud, upright) *modu* (manner): "Proud/upright manner."

Koresand, korru-sant, *korru* (circle) *santujale* (devout, religious): "Holy (stone) circle?" Was this one of the many pre-Christian stone circles found all over the Atlantic coast of Europe and North Africa?

Kilsand, kil-sant, *kili* (gentle) *santujale* (devout): "Gentle and devout" (owner?)

Fanø, *fano* (horsepasture): "Horse pasture."

Skallingen, ska-al.-ling-en., *sikatu* (dry out) *alik ondoen* (as well as possible) *lingirda* (seaweed) *-enetan* (always): "Always dry out the seaweed as well as possible."

Ho Bugt, ho-bukat, *aho* (mouth) *bukatu* (inlet): "Mouth of the inlet (this is a channel)."

Blåvands huk, bla-band-huk, *bila* (searching for) *banda* (direction) *hukiketa* (point of contact): "Searching for direction to our point of contact."

Some other Friesian names.

Bolsward, bol-su-ard, *bolada* (occasion) *su* (fight, brawl) *ardo* (wine): "On occasion a drunken brawl."

Franeker, f.-.ran-neker, *afa* (happy) *arran* (bells) *nekarazi* (tired of): "I'm tired of the happily tingling bells."

Harlingen, (the main harbour): har-ling-en, *harri* (stones) *lingirda* (slime, seaweed) *-enetan* (always): "The stones are always slimy."

Lemmer, (harbour on the south-west coast), *lemar* (helmsman).

Ljouwert, L-jau-ert, (L:?) *jaundu* (to dominate) *erd* (centre): "Dominates the centre."

Marknesse, mark-neska, *markatu* (to wave) *neska* (unmarried young woman): "A young woman is waving."

Sneek, sine-ek, *sinesgarri* (testimony) *ekinaldi* (persistence): "Testimony to persistence."

Ulrum, uler-um, *uler* (to understand) *ume* (child): "I understand the child."

Wirdum, uhir-du-um, *uhir* (naughty) *du* (he has) *ume* (child): "She has a naughty child."

Zurich, *zurik* (flatterer): "Flatterer."

THE ORIGIN OF GERMAN

What we call the "German language," the Germans call "Deutsch." Where did the word "Deutsch" come from? It should come as no surprise that monks, being religious types, hid biblical phrases in important words. As they used the VCV vowel interlocking formula for word-agglutination, vowel-linking was required. In this case the diphthong (double vowel) of both words overlaps:

"deu – eutsch,"
deun (Lord) – *eutsi* (to keep)
"The Lord keep you."

This is obviously an abbreviation of "May the Lord bless you and keep you" (Numbers 6:24). The word "Deutsch" may have been designed at first as a greeting (In Basque the "s" is always pronounced with a slight "sh"). The Dutch language is called "Diets" in Holland and is said to be a derivative of "deutsch," but no, it comes from *.di-its.*, *adi-itze*: *adibegiratu* (pay close attention to) *itzeman* (promise): "Pay close attention to your promises" or **"Be true to your word,"** or as they sing in Holland: "Een man, een man, een woord, een woord."

FIRST SOME GEOGRAPHICAL NAMES

Consider the name of the river Rhine. The Germans write it **"Rhein"** (same pronounciation). The river was renowned as the world's most productive salmon river. So much salmon was caught in the Rhine until one century ago that many domestic servants in cities along the river had clauses in their contracts saying that the servant would not be obliged to eat salmon more than twice a week. It is not surprising that the Basque word for **fish** is *arrain*. Put "ar" in front of

"Rhine" and you know where the name came from.

The name **"Berlin"** is slightly more complicated. The monks assembled it from three words:

.be-erli-in.
abe-erli-inu
abergikor – erlijiozale – inurritze
hospitable – pious – inspiring
"A hospitable, pious and inspiring town."

These words sound like they belong on the town's coat of arms, which happens to depict a bear. "Berlin" does sounds like a little bear, however; bear in Basque is *hartz*, which is the name of the well-known mountainous area west of Berlin.

Lorelei:

.lo – ore – ele – ei
lotsagabeki – orekatu – eleztatu – eia
brazenly – to balance – to call – come here!
"Brazenly balanced (on the cliff) they call: Come to us."

The name of the fortified city of **"Stettin"** takes more time to decode but still conforms strictly to the VCV formula:

.s.-.te-et.-.ti-in.
asa-ate-eta-ati-inu:
asaldatze – aterpe – eta – atxikitzaile – inurritu
rioting – refuge – and – supporter – to inspire
"A refuge from the rioting and inspiration for our supporters."

On the other hand the name **"Lübeck"** falls quickly into place:

lu-ube-ek.,
lu-ube-eka
luzarotu – uberka – ekaizte
to last a long time – water reservoir – rain storm
"The reservoir will last for a long time (after) a big rain storm."

Tirol is an easy one:

tiro-ol
tirokaldi (shooting) *oldartu* (to begin, to start)
shooting – to begin/start
"Start shooting" or "Shoot."
This may have something to do with Wilhelm Tell's legend.

Or **Yodel**,

jo-del
jo – delako
to sing – supposed to be
"It's supposed to be singing."

BASQUE IS HEARD EVERYWHERE IN GERMANY

Wherever we go in Germany, it is impossible to get away from Basque-related language, the place names, the family names, the mountains, even in music. In the well-known song "Ein Heller und ein Batzen," the Heller buys a drink of water, the Batzen buys a glass of wine. Heller comes from *ele-er*, *ele* (story) *erdi* (half): "half a story," we would say **"for a song."** Batzen comes from *bat-zen*: *bat* (one) *zenbatu* (to count): **Count one.** In the past, several German and other European students in linguistics have pointed out this unexplained relationship between Basque and German, especially in southern Germany, closer to the Alps where the pre-Christian language survived the longest and still is used in several isolated valleys in a number of dialects called Rhaeto-Romance or Ladin. However, like everywhere else in Europe and North America, the suggestion that the Germans spoke Basque before they spoke German was always squashed by more senior academics with the words: "That relationship has been looked into so many times and it doesn't exist." But none of them has been able to show where the results of this "looking into" was published. Things haven't changed; ask at any university and you will find that similar answers are still given. To these people the suggestion that German is an invented language, and created by the Benedictine monks with formulaic manipulation of Basque, is heresy. In an effort to overcome this problem I will show the Basque origin of a large number of German words.

THE MONKS HAD FUN DOING THEIR TASK

The monk-grammarians, assembling these words, had a lot of fun doing their work. Their number one rule was to create words which were totally unlike Basque. This was done by building into the new language peculiarities which would make the artificiality unrecognizable from Basque. In this assignment they succeeded admirably. As shown in my comments on the Auraicept, they themselves admitted to having great pride in new word construction and introducing their creations to the public. They also liked their beer and wine as the

German word **"Kanne"** (jug, can) shows, from *.ka-anne, aka-anu, akabu* (sublime) *anu* (passing out, bliss): **sublime bliss.** Consider **"Kugel"** (bullet): *.ku-ugel, uku* (awry) *ugalpen* (reproduction): **"reproduction gone awry"**; they couldn't be more right because that's what a bullet is supposed to do! Or German **"Fest"** (feast), from *f.-est, afa* (pleasing) *este* (intestine): **Pleasing the intestine.** The German vocabulary is full of such hidden wise-cracks.

In Basque very few words start with "f," none start with "r" and none end with "m." These were peculiarities which the grammarians could exploit. Our English and German dictionaries are balanced, with the first 13 letters (A-M) taking up half of the dictionary and the last 13 (N-Z) the other half. The Basque dictionary is quite different in that about 80% of all Basque words are found in A-M. The grammarians made every effort to tidy up this imbalance with the result that most European dictionaries are now balanced.

THE USE OF THE LETTER "F"

The early grammarians made prolific use of the letter "F" by creating many words which made the letter more prominent. The word most often selected to provide the "f" was *afa* or *fa* meaning "happy" or "pleasing." Words that could remotely be associated with happiness or pleasing, were then started with "f." An idea about the monks' attitude toward women is seen in "Frau," fa – arau, meaning **"Happy (under/with) discipline."** I have a feeling that the meaning of the word "Weib" (see below) is much more acceptable to modern women. Almost without exception, the letters following the "f" were clearly recognizable Basque words, easily translated. In the case of "Freund," the English equivalent "friend" is closer to Basque; Freund was likely adapted from English. Note that for many of these agglutinations the standard vowel-linking rule has been ignored.

Fabel (fable): *fa-abel, afa* (happy) *abel* (herdsman): "Happy herdsman."
Faden (string): *fa-adin, fabore* (help, relieve) *adinagin* (wisdom tooth): "Relieve the wisdom tooth."
Fabrik (factory): *fa-abriko, afa* (happy) *aberriko* (patriotic): "Happily patriotic."
Fahne (flag): *.fa-anai, afa* (happy) *anaiti* (united): "Happily united."
Fakkel (flare, torch): *fa-akkel, faltadun* (guilty) *akelarre* (witch): "Guilty witch." She had to be torched.
Feier (celebration): *.f.-aier, afa* (happy) *aier* (tendency): "Tendency to be happy."
Feld (field): *.f.-eldu, afa* (happy) *eldu* (to ripen): "Happy (to see it) ripen."
Fest (feast): *.f.-este, fa* (pleasing) *este* (glut, intestine): "Pleasing the intestine."
Festung (fortress): *f.-estun, familiar* (familiar) *estune* (narrow street): "Familiar narrow streets."
Feuer (home fire): *f.-eur, familiarki* (familiarly) *euren* (theirs, their own): "Familiarly their own."

Finger (finger): *f.-ingur, fabore* (help) *inguratu* (grip): "Helping hand/grip."

Fish (fish): *.f.-ish, afa* (happy) *isho* (quiet): "Happy and quiet."

Fjord (fiord): *.f.-jor-di, afa* (happy) *jori* (abundance) *-di* (place of): "Happy place of abundance."

Flagge (flag): *.f.-.laig, afa* (happy) *alaigarri* (comforting): "Happily comforting."

Flucht (escape): *f.-.luk-et, faltsu* (deceptive) *alukeria* (stupid action) *et* (warning): "Warning: a deceptive and stupid action."

Forst (forest): *.f..orritz, afa* (happy) *orritza* (foliage): "Happy foliage."

Fort (stronghold): fa-ort, *faboredun* (favoured) *ortzeune* (heavenly peace): "Favoured heavenly peace."

Forum (tribunal): *f.-orru-um, afa* (happy) *orru* (roaring) *umeki* (childish): "Happy childish roaring."

Fossil (fossil): *f.-osi-il, farra-farra* (profusely) *osi* (deep down) *il* (dead): "Profusely deep down but dead."

Frage (question): *.f.-.rag., afa* (happy) *aragitu* (to assimilate, to join): "Happy to join."

Frass (feed): *f.-.ras, familiar* (familiar) *arasa* (cupboard): "Mother's cupboard."

Fratz (naughty child): *f.-.ratz, fa* (happy) *aratz* (brilliant, bright): "Happy and bright."

Frau (wife): *f-rau*, fa-arau, *fa* (happy) *arau* (discipline): "Happy with/under discipline."

frech (cheeky): *f.-.rek, fa* (happy) *arek* (that one): "That one is happy."

Fremd (foreigner): *f.-.rem-d, afa* (happy) *arreman* (relationship) *da* (he has): "He has a happy relationship."

Freund (friend): *.f.-.rend, afa* (happy) *arrendu* (to call upon): "Happy to call upon."

Friede (peace): *.f.-.rid., afa* (happy) *arridu* (surprise): "Happy surprise."

frölich (joyfull): *f.-.ro-olig, afa* (happy) *aro* (everybody) *oligetan* (joking): "Everybody happily joking."

fromm (pious): *f.-.ro-om, afa* (happy) *arroki* (proudly) *omendatu* (to praise): "Happy and proudly praising."

Fron (enforced labour): *f.-.ron, famababe* (infamous) *arronategi* (stony place): "Infamous stony place."

Fuchs (fox): *f.-uk.-.s., afa* (happy) *ukatu* (to deny) *asekeria* (gluttony): "Happy to deny his gluttony."

Fuchtel (whipping): *f.-ukat-el., faltsuki* (falsely) *ukatz* (deny) *ele* (story): "He falsely denied the story."

Fug (justly): *.f.-ug., afa* (happy) *ugal* (abundance): "Happy abundance."

Fuhre (cartload): *.f.-urre, afa* (happy) *urreko* (nearby): "Happy it's nearby."

führen (to lead): *.f.-urren, afa* (happy) *urrengo* (following): "Happy to follow."

Führer (leader): *f.-urrer, afa* (happy) *urreratu* (to draw near, come close to): "Happy to come close to."

Fülle (abundance): *f.-ule, afa* (happy) *ule* (hair): "Happy full head of hair."

Funk (spark): *f.-unek, faro* (flash) *uneko* (instantaneous): "Instantaneous flash."

Funsel (miserable lamp): *f.-untzil, farol* (lantern) *untzil* (crewman): "Crewman's lantern."

Furcht (fear): *f.-urkat, famagabe* (vile) *urkatze* (hanging, execution): "Vile hanging."

Furore (sensation): *f.-ur-ore, faltsuki* (falsely) *ur* (water) *ore* (bread, dough): "Falsely on water and bread."

Furz (fart): *f.-urez, faltatsy* (faulty, accidentally) *urezko* (watery, wet): "Accidentally watery."

Füsilier (fusilier): *f.-uz-eliker, afa* (happy) *uzkali* (to vanquish) *elikera* (food): "Happy to vanquish the food."

Fuss (foot): *f.-us, afa* (happy) *ustikatu* (to kick): "Happy to kick."

Fussel (fluff): *f.-utsal, afa* (happy) *utsaldi* (nothingness): "Happy nothingness."

Words Starting With "R"

No Basque word starts with "r," instead this letter is always preceded by a vowel or a vowel combined with a second "r," e.g. *aran* (plum), *arran* (cattle bell), *eri* (illness), *erri* (village), *iri* (city) *irri* (laugh, joke), *ore* (dough) *orre* (juniper tree), *ura* (this), *urra* (gold). The "rr" must be rolled, like the Scottish "r."

Rabulist (hairsplitter): *.ra-abu-uli-ist.*, *arra* (always) *aburu* (opiniated) *uli* (fly) *istilu* (disturber): "Always the opiniated fly disturber."

Rad (wheel): *.ra-ad.*, *arra* (repetitious) *ada* (noise): "Repetitious noise."

radikal (radical, utterly): *ra-adi-ika-al*, *arra* (repetition) *adi* (watch) out) *ikara* (terror) *al* (power): "Watch out for the terrorist's power."

Ramm (ram, batterer): *.ram*, *arramaska* (rush , haste): "Rush."

Reede (at anchor): *.redu.*, *aredun* (sandy): "Sandy (beach)."

Regel (rule): *.re-egil*, *arrendu* (to ask) *egile* (author): "Ask the author."

Regen (rain): *.re-egun*, *arre* (grey, bleak), *egun* (day): "Bleak day."

Regierung (government): *.re-egi-iri-ing*, *arrendu* (to request) *eginak* (works) iri (city) *ingurumari* (neighborhood). "Request the city to do works in our neighborhood."

Regiment (regiment): *.re-egi-mend*, *arean* (real) *-egi* (overwhelming) *mende* (authority): "Overwhelming authority."

Rettung (salvage): *.ret.-un.-.ng*, *arreta* (concern) *uni* (general) *inguru* (vicinity, nearby): "General concern nearby."

Ritter (knight): *.rit-tar*, *arritze* (admiration) *-tar* (member): "Admired member."

Roggen (rye): *.ro-ogun*, *arro* (soft) *ogun* (wheat): "Soft wheat."

Ruder (rudder): *.ru-udar*, *arrunt* (simple) *udare* (pear): i.e. lee-board. "Simply shaped like a pear."

Ruin (decay): *.ruin*, *urruin* (contempt, reject) "Reject."

Rüste (rest): *.ru-uste*, *arrunt* (simple) *uste* (trust): "Simple trust."

The Use of "V": A New Letter

The letter "v" does not exist in Basque. In German and Dutch the Latin "v" was introduced to displace the original "b" as was also done in the Romance languages.

veranker (to anchor, to moor): *ber-anker*, *ber* (repeat) *ankerkeria* (cruelty): "Repeated cruelty."

Verbau (rebuild): *ber-abaunza*, *ber* (repeat) *abaunza* (mass of branches): "Again get a mass of branches."

verbergen (to hide): *ber-berga*, *ber* (repeat) *berga* (rod, switch): "Again beaten with a rod."

verbiegen (to bend): *ber-bigun*, *ber* (repeat) *bigun* (malleable, bendable): "To bend again."

Verbund union (from Dutch verbond): *ber-bon-ond.*, *berezko* (spontaneous) *abonau* (to speak well of) *ondore* (future): "(He) will speak well (of it)."

verboten (to forbid): *ber-bota*, *bereala* (quickly) *bota* (to throw out): "Throw him out quickly."

verzerren (deformed): *bertzeren, bertzeren* (happens to someone else): "It happens only to someone else."

Volk (people, folk): *boladak, bolada* (group of people) *-ak* (plural): "Groups of people."

Vollmacht (full of power): *bol-makat, bolada* (group of people) *makatz* (wild): "Wild bunch of people."

Vollstange (bar): *bol-sut-ang, bolada* (group of people) *sutan ipini* (provoked) *ango* (local): "Provoked group of local people."

"W": The Letter Without Meaning

The "w" does not occur in Basque; it is an invention we could have done without. The invention of the "w" was another way to confuse the words borrowed from Basque. In general the "w" represented "u" or proved to be meaningless, however, it sometimes makes the new word sound and look quite different. The word "Welt" (world), "wereld" in Dutch, comes from Basque *eraldu* meaning: "to be reformed, to be renewed," which, no doubt, was the church leaders' stated religious and political objective. The "w" words were easier to sort out than the "v" words, almost as if the grammarians who made the "v" words had more detailed knowledge of the original language.

wachsen (to grow): *ak-zen, akuilu* (to spur, to grow up) *izan* (to be): "To be growing up."

Wald (forest): *ald., aldaerazi* (to transform): "To transform (into fields)."

Wasser (water): *ater, atera* (to go for, to get). "Go get it" (from Dutch water).

Webe (weaving, web): *eba, ebaki* (to make decisions). "Making decisions."

Welle (wave): *el.-.le, ela* (story) *alegera* (rejoicing): "Story of rejoicing."

Welt, from Dutch "wereld" (world): *erald, eraldatu* (to reform, renew, transform): "Reform (the world)."

Wende (turn): *ende, endekoi* (friendly): "Friendly (turn)."

Werk (work): *erak, erakarpen* (contribution): "Contribution."

Wetter (weather): *etor, etorki* (expecting, forecast): "Weather forecast."

Widder (battering ram): *idor, idor* (insensitive): "Insensitive."

Wiege (cradle): *ige, iges* (refuge): "Safe place."

Wind (wind): *ind., indar* (strength, force): "Force."

Wirt (host): *irte, irteera* (arrangement): "Arrangement."

Witz (joke): *itz, itzalgabe* (irreverent), "Irreverent."

Wolk (cloud): *olak, olako* (resemblance): "It looks like..."

Wonne (delight): *one, onen* (the best): "The best."

Wort (word): *ord, ordainbide* (promise): "Promise."

Wunder (wonder, surprise): *ondar, ondare* (inheritance): "Inheritance."

würgen (to choke): *urgain, urgain* (to float to the surface): "To float to the surface."

Some "EME" Words

eme, meaning "female," "woman," "child" or "peaceful," was usually abbreviated to *me* and used in a number of German and Dutch words. Here follows a small selection:

melden (to report): *.me-eldu-un.*, *eme* (woman) *eldu* (to arrive) *une* (place, here): "The woman is to arrive here."

Menge (amount, number): *.me-engai*, *emendatu* (to increase, overestimate) engainatu (to cheat): "To cheat by overestimating the amount."

merken (to notice): *.me-erka-an*, *eme* (woman) *erkatu* (to compare) *andika* (bulk, volume): "The woman compares the volume."

Mesner (sacristan): *.me-esnaer*, *eme* (woman) *esnaerale* (awakener): "Female awakener."

Messer (knife): *.me-eser*, *ume* (child) *eseri!* (sit down!): "Child, sit down!"

A similar list can be made up with words starting with **ama** or *ma*, meaning "mother," "priestess" or "goddess." Here are a few:

Magd (servant girl): *ma-agud*, *ama* (mother) *agudo* (diligent, active): "Diligent mother."

Magdalena (woman's name): *.ma-aguda-alen-a*, *ema* (mother) *agudota* (diligent) *alen* (totally) *a* (the): "The totally diligent mother."

Mahagony (mahogany, mahogoni): *.ma-ahogo-oni*, *ama* (mother) *ahogozo* (in good taste, favourite) *oniraun* (long lasting, durable): "Mother's favourite and durable wood."

Maid (maid): *.ma-aid*, *ama* (mother) *aide* (relative): "Mother's relative."

Mammut (mammoth): *ama-amu-ut*, *ama* (mother) *amure egon* (suspicious) *uts* (absence): "Mother is suspicious about its absence."

Words Used in German and Dutch, But Not in English

In the following pairs, German comes first, followed by Dutch:

Ärger – ergernis (annoyance): *erge-era-aniz*, *ergel* (foolish) *-era* (behaviour) *anitz* (frequent): "Frequent foolish behaviour."

Begriff – begrip (idea, conception): *begirap* (discretion), "Discretion."

Besen – bezem (broom): *besom*, *besomotz* (short arms): "Short arms."

Futsch – foetsie (poof, gone): *futz* (puff of air), "Puff of air."

frok – Frack (outer garment, dress coat): *fraka* (trousers), "Trousers."

gesund – gezond (healthy): *gizondu* (to grow up), "To grow up."

grob – grof (rude): *g.-.ro-ob*, *aga* (blow) *arozgo* (blacksmith) *obe* (better than): "Better than a blow from the blacksmith."

kahl – kaal (bald): *kalpar* (bald spot), "Bald spot."

Kitzler – kittelaar (used to be "kiddelaar": clitoris), *ki-ide-edi-ila-ar.*, uki-ide-edi-ila-ari; *ukitu* (to touch) *idekidura* (opening) *ediren* (hidden) *ilaje* (hair) *arin* (lightly/gently): "Gently touch the opening hidden by hair."

kauf (1)- koop (2) (purchase): 1) *kau-auf*, *kausitu* (to find) *aufa* (cry of happiness): "Happiness is finding." (2) *kopuru* (quantity): "Quantity."

Korb – korf (beehive, basket work): *kofau* (beehive), "Beehive."

Kraft – kracht (strength): *.k.-.ra-ak.-.t.*, eka-arra-aka-ata, *ekandu* (to be used to) *arranditsu* (boastful) *akabu* (superior)*atarramendu* (advantage): "Used to boasting about a superior advantage" (a show-off).

krachen (to crack, to burst): **kraken** (to crack, to crunch): *.k.-.ra-ake-en.*, aka-ara-ake-ene; *akabu* (the end of life) *aragikoi* (lustful) *akela* (witch) ene (screams of pain): "The life of the lustful witch ended in screams of pain."

Laster – laster (depravity, slander): *laster* (to press, push, force): "To force."

leiden – lijden (to suffer): *lai-aide-en*, *laida* (insult) *aide* (kinship) *-en* (superlative suffix, e.g. grievously): "Grievously insulted kinship."

Magen – maag (stomach): *.ma-aga*, *ama* (mother's) *aga* (abundance): "Mother's abundant (food)."

Messer – mes (knife): *.me-ese-er*, *ume* (child) *eseri* (sit down) *erabaki* (decision, order): "Child, Sit down!"

Mist – mest (manure): *me-est*, *mehatxu* (menace, threat) *estaldu* (to cover up): "Cover up the menace."

unartig – onaardig (rude, despicable): *un-arti-ig*, una-arti-iguin, *unagarri* (annoying) *artikulu* (article) *iguindu* (despicable): "Annoying despicable article."

Untat – ondaad (crime): *ondatu* (to ruin, to destroy), "To ruin, to destroy."

plötzlich – plotseling (suddenly): *.pi-ilo-otsa-ali-ing*, ipi-ilotz-otza-ali-ing, *ipini* (to throw) *ilotz* (cadaver) *otza* (wolf) *alienatu* (to destroy) *ingira* (composure): "Throw the cadaver of a wolf to destroy his composure." (What would his horse do?)

reigen – rijgen (to thread at a folk dance): *.rai-.gun*, *arraia* (line-up) *egun* (today): "Dance today."

Stadt – stad (city): *.stat*, *ostatu* (inn, hotel): "Inn."

Zweifel – twijfel (doubt): *tzai-aifel*, tzu-ufal, *tzu* (several) *ufaldi* (sighing): "Several are sighing. (That happens often when in doubt)."

Vieh – vee (cattle): *bei*, vei (cow): "Cow."

Verbesserung – verbetering (improvement): *bera-abe-bete-erri-ing*, *berarizko* (special) *abeltalde* (herd) *betekor* (productive) *erritartu* (to become naturalized/adapted) *ingurumen* (environment): "An especially productive herd to become adapted to our environment."

Wirt – waard (host): *irte*, *irteera* (arrangement): "Arrangement."

Wunder – wonder (surprise): *ondar*, *ondare* (inheritance): "Inheritance."

A RANDOM SELECTION OF GERMAN WORDS

Abend (evening): *abend.*, *abendu* (Advent): "Season before Winter Solstice."

Arbeit (work): *ar.-.be-it*, *arrastakari* (hard-working person) *abe* (family support) *itxaro* (to hope for): "I hope for a hard-working person as family support."

aufheben (to lift up): *aufa-eban*, *aufa* (cry of happiness) *ebanjelari* (evangelist): "Evangelist's cry of happiness."

auskerben (to indent, to notch): *auskor-ben*, *auskor* (fragile, easily dented) *benturaz* (perhaps): "Perhaps fragile."

Bakel (teacher's cane): *bakeal.*, *bakealdi* (to make peace): "It makes peace."

bauen (to build): *.baun*, *abaunza* (mass of branches): "Mass of branches (to build wicker walls)."

beherrschen (to control): *beher.-xe-en*, *behera* (under, below) *xedaketa* (limitation) *enetan* (always): "Always under limitation/control."

dunkel (dark) from Dutch "donker," *donker*, *donkeria* (evil, bad): "Bad."

Eber (boar): *eber.*, *ebertar* (Hebrew): "Wild boar."

euch (you, to you): *euk*, *euk* (you yourself): "You."

Eule (large moth): *eule, euli* (fly): "Fly."

gesund (healthy) from Dutch "gezond," *gizond, gizondu* (to mature, to grow older): "Growing older."

Gurgel (throat): *gurge, gurketa* (adoration, reverence): "Adoration."

Hand (hand): *handi, handiera* (extension): "Extention."

Haus (dwelling): *hau-aus, haundi* (large) *ausarki* (more than enough): "More than large enough."

Heim (home): *hei-im, hei* (shelter) *imaz* (place of woven branches): "Shelter of woven branches." (i.e. a wattle shelter.)

Himmel (heaven): *im.-.me-el., imaginatu* (to picture, image) *ametz* (dream) *ele* (story): "I pictured the story in my dreams."

Herzog (duke): *herts-og, hertsatu* (to coerce, extort) *ogi* (wheat): "He extorts wheat."

horch (hearken): *hork, horko* (pertaining, relevant to): "Relevant to."

Kamin (fireside): *kamain, kamaina* (miserable place to sleep, cow shed): "Miserable place to sleep."

Kanne (tankard): *aka-anu, aka* (sublime) *anu* (passing out, bliss): "Sublime bliss"

Karte (card): *karta, karta* (letter): "Letter."

Klage (complaint): *kla-age, klaskada* (snapping, swooshing) *age* (rod): "Swooshing rod."

klug (smart, shrewd): *kalku-uga, kalkulatzaile* (calculating) *ugari* (abundant, very): "Very calculating."

krank (ill): *ka-aran-ak, akabu* (final) *aran* (bell) *-ak* (plural): "Final bells."

Kummer (grief): *ku-umor, uku* (gone bad) *umor* (sense of humour): "Sense of humour is gone bad."

König from Dutch "koning" (king): *kon-ing, konde* (nobleman's) *ingira* (disposition): "Nobleman's disposition."

Kugel (bullet): *ku-ugal, uku* (gone bad, awry) *ugal* (reproduction): "Reproduction gone awry."

Küste (coast): *ku-uste, ekuru* (quietly) *uste* (hopeful): "Quietly hopeful."

Kutsche (carriage): *kutsha, kutxa* (trunk, chest): "Trunk."

Lage (situation): *laga, lagatze* (tolerable): "Tolerable."

Last (freight): *last, laster* (quickly): "Quick transport."

Lust (pleasure): *luzat, luzatu* (to prolong, to stretch out): "Make it last."

Leute (crowd): *letu, eletu* (to talk loudly): "Loud talk."

mein (mine): *.mai-ain, emai* (gift) *ainbat* (many): "Many gifts."

meinen (to believe): *.mai-ain-en, emai* (gift, own) *aingeru* (angel) *ene* (my): "My own angel."

Metall (metal): *eme-eta-al, emendatu* (to increase) *eta* (amount) *al* (power): "To increase the amount of power."

Meteor (meteor): *me-ete-eor, mendi* (mountain) *ete* (perhaps) *ehortzi* (to bury): "Perhaps to bury itself in the mountain."

Muhme (grandmother): *.mu-ume, amultsu* (affectionate) *ume* (child): "She is affectionate towards the child."

Mutter (mother): *mutu-ur, muturka ibili* (she is annoyed) *ura* (she): "She is annoyed."

neigen (to bend): *naiga-an, naigabe* (suffering, afflicted) *anatomia* (anatomy, body): "Suffering body."

Ober (waiter): *obr., obra* (action): "Action!"

Opera (opera): *ope-era, opetsi* (to offer) *erakarpen* (attraction): "To offer an attraction."

Orden (order): *orde-er, ordenamendu* (organizing) *erabide* (method): "Method of organizing."

Ostern, pronounced with clear "oh" or "oo": o.o-oste-ern., oho-oste-erne, *ohoratu* (to glorify, to worship) *ostera* (return) *ernebizitu* (to excite): "Worship His exciting return."

Pantzer (armour): *pa-antza-ar*, *paketu* (to make peace) *antzatu* (to get ready) *araubide* (discipline): "Get ready to make peace (by using) discipline."

Pferd from Dutch "paard" (horse): *pard*, *pardel* (pack, load, parcel): "Pack (horse)."

rau (raw), *.rau*, *araubide* (discipline): "Disciplined."

Reiter (rider): *rai-tor*, *arrai* (gentle) *aitor* (legendary patriarch): "Gentle legendary patriarch (possibly St. Bonifacius)."

Saltz (salt): *saltze*, *gesaltze* (to melt): "It melts."

Schwester from Dutch "zuster" (sister): *zuzter*, *zuzter* (growing up fast): "She is growing up fast."

singen (to sing): *zing-en*, *zingle* (fragile) *enegana* (to attract): "The fragility is attractive."

Spinne (spider): *zepi-in*, *zepilu* (to brush against) *inon* (somewhere): "I brushed against it somewhere."

Stein (stone): *estai-in*, *estai* (stay, stay put) *indar* (strong, firm): "Stays firmly put."

Strasse from Dutch "straat" (street): *sta-arrat*, *asta* (donkey) *arrate* (narrow passage): "Donkey's narrow passage."

Tante (aunt): *tante*, *tantai* (large hefty log): "Big and hefty woman."

Tier (animal): *tir.*, *tiro* (shot): "Shoot!

Tochter (daughter): *toktu-ur*, *tokatu* (to behave properly) *ura* (she): "She is to behave properly."

trau (faithful): *ta-arau*, *ta* (slap) *arau* (discipline): "Slapping discipline."

übel (evil): *ubel*, *ubel* (purple): "Purple." (It was the official color of the pre-Christian priestess and therefor despised).

zeigen (to display): *zai-gen*, *zaildura* (persistence) *genuen* (we had): "We had persistence."

DESTROYING AN EGALITARIAN SOCIETY

In the early days, the magical reproductive and child-nurturing abilities of the woman were even more a matter of awe than the wonderfully productive sea and land. It was this high position of respect accorded the women that the proponents of male dominance set out to destroy in the hope that the same level of respect would be transferred to them. To begin with they made up the word "man" for themselves (German: "Mann") which came from *manatu*, meaning "to decide" or "to give orders." The men went to great lengths to make up disparaging names for the women, with the obvious intent to corrupt the position of honour which the women had occupied since times immemorial.

The wearing of jewelry and beautiful clothes was associated with female authority. The Basque word for "adorned" is *adelu* which later became the German word "Adel" (nobility). However, with the coming of male domination, the word *adelu* was attached to *haidur* (malicious), creating the derogatory girls' name **adel-haidur** or "Adelheid" meaning "maliciously adorned," which was used originally by the missionaries for the Priestess and her ladies in waiting. The name "Adelheid" is still used as a given name for girls, only today the original negative meaning has been forgotten. The general rule, clearly expressed in the Old Testament, was to portray all females as untrustworthy and in urgent need of male supervision and discipline. The proper word for a married woman in German is "Weib" (English "wife") from *ai-be*, *ai* (strong desire) *be'ar* (necessity): "strong desire for the necessity," which very good word the men made unacceptable by attaching "Fish" to form "Fishweib" in German, "viswijf" in Dutch, someone smelly. At the same time the word "Weib" was replaced with "Frau" (*f.-.rau*): agglutinated from *afa* (happy) and *arau* (discipline): therefore meaning "happy discipline" or "happy with/under discipline." There is no indication whether the word refers to her disciplining the children or that she is supposed to be happy under her husband's discipline, but there is no doubt that the German men accepted the meaning given in the Old Testament. This name-change alone must have caused a great deal of misery and, no doubt, violence in the family. To this day women may not be without a man's supervision. She is taken bodily to the altar by her father and officially handed over to her new owner, whose name she then takes. How long will women put up with this degrading tradition?

It is difficult to imagine what it was that made someone coin a name like Brunhilda, from *burun* (insanity) *hildako* (death): "deathly insane," but there is little doubt that the object was to put down an independent thinking woman. Similarly, the making of a name like Rhonda, *ro-onda*, arro-ona: *arrotasun* (pride) *ondagarri* (ruinous, destructive): "ruinous pride" or Tamara, *tama-ara*: *tamal* (bad luck) *arrabeteko* (handful): "handful of bad luck" or: Wietska, *itz* (talk) - *ka* (incessant): "She talks incessantly." These names certainly do not indicate respect, but instead prove that the women were being used and "put in their place," not honoured as before. As a result Germany ended up with an odd assortment of girls' names which had never existed before, courtesy male dominance run amok. Here are some more:

Albine: *albinu* (threaded needle): "Seamstress."
Alida: *ali-da*, *alik* (possible, suitable) *-da* (for me): "Suitable for me."
Barbara: *barba-ara*, *barbail* (trouble making) *arra* (repeated): "Time and again she makes trouble."
Bianca: *bi* (two) *anka* (leg): "Two legs."
Charlotte: xa-arlote, *xafratu* (to scrub) *arlote* (dirty): "Scrub the dirt."
Doris: *dor-iz*, *dorpeki* (clumsy) *-izan* (to be): "She is clumsy."
Else, Ilse: *eltze* (stewpot): "Stewpot."
Erika: *eri-ika*, *eri* (sickness) *ikara* (fear of): "Afraid of illness."
Eva: *eba*, *ebasle* (thief): "Thief"; (she stole the apple).
Inge: *ingi*, *ingiratu* (to make ready, to serve): "Servant girl."
Irmgard: *irm-gard*, *irme* (steady, stable) *gardari* (one who cards wool): "Steady carder."
Jolanda: *jo-landa*, *jo* (to go) *landa* (outside): "Go outside."
Karen: .*ka-aren*, *akatsbako* (perfect) *arengana* (for him): "Perfect for him."
Liese: *lisiba* (washing clothes): "Washer woman."

Linnie: *lina-ani, linburketa* (obscene, offensive) *anitzetan* (often): "Often offensive."
Margo: .*ma-argo, emakume* (woman) *argo* (sex starved): "The woman is sex starved."
Odette: *odeitu* (overcast, storm on the way): "Stormy weather."
Tamara: *tama* (bad luck), *arra* (handful): "Handful of bad luck."
Renate: .*ren-ate, arren* (please) *ate* (door): "Please (shut) the door."

SOME NAMES FOR MEN, THE LORDS OF CREATION

As derogatory as some of the names for women were, as heroic the names for men were. In cases where two names have the same initial letters such as Herbert and Herman, this does not mean that they mean the same thing; the meaning depends to a great extent on what follows, as shown below. First some male designations:

Ehemann (husband): *ehi-man, ehiztari* (hunter) *manatze* (commanding): "Commanding hunter."
Gatte (husband): *gatte, gate* (chain): "He (feels) chained."
Gemahl (husband): *ge-mal, gehi* (supreme) *malerus* (unhappy): "Supremely unhappy."
Germane (German): *ger-mana, gerai* (tall) *manatu* (commanding): "Tall and commanding."
Held (hero): *heldu* (maturing, healing of wound): "The wound is healing."
Herr (Sir): *herr, herriko* (popular): "Popular."
Mann (man): *man, manatze* (giving orders). "He gives the orders!"
Mensch (person): *men-sh, men* (power) *sh* (diminutive); "A little bit of power."
Onkel (uncle): *onk.-.le, onkote* (easy going) *oles egin* (to call upon): "Call upon easy going."
Oheim (uncle): *ohe-eme, ohe* (bed) *eme* (female): "In bed with a woman."
Sohn (son): *sondatu* (to inquire, to explore): "Exploring."
Vater (father): *fa-ater, fa* (happy) *aterpe* (refuge): "Happy refuge."

The boys received tough and heroic names under the new management:

Adolf: *ado-dol-f, adoretsu* (courageous) *dolo* (pain) *ufakari* (scornful of): "Courageous and scornful of pain."
Bernhardt: *bern-hart, bernoker* (bowlegged) *hartz* (bear): "Bowlegged bear."
Dietrich: *di-etor-ik, dit* (he has..to me) *etor* (come) *ikara* (fear): "He came to me out of fear."
Eberhart: from Aberhart, *aber-hart, abere* (brute) *hartz* (bear): "Brute bear."
Fritz: *fa-aritz, afa* (happy) *arritze* (admiration, praise): Happy with praise.
Heinrich: *hein-rik, hein* (large measure, many) *arrikari* (thrower of rocks): "Thrower of many rocks."
Helmken: *helm-ken, helmuga* (goal) *kendu* (to charge towards): "Charges towards the goal."
Helmut: *hel-mut, heldura* (to mature) *mutil* (boy): "The boy will mature. (i.e. give him a chance)."
Herbert: *her-bert, herriko* (popular) *bertute* (virtuous): "Popular and virtuous."
Herman: *herrausle* (destroyer) *manatzaile* (giver of orders): "Gives orders to destroy."
Horst: *horztun* (having teeth): "Has teeth, (will bite)."
Johan: *jo-han,* jokari (player) handi (important, famous): "Famous (ball) player."
Kaspar: .*kats-par, akatsbako* (perfect) *paregabe* (unequalled): "Perfect and unequaled."

Karl: *ekarle* (messenger): "Carrier of messages."
Norman: *nor-man, nor* (worthy of) *manatu* (command): "Worthy of command."
Roland: *.ro-land., arro* (arrogant) *lander* (indignant): "Arrogant and indignant."
Rotbart: *.rot-bart, arroti* (boastful) *bart* (last night): "He was boasting last night."
Rudolf: *.ru-dol-.f, arrunt* (completely) *dolo* (pain) *ufakari* (scornful): "Completely scornful of pain."
Siegbert: *zig-bert, zigor* (whip) *bertan* (right there): "Whip right there!"
Sigismund: *zigi-iz-mund, zigilu* (stamp, seal) *izudura* (fear) *mundu* (world): "He put his stamp of fear on the world."
Uwe: *uhe, uher* (naughty): "Naughty."
Werner: *erner, ernera* (fertile): "Fertile." (girls watch out! Danger!)
Wolf: *ulu-uf,* ulu (howl) *ufakari* (scornful): "Scornful howl."
Wulfgang: *ulu-uf-gang,* ulu (howl) *ufakari* (scornful) *gangar* (vain): "Vain and scornful howl."

And then there were some non aggressive names like **Hans**, from *hanzkor/ahantzkor* meaning 'forgetful,' or **Haiko** from *haiko maikoka*, meaning 'making excuses,' for the timid boys.

Many German Family Names are Derived From Basque

A great deal of linguistic effort went into replacing the early spoken language, however, less went into changing the original family names. "von" is supposed to indicate nobility but the translation does not support this. The "v" is always written as "b" in Basque therefore "von" becomes "bon," which is derived from *bonbon* (lavish spending) while the abbreviation "bon" indicates "rich." This is confirmed by some of the names like "von Baillou" ("rich, indeed miserly"), "von Grad" ("hankering for riches") or "von Sydow" ("riches are your misfortune"). Rich must therefore be placed (in most cases) before the following translations e.g. rich lancer, rich and concerned, rich and thoughtful etc. This does not apply to names such as "von Anrep" (a military command) or "von Goertz" (cross) in which cases "von" must have been added to the name after the original meaning had been forgotten and meaning of "von" was altered to mean "nobility."

von Aderkas: *aderkatz, aderkatze* (act of goring): "Lancer."
von Aesch: *ash, ashola* (care, concern): "Concerned."
von Anrep: *an-re-ep, anai* (brother) *arre* (advance) *ep* (carefully): "Brothers advance carefully."
von Baillou: *bai-lu, bai* (yes, indeed) *lukur* (miserly): "Indeed miserly."
von Barr: *barrast, barrastatu* (to distribute): "He distributed his riches."
von Bartko: *bart-ko, bart* (last night) *kokolo* (foolish): "Last night he made a fool (of himself)."
von Berner: *bern-er, berna* (calf of the leg) *-era* (action of): "Runner?"
von Borck: *borrok, borrok* (beligerent): "Beligerent."

von Escholtz: *esholatz, asholatz* (thoughtful): "Thoughtful."

von Faulhaber: *fa-aul-aber, famadun* (famous) *aul* (feeble) *aber* (rich): "Famous, feeble and rich."

von Ferber: *fa-eraber, fa* (happy) *eraberri* (changes, reform): "Happy with the changes."

von Gaza: *gaza, gaza* (dull, insipid): "Rich and dull."

von Goertz: *gurutz, gurutz* (crucifix, cross): "Of the Cross."

von Grad: *gura-ad, guratsu* (wishing) *adurtsu* (lucky): "Wishing to be lucky."

von Hahn: *ahan, ahanzkor* (forgetful): "Rich and forgetful."

von Haimberger: *hei-im-berga-ar, hei* (shelter) *imaz* (place of woven branches) *berga* (twigs, coppice) *arrunt* (simple): "Simple shelter made from woven branches."

von Hockauf: *ok-auf, okin* (baker) *aufa* (happy): "Happy baker."

von Kaldenberg: *kalda-an.-berga, kaldatu* (to heat with) *anitzetan* (often) *berga* (twigs, branches): "Often heats with branches."

von Kanel: *.ka-ane-el., ukan* (to have) *ane* (measure, supply) *elikagai* (food): "He has a supply of food."

von Katzler: *ka-atzelar, kabu* (hit) *atzelari* (backplayer of jai-alai ballgame): "The backplayer hit the ball."

von Maltzahn: *maltz-an, maltz* (tricky, deceiptful) *anai* (brother): "Tricky brother."

von Rudloff: *.ru-ud.-.lo-ob.-.b.,* oru-uda-alo-obe-eba: *orubeketa* (piece of land) *udalarre* (summer pasture) *alordun* (farmer) *obeki* (better) *ebaluatu* (to evaluate, consider): "The farmer considers the lower part of the summer pasture to be better."

von Sacken: *sakon, sakan* (deep ravine, gorge): "By the gorge."

von Schalburg: *shal-burg, shalo* (frank, candid) *burgoi* (arrogant): "Frank and arrogant."

von Schellwitz: *shel-u'its., shelebre* (funny) *uitsu* (tarred): "He looked funny tarred (and feathered?)."

von Schilling: *tshilin, txilin* (little bells on animals): "He has little bells on (his) animals."

von Schlabbrenberg shal-laber-en-berg: *tshal* (calf) *laberatu* (to put in the oven) *-enetan* (always) *berga* (twigs, dry branches): "Always put the calf in the oven with dry branches"?

von Sydow: *zu-doa, zu* (you, your) *doakabe* (misfortune): "Riches are your misfortune."

von Totossy: *toto-osi, tot* (round) *osin* (moat): "Moat all around."

von Welarp: *el-arp, ele* (story) *arpa* (harp): "Story sung with the harp."

von Zuben: *tsu-ben, tsu* (abundance, very) *ben* (honest, serious): "Very serious."

THE BENEDICTINES

LANGUAGE INVENTORS SUPREME

EARLY HISTORY OF THE BENEDICTINES

Gnathberla: Under the protection of the religious order we assemble perfectly adapted words (Auraicept 1053)

When St. Benedict of Nursia was asked by Pope Felix IV (526-530 A.D.) to establish an order of highly motivated and well educated monks to evangelize Western Europe, this involved the introduction into these lands of a new culture, a foreign religion and many new languages. It was a very tall order, because each group of monks was instructed to:

1) locate a site and build a monastery which was to be the centre of the evangelization effort,
2) build, equip and staff a scriptorium with a library where the new regional language was to be developed,
3) do Christian outreach work to overcome local prejudices and then
4) introduce the newly invented language to the population.

This extraordinary assignment was the Church's response to a serious challenge.

A Church Under Siege

The task assigned to Benedict was to train monks to go out into western Europe and create a Roman Catholic presence in areas where many Gnostic Christian missionaries from Ireland had long been active. After the Benedictine monks had established themselves in secure monasteries they were to do everything within their power to destroy not only the deep-rooted belief in the very ancient Ashera religion with its supreme Goddess, but also to re-evangelize the areas where Gnostic evangelists from Ireland had spread their own Gospels, most of them very different from those in the New Testament. (See "The Gnostic Gospels" by Elaine Pagels). The name **'Gnostic'** is shorthand for five agglutinated words, one for each consonant:

.g. – .no – os. – .ti – ik.
igo – ono – osa – ati – ika
igoarazi – onon – osatasun – atxikigarri – ikaskai
to lift up – exquisite – perfection – faithfulness – teachings
"Lift up to exquisite perfection our teachings in faithfulness."

The only thing the two forms of Christianity could agree on was the teachings of Christ, and even here were differences; all other aspects were at odds. It was considered of great urgency to teach orthodox Christianity because the Gnostic missionaries had already converted all of Ireland to their particular type of worship and were having great success in large parts of the continent. These evangelists had no real disagreement with the ancient Goddess faith, its culture or its language. They were on talking terms with the abade, the male clergy of the Ashera religion, many of whom they converted to Christianity to become the most dedicated and enthusiastic evangelists of the Gnostic Christian church. In a short time they spread their form of Christianity over much of western Europe, establishing numerous monasteries in England, Germany, Switzerland, Austria, France, Italy and Spain.

One of the best known Benedictines, **Bonifacius**, was disgusted with the looks of these energetic and incorruptible Irish monks. In the style of the abade, they painted their upper eyelids purple, shaved the front half of their heads from ear to ear (instead of a circle on top like the Benedictines) and wore long white sheepskin cloaks, which made them recognizable and highly respected among the peoples they set out to convert.

Bonifacius
.bo – oni – ifa – aki – us.
abo – oni – ifa – aki – usa
aboskatu – onibilera – ifartar – akigabe – usa
to proclaim – success – northerner – tireless – holy man
"The tireless holy man proclaimed success with the northerners."

The free-spirited Gnostic Christianity they preached was abhorrent to Bonifacius who complained to the Pope and asked him to place two of them, the respected monks Adalbert and Clement the Irishman, into solitary confinement. At the same time these two gentlemen reported Bonifacius to the same Pope asking that Bonifacius be removed because of his inconsiderate and ruthless behaviour. The Pope was caught in the middle. The R.C. church could not do without either of the complainants because the Irish monks would preach in the universal (Saharan/Basque) language of the people and introduce a basic Christianity to the people. These Gnostic evangelists were very welcome wherever they went and, most important of all, they never had to worry about personal safety. On the contrary, many of the dogmatic orthodox missionaries, Bonifacius among them, were martyred in the evangelizing process in areas where the Gnostic monks had not done their "softening-up" work first.

The town where St. Boniface was murdered is said to be Dokkum in Friesland. However, the translation of the name of the nearby town of Drachten appears to indicate that he may have been killed there. Like Gnostic, **Drachten** is shorthand for a sentence of five words:

.d. – .ra – ak. -.te – en:
ada – ara – aka – ate – ent
adarka – arakintzo – akabatu – atezatu – entzute
by goring/stabbing – massacre – to end a life – to live on – fame
"The stabbing massacre ended his life but his fame lives on."

Irish Gnostic Christianity proved to be popular among the people of the continent and was considered to be a refinement and natural growth of the ancient religion. The monks also promised to end the voluntary sacrifice of a worthy young man. The ease with which the Gnostic monks successfully converted the people of Western Europe was a most unnerving threat to the ambitious Roman Catholic Church. The church fathers' plan to bring Orthodox Chistianity to this huge area was being pre-empted by this "heretical cult." The word **"heretic"** was especially coined for them by a church-grammarian and means:

he – ere – eti – ik.:
helburu – erretxindura – etikaezin – ikaraz
destination – exasperation – unethical – frightfully
"destined to be a frightfully unethical exasperation."

a most unfair label for these selfless and dedicated followers of Christ. The Roman Catholic leadership decided it had to do something drastic and proceeded with an aggressive and far-reaching solution.

THE SCHOLARLY COMMANDOS

The search was on for a highly educated, strong-minded and absolutely devoted man to organize a monastic Order of disciplined, scholarly commandos to thrust into the opponents' territory, to courageously and aggressively establish monasteries and to bring the "right" form of Christianity to the "heathens" of the Ashera religion. The search for this super apostle ended in 528 when Benedict, who was then approximately 48 years old, was found. He was quickly given all necessary resources and support to build and staff the headquarters for his new Order. He was to train monks for the dangerous and almost overwhelming task of evangelizing all of western Europe. The name he was given by the Pope was **"Benedict of Nursia,"** analyzed with the VCV formula:

.be-ene-edi-ik.-.t.
abe – ene – edi – ika – ate
abe – eneganatu – ediren – ikasgintza – ateratu
cross – to come to me – to find – learning – to take with you
"Come to me under the cross and find learning to take with you."

.nu- ur. -.si – i.a
inu – ura – asi – iha
inurritze – urragarri – asiberri – ihardetsi
inspiring – touching – beginner – to respond
"He inspires and touches beginners to respond."

Benedict's new monastic order was awarded a distinctive habit, which was a loose black gown tied around the waist with a rope, with large wide sleeves and a cowl on the head, similar in design to what had been worn by the Gnostic St. Pachomius and his anchorite brothers of the Sinai monastery some centuries before. Black was chosen to clearly distinguish the Benedictines from the white-robed Gnostic monks. Black clothes had also been adopted many centuries before by the Luwian pre-Hebraic clergy, who wanted to be distinguished from the white-gowned abadeak (priests) of the Ashera religion, who later were given the derogatory title: **druids**.

.d. – .ru – id.
udi – iru – ido
udikan – iruzurtsu – idolgurtzaile
get out – deceitful – idolator
"Get out, you deceitful idolator."

Benedict's first action was to get organized in the area of **Subiaco**, east of Rome, while he searched for a suitable headquarters site.

.su-ubi-ako
isu – ubi – ako
isurikatu – ubil – akorduan euki
to waste a life – whirlpool – to remember
"Remember the waste of life in the whirlpool."

This waste of life referred to the voluntary sacrificial death of a young man by drowning, first in the First Cataract of the Nile, and later also in the whirlpool of Corrivreckan, 70 km west of Glasgow. This event, which occurred once every eight years, was of course unacceptable to the Christian religion and Subiaco became the Benedictines' rallying cry. They even carved it on pre-Christian standing stones in Ireland, using Ogam characters (e.g. Llominaca #121, Litubiri #131, Lubbais #152, Corbi #244, Caveti #433, see Macalister). The task was of such importance that the Pope ordered Benedict not to deal with any bishops or other intermediaries but to report directly to him on all matters. The general had given his marching orders and the commando units would soon fan out over Western Europe to spread their own, more recent, variety of Christianity, which had married Christianity to Judaism. The Pope's order to have Benedict report directly to him applied to every Benedictine Abbot from then on, until rescinded in 1893 by Pope Leo XIII who created the office of the Abbot Primate of the Federation of Autonomous Congregations.

BENEDICT'S FORMATIVE YEARS

No reliable information exists about Benedict's birth but it is estimated that he was born in 480 and lived until 547. As an educated young man from a well-to-do family, he had observed the shocking licentiousness of life in Rome. In his early twenties he decided upon a life as an ascetic and then spent three years living the life of a hermit, first near Enfide in the Simbruinian Hills, later to move into the cave of Sacro Speco, above the lake then existing near Nero's ruined palace at Subiaco, some 65 km east of Rome. **Sacro Speco** decodes as:

.sa-ak.-.ro .spe-eko
usa – aka – aro   aspe – eko
usa – akabu – arroztu   asperkeria – ekoiztu
dove/holy man – ultmate – to exile   boredom – to produce
"Holy man in ultimate exile, which produces boredom."

There were several small monasteries near Subiaco and he was asked to become abbot of one of these. Although bored stiff, the young man refused the offer and returned to his cave, where he then came to the conclusion that self-torment in solitude was not nearly as constructive as group living, communal worship and doing good works. By now the fame of his sanctity was spreading and disciples started to flock to him. To take care of his many devoted followers he organized twelve monastic homes, each with 12 novices, patterned after Christ's 12 apostles, with himself in general control. Senators and other influential people came from Rome to offer their sons to be trained as monks under his direction and two of these young men, Maurus and Placid, became his lifelong trusted disciples. **Maurus** is a contraction of **Marurus**:

.ma – aru – uru – us.
ema – aru – uru – usu
eman – aruntz onuntz ibili – urrun – usu
to teach – to wander – far away – often
"(He) often wandered far away to teach."

Placid
.p. – .la – aki – id.
apa – ala – aki – ide
apaiz – alai – akigabe – -ide
priest – happy – tireless – partner
"A happy priest and a tireless partner."

Many of his associates followed him to Monte Cassino. To this day Subiaco is considered the mother-house of the Benedictine Order, but the use of the name as a rallying cry has been forgotten.

The militant aspect of the new Order was clearly demonstrated in the type of site chosen for their main monastery. The summit of a rocky hill located between Rome and Naples was selected, which had been a major holy Ashera site of the Volski people. At one time the town of Casinum had existed there in the 5th century B.C. This action set the example for all future monasteries to be established; when entering a new region, it became a tradition for the monks to conquer the most important religious centre of Ashera, devastate it, desecrate the holy well and cave, cleanse the site by prayer and build a monastery on the ruins. The original home of the Great Goddess had been at the 2100 metre level of the Hoggar mountains in SE Algeria, close to the centre of the Sahara. When the population of that area had to flee to Europe because of desertification, the population looked for other prominent high places for their priestess sites, to imitate their oldest most holy centre. It was these high places, the former centres of the old religion, which the Benedictines aggressively occupied.

On the mainland these sites had been on prominent rocky hills, but on the ocean they were on centrally located islands, preferably near a year-round flowing well and sacred cave. On the Atlantic islands the Sea-Peoples had chosen similar sites, if they were available, such as Mont St. Michel in Normandy, Mount St. Michael in Cornwall (England) and Talamhantu on Barra, Scotland. Where such prominent sites were not available, small and centrally located islands had become the domicile of the priestess, with the result that a few of the new Benedictine monasteries ended up in some of the most out-of-the-way places, only accessible by boat, which created problems for the landlubbers among the monks, e.g. on Iona (Scotland) and Griend (Friesland). There was a practical side to this aggressive action, because these were the sites where very large stone monuments, such as barrow tombs, had existed, the stones of which were then put to use in the new monastery construction. On Iona, in the huge barrow tomb there had been far more stones than were needed for the monastery construction so the remainder was laid down around the buildings, and covered with sand, so that the land was raised at least one metre. The other major Ashera sites, which had not been used by the monks, were leveled with the ground and the access road blocked or removed, e.g. the Talamhantu centre on the Isle of Barra. Benedict named his first monastery: Monte Cassino. It is desirable to explain this name because the theme expressed in it would be repeated over and over in many of the later establishments. **"Monte Cassino,"**

.mo – on. – .te
amo – ona – ate
amodiotsu – onarketa – aterpe
loving – welcoming – refuge
"A loving and welcoming refuge."

.ka – as. – .si – ino
ika – asa – asi – ino
ikasleku – asagutu – asi – inora
learning centre – go far away – to start – somewhere
"Go far away and start a learning centre somewhere."

The word "monte" therefore means a "welcoming refuge," which later was used for the French word "mont" and English "mount and mountain." Benedict's sister, **Scholastica**, established a convent near Monte Cassino and was allowed to adopt for her nuns the same habit as the monks wore. Her name comes from:

.skola-asti-ika
eskola – astiro – ikasle
to teach – calmly – student
"She calmly teaches the students."

Another major Benedictine monastery using "mont" was built in NE Spain called **Mont Serrat**, also built on a high rock outcrop.

.mo-on.-.t.
amo – ona – ate
amodiotsu – onarketa – aterpe
loving – welcoming – refuge
"A loving and welcoming refuge."

.se – er. – .ra – at.
ase – era – ara – ati
asezindaki – erakuste – arrazi – atxikitzaile
craving – education – to encourage – faithful
"We encourage the faithful to get a craving for education."

In the above text I have translated some of the important names of the Benedictines. All of their names can be readily translated with the use of the VCV formula and the modern Basque dictionary which means that this language has changed very little over the last 1500 years. Even the name **"Vatican"** proves to be pure Basque when analyzed with the VCV formula:

.ba – ati – ika – an.
aba – ati – ika – ana
abadeburu – atxiki – ikasgiro – anaiarte
head priest – faithful – learning environment – brotherhood
"The faithful head priest's learning environment for the brotherhood."

The fact that the pre-Christian, universal language is still clearly discernable in the majority of words and names we speak, means that an important element of the Neolithic civilization is still with us in a very fundamental way.

DAILY LIFE OF THE BENEDICTINE MONKS

After some years on the job, Abbot Benedict realized that much greater discipline among the monks was required if the Pope's enormous ambitions were to be realized. In about 535 A.D. he wrote his "Little Rule for Beginners" known as the "Rule of St Benedict," which provided complete instructions for monastic government, spiritual and material well-being. The "Little Rule" dictated a routine which filled day and night and established a highly disciplined pattern, later adopted by other monastic orders. The Rule divided the day into strict periods of prayer, sleep, intellectual and manual work. It wasn't long before the Monte Cassino monastery was renowned for its teaching, scholarship, devoutness and above all, its discipline. The novices were put through a tough training course and had to perform as was expected of them or else they were punished, often with floggings. It was the first Orthodox Christian place of higher learning in western Europe and its methods of corporal discipline carried on into later secular institutions.

The activities in the scriptorium section of the monastery were two-fold, one was public and the other secret. To outsiders it was a workshop where monks preserved, studied and multiplied Christian writings and where the ancient legends and myths of the people were written down, to be preserved for eternity.

Scriptorium:

.s. – .k. – .ri – ip. – .to – ori – um.
ese – eka – ari – ipa – ato – ori – ume
esegeini – ekarpen – arrigarri – ipartar – atondu – orrits – umekoi
to offer – contribution – marvelous – northerner – to arrange – feast – prolific
"We offer a marvelous contribution to the northerners by arranging a prolific feast."

What the public did not find out about until later was the work the "grammarians" did. These highly skilled professional linguists, some were monks, others were Ligurian scholars, were hard at work at Monte Cassino developing Latin as the Christian liturgical language, to replace the Ligurian tongue which was still spoken by a majority of inhabitants of Italy. They also trained specialists in the art and science of language invention, to be put into practice in areas the monks were evangelizing in the north. To make up new Latin words, they made use of the neolithic language, which in reality was the Saharan/Basque/ Ligurian language. The scriptorium was the only place in the monastery where the ancient language was allowed to be spoken and consequently was out-of-bounds to all those not involved in language invention. The name **Ligurian** tells us what was in store for it:

li – igu – uri – an
libratu – iguindu – urritu – andeatu -
to purge – to despise – to dwindle – to corrupt
"To be purged, despised, dwindled and corrupted."

The church was not entirely successful in reaching this goal in northern Italy because Rhaeto-Romance, also called Ladin, is the last remnant of Ligurian still spoken in a few out-of-the-way valleys in the Alps (Lahovari).

CLEANSING THE PRE–CHRISTIAN LITERATURE

Another task assigned to the Order was the gathering, translating and censoring of large numbers of classical Greek and Roman writings. In the process of translating, these documents were cleansed of all references to the global pre-Christian civilization and religion, its elaborate rituals, celebrations, sacraments and other unwanted wisdom, all aimed at wiping out any memories of this very early and peaceful civilization. Those references to the Ashera religion that remained, were twisted routinely to put the ancient religion in a cruel or decadent light, always referring to it as pagan, heathen, idolatrous, savage, barbaric, cruel etc. often followed by "cult," something despicable. Many years later Charlemagne re-enforced this policy by making it an official order in his Edict #78, dated March 23, 789. It read:

> *#78. "Let no false writings and doubtful narratives, records which entirely con-*
> *tradict the Catholic Faith,... let not such documents be believed or read, but be*
> *destroyed by fire, lest they lead people into error. Only the canonical books and*
> *Catholic treatises and the sayings of sacred writers are to be read and delivered."*
> *(Duckett p.122).*

After the censor's work was done, the original document containing the objectionable passages was burned as ordered, even if it had been borrowed from elsewhere, in which case a cleansed copy was returned. The censored manuscript was then sent to the copiers in the scriptorium for multiplication. Epics like Homer's Iliad and Odyssey, Apollonius' Voyage of the Argo and many others were thus censored and shorn of any favourable references to the previously omnipresent supreme Goddess and her civilization. This savage censoring has done enormous harm to the wonderful classical and ancient literature which had been passed on by word of mouth for many centuries without change. Much of this historical information was located in several world class institutes of learning such as the famous library of classical antiquity at Alexandria, founded by the Ptolemies about 300 B.C.

Another famous library was started by Ptolemy III in the Temple of Saragis. The knowledge contained in these institutes left no doubt that a world-wide civilization with one deity, speaking a universal language (Genesis 11:1), had existed before the coming of Judaism, and the library's existence was a major irritation for the Christian church in Rome, which had decided to deny the existence and destroy any evidence of this Neolithic civilization. As the church had no direct control over these educational facilities, special action was necessary. The oldest and best library was targeted first and burned just before 300 A.D. The satellite library in the Temple of Saragis was attacked and burned in 391 A.D. The confusing inconsistencies, the invented mythologies of Mesopotamia, Anatolia and Greece, and the glaring gaps in the Odyssey and the travelogue of the Argonauts are obviously the work of crude censorship. But the ancient oral traditions were never completely eradicated and to this day are remembered as folklore and myths which make it possible to get some idea what the early civilization of our ancestors was like.

Any "heathen" population was invariably described in these censored documents as having its own primitive and distinct language, which covered up the fact that they had all been speaking exactly the same highly evolved universal language. Many early personal and geographical names, even words, managed to survive unaltered, which allowed me to prove that the tribes had spoken the same language. It is true that, after Emperor Charlemagne's reign, no more classical literature was lost due to fire, wars or neglect, however, it is also true that all the surviving literature which had gone though Charlemagne's cleansing sieve was severely mutilated, much of it eliminated, rewritten or rendered useless and rewritten with totally phony legends. Not until archaeologists discovered the huge libraries of clay tablets in long-ruined palaces of the Near East, dating from classical and ancient civilizations, would we have access to authentic, unaltered original literature. Even so, when documents such as the Dead Sea Scrolls and the Nag Hammadi library were discovered early in the 20th century, the church managed to assign control over the documents to trusted censors, often Dominican monks, who succeeded in delaying and obstructing release for many decades, to the point where we do not know today how much of the literature disappeared or was mutilated before the remainder was made public.

THE BENEDICTINES' OPERATIONS MANUAL

We would not have known about the activities inside the protecting walls of the scriptorium, were it not for an amazing book called the **"Auraicept na n'Ecez,"** the Benedictines' operational manual (see my Ogam chapter). The book was assembled over the centuries, the earliest parts we have could be from about 700 A.D., but it must have been first initiated the moment language invention was started and taught in Monte Cassino. There is little doubt that this manual was confidential and should not have been released to the public. However, some parts of it found their way to the British Museum in London and Trinity College in Dublin and are now available in print (Calder). Because of increased demand it was reprinted recently in Ireland. Irish scholars insisted that the book was written in "Celtic" but were unable to provide a single translation that made sense, although they tried very hard. Elsewhere I explain that the language of the Auraicept is Basque, more accurately: coded Basque, which can be decoded by using the VCV formula and a modern Basque dictionary, as shown. In the Auraicept it is described how the grammarians made up languages and that they took a great deal of pride in their work as for instance the Auraicept indicates in: **Beithe-luis-nin** (Auraicept lines 1057, 1134, 4013)

.be – ite ' lu – is. _ ni – in.
obe – ite _ lu – isi ' ni – in
obetoezin – itegun _ ludi – isilean _ ninikatu – inguru
perfectly – work performed ' world – hidden from ' to take root – vicinity
"Perfectly performed work, hidden from the world, will take root in the vicinity."

Some of the linguists who knew the universal language best, created specially organized dictionaries for the use of the grammarians, the creative minds who assembled the words using pre-determined linguistic rules. For a short time, the Benedictine monks in Ireland made good use of the early Gnostic Ogam writing system. Between 500 and 1500 A.D. these hard working Basque-speaking grammarians created and introduced all west- and central European languages, including Celtic, French, Spanish, German, Hungarian, Scandinavian, even Finnish, Russian and Polish, an absolutely unique and incredible accomplishment.

Go Far Away and Start a Learning Centre

In order to get an idea of the enormity of the Benedictine effort and the extraordinary time period over which their efforts were spread, I will first name some of the most important monasteries and scriptoria, complete with details of establishment, where these are available to me.

Date	Monastery	Details
529	Monte Cassino (Italy)	Established by St. Benedict himself.
550	Luxeuil (France)	Established originally by the Irish St. Columbanus; library taken to Vatican in 15th century.
597	Canterbury, (England)	Established by papal librarian Augustine and 40 Benedictines.
612	Bobbio (Italy)	First established by the Irish evangelist St. Columbanus.
635	Holy Island, NE England.	Established by Irish St. Aidan. The name was changed to Lindisfarne in 793 after the Vikings burned Aidan's monastery.
674	Wearmouth (England)	Founded by Biscop Baducing.
681	Jarrow (England)	Where Bede grew up and wrote many books.
724	Reichenau (Germany)	Est. by Karl Martell, first abbot: Pirmin.
727	Murbach (France)	Est. by St. Pirmin from Reichenau. Alcuin visited here to borrow books.
744	Fulda (Hessen,Germany)	Est. by Sturmi, disciple of St. Bonifacius.
769	Aachen (Germany)	First it was a Pfaltzkapelle, then royal palace with added scriptorium
785	Westminster (England)	Small monastery on island in the Thames, enlarged by St.Dunstan 960.
822	Corvey (Germany)	
888	Mont Serrat (Spain)	Officially est. 888 but functioned covertly in early Moorish times, their language research done in Arab characters.
889	Andechs (Austria)	
910	Cluny (France)	Founded by William of Aquitane. Main centre for the invention of the French language.
922	Egmond (Holland)	Est. by the burial place of St. Willibrordus in North Holland, west of the city of Alkmaar.
934	Ebersberg (Germany)	The amazing Willeram was written here in 1060.
934	Einsiedeln (Switzerland)	
985	Melk (Austria)	Benedictine presence officially est. in 1089.

996   Pannonhalma (Hungary) In 1996 1000 years old, meeting of eastern and western
                               prelates which didn't materialize because of illness.

1006 Lysa Gora (near Kielce Poland) Est. by King Boleslaw

1040 Pecherska Lavra (Kiev, Ukraina.) Est. by Yaroslav the Wise; with linguistic help from
                               the Benedictines in Pannonhalma.

1044 Tyniec (Poland)   Burned down in 1839. Again an active monastery since 1939.

1044 Sofiyiskaya Storna (Rus.)   Linguistic assistance from Benedictines only.

1083 Göttweih (Germany)

11th century. Alba Iulia (central Romania) Formerly Karlsburg: its famous library now
                               housed in Batthyaneum Library, which includes
                               famous "Codex Aureus."

ATTEMPT AT BENEDICTINE ESTABLISHMENT IN POLAND

It appears that the very first monasteries created by the Benedictines were small establishments with limited staff, similar to the monastic houses which Benedict had established near Subiaco. These were well-suited for initial take-over of the old established centres of the pre-Christian clergy, for exploratory evangelical work and for scouting out of new locations and attitudes, but inadequate for sustained religious and social development, language invention and language introduction, which required a much larger, more secure and more diverse establishment.

In the Polish "Historiae Poloniae" Jan Dlugosz (1415-1480), high official of the court of king Kazimierz Jagiellonczyk wrote that the first Benedictine monastery was established in 1006 A.D. in the Gory Swietokrzystkie (Mountains of the Holy Cross) on top of Lysa Gora (the Bald Mountain).

Lisa Gora
eli – isa   ego – ora
elizlur – izadi   egoitza – orraztu
holy ground – creation   establishment – to dispossess
"We created holy ground after dispossessing the establishment."

This name tells us that these monks did the same to the holy site of the previous Goddess religion as they had done at Pannonhalma in Hungary and many other places in western Europe. King Boleslaw had brought twelve monks from Monte Cassino and their first task had been to occupy the existing holy site of the pre-Christian religion, a place with many stone circles, a holy well and megalithic works, which may still be seen there. It is only natural that the local population objected to the desecration of their holy site and the monks were not heard from again. It was not until 1044 that another attempt was made to establish a Benedictine presence in Poland, this time at Tyniec where a large monastery developed and thrived until the roofs burned off the buildings in 1839 and the monastery became a ruin. In 1939 eleven monks from the Belgian Abbey of St. Andrew started reconstruction and in 1947 the monastery came back into the rank of an abbey. Such is the history of many Benedictine abbeys.

DOING GOOD IN HUMBLENESS

Benedictine establishments were known as "missions," which word expresses the purpose of the order, seen from the monks' point of view. The following analysis shows that "**mission**" was originally written with one "s,"

.mi – isi – on.:
umi – isi – one
umiltasun – isilka – onegite
humbleness – quietly – doing good
"Quietly doing good in humbleness."

These dedicated men really believed that changing the peaceful, egalitarian and active society of their ancestors into a male dominated and strictly disciplined civilization, was their God assigned duty.

THE BENEDICTINES IN ENGLAND

Credit: Most of the historical information about Alcuin is obtained from
Alcuin, Friend of Charlemagne by Eleanor Shipley Duckett.

THE MONKS COME TO ENGLAND

In 597 A.D. the papal librarian Augustine and forty scholarly Benedictine monks arrived in England. They had been sent by Pope Gregory the Great, to begin the conversion of the local people to orthodox Christianity. They brought enough books with them to form the nucleus of the scriptorium library which they included in their monastery built at **Canterbury** in Kent. In line with their teaching duties they named their establishment **Kanterburi**, analyzed as .ka – an. – .te – er. – .bu – uri:

.ka	ika	*ikasi*	learned
an.	ana	*anaia*	brothers
.te	ate	*ateratu*	to take advantage of
er.	era	*erabide*	education
.bu	abu	*aburu eman*	to express (opinion, idea)
uri	uri	*urrikimendu*	repentance

"Take advantage of an education from the learned brothers and express repentance."

Once the buildings were finished, monks and grammarians settled down to the demanding but creative task of laying the foundation for the new English language. Little is known about the amount of progress achieved during the next decades until the year 635 A.D. In that year King Oswald of Northumbria offered his help to establish a new monastery in the NE of England on an island near the mouth of the Humber river, long known as Holy Island. He asked the Irish St. Aidan, who had built the monastery on Iona, to send priests to build a new monastery on the island in a location which was within sight of his fort at Bamburgh. St. Aidan decided to lead the delegation himself and the monastery buildings were started, as was the habit at the time, on the ruins of the previous sacred site of the Ashera or Goddess religion.

The ruins visible there today are those of the subsequent monastery built by the Benedictines in 1083. The island is about 2 km off shore and can be reached on foot at low tide. After the Vikings burned the monastery in 793 the island was known as Lindisfarne. Some other early monasteries were built in England such as Wearmouth in 674, Jarrow in 681 and Rochester in about 780, to expand the language creation effort. The principal language centre became York, not far from Holy Island, where a scriptorium was attached to the Cathedral school. Around 1100 a large Benedictine monastery was also built near the Cathedral, the ruins of which are now in the museum garden. Contact between these centres of learning was regular and frequent, as remaining records show. The name Holy Island was changed to **Lindisfarne** after the Viking raid of 793. With the VCV formula the name breaks down to:

.li – in. – .di – is.- .fa – arne:

.li	ili	*ilintu*	to set fire
in.	inu	*inular*	sundown
.di	udi	*udikan*	get away!
is.	isi	*isilume*	bastard
.fa	ifa	*ifar*	northern
arne	arne	*arnegatu*	cursed

"Get away from here! At sundown the cursed northern bastards have set fire!"

Alcuin, The Bendictines' Teacher

If any person can be identified as having had the greatest influence upon the formation of English and the other Germanic languages, this person must be Alcuin. His absolute dedication to the task, his organizing ability and his tireless work during a long life had such an influence that he must be regarded as the greatest of west European language teachers. The name **Alcuin** was apparently given to him at the time that he became head of the Cathedral school in York and is composed of three words: *al . -.ku – in.*

al.	ala	*alaiki*	happily
.ku	aku	*akuilatu*	to stimulate
in.	inu	*inurritu*	to tingle, to inspire

"Happily stimulating and inspiring."

Alcuin was born around 732, in or near **York** and grew up at the Cathedral school of which Egbert was the head master. The Little Rule of St. Benedict provided for child oblates to be accepted by the monasteries, and probably at the age of seven or eight Alcuin became one of them.

.jo – or. – .k.
ajo – ora – aku
ajola izan – orain – akuilatze
to care – always – stimulating
"Always caring and stimulating."

This was a residential school where the boys would stay year-round with only occasional visits home. Parents would give these children because they were certain that the boys would receive an excellent education. They were, of course, thoroughly indoctrinated into the Roman Catholic faith and became a valuable reservoir from which the church could draw future monks and deacons. The speaking of their mother tongue was punished severely and even the slightest hint of pre-Christian religious observances was considered abhorrent and beaten out of them. Egbert was especially concerned to carry on the tradition of learning which he had known under his master Bede, a tradition already founded by its former bishops Bosa, John of Beverley and Wilfrid the Second.

Egbert

eg.	ega	*egapetu*	to protect
.be	abe	*abegi egin*	to welcome
er.	era	*eraspen*	devotion
.t.	ati	*atxikitasun*	faithfulness

"He welcomed and protected (the boys) with devotion and faithfulness."

These bishops had been trained in Irish Gnostic discipline of books under Abbess Hild of Streanaeshalch, the later Whitby. **Streanaeshalch** is made up of five words:

.st.-.re-ana-esha-alk:

.st.	ezta	*eztabaidazale*	fond of discussions
.re	are	*arrerazko*	hospitable
ana	ana	*anaiak*	brothers
esha	esa	*esalditu*	to talk (the "s" is pronounced as "sh")
alk	alk.	*alkarbatu*	to get together

"Fond of discussions, the hospitable brothers get together to talk."

Under Egbert, the York Cathedral school became the most famous centre of learning in England which attracted young men not only from nearby Northumbria, but also from the rest of England and the continent. Although at first the school had concentrated on religion, Egbert expanded the curriculum to include the liberal arts and secular literature and science, such as Bede had written down at Yarrow. It was in this energetic atmosphere that Alcuin grew up. Egbert loved all his boys but he took a special interest in Alcuin, who would run errands for him in the streets of York, learn about its history from the pages of Orosius and Bede and roam the Roman ruins on the banks of the river Ouse.

He learned how the Roman Emperor Severus had come to crush the northern Picts and the Caledonian Scots. Emperor Constantius had come to see Britain under his power and here he had also died. Here his son Constantine had started his reign which had been of such importance to Christianity. The city was already old at the time of the Romans, having been a trading center and important harbour on the navigable Ouse, dating back to long before Christ was born. The first Church had been built in 627 by Bishop Paulinus who had dedicated it to St. Peter. This little wooden building was soon replaced by Paulinus' successor, King Oswald, who completed a splendid structure of stone.

As Alcuin grew up, another teacher became even more important to him than Egbert had been. His name was Aelbert, whose special interest was in books and teaching. The name Aelbert cannot be translated and should be spelled **Ailbert,** ai – il. – .be – er. – .t.

ai	ai	*ai*	strong desire
il.	ila	*ilarteko*	lifetime
.be	abe	*abegikortasun*	hospitality
er.	ere	*errez*	simple
.t.	ete	*etengabe*	ceaseless

"A strong desire for a lifetime of simple, ceaseless hospitality."

It was Aelbert who allowed Alcuin to teach the younger students. Alcuin said later about Aelbert: "My master told me to rise with all that was in me to the defense of the Catholic faith if anywhere I should hear of the springing up of strange sects, opposed to Apostolic doctrines." Aelbert introduced more advanced studies such as Latin grammar, language and prose, rhetoric, mathematics, arithmetic, geometry and astronomy.

Natural sciences were also taught including eclipses of the sun and moon, tides, earthquakes and the laws that govern the lives of men, beasts and birds as written by Pliny, Isidore and Bede. Alcuin also encouraged these teachings and gave credit to pre-Christian teaching, saying: "They were the wisest men who discerned these arts in nature. It is a great disgrace to us to let them die out in our time." Canon law was required by those who wished to enter the priesthood which also required knowledge of music such as the Gregorian chant as composed by Pope Gregory himself. Every minute Aelbert could spare he spent in his beloved Cathedral library, which expanded rapidly under his devoted care. Alcuin then assembled for him a list of all the books and documents in the library, the first library catalogue in Britain.

When time permitted Aelbert would travel to the continental monasteries to borrow more books to be copied in the scriptorium. On one of these trips he took Alcuin along with him to Rome and Pavia and visited Frankish monasteries like Murbach on the way back.

"Murbach" comes from: *.mu-ur.-.ba-ak.*:

.mu	amu	*amultsu*	tender
ur.	uri	*urrikitu*	to show compassion
.ba	iba	*ibarretxe*	house in the valley
ak.	aki	*akitu*	to be exhausted

"At the house in the valley the exhausted find tender compassion."

All these travels and activities resulted in more knowledge being accumulated and raised the profile of the school and of its master to new heights and it generated a desire in Alcuin to do the same if and when he became master of his own school.

When Alcuin was 35 years old, he was ordained a deacon, which was one step lower than a priest, as the analysis of the word **"deacon"** shows: *.de-ako-on.*

.de	ide	*-ide*	companion
ako	ako	*akordiozko*	traditional, conventional
on.	one	*oneskarri*	worthy of respect

"Traditional companion worthy of respect."

The title **"priest"** is agglutinated from: *.p.-.ri-ist.*:

.p.	apa	*apaiz*	priest
.ri	ari	*ariketa*	assignment, task
ist.	istu	*iztun*	speaker, persuader

"The priest's task is to persuade."

The task assigned to Alcuin was to establish and run a college where monks and priests were taught the new language and learned how to introduce and teach this to the people. He became therefore the educator of the clergy. It is likely that it was one of the local grammarians who coined the word **"Library,"** when he painted or carved the word on a sign which he hung over the door giving access to the study hall:

"library" from *.li – ib. – .ra – ari*

.li	eli	*elizdiru*	religious duty
ib.	ibi	*ibili*	to acquire
.ra	ira	*irakaskuntza*	education
ari	ari	*arrigarri*	marvelous

"It is your religious duty to acquire a marvelous education."

ALCUIN MEETS CHARLEMAGNE

Alcuin believed that the creation of the new English language had started in earnest with Venerable Bede, acknowledged the most learned man of the time and the earliest church historian of England. Bede was Alcuin's hero and role-model and he tried to pattern his life after him. Shortly before his death in 735, Bede had written a severe critique of monastic living in England: "within very many of these 'houses of God' monastic doors concealed homes of lust and luxury, free from discipline, to which crowded all who gladly shook off for comfort and idleness the burden of an honest life in the world." Alcuin always remembered these words and warned his students never to give in to temptation. The name **"Venerable Bede"** deserves to be translated because it is exactly in line with the other Benedictine names.

It analyses as: *.be-ene-era-ab.-.le be-ede*:

.be	obe	*obeagotu*	to improve
ene	ene	*ene*	come to me
era	era	*erabide*	education
ab.	abe	*abe*	cross
.le	ele	*eleiza*	church
be	be	*bedeinkagarri*	blessed one
ede	ede	*ederki*	brilliant

"To improve yourself, come to me for an education under the church' cross. The Blessed and brilliant one."

In 781 Aelbert sent Alcuin to Frankland on a mission to king Charlemagne and, just before Easter on his way to Parma, he had caught up with the king's party. It was the second time he met the king of the Franks and king Charles had not forgotten the brilliant young man, because by that time Alcuin's scholarship was known throughout western Europe. Charles was looking for outstanding scholars to staff the palatine school he was developing in Aachen (Aken), attached to his Court. The Frankish king had great plans for the education of his people and not the least of his goals was the replacement of the indigenous "heathen" language of the Germans with an acceptable Christian one, free from verbal imagery associated with the still omnipresent Ashera religion. Alcuin refused Charlemagne's offer to become head of the palatine school at Aachen, a refusal which the king did not accept. He was in urgent need of an outstanding and strong-minded scholar with organizing ability and he knew he had found his man.

Associated with the school, Charles planned to start an Academy to train missionaries, priests and scholars, people badly needed if Roman Catholic Christianity was to prevail. With Alcuin at the head of this educational institute, Charles was sure that his dream would become a reality. Alcuin's refusal caused the king to change his approach and he then contacted co-workers of Alcuin such as Eanbald, Elfwald and Willehad, who had no reservations about leaving York and willingly accepted. His co-workers having taken the big step to Aachen, this caused Alcuin to overcome his objections and he agreed to leave his comfortable life in England, his many friends and his beloved library to join the monarch. He had helped Aelbert build the best academy and library in Europe and the thought of leaving all that behind for the uncertainties of Charles' court was unnerving to him. He spent his last days in York writing his "Verses on the Saints of the Church of York" a long poem honoring the history of the great men in York's history in church and state. After that was done he declared himself ready to go. It was the year 782, Alcuin was 50 years old and a whole new life lay ahead of him.

---

[1] Much of the historical information concerning the Benedictines and Alcuin was borrowed from "Alcuin, Friend of Charlemagne" written by Eleanor Shipley Duckett Ph.D, D.Litt, LHD.

The Benedictines in Germany

Evangelizing Germany

Alcuin came to Charlemagne's court to bring the very best of English learning to a country where most knowledge was still retained in oral form. As in York, there was no regular Benedictine monastery in Aachen (or Aken) and therefore the large scriptorium was attached to the Palatine School of Charlemagne. The Benedictine monks who lived there were all linguists who worked with the grammarians to develop the German language. Already during the reign of Charles Martel and Pepin the Short a simple version of the Palace school had existed, but training had been restricted to court manners, procedures and protocol.

Irish monks had come to the continent of Europe in about 500 A.D. to bring their brand of simple Gnostic Christianity and had brought along their own Gnostic Gospels. The Irish St. Columban had established monasteries in Luxeuil, Sanct Gallen and Bobbio and assisted in monastery construction at Faremontiers, Jouarre and Rabais. St. Gall had taken over at Sanct Gallen which was named after him. Virgil the Geometer, the nemesis of Bonifacius, had been bishop in Salzburg for many years. The scholar Donatus had been elected bishop of Fiesole and ruled there for nearly 50 years. St. Pirmin built the Reichenau, Murbach and Amorbach monasteries. Many other religious houses had been started by the Irish such as Lumièges, Auxerre, Laon, Liège, Trier, Würzburg, Regensburg, Rheinau, Vienna, Lucca and many others, but none had taught secular or worldly learning.

The Irish monks had brought the simple message of Jesus, of peace and love, decency and caring, without applying coercion. Gnostic Christianity had evolved directly from the **Ashera** religion, from ash-era, asho-era: *axola* (care) *-era* (ing): **"Caring"** and had retained the loving, caring deity of that religion, as opposed to pre-Hebraic Judaism in which a jealous and cruel tribal god-king had married the chief priestess and placed her in an inferior position (see Raphael Patai, "The Hebrew Goddess"). The Gnostic type of Christianity was egalitarian and unstructured and therefore had no hierarchy of deacons, priests, bishops and pope. The people prayed directly to their Deity, a right which was denied the people by the Roman Catholic missionaries. The Irish monks had made great strides in introducing a peaceful renaissance in the Ashera religion, aimed at modernizing the age-old habits and eliminating the human sacrifice of a young man, of which Jesus may have been the last one in Palestine (see Tammuz in: Ezekiel 8:14). As such, the Irish monks, mostly converted "abade" or male clergy of the Goddess, had fitted in well, were welcomed wherever they went and had been given all help needed to establish their monasteries. The Gnostic Gospels they brought along did not include the Old Testament accounts of the brutal assault on the "Land of Milk and Honey" as documented in such graphic and gruesome detail in Numbers, Kings, Joshua and Judges.

This all changed with the coming of the missionaries of Orthodox Christianity, whose avowed duty it was to destroy the old order with all means at their disposal and to introduce Judeo-Christianity. Theirs was a belief which talked about love but did not accept a refusal of it. Charlemagne had even issued an Edict, some time between 782 and 785, which laid down his law among newly conquered people. The death penalty was prescribed for anyone refusing Christian baptism, for burning a Catholic church, stealing any of its contents, conspiring against Christian men and for disloyalty towards the King. No wonder the independent Germans and Friesians were disgusted and fought back, in the process creating a fair number of martyrs, Bonifacius among them.

The Benedictines had learned from the Irish experience and as soon as it was humanly possible to do so, the Reichenau monastery was taken over from the Gnostic monks who had built it on an island in lake Constance, again on an ancient holy Ashera site. As did the name Monte before, the name **Reichenau** reflected the traditional Benedictine hospitality:

.re – ike – ena – au
are – ike – ena – au
arreraegin – ikertzaile – ena – aupatu
to welcome – visitor – that – to give praise
"We welcome visitors that give praise."

St. Willebrord built at **Echternach**, in Luxemburg:

ek. – .te – er. – .na – ak.
eka – ate – era – ana – ako
ekarri – aterpe – eramankizun – anaidi – akordiozko
to provide – refuge – suffering – brotherhood – traditional
"Traditional brotherhood which provides a refuge from suffering."

St Chrodegang built at **Lorsch** near Mainz, a name which may come from:

.lo – ors.
alo – ortz
alondegi – ortzeko
wine storage – heavenly
"Heavenly wine cellar."

St. Bonifacius established his monastery in **Fritzlar** in Hesse:

.f. – .ri – itz. – .la – ar.
afa – ari – itza – ala – are
afa – ari – itza eman – alaitzaile – arrera
happy – mission – to give a promise – joyous – to welcome
"Happy mission which promises a joyous welcome."

Bonifacius' other favourite was **Fulda** in Hesse-Nassau:

fu – ul. – .da
fu – ule – eda
funtsatu – ulerketa – edagale
to create – understanding – thirst
"We create a thirst for understanding."

Bishop Butchard's monastery was at **Würzburg:**

urtz ' bu – urg
urtzeko – buruargi – urgatza
heavenly – ingenious – protection
"Ingenious, heavenly protection."

It was the same place where the Irish monk **Kilian** had built:

.ki – ili – an.
eki – ili – ana
ekinkor – ilinti – anaia
active – high spirited – brother
"The active, high-spirited brother."

ALCUIN'S CO–WORKERS IN GERMANY

When Alcuin arrived at the Court in Aachen he met there the deacon Peter of Pisa, a specialist in grammar and correct usage of words, as shown in Greek and Latin texts. Peter also was one of the main grammarians of the German language. Alcuin had been hired to train the monks to bring the newly invented language to the people and soon wrote a textbook "for the use of his pupils and for the love of his lord" meaning Charles. Where the serious Alcuin became Charles' advisor in matters of education, civilization and government, Peter advised the king for a variety of less serious topics and wrote a number of poems under Charles' name. When Alcuin met Peter, he was already aging and declining fast in health and influence but his humorous streak stayed with him until the end.

Another teacher of grammar in the palace school was Paul the Deacon, who was also learned in Latin and Greek. To please Princes **Adelga**, the daughter of **Desiderius** (king of Lombard Italy), he translated and censored into suitable Christian language the "Roman History" written by Eutropius.

ade – el. – .ga
ade – ele – ega
adeitsu – ele – egapetu
gentle – story – to favour
"She favours gentle stories."

Desiderius
.de – esi – ide – eri – us.
ede – esi – ide – eri – usa
ederrak hartu – esiketa – ideki – eriotze – usain
"o be defeated – siege – to open – death – stench
"He was defeated by the siege and opened up to the stench of death."

Paul also wrote the first commentary on the "Little Rule" of St. Benedict. In spite of being very productive and appreciated, Paul was quite unhappy at the Court and he eventually left to live and die at Monte Cassino. His unhappiness pours out of a letter he wrote to Abbot Theodemar:

> *"They are Catholics here, it is true, and they practice Christian ways; they welcome me, all of them and are kind to me, for the love of our Father Benedict and your own high fame. But in comparison with your monastery this Palace is a prison and when I think of the peace there, life here is one hurricane! Only in body I am here. Please dear brothers, please keep on asking our blessed common Father and Teacher St. Benedict that by his merits he may prevail with Christ and send me back without delay."* (Duckett, p. 100).

Under Charles' constant urging, life in Aachen must have been like living in a pressure cooker, there was so much to do, so little time and so few of them to do it. Burnout was taking its toll. However, before Paul left for Monte Cassino, he abridged for king Charles the Roman "On the meaning of words" by Pompeius Festus. He also wrote many little riddles, fables, reflections and happy guessing games all designed to familiarize the students with the newly created German language. He and Peter of Pisa exchanged poems and problems of the imagination, many of them written under the name of Charles. Of interest are Paul's fables on the sick lion, the vengeful fox, the hungry calf, and the thin-legged stork. He even wrote on gout and fleas and how to stop these plagues.

One of Alcuin's closest friends was Paulinus, a teacher of literature who had been in Aken for several years before Alcuin came. When Paulinus had gone to live in Aquileia, Alcuin wrote:

> *"I have always loved you dear friend, ever since I came to know you. I have inscribed the name of my Paulinus, not on waxed tablets where it could be rubbed out, but in my heart for always. Do not forget the name of your Alcuin in your prayers."*

Peter, Paul and Paulinus had been full-time teachers, leaders of discussions in the humanities, but there were others such as Angilbert, a young lad who became a Court poet and close associate of Charles.

Angilbert
an. – .gi – il. – .be – er. – .t.
ana – agi – ila – abe – era – ate
anaia – agindugarri – ilarteko – abe – eraspen – atxikitzaile
brother – obedient – lifetime – cross – devotion – faithfulness
**"Obedient brother (who gave) a lifetime of devotion
and faithfulness under the cross."**

St. Riquier
.ri – iku – i.e – er.
uri – iku – ihe – ere
urrikalkor – ikustatu – ihesleku – errezibimendu
merciful – to visit – shelter – welcome
"It is merciful to visit our welcoming shelter."

Angilbert loved learning, the arts, the beauty of the world, but above all he loved king Charles' daughter. Charles did not approve and sent him to the abbey of **St. Riquier** near Amiens as abbot, where he contributed greatly to the glory of its architecture and the books with which he endowed the abbey at Centula.

Centula
.ke – en. – .tu – ula
ike – ena – atu – ula
ikertu – -ena – atutxa – ulatu
to visit – superlative/wonderful – evergreen oak forest/heavenly place – to welcome
"Visit our wonderful heavenly place and be welcome."

CHARLEMAGNE, FEARED AND RESPECTED

Charlemagne proved to be a master of strong-handed tactics. He massacred tens of thousands of honest free people who had severe reservations about his aggressive form of Christianity. Had Christ been with King Charles on those forays, he certainly would not have recognized his own religion and would have been horrified by what had happened to the cause he voluntarily gave his life for. But Alcuin said nothing and took these brutalities in stride as an unavoidable evil necessary to force the people to accept Christianity. A look at the meaning of Charlemagne's name is worth while. The name **Charlemagne** comes from Latin: **Caroli magni rex**; or written with the VCV formula:

.ka-aro-oli .ma-ag.-.ni .re-ek.-.s.:

.ka – aro – oli
aka – aro – oli
akatsbako – arro – oliotu
perfect – proud – holy
"Perfect, proud and holy…

.ma – ag. – .ni
ema – agu – uni
eman – aguregin – unibertsal
to be devoted – to worship – general
… devoted to general worship,…

.re – ek. – .s.
are – eko – osa
arretatu – ekonomia – osasundun
to foresee –economy – health
… foresaw a healthy economy."

King Charles tried to be everywhere and be all things, a super-human effort in which he succeeded because of determination, a brilliant mind and an iron constitution. Barely back from his military campaigns he would attend to his school, asking questions, encouraging, criticizing, always full of new ideas. If he had been near an established monastery he would bring rare books and ancient poetry of his people which he ordered copied. At the king's request the Benedictine grammarians were busily preparing a book of instruction in grammar for the new language. As semi-literate as he was, he even took a personal interest in the word-invention process when he designed new names for the 12 months of the year and the directions of the winds.

Charlemagne's names for the months:		Charlemagne's names for the winds:	
January:	wintarmanoth	east wind:	ostroniwint
February:	horning	south-east	ostsundroni
March:	lentzinmanoth	south-south-east	sundostroni
April:	ostarmanoth	south wind	sundroni
May:	winnemanoth	south-south-west	sundwestroni
June:	brachmanoth	south-west	westsundroni
July:	heuimanoth	west wind:	westroni
August:	aranmanoth	north-west:	westnordroni
September:	witumanoth	north-north-west	nordwestroni
October:	windumemanoth	north wind	nordroni
November:	herbistmanoth	north-north-east	nordrostroni
December:	heilagmanoth.	north-east	ostnordroni

Introducing the New Language

On March 23, 789 Charlemagne sent out a "General Admonition," a series of Edicts. They dealt with the duties and behaviour of the bishops, priests, deacons and monks. There is no doubt that Edict #72 was written by Alcuin who had long advocated the establishment of schools for the common people throughout the land. It was an expansion of the system of cloister schools of which he himself was a product. The Edict created the church-run educational system which is still with us today. The new German language, having advanced enough so that simple sentences could be spoken, King Charles decided that it was time to rule that:

> *"... there be schools to teach boys to read. Correct, we command you, with due care the copies of the psalms, the written signs, the chants, the calendar, the grammar in each monastery and diocese, and the Catholic books, because often people wish to pray to the Lord, but do so badly, because the books are at fault. And do not allow your boys to corrupt the books by their own reading or writing"*
>
> (Ducket p122).

Alcuin's schools proved to be very effective in spreading the new language and religion. The boys were like prisoners and often brutally and degradingly treated, especially if they tried to speak their mother tongue, or reverted to "pagan" practices. This system of education was so successful that it continued in use. Many centuries later the colonial powers applied it throughout the world by giving the churches the right to have monks, nuns and deacons "educate" native children. The mere speaking of their native language, until very recently, resulted in corporal and other punishment. Until the 1980's Canada used this abominable system to force a Christian education onto its large native population. Church control over the children was only abandoned after the boys' and girls' long ignored complaints of sexual harassment and gross indecency by many of the live-in clergy were finally taken seriously.

As literacy spread among the people living near priests who had been trained by Alcuin, Charles' enthusiasm for the new language became infectious and popular. Many persons who still had knowledge of the universal language, started to use it to invent new words and names, but like Charlemagne, only rarely following the strict rules by which the Benedictine linguists and grammarians worked. For many years to come, this word and name invention game would be a popular pastime until the new language was saturated with acrostically mutilated words and names, and the population in the main centres was reasonably comfortable with the new language. However, the German language always remained an unstable invention.

KING CHARLES' WIVES

Name	Married	Children	End of marriage.
Himiltrude	767		Discarded 770
		Pippin the Hunchback (769)	
Desiderata	770	None	Discarded 771
Hildegarde	771		Died 783 at age 25
		Charles (772)	
		Adelheid (774)	
		Hrotrud (775)	
		Pippin (775)	
		Louis the Pious (778)	
		Lothar (778)	
		Bertrada (779)	
		Gisila (781)	
		Hildegarde (782)	
Fastrada	785		Died 796.
		Hiltrud (785)	
		Theodrada (787)	
Liutgard	796	None	Died 800

Sadness fell over the entire Palatine school when it was announced that the young Queen Hildegard had died. She was king Charles' third wife and had been only 12 years old when he married her and in the 12 years of married life had given birth to 9 children of which 3 had died in infancy. Alcuin had much appreciated the beautiful young woman. Her charming personality had enlivened the Court: **Hildegard**:

il. – .de – ega – ard.
ile – ede – ega – ard
ilezkor – ederreztatu – egapetu – arduradun
always – to beautify – to protect – responsible
"Always beautiful, protective and responsible."

Charles did not remain single for long. A year later he married an eastern Frank known now as Fastrada. As beloved as Hildegard had been, as disliked Queen Fastrada became. Einhard, Charles' biographer, relates stories about her cruelty which even made her own people, the eastern Franks, rise in revolt. **Fastrada** was obviously not the name by which she called herself:

fa – aztra – ada
farranda – aztura – adarra sartu
ostentatious – habit – to deceive
"Of deceiving ostentatious habit."

Although the uprising of her people was quickly suppressed, a second, potentially more serious one started soon after. It was prompted by Charles' own son Pippin the Hunchback, because he and the Frankish nobles could no longer bear the cruelty of the Queen. Charles was warned in the nick of time about the revolt and the leaders died by the sword and the gallows. Charles could not kill his own son but banished him to the monastery of Prüm in Lorraine. Fastrada died after 11 years of marriage. She had given birth to two daughters, Hiltrud and Theodrada, both of whom became abbesses in France. The fifth queen of Charles was Liutgard, of German origin, according to Theodulf a gracious, courteous and generous person, delighting in books and the arts. The analysis of **Liutgard**'s name confirms this:

.li – ut. – .ga – ard
eli – uto – oga – ard
elizkoi – utopikera – ogasun – ardura artu
pious – idealistic – wealthy – caring
"Pious, idealistic, wealthy and caring."

Where Queen Hildegard had been a much appreciated student of Alcuin, Queen Liutgard became his friend and confidante. They helped each other whenever in need and he admired her greatly during the few years of her life at the Court.

ALCUIN'S TEACHING METHOD

Alcuin was an extremely devoted teacher, administrator and disciplinarian and a stimulator of young and old but he was neither an original thinker, a poet, nor a philosopher. He was content to compile his lessons by borrowing from established authorities, which often made his treatises dull and dry. However, he was rich in experience and knowledge of human nature and had an encyclopedic knowledge of available information and knew exactly in which books this was to be found. Through prolific correspondence with his many friends, all over western Europe, he was knowledgeable about all that was going on in monasteries and schools and even in Rome.

To teach the new German language, Alcuin had adopted the method of dialogue, question and answer. He insisted on proper pronunciation in reading and gave careful instruction in the mysteries of metre and rhythm. In his book *"On Orthography"* he lists many words in alphabetical order and teaches proper form, declension and usage so that his students would write and speak correctly. He pointed out pitfalls in Latin such as the initial "a" in *ara* (altar) and *hara* (pigsty); the confusion of "b" and "v" in *bile* and *vile*, *acerbus* (harsh) and *acervus* (heap). His sources were Bede, Priscian and Cassiodorus with a little Alcuin added. He also compiled a long list of simple questions and not so logical answers, especially designed to increase the student's vocabulary and usage of the new language. The answers he devised were not so much intended as a good response to the questions as to familiarize the students with the usage of the newly invented words.

1. What is writing?	the guardian of history
2. What is speech?	the revealer of the spirit
3. What gives birth to speech?	the tongue
4. What is the tongue?	the lash of the air
5. What is air?	the guardian of life
6. What is life?	the joy of the blessed
	the sorrow of the sad
	the looking for death
7. What is death?	an inevitable happening
	an uncertain pilgrimage
	the tears of the living
	the basis of last wills and testaments
	the thief of man

8. What is man?	the bondsman of death
	a passing wayfarer
	a guest sojourning on earth
9. To what is man like?	to an apple on a tree
10. How is he placed?	like a lantern in the wind
30. What are the lips?	the doors of the mouth
31. What is the throat?	the devourer of food
39. What is the stomach?	the cook of food
49. What is day?	the stimulant of toil
51. What is the moon?	The eye of the night, the giver of dew
	the foreteller of storms
65. What is spring?	the painter of the earth
67. What is autumn?	the barn of the year

Alcuin used a great many riddles for the same purpose, knowing that they had to be memorized by heart to be remembered, such as his #42:

A ladder has 100 steps. On the first sits one pigeon, on the second two, on the third three, and so on up to the 100th. How many pigeons in all? Alcuin's answer was:

Step 1 plus step 99 = 100, step 2 plus step 98 = 100 and so on to come up with: 49 x 100 + 50 + 100 = 5050.

Working out their own solutions to the problem this forced the students to use many words and numbers, many new or not in common use, others were suggested as yet to be invented.

It was just like the grammarian wrote in the Auraicept: **Berlan-etarscartha**:

.be-er.-.la-an. eta-ar.-.s.-.ka-ar.-.ta (lines 1317, 2526, 4635):

.be – er. – .la – an.
obe – ere – ela – and
obetoezin – ereduztatu – ela – andana
perfectly – adapted – word – in groups
"Perfectly adapted words in groups (are)"

eta – ar. – .s. – .ka – ar. – .ta
eta – ara – asi – ika – are – eta
-eta – arazoi – asi – ikaskintza – arretazko – eta
abundant – reason – to begin – instruction – careful – afterwards
"abundant reason to begin careful instruction afterwards."

It was the questions and riddles which provided the grammarians with goals to work towards, designing groups of words which could accommodate the discussions associated with the key-words in the riddles. This must have lead to endless testing among the grammarians to ensure that the riddle-solving could be done with all the necessary words in place before the group of words was released. Charlemagne also needed Alcuin to eliminate the ancient oral traditions of the people by replacing them with literacy. Written records could be easily manipulated, censored, copied and hidden or destroyed. They were far easier to influence than the age-old tradition of memorizing by professional memory-men. Where memorizing had been a highly respected art, it now became a hazardous vocation, because after the priestesses and clergy had been disposed of by the church, the memory-men came next.

The strictly maintained oral tradition had created the great stability of the ancient language. Its demise would leave a vacancy which could only inadequately be filled by the introduction of writing. Alcuin was brought in to bring this change about and in the process he was to get rid of the persistent native language. Alcuin had started this task by vowing that he himself would never again speak the universal language of his ancestors and urged others to do the same. Being a man of high principles and great determination, he succeeded where everyone else had failed, but only after Charlemagne had extracted an incredible price in blood. Those who did not perceive reality in the prescribed way were killed or converted. Finally his efforts resulted in the Germans, Danes and Friesians accepting new and highly immature languages against their will, while the speaking of their own beautiful and mature language was forbidden.

When Benedictine abbeys had been established in farther out-of-the-way places such as Pannonhalma in Hungary, Nidaros in central Norway and Tyniec in Poland, the basic acrostic word-invention processes, proven so effective in England and Germany, were repeated there, only with drastic changes in basic syntax, characters and pronounciation. The methods Alcuin had developed were put to good use, when the Benedictines became established in these places. But what did the grammarian who made up the word "acrostic," tell us what he meant? The English word "acrostic," when analyzed, only makes partly sense because it is incomplete. The word must therefore have originated outside of England. In German and Greek the word is: **"akrostichon,"** which is much more promising. When each consonant of this word is arranged with the VCV formula, it reads as follows:

ak. – .ro – os. – .ti – ik. – .ho – on.:

ak.	aka	*akabu*	perfect
.ro	aro	*aroztegi*	forged
os.	osa	*osagai*	component

.ti	ati	*atxiki*	to agglutinate
ik.	ika	*ikaskizun*	lesson to be learned
.ho	aho	*ahohizkuntza*	spoken language
on.	one	*oneratu*	to improve

"Perfectly forged agglutinated components are the lesson to be learned to improve the spoken language."

This is not exactly a definition of acrostic as is taught today, but it tells us something; it does admit that acrostics were used to create a spoken language. In any case, it is usually possible, like the examples above, to identify the words which were used to assemble the new word.

It was the awesome task given to the Benedictines to re-make the culture, religion and language of this ancient and happy society of Ireland which had a highly disciplined civilization, no weapons or fortifications, had a marvelous work-ethic and led a life of caring communal solidarity. It was a foregone conclusion that the dogmatic Benedictines would not be welcome. Literally every aspect of the old order was overturned by them with enormous and tragic consequences for the population. It may be said that the Benedictines tore down a vibrant society, then re-organized, re-built and re-inspired it, just like the Ligurian/Basque word *erald* expressed: from *eraldatu* (to transform) the first part *erald* then became the Dutch word "wereld" and, slightly manipulated, the English word "world," "Transform the world."

5200+ YEARS OF LINGUISTIC RESEARCH

The profession of the language inventor was already extremely ancient by the time Benedict of Nursia built his monastery on the rocky hill half way between Rome and Naples. Long before Benedict, Plato had described Homer as a "daemiourgon onomaton" (craftsman of words) and Homer's two epics give ample evidence that he was one of the most influential inventors of the Greek language. Language invention had always been the manipulation of the magical Old Egyptian or Saharan. This manipulating of morphemes must have started well before the time of the first pharaoh who lived some 3,200 B.C., in an effort to create a magical form of writing which would be the preserve of scholars, not to be read by the vulgus. The genius who invented the VCV agglutinating system created something very special that endures unaltered to this day. The word construction system was taken over by those who wanted to destroy the Ashera religion because it was the most ingenious and versatile system available, and they used it to create a plethora of unstable languages. Where the ideology used to be "make love, not war," this was turned around to "make war, not love" when creating the new polytheistic proto-Judaic religion. This "down with the woman" syndrome was then built into all new languages, sometimes using objectionable and repulsive language, and is with us to this day, as pointed out in several chapters of this book.

In those early days proto-Judaism was a missionary religion. Groups of monk-linguists and clergy followed the trade-routes to far-away places and created new languages with associated scripts. Just like was done later in western Europe, the plan was to create a new language for each area and one liturgical language was needed as an umbrella language so the many different groups doing the language creation, could talk to each other. Some of these early umbrella/liturgical languages are: Akadian (Mesopotamia), Sanskrit (India), Tocharian A (China), Iberian (Spain), Etruscan (Italy), Greek (Greece), Gothic (Eastern Europe), Arab (North Africa), Ge'ez (Ethiopia), Hebrew (Palestine) and possibly even Japanese and Quechua (the Inka language; *ainkoa* is Basque for "the god"), This enormous linguistic effort had already created many languages by the time Benedict set up his linguistics training centre at Monte Cassino abbey. The patriarchal insistence on confusing the one and only universal language had been repeated later in Genesis 11:7: "Come, let us go down and there confuse their language, that they may no longer understand one another's speech" and was closely tied in with the patriarchs' determination to destroy the ancient pre-Christian religion, so clearly expressed in the Bible. The decision to invent names for pharaohs was possibly made some 5200 years ago, well before Christ was born. When the Benedictine monks invented English, they used the same system and created a winner; it became England's most successful export because 1) its grammar can be greatly simplified without much loss of meaning, and 2) because England, later the U.S.A. were great empire builders.

One of the more recent invented languages was Latin, which may have been pioneered originally by a highly educated missionary group of Luwian clergy who had settled in central Italy and had started what later became known as the Etruscan culture. They brought the proto-Judaism of the jealous sky gods to their new homeland of Tuscani and along with this they created a form of writing which still defies complete deciphering. This development work was going on when the Romans, who originally spoke Ligurian-Basque, took over Tuscani and adopted the new and still immature Latin as their own language of state and general use to replace the original Ligurian language spoken until then. They also introduced a different type of script, possibly borrowed from the Phoenicians, which we still use today.

The meaning of the word **"Latin"** tells a story:

.la – ati – in

ela – atxiki gogoz – indar egin

word – to memorize – to make an effort

"Make an effort to memorize the words."

Their linguists exploited the unique characteristics of the Ligurian/Basque language, still spoken in Northern Italy, and added the invented VCV vocabulary to it. They then made sentences in Basque/Ligurian which were reduced to words with the use of vowel-interlocking formula, as described in my previous articles. The result was a beautiful sounding and elegant language which was considerably easier to learn than the complicated but very logical Ligurian language. The highly structured Latin language, which appeared and sounded quite different from the "pagan" language it originated from, appealed to the newly established Christian community in Rome. The church leadership then ordered it and its script to be adapted for use as their own liturgical language and eventually Benedict was given the task to use the same agglutinating formula as the basis for developing the Romance group of languages including Spanish and Catalan, French and Provençal, Italian and Rumanian. Thus Latin became the communication language of the Benedictines and also the uniform language of science. This was a very necessary decision because the efforts to create new regional languages, which only the local Benedictines could understand, were not suited for international communication between the many monasteries and Rome. Many centuries later Latin was formally adopted as the scientific language of the western world and all plants and animals were renamed in that language, except for those which already had Greek or Basque names.

Name Translations of Some Other Monasteries

Cluny (S.E. of Paris)

.k. – .lu – uni
eki – ilu – uni
ekinaldi – ilun – unibertsal
perseverance – darkness – general
"Perseverance (amid) general darkness."

Corbie (northern France)

.ko – or. – .bi – i.e
ako – ora – abi – ihe
akorduan euki – orain – abialeku – ihestoki
remember – always – place of departure – safety
"Always remember the safety of your place of departure."

Medehamstede (Benedictine monastery in East Anglia)

.me – ede – eha – am. – .s. – .te – ede
eme – ede – eha – ame – ese – ete – ede
emekiro – eder – ea – ameslari – esetsi – etengabe – ederbera
peaceful – beautiful – (emphasis) – idealist – to debate – constantly – aesthetic
"In this peaceful and very beautiful place the idealists constantly debate aesthetics."

Montéliou (southern France)

mo – on. – .te – eli – ou
amo – ona – ate – eli – ou
amodiozko – onartu – aterpe – elikadura – (French ending?)
loving – welcoming – refuge – food – (French ending?)
"A loving, welcoming refuge (serving) food …?"

Nidaros (Trondheim, Norway)

.ni – ida – aro – os.
ani – ida – aro – osa
anitzetan – idatzi – arrotzen– osaera
often – to write – strangest – composition
"(We) often write the strangest compositions."

Nonantola (Lombardy)

.no – ona – an. – .to – ola
ono – ona – ana – ato – ola
onon – onarketa – anaiak – atondu – ola
wonderful – welcome – religious brothers – to prepare – cabin
"The religious brothers prepare a wonderful welcome in the cabin."

Pavilly (northern France)

.pa – abi – il. – .li
apa – abi – ile – eli
apaiz – abia – ilezkor – eliza
priest – home – immortal – church
"The priests' home in the immortal church."

Pesherska Lavra (in Kiev, Ukraine.)

.pe – es. – .he – er. – .s. – .ka   .la – ab. – .ra
ope – esi – ihe – era – aska   ila – abe – era
opetsi – eziketa – ihesleku – eraspen – askamen   ilarteko – abegion – erantzun
to offer – education – shelter – devotion – pardon   lifetime – hospitality – to fulfill
"We offer education, shelter, devotion and pardon.
Ours is a lifetime of hospitality and fulfillment."

Ramsey, (West Midlands of England)

.ra – am. – .se – ei
era – ame – ese – ei
eraspen – ametsetsi – esetsi – eia
devotion – to idealize- debate – come and participate
"We are devoted to idealistic debate. Come and participate."

Rievaulx (Cistercian monastery in France)

.ri – eba – au – ul. – .k. – .s.
uri – eba – au – ula – aka – ase
urrikaldor – ebanjelari – aurkileku – ulatu – akatsbako – ase
to be merciful – evangelist – meeting place – to welcome – perfect – fill up/meal
**"You are welcomed with a perfect meal to the
meeting place of the merciful evangelists."**

Sahagun (Cluniak abbey in Spain)

.sa – aha – agu – un.
osa – aha – agu – uni
osatasun – ahalguzti – aguregin – unibertsal
perfection – almighty – to worship – universal
"The perfection of the Almighty is universally worshiped."

St. Emmeram (Regensburg, south Germany).

em. – .me – era – am.
emo – ome – era – ame
emon – omenaldi – eraspen – ameslari
to give/to pay – tribute – devotion – idealist
"Pay tribute to this devoted idealist."

IV

LANGUAGES INVENTED BY OTHER RELIGIOUS SCHOLARS

THE ORIGIN OF GREEK

INTRODUCTION

That the Greek language was invented was already known to Plato and described in his "Kratylos" when he calls Homer a "daemiurgon onomaton" (master of the art of forming words) and adds that not just any sound will do for a word but "onoma homoion to pragmati" (the word resembles the thing) and "stoicheia homoia tois pragmasin" (the sounds, i.e. the stoicheia, be similar to the thing also). In the same book Plato talks about the connection of words and namings, meanings and sounds, which today would be called a discussion of semiotics. Plato's writing gives the impression that he wanted to preserve some ancient science that even he, one of the most knowledgeable men of his time, had only a dim recollection of, so it would not be lost to posterity. (A.Goppold). What he did not divulge was the formulaic manner in which Greek vocabulary and names were assembled. He must have known this because his own name tells about the system:

Plato(n)
.p. – .la – ato – on.
ope – ela – ato – onu
opetsi – ela – atondu – onutski
to offer – words – to assemble – perfectly
"I offer perfectly assembled words."

There is little doubt that Plato is one of the main word-smiths of the Greek language and that he knew more about the Magic Egyptian VCV language than he wanted to be let known.

First a Few Well Known Names

Hellas (Greece) he – el. – .la – as.

he – ele – ela – asi
herri – eleizako – ela – asiera
nation – sacred – story/legend – origin
"Our nation's sacred legends (tell) our origin."

This is the name the Greeks use for their own country. It also tells us that the priesthood in charge 3000 years ago wanted the people to accept their heroic kingship version of early history. This means that all traditional memorized epics had to be abandoned or destroyed or re-written into pure nonsense. This is exactly what Homer did to the original Odyssey and the Iliad and also what religious linguists have been doing ever since to all writings unapproved of by the new religious leadership throughout history, until today. As Michael Wood wrote in "In Search of the Trojan War":

> *"The ideals and the way of life portrayed in early Germanic epic had much in common with Homer, and that the later Norse, Celtic and Anglo-Saxon traditions were very similar... historians and anthropologists now tend to see these "heroic traits" as literary creations, characteristic of periods of nostalgic decay."* (p. 156)

Whenever clergy of the patriarchal religions entered a new territory of the Goddess, the endemic epics were trashed and turned around to depict the traditions of a warlike, male-dominated society. Wherever this happened, Anatolia, Mesopotamia, Greece, Germany, Ireland, Norway, a totally invented set of heroic legends replaced the old peaceful ones. Especially in Norway, the monks at the Nidaros monastery really outdid past efforts by "discovering" some 700+ Norse and Icelandic sagas, very few of them with any truth in them. The monks admit this themselves when they named their monastery in Trondheim Nidaros, meaning: "We often write the strangest compositions." Today even many Norwegian academics believe the sagas to represent a realistic past.

Greece (grique, griek, grike), a Latin name.

.g. – .ri – ike
iga – ari – ike
igaro – arritzeko – ikertaldi
to travel – fantastic – visit
"Travel (there) for a fantastic visit."

Akropolis ak. – .ro – opo – oli – is.

ake – ero – opo – oli – iza
akela – erotiko – opor egin – olio – izarmoltzo
Great Goddess – erotic – to create – constellation
"The erotic Great Goddess created the constellations."
or by using: *izadi* (nature):
"The erotic Great Goddess created (all of) nature."

Parthenon .pa – art. – .he – eno – on.

apa – arte – ehe – eni – onu
aparta – artelan – ee – eni – onuts
special – work of art – to call attention – my – perfect
"This special work of art draws the attention (to its) perfection."

Homer, ho – ome – er.

ho – ome – era
hoberen – omentsu – erakutsi
the best – honourable – to teach
"The best of the honourable teachers."

Odysseus odi – is. – .se – us.

odei – ise – ese – uste
odeiertz – iseka egin – ezezagun – ustekabe
horizon – to joke about – unknown – unforeseen
"He jokes about the unforeseen and unknown (beyond) the horizon."

Cassandra .kas – andr. – a

akas – andre – a
akasgabeko – andre – a
flawless/perfect – woman – the
"The perfect woman."

Knossos .k.-.no-os.-.so – os.

eka – ano – osa – aso – ose
ekarri – ano – osakor – azoka – ozen
to provide – food supplies – healthy – open air market – noisy
"The noisy open-air market provides us with healthy food supplies."

Mukaenai (Mycena) .mu – uka – ena – a.i

amu – uka – ena – ahi
amultsukeria – ukan – ena – ahiniztasun
excessive affection – possessions – (superlative) rich – large quantities
"Excessive affection for large quantities of rich possessions."

Iraklion ira – ak. – .li – on.

ira – aki – ili – one
iraun – akidura – ilinti – oneraegin
to suffer – exhaustion – firebrands – to recover
"We recovered from the suffering and exhaustion of the firebrands."

AND SOME RANDOMLY CHOSEN WORDS FROM THE GREEK DICTIONARY

agathon (beauty) aga – at. – .ho – on

aga – ato – oho – ono
-aga – atondu – ohore eman – onon
abundance – ornamentation/makeup – to glorify – wonderful
"An abundance of make-up glorifies wonderfully"

agroktima (farm) ag. – .ro – ok. – .ti – ima

aga – aro – oki – iti – ima
aga – arrotsu – okitu – itxi – imatz
abundance – proud – completely – to enclose/store – wicker shelter
"Proud that the abundance is completely stored in the shelter."

akhortagos (greedy) ak. – .ho – or. – .ta – ago – os

ako – oho – ora – ata – ago – oso
akorduan euki – ohoin – orraztu – ataldu – agorrune – oso
to remember – thief – to rob – to take advantage – scarcity – total
"Remember the thief who robbed and took advantage of the total scarcity."

akrostichon (acrostic) ak. – .ro – os.- .ti – ik. – .ho – on

aka – aro – osa – ati – ika – aho – one
akabu – aroztegi – osagai – atxiki – ikaskizun – ahohizkuntza – oneratu
perfect-forge-component -agglutinate-lesson to be learned-spoken language-to improve
**"Forging perfectly agglutinated components to improve
the spoken language is the lesson to be learned."**

alogo (horse) alo – go

alor – goldatu
farmer – to plow
"The farmer is plowing."

bakaliko (food store) ba – aka – ali – iko

banakatzaile – akatsbako – alik – -iko
distributor – excellent – possible – that
"It is possible that the excellent distributor (has it)."

demos (people) .de – emo – os

ide – emo – ozt
idekotsu – emonkor – ozte
all alike – prolific – crowd
"That prolific crowd looks all alike."

eklisia (church) ek. – .li – isi – i.a

eka – ali – isi – iha
ekarri – alik – isilka – iharduki
to come – possible – in a low voice – to talk
"When possible come and talk in a low voice."

elatoma (fault) ela – ato – oma

elaberritu – atondu – oma
to tell – come – grandma
"Come, I'll tell grandma."

ema (blood) ema

emalege
"menstruation."

epivatis (passenger) epi – iva – ati – is

epi – iba – ati – isu
epiza – ibaiontzi – atxiki – isurbide
short of time – ferry – to catch – canal
"You are short of time to catch the ferry across the canal."

ethafos (ground) et. – .ha – afo – os

eta – aha – abo – osto
-eta – ahaskeria – aboskatu – ostolaza
abundance – dirt/soil – to declare – grassland
"They declared the abundance of soil in the grassland (their own)."

falakros (bald) fa – ala – ak. – .ro – os

fa – ala – ako – oro – osa
farre egin – alabearreko – akordoizko – oroz – osaezin
to poke fun of – unavoidable – traditional/normal – totally – incurable
"Poking fun of the unavoidable, normal and totally incurable."

flidzani (cup) f. – .li – id. – .za – ani

fe – eli – idu – uza – ani
festa – elikadura – iduki – usaingozo – anitz
feast – nutrition – to have – aroma – much
"To have pleasing nutrition with much aroma."

fonazo (call) .fo – ona – azo

abo – ona – azo
aboskatu – onaldi – azokalari
to shout out – prosperity/sales pitch – merchant
"The merchant shouts out his sales pitch."

friktos (horrible) f. – .ri – ik. – .to – os

fa – ari – ika – ato – os
fanatiko – arimagalduko – ikararazi – ator – ospa egin
fanatic – ruthless – to terrorize – come! – to escape
"The ruthless fanatics are terrorizing. Come, let's escape!."

glendi (party) gale – endi

gale bizia – endikoi
strong desire – sociable
"Strong desire to be sociable."

isegoria (right to have your say) ise – ego – ori – i.a

isekatu – egokiera – ori – ihadetsaldi
to satirize – opportunity – that – response
"Your opportunity to satirize that response."

kakos (bad) ka – ako – os

kaldar – akordiozko – osasungaitz
thief – habitual – incurable
"He is a habitual and incurable thief."

kalathi (basket) ka – ala – at. – .hi

kaiola – alabeharreko – atxiki – ihi
cage/container – necessary – to grab/gather – rushes
"Container made out of rushes, necessary to gather."

kalispera (good day) ka – ali – is. – .pe – era

ka – ali – ise – epe – era
kanpoan – alik – iseka egin – epel – errainuketa
outside – if possible – to rejoice – warm – sunlight
"Outside one rejoices in the warm sunlight."

kalos (good) ka – alo – os

> ka – alo – oso
> *kargu hartu – aloger – osoro*
> to be responsible for – wages – total
> **"He is totally responsible for the wages."**

kataskinono (camp) ka – ata – aski – ino – ono

> *kanpadenda – atalgabeko – askiki – inon – onon*
> tent – simple – adequate – some place/spot – wonderful
> **"A simple but adequate tent in some wonderful spot."**

kathethrikos naos (cathedral)

> ka – at. – .he – et. – .h. – .ri – iko – os. _ na – a.o – os.
> ka – ati – ihe – eto – ohi – iri – iko – os. _ na – aho – os.
> *kanpaialdi – atxikitzaile – ihesleku – etorri – ohibezala – iritsi – iko – osakera*
> _ *nabarmen – ahoeder – ospatu*
> ringing of bells – faithful – refuge – to come – as usual – to obtain – (verbal adj.) – healing
> _ to excel – eloquent – to glorify
> **"When the bells ring, the faithful come to the refuge as usual to obtain healing.**
> **They excel in eloquent glorifying."**

katsika (goat) ka – at. – .si – ika

> ka – ate – esi – ika
> *katetu – ateratu – esi – ikastobi*
> to chain – to take outside – fence – opening in the forest
> **"Chain (the goat) outside the fence in the forest opening."**

keo (burn) ke – e.o

> *ketu – eho*
> to smoke – to grind, rub
> **"Rub (until) it smokes."**

khina (goose) k. – .hi – ina

> ke – ehi – ina
> *-kera – ehizaldi – inauguratu*
> **"Nesting season inaugurates the hunt."**

khora (country) .k. – .ho – ora

> ako – oho – ora
> *akorduan euki – ohorarazi – orain*
> to remember – to honor – always
> **"Remember to honor (it) always."**

khrisos (gold) .k. – .h. – .ri – iso – os

ka – aho – ori – iso – oso
kaldatu – ahoziritu – oribizi – isolamendu – osoilik
to smelt – to deceive – gold – secret place – simply
"Simply deceive by smelting the gold in a secret place."

khivernisi (government) ki – ive – er. – .ni – isi

ki – ibe – era – ani – isi
kide – ibeni – eraberri – anitz – isilki
member – to introduce – reform – many – calmly
"The members calmly introduce many reforms."

khorevo (to dance) k. – .ho – ore – evo

ko – oho – ore – ebo
kolokari – ohoretu – orekatu – eboluzionatu
swinging – to celebrate – balance – to develop
"While swinging and celebrating you develop balance."

khoros (dance) k. – .ho – oro – os

ko – oho – oro – ospe.
kolokari – ohoretu – oro – ospetsuki
swinging – to celebrate – all – in a stately manner
"All are celebrating and swinging in a stately manner."

khortari (grass) k. – .ho – or. – .ta – ari

ko – oho – ori – ita – ari
kokatu – oholtza – orri – itaitu – arrigarriki
to place – wooden rack – leaves – harvest with a scythe – marvelously
"Place the leaves, so marvelously harvested with a scythe, on the wooden rack."

kipos (garden) ki – ipo – os.

kimatsu – ipo – osasundun
full of sprouts – dwarf/small – healthy
"It is full of healthy small sprouts."

kithara (guitar) ki – it. – .ha – ara

ki – itu – uha – ara
kitzikatu – itun – uhain – arrantza egin
to provoke – sadness – wave – to weep
"It provokes a wave of sadness and weeping."
The Greek spelling of 'guitar' tells us where this word really came from.
It was not from Arabic!

kori (daughter) ko – ori

> *koskortu – oritu*
> to grow up/develop – to turn pale
> **"She is growing up and turning pale."**

kore (girl)

> ko – ore
> *konkordura – oreztu*
> swelling/hard-on – to fill a hole
> **"Fill (her) hole with (your) hard-on."**

kosmos (crowd)

> ko – os. – .mo – os.
> ko – oza – amo – osa
> *kontraekintza – ozar – amorratu – osatu*
> opposition – arrogant – furious – united
> **"The opposition was arrogant, furious and united."**

kouros (boy)

> ko – uro – os.
> ko – uro – oso
> *konkortu – uroditza – oso*
> to swell up – water pipe – simple
> **"Simple inflated water pipe."**

ko'yenia (family)ko' je – eni – i.a

> *koipetsu – jendaki – eni – iharduki*
> adulatory/flattering – kinship – to/for me -to be busy with
> **"Flattering kinship for me to be busy with."**

kratos (power)   .k. – .ra – ato – os.

> oke – era – ato – ospa
> *oker – eraso – atoitu – ospa egin*
> bad – storm – to tow – to escape
> **"Being towed to escape from a bad storm."**

krevati (bed) k. – .re – eva – ati

> ka – are – eba – ati
> *kargu hartu – are – ebatura – atxikitzaile*
> take care of – his/her – surgery/wound – faithfully
> **"Take care of his wound faithfully."**

labyrinth (labyrinth), la – abi – iri – in. – .t. – .h.

la – abi – iri – inu – uti – ihe
larde izan – abiadan – irrikitan – inular – utikan – ihesegin
to be afraid – fast – anxious – sunset – to get out – to escape
"I am afraid and anxious to get out fast and escape at sunset."

lemoni (lemon) .le – emo – oni

ale – emo – oni
ale – emankor – onizan
fruit – prolific – useful
"Prolific and useful fruit."

lexicon (speech) le – ek. – .si – iko – on.

le – eka – asi – iko – onu
lenbiziko – ekarpen – asierako – -iko – onuratsu
initial – contribution – elementary – that – useful
"Initial elementary contribution that is useful."

makria (far) ma – ak. – .ri – i.a

ma – aka – ari – iha
marineleria – akabu – arriskuan egon – ihardun
fishermen – the far end/far away – to be surrounded by danger – to spend time
"Far away our fishermen spend their time, surrounded by danger."

mera (day) me – era

mementoan – errainuketa
in a moment – sunlight
"In a moment we'll have sunlight."

miga (fly) mi – iga

minkor – igarokabe
offensive – intollerable
"Offensive and intolerable."

moro (baby) mo – oro

morkona – orrokatu
dirty/soiled – to scream/to cry
"When soiled it cries."

onomatopoiia (onomatopoeia)

ono – oma – ato – opo – o.i – i.i – ia
ono – oma – ato – opo – oi – ihi – ia
onon – oma – atondu – opor – oinordetzia – ihite – ia
wonderful – grandma – to arrange – time off – inheritance – resemblance – almost/close
**"Our wonderful grandma arranged in her spare time
an inheritance of close resemblance."**

oreos (fine weather) ore – os.

oreka – osoro
stable – perfectly
"Perfectly stable (weather)."

paralia (beach) pa – ara – ali – ia

pantoka – arrastakatu – alik – ihartu
forward part of the boat – to drag – possible – to dry out
"If possible drag up the forward part of the boat to dry out."

pirkaya (fire) pi – ir. – ka – aia

pi – ira – aka – aia
pinu orri – irazeki – akabu – aiaia
pine branches – to ignite – death – sorrow
"Igniting the pine branches (caused) death and sorrow."

plio (passenger boat) p. – .lio

pi – ilio
pisugain – iljo
overloaded – death knell
"Being overloaded is a death knell."

poli kalitera (much better)

po – oli _ ka – ali – ite – era
poto – oli _ kalipu – alizan – itegun – eraspen
container – olive oil _ vitality – to be capable of – work performed – devotion
**"A container full of olive oil. (He is) capable of vitality
and devoted to the work performed."**

porneia (fornication), .po – or. – .ne – eia

apo – ora ' ne – ia
apokeria – orraztu ' neskaso – iarduki
filthy deed – to despoil ' virgin – to resist
"It is a filthy deed to despoil a resisting virgin."

pothi (leg) po – ot. – .hi

po – ota – ahi
pot egin – otalurmendiak – ahitzinatu
to tire out – wild mountains – to make progress
"It is tiring to make progress in the wild mountains."

proethros (president) p. – .ro – et. – .h – .ro – os.

pa – aro – eti – iha – aro – oso
pakegile – arro – etika – iharduki – aro – osoki
peacemaker – dignified – ethical issue – to discuss – time for – thoroughly
"Dignified peacemaker who has time to thoroughly discuss ethical issues."

protomi (bust) p. – .ro – oto – omi

po – oro – oto – omi
porrokatu – oroitarri – otoikatu – omia saindu
to destroy – monument – to pray to – hallowmass
"Destroy the monument (the pagans) pray to at hallowmass."

psilos (flea) p. – .si – ilo – os.

pa – asi – ilo – osa
pairaezin – asikidura – ilordu – osasungabe
unbearable – to bite – agony – sickness
"Unbearable bites cause agony and sickness."

sika (figs) si – ika

siku – ikaza
dry – place of the fig trees
"Dried figs."

sinkharitiria (congratulations)

si – in. – .k. – .ha – ari – iti – iri – ia
si – ina – aka – aha – ari – iti – iri – ia
sineskuntza – inaugurata – akatsgabeko – ahalguzti – arrigarri – itxi – irri – iaio
with reverence- to introduce – pure- almighty- marvelous- to permit- laughter-cheerful
**"With reverence he introduced the pure and marvelous
Almighty who permits cheerful laughter."**

skotinos (dark) .sko – oti – ino – os.

oskorri – otzikaratu – inolaz – oztasun
daybreak – to shiver – somehow – coldness
"It is daybreak and somehow I am shivering from coldness."

soma (body) so – oma

> *soin – oma*
> bosom – grandma
> **"Grandma's bosom."**

tebelis (lazy) te – ebe – eli – is.

> *tentakari – ebertar – elizkoi – isekatu*
> tempting – Jew – pious – to ridicule
> **"It is tempting to ridicule the pious Jew."**

thanatos (death) t. – .h. – ana – ato – os.

> ta – aha – ana – ato – osa
> *talkan – ahalkegabe – anai – ator – osalari*
> blow on the head – bold – brother – to come – doctor
> **"He (received) a bold blow on the head from his brother.**
> **The doctor is coming."**

thriskia (religion) .t. – .h. – .ri – is. – .ki – ia

> ita – aha – ari – isu – uki – ia
> *itxarokizun – ahalgustidun – -ari – isuri – ukitu – iaio*
> to have faith in – Almighty – mission – to inspire – to touch – cheerful
> **"We have faith in the Almighty and in our mission to inspire with a cheerful touch."**

timios (honest) .ti – imi – os.

> eti – imi – oso
> *etikoa – imintzio – osotasun*
> ethical – gesture – integrity
> **"Ethical gesture of integrity."**

trofiki (food poisoning) t. – .ro – ofi – ki

> te – ero – obi – -ki
> *tentaketa – erori – obiratze – -ki*
> temptation – to succumb – burying – piece of meat
> **"He succumbed to the temptation of the meat and was buried."**

vivliothiki (library) .vi – iv. – .li – ot. – .hi – iki

> .bi – ib. – .li – ot. – .hi – iki
> abi – ibe – eli – oto – ohi – iki
> *abiatu – ibeni – elizlegedi – otoi – ohitu – ikasbide*
> to begin – to introduce – collection of church laws – please – to get used to – doctrine
> **"We begin by introducing the collection of church laws**
> **so please get used to the doctrine."**

yefira (bridge) ye _ fi – ira

> *je _ fi – ira*
> *jeinutsu _ finkatu – iragaile*
> ingenious _ to establish/build – crossing
> **"(He) built an ingenious crossing."**

yimnasterio (gym) ji – im. – .na – as. – .te – eri – o

> ji – imi – ina – asa – ate – erri – o
> *jipoitu – imitagarri – inarroskatu – asaldaketa – atezu – erri – oh!*
> to strike/hit – exemplary – to stir up – excitement – tension – public – oh!
> **"An exemplary strike stirred up excitement and tension among the public; oh!."**

zevgari (couple) ze – eb. – .ga – ari

> ze – ebe – ega – ari
> *zentzudun – ebertar – egape – arrisku*
> sensible/prudent – patriarchal – protection – danger
> **"Sensible patriarchal protection from danger."**

CONCLUSION

The above Greek words, decoded via Basque and translated into English, leave little doubt that **the Greek language was the product of intelligent design. The words and names were made up** by professional linguists who used the Magical Language of the ancient Egyptians in their invention process.

BASQUE AND LINEAR–B

INTRODUCTION

While digging in Knossos on the isle of Crete, the famous archaeologist Arthur Evans found a number of tablets and seal stones which were inscribed. He identified three different types of script which he called hiero-glyphic, Linear A and Linear B. At the time no attempt at decipherment could be made because there was too little material to work with. Not until many more clay tablets with Linear-B writing had been found in subsequent digs on Crete and on the Greek mainland, did it become possible to make an attempt at deciphering. Michael Ventris, a young English architect, announced in 1952 that he had succeeded in deciphering Linear B and had proven that this old writing was archaic Greek. He identified 89 Linear B characters and established phonetic values for most of them, which he decided, was adequate to translate many of the tablets.

The majority of the tablets he worked with had come from a once beautiful mansion at Pylos, on the west coast of the Peloponnisos in south Greece, which had been destroyed through violent human activity and a very hot fire. The heat of the fire had baked the recently written soft clay tablets into indestruct-ible pottery tablets. The deciphering of the writing gave Ventris no idea about the circumstances of the attack, and the fate of the inhabitants remained un-known to him. The archaeologist in charge of the dig had suggested that this was the palace of king Nestor, of Homeric fame. However, he wondered why this was the only palace in Greece which had not been prepared for the war they obviously knew was coming, in fact the building had no defenses at all. Was it really Nestor's palace? Almost all of the Pylos tablets appeared to relate to one village, in which the majority of the landholders had religious titles. This indicated to Ventris that he was dealing with a very unusual settlement. To me, the writer of this book, the establishment he described appeared similar to later religious centers, the Benedictine monasteries of western Europe, established to introduce a new religion and social order in areas where the older religion of the Goddess had been practiced since time immemorial. Could "Nestor's palace" possibly have been the monastery of the priest-linguists who had come to Greece to bring the new male-dominated religion to a place where the Goddess had reigned before, and to destroy her language by inventing and introducing a new one?

SOLVING THE LINEAR–B PUZZLE

The 89 characters used in the writing had told Ventris that he was dealing with a syllabic script, most of the phonetic values were represented by one consonant and one vowel e.g. in-di-vi-du-al or Ca-na-da. This in contrast to a pictographic or ideographic script in which one symbol represents one word, like in Chinese with thousands of characters, or an alphabetic script like English in which a small number of characters represents the sounds which make up the words. To find out how Ventris deciphered the script, see: John Chadwick's "The Decipherment of Linear B." By assembling the phonetic values he had obtained, Ventris was able to show that the language used was an early form of Greek. The job of deciphering was still not completely finished when Ventris was tragically killed in a car accident and his work was written up for popular consumption by his co-worker John Chadwick.

The syllabic system of writing made up mostly of CV, reminded me of the early Ogam inscriptions of Ireland, written on stone and also of the Benedictines' manual the "Auraicept na n'Eces," in which most syllables had been made up of consonant-vowel. This possible similarity urged me to apply the Basque language to the sentences which Ventris had worked out. In the back of his book, Chadwick provided me with some tablets in transcription and of these I selected a few. The result was fascinating:

PYLOS TABLET PY Fr 1184.

Transcribed text: ko-ra-ro a-pe-do-ke e-ra-wo to-so e-u-me-de-i pa-ro i-pe-se-wa ka-ra-re-we.

Ventris' translation: Kokalos repaid the following quantity of olive oil to Eumedes: 648 liters of oil. From Ipsewas, thirty-eight stirrup jars (?).

Nyland's translation:

ko	ko	*kontrako*	enemy
ra	ora	*oratu*	to grab

ro/	aro/	-aro	all
a-pe	ape	apez	priest
do	edo	edonongo	from everywhere
ke	oke	oker	unjustly, without reason
e-ra	era	erailketa	murder
wo/	awo/	aopetic	secretly, out of sight
.to	ito	itoaldi	drowning
so/	oso/	oso	simple
e-u	eu	eupakada	calling out to
me	ume	ume	child, offspring, descendant
de	ede	edesti	history
i	ei	ei	they say, I am told
pa	ipa	ipartar	northern
ro/	aro/	arrotz	stranger
i-pe	ipe	epe luzatu	to prolong, continue
se	ese	esetsaldi	attack
wa/	ewa/	ea	(emphasis) e.g. terrible
.ka	ika	ikararazi	to terrorize
ra	ara	arrapakatu	to plunder
re	are	arestian	a short time ago
we	?		

"The enemy grabbed all the priests from everywhere and without reason murdered them, out of sight, by simple drowning. I am calling out to our descendants in history. I am told that the northern strangers continued their terrible attack, terrorizing and plundering (until) a short time ago."

Within each word made up with the symbols, the vowel of the preceding syllable is the same as the first vowel of the following syllable; this is called vowel-interlocking. When the archaic Greek word starts with a consonant, the first vowel is often missing and must be recovered by testing all five vowels, in which case a dot has temporarily been placed in the spot of the missing letter. A slash indicates where the vowel-interlocking is broken. This process is shown in much greater detail in the Ogam chapters.

The above translation is very different from what Ventris came up with. Why was it so different? The answer probably lies in the suggestion that we are dealing here with the first hesitant steps of monk-linguists who were experimenting with the foundation of a new language, in this case the Greek language. Based on the tablets found in Knossos I suggest that the Greek language does not date back farther than about 1,300 B.C.

PYLOS TABLET PY Ta722.

Transcribed text: ta-ra-nu a-ja-me-no e-re-pa-te-jo a-to-ro-qo i-qo-qe po-ru-po-de-qe...

Only the first part of this tablet could be translated with this method, so far..

Ventris' translation: One footstool inlaid with a man and a horse and an octopus and a griffin in ivory.

Nyland's translation:

ta	eta	-eta	abundance, huge
ra	ara	arakintza	massacre
nu/	anu/	anu egin	fall back in fear
a-ja	aia	aiaia	grief, suffering
me	ame	ameskaitz	nightmare
no/	eno/	enora	wart, inflicted, afflicted
e-re	ere	erremindu	to burn
pa	epa	epaitu	to decide
te	ate	aterpe	refuge
jo/	ejo/	ejo/eho	to beat
a-to	ato	atoitu	to drag
ro	oro	oro	all
qo/	oko/	okolu	stall, stable
i-qo	iko	iko ukaldi	hammer blow
qe/	oke/	okertu	to be done evil
.po	apo	apokeria	filthy deed
ru	oru	orubekatu	place, piece of land

"I fell back in fear from the (huge) massacre inflicted on us during this nightmare of suffering. They decided then to burn our refuge and to beat us. All were dragged from the stable and done evil with hammer blows. This filthy deed…"

PYLOS TABLET PY Sa 794.

Transcribed text: ka-ko de-de-me-no no-pe-re-e.

Ventris' translation: One pair of wheels, bound with bronze, unfit for service.

Nyland's translation:

.ka	ika	ikara	terror
ko/	ako/	akorduan euki	remember
.de	ide	idekotu	to adjust, recover
de	ede	ederrak hartu	to defeat
me	eme	emeki	gently
no	eno	enora	wart, afflicted
no	ono	onon	very good
pe	ope	operatu	to perform surgery
re	ere	erremusina	to care, charity
e	?		

"While remembering the terror, we had to recover from the defeat by gently giving very good care to the afflicted and performing surgery."

KNOSSOS TABLET KN Gg 702.

Transcribed text: pa-si-te-o-i me-ri da-pu-ri-to-jo po-ti-ni-ja me-ri.
Ventris' translation: To all the gods, one amphora of honey. To the mistress of the Labyrinth (?), one amphora of honey.

Nyland's translation:

.pa	ipa	*ipartar*	northerner
si	asi	*asi*	to start
te	ite	*itegun*	work performed
o	eo	*eortziri*	to bury
i/	oi/	*oian*	forest
.me	ame	*ameskaitz*	nightmare
ri/	eri/	*erioaldi*	agony
.da	ada	*adazkatu*	to gore
pu	apu	*apurtu*	to destroy
ri	uri	*urrikalgabe*	mercilessly
to	ito	*itoarazi*	to drown
jo	ojo/oho	*ohoindu*	to rob
po	opo	*opor*	time off, to be left alone
ti	oti	*otzikaratu*	to shiver
ni	ini	*initz/ainitz*	many
ja	ija	*iabali*	frightened
me	ame	*ameskaitz*	nightmare
ri	eri	*erioaldi*	agony

My translation:
**"The northerners have started the work of burying in the
forest after a nightmare of agony during which they gored and
destroyed and drowned mercilessly while robbing. When we
were left alone many were still shivering and frightened after
this nightmare of agony."**

This last tablet came from Knossos and was probably written 200 years before the other three from Pylos. In this case the northerners may well have been the Achaeans themselves who are thought to have conquered Crete at that time. It looks like the Achaeans received in Pylos what they had dished out, two centuries earlier, in Knossos.

Then there is that odd name **"Pylos,"** analyzed with the vowel-interlocking formula as:

pi-ilo-os.
epi-ilo-oso
epika- ilordu – oso
epic – agony – total
"Epic of total agony."

This is the name Homer used. Homer lived some 400 years after the destruction and he must have used the name current at his time. We do not know the name of the town before the massacre by the Sea Peoples.

The name **"Knossos"** appears to be the original one:

.k. – .no – os. – .so – os.

eka – ano – osa – azo – oze

ekarri – ano – osakor – azoka – ozen (noisy)

to provide with – food supplies – healthy – open air market provide with

"The noisy open air market provides us with healthy foodsupplies."

The name **Mukaenai** (Mycenae) tells a story which has been verified by Schliemann:

.mu-uka-ena-ahi

amultsukeria – ukan – ena – ahiniztasun:

excessive affection – possessions – superlative, rich – large quantities

"Excessive affection for large quantities of rich possessions."

What would they have called their own town?

The Town of Pylos was Prepared for the Attack

Many of the tablets found at Pylos described preparations for an attack which had obviously been expected from the direction of the sea. Michael Wood in his book "In Search of the Trojan War" wrote the following:

> *"One of the most important tablets is entitled: 'Thus the watchers are guarding the coasts' : command of Maleus at Owitono... 50 men of Owitono to go to Oikhalia, command of Nedwatas... 20 men of Kyparssia at Aruwote, 10 Kyparissia men at Aithalewes... command of Tros at Ro'owa: Kadasijo a share-holder, performing feudal service... 110 men from Oikhalia to Aratuwa. Some of the last tablets written at Pylos speak of rowers being drawn from five places to go to Pleuron on the coast. A second list, incomplete, numbers 443 rowers, crews for at least fifteen ships. A much larger list speaks of 700 men as defensive troops; gaps on the tablet suggest that when complete, around 1000 men were marked down, the equivalent of a force of 30 ships."*

It was all to no avail because the attack had been totally overwhelming. The first wave of attackers appears to have targeted the priests but did no burning. This allowed the scribes enough time to describe the attack on their tablets when the second wave of attackers arrived who devastated the palace with fire and beat anyone they could find. The old story that some Dorians came over land from the north and devastated the palaces may well be true, but they must have done it in cooperation with the overwhelming Sea Peoples' attacks in boats. The only strangers for which we have good evidence are the Sea Peoples from the Atlantic ocean and their main goal was to stop the advance of the new

cult of the jealous and cruel patriarchal gods. The attacks were successful because, like the Hittite empire, we know that the Achaean civilization came to an
abrupt end. Only Athens was apparently strong enough to ward off the attacks.
I now must digress to put the happenings into perspective.

WHY THE VICIOUSNESS OF THE ATTACK?

There must have been a very good reason for the northern peoples from the
islands in the Great Green Sea to mount such a massive attack so far away from
home. These people came from a peace-loving, caring society and they must
have reached the end of their patience to decide to do something so unbeliev-
ably drastic. Allow me some educated speculation, that's all I have so far.

The spread of the aggressive patriarchal cults with their cruel gods in the Near
East must have been well-known to the peoples of the Atlantic islands, because
they did much of the trading in the east. The name Atlantis most likely has
nothing to do with the Atlantic ocean because it tells us something about a
frightening tidal wave, probably caused by the eruption of the Thera volcano,
that devastated the entire eastern Mediterranean about 1420 B.C. Plato has
some explaining to do.

Atlantis
at. – .la – an. – .ti – is.
ato – ola – ani – iti – izi
atontze – olatualdi – aniztu – itxi – izugarrikeria
get ready! – large waves – to increase – to abandon/get away – terrible happening
**"Get ready to go! Large waves are increasing in size.
Get away from this terrible happening!"**

As long as this was going on in Mesopotamia, Persia, Anatolia or Assyria there
was little the Sea Peoples could do about it. But when the decision was made to
venture out to the countries farther west in the Mediterranean, the culture- and
religion-destroying missionaries were within easy striking range of the mobile
Sea Peoples. One of the educated groups of proto-Judaic missionaries and their
monk-linguists went probably from Anatolia to Pylos in Greece. It was an especially good vantage point from where to cast out to places further west. For
their next team's location they decided to go to what later became Tuscany on
the west coast of north central Italy, where the priest-linguists worked on the
Etruscan language and probably also on Latin. Then another team of missionaries was sent to the east coast of Spain where work on the Iberian language was
started (Iber or ibar means lowland or river valley land). All this aggressive
religious activity was closely observed by the Sea Peoples who decided that

something had to be done before it was too late. A war council was called of all the west European nations, which was likely held on the Isle of Barra, the location of the only Chief Priestess of the Atlantic, in the Holy Land of antiquity. The seriousness of the situation called for a holy war because it was clear that the survival of their ancient religion was threatened by the ever advancing forces of male domination.

When the fleet was finally assembled and the cooperation of the allies around the Baltic and Black Sea had been assured, their first target was probably the Iberian monastery in Spain, but we have no record or archaeological evidence for this. If it had been built near the coast it would have been easily eliminated, never to rise again. The Etruscans were more difficult to reach because they had established themselves farther inland. They must have had advance warning because their civilization survived the onslaught, in spite of the losses. For their next target, Pylos, we are on more solid ground because we have the tablets (above) which tell us some of what happened. The attack on Pylos and the other pirate states of Greece was so dreadfully effective that for the next 550 years Greek civilization came to a halt and writing was forgotten.

The Sea Peoples' most important attack was then aimed at the Luvian religious control centre of the patriarchal religion, located in the province of Kizzuwadna, Anatolia. This attack is likely to have been coordinated with the Scythians of the Ukraine, the Kirrukaska (or Kaska) of NE Turkey and the people of **Colchis**, now Georgia.

.ko – ol.- .txi – is.
ako – oli – itxi – isi
akorduan euki – oliotu – itxi – isilpetasun
to remember – to anoint – to leave – secrecy
"Remember the anointed one who left in secrecy."

This probably refers to the priestess Medea who left with the Argonauts, taking her father's golden fleece, then fled up the Dnjepr river to the Baltic and on to Kirke on Barra, Scotland.

A massive assault from both the land and the sea totally obliterated the Hittites, their allies and all the cities and towns in Kizzuwadna. We have no written records of this but we can be assured that it was a horrible massacre. Next, the attackers trekked and sailed south, doing the same to all the cities along the Levantine coast, an action of which several eye-witness descriptions have survived. That was the end of the Sea Peoples' string of successes because their next move was to Egypt where Ramesses III was ready for them. Much of the huge fleet sailed up the Nile and the pharaoh's fleet then closed off the mouth of the river behind them, imprisoning the entire attacking fleet. Thousands of the pharaoh's soldiers with long-bows lined the river banks and dealt out death and drowning. The attackers had only swords, spears and small bows, none of which reached the shore. The massive defeat of the great armada from western Europe spelled the beginning of the end for the civilization of the Goddess. (see detailed description on Ramesses III's temple at Medinet Habu in *The Sea Peoples* by Sandars.)

THE BASQUE CONNECTION

In a number of these chapters I explain, with many examples, how the Saharan-Basque language was spoken in all of Europe as the universal language, because almost the entire population of Europe had migrated from the unilingual Sahara when the formerly productive land became a desert. With the coming of the new cults of the sky gods from Anatolia, all of them promoting male domination, priests had been sent out to far away places with orders to destroy the ancient religion of the Goddess, introduce male domination, wipe out the tribal system and create nations, introduce private landownership and invent new languages with different scripts for each new nation. This meant that every new language had to be based on the old Saharan language because there was no other to work from. The newly created languages are known today as the Indo-European "family" of languages. The old Saharan language survives as Basque in Europe and in an earlier form of the language as Dravidian in India and Ainu in Japan.

With this background it is not difficult to suggest that the tragic destruction in the eastern Mediterranean was the result of a major religious war. The aggressively expanding new religion of the patriarchy had to be stopped and the peoples of the Goddess united in one massive effort to eliminate the culprits once and for all, an effort which involved more than 1000 ships and possibly as many as 100,000 fighters. The Egyptians documented a great deal of this war on the walls of Ramesses III's temple at Medinet Habu and other places. According to these records, the Sea Peoples had come from their islands in the midst of the Great Green Sea, now known as the Atlantic Ocean. The travels of Odysseus by Homer describe the homecoming of one or more of these groups, which may have been composed of Irish, Scots, Phaikians (Vikings), Danes, Berbers and Canary Islanders. Without Homer we would not have known about this enormous effort with its tragic ending, inflicted on Britain and its allies. The memories of this awful defeat and loss of a whole generation of young men must have raised years of wailing but eventually even that was forgotten after the millennia had gone by. Homer hints at this tragedy when he called the Isle of Barra: "Aiaia" meaning "suffering." (Book X:135 in the Odyssey.)

DOUBLE–SPEAK IN BASQUE AND GREEK

One amazing characteristic of the syllabic system is that it allows the linguist to apply one language, Basque, to the script and come up with one translation, while another language, Greek, may produce a quite different story from the same characters, as the examples above show in Ventris' and my translations. I have earlier described the same technique in "Olla Vogala" in which two lines of the writing are in Latin, which were then translated into two lines of archaic Dutch, both telling the same story about birds. Applying Basque to all four lines, produced a quite different and coherent bird story. That Basque was involved in Linear A and B has been proposed long ago. In 1931 a booklet was published by the Oxford University Press entitled "Through Basque to Minoan" in which the author, F.G. Gordon, tried to interpret the script with the use of Basque. He identified each sign as an object and then gave its name in the language assumed. His incomplete research and prematurely published efforts had a negative influence upon future linguists, which reinforced the church-held idea that Basque was a trash language, which had to be avoided at all cost. Yet Gordon had taken the first steps on the right track; all Indo-European and Semitic languages and also Sumerian and Akkadian, are based on the old Magic Egyptian VCV language, which survives today in mostly unaltered form as part of the Basque language.

THE ORIGIN OF SLAVIC NAMES

INTRODUCTION

Some linguists have suggested that elements of Basque words can be detected in many East European names and words. In the following analysis of a number of Ukrainian, Russian and Polish names I searched for the Basque element and found that virtually all Slavic names are agglutinated using Basque vowel-consonant-vowel (VCV) roots with frequent use of VCCV endings, and with the vowels interlocking. This form of word agglutination was done with what I called the "VCV vowel interlocking formula." The formal decoding notation is used for greater clarity because many of the names are long.

Contrary to popular belief, the word **"Slav"** has nothing to do with slavery. Look up the meaning of the name "Yaroslav" below and your will see that "Slav" means: **"I swear to unite my fellow-countrymen."**

No vocabulary is included here. Slavic words are also assembled from Basque, but the process used by the monks in Kiev will need more experimentation, for future study.

NAMES ENDING IN "SKI"

A large number of names end in -ski, so let us look at the suffix "-ski," an ending common to Polish, Ukrainian, Serbian and Russian family names. The suffix "-ski" can have many meanings in Basque. The reader must keep in mind that the English "s" in Basque is spelled as "z" while the letter "s" in Basque is pronounced as a soft "sh." This means that the Slavic suffix "-ski" may have originated from "-ski or -zki." These two suffixes have a number of meanings in Basque:

aski	revenge, sufficient, frequently
azki	N.A.
eski	stairs, ladder, to offer
ezki	linden tree, irritable, small bell, belltower, bellringer
iski	pin, needlecase, weapon, joke, mockery
izki	shrimp, letter of alphabet, to write
oski	shoes, cobbler, coward, afraid
ozki	susceptible to the cold
uski	N.A.
uzki	anus, get lost!, remains, leftovers

SOME EXAMPLES OF–SKI NAMES

The "v" in Slavic names is always represented by a "b" in Basque, the "c" by a "k."

Bogolyubski, bog-oli-ub.-.ski,

bog	bog	*boga*	rower, boatman
oli	oli	*oliodura*	anointed, holy
ub.	ubi	*ubil*	whirlpool
.ski	iski	*iskirio*	mockery, joke

"(He made) a mockery of the holy boatman in the whirlpool."
This refers to the annual voluntary sacrifice of a young man in the whirlpool of Corryvreckan.

Gzovski, .g.-.zo-ob.-.ski,

.g.	ega	*egarri* strong	desire
.zo	azo	*-azo*	to bring about, to make happen
ob.	oba	*obakuntza*	improvement
.ski	aski	*askietsi*	sufficient, adequate

"He has a strong desire to bring about adequate improvements."

Keluski, .ke – elu – us. – .ki

.ke	ke	*kendu*	to get away from
elu	elu	*elur*	snow
us.	usu	*usu*	often
.ki	uki	*ukitu*	to refer to/to mention

"He/she often mentioned to get away from the snow."

Khmelnitsky, Bogdan, .bo-og.-.da.-an. .k.-.h.-.me-el.-.ni-it.-.ski,

.bo	abo	*aboskatu*	to proclaim
og.	oga	*ogasun*	property, land
.da	ada	*adarkadura*	ramification
an.	ana	*anaiguda*	civil war
.k.	ako	*akordio*	agreement
.h.	oho	*ohoragarri*	honorable

.me	ome	*omenaldi*	tribute
el.	ela	*ela*	talk, negotiation
.ni	ani	*anitz*	many
it.	itxi	*itxi*	to abandon, to lay down
.ski	iski	*iskilo*	weapon

"Proclaim our land at the outcome of the civil war. The honorable agreement is a tribute to the many negotiations (achieving) the laying down of weapons."

Orlovski, or.-.lo-ob.-.ski,

or.	ora	*oraindanik*	from now on
.lo	alo	*alokairu*	salary
ob.	oba	*obakuntza*	improvement
.ski	aski	*askiki*	adequately

"From now on my salary is adequately improved."

Pavlovski, .pa-ab.-.lo-ob.-.ski,

.pa	opa	*opa izan*	longing for
ab.	aba	*abadune*	opportunity
.lo	alo	*alokairu*	salary, earn money
ob.	oba	*obakuntza*	betterment, improvement
.ski	aski	*aski*	sufficient, enough

"I am longing for an opportunity to earn a salary sufficient for improvement."

Palubiski, .pa-alu-ubi-is.-.ki,

.pa	ipa	*ipartar*	northern
alu	alu	*alukeria*	repulsive action
ubi	ubi	*ubil*	whirlpool
is.	isu	*isuri*	to inspire
.ki	uki	*ukitu*	to touch, to move

"The repulsive action (i.e. sacrifice) in the northern whirlpool inspired and touched me."

Prezewalski, .p.-.re-eze-al.-.ski, (the "w" is usually meaningless)

.p.	ape	*apellaniz*	pasture
.re	ere	*erreka*	stream
eze	eze	*ezeizabarrena*	under the fir trees
al.	ale	*aleketa*	grain in abundance
.ski	eski	*eskindu*	to offer

"In the pasture by the stream under the firs we offered them grain in abundance."

Starokadomski: .sta-aro-oka-ado-om.-.ski,

.sta	esta	*estali*	to shelter
aro	aro	*aro*	weather
oka	oka	*okaztagarri*	disgusting
ado	ado	*adoretasun*	courage
om.	ome	*omen egin*	to pay tribute
.ski	eski	*eskini*	offering, devotional

"Sheltered from the disgusting weather we paid tribute (to their) courage with a devotional."

Stravinski, .s.-.tra-abi-in.-.ski,

.s.	asa	*asarredun*	angered
.tra	atra	*atrapala*	noise, sound
abi	abi	*abiatsuki*	impulsively
in.	ina	*inarrosketa*	to shake
.ski	aski	*askitan*	frequently, often

"When angered by the sound, he often shook impulsively."

Riasanovski, .ri-asa-ano-ob.-.ski,

.ri	iri	*irritsatu*	to yearn for
asa	asa	*asagotu*	to go far away
ano	ano	*ano*	food supply
ob.	oba	*oba*	better
.ski	aski	*askiki*	plentiful

"He yearned to go far away with a better and more plentiful food supply."

Tchaikovski, txai-aiko-ob.-.ski,

txai	txai	*txairo*	graceful
aiko	aiko	*aiko maikoka*	making excuses
ob.	oba	*obakuntza*	improvement
.ski	aski	*aski*	enough, satisfactory

"Gracefully making excuses (and showing) satisfactory improvement." It is safe to assume that all -ski names have such sentences written in them, although not all yield their hidden sentence as readily as the ones above did.

NAMES ENDING IN "ITCH"

The ending "-itch" can also have several meanings. In Basque the sharp "sh" is written as "x," which spelling will be used here:

itxa	to await, to hope, to trust, expectation, sea
itxe	N.A.
itxi	to shut in, to close, to abandon, to denounce, to permit
itxo	to wait, waiting room

itxu   aspect, appearance, absurd, similar, to simulate, hypocrite, imposter, pretense, to transform

Adamovitch, ada-amo-obi-itx.

ada	ada	*adatz*	long hair, long braids
amo	amo	*amona*	grandmother
obi	obi	*obi*	grave
itx.	itxi	*itxiarazi*	to enclose

"Grandmother's long braids were enclosed in her grave."

Kazanovitch, .ka-aza-ano-obi-itx.

ka	ka	*katabuta*	coffin
aza	aza	*azalkeratu*	to discover
ano	ano	*anonimo*	unmarked
obi	obi	*obi*	grave
itx.	itxi	*itxi*	to abandon

"He discovered the coffin in an unmarked, abandoned grave."

Mostovitch, .mo-os.-.to-obi-itx.,

.mo	amo	*amona*	grandmother
os.	oso	*oso*	simple
.to	oto	*otoi*	prayer
obi	obi	*obi*	grave
itx.	itxi	*itxi*	to close

"(After) grandmother's simple prayer the grave was closed."

Rabinovitch, .ra-abi-ino-obi-itx.

.ra	era	*erauntsi*	violent storm
abi	abi	*abiatu*	to begin
ino	ino	*inon*	somewhere
obi	obi	*obiratu*	to bury
itx.	itxa	*itxaso*	sea

"A violent storm is beginning; bury (him) somewhere at sea."

Salamuneovich, .sa-als-amu-une-obi-itx.

.sa	asa	*asagotu*	to go away
ala	ala	*alargun*	widow
amu	amu	*amultsurikatu*	to grieve
une	une	*une*	instant
obi	obi	*obi*	grave
itx.	itxi	*itxi*	to close

"His grieving widow went away the moment the grave was closed."

Topalovitch, .to-opa-alo-abi-itx.

.to	ato	*ator*	Come!
opa	opa	*opari egin*	to give
alo	alo	*alorgizon*	farmer
obi	obi	*obiratze*	burial
itx.	itxu	*itxurazko*	decent

"Come, let's give the farmer a decent burial."
'alo' could also stand for *alogereko* (mercenary):
"Come let's give the mercenary a decent burial."

NAMES ENDING WITH "KO"

Another common ending is -ko which may come from:

ako:	agreement, contract, tradition, memory
eko:	to produce, fertile, ecology, economy, administrator
iko:	lump, swelling, stonemason's hammer
oko:	cattle stable, pasture next to the house, chin, dewlap
uko:	refusal, negative, elbow

Bracco, .b. – .ra – ak. – .ko,

.b.	abe	*abe*	cross
.ra	era	*erakaserazi*	teacher
ak.	aka	*akatsbako*	perfect
.ko	ako	*akorduan euki*	to remember

"Remember our perfect teacher of the cross."

Atamanenko, ata-ama-ane-en-.-ko,

ata	ata	*ataldu*	to divide
ama	ama	*ama*	mother
ane	ane	*anega*	measure of grain
en.	ena	*-ena* plural	possessive suffix
.ko	ako	*akordiozko*	according to tradition, as usual

"Mother divided our measure of grain according to tradition."

Macarenko, .ma-aka-are-en.-.ko,

.ma	ama	*ama*	mother
aka	aka	*akabu*	perfect
are	are	*arrera*	reception, welcome
en.	ene	*enetan*	always
.ko	eko	*ekoizkor*	productive, lavish, generous

"Mother's perfect welcome was always generous."

SOME OTHER TYPICALLY SLAVIC NAMES

Baranof, .ba-ara-ano-ob.,

.ba	aba	*abade*	priest
ara	ara	*arrapatu*	to get drunk
ano	ano	*ano*	wine
ob.	oba	*obaez*	of course

"The priest got drunk, on wine of course."

Baryluk, .ba-ari-ilu-uk.,

.ba	eba	*ebaskindegi*	hide-out
ari	ari	*arinari eman*	to escape
ilu	ilu	*iluntasun*	darkness
uk.	uka	*ukan*	to have

"He escaped from his hiding place during darkness."

Boyar, .bo-oia-ar.,

.bo	ebo	*eboluzionatu*	to develop, cultivate
oia	oia	*oian*	forest
ar.	ara	*arazo*	task

"Cultivating the forest (is their) task."

Cossack, ko-os.-.sa-ak.,

ko	ko	*kontaezinbesteko*	innumerable, all the people
os.	osa	*osatu*	to unite
.sa	asa	*asaben*	ancestral
ak.	ako	*akordu*	tradition

"Unite all the people in the ancestral tradition."

Dmitriev, .d.-.mi-it.-.ri-eb.,

.d.	idu	*iduki*	to have
.mi	umi	*umiltasun*	humility
it.	ita	*itxaro*	to trust
.ri	ari	*-ari*	mission
eb.	eba	*ebanjelari*	evangelist

"Have humility, and trust in the evangelist's mission."

Dumala, .du-uma-ala,

.du	idu	*iduki*	to have
uma	uma	*uma*	child
ala	ala	*alaitu*	to fill with joy

Having a child fills (me) with joy.

Dzogan, .d.-.zo-oga-an.,

.d.	ida	*idatziz*	to record

.zoazo	*azokalari*		merchant
oga	oga	*ogasun*	wealth
an.	ane	*anega*	grain measure, supply

"He records the wealthy merchant's grain supply."

Gorbachov, .go-orba-axo-ob.,

.go	ego	*egoera*	manner of behaving
orba	orba	*orbaingabe*	pure
axo	axo	*axoladun*	careful, diligent
ob.	obe	*obengabe*	blameless

"His behaviour is pure, diligent and blameless."

Gulag, ,gu-ula-ag.

.gu	egu	*egur*	punishment
ula	ula	*ulaka/uluka*	wailing, crying out
ag.	aga	*agaka*	hitting with a stick

"He cried out after being hit with a stick in punishment."

Karasik, .ka-ara-asi-ik.,

.ka	ika	*ikaserazi*	to teach
ara	ara	*arrai*	gentle
asi	asi	*asialdi*	beginning
ik.	ika	*ikasgale*	desire to learn

"Gentle teaching creates a desire to learn."

Korelus, .ko-ore-elu-us.,

.ko	ako	*akorduan euki*	to remember
ore	ore	*orekan*	to keep your balance
elu	elu	*elurlera*	sled
us.	usa	*usatu*	to get used to

"Remember to keep your balance when getting used to your sled."

Korolef, .ko-oro-ole-eb.,

.ko	ako	*akorduan euki*	to remember
oro	oro	*oroegile*	Creator
ole	ole	*oles egin*	to call upon
eb.	ebe	*ebertar*	Hebrew, Jesus

"Remember the Creator by calling upon Jesus."

Kowalchuk, .ko-al.-.txu-uk.,

.ko	ako	*akorduan euki*	to remember
al.	ala	*alaitasun*	happiness
.txu	atxu	*atxuri*	newborn lamb
uk.	uki	*ukitu*	to touch

"Remember your happiness when you touched the newborn lamb?"

Landau, .la-an.-.da-au

.la	ala	*alabeharreko*	unavoidable
an.	ana	*anarkia*	anarchy
.da	ada	*adarkadura*	ramification
au	au	*auhen*	lament, suffering

"The unavoidable ramification of anarchy is suffering."

Ligachev, .li-iga-atxe-eb,

.li	ili	*ilinti*	fiery
iga	iga	*igartze*	prophesying
atxe	atxe	*atxeki*	to adhere to, to be determined
eb.	eba	*ebanjelari*	evangelist

"Fiery, determined, prophesying evangelist."

Mazowsze (Mazovshe), .ma-azo-ob.-.xe, (Polish singing/dancing group)

.ma	ama	*amaikatxo*	many
azo	azo	*azoka*	market day
ob.	obe	*obeki*	good
.xe	exe	*exeri*	to sit (and listen)

"Many market days it is good to sit (and listen)."

Monomakh, .mo-ono-oma-ak.-.h.,

.mo	amo	*amodiotsu*	loving
ono	ono	*onon*	wonderful
oma	oma	*oma*	grandmother, tribal mother
ak.	ako	*akorduan euki*	to remember
.h.	oha	*ohardun*	thoughtful

"Remember our wonderfully thoughtful tribal mother."
Vladimir Monomakh was the grandson of Yaroslav the wise, the
Great Lawgiver; from his name I deduct that Yaroslav the Wise
must have been a woman. See below.

Pashnik, .pa-ax.-.ni-ik.,

.pa	opa	*opa izan*	longing for
ax.	axo	*axolagabetsu*	carefree
.ni	oni	*onik*	safe
ik.	ike	*ikertaldi*	visit

"Longing for a carefree and safe visit."

Pecheneg, .pe-eche-ene-eg.,

pe	pe	*pena ukan*	to suffer
exe	exe	*exeri*	to sit
ene	ene	*-enerako*	before
eg.	egu	*egur*	punishment

"(Let them) sit and suffer before punishment."

Pierzchala, .pi-er.-.z.-.txa-ala,

.pi	ipi	*ipini*	to acquire
er.	era	*erakuste*	education
.z.	azi	*aziarazi*	to raise
.txa	itxa	*itxaro*	hope
ala	ala	*alaitasun*	happiness

"Acquiring an education raises the hope for happiness."

Polovtsy, .bo-olo-ob.-.tsi,

.bo	ebo	*eboluzionatu*	to develop, process
olo	olo	*olo*	oats
ob.	oba	*oba*	better
.tsi	atsi	*atximurkari*	pincher, roller

"You process the oats better in a roller."

Pravda, (justice) .p.-.ra-ab.-.da

.p.	opa	*opatu*	to give
.ra	ara	*arausail*	Code of Laws
ab.	abe	*abe*	support, stability
.da	eda	*edangura*	thirsting for

"Give us a Code of Laws; we are thirsting for stability."

Prokopchuk, .p.-.ro-oko-op.-.txu-uk.,

.p.	opo	*oporrak*	vacation
.ro	oro	*oroitu*	to remember
oko	oko	*okolu*	stable
op.	opa	*opa izan*	to long for
.txu	atxu	*atxuri*	newborn lamb
uk.	uki	*ukitu*	to touch

"Remember the stable on our vacation where you longed to touch the newborn lamb?"

Ranogajek, .ra-ano-oga-aje-ek.,

.ra	ara	*arrapatur*	to get drunk
ano	ano	*ano*	wine
oga	oga	*ogasun*	homemade
aje	aie	*aiene*	grief, suffering
ek.	eka	*ekarrarazi*	to cause

"Getting drunk on home-made wine causes grief."

Rasputin, .ra-as.-.pu-uti-in.,

.ra	ara	*arakintza*	massacre
as.	asa	*asarrekeria*	shocking
.pu	apu	*apurtzaile*	destructive

uti	uti	*utikan*	go away, get out!
in.	ino	*inola*	in any way possible

"A shocking and destructive massacre! Get out in any way possible."

Razin, .ra-azi-in.,

.ra	ira	*iraultzatu*	to revolt
azi	azi	*azitoki*	birthplace
in.	ine	*inertzia*	downtrodden

"Revolt for our downtrodden birthplace."

Sabatinovka, .sa-aba-ati-ino-ob.-.ka

.sa	asa	*asaba*	ancestor
aba	aba	*abade*	priest
ati	ati	*atxiki*	faithful
ino	ino	*inoiz ere ez*	ever
ob.	oba	*oba*	better
.ka	aka	*akabu*	end

"The priest tells us to be ever faithful (to achieve) a better end."

Shatalin, xa-ata-ali-in.

xa	xa	*xalo*	open/frank
ata	ata	*atalgabeko*	uncomplicated
ali	ali	*alizan*	capable
in.	inu	*inuritze*	inspiring

"Uncomplicated, capable and inspiring."

Skorepa, .s.-.ko-ore-epa,

.s.	asa	*asagotu*	to go away
.ko	ako	*akorduan euki*	to remember
ore	ore	*oren*	hour
epa	epa	*epaialdi*	trial

"If you go away, remember the hour of the trial."

Slutskaya, .s.-.lu-uts.-.ka-aia,

.s.	asa	*asaldagarri*	shocking
.lu	alu	*alukeria*	repulsive action
uts.	utsi	*utziezin*	unavoidable
.ka	ika	*ikara*	terror, horror
aia	aia	*aiaia*	grief, suffering

"The shockingly repulsive action caused unavoidable horror and suffering."

Stalin, .sta-ali-in.,

.sta	asta	*astapotro*	brutish, in a brutish way
ali	ali	*alienatu*	to kill a person

in.	ino	*inola*	in any way possible

"In a brutish way he kills people any way possible."

Tarasof, .ta-ara-aso-ob.,

.ta	ita	*itxaro*	to hope for
ara	ara	*araberatasun*	agreement
aso	azo	*-azo*	to bring about
ob.	oba	*obakuntza*	improvement

"We hope for agreement to bring about improvement."

Volnitza, .bo-ol.-.ni-itza,

.bo	abo	*aboskatu*	to proclaim
ol.	ole	*oleazio*	destiny
.ni	eni	*eni*	to me, us
itza	itza	*izaldun*	honorable

"Proclaim an honorable destiny for us."

Vsevolod and Mikhalko (brothers), .b.-.se-ebo-olo-od. .mi-ik.-.ha-al.-.ko,

.b.	oba	*obakuntza*	improvement
.se	ase	*aseguratu*	to insure
ebo	ebo	*eboluzionatu*	the develop, produce
olo	olo	*olo*	oats
odi	odi	*odi*	tube, drum, roll

"The improvement insured the production of rolled oats."

.mi	ami	*amilura*	falling water
ik.	ika	*ikaserazi*	to teach
.ha	aha	*ahalizan*	to make possible
al.	ale	*aleketa*	abundance of grain
.ko	eko	*ekoiztu*	to produce, to process

"He teaches how falling water makes it possible to process grain in abundance."

The translation of these names tell a very different story from that in the history books.

Yaroslav the Wise, .ja-aro-os.-.la-abe,

.ja	oja	*oian*	forest
aro	aro	*arroztu*	to exile
os.	osa	*osatu*	to unify, to unite
.la	ala	*alafede*	I swear to
ab.	abe	*aberkide*	fellow countrymen, patriots

"The forest exile swore to unify the patriots."

From the name of her grandson, Monomakh, I deduct that Yaroslav was a wise tribal mother. The true meaning of **Slav**, os. – .la – av, osa – ala – abe is here revealed. It has nothing to do with slavery, instead it means: **"I swear to unite my fellow countrymen."**

Zadaprushki, .za-ada-ap.-.ru-uxki,

.za	aza	*azaluts*	insincere
ada	ada	*adarra sartu*	to deceive
ap.	ape	*apeta*	tendency
.ru	eru	*errukigabe*	cruel, pitiless
uxki	uxki	*uxkia miazkatzera*	get lost!

"(You are) insincere and deceiving (and have) a tendency to be cruel; Get lost!: (what a name!)

Zaporogian, .za-apo-oro-ogi-an.,

.za	oza	*ozar*	arrogant
apo	apo	*apokeria*	insult
oro	oro	*orobatu*	to unify
ogi	ogi	*ogipuska*	easygoing
an.	ana	*anaitasun*	brotherhood

"Arrogant insults united the easygoing brotherhood."

SOME SLAVIC GEOGRAPHICAL NAMES

Chernobil, txer.-.no-obi-il.

txe	txerri	*txerrizain*	swineherd
.no	ino	*inor*	no-one
obi	obi	*obi*	grave
il.	ile	*iletu*	to mourn

"No-one mourned at the grave of the swineherd."

Dniepr, d.n-ie.p-.r

d.n	don	*donetsi*	to bless, the blessed one
ie.p	ihesp	*ihespideto*	means of escape
.r	ur	*ur*	water

"The blessed one's means of escape was by water."
(Probably referring to the Priestess Medea who escaped with Jason up the Dniepr river after taking the golden fleece from King Aietus. See "The Voyage of Argo" by Apollonius of Rhodes).

Donetz,

donetz		*donetzi*	to sanctify

"The sanctified one."

Irkutsk, ir.-.ku-utsik,

ir.	iri	*iri*	city
.ku	iku	*ikustatu*	to visit
utsik	utsik	*utsik*	deserted

"I visited the deserted city."

Kamchatka, .ka-am.-.txa-at.-.ka,

.ka	ika	*ikaragarri*	frightening
am.	amo	*amorro*	fury
.txa	otxa	*otxoa*	wolf
at.	ate	*aterbegabe*	unprotected, out in the open
.ka	eka	*ekantze*	to get used to.

"Out in the open, the frightening fury of the wolves takes getting used to."

Kiev, .ki-eb.,

.ki	oki	*okitu*	totally, completely
eb.	eba	*ebanjeliotu*	to evangelize

"Completely evangelized."

Okhotsk, ok.-.ho-otsk

ok.	oka	*okaztagarri*	disgusting
.ho	aho	*ahozagarri*	astonishing
otsk	otsok	*otsok*	brutality

"Astonishingly disgusting brutality."

Taymyr, tai.-.mi-ir.,

tai.	taiu	*taiuera*	size, appearance
.mi	umi	*umildu*	to humble
ir.	ira	*iraganaldi*	migration, migrating herd

"The size of the migrating herd is humbling."

Vladivostok, .b.-.la-adi bo-osto-ok.,

.b.	aba	*abaroan egon*to	take refuge
.la	ala	*alabearreko*	necessary
adi	adi	*adi*	watch out!
bo	bo	*bortxakeria*	violence
osto	osto	*ostosketa*	rolling of the thunder
ok.	oki	*okildu*	to be frightened

"Watch out! It's necessary to take refuge. The violence of the rolling thunder is frightening."

WHO MADE UP THESE NAMES?

It is obvious that these names could not have been invented by the people themselves. The system of agglutination is exactly the same as was used by the Benedictines and their grammarians in western Europe. It is well-known that there was close cooperation between the eastern and western Christian churches in the 10th and 11th centuries, especially between the Pannonhalma Benedictines in Hungary and the monks from the Tyniec monastery in Poland and those in Kiev. The Kiev monastery of **Pecherska Lavra** was established in 1040, a few decades after these other two monasteries and some qualified linguists were apparently sent from there to Kiev to train the Eastern monks in the use of the Basque language.

Pesherska Lavra

.pe – es. – .he – er. – .s. – .ka   .la – ab. – .ra

ope – esi – ihe – era – aska   ila – abe – era

opetsi – eziketa – ihesleku – eraspen – askamen   ilarteko – abegion – erantzun

to offer – education – shelter – devotion – pardon   lifetime – hospitality – to fulfill

**"We offer education, shelter, devotion and pardon.
Ours is a lifetime of hospitality and fulfillment."**

The early cooperation is still remembered because in the summer of 1996 the head of the Russian church planned to attend, with the Pope, the 1000 year celebrations at Pannonhalma. Unfortunately, illness prevented the historic meeting from happening. In 1040 AD there was probably no longer a source of educated Saharan/Basque speakers in Russia, so either these specialists were recruited in Liguria (northern Italy) and Euskadi (northern Spain) and sent east, or the linguists worked from Basque dictionaries, without being able to speak the language. Likely some of both happened.

SANSKRIT

INTRODUCTION

After having tested many "Indo-European" languages for Basque content and reported on the results in these chapters, several correspondents have asked me to do the same with Sanskrit, which was said by some to be one of the oldest languages of them all. It was a lucky choice that the first word tried, **niire** (water), was clearly assembled with Basque words in the VCV manner but without vowel interlocking:

ni – ire

ni – irensle

I – to swallow/to drink

"I drink."

This made good sense and was done in the same manner in which Latin, Greek, English etc. vocabulary was composed, except that a CV word was used for the first morpheme. However, Sanskrit vocabulary turned out to be not quite as easy to decode as the European languages and several words did not respond to the decoding process. There may be two reasons for that: 1) because the early Saharan language, used by the Brahmin priests to construct the words, was somewhat different from the modern Basque language used by the Benedictine monks one millennium later, and 2) there may have been a local language in use which contributed words to the newly invented Sanskrit, just as it did to the modern Dravidian languages. I expect both reasons have something to do with those Sanskrit words that have proven difficult or impossible to decode. An interesting observation is that in the word-invention process, mostly that half of the Saharan/Basque vocabulary was used which begins with vowel-consonant-vowel (VCV). The first three letters of the selected Saharan words were inserted into the VCV vowel-interlocking formula, after which many of the vowels were removed, especially the first, to create the final word. In the above example the vowels match, but both 'i's were retained independently. Let us first look at a few old Sanskrit names.

Punjab

.pu – un. – .ja – ab.
ipu – uni – ija – abe
ipuinezko – unibertsal – iaio – abegion
legendary – universal – cheerful – hospitality
"Our cheerful hospitality is legendary and universal."

Kashmir:

.ka – ash. – .mi – ir.
ika – axo – omi – ira
ikasbide – axoladun – omia santu – irakitu
teachings – caring – holy – fired with passion
"Our teachings are holy, caring and fired with passion."

Taxila, the oldest university in India:

.ta – ak. – .si – ila
ata – aka – asi – ila
ataurre – akatsbako – asi – ilarteko
introduction – perfect – to begin – lifetime
"Perfect introduction to begin a lifetime."

When the British arrived in India they continued this system of naming e.g:
India:

in. – .di – ia
ina – adi – ia
inarroskatu – adiskidegarri – iaio
to excite – friendly – cheerful
"Exciting, friendly and cheerful."

The oldest documents in Indo-Aryan writing are thought to be the "Vedic" texts, reputedly composed and memorized in the Sanskrit language in the latter half of the second millennium B.C., but not written down until ca 500 B.C. In these texts the Sanskrit language is called **"samskrta"** which obviously is an agglutinated name with several vowels removed. These missing vowels are shown here as dots and arranged according to the VCV formula: **.sa-am.-.s.-.k.-.r.-.ta.** Using a more systematic form of notation from the one shown above (because of the length of some of the words), the meaning therefore decodes as:

.sa	esa	*esaldi*	language
am.	ama	*amaitu*	to destroy
.s.	asa	*asaba*	ancestor
.k.	ako	*akordiotu*	to agree
.r.	ora	*oraingoera*	renewal, modernization
.ta	ata	*ataurre*	to introduce

"Destroy the language of our ancestors by agreeing to introduce renewal."

Again we run into remarks that the language of the Goddess religion (the Basque-related Dravidian language) had to be destroyed and replaced by an invented language. If all the vowels were re-inserted into Samskrta, the name would read: Asamasakorata which shows that the person who invented the name Sanskrit guessed wrong when he inserted an "i." The language could more accurately be abbreviated to **"Samskrat."** The dictionary I used to rediscover the hidden sentence in the **Samskrta** words is the Basque-English one by Gorka Aulestia. Saharan/Basque may well be the language referred to in Genesis 11:1 as the Universal language: "Now the whole world had one language." The words "language of our ancestors" mentioned in the above translation must therefore have referred to the Universal language mentioned in the Bible. If the above analysis is correct, then virtually all, or at least a good part of the Samskrta language, must have been invented. This invention theory can be proven by using the same VCV formula to test a large number of Sanskrit words.

Let us start with a few of the most common words and immediately we see that we are dealing with a patriarchal society in which the women had to behave as the men dictated or else.

abizarika (housewife): abi-iza-ari-ika,

abi	abi	*abia*	nest, home
iza	iza	*izan*	to be
ari	ari	*ari*	her
ika	ika	*ikaskari*	assignment, task

"The home is her assignment."

bharya (wife): .b.-.ha-ari-i.a,

.b.	abi	*abia*	nest, home
.ha	iha	*ihardun*	to spend time
ari	ari	*ari izan*	to be busy
i.a	ia	*iaio*	cheerful

"She spends (her) time in the home, is busy and cheerful."

brahmin, .b.-.ra-ah.-.mi-in.

.b.	ebe	*ebertar*	patriarch
.ra	era	*eraspen*	devotion

ah.	aha	*ahalguzti*	almighty
.mi	ami	*amildu*	to oust
in.	ine	*inertzia*	passiveness

"The devoted patriarch of the Almighty will oust passiveness."

duhitr (daughter): .du-uhi-it.-.r.:

.du	adu	*adurajausi*	charming
uhi	uhi	*uhintsu*	wavy, curley
.t.	ito	*itoaldi*	disgrace
.r.	ora	*oraingoz*	sometimes

"Charming curls but sometimes a disgrace."

manus (man): man-us.

| man | man | *manatu* | to give orders |
| us. | usa | *usaiako* | habitually, by nature |

"It's his nature to give orders."

nara (man): .na-ara,

| .na | ona | *onartu* | to welcome |
| ara | ara | *aragiztatu* | to become a man |

"He welcomes becoming a man."

pati (master, husband): .pa-ati,

| .pa | opa | *opa izan* | to desire |
| ati | ati | *atxikitasun* | faithfulness |

"(He) desires faithfulness."

pitr or pitar (father): pi-ita-ar.

pi	pi	*pindartu*	to get angry
ita	ita	*itaun egin*	to demand
ar.	ara	*arau*	discipline

"When angered he demands discipline."

putra (son): .pu-ut.-.ra,

.pu	ipu	*ipurterre*	impatient
ut.	uti	*utikan*	to go, to get away
.ra	ira	*irabazi*	to grow up

"Impatient to grow up and to get away."

vipra (Brahmin): .bi-ip.-.ra,

.bi	ibi	*ibili*	to be
ip.	ipu	*ipurgarbitu*	to adulate, to venerate
.ra	ura	*ura*	he

"He (is) to be venerated."

DE BASALDUA NOTED A RELATIONSHIP BETWEEN SANSKRIT AND BASQUE

Florencio Canut de Basaldua in his book "Historia de la Civilizacion Indigena de Amerika" (1925) showed that Samskrta words could be translated with Basque (pages 52-70). However, he recognized only complete Basque words, did not stick closely to the Samskrta spelling and did not reduce the Samskrta words to their VCV roots. Here follow a few of the words he explained with Basque:

ABARADHA (adultery) he translated as: *abar* (branch) *ramera* (whore) probably referring to a beating of the woman. However, a more convincing translation is obtained by using the VCV formula:

abaradha (adultery): aba-ara-ad.-.ha

aba	aba	*abagadune*	on occasion
ara	ara	*aragiztatu*	to be lustful
ad.	ada	*adarra sartu*	to deceive
.ha	aha	*ahalkegarri*	shamefully

"To be lustful on occasion is to deceive shamefully."

ABAROHA (hanging branch) he translated as: abar-oha, *abar* (branch) *oha* (finish) but a better translation is obtained with the VCV formula:

abaroha (hanging branch): aba-aro-oha

aba	aba	*abar*	branch
aro	aro	*arotu*	to break off
oha	oha	*ohar*	caution, advice

"Caution, break off that branch."

ABIJANA (family) he translated as: abia-gana, *abia* (nest, home) *gana* (movement towards); not bad, but now try:

abijana (family): abi-ija-ana

abi	abi	*abia*	nest, home
ija	ia	*iaio*	happy, cheerful
ana	ana	*anaitu*	to get together

"Happy to get together in the home."

ABIRA (pastor) which de Basaldua translated as 'rebaño vacuno' (flock bovine), according to him coming from Basque: *abere* (beast) *idizko* (bovine), which is neither flattering nor close. Now try it the VCV way:

abira (pastor): abi-ira

abi	abi	*abil*	talented
ira	ira	*irakasle*	teacher

"Talented teacher."

ABYADANA (beginning of something), which he explained as adia-dana, *adia* (intelligence) and *dana* (all); he was way off the mark this time:

abyadana (beginning of something): abi-ija-ada-ana

abi	abi	*abiatu*	to begin
ia	ia	*iaio*	happy
ada	ada	*ada*	noisy
ana	ana	*anaitu*	to gather, get together

"A happy beginning (in) a noisy gathering."

Florencio de Basaldua gives several more such examples, which show that he was aiming in the right direction, but did not realize that Samskrta was a formulaically agglutinated language. However, as he was the first one, to my knowledge, to point out a very close relationship between Basque and Samskrta, he deserves some credit. To prove my VCV theory, it is now necessary to list some randomly chosen Samskrta words and show the manner in which these words were agglutinated.

SANSKRIT WORDS AND THEIR DERIVATION FROM SAHARAN BASQUE

abidarma (meta-physica): abi-ida-ar.-.ma,

abi	abi	*abil*	skillful
ida	ida	*idatzi*	to write
ar.	aru	*arrunt*	simple
.ma	uma	*umaketa*	procreation

"Skillful writing about simple procreation."

abita (secure, without fear): abi-ita,

| abi | abi | *abia* | nest, home |
| ita | ita | *itxaro* | to trust, have faith in |

"Have faith in your home."

açita (food, meal): asi-ita,

| asi | asi | *asiki* | bite to eat |
| ita | ita | *itaundu* | to ask |

"Ask for a bite to eat."

adyayana (study): adi-ia-aja-ana,

adi	adi	*adi*	attentive
ia	ia	*iaio*	dexterous, mentally adroit
aja	aja	*ajaja*	happy

ana	ana	*anaia*	religious brother

"Be attentive and mentally adroit with the happy religious brother."

adyopatya (Lordship), adi-io-opa-ati-ia

ad.	adi	*adiera*	hearing
io	io	*iortziri*	thunder
opa	opa	*opari*	offering
ati	ati	*atiki*	to be faithful to
ia	ia	iaio	cheerful

"Upon hearing the thunder, offer faithfully and cheerfully."

agnis (fire): ag.-.ni-is.:

ag.	aga	*agakatu*	to hit, to strike
.ni	ani	*anitzetan*	often
is.	isa	*izar*	star, spark

"Strike often (to get) sparks."

ajras (field): aj.-.ra-as.

aj.	ajo	*ajola izan*	to take care
.ra	ora	*oraintxe*	right now
as.	ase	*asetasun*	abundance

"Right now take care of the abundance."

anala (fire, hearth): ana-ala,

ana	ana	*anaitu*	to get together
ala	ala	*alaitu*	to fill with joy

"Getting together fills us with joy."

analena (by the fire), ana-ale-ena,

ana	ana	*anaitu*	to get together
ale	ale	*alegeratu*	to be happy
ena	ena	*ena*	(superlative) very

"Very happy to be together."

anila (wind): ani-ila,

ani	ani	*anitzetan*	often
ila	ila	*ilaundu*	to destroy

"Often destructive."

anityam (temporary): ani-iti-ia-am.,

ani	ani	*anitz*	many
iti	iti	*itxi*	to close up
ia	ia	*iardun*	to spend time
am.	ama	*amabostaldi*	two weeks

"Many close up to spend 2 weeks time." (holidays, religious festivity?)

aniyamita (irregular): ani-ija-ami-ita,

ani	ani	*anitz*	many
ija	iha	*ihabali*	frightened
ami	ami	*aministrator*	administrator
ita	ita	*itaunketa*	interrogation

"Many are frightened of the administrator's interrogation."

anugraha (grace, favour): anu-ug.-.ra-aha,

anu	anu	*anu egin*	to faint
ug.	uga	*ugaru*	bountiful
.ra	ara	*aratz*	pure
aha	aha	*ahalguzti*	almighty

"To (feel) faint (before) the bountiful and pure Almightly."

dahati (to burn): .da-aha-ati,

.da	ada	*adarki*	firewood
aha	aha	*ahala*	as much as possible
ati	ati	*atxiki*	to grab, to gather

"Gather as much firewood as possible."

giris (mountain): .gi-iri-is.:

.gi	egi	*egilaz*	summit
iri	iri	*iritsi*	to reach
is.	isu	*izugaitz*	daring

"It is daring to reach the summit."

khadati, (to eat): .k.-.ha-ada-ati,

.k.	eki	*ekin*	to keep on
.ha	iha	*ihaurri*	in abundance
ada	ada	*adarki*	firewood
ati	ati	*atxiki*	to gather

"Keep on gathering firewood in abundance."

kiirtii (fame): .ki-ir.-.ti

.ki	aki	*akigarri*	aged
ir.	ira	*irakasle*	teacher
.ti	ati	*atiki*	faithful

"Aged faithful teacher."

kumaarah (boy, adolescent): .ku-uma-ara-ah.,

.ku	aku	*akuilatu*	to stimulate
uma	uma	*uma*	child
ara	ara	*aragikoitasun*	sexual desire
ah.	aho	*ahopean*	secretly

"The child stimulates his sexual desire secretly."

kumaarikaa (girl): .ku-uma-ari-ika-aha,

.ku	aku	*akuilatu*	to stimulate
uma	uma	*uma*	child
ari	ari	*ari*	to her, her
ika	ika	*ikasi*	to learn
a.a	aha	*ahalegin*	attempt, trial

"The (boy?) child stimulates her in a learning attempt."

kumara (prince): .ku-uma-ara,

.ku	iku	*ikusgarriki*	visibly, obviously
uma	uma	*umaldi*	birth
ara	ara	*aratz*	pure

"Obviously of pure birth."

kutsya (despicable): .ku-ut.-.si-ia,

.ku	uku	*ukurtzaile*	perverter
ut.	uti	*utikan*	go away
.si	isi	*isilume*	bastard
i.a	iha	*iharduko*	to argue, to talk fast

"Perverter go away, you fast talking bastard."

nagara (city, town): .na-aga-ara,

.na	ana	*anaitu*	to gather
aga	aga	*-aga*	abundance
ara	ara	*arraginlan*	masonry

"They gather in an abundance of masonry."

punar (again): .pu-una-ar.,

.pu	ipu	*ipuin*	story
una	una	*unagarri*	annoying
ar.	ara	*arrakor*	repetitious

"Annoying repetitious story."

putra (son): .pu-ut.-ra,

.pu	ipu	*ipurterre*	impatient
ut.	uti	*utikan*	to go away, to leave home
.ra	ira	*irabazi*	to grow up

"Impatient to grow up and leave home."

rohati (to grow): .ro-oha-ati,

.ro	uro	*uroditu*	to irrigate
oha	oha	*ohartu*	to take care
ati	ati	*atxikigarri*	faithfull

"Take care to irrigate faithfully."

sukha (happiness): .su-uk.-.ha,

.su	asu	*asuri*	newborn lamb
uk.	uki	*ukitu*	to touch
.ha	iha	*ihaio*	cheerful, happy

"Happiness is touching a newborn lamb."

Sanskrit is an Invented language

The above examples show that the Sanskrit words examined above were composed with the use of the ancient Saharan/Basque vocabulary. Almost all these Sanskrit words were manufactured from the VCV half of the Basque language. Only if the right word was not available, such as in *pitar* (father) or *manus* (man) or *niire* (water), would the linguist go to the CV half of the vocabulary, just as was done in English. Sanskrit is no different from Latin, Spanish and English, only other hidden sentences were used.

THE ORIGIN OF YIDDISH

Yiddish, the speech of the Ashkenazim Jews of Eastern Europe, is usually considered to be an offshoot of German, although it is not intelligible to most German speakers. Leo Rosten, a well-known Jewish author and linguist, wrote "The Joys Of Yiddish," a relaxed lexicon of Yiddish, replete with Jewish humor, folklore, history etc. His book is used extensively in this article to provide the Yiddish words and their current meanings. After a short exploration of the make-up of the words it appeared that there was a close but artificial relationship with Basque.

The inventors of the Romance languages and English used only that half of the Basque language which begins with vowel-consonant-vowel (VCV and VCCV), but the linguists making up Yiddish used the entire Basque vocabulary (CV and VC words), which allowed more flexibility in word invention. Vowel-linking was not always maintained. It turned out that all Yiddish words, supplied by Rosten, could be broken up into Basque roots, sometimes with surprising results. In most words the meaning thus obtained was related to the translation shown in Rosten's book. A few of the Yiddish words in my translation turned out to be highly undesirable language, however, that is no reason to omit them here.

What is surprising is the ease with which many Yiddish words were translatable via Basque, as shown below. Some words took more time or defied the decoding process entirely, which is understandable because, with popular use over centuries, some words do change. Many of the Yiddish words were the same as in Hebrew or showed only slight changes in spelling. How old Yiddish is, is a good question, but it appears that Yiddish is considerably older than German, possibly dating back to the time that the blond Khazars of the lower Wolga region accepted Judaism, which would date the formation of the language to around or just before the time of Christ. It is reasonable to deduce that the linguists who made up the Yiddish language were Jewish scholars. Therefore Yiddish belongs to the Semitic languages not to the Germanic group. The Benedictine linguists then used Yiddish and Hebrew vocabulary and syntax to help them with the creation of the Germanic languages during the 9th and 10th centuries.

We can draw one firm conclusion from the following list of translations which is that Yiddish was 100% assembled out of the astonishingly versatile Basque language, which was distorted and manipulated in the process. My list gives first the Yiddish word, followed by the English translation in brackets as supplied by Leo Rosten. After this I show the components of the word, separated by hyphens, and the Basque words these components represent, with their translations. Any vowels and "h's" removed in the language invention process are shown as dots. The "sh" in Basque is spelled "x."

Some Yiddish Words Decoded with the Basque Dictionary

The best notation of showing the derivation of a word is:

Ashkenazim
ash. _ kena – azim
axola _ kena – azima
caring/worrying _ to take away/lose – identity
"Worried about losing our identity."

However, when dealing with large numbers of words, this format would take too much space, so a shorthand form of notation is used for the following words.

am ha-aretz (ill-mannered person), *am.-.ha-aretz: ama* (mother, Priestess) *ahalgegabe* (shameless) *arretzin* (unacceptable): "The Priestess' shamelessness is unacceptable."
apikoros (skeptic, atheist), *apik-iku-oroz: apika* (perhaps) *ikur* (sign) *orozale* (ambition): "Perhaps a sign of ambition."
Ashkenazim (Germany), *ash.-kena-azim: axola* (caring, worrying) *kena* (to take away, to lose) *azima* (character, identity): "Worried about losing our identity."
averah (unethical act), *abera: aberats* (wealthy): "Wealthy."
aydem (son-in-law), *aide-em: aidetu* (to become a relative of) *eme* (female): "He became a relative of the female (member of the family)."
ayin harah (evil eye), *aien-aharra: aiene* (lament) *aharra* (disturbance): "(We) lament the disturbance."
baalshem (Master of the Good Name), *bala-shem: balakatu* (to flatter) *xeme* (native son): "To flatter the native born son."

badchanim (jester, entertainer), *bad.-.ka-anim*: *badaezbada* (eventual) *akabu* (death) *animalia* (animal): "The eventual death of the animal." (just what did that "jester" do?)

balbatim (master of the house), *bal.-.bant-im.*: *balaztatu* (to control) *abantaila* (privileged) *imatz* (dwelling, house): "Privileged to control the house."

balabatish (responsible), *bala-aba-ati-ix*: *balaztatu* (to control, operate) *abantaila* (privileged) *ateka* (small door) *ixi* (quietly): "Privileged to open and close the small door quietly."

baleboss (head of the household), *bala-abots*: *balaztatu* (to control) *abots* (voice): "The voice controls."

balmalocha (craftsman), *bal-.ma-aloka*: *baliarazu* (to make valuable) *ama* (mother) *alokai* (payment): "He makes something valuable for mother as payment."

bar mitzva (man of duty), *bar-imi-itz-.ba*: *ibarretshe* (house in the valley) *imini* (to place) *itz* (obligation) *-aba* (work): "He has a work obligation at the house in the valley."

batlanim (misfit, lazy person), *bat-lan-im*: *bat* (one) *lan* (work) *imatz* (house): "One for the work house."

behama (ignorant person), *beha-ama*: *beha* (to observe, to stare at) *ama* (mother): "He stares at mother."

ben (son), *ben*: *ben* (honest, trustworthy): "Trustworthy."

bentsh (to bless), *ben-tsh*: *ben* (honest) *tshalo* (applause): "Honesty is applauded."

berrieh (woman with remarkable energy), *berri-eh.*: *berri* (new) *ehule* (weaver): "New weaver."

besdin (house of judgement), *bes-din*: *bestemunduku* (exceptional) *adin* (judgement, justice): "Exceptional justice."

bes midrash (house of study), *bes-imi-ido-orraz*: *bestemunduku* (outstanding) *imitatu* (to imitate, to copy) *idoro* (to discover) *orraztari* (editor, collection): "Outstanding copy of the discovered collection."

blintzeh (filled pancake), *balintz-eh*: *balintz* (requirement) *ehotza* (act of eating): "Must be eaten" (come and get it!).

bnai brit (sons of the covenant), *ben-.nai-barrit*: *ben* (honest) *anaiarte* (brotherhood) *barritu* (to reform): "Honest brotherhood (promoting) reform."

borderkeh (female boarder), *border-ke*: *bordari* (settler, colonist) *kementsu* (energetic): "Energetic settler."

bonditt (bandit), *bon-.dit*: *bonbon* (lavish spending) *aditugabe* (unheard of): "Unheard of lavish spending."

cabala (tradition), *kabal-la*: *kabal* (cattle) *-la* (like): "Like cattle."

chasidim (pious man), *kasi-idi-im.*: *kasik* (almost) *idi* (ox) *imintziogabe* (expressionless): "Almost like an expressionless ox."

chassen (man-of-the-hour), *kasu-un*: *kasu* (circumstance) *une* (moment): "Momentary circumstance."

chasseneh (wedding), *kasu-une*: *kasu* (pay attention) *une* (a moment): "Pay attention for a moment." (Surely this event is more important than that?)

chaver (friend, comrade), *kabe-er*: *kabe* (without) *eragozkor* ((hindering, obstruction): "Without obstruction."

chazzen (a seer), *gaz-zen*: *gaz* (with) *zentzu* (common sense): "With common sense."

chedar (room), *kedar*: *kedarketa* (smoke stained): "Smoke-stained."

chevra (comradship), *keb-bara*: *kebelar* (tobacco) *bara* (slow): "Smoking slowly."

chillul chashem (profaning God's name),

chillul: *.kil.-.lu-ul.*: *akilarre* (witch) *alu* (vulva) *ule* (hairy): "The witch's hairy vulva."

chashem: kash-em: *kashkartu* (to degrade oneself) *ema* (prostitute): "Self-degrading prostitute."

chloppeh (to knock, to bang), *kalo-ope*: *kalonje* (priest) *oper* (time off, away): "When the priest is away." (the cat is away the mice will play.)

chmallyeh (severe blow), *kamel-li-eh.: kamelu* (camel) *libratu* (to set free, to run away) *ehizibilatu* (to beat): "To beat the run-away camel."

choleria (plague), *kol-eri-a: koldar* (coward) *eri* (illness) *a* (the): "The coward's illness."

chollileh (God forbid that should happen), *koli-ile: kolitza* (belltower) *ilintitu* (To set on fire): "Burning of the belltower."

chometzdik (fermented), *kome-etz.-.dik: komenigarri* (beneficial) *etzaldi* (rest) *adikor* (understandable): "That he needs beneficial rest is understandable." (Needs to sleep it off).

chozzerai (junk, trash), *koz-erai: koz* (intended for) *erain* (scattering, disposal): "Intended for disposal."

chutzpa (audacity), *kutz.-.pa: kutzaketa* (profanity) *apalatu* (to humiliate): "Using profanity to humiliate."

cockamamy (mixed up), *kok-ama-mi: kok* (bellyfull) *ama* (mother) *mi* (my): "Bellyfull from my mother."

darshan (preacher), *darj-anai: adarjo* (to pull one's leg, tease) *anaia* (religious brother): "To tease the preacher."

dayan (rabbinical judge), *dai-an.: daiteke* (he can be) *anaia* (religious brother): "He can be a religious brother."

diaspora (exile, dispersion), *.di-as.-.po-ora: adibide* (advice) *asagotu* (to go far away) *apokeria* (filthy deed) *oraintxe* (right now): "The advice is to go right now, far from the filthy deeds."

dovid ha Melech (expected Messiah), *.do-obid/.ha/me-ele-ek.: adoratu* (to worship) *obidientzia* (obedient) *ahal* (I hope) *Mesias* (Messiah) *ele* (story) *ekarri* (to bring): "With obedient worship I hope to bring the story of the Messiah."

dreck (wet dirt, crap), *.d.-.re-ek.: adarka* (goring) *areztatu* (to cover with sand) *eki* (as much as possible): "Cover the gore with sand as much as possible."

dresske (hand-me-down garment), *dar-eske: darama* (to take) *eske* (alms): "Taking alms, begging."

elohim (YHVH), *elo-ohi-im: elorritsu* (troublesome) *ohitu* (to be accustomed to) *imitapen* (imitation): "He is accustomed to troublesome imitation." (He is jealous: Exodus 34:14).

eppes (a little, something), *epe-ez: epe* (time limit) *eza* (shortage): "Shortage of time."

eretz Yisroel (the land of Israel), *eretz-Israel: eretz* (on the side of): "On the side of Israel."

farbissen (unpleasant), *.far-bizi: ifar* (north) *bizi* (to live): "To live in the north."

farblondjet (wandering aimlessly), *.far-.bel-ond.-jet: ifar* (northern) *abel* (herdsmen) *ondo* (harvest colored) *jetshi* (descend): "The straw-haired northern herdsmen descend (on us)."

farchadat (dizzy, confused), *.far-kada-at.: ifar* (northern) *-kada* (to hit) *-at* (direction, from): "Northern storm hits us."

farshtinkener (all stunk up, farting), *.far-tink-ener: ifar* (north) *tinkatu* (to press, to push) *ener* (when): "When the north (wind) pushes, blows."

flayshedig (meat of all sorts), *.f-.lai-shede-ig: afa* (happy) *alai* (rejoicing) *shede* (to reach the goal) *iges* (shelter); "Happy rejoicing when the shelter is reached."

folks-mensh (man of the people), *bolk-men-sh: boladak* (groups of people) *men* (power) *sh* (little bit): "A little bit of power to the people."

fress (to gorge, devour), *.fa-arrez: afa* (happy) *arrezkero* (from then on): "Happy from then on."

frosk (slap), *.f.-.rotz-k.: afa* (happily) *arrotsu* (jovial) *-ko* (slap): "Happy jovial slap."

frum (pious), *.f.-.ru-um.: afa* (happy) *arrunt* (simple) *ume* (child): "(Like a) simple happy child."

galitzianer (Jew from Galicia), *gali-itz-ia-ner: gali* (wheat) *itz* (promise) *iaio* (cheerful) *onera* (maturing): "The cheerful promise of the maturing wheat."

galut (exile), *gal-ut: galdos* (pasture ground) *utzi* (to leave behind): "To leave the pasture ground behind."

Gan Eden (Garden of Eden), *gan-eden*: *gandoa* (pasture) *eden* (poison); "Pasture of poison."

ga'on (genius), *ga-on*: *garai* (outstanding) *onbide* (example): "Outstanding example."

gelt (money), *geld*: *geldi* (little by little): "(Saving) little by little."

gesundheit (health), *gizond.-haiet*: *gizondu* (to grow up, old) *haietara* (to them): "Good growing old to you."

get (divorce), *ge-et*: *gehitu* (to reproduce) *eten* (to cut): "Cut reproduction."

golem (shapeless), *gol-em*: *golo* (goitre) *emendatu* (to enlarge): "The goitre enlarges."

goniv (thief), *ganib*: *ganibetada* (knifing): "Stick-up with a knife."

gott (god), *gotor*: *gotor* (support, strength): "Support and strength."

goy (nation), *goi*: *goian* (in heaven, on high): "On high."

gozlin (swindler), *goz-lin*: *gozagaitz* (disagreeable) *linburtu* (flatterer): "Disagreeable flatterer."

graub (uncouth), *g.-.raub*: *gabe* (without) *araubide* (discipline): "Without discipline."

habdala (separation), *abe-edala*: *abere* (brutal) *edalari* (alcoholic): "Brutal alcoholic."

haftarah (end, conclusion), *af.-.tera*: *afa* (happy) *atera* (to pull out): "Happily (to have been) pulled out."

haggadah (tale telling), *aga-ada*: *agariz* (publicly) *adarjo* (to make fun of): "Publicly made fun of."

haimish (home), *hei-im-ish*: *hei* (shelter) *imatz* (woven branches) *ishi* (quiet): "Quiet shelter of woven branches."

halakha (law), *ala-aka*: *alabear* (destiny, fate) *akabu* (ultimate): "Ultimate fate."

halevai (I wish I had), *aleba-ai*: *alebanatu* (to shell out grain) *ai* (grief, suffering): "Give out grain to ease the suffering."

hamantash (pocket), *amanta-ash*: *amantal* (apron) *ashola* (caring, collecting): "Collecting apron."

haskalah (education, knowledge), *aska-ala*: *askar* (bright) *alabear* (future, destiny): "Bright future."

hatikva (the hope, national anthem), *.atik-ba*: *batik* (special) *abagadune* (occasion): "Special occasion."

hok a tshynik (to talk nonsense), *oka-tshai-nik*: *oka* (overflowing) *tshaire* (air) *onik* (harmless): "Bubbling with harmless air."

hotzeplots (God only knows where), *hotz-pilotz*: *hotz* (cold) *pilotz* (plenty): "Plenty cold."

Jehova (YHVH, YHBH), *YHaBaliH/ihabali* (to be afraid of): "To be afraid of."

judesmo (Ladino Jew), *jud-esmo*: *judas* (traitor) *esmoil* (cruel): "Cruel traitor."

kabotz (to beg), *kabe-otz*: *kabe* (without) *otzan* (shame, humility): "Without shame."

kaddish (holy), *kad-itz*: *kada* (blow, hit, killing) *itzi* (denounce): "Denounce the killing."

kalikeh (cripple), *kali-ike*: *kalifikaezin* (unknown) *ikergai* (topic of investigation, cause): "Unknown cause." (Why would that be?)

kalleh (bride), *kale*: *kaleratu* (to throw out into the street): "Throw her out into the street!"

kaporeh (forgiveness), *.ka-apo-ore*: *ekandu* (to be used to) *apokeria* (insult) *orrelako* (like that): "He is used to insults like that."

kasheh (difficult), *kash-eh*: *kashako* (abandon) *ehi* (hunt): "Abandon the hunt."

kibutzim (collective), *.kip-utzi-im*: *akipen* (exhausted) *utzi* (to leave) *imatz* (home): "Too exhausted to go out."

kibbitzim (criticizing), *akip-itzi-im*: *akipen* (exhaustion) *itzi* (to denounce) *imintzio* (gesticulating, arm waving): "Denounce the exhausting arm waver."

kiebitz (lapwing, meadow bird), *ki-ibitz*: *kidetu* (to be alike) *ibitzale* (fond of walking): "(Male and female) look alike and are fond of walking."

kibosh (nonsense), *.ki-ipo-oz*: *akipen* (exhaustion) *ipo* (little fellow) *ozar* (insolent): "Insolent and exhausting little fellow."

kiddush (sanctification), *kid-dutsh*: *kidetu* (to be like one of us) *dutsha* (shower, dunking): "A dunking to become like one of us." (A baptism?)

kinder (children), *aki-indar*: *akigabe* (tireless) *indar* (vitality): "Endless vitality."

kinderlach (little children), *ki-indar-lak*: *akigabe* (tireless) *indar* (vitality) *laket* (pleasure giving): "Pleasure giving, endless vitality."

klezemer (musical instruments), *oke-elez-emer*: *oke* (plentiful, lots of) *elezun* (adulation) *emer* (woman who recently gave birth): "Lots of adulation for the young mother who recently gave birth."

klutz (bungler, oaf), *.k.-.lu-utz*: *aka* (ultimate) *alu* (vulva) *uts* (useless, faulty): "The ultimate useless vulva."

knish (small dumplings), *k.-.nitz*: *kako* (little turds) *anitz* (many): "Many little turds."

kochalayn (room with cooking), *koka-alai-in*: *kokaldi* (bellyfull) *alai* (joyous) *indar* (vitality): "Bellyfull gives joyous vitality." (Compare with name of Irish hero: Cuchulainn).

kohen (Hebrew priest), *.ko-ohe-en.*: *okolu* (pasture next to house) *ohe* (bed) *ene* (my): "My bed is in the pasture." (Why would that be?)

kosher (proper), *ko-sherra*: *koilarakada* (spoonful) *sherra* (little bites): "Spoonfuls of little bites."

koved (honor, glory), *.ko-obe-ed*: *uko egin* (to refuse) *obe* (preferable) *ederrak hartu* (to be defeated): "I refuse; it is preferable to be defeated."

krechtz (grunt, moan), *.k.-.rek-tz*: *akabu* (the end) *arek* (that one) *tz* (suffix): "It's the end for him."

krenk (sick), *.k.-.renk*: *akatz* (defect) *arrenka* (limping): "Some defect makes him limp."

kurveh (prostitute), *.ku-urbe*: *uku* (gone bad, stinking) *urbelar* (scum): "Stinking scum."

kvell (pride, swell), *kabe-el.*: *kabe* (without) *ele* (words): "Without words."

kvetsch (to sqeeze), *kabe-ebatz*: *kabe* (without) *ebatzaile* (bruising): "Without bruising."

kvitch (to yelp, to squeal), *kabe-itsh*: *kabe* (without) *itsharo* (trusting): "Without trusting."

ladino (familiar with), *.la-adino*: *alabehar* (destiny) *adinaro* (attaining full rights): "Our destiny is to attain full rights."

latke (pancake), *.lat-ka*: *alatu* (to eat) *kalda* (hot): "Eat while they are hot."

l'chayim (here's to life!), *ele-ekai-im*: *ele* (story) *ekai* (job, accomplishment) *imitagarri* (exemplary): "Story of an exemplary accomplishment."

letz (life of the party, wit), *laitz*: *laitzin* (in front of everybody): "Stand-up comic."

levaya (funeral), *le-ebanja*: *ele* (story, speech) *ebanjalari* (preacher): "Preacher's sermon."

litvak (pedantic type), *li-ito-obak*: *eli* (to nourish) *ito* (quick) *obakuntza* (improvement): "Nourishment resulted in quick improvement."

loch in kop (hole in the head), *lok-in.-kope*: *alokari* (renter) *inozo* (stupid) *kopetadun* (shameless): "Shameless stupid renter."

loksh (skinny person), *lok-sh*: *lokarri* (rope) *sh* (diminutive): "Thin rope."

lox (salmon), (German: lax), *lok-is*: *lokaldi* (spawning) *izokin* (salmon): "The salmon are spawning."

luft (air), *ulu-ufat*: *ulu* (howling) *ufatu* (to blow): "Howling wind."

maggid (teacher, preacher), *ma-agi-id*: *maisugoko* (pertaining to teaching) *agian* (I hope) *idatzi* (to write): "I hope he teaches me to write."

mah nishtana (distinguishes), *.ma-aniz-tan-na*: *mazaltasun* (decency) *anitz* (many) *-tan* (times) *nahi* (desirous): "Decency is many times more desirous."

mairev (evening prayer), *.ma-aireb*: *maiz* (often) *aireberritu* (to expose to air, open air): "Often in the open air."

marrano (secret Jew), *marra-ano*: *mara mara* (quietly) *anonimo* (anonymous): "Quietly anonymous."

matzes (unleavened bread), *ma-atzez*: *mahai* (table) *atzezka* (face-up, good side up): "Good side up on the table."

mavin (expert), *ma-abi-in*: *maixu* (expert) *abiadan* (fast) *indartsu* (strong): "The expert is fast and strong."

mazel (luck), *.ma-aze-el*: *ama* (mother) *azentuata* (to emphasize, often repeat): *ele* (story): "Mother often repeated the story."

mazik (clever child), *ma-azik*: *ama* (mother) *aziketa* (upbringing): "Mother's upbringing (did it)."

mechaiek (pleasure), *.me-ekai-ek.*: *eme* (female, woman) *ekarkortasun* (fecundity) *ikertu* (to explore): "To explore the woman's fecundity."

mechule (finished), *me-eku-ule*: *eme* (female) *ekuru* (quiet) *ulerketa* (understanding): "The woman's quiet understanding."

medina (country), *medi-ina*: *medio* (by means of) *inarrosketa* (agitation): "By means of agitation."

melchik (milky), *me-elki-ik*: *emeta* (gently) *elki* (to empty) *ik* (you): "You (must) empty it gently," (i.e. milking).

menorah (candalabrum), *men-ora*: *menpegabe* (emancipated, free) *orregatik* (because of, in appreciation of): "In appreciation of our freedom (or emancipation)."

meshogge (crazy), *me-esho-oge*: *eme* (woman) *exotiko* (exotic) *oge* (bed): "An exotic woman in bed."

metsieh (find), *me-etsi-ehi*: *mendizain* (forest ranger) *etsi* (to abandon) *ehi* (hunt): "The forest ranger abandoned the hunt."

midrash (to study), *.mit.-.raz*: *imitapen* (to copy) *arrazoi* (to be right, correct): "Copy it correctly."

I could add hundreds more but this will suffice to prove that Yiddish is basically distorted Basque.

HEBREW

THE HEBREW–BASQUE RELATIONSHIP

It has been suggested by many Basque scholars, such as Abbé Dominique Lahetjuzan, Abade Erroa and Abbé Diharce de Bidassouet, that the words and names of the Hebrew language, and those used in the Bible, were made up from a Basque-related language, using a form of shorthand writing. The linguists developing Hebrew indeed used the first letters of Saharan/Basque words starting with VCV in their manipulations, but they also used words starting with CV, especially in the first syllable of the new word. Hebrew is a consonantal language, just like Old Egyptian, which means that all vowels were removed when the word was written down. To begin my research, I chose the central pillar of Judaism, the Talmud for examples because this document retained the vowels and had been passed on orally to posterity with extreme care:

Tal-mud
tala – mudapen
look out – alteration
"Look out for alteration" or "Pass on unaltered"

This definition makes sense because the Talmud is the summary of the Oral Law of the Jews and the only way to preserve an oral law throughout the ages is to make sure that it is passed on by rote in unaltered condition. The Talmud has two main components: the Mishnah, a book of law (halakhah), and the Gemarah, which is the commentary on the Mishnah. The Torah is the Pentateuch or law contained in the Old Testament. As the many words associated with these books have been passed on quite faithfully in the original pronounciation, I decided to make an effort to work with them first:

Gemara (to expand the mind)
.ge-ema-ara
age-ema-ara
ageri – eman – aratz
revelation – to teach – pure
"Pure teachings of the Revelation."

Mishna (instruction)
mi-ix.-.na
umi-ixa-ana
umiltasun – ixartu – anaitegi
humbleness – to wake up – congregation
"In humbleness waking up the congregation."

Torah (teaching)
.to-ora-ah,
oto-ora-aha
otoitzegin – orain – Ahalguzti
to pray to – always – Almighty
"Always pray to the Almighty."

The vowel-interlocking of the VCV syllables is clearly maintained in many of these words, proving that this linguistic trick was already in common use around 600 B.C.

EXAMPLES

A large number of names and words are associated with these books, a small sampling follows in alphabetic order, with their present meanings in brackets.

Avo'dah Zarah (keeping one's distance from idolaters)
abo _ da   za – ara – ah.
abonau _ damu   zapuzkarri – araokari – ahalkegabe
proclaim _ repentance   stay aloof/clear – idolater – bold
"Proclaim your repentance and stay clear of the bold idolater."

Avot (ethics)
abo – ot.
abonau – otoi
to voice – prayer
"Voice your prayers."

Baba Batra (laws on partnership and sales)
.ba – aba .ba – atra
ba – aba eba – atra
babesegin – abantaila ebatzi – atralaka

to protect – advantage to decide – dispute
"Protect your advantage. Decide the dispute."

Baba Kama (direct and indirect damages)
ba – aba ka – ama
ba – aba ka – ama
babesegin – abantaila. kanpoaldi – ama
to protect – advantage. away – mother
"Protect your advantage. Mother was terrorized."

Baba Metzia (laws on losses, loans and work)
ba – aba .me – et. – .zi – i.a
ba – aba ame – ete – ezi – iha
babesegin – abantaila amestu – etekin – ezinobe – ihalozkatu
to protect – advantage to dream – profit – excellent – to wallow in
"Protect your advantage. I dream about excellent profits to wallow in."

Berakhot (prayers)
.be – era – ak. – ho – ot.
be – era – aka – aho – oto
bedeinkapen – eraspen – akabu – ahoeder – otoi
blessing – devotion – perfect – eloquent – prayer
"Blessings (through) perfect devotion and eloquent prayers."

Betza (general festival laws)
.be – et. – .za
ebe – eti – iza
ebertar – etika – izan
Hebrew – ethics – nature
"The nature of Hebrew ethics."

Demai (doubtfully tithed produce)
.de – ema – ai
ide – ema – ai
idetu – emaitza – ai
to compare – produce – I want
"I want to compare the produce."

Eduyot (testimonies on various subjects)
edu – ujo – ot.
edukitsu – uiol – otalurmendiak
powerful – flood – wild mountains
"A powerful flood from the mountains."

Gittin (divorce)
.gi – it. – .ti – in.
egi – itu – uti – ino
egingabe – itun – utikan – inorenganatu

undone – agreement – go away! – to alienate/reject
"The agreement is undone, go away, I reject you."

Hagigah (rules for pilgrimage festivals)
.ha – agi – iga – ah.
iha – agi – iga – aha
ihaute – agindu – igandetu – ahalegindu
festival – to promise – to dress up – to try
"I promise to try to dress up for the festival."

Horayot (erroneous rulings of the courts and their rectification)
.ho – ora – aio – ot.
uho – orra – aio – ota
uholdesko – orratio – aiol – otalurmendiak
torrential rain – surprise – flood – wild mountains
"Torrential rains (caused) a surprise flood (from) the wild mountains."

Iruvin (laws of permissible limits)
iru – ubi – in.
iru – ubi – ino
irudigurtza – ubil – inolaz
worshiping of idols – whirlpool – absolutely unacceptable
"Worshiping of idols and the whirlpool is absolutely unacceptable."

The whirlpool refers to the tidal race of Corrivreckan, Scotland, where every eight years in pre-Christian times a voluntary human sacrifice used to take place on Hallowmass (November 1, see Tammuz, Ezekiel 8:14).

Karmelit (semi-developed areas on which there are certain restrictions)
.ka – ar. – .me – eli – it.
uka – are – eme – eli – ita
ukan – arrera – emekiro – elizlur – itxaro
to have – welcoming – quiet – piece of holy ground – to wish, hope
"I hope to have a welcoming, quiet parcel of holy land."

Kelim (types of utensils)
.ke – eli – im.
ike – eli – imi
ikertu – elikadura – imini
to examine – food – to serve
"Examine the food to be served."

Keritot (sins requiring extirpation)
.ke – eri- ito – ot.
ike – eri – ito – oto
ikertu – eriozkortasun – itotzaile – otoikatu
to examine – fatality – murderer – to beg
"The murderer begged to have the fatality (re)examined."

Kiddushin (Marriage Act)
.ki – id. – .du – us. – .hi – in.
uki – ide – edu – utzi -ingu
ukigabe – ide – eduki – utzi – inguratu
untouched/virgin – companion – to hold – to authorize – to embrace
"You are authorized to hold the virgin for companion and to embrace her."

Kinim (mixing of sacrifices)
kini – im.
kiniela – imintze
betting/taking chances – the act of sacrificing
"Taking chances with the sacrificing."

Knesset Gedolah (Great Assembly)
k. – .ne – es. – .se – et.
ke – ene – ese – ese – eta
-keto – eneganatu – eseri – esetsi – etapa
(denoting action) – come to me – sit down – to argue – stage
"Come to the action, take a seat and argue from the stage… "

ge – edo – ola – aho
gerizatu – edonolako – ola – aholkularitza
to help/speak for – the common man – cabin/house – council
"to speak for the common man in the Council's house."

Ma'aseh Bereshit (act of creation)
.ma – ase – eh.   be – ere – esi – it.
emaitza – ase – ehi   bedeinkagarri – eredu – ezinobe – itxaro
produce – abundance – they say   blessed – example – supreme – faith
"An abundance of produce, they say, is a blessed example of supreme faith."

Ma'aseh Merkavah (Divine Chariot)
.ma – ase – eh.   merka – aba – ah.
emaitza – ase – ehi   merkatalgo – abantaila – ahal
produce – abundance – they say   commerce – advantage/promote – I hope
"I hope that an abundance of produce will promote commerce."

Ma'aserot (tithes for the Levites and the poor)
.ma – ase – ero – ot.
ama – asetu – erozgai – otzara
mother – to feed – groceries – basket
"Mother feeds us with a basket of groceries."

Ma'aser Sheni (the second tithe and bringing it to Jerusalem)
.ma' ase – er. ' xe – eni
ama – ase – eri ' xe – eni
ama – asetu – erri 'xede – eni
mother – to feed – common people – objective – to me
"Mother (said): to feed the common people is my objective."

Makot (punishment by flagellation)
.ma – ako – ot.
ema – ako – oto
eman – akorduan euki – otoi
to hit/whip – to remember – prayer
"When whipped, remember your prayers."

Megillah (laws of Purim)
.me – egi – il. – .la
ome – egi – ila – ala
omen – egia – ilarteko – alabehar
honour – truth – lifetime – destiny
"A lifetime of truth and honour is your destiny."

Me'ilah (sins against temple property)
.me – ila – aho
mesprezuzko – ilargijo – ahogaizto
disrespectful – lunatic – bold
"Disrespectful bold lunatic."

Mekom petur (exempt location):
.me – eko – om.   .pe – etu – ur.
ome – eko – ome   ape – etu – urra
omenka – ekonomo – omenezko   apez – edukitza – urratu
according to – administrator – honourable   priest – possession – to violate
**"According to the honourable administrator you
are violating the priest's possession."**

Menahot (meal offerings)
.me – ena – aho – ot.
ome – ena – aho – oto
omendatu – -ena – ahoeder – otoi
to praise God – (superlative) – eloquent – prayer
"Praise God greatly with eloquent prayers."

Midot (measurements of the temple).
mi – ido – ot.
mi – ido – oto
miatu – idoro – otoiztegi
to examine – to discover – place to pray/temple
"Examine the discovered temple."

Nashim (restrictions on marriage)
.ne – asi – im.
ona – asi – imi
onarpen – asialdi – imitagarri
recognition – beginning – exemplary
"Recognition for an exemplary beginning."

Nazir (nazirite laws)
.na – azi – ir.
ena – azi – ire
-ena – azienda – irestzaile
(superlative) – wealth – destructive
"Great wealth is destructive."

Nedarim (types of vows)
ne – eda – ari – im.
neurritasun – edan – ariarazi – imitagarri
moderation – to drink – to be doing something – exemplary
"Moderation in drinking is setting a good example."

Nezekin (laws on damages)
.ne – eze – eki – in.
ene – eze – eki – ina
-enea – ezereztu – ekinalean – inarroskatu
possession – to destroy – as much as possible – to agitate
"Property destroyed? Agitate as much as possible."

Nidah (ritual impurity of the woman)
ni – ida – ah.
nirekiko – idatzi – ahalke
for myself – to document/keep record – shame
"I keep record of this shame for myself."

Oholot (laws of the uncleanliness of the dead)
oho – olo – ot.
ohoratu – oliotu – otordu
to praise – to anoint/anointed – mealtime
"Praise the anointed at mealtime."

Orlah (prohibition against harvesting trees)
or. – .la – ah.
ori – ila – aha
orritza – ilaundu – ahai
foliage – to destroy – anger
"Angry about the destruction of the foliage."

Purim (festival)
.pu – uri – im.
ipu – urri – imi
ipuinondore – urrikalmendu – imitagarri
morality – mercy – examplary
"Be an example of morality and mercy."

Reshut ha'rabim (public domain)
.reshu – ut.   ha – ara – abi – im.
erresu – uti   oha – arra – abi – imi
erresuma – utikan   ohar – arrapaladan – abiatu – imintzio
the King's domain- get out!   warning – immediately – to depart – gesture
"Get off the King's land. Warning with gesture: immediately depart!"

Reshut ha'yahid (private domain)
reshu – ut.   ha ' .ja – ahi – id.
erreshu – uti   ha ' oja – ahi – idu
erresuma – utikan   hainbanatu ' ojanguren – ai – iduki
the King's domain – get out! to subdivide – edge of the forest – desire – to have
**"The King's land, get out! I have a desire to subdivide the land
up to the edge of the forest."**

Shekalim (shekel dues for the temple)
xe – eka – ali – im
xedatu – ekarpen – alik – imini
to decide – contribution – possible – to deposit/to give
"Decide what contribution it is possible to give."

Sofer (writer)
.so – ofe – er.
eso – obe – eri
esonde – obeagotu – erri
advice – to improve/inform – common people
"He gives advice to inform the common people."

Taanit (fast days)
.ta – ani – it.
ota – ani – itxi
otamen – animalia – itxi
mouthful/eating – animal – to stop
"Stop eating animal (meat)."

Toharot (purity)
.to – oha – aro – ot.
ito – oha – aro – oto
itoi – ohar – -aro – otordu
filthy/impure- warning – all – meal/food
"Warning (against) all impure foods."

Tohorot (various laws of purification)
.to – oho – oro – ot.
eto – oho – oro – oto
etor – ohoratu – oroegile – otoi
come! – to praise – Creator – prayer
"Come and praise the Creator with prayers."

Uktz'kin (things susceptible to uncleanliness)
uk. – .tz ' kin
uku – utzi ' kin
ukurtu – utzi ' kinella
go bad/unclean – to leave it ' betting/taking chances
"It is unclean, leave it alone, you are taking chances."

Vedok (continue to examine the matter)
ve – edo – ok.
be – edo – oki
beharbada – edonoiz – okitu
perhaps – some time – to complete.
"Perhaps sometime to be completed."

Yadaim (unclean hands)
.ja – ada – im.
jakinezin – adarrasartu – imintze
unknowingly – deceived – offering
"Unknowingly deceived by the offering."

Yoma (sacrifices and the fast of Yom Kippur)
.jo – oma
ajolatu – oma
to be concerned – grandmother
"Grandmother is concerned."

Zavim (gonorrhea)
aza – abi – imi
azalkeratu – abiatu – imintze
to become evident – to begin – act of offering
"When it (the gonorrhea) becomes evident, begin the act of offering."

Zevahim (laws of sacrifice)
.ze – eba – ahi – im.
ize – eba – ahi – imi
izeki – ebakin – ai – imini
to burn – cut grass/harvest – strong desire – to serve/sacrifice
"I have a strong desire to sacrifice some of the harvest by burning."

AND SOME RANDOMLY SELECTED WORDS, NOT IN THE TALMUD

Kibutzim (collective)
.ki-ib. ' utzi-im
aki-ibi ' utzi – imi
akiarazi – ibili ' utzi – imatz
to exhaust – to work ' to leave – home
"Too exhausted from work to go out."

Mosad (institution, secret service)
.mo-osa-ad.
amo – osa – adi
amoltsu – osalari – adibide
caring – doctor – advice
"The caring doctor gives advice."

Jezebel,
je – eze – ebe – el.
je – eze – ebe – ele
jentil – ezetsiz – ebertar – eleizakoak
pagan – disdainful – Hebrew – sacraments
"(This) pagan is disdainful of Hebrew sacraments."

Jerusalem,
je – eru – usa – ale – em.
je – eru – usa – ale – ema
jentil – errukigabe – usadio – alegia – emankortasun
pagan – cruel – custom – fake – fertility
"Cruel pagan custom (to achieve) fake fertility."
(refers to crucifixion, see Ezekiel 8: 14).

Bethlehem,
.be – et. – .h. – .le ' he – em.
abe – eto – oha – ale ' he – emo
abelaska – etorberri – ohartzaile – alegera ' heben – emoi
manger – newborn – councillor/wise man – rejoicing/glorifying ' here – gift
"The newborn is in the manger. The wise men are here glorifying with gifts."

Apocalypse,
apo – oka – ali – ipu – use
apokeria – okastagarri – alienazio – ipuinezko – usario
filthy deed – disgusting – the killing of a person – legendary – tradition
"The disgusting and filthy killing of a person in legendary tradition."

zene (music)
ze – ene
zentzubizgarri – enegana
stimulating – to me
"It's stimulating to me."

Halle'lujah
.ha – al. – .le ' lu – uja – ah.
aha – ala – ale ' lu – uja – aho
ahalguzti – alaiki – alegera 'luzatu – uja – ahostaku
Almighty – happily – rejoicing – to prolong – shout of joy – to utter
"Happily rejoicing in the Almighty by uttering prolonged shouts of joy."

Amen,
ame – en.
ame – en.
ametsetsi – ene
to idealize – exclamation
"Exclamation of idealization."

CONCLUSION

Every Hebrew word or name appears to have a built-in hidden sentence written in the Basque/Saharan language, almost always having some relation to the present meaning. Many words in the daily language have been distorted over time and can no longer be translated with confidence, but the majority can still be decoded and translated. The words in the Talmud are in a different class, having been carefully memorized century after century and were passed on virtually unaltered. This means that every one of them can be decoded with the Basque dictionary. There is little doubt that the Hebrew language was constructed by skilled linguists applying formulaic manipulation to the Saharan/ Basque vocabulary, which may well have been the language of the Jews as they came from Arabia ca 3100 years ago. It is well possible that work on the new Hebrew language was started when they were captives in Babylonia. Lahetjuzan and the other early Basque scholars were right after all; there is no doubt that **Hebrew is basically manipulated Saharan-Basque.**

The Names of Egypt

"Naming represents a first step in language, a first sign that mankind stands apart from the world around. Giving things names permits us to order our world by distinguishing each item in our experience: without names the material world would become an uncontrolled sea of matter."

(Stephen Quirk in *Who Were The Pharaohs?*)

The Magical Language

The Old Egyptians saw magic in their mathematics, in the moon and the stars, in everything they studied. It is therefore not surprising that the priesthood created a magical language containing a relatively small number of carefully selected words with which, in combination, they could say almost anything. Using these words, they would first make up a sentence to describe a person or object or idea, then they took the first three letters of each selected word and agglutinated them into a new name or word, which is a shorthand form of writing the sentence. Mirror-imaged numbers were often considered magic, 121, 797, 12521 etc. and they built the same system into the new magic language. Four basic rules were set for name and word creation.

1) Only words starting with vowel-consonant-vowel (VCV) were used in the to-be-agglutinated sentence e.g. ama, opa, use. As they used 16 consonants, each consonant had 25 VCV possibilities, or 400 in total (see Appendix 1).

2) The words in the sentence had to be chosen in such a way that the adjoining vowels were the same, a system I called vowel-interlocking e.g. apo-opi-iz., the name of pharaoh Apopiz, 17th dynasty.

3) Under no circumstance shall the new word or name resemble the original language in sound or format.

4) The new word or name must then be finished or simplified by removing some of the vowels.

Only words starting with VCV made up the new magic vocabulary. It is amazing to me that this very ancient invented language was word for word incorporated into modern Basque, which now is half composed of the original Paleolithic language and the other half of the invented Egyptian magic language. Some of the magic words fell out of use in Basque but were maintained in other languages such as '*ulatu*' (to welcome) which is still found in the Polynesian languages. Visitors to Hawaii are still welcomed by dancing girls wearing hula or ula grass skirts.

WHO DID THE NAMING?

Naming has traditionally been the preserve of priest/linguists. They assembled the many words needed for the ever evolving first civilization in North Africa and also for the names of people, including the monarch. If the monarch was in tune with the priesthood, the names expressed respect and appreciation. If at odds with the priests, the names they gave expressed their negative feelings, often in colourful language. Take for instance the name of the Persian king Cambyses, which means "Our perfect administrator is famous and wise" a most respectful name given to him in Persia. Cambyses had dreamt of being eternalized in stone as one of the many illustrious god-kings of Egypt, therefore, when he conquered Egypt in 525 B.C., he asked the Egyptian priest/ linguist Wedjahorresnet to create for him a true Egyptian pharaoh's throne name which the priest did: Mesutira, meaning "You skinny dreamer, go away and suffer." He became the first king of the 27th dynasty, and was told that the name meant something like "Conqueror of two lands" (Upper and Lower Egypt) and he was pleased with it. Wedjahorresnet then had a magnificent statue carved of himself (now in the Vatican museum) on which he recorded the highlights of his career, including the making of royal names for Cambyses. In doing so he became, to my knowledge, the only person, in over 5000 years of name invention, to admit to having the skill to do so. All the other linguists creating names chose to remain anonymous, which was probably a wise decision. If Cambyses had known what the priest had done to him, the priest's career would likely have been terminated very abruptly.

The same system of naming has been in use throughout more than five millennia and the capability still exists without any change. For instance, the person who made up Stalin's name told him that it meant "Man of Steel," but in the secret encoding language it meant "He kills people indiscriminately." The person who did this was likely a learned monk of the Eastern Orthodox monastery in Kiev, Ukraine. Lucky for him, Stalin never found out the true meaning. Similarly, one of these monks must have been disgusted with personal cleanliness of the people when he made up the name Ukraina, from *uku-araina*, meaning "They smell like rotten fish," possibly because of the proverbial distaste of the early Ukrainian horsemen for washing, commented on even by Herodotus. The people who accepted this agglutination as their country's name cannot have had the slightest idea what it really meant.

If, on the other hand, a good relationship existed between priesthood and monarch, the names given were very appropriate, such as the family name of British royalty: Windsor, meaning "Bequeath a thoroughly united nobility." They accepted this name early in the 20th century and they must have known exactly what they were doing. Even though none of the family probably had any idea about the encoding language or the technique involved, they trusted the linguist who selected the name for them. These examples show that the ability to create names and words is still secretly preserved and practiced in private or religious institutions, many millennia after it was invented.

Translating the pharaohs' names, one is struck by some of the strange hidden sentences. Most pharaohs had five different names, some to do with his greatness or prowess in war, some with his health or actions, some heralding his piousness and others telling about natural disasters. Even repeated attacks by the Hebrews, coming out of the Arabian desert, are recorded.

Consonantal Writing

Ancient Egyptian writing does not record the vowels. To the normal educated person living at that time, the vowels could be filled in from knowledge of the language, just like Hebrew and Arabian is completed today. To us the missing vowels must be sought in the quite similar Coptic language or from the literature of nearby nations such as Greece and Assyria.

The scribes creating the inscriptions gave themselves appropriate names such as: **Nesmeterakhem,** son of Nesmeterpanakhet at the time of Hadrian, AD 117-138 (Parkinson p.178)

.ne – es. – .me – ete – era – ak. – .he – em.
ene – esa – ame – ete – era – ako – ohe – ema
ene – ezangarri – ameskile – etengabeko – erran – akordiozko – ohetoki – emai
my – symbols – fanciful – continuous – saying/epigram – traditional – burial chambre – gift
"My fanciful symbols (form) a continuous epigram,
a gift for the traditional burial chamber."

His father, **Nesmeterpanakhet**, used the same introductory sentence, then adds:

.pa – ana – ak. – .he – et.
apa – ana – ako – ohe – ete
apaindu – anaia – akordiozko – ohetoki – etengabetasun
to make up – religious brother – traditional – burial chambre – in perpetuity
"My fanciful symbols (form) a continuous epigram,
made up for the religious brother's traditional burial chamber in perpetuity."

THE ROSETTA STONE

The meaning of the name **Rosetta** came to me as a surprise:

.ro – ose – et. – .ta
ero – ose – ete – eta
erotegi – ozen – etengabeko – -eta
insane asylum – penetrating voice/cry – incessant – overpowering
"The incessant penetrating screams from the insane asylum are overpowering."

In contrast to the VCV method used to agglutinate the names, the Egyptians' writings on stone, papyrus etc. made use of all words in the ancient vocabulary, as shown here in a sentence borrowed from the Rosetta stone. Parkinson in his book "Cracking Codes, the Rosetta Stone and Decipherment" (p. 54) supplies us with the pronunciation of the transliterof the last sentence on the Rosetta Stone. I show the corresponding Basque words and *my translation* underneath (English 'sh' = Basque 'x'):

Rosetta: her   ahay   neti   aat   rudj   em   sech
Basque: *herrikatu ahaide   netik   atx   rudipetu eman   sekretu*
English: proclamation–our people–from this date on–stone–to symbolize–the above–secret script
Translation: "Proclamation to our people. From this date on the stone will symbolize the above in the secret script… "

ni medu   netcher   sech   ni   hay   sekhay ni hau-nebu
? eme'edukitsu   txera   sekretu   ?   xeheki   asekhai ? hau-uneburu
?–female'powerful–intelligent–secret script–?–in great detail–abundant–?–this–important place
**"... of the Goddess in intelligent secret writing in great and abundant
detail in this important place."**

My translation differs considerably from the *translation shown by Parkinson*
in his book which reads: **"Upon a stela of hard stone in hieroglyphic writing, in demotic writing, and in the script of the Aegians."**

It seems that our modern linguists who did the translations, often had little
idea what they were doing e.g. the name of king "Aha" was translated by them
as "the fighter," when it means "the omnipotent" (*ahalguzti*).

WHO MADE UP THE TITLE "PHARAOH"?

The title **"pharaoh,"** more accurately spelled **"faraoh,"** is no Egyptian invention because it is appropriate for males only:

.fa – ara – a.o – oh.
afa – ara – aho – oha
afa – aragikeria – ahokatu – ohaide
pleasing – fornication – to engage in – concubine
"Engaged in pleasing fornication (with a) concubine."

Stephen Quirke in "Who were the pharaohs?" p.33 tells us: **"The Hebrew
version of "per 'aa" in the Bible gives us our word Pharaoh."** This, I find
very hard to accept, so hard that I will call it nonsense. The traditional translation of the name as "Great House" cannot be taken seriously either.

Otto Muck in "Cheops et la Grande Pyramide" (1978) p.114, claims that the
Shepherd Philitis brought the title to Egypt from the north, witness Stone-
henge in England. Diop calls this an insipid notion and so do I. Pharaoh is an
agglutinated title, likely of Latin origin; neither the Egyptians nor Greeks pronounced the 'ph' as 'f.'

Nile
.ni – ile
uni – ile
unibertsal – ilezkor
universal – immortal
"Universal and immortal."

Pyramid
.pi – ira – ami – id.
epi – ira – ami – ide
epika – iragartzapen – amildu – ideadura
epic – to prophesy – destruction – ideology
"The epic prophesied the destruction of our ideology."
That's why they built for eternity.

Egypt
egi – ip. – .t.
egi – ipu – uto
egin – ipuin – utopia
to create – legend – utopia
"They created the legend of utopia."

Dynasty
.dina – asti
adina – astiz
so many – bright future
"So many bright futures."

Some Etyptian Gods

Amun
amu – un.
amultsu – unibertsalki
affectionate – universally
"Universally affectionate."

Aten
ate – en.
aterpe – ene
refuge – my
"My refuge."

Ra. There at least four possible origins for Ra. My guess is that #1 is right.
a**Ra** meaning **pure** (*aratz*)
e**Ra** meaning **devotion** (*eraspen*)
ir**Ra** meaning **radiating** (*irradiatu*)
o**Ra** meaning **for ever** (*orain*)

Re. Also has a few possible derivations, the most likely being:
ar**Re** meaning **Redeemer** (*arrerosle*)

The Four Children of the Sun God Ra

Geb, (the Earth, a male principle)
.ge – eb.
age – ebo
agerian – eboluziozko
evidently – evolving
"Evidently evolving."

Shu, (the Air).
.xu, *uxu* (**yodel cry of happiness**)

Tefnut, (the Water)
.te – ef. – .nu – ut.
ete – ebo – onu – uto
etengabeki – eboluzionatu – onurakor – utopia
constantly – to evolve – beneficial – utopia
"Constantly evolving beneficial utopia."

Nut (the Heaven, the Stars and the Ether; a female principle)
.nu – ut.
onu – uto
onuts – utopia
perfect – utopia
"Perfect utopia."

Geb and Nut had Four Children

Osiris, (personification of all that is good)
osi – iri – is.
osintsu – irrikitasun – izate
very deep – desire – life
"Very deep desire for life."

Isis,
(the Goddess who introduced immortality of the soul and individual salvation)
isi – is.
izi – izi
izigarri – izigarrikeria
terrible – atrocity
"Terrible atrocity."
This must refer to the dreadful killing of her brother – husband.

Seth, (introduces evil)
.se – et. – .h.
ase – eta – aha
asegaitz – -eta – ahalmen
craving – abundance – power
"He craves an abundance of power."

Nephthys/Nefthis, (introduces evil with Seth).
.ne – eb. – .t. – .hi – is.
ene – ebe – eto – ohi – izu
enetan – eberu – etorri – ohinazestatu – izugarriki
every time – Hebrews – to come – to suffer – horribly
"Every time the Hebrews came we suffered horribly."

The name Nephthys is extremely old, possibly predating the first known pharaoh. This name and many of the pharaohs' personal names tell us about the suffering caused by the attacks of the Hebrews on the Egyptians. It appears that the Hebrews tried for many millennia to conquer the land of Egypt and finally gave up and turned to the "Land of Milk and Honey," which their god had assigned to them.

Horus, (son of Isis and Osiris)
.ho – oru – us.
eho – oru – usa
ahopeko – orube – usa
secret – site/place – dove/holy man
"Secret (burial) place of the holy man." (?)

Abydos, burial place of the head of Osiris.
abi – ido – os.
abia – idolo – oso
nest/home – idol – simple
"Simple home for the idol."

HISTORY IN PHARAOHS' NAMES

A great deal of previously unknown historical information is hidden in the Pharaohs' names. They tell us about attacks by the Sea Peoples from Libya and from the Islands in the Great Green ocean, and of the many attacks by the Hebrews from Arabia. They tell of dreadful floods of the Nile and of tidal waves from the ocean. We now know that some of the earlier pharaohs participated in the Sacred Marriage (as Tammuz) after which they were ritually sacrificed by drowning in the First Cataract of the Nile.

Cataract
.ka – ata – ara – ak. – .t.
ika – ata – ara – aka – ate
ikaragaitz – atano – arauzaletasun – akabatu – aterriki
fearless – hereafter – respect for the law – to end a life – calmly
"Fearlessly and in respect for the law of the hereafter, he calmly ended his life."

The pharaoh's body was recovered and then taken to the little island of Abu just downstream from the cataract. The name Abu comes from 'aburukide' meaning 'person who agrees' (to be sacrificed). It was later renamed Elephantine by the Greeks. The Hebrews then built a replica of Solomon's temple on the holy site, the foundations of which can be visited.

In some literature this sacrifice is erroneously called regicide, the murder of a king. This was not a murder in Egypt because he went voluntarily and proudly to his death, proving his absolute faith in the Goddess, in the full knowledge that resurrection in her womb was waiting for him, just as was done in Scotland in the whirlpool of Charybdis (Corryvreckan). In pre-pharaonic years it could have been regicide, when the king was cut to pieces, as had happened to Osiris (see Joseph Campbell, *Primitive Mythology* p.425-26). The same happened in other parts of Africa and India where the people attending the sacrifice would receive a piece of the body which would then either be eaten or be buried in the field of the family to assure a good harvest, health and happiness. Today the Christian churches continue this sacrament symbolically by cutting a loaf of bread into small pieces after which the tray is passed around from person to person with the words: "The body of Christ." The wine is then passed around in a goblet with the words: "The blood of Christ." The sacrifice of a king was continued well into pharaonic days but it is highly unlikely that the body was cut up.

In Greek the practice of the Sacred Marriage, which preceded his death, is called Hieros Gamos. Where the Sacred Marriage may have taken place every year, the sacrifice is thought to have been held once every eight or so years but little information is available about the duration of Tammuz' reign. It is hinted that when his wives complained about his declining virility that the priests decided that it was time for him to go, but this is not verified. It is obvious that the person, who made up the name, condemned the practice of the Sacred Marriage in the strongest terms:

Hieros Gamos
hi – ero – os.   ga – amo – os.
higuindu – erokeria – osin   gaitzesgarry – amodio – ospatze
to detest – insanity – abyss   disgusting – love – celebration
"Detestable insanity in the abyss (after) a disgusting love celebration."

The first pharaoh we know of who was sacrificed in the waves was Hotepsekhe'mui (2ⁿᵈ Dynasty), the last three letters 'mui' or 'mu-uhi' tell us that he drowned in the waves (*murgilarazi – uhin* or: to drown – waves). Others were Kha'sekhe'mui (2ⁿᵈ), Merytawy (known as Pepi, 8th), Wadjkara Demedjibtawy (8ᵗʰ) and Nebtawyrat Mentuhotep (11ᵗʰ). It is likely that many of the pharaohs of the first eleven dynasties died in this manner. Another surprising, and previously unknown, bit of history is the record of the many attacks by the Hebrews. Several pharaohs' names refer to the attacks and the horrible consequences. Historically the Jews themselves reported to have suffered a great deal from the cruelty of the Egyptians who enslaved them, as told in the Jewish writings in the Old Testament Bible. However, translation of the names of the pharaohs, and of the name of the Goddess Nefthys, tells a very different story. It is good to hear what the other side had to say about this subject.

PHARAOH'S NAMES TRANSLATED

FIRST DYNASTY (C.3100-2890 B.C.)

(The names and the dates of the dynasties are taken from "Who were the Pharaohs?" by Stephen Quirke, Dover Publications, 1990.)

Menes, (probably his funeral name).
.me – ene – es.
ome – ene – esa
omendu – -enetan – ezarle
to honour – always – founder
"Always honour our founder."

Narmer, (same person as Menes).
.na – ar. – me – er.
ana – aro – ome – ere
anaitu – -aro – omenezko – erreinu
to unite – all – honourable – kingdom
"He united all into an honourable kingdom."

Hor-aha
.ho – or. – aha
oho – ora – aha
ohoratu – orain – ahalguzti
to praise – always – almighty
"Always praise the Almighty."

Berner-Ib, wife of Hor-aha.
(Note that the name is hyphenated at the interruption of vowel-interlocking)
.be – er. – .ne – er. ' ib.
abe – ere – ene – ere ' ibi
aberaski – erregina – enetan – erregekiro ' ibili
elegant – queen – always – royally ' to act
"My elegant queen always acts royally."

Zer
.ze – er.
eze – ere
ezezagun – errege
unknown – king
"Unknown king."

Meryet-nit
.me – eri – i.e – et. ' .ni – it.
ume – eri – ihe – ete ' uni – itu
ume – eriotze – ihesezin – etenkor ' unibertsal – itundu
child – death – unavoidable – fragile ' general – sadness
"The death of her fragile child was unavoidable. (There was) general sadness."

Uadji
u.a – ad. – .ji
uha – adi – iji
uhaldu – adi – ijito
to fasten down – watch out – Gypsy
"Fasten (everything) down; watch out for the Gypsies."
This must be the strangest name of all. Hard to believe that this is a pharaoh's name.
Was Uadji really a pharaoh's name?

Udimu, to translate this name it must be written:
Udi ' mu:
udi ' amu
udikan ' amure egon
get out ' to be distrustful
"Get out! I don't trust you."
What is going on here? It appears that the early Egyptians had a serious problem with Gypsies, as both Uadji and Udimu seem to indicate, but why write this in the king's name?

Hemaka (Udimu's chancellor).
.he – ema – aka
hegaztiazti – emankizun – akatsbako
diviner/augur – performance – perfect
"Diviner of perfect performance."

Semti, name somehow associated with Udimu.

.se – em. – .ti

ase – ema – ati

asete – eman – atxikidura

period of abundance – to celebrate – unity

"In this time of abundance we celebrate unity."

Enezib

ene – ezi – ib.

-enetan – eziakin – ibildari

always – illiterate – nomad

"Always an illiterate nomad."

Semerkhet (same person as Sozer-Teti)

.se – eme – er. – .k. – .he – et.

ese – eme – ere – eki – ihe – ete

ezezagun – emeki – errege – ekile – ihesegin – etendura

anonymous – peaceful – king – enterprising – to escape/to be missed – lineage

"Anonymous peaceful and enterprising king who was missed from the lineage."

Sozer-Teti, alternate name for Semerkhet)

.so – oze – er. ' .te – eti

eso – oze – era ' ate – eti

esonde – ozen – erran ' aterbe – etika

advice – penetrating voice – to say/speak ' safety – ethics

"He speaks his advice about safety and ethics with a penetrating voice."

Zezer'kerasonb

(his dynasty and place in it is uncertain to me at this time).

.ze – eze – er. ' .ke – era – azo – on. – .b.

eze – eze – ere ' ake – era – azo – ona – abe

ezezagun – ezegin – errege ' akela – eraspen – -azo – onaldi – aberatstasun

anonymous – to omit – king ' Goddess – devotion – to bring about – prosperity – riches

**"Anonymous, omitted king." "His devotion to the Goddess
brought about prosperity and riches."**

SECOND DYNASTY (C.2890-2686)

Hotepsekhe'mui

.ho – ote – ep. – .se – ek. – .he ' emu – u.i

oho – ote – epe -eze – eki – ihe ' mu – uhi

ohoratu – otseinketa – epetu – ezezagun – ekin – ihesezin ' murgilarazi – uhin

to honour – service – set time limit – to persevere – unknown ' to drown – waves

**"We honour his service for the set time period. He persevered
into the unknown and drowned in the waves."**

The "set time period" for a king who had participated in the "Sacred Marriage" may have been about seven years. He reigned as a semi-god, the bridge

between the people and the deity, and when his time was up he was sacrificed by drowning in the waves, possibly in the First Cataract. Joseph Campbell in Primitive Mythology records many instances of death of the reigning king e.g.:

> ... the archaeic regicide comes out cruelly the moment we focus on the royal ritu-
> als traditionally practiced, until recently, in the Sudan. Among the Shilluk, the
> priests, who were the only ones knowing the will of God (whom they called Nyakang),
> saw to it that the king was killed after a term of seven years, or, if the crops or
> prosperity of the herds failed before that time, even earlier. (p. 156)

This human sacrifice was also practiced in Scotland in the whirlpool of Corrivreckan, until Christianity arrived. The bodies were buried on the holy Isle of Iona and the memory of this event still lives on in folk legends. The above name of the Egyptian pharaoh now confirms that the human sacrifice was also practiced in early Egypt during his dynasty. The pharaohs had several names assigned during their lifetime and only his funeral name would tell about the manner of his death. We do not know all the names given to the pharaohs. The following names are probably earned during his life.

Nebra (Ra-Neb)
.ne – eb. – .ra
ene – ebe – era
enetik – ebertaren – erasan
from that time on – Hebrews – to attack
"From that time on the Hebrews attacked."

Neteren
.ne – ete – ere – en.
one – ete – ere – -ena
onegite – etengabeki – errege – -ena
doing good – constantly – king – 'superlative'
"Our 'wonderful' king was constantly doing good."

Netermu, same person as Neteren
.ne – ete – er. – .mu
one – ete – era – amu
onegite – etengabeki – eraspen – amultsutasun
doing good – constantly – devotion – tenderness
"Constantly doing good with devotion and tenderness."

Sekhemib. The name tells us that this was a queen, not a king as is stated. Archaeologists have long wondered why she abandoned her allegiance to the god Horus and switched to Set. Her name tells us why. The name should be spelled:

Sekhem – ib
separated because the vowel-interlocking is interrupted.
.se – ek. – .he – em. ' ib.
ese – eki – ihe – ema ' ibi
esetsi – ekimendu – ihesari eman - emarrapaketa ' ibili
to attack – to take the initiative – to escape – abduction of a woman – to go along
**"She was attacked and took the initiative to escape
by going along with her abductors."**

Perabsen, same person as Sekhem-ib.
.pe – era ab. – .se – en.
pe – era – aba – ase – ena
petralkeria – erasan – abade – aserrekor – -ena
villainy – to attack – priest – infuriating – 'superlative'
"The villainy of the priests' attack was 'extremely' infuriating."

Sendji
.se – en. – .di – .ji
ase – ena – adi – iji
azeri – -ena – adi – ijito
shrewd – 'superlative' – watch out – Gypsy
"Gypsies are 'extremely' shrewd, watch out."

Neterka
.ne – ete – er. – .ka
one – ete – era – aka
onegite – etengabeki – eraspen – akatsbako
doing good – constantly – devotion – perfect
"Constantly doing good with perfect devotion."

Neferkara
.ne – ebe – er. – .ka – ara
ane – ebe – era – aka – ara
añendu – eberu – erratu – akargarritu – arakintzatu
to curse – Hebrews – to wander – to infuriate – to massacre
"The cursed wandering Hebrews infuriated and massacred."

Kha – sekhe'mui
.k. – .ha ' .se – ek. – .he ' mu – u.i
ako – oho ' ase – eki – ihe ' mu – uhi
akorduan euki – oharti ' asezin – ekin – ihesezin ' murgilarazi – uhin
to remember – thoughtful ' craving – to persevere – inevitable ' to drown – wave
**"Remember his thoughtful craving to persevere in
the inevitable and be drowned in the waves."**
Another courageous Tammuz went honorably to his sacrificial death.

THIRD DYNASTY (C.2686-2613)

Djoser, builder of the step pyramid.
.d. – .jo – ose – er.
ida – ajo – ose – era
idazlan – ajola – ozen – erran
writing – interest – penetrating voice – to say/to speak
"He speaks his interest in writing in a penetrating voice."

Imhotep, architect and physician and everything else of Djoser.
Vowel-interlocking is interrupted; the name should be spelled:
Im-Hotep.
im. ' .ho – ote – ep.
ima ' oho – ote – epa
imajina ' ohoratu – otseinketa – epaile
statue ' to honor – service – judge
"This statue honors his service as a judge."

Khaba, (of the Layer Pyramid)
.k. – .ha – aba
aka – aha – aba
akabu – ahalguzti – abade
high/superior – almighty – priest
"High priest of the Almighty."

FOURTH DYNASTY (C.2613-2494)

Seneferu
.se – ene – ebe – eru
ese – ene – ebe – eru
esetsi – -enetan – eberu – errukigabe
to attack – every time – Hebrews – cruel
"Every time he attacked the cruel Hebrews."

Djedefre,
.d. – .je – ede – eb. – .re
ada – aje – ede – ebe – ere
-ada – ajene – ederrakhartu – eberu – eremu
noise of the action – lament – to be defeated – Hebrews – desert
"The Hebrews lamented loudly when they were defeated in the desert."

Nebka
.ne – eb. – .ka
one – ebe – eka
onera hartu – ebertaren – ekarri
to accept – patriarchy – to bring
"Accept the patriarchy I bring."

FIFTH DYNASTY (C.2494-2345)

THE KHU'FU FAMILY.

Snofru, father of Khu'fu
builder of the Bent Pyramid
.s. – .no – ob. – .ru
aso – ono – obi – iru
-azo – onon – obi – irudi
to bring about/create – wonderful – tomb – symbol
"He created his wonderful tomb as a symbol."

Hetepheres, mother of Khu'fu.
.he – ete – ep. – .he – ere – es.
ihe – ete – epo – ohe – ere – esa
ihezin – etenkor – epotu – ohealdi – erregina – esaeratsu
inevitable/fated – fragile – to loose weight – time spent in bed – queen – wise
"Fated to be fragile and losing weight, our wise queen spent her time in bed."

Cheops. This is the Latin spelling because neither Egyptian nor Greek possesses the 'c.' The name should be spelled: **Keops**, the 'h' had to be added when the 'k' was changed to 'c' otherwise the name would have been pronounced Seops.

Keops
.ke – e.o – op. – .s.
ake – eho – opa – asa
akela – ehortzetak – opakuntza – asaba
Goddess – funeral – offering – ancestor
"The Goddess' funeral offering to the ancestors."

This translation tells us that Keops cannot have been the name of the pharaoh but instead must have been the name of the Great Pyramid itself. This, the most impressive stone building ever constructed on earth was not built as the tomb for just one king, but instead contained the womb of the Goddess for reincarnation of all the people. The people who worked so enormously hard to build it were not building for the pharaoh but instead they were building their own edifice. The mighty sarcophagus always stands open and was intended to be available for all the beloved departed of the Goddess world. Strabo in his "Geographica" tells about a stone in the side of the pyramid which may be taken out. Petrie interpreted this statement to mean that there was a flap-door composed of a single slab of stone (Edwards). It could have been there to allow access to the sarcophagus for the funerals of the people. This explains why the great pyramid has no decorations to show scenes of the dead pharaoh's life. The huge sarcophagus was never intended for the pharaoh alone, although it is possible that he was the first one to use it. His real grave may yet be found, hidden deep under the pyramid, where his personal life would have been depicted on the walls. If this is indeed the case, the grave may yet be found intact, the most elaborate and costly grave ever constructed. Herodotus tells about subterranean chambers where vaults were constructed on an island, surrounded by water brought from the Nile by tunnel. On this island, he was told, the body of Khufu lies. Nothing of that description has ever been found. It is interesting that a Japanese expedition has recently found evidence of just such underground caverns while sounding the deep underlying rock with sophisticated equipment.

The name "Akela'," meaning "Great Goddess," is still used in many Indo-European languages but now it has been twisted into 'witch' or a boy-scout's cry, a meaning-change enforced by the Christian and Judaic clergy. As male domination throughout the following millennia has made every effort to eliminate the memory of the Great Goddess, this is likely the reason why the spelling of the name Keops was changed to Cheops, to hide the '.ke' of 'ake.'

Khufu. This must be the real name of the "great pharaoh" Keops because Khufu'khaf was the name of his son who died in infancy. The final letters 'ufu' are untranslatable therefore an interruption of the vowel-interlocking must be assumed. The 'f' is interchangeable with 'b':

Khu'fu
.k. – .hu ' fu,
aka – ahu ' bu
akabu – ahurrelaritza ' bukatu
perfect – leadership ' to bring to a finish
"Perfect leadership brought (the pyramid) to a finish."

Rekha'ef, alternate name for Khu'fu.
.re – ek. – .ha ' ef.
ere – eki – iha ' eba
errege – ekinaldi – ihaiotasun ' ebatzizko
king – perseverance – expertise ' decisive
"The king's perseverance and expertise were decisive."

Hardjedef, son of Khu'fu
.ha – ar. – .d. – .je – ede – ef.
oha – ari – ida – aje – ede – ebe
oharrezko – arrisku – idatzi – ajeru – edendun – eberu
to warn – danger – to write about – suspicion – poisonous – Hebrews
**"He warned about the danger and wrote about his suspicions
of the poisonous Hebrews."**

Redjedef, son of Khu'fu
.re – ed. – .je – ede – eb.
are – eda – aje – ede – ebe
arrenkuratu – edangabetu – ajenatu – ederrak eman – eberu

to become impatient – to deprive of water – to drive away – to defeat -   Hebrews
**"He was impatient to deprive the Hebrews of water,
then to defeat and drive them away."**

Khufu'khaf, infant son of Khu'fu
Khufu ' .k. – .ha – ab.
Khufu ' ki – iha – aba
Khufu ' *kirikaldi – ihar – -aba*
Khufu ' period of vigilance – to waste away – family relation/heir
"(During) Khufu's period of vigilance his heir wasted away."

Khnumbraf, infant son of Khu'fu.
.k. – .h. – .nu – um. – .b. – .ra – af.
ako – ohi – inu – uma – abo – ora – afa
akorduan euki – ohihaldu – inudetu – uma – abots – orain – afa
to remember – wrapped in diapers – to nurse – child – voice – always – happy
"Remember the nursing child in diapers, whose voice was always happy."

Hetephras, daughter of Khu'fu.
.he – ete – ep. – .h. – .ra – as.
ohe – ete – epe – ehi – ira – asu
ohekoi – etenkor – epel – ehihargarri – iragan – azurruts
tends to sleep a lot – fragile – weak – wilting – to suffer – very skinny person
"She tends to sleep a lot, is fragile, weak and wilting, and very skinny."

Meresankh
(daughter of Khu'fu, wife of Khephren), obviously a funeral name.
.me – ere – esa – an. – .k. – .h.
ome – ere – esa – ana – aka – ahi
omendatu – erregina – esaeratsu – anaitu – akabu – ahienekatu
to honour – queen – wise – to gather – death – to lament
"To honour the wise queen we gather for a death lament."

Kawaat, eldest son of Khu'fu.
.kawa – a.a – at.
akawa – aha – ate
akabatu – ahalguzti – aterpe
to end a life – almighty – refuge
"His life ended in the refuge of the Almighty."

Menkhaf, (son of Khu'fu)
.me – en. – .k. – .ha – af.
ume – ena – ako – oha – afa
ume – -ena – akorduan euki – oharkabetasun – afa
child – 'superlative' – to remember – innocent – happy
"Remember this 'wonderful' child, so innocent and happy."

Kephren (Khaef – Re)
.ke – ep. – .h. – .re – en.
ake – epa – ahe – ere – ena
akela – epaitu – aherentzia – errege – -ena
Goddess – to decide – inheritance – king – 'superlative'
"The Goddess decided the great king's inheritance."

Khaef – Re, same person as Kephren.
.k. – .ha – a.e – eb. ' .re
aka – aha – ahe – eba ' ere
akabu – ahalguzti – aherentzia – ebatzi ' errege
ultimate/great – Goddess – inheritance – to decide ' king
"The Great Goddess decided the inheritance of the king."

Mycerinus (Men-kau-Re)
.mi – ike – eri – inu – us.
umi – ike – eri – inu – uso
umilki – ikertu – eri – inurritze – uso
humbly – to examine – sickness – inspiring – holy man
"(The doctor) humbly examined the illness of the inspiring holy man."

Men – kau – Re, same person as Mycerinus.
.me – en. ' kau – ' .re
ome – ene ' kau ' are
omendatu – enetan ' kauta ' arrerosle
to honour – always ' obligation ' Redeemer
"Always honour your obligations to the Redeemer."

Khamerernebti, queen of Mycerinus
.k. – .ha – ame – ere – er. – .ne – eb. – .ti
aka – aha – ame – ere – era – añe – ebe – eti
akargarri – aharrari – ameskaitz – errege – erasan – añendu – eberu – etikagabe
infuriated – troublemaker – nightmare – king – to attack – to curse – Hebrew tribe – unethical
**"Infuriated with the nightmare caused by the troublemakers,
the king attacked and cursed the unethical Hebrew tribe."**

Khentkaues, mother of Userkaf
.k. – .he – en. – .t. ' kau ' es.
aki – ihe – ene – ete – eka ' kau ' es.
akitu – ihesezin – enetan – etenkor – ekarri ' kauta ' esaeratsu
to be tired – fated – always – fragile – to bring ' responsibility ' wisdom
**"She was fated to always be tired and fragile, but
she brought responsibility and wisdom."**

Userkaf
us. – er. – .ka – ab.
uste – ere – eka – abo

uste oso – errege – ekarpen – aboskatu
complete faith – king – contribution – to proclaim
"The contributions of the king with his complete faith were proclaimed."

Sahure

.sa – ahu – ure
asa – ahu – ure
asaba – ahutoizendatu – urentasun
ancestor – to appoint oneself – nobility
"Ancestor who appointed himself to nobility."

Unas

una – as.
una – asa
unai – asaba
cowherd – ancestor
"His ancestors were cowherds."

Neferefre

.ne – ebe – ere – eb. – .re
ane – ebe – ere – eba – are
añendu – eberu – eremutu – ebatsi – arestian
to curse – Hebrew tribe – to depopulate – to plunder – a short time ago
"The cursed Hebrews depopulated and plundered a short time ago."

Nuserre

.nuse – erre
inuze – errege
mentally defective – king
"Mentally defective king."
Another name made up by a historian, possibly Manetho.

Neferirkere

.ne – efe – eri – ir. – .ke – ere
ene – ebe – eri – ira – ake – ere
enerako – ebertaren – erioaldi – irakitu – akela – errespedatu
before – patriarchy – agony – to fire with compassion – Goddess - to respect
"Before the agony of patriarchy our passionate Goddess was respected."
It is known that the Goddess religion reestablished itself every once in a while.

Djedkare Izezi

.d. – .je – ed. – .ka – are   ize – ezi
ida – aje – ese – eka – are   ize – ezi
idatzi – ajenatu – esesti – ekarpen – aren   izen – ezinirakurrizko
to document – to be lost – history – contribution – his   name – illegible
"Documented (because) his contribution to history may be lost. Name illegible."
This is probably Manetho's comment.

Menhauhor

.me – en. – .ha – au – uho – or.
ame – ena – aha – au – uho – ora
ameskaitz – -ena – ahazte – aundi – uholde – orraztu
nightmare – 'superlative' – action of trying to forget – enormous – flood – to despoil
**"He tried to forget the 'terrible' nightmare of the enormous flood
which had despoiled (the country)."**

Shepseskaf, last pharaoh of the Fifth Dynasty.
.s. – .he – ep. – .se – es. – .ka – ab.
uso – ohe – epe – eze – ezu – uka – abi
uso – ohealditu – epel – ezeuskor – ezurruts – ukan – abiatu
dove/holy man – to spend time in bed – weak – fragile – very skinny – to have – to depart
**"Our holy man, who spent his time in bed, weak,
fragile and very skinny, has departed."**

SIXTH DYNASTY (C.2345-2181)

Teti

.te – eti
ete – eti
etengabe – etikoa
constantly – ethical
"Always ethical."

Maryra Pepi

.ma – ari – ira   .pe – epi
ema – ari – ira   epe – epi
emakoi – arrigarri – irakasle   epetu – epika
generous – marvelous – teacher   to set a deadline – epic of utopia
"Generous and a marvelous teacher. The end of the epic of utopia is coming."

Nefersahor (Pepi)

.ne – ebe – er. – .sa – aho – or.
ane – ebe – era – asa – aho – ora
añendu – eberu – eraso – asaldagarri – ahozuritu – orratio
to curse – Hebrews – attack – shocking – deceit – surprise
"The cursed Hebrews' shocking attack came by surprise and deceit."

Merytawi (Pepi's Horus name)

.me – eri – ita – au – u.i
imi – eri – ita – au – uhi
imintze – erio – itxaro – aukeramen – uhin
act of offering – death – to have faith – free will – waves
"A faithful death offering out of free will in the waves."
(Another Tammuz went courageously to his death.)

Ibi
ibi from *ibildari* (nomad)
"Nomad."

Merenre
.me – ere – en. – .re
ome – ere – ene – ere
omendatu – errege – enetan – erregetza
to honor – king – always – royal power
"Always honor the king's royal power."

EIGHTH DYNASTY (C.2181-2130 B.C.)

Wadjkara Demedjibtawy
u.a – ad. – .j. – .ka – ara
uha – ada – aje – eka – ara
uhalde – adaskadura – ajene – ekarri – arrailagarri
flood/cataract – being swallowed – lament – to cause – heartbreaking
"Being swallowed up by the cataract caused lament and heartbreak."
Another voluntary sacrifice was drowned in the Cataract.

.de – eme – edi – ib. – .ta – au – u.i
ade – eme – edi – iba – ata – au – uhi
adelatu – emekiro – ediren – ibar – atano – aukeramen – uhin
to prepare – venerably – to find – river – evergreen forest/hereafter – free will – wave
**"Venerably he prepared to find the hereafter in the waves
of the river on his own free will."**
Obviously the sacrifice of a king was still practiced at this time.

Qakara Iby
.ka – aka – ara / ibi
ika – aka – ara / ibi
ikaserazi – akatsbako – aratz / ibili
to teach – perfect – pure / to be
"His teachings are pure and perfect."

Min
in pain
"In pain."

NINTH AND TENTH DYNASTY (C.2130-2040 B.C.)

Kheti
.k. – .he – eti
oki – ihe – eti
okitu – ihesleku – etikoa
completely – safe place to live – ethical
"A completely safe and ethical place to live."

Ankhtify

an. – .k. – .h. – .ti – .bi
ana – ako – ohi – iti – ibi
anaiarte – akorduan euki – ohinaze – itxiki – ibildari
gathering/everybody – to remember – suffering – faithfulness – nomad
"Everybody will remember the suffering and the faithfulness of the nomad."

Neferirkare

.ne – ebe – eri – ir. – .ka – are
añe – ebe – eri – ire – eka – are
añendu – eberu – eriotza – irentsi – ekarri – arrenguratsu
to curse – Hebrews – death – to destroy – to bring – lamenting
"The cursed Hebrews brought death and destruction and lamenting."

ELEVENTH DYNASTY (C.2130-1991 B.C.)

Nebtawyrat Mentuhotep

.ne – eb. – .ta – au – u.i – ira – at.
ine – eba – ata – au – uhi – ira – ate
inertzia – ebatzi – atano – aukeramen – uhin – iraun – ateri
passive – to decide – evergreen oak forest/hereafter – free will – wave – to endure – calm
"He passively decided to endure the waves calmly on his own free will (to enter) the hereafter."

.me – en. – .tu – uho – ote – ep.
ame – eni – itu – uho – ote – epa
ameskaitz – eni – itxuragabe – uhol – ote – epai
nightmare – to me – senseless – flood/cataract – perhaps – judgment
"To me the senseless nightmare in the Cataract is perhaps a judgment."

TWELFTH DYNASTY (C.1991-1786 B.C.)

Amenemhet

ame – ene – em. – .he – et.
ame – ene – emo – ohe – etsi
amesgaitz – enetan – emon – ohe – etsitu
nightmare – always – to produce – bed – to despair
"His nightmares always produced despair in bed."

Sobekneferu, (Queen)

.so – obe – ek. – .ne – ebe – eru
oso – obe – eka – añe – ebe – eru
osoro – obendun – ekanduak – añendu – eberu – errukigabe
absolutely – sinful – customs – to curse – Hebrews- merciless
"The absolutely sinful customs of the cursed Hebrews were merciless."

Sesostris, (Amenemhet's successor)
.se – eso – os. .t. – .ri – is.
ase – eso – osa – ate – eri – isu
asetu – esonde – osalari – atera – erioaldi – izugarri
to crave – advice – doctor – to get – agony – terrible
"He craved to get advice from the doctor for his terrible agony."

Sesostris III ordered his engineers to cut a channel 260 feet long and 34 feet wide through the granite of the First Cataract. This action not only allowed his war-galleys to sail farther up river, but he also removed the whirlpool in which earlier pharaohs had gone to their voluntary death. In doing this he may have put a permanent stop to this human sacrifice in Egypt, because none are mentioned after that marvelous engineering feat. There was one other whirlpool, which continued to be used for the same purpose and this was in Scotland, at the north tip of the Isle of Jura, 70 km west of Glasgow.

Amenemes
am. – .me – ene – eme – es.
ama – ame – ene – eme – eza
ama – ametsetsi – enetan – emekiro – ezagutze
Goddess – to idealize – always – peaceful – all knowing
"Always idealize (our) Goddess; she is peaceful and all-knowing."

THIRTEENTH DYNASTY (C.1786-1674 B.C.)

Khendjer. This is a funeral name.
.k. – .he – en. – .d. – .je – er.
aka – ehe – -ena – -ada – aje – ere
akabu – ehe – -ena – -ada – ajene – errege
death – call attention – 'superlative' – sound of the action – lament – king
"Calling attention to the king's death with 'loud' sound of lament."

FOURTEENTH DYNASTY (C.1700-1674 B.C.)

Aasehrat Nehesy (funerary name)
a.a – ase – eh. – .ra – at.
aha – ase – eha – ara – ata
ahaltsu – asegaitz – ea – aratz – atutxa
powerful – craving – emphasis – pure – evergreen forest/ hereafter
"His powerful craving for a pure hereafter was emphasized."

Nehesy
.ne – ehe – esi
enetan – ee – eziakintasun
always – pay attention – illiteracy
"Always pay attention to illiteracy."

FIFTEENTH DYNASTY (C.1674-1567 B.C.)

Seuserenrat Khyan
.se – use – ere – en. – .ra – at.
ase – use – erre – ene – era – ati
asezindako – usei – errege – enetan – eraspen – atxikigarri
craving – sneeze – king – always – devotion – faithful
"(In spite of) his craving to sneeze, the king was always devoted and faithful."

.k. – .hi – an.
ako – ohi – ana
akorduan euki – ohinaze – anaia
to remember – suffering – religious brother
"Remember our suffering religious brother."

SIXTEENTH DYNASTY (C.1674-1567 B.C.)

Anather
ana – at. – .he – er.
ana – ati – ihe – ere
anaia – atxikigarri – ihesezin – erren
brother – faithful – unavoidable – cripple
"Faithful brother, unavoidable cripple."

Yakobaam
.ia – ako – oba – a.a – am.
iaio – akorduan euki – oba – ahal – aministralgo
cheerful – to remember – improvement – strength – administration
**"He is cheerfully remembered for the improvement in
the strength of his administration."**

SEVENTEENTH DYNASTY (C.1674-1567 B.C.)

Apopis
apo – opi – is.
apo – opi – isu
apokeria – opio – izurreztatu
morally corrupt – opium – to be addicted to
"It is morally corrupting to be addicted to opium."

Sekhemra Wadjkhaut Sobe'kemsaf
.se – ek. – .he – em. – .ra
ese – eki – ihe – eme – era
esetsaldi – ekin – ihesezin – emen – erasan
battle – to persevere – inevitable – here – to attack
"He persevered in the inevitable battle and attacked here."

u.a – ad. – .j. – .k. – .ha – au – ut.
uha – ada – aje – eki – iha – au – uti
uhalde – -ada – aienekatu – ekinaldi – ihabali – aurki – utikan
flood – being swallowed – lament – to persevere – fright – soon – get out
**"He was swallowed up by the flood (which caused) lament;
but he persevered and frightened, he soon got out."**

.so – obe   .ke – em. – .sa – af.
oso – obe   ake – eme – esa – aba
oso – obedientza   akela – emekiro – esaeratsu – abade
perfect – obedience   Goddess – peaceful – wise – priest
"The peaceful and wise priest (acted) in perfect obedience to the Goddess."

Kamose, either he or Seknerre drove out the Hyksos
and became the last pharaoh of the dynasty.
.ka – amo – ose
eka – amo – ose
ekandu – amorratu – osen
to be used to – to rage – penetrating voice
"He used to rage with a penetrating voice."

Seknerre, relative of Kamose
.se – ek. – .ne – erre
ase – eko – one – erre
asete – ekoizpen – onesan – errege
period of abundance – production – to praise – king
"Praise the king for a period of abundant production."

EIGHTEENTH DYNASTY (C.1567-1320 B.C.)

Ahmosis
ah. – .mo – osi – is.
aha – amo – osi – ize
ahalguzti – amodio – osin – izenandiko
Almighty – love – very deep – celebrated
"The Almighty's very deep love is celebrated."

Amenhotep
ame – en. – .ho – ote – ep.
ame – ena – aho – ote – epo
amesgaitz – -ena – ahomoteldu – ote – epotu
nightmare – that – to stutter – perhaps – to grow a little
"It is a nightmare that he stutters and perhaps he will grow a little."

Nibmuaria
(praenomen of Amenhotep III; Parkinson p.54)
.ni – ib. – .mu – u.a – ari – i.a
ani – iba – amu – uha – ari – iha

aniztu – ibai – amure egon – uhalde – arritu – ihabali
to increase/to rise – river – be suspicious – flood – to surprise – frightened
"Be suspicious of the rising river; a surprise flood is frightening."

Tuthmosis
.tu – ut. – .h. – .mo – osi – is.
atu – uto – oha – amo – osi – isa
atutxa – utopia – ohartasun – amodio – osintsu – izan
evergreen forest – utopia – thoughtfulness – love – very deep – to exist/live on
**"In the evergreen forest of utopia his thoughtfulness
and very deep love will live on."**

Menkheperre, same person as Tuthmosis
.me – en. – .k. – .he – epe – erre
ame – ena – ako – ohe – epe – erre
amesgaitz – ena – akorduan euki – ohealdi – epegabeko – errege
nightmare – 'superlative' – to remember – time spent in bed – continuous – king
**"We remember his 'dreadful' nightmares and the continuous time
spent in bed by the king."**

Hatshepsut
.ha – at. – .s. – .he – ep. – .su – ut.
aha – ata – ase – ehe – epi – isu – uto
ahalguzti – atano – asegaitz – ehe – epika – isurialdi – utopia
Almighty – evergreen forest – craving – call attention – epic – inspiration – utopia
**"Craving for the evergreen forest of the Almighty she called attention
to the inspiration (offered) in the epic of utopia."**

It was very likely during the reign of Amenophis III that the enormous Thera vulcano erupted (c 1420 B.C.), bringing the Cretan civilization to its knees and wreaking untold grief on Egypt and most other countries around the eastern Mediterranean with tidal waves and volcanic ash fall. (see Diop, p.79-83).

Amenophis
ame – eno – op. – .hi – is.
ame – eno – opo – ohi – isu
amesgaitz – enoradun – oposagaitz – ohil – isurduhin
nightmare – afflicted – unopposable- savage – tidal wave
"Afflicted by the nightmare of a savage unopposable tidal wave."

Akenaten
ake – ena – ate – en.
akela – -ena – aterpe – ene
Goddess – superlative/great – refuge – my
"The Great Goddess, my refuge."

Nefertiti
.ne – efe – er. – .ti – iti

ane – ebe – era – ati – iti
añendu – ebertaren – eraberritu – atikitasun – itiki/idiki
to curse – patriarchy – to reform – faithfulness – to discover
"Reform the cursed patriarchy and discover faithfulness."

Tutankhaten
.tu – uta – an. – .k. – .ha – ate – en.
itu – uta – ana – ake – eha – ate – ene
itxuragabe – utsa – anaiarte – akela – ea – aterpe – ene
senseless – to dispossess – priesthood – Goddess – 'emphasis' – refuge – my
"It is senseless to dispossess the priesthood of the 'Great' Goddess, my refuge."

Ankhesenamen, queen of Tutankhaten
an. – .k. – .he – ese – ena – ame – en.
ana – aki – ihe – ese – ena – ame – ena
anai – akigarri – ihesezin – esetsi – ena – amesgaitz – ena
religious brother/priest – exhausted – to escape – to attack – 'superlative' – nightmare – 'superlative'
**"The exhausted priest escaped from the 'vicious' attack
like from an 'awful' nightmare."**

Keftiu,
This was the name used for the island of Crete, but only during the 18th Dynasty.
.ke – eb. – .ti – i.u
ake – eba – ati – ihu
akela – ebakin – atxikilotu – ihuodei
Goddess – harvest – to arrest/hold back – thunderclouds
"The Goddess of the harvest holds back the thunderclouds."

NINETEENTH DYNASTY (C.1320-1200 B.C.)

Horemheb
.ho – ore – em. – .he – eb.
oho – ore – eme – ehe – eba
ohoratu – orrek – emekiro – ehe – ebakin
to praise – that – peacefulness - pay attention – harvest
"Praise the peacefulness that we have (so we can) pay attention to the harvest."

Ramesses
.ra – ame – es. – .se – es.
ura – ame – ese – ese – esi
urabazter – amesgaitz – esetsi – ezereztu – ezigabe
bank of the river -nightmare – to attack – to annihilate – savage
**"(During) the nightmare on the banks of the river
we attacked and annihilated the savages."**

This huge battle is usually said to have taken place ca. 1186 B.C., during Ramesses III's reign (see Sandars for description of the battle at Medinet Habu).

This is at odds with the dates supplied by Quirke for the dynasty. There were several earlier attacks by the Sea Peoples during the reign of Ramesses I and II also, but probably none after Ramesses III defeated the Sea Peoples decisively.

Usermaatra (Ramesses II and III)
use – er. – .ma – a.a – at. – .ra
use – era – ama – aha – ato – ora
usei – eraso – amaitu – ahalguzti – atorri – orain
to sneeze – attack – to end – almighty – to come – always
"To end the sneezing attack, always come to the Almighty."

Merneptah
.me – er. – .ne – ep. – .ta – ah.
ame – eri – ine – epe – eta – ahi
amesgaitz – eri – inertzia – epel – eta – ahi
nightmare – sickness – debility – to weaken – and – cause sorrow
"Having nightmares is a debilitating illness which weakens and causes sorrow."

Siptah
si – ip. – .ta – ah.
si – ipi – ita – aha
sinestu – ipini – itxaro – ahalguzti
to believe – to place – trust – Almighty
"To believe is to place your trust in the Almighty."

Meryptah (Parkinson p.83)
.me – eri – ip. – .ta – ah.
ame – eri – ipi – ita – aha
amesgaitz – eri – ipini – itxaro
nightmare – agony – to place – trust – almighty
"During the agony of a nightmare, place your trust in the Almighty."

Setnakht
.se – et. – .na – ak. – .h. – .t.
ase – eta – ana – aka – aha – ate
asetu – -eta – anaitu – akatsgabeko – ahalguzti – aterbe
to crave, pray – expresses an abundance – to gather – perfect – almighty – protection
"We pray that the abundant harvest is gathered under the protection of the Almighty."

TWENTIETH DYNASTY (C.1200-1085 B.C.)

Nesubenebded
.ne – esu – ube – ene – eb. – .de – ed.
añe – esu – ube – ene – ebe – ede – eda
añendu – ezurruts – ubeldu – -enerako – eberu – ederrak hartu – edagale
to curse – very skinny – to bruise - as before – Hebrews – to be defeated – thirst
"As before, the cursed skinny and bruised Hebrews were defeated by thirst."

TWENTY FIRST DYNASTY (C.1085-945 B.C.)

Herihor

.he – eri – iho – or.
ihe – eri – iho – ora
ihesleku – eriotzaldi – ihortziri – orain
to seek shelter – agony – thunder – always
"He always sought shelter from the agony of the thunder."

Psusennes

.p. – .su – use – en. – .ne – es.
ape – ezu – use – eno – one – ezo
apez – ezuster – usei – enoradun – onetsi – ezongialdi
priest – unexpectedly – to sneeze – afflicted – to bless – indisposition
"The priest unexpectedly was afflicted by sneezing (so we) blessed his indisposition."

Amenemope

ame – ene – emo – ope
amegaitz – enetan – emonkor – operatu
nightmare – always – generous/prolific – to perform surgery
"Surgery was performed on his always prolific nightmares."

Pinudjem

.pi – inu – ud. – .je – em.
pi – inu – uda – aje – eme
pizkanaka – inular – uda – aienatu – emeriko
slowly – sunset – summer – to slip away – peacefully
"Slowly the summer sunset slips away peacefully."

Siamon

.si – i.a – amo – on.
isi – iha – amo – one
isilki- ihardun – amodio – onesan
quietly – to take time – love – to praise
"Quietly take time to love and praise."

Osorkon

oso – or. – .ko – on.
oso – ora – ako – ona
oso – orain – akordiozko – onarketa
sincere – always – traditional – welcome
"Always give a sincere traditional welcome."

TWENTY SECOND DYNASTY (C.945-715 B.C.)

Alara

ala – ara
alaitasun – aratz
joy – pure

"Pure joy."

Kashta

.ka – as. – h. – .ta
uka – ase – eha – ata
ukan – asegaitz – eha – atano
to have – craving – 'emphasis' – evergreen forest/hereafter
"I have a craving for a 'wonderful' hereafter."

Amonirdis

amo – oni – ir. – .di – is.
amo – oni – ira – adi – iza
amodio – oniraun – iradoki – adiskidego – izaera
love – goodness – to elicit/inspire – friendship – character
"Love and goodness inspire friendship and character."

Shoshenk. We have two spellings, both tell about the same story. But what really happened? Compare: Psalm 106:9 ... *"the Red Sea became dry and he led them through ..."* and Psalm 106:11 *"...and the waters covered their adversaries... "* The translation of the pharaoh's name sounds like a tsunami or tidal wave. But where would it have come from? The Indian Ocean?

Shoshenk

.s. – .ho – os. – .he – en. – .k.
isu – uho – osi – ihe – ena – aka
isurialdi – uholatu – osin – ihesezin – ena- akabu
overflowing/cascading – flood wave – very deep – unavoidable – 'superlative' – death
**"The overflowing flood (or tidal wave) was very deep and
unavoidable (and caused) dreadful death."**

Sheshonk. Second spelling.

.s. – .he – es. – .ho – on. – .ka
isi – ihe – esu – uho – onda – aka
isilpetu – ihes egin – ezustez – uholatu – ondartu – akastun
to hide – to escape – unexpected – tidal wave – to come ashore – defective/impossible
**"To hide or escape was impossible, when the unexpected
flood (or tidal wave) came ashore."**

TWENTY THIRD DYNASTY (C.818-715 B.C.)

Piankhi

.pi – i.a – an. – .k. – .hi
opi – iha – añe – eka – ahi
opiozale – ihardun – añendu – ekandu – ahi
being fond of opium – spend time – to curse – habit – strong desire/addiction
"Being fond of opium to spend the time is a cursed habit (leading to) addiction."

Shabaka

.sa – .aha – aba – aka
esa – aha – aba – aka

esaeratsu – ahalguzti – abade – akabu
wise – almighty – priest – high
"Wise priest of the Almighty."

TWENTY FOURTH DYNASTY (C.727-715 B.C.)

Tefnakhte
.te – eb. – .na – ak. – .h. – .te
ite – eba – ana – aka – aha – ate
itegun – ebakin – anaitu – akatsgabeko – ahalguzti – aterbe
work performed – harvest – to gather – perfect – Almighty – protection
**"The gathering of the harvest is work performed under
the protection of the Almighty."**

Piakhi
.pi – i.a – ak. – .hi
epi – iha – ake – ehi
epika – iharduki – akela – ehite
epic – to discuss – Goddess – aspect
"He discussed the epic of the Goddess in all its aspects."

Bokkhorus
.bo – ok. – .k. – .ho – or. – us.
abo – oki – ika – aho – oru – usu
aboskatu – okilaso – ikasbide – ahozpetu – orube – usu
to proclaim – great grandfather – catechism/doctrine – kneeling down – place – usual
**"Great grandfather proclaimed the catechism while kneeling down in his usual
place."**

TWENTY FIFTH DYNASTY (C.747-656 B.C.)

Sheb'iku
xe – eb ' iku
xeratsu – ebazle ' ikusgarrizko
kind – judge ' admirable
"Kind and admirable judge."

Taharka
.ta – aha – ar. – .ka
ita – aha – ara – aka
itxaro – ahalguzti – aratz – akatsbako
to trust – almighty/deity – pure – perfect
"Trust the Almighty, pure and perfect."

TWENTY SIXTH DYNASTY (C.664-525 B.C.)

Psamtik
.p. – .sa – am. – .ti – ik.
ape – esa – ama – ati – ika

apez – esaeratsu – amaigabeko – atxikitasun – ikasbide
priest – wise – endlessly – faithfulness – to teach
"The wise priest endlessly taught faithfulness."

Nitocris
.ni – ito – ok. – .ri – is.
ani – ito – oke – eri – iso
anitz – itoarazi – okerkeria – erioaldi – isola
many – to drown – injury – agony – torrential rain
"Many were drowned or injured during the agony of the torrential rains."

Necho (son of Psamtik)
.ne – exo
nekebide – exorzizatu
cause of suffering – to eliminate
"Eliminate the causes of suffering."

Harmachis
High priestess who crowned Ptolemy V (Parkinson p.31).
.ha – ar. – .ma – ak. – is.
aha – ara – ama – aki – isi
ahaldun – aratusteldu – ama – akigabeki – isiljokatu
powerful – to corrupt – priestess – tirelessly – to scheme
"Powerful (but) corrupt priestess, tirelessly scheming."

Anemhor
Mother of Harmachis (Parkingson p.31).
ane – em. – .ho – or.
ane - ema – aho – ora
añendu – ematxar - ahoruritu – orain
to curse – prostitute – cheating – always
"Cursed prostitute who is always cheating."

TWENTY SEVENTH DYNASTY (525-404 B.C.)

Cambyses (his Persian name)
.ka – am. – .bi – ise – es.
aka – ami – ibi – ize – esa
akatsbako – aministratu – ibili – izenandiko – esaeratsu
perfect – administrator – to be – famous – wise
"Our perfect administrator is famous and wise."

Mesutira (Egyptian name for Cambises)
.me – esu – uti – ira – at.
ame – esu – uti – ira
ametsegile – ezurruts – utikan – iragan

dreamer – very skinny – go away – to suffer
"You skinny dreamer, go away and suffer."

Wedjahorresnet
(priest who made up the name Mesutira)
ed. – .ja – aho – or. – .re – es. – .ne – et.
ede – eja – aho – ore – ere – eso – one – eti
eder – -ea – ahohizkuntza – orrek – errege – esonde – oneste – etikoa
beautiful – emphasis – spoken language – that – king – advice – honest – ethical
**"It is with emphasis on beautiful spoken language that
I give honest and ethical advice to the king."**

TWENTY EIGHTH DYNASTY (404-399 B.C.)

Amyrtaeus
ami – ir. – .ta – e.u – us.
ami – iri – ita – ehu – usa
aministratu – irrikagarri – itxaro – eutsi – usario
administrator – ambitious – to be faithful – to maintain – tradition
"Our ambitious administrator was faithful and maintained the traditions."

Amenirdis
ame – eni – ir. – di – is.
ame – eni – ira – adi – isa
ameskaitz – eni – iragarpen – adi – izuarazle
nightmare – to me – warning – watch out – terrorist
"To me that nightmare was a warning to watch out for terrorists."

TWENTY NINTH DYNASTY (399-380 B.C.)

Maatibrat Hakor (queen)
.ma – a.a – ati – ib. – .ra – at.
ama – aha – ati – ibi – ira – ati
ama – ahalguzti – ibili – atxigarri – irakitu – atxiki
priestess – almighty – to be – faithful – fired with passion – loyal
"(Our) priestess of the Almighty is faithful, fired with passion and loyal."

.ha – ako – or.
aha – ako – ora
ahalguzti – akorduan euki – orain
Almighty – to remember – always
"Always remember the Almighty."

Nectanebo (army general)

.ne – ek. – .ta – ane – ebo
ene – eki – ita – ane – ebo
enetan – ekineztu – itxaro – añendu – eboluzio
always – to persevere – to keep faith – cursed – development
"Always persevere and keep faith (during these) cursed developments."

Sebennytos (town of general Nectanebo)
.se – ebe – en. – .ni – ito – os.
ese – ebe – ena – ani – ito – osi
esetsi – eberu – -ena – anitz – itoa – osintsu
to attack – Hebrews – (superlative) – many – drowned – very deep water
"The Hebrews attacked and a great many drowned in very deep water."

THIRTIETH DYNASTY (380-343 B.C.)

Djedhor
.d. – .je – ed. – .ho – or.
-ada – aje – edu – uho – ora
-ada – aienatu – edukitsu – uhol – orraztu
action of being swallowed – to be frightened away – powerful – flood – to devastate
"We were being swallowed and frightened away by a powerful and devastating flood."

THIRTY FIRST DYNASTY (343-332 B.C.)

Darius
.da – ari – us.
ada – ari – usa
adarra sartu – arimagalduko – usantza
to deceive – ruthless – habit/character
"A deceiving and ruthless character."

Khababash
.k. – .ha – aba – aba – ax.
aka – aha – aba – aba – axo
akabu – ahalguzti – abade – abailtuta – axolazko
superior/high – almighty – priest – weary – grave
"The high priest of the Almighty was weary and grave."

KINGS OF MACEDON IN EGYPT (332-305 B.C.)

Meryamunt – Setepenrat
(Alexander the Great)
.me – eri – i.a – amu – un. – .t.
ame – eri – iha – amu - uni – ito
amesgaitz – eriotzordu – ihar – amure egon – unibertsal – itobehar
nightmare – agony – weakness – distrust – general – anxiety

"The agony of nightmares weakened him (causing) general distrust and anxiety."

.se – ete – epe – en. – .ra – at.
ese – ete – epe – ene – era – ata
esetsaldi – etengabeko – epe – enetan – erakarri – atalbanaketa
battle – continuous – period of time – always – to cause – discent
"Continuous battles over a long period always cause dissent."

Haaibra – Setepenamun
(Philip Arideus)
.ha – a.a – a.i – ib. – .ra
iha – aha – ai – ibe – era
iha – ahalguzti – aiherkuntza – ibeni – erasoketa
almost – unlimited power – hatred – to introduce – aggression
"Almost unlimited power introduces hatred and aggression."

.se – ete – epe – ena – amu – un.
ese – ete – epe – ena – amu – uni
esetsaldi – etengabeko – epe – ena – amure egon – unibertsal
battle – continuous – period of time – 'superlative' – distrust – general
"Continuous battles over a long period (caused) serious and general distrust."

THE PTOLEMIES (305-30 B.C.)

Arsinoe (mother of Ptolemy V)
ar. – .si – ino – o.e
ari – isi – ino – ohe
arimagalduko – isilerazi – inor – ohe
merciless – to silence – someone – in bed
"Someone mercilessly silenced her while in bed."

Cleopatra
.k. – .le – e.o – opa – at. – .ra
uki – ile – eho – opa – ata – ara
ukitu – iletari – ehorzleku – opa izan – atano – arraitasun
to touch – mourners – funeral – to desire for – hereafter – happiness
**"The mourners at her funeral were touched by
her desire for happiness in the hereafter."**

THE ORIGIN OF SUMERIAN

A SOCIETY TURNED INSIDE OUT

The long era of the tribal, egalitarian society of the Neolithic in Mesopotamia came to an end between 4,400 and 3,000 B.C. Archaeologists and
anthropologists have documented that the early society of Mesopotamia had
been guided by women and had a Goddess as deity. During the Neolithic the
men had been in charge of all the work outside the tribal area, often away for
long periods of time busy with herding, hunting, fishing, exploring etc. This all
changed because of a number of advances and happenings. The rapid
desertification of the Sahara caused an enormous exodus of the tribes living in
these formerly productive grazing lands. Many migrated to areas of excellent
soils where high quality agriculture was possible, such as the floodplains of the
Fertile Crescent and the Indus valley, and the loess areas of southern Russia.
Metal working and mining were invented, the camel and horse were domesticated, star navigation and ocean travel were perfected and all continents of the
world had been discovered. The growing populations demanded improvements
in food production with a result that over-population pressures and conflicts
over land and resources developed. The settlement of the Saharan tribes in
areas of agricultural potential kept the men at home, demanding more control
over the running of the tribe. Centralized religious control from the Sahara had
become difficult or impossible to maintain and a breakdown of the old gylanic
society was inevitable.

The first change made by the men, who were now in charge of the tribe, was
to dispose of the annual voluntary sacrifice of a special young man (Tammuz),
which had been felt essential to bring back the summer and nature's productivity. He had experienced the exalted position of king, a bridge between the deity

and the people, wearing the purple robe for a number of years after participating in the Sacred Marriage and was supposed to have gone to his death but refused, as was so well documented in the Gilgamesh epic. This human sacrifice apparently was the beginning of the end of female leadership. The following quote in "In the Wake of the Goddesses" by Frymer-Kenski tells about this end:

> *"The dynasty of Kish was founded by Enmebaragesi, a contemporary of Gilgamesh, who it now appears may have been a woman"* (p. 79)

The "name" **Enmebaragesi** tells us a story. When separating this "name" into its VCV components it becomes immediately clear that in this Sumerian "name" we are dealing with a scholarly manipulated statement in the Saharan/Basque language:

en. – .me – eba – ara – age – esi
ene – eme – eba – ara – age – esi
enetik – eme – ebakin – aragikor – ageriko – ezi
from that time on – female – harvest – lustful – notorious – to domesticate
"From that time on the lustful, notorious harvest female was domesticated."

The 'harvest female' mentioned was no queen, and she did not found a dynasty, but she was a priestess associated with agriculture, a real historical person. Her "name" tells us in no uncertain terms that the time of the Goddess was on the decline, because male domination had arrived. With this change in society and abundant agricultural production came an astonishing outburst of scholarly inventiveness. Some educated people were now able to devote their lives to pursuits other than survival. They decided that the time had come to disband the tribal system and to create city states and nations. The old, highly evolved, language of the Sahara was considered too closely associated with the Goddess religion and had to be changed, as is clearly shown in the creation of new languages such as Sumerian and Akkadian.

INVENTING NEW LANGUAGES

Somewhere in the Sahara the centre of the first civilization on earth had developed and all people were taught the same highly developed language which I call Saharan. Those migrants who subsequently settled in the Fertile Crescent, Anatolia, the Ukraine and the Indus valley therefore all spoke the same Saharan language. In the areas where male domination had taken hold priest/scholars were assigned to develop new languages such as Sanskrit which had no likeness to the original Saharan. The first efforts of manipulating the foundation language were very likely made in Egypt, followed by Sumeria, Akkadian etc. some using the original Saharan vowel-interlocking agglutination formula while others just put original words together, or combinations of both systems. Examples of vowel-agglutination are the new words invented for **king** shown here in several extinct Near-Eastern languages:

Lugal (Sumerian)
.lu-uga-al.
ilu-uga-ali
ilundu – ugazaba – alienatu
to get angry – master – to kill a person
"When the master gets angry he kills."

Sharru (Akkadian)
sha – ar. – .ru
xa – are – eru
xahutu – arerio – errukigabeki
to destroy – enemy – mercilessly
"He destroys the enemy mercilessly."

Hasshu (Hittite)
ha – as. – .xu
ha – ase – exu
handizki – aserretu – exustez
majesty/aristocrat – to anger – unexpectantly
"(His) majesty angers unexpectedly."

Ereli (Urartaean)
ere – eli
errege – elizatiar
king – pious
"Pious king."

Ivri (Hurrian)
iv. – .ri
ibi – iri
ibili (to be) – irrikan
to be – ambitious
"He is ambitious."

An example of assembling parts of Saharan/Basque words into new words and names without the VCV formula is: **Nunbarsegunu**, (an alternate name for the Goddess Nisaba, mother of Ninlil):

nun – bar – segunu
nunbait – barnatu – segundu
from nowhere – to come in/appear – second/instant
"In an instant she appeared from nowhere."

From these and following translations I show that both Sumerian and Akkadian words and names are assembled by scholarly manipulation from Saharan/Basque vocabulary. The modern Basque-English dictionary by Gorka Aulestia is still perfectly suitable to translate these ca 4,800 year old names and words. This means that the modern Basque language has changed very little since that time.

Other vowel-interlocking names are:
Sumer, which tells of the peoples' arrival in Mesopotamia:

su – ume – er.
su – ume – era
sustraitu – ume – eraspen
to settle down – child – devotion
"The devoted children settled down."

Akkadia, the nation of builders:

ak. – ka – adi – ia
aki – ika – adi – ia
akigabe – ikasgo – adibide – iaio
tireless – teaching – advice – expert
"Tirelessly teaching with expert advice."
Could it be that the Sumerians and Akkadians were the same people?

All school children are taught that **Mesopotamia** is 1) a Greek word and 2) that it means "land between the rivers." Both statements are obviously incorrect:

.me – eso – opo – ota – ami – i.a
eme – exo – opo – ota – ami – iha
emen – exorzizatu – oporrez – otalurmendiak – amiltze – ihardunaldi
here – to flow out – lazily – wild mountains – tumbling down – period of activity
"Here (the rivers) flow lazily (after) a period of tumbling down the wild mountains."

In the flat land the two rivers are usually sluggish but in the mountains both are wild. The name Mesopotamia is agglutinated from pure Saharan/Basque vocabulary, not Greek. The proper pronunciation of Mesopotamia has to be Me**sh**opotamia because *eso* (advice) makes no sense in the description, *exo* does.

The names of the Rivers

Two large rivers dominate Mesopotamia, the Euphrates and the Tigris, the pre-historic names of which are reported to have been **Buranun** and **Idiglat**. Both names are obviously made up out of Saharan/Basque:

Buranun (Euphrates)
bu – ura – anu – un.
bu – ura – anu – une
burrundara – uraldi – anu egin – unean
deafening noise – flood – fall back in fear – instantly
"The deafening noise of the flood made me fall back in fear instantly."

Idiglat (Tigris)
idi – ig. – .la – at.
idi – igo – ola – ato
idiki – igon – olatu – ator
to discover/observe – to get higher – wave – Come!
"I observed that the waves are getting higher, Come!"

When male domination arrived, new languages were created and all geographical features renamed, but the new names carry the same message as the old ones:

Euphrates
eu – uf. – .ra – ate – es.
eu – ufa – ara – ate – ezi
eurizaparrada – ufatu – arao – aterperatu – ezinjasanezko
downpour – blowing/wind – curse – let's get out of the rain – unbearable
"The downpour and the wind are a curse, let's get out of this unbearable rain."

Tigris
.ti – ig. – .ri – is.
uti – ige – eri – iso
utikan – iges egin – erioaldi – isola
get away from here – to escape – agony – torrential rain
"Get away from here and escape from the agony of the torrential rain."

THE EARLIEST WRITING

Notations on stone, bone and clay have been known from as far back as 18,000 years B.P., according to Marija Gimbutas in "The Language of the Goddess," but true writing did not come into being until the oldest known clay tablets were written in the City of Uruk some time before 3000 B.C. in a pictographic script. This script evolved into the extremely durable cuneiform script by 2,800 B.C., which was used on clay for close to 3,000 years. The first translation efforts were made around 1850 but no real progress was made until 1923 when the first Sumerian grammar appeared. In the intervening period, masses of clay tablets had been found and distributed to museums around the world. Many were treated as curiosities, carelessly dug up, stored without protection and often separated from the ones they were found with and even knocked in half to bring in more money. Much effort has now gone into reading them, but there still remains a massive amount to be done. In the meantime, the present political uncertainty in Iraq has seen to it that excavation was effectively stopped, but whole libraries are still thought to await the spade, to be brought to light by the next generations of students. The Goddess **Nisaba** is given credit for the invention of writing and the translation of her name agrees:

Nisa'ba,
ni – isa ' ba:
ni – isa ' ba
ni – izaditu ' baimenagiri
I – to create ' written document
"I create written documents."

Sumerian is closely tied in with the Akkadian language, which is supposed to be a Semitic language. Akkadian myths were told in Sumerian, Hittite, Hurrian and Akkadian. Sumerian words have few, or no, vowels, but Akkadian words have vowels, which seems to be the only distinguishing characteristic. The Akkadian writers appear to have considered Sumerian to be a classical language, similar to our academics using Latin. People in positions of command had their names designed in Sumerian, such as King

Sargon (born ca.2335 B.C.)
.sa – ar. – .go – on.
esa – ara – ago – one
esaeratsu – arautzaile – agorgaitz – onegite
wise – lawgiver – tireless – doing good
"Wise lawgiver, tirelessly doing good."

Nin'Hursag was known as the Mountain Lady, Lady of the Foot-hills, Ninmah the Supreme Lady, Mother of all Children, Mistress of the Gods etc. The name **Hursag** is traditionally translated as either 'foothills' or 'mountains,' however, although she had something important to do in the hilly country beyond the valley, this was not the translation. In order to supply the people in the valley with an adequate and reliable, potable water supply, an astonishing 80 km conduit was built from lakes existing in the eastern hills, much of it a tunnel, deep underground, cut through living rock. It still functions to this day, as planned so long ago. The translation of her name tells us what she did:

Nin'Hursag
.ni – in. ' .hu – ur. – .sa – ag.
oni – ina ' hu – uro – osa – ago
onibilera – inauguratu ' hura – uroditza – osatu – ageriko
prosperity – inauguration ' she – watertunnel/conduit – to complete – public
"She inaugurated the completed water tunnel for public prosperity."

THE NAMES OF THE MAN WHO BUILT THE ARK

Stephany Dalley, in her "Myths from Mesopotamia" (p. 2) provides us with seven different names for the man who survived the great flood by building a boat. The Sumerian name is thought to be the oldest:

Ziusudra:
.zi – i.u – usu – ud. – .ra
izi – ihu – usu – udi – ira
izigarri – ihurtziri – usu – udikan – iragaile
frightening – thunder – persistently – to go/sail away – boatman
"The bargeman sailed away during the frightening and persistent thunder."

Atrahasis (Akkadian):
atra – aha – asi – is.
atrakaleku – ahalik – asi – isola
pier – as soon as possible – to start – torrential rain
"He left the pier as soon as possible after the torrential rain started."

Utnapishtim, the wise priest of Shuruppak, mentioned in the Gilgamesh Epic (ca 2700 B.C.). This name is also thought to be Akkadian, however, the translation of his name appears to have nothing to do with the big flood or the ark. However, what Ms. Dalley thought to be his hologram: **Ud.Zi** could very well refer to the flood: udi-izi, *udikan-izi* (go away – it's frightening).

Utnapishtim:
ut. – na – pish – ti – im.
uti _ na _ pix _ ti – imi
utikan _ nabarmen _ pix _ tirriatu – imiña
get away _ immoral _ urine/menstruation _ to want – a measure, bit
"Get away from here! To want some menstrual blood is immoral!."
(Menstrual blood was collected from the priestess for religious
purposes in Sumer as well as anywhere else in the wide world of
the Goddess religion, including Ireland and Scotland.)

Shuruppak:
xu – uru – up. – .pa – ak.
xu – uru – upa – apa – ako
xurugatu – urruindu – upa – apaiz – akordiozko
to gulp – to despise – beer cask – priest – traditional
"The traditional priest despised the gulping of beer from the cask."
Here we may have the first admonition against public drunkenness.

Xisuthros(Babylonian):

This name was used by the Babylonian priest Berossus in his book "Babyloniaca" (third century B.C.) to tell the history of the flood. It seems to be an alternate for Ziusudra or Atrahasis. The first letter X has to be a contraction of KS or more accurately: KZ:

Kzisuthros
k. – .zi – isu – ut. – .h. – .ro – os.
ke – ezi – isu – utu – uho – oro – osi
keinatu – ezinjasanezinez – izubera – utxu – uholde – orroe – osintsu
to threaten – unbearably – frightening – loud cry – flood – roar – very deep
**"The unbearably frightening loud cries and the roar of
the very deep flood are threatening."**

Noah, (Palestinian):

noa is modern Basque and simply means: **"I go"** or **"I am going."**

Of the above seven names for the boatman who survived the flood, listed by Stephany Dalley, Utnapishtim and Shuruppak do not appear to belong in the story of the Ark. Atrahasis, Ziusudra, Noah, Kzisuthros and even UdZi qualify as authentic flood names.

A first millennium lamentation which refers to the flood is the **"Uruamirabi** Congregational Lament."** (Mark Cohen in "The Canonical Lamentations of Ancient Mesopotamia" Potomac Md, 1988.)

uru – uha – ami – ira – abi
urrutiratze – uhalde – amilura – iragaile – abiaduran
getting away – deluge – waterfall – bargeman – in a hurry
"Get away from the deluge like a waterfall, the bargeman is in a hurry."

A Random Selection of Sumerian and Akkadian Names

Ama'ushumgalanna, supposedly the name by which the Priestess called the king who was her partner in the Sacred Marriage feast (Frymer-Kenski p.59). Instead it is the traditional cry uttered by the Priestess at the start of the sexual union:

ama _ ushu – ume – galan – na
Ama _ uxu – ume – galant – -nahi
priestess _ cry of happiness – youth – handsome – desirous
**"The priestess' cry of happiness upon seeing
the handsome and desirous youth."**

Ammisaduqa (king of Babylon):

am. – .mi – isa – adu – uka
ama – ami – iza – adu – uka

amaitu – amildu – izadi – adurtsu – ukan
to destroy – to oust/avoid – creation/engineering – fortunate – to possess
"We avoid destruction (because) we are fortunate to possess engineering."

Anduruna (home of the gods), andu – uruna

andu – urunna
pasture – distant/far away
"Far away pastures."

Aruru (mother goddess):

aru – uru
aruntz onuntz ibili – urru
to wander – far away
"She wanders far away."

Assurbanipal (king of Assyria who succeeded king Esarhaddon and then extended the Assyrian empire to reach from the Persian Gulf to the Mediterranean and the Caucasus):

as. – .su – ur. – .ba – ani – ipa – al.
asi – isu – uri – iba – ani – ipa – alu
asi – izuikaratu – uri – ibar – anitz – ipar – alukeria
to start – to terrorize – city – valley – many – northern – repulsive actions
"He started to terrorize many cities in the northern valley with repulsive actions."

Astarte (one of the three prominent goddesses of Ugarit):

asta – arte
astalarossa – -arte
wild rose – among us
"A wild rose among us."

Badtibira (early city, rival of Uruk?, hardly):

bad _ ti _ bira
badaezbadako _ -ti _ biraobota
rude _ habit _ to curse
"Rude habit of cursing."
Whatever that referred to.

Enheduanna, (daughter of Sargon):

en. – .he – edu – u.a – ana
ene – ehe – edu – uha – ana
enegana – ee! – edukitsu – uhalde – anaitu
come to me – Attention! – powerful – flood – to unite/to gather
"Attention! Come to me, a powerful flood is gathering."

Enki (god of pro-creation):

> en. – .ki
> ene – eki
> *ene – ekinbide*
> my – initiative
> **"My initiative."**

Geshtinanna (goddess who sang laments for the return of her brother Dumuzi (Tammuz) from the underworld:

> gestina – ana
> *gestionatu – anaia*
> to negotiate – brother
> **"She negotiated for her brother's (return)."**

Gudea (king of Lagash, ca 2200 B.C.):

> gud. – ea
> *guda – ea*
> warrior – emphasis/the best
> **"The best warrior."**

Hammurabi (early Babylonian king and law-giver):

> ham. – mu. – ura – abi
> *hamai – muga – ura – abiarazi*
> many – restriction/law – he – to promulgate
> **"He promulgated many laws."**

Kazallu (early city?):

> kaz – alu
> *kazeta – alukeria*
> writing on clay tablet – objectionable
> **"Objectionable writing on clay tablet."**
> (What would that refer to?)

Lugal'zaggesi, (king of Umma who laid siege to the city of Lagash and destroyed it. The following translation is obviously not his real name, but instead was written by one of his victims.)

> .lu – uga – al. _ .za – ag. – .ge – esi
> ilu – uga – ali _ za – agi – ige – ezi
> *ilundu – ugazaba – alienatu _ zaildu – agian – igesegin – esiketa*
> to get angry-master-to kill a person _ to be difficult-I hope-to escape-siege
> **"When the master gets angry he kills.**
> **It may be difficult but I hope to escape the siege."**

Meskiaggasir (possibly the first king of Uruk):

.me – es. – .ki- ag.-.ga – asi – ir.
ome – esa – aki – age – ega – asi – iri
omenezko – ezalari – akigabe – ageriko – egapetu – asi – iri
honorable – founder – tireless – public – to protect – to start – city
"Honorable founder, tireless public protector, who started the city."

Urukagina (king of Lagash who protected his citizens from bureaucratic injustice.)

uru – uka – agi – ina
urruindu – ukan – agintza – inarrosketa
to despise – to have – legacy – fomentation/chaos
"He despised to have (inherited) a legacy of chaos."

Zabalam (early city):

zabal – am.
zabal – amodiozko
generous – loving
"Generous and loving."

Zulummar (goddess who dug the clay for Enlil to create humanity):

.zu – ulu – um. – .ma – ar.
azu – ulu – ume – ema – ari
azukre – uluka – ume – emarazi – arin
sugar/sweet – crying – child – to calm down – quickly
"With a sweet she quickly calmed down the crying child."

FOOTNOTE

It is astonishing to me that the neolithic language of the Sahara has survived the millennia almost intact, while all of the later languages, derived from Saharan, were greatly altered over time or by design, or have not survived the test of time. The fact that the very early Saharan language is still spoken by the Basque people, not all that different from what it was in Egypt and Sumer more than 5,000 years back, must have a very special reason behind it. This has possibly something to do with the incredibly accurate oral transmission of the legends and literature, which required a very high standard of education. Another reason may be that the vowels are very stable in Saharan/Basque, while the consonants are stable in Indo-European and the vowels very unstable (e.g. sing –sang–sung), which may well have been done on purpose in the 'turning around' process.

The migrating peoples from the Sahara may have created the high civilizations of Egypt, Mesopotamia, Anatolia and the Indus valley. Several archaeologists working in Sumeria commented on the fact that the Sumerian and Akkadian civilizations appeared to have no primitive base locally i.e. the people arrived there from elsewhere with all the knowledge of how to build such a civilization. They therefore must themselves have experienced this civilization in their place of origin, possibly somewhere near Egypt. In some locations of the Sahara extensive irrigation canal systems have been spotted (NASA photography) and standing stones are still prominent in out-of-the-way places. The original Saharan language is clearly detectable in all four early civilizations, as is shown above for Sumer and Akkad and elsewhere in this book for Hebrew, Sanskrit and Dravidian.

V

THE LANGUAGE OF GENESIS 11:1

The Astonishing Basque Language

The origin of the beautiful, logically constructed, Basque language is hidden behind long millennia, dating back into the Palaeolithic. In its early stages, this language couldn't have been anything but a gradually evolved language. Then the Neolithic came along with a growing population and a fast evolving civilization with simple agriculture and irrigation. This civilization then developed so greatly that the old palaeolithic language was no longer adequate to describe their enormous achievements in astronomy, architecture, mathematics, medicine, acoustics, navigation, religion etc. and a logical system had to be found to expand the language. Some genius developed the VCV system, assigning carefully selected meanings to each VCV, which could be agglutinated into a decodable shorthand (Appendix 1). The VCV language was then artificially enhanced by skillful priest-linguists to accommodate the changing times with enriched communication. The names and words they made up were formulaically assembled with the use of this artificial language, which seems to have been originally designed as a holy or magical language and therefore the preserve of the priesthood. In Egypt this magical language was used not only to name all the pharaohs, the clergy, officials and geographical features, but also to enrich the spoken language to make it more versatile. The astonishing fact about the early language is that at one time both *the original palaeolithic and the invented neolithic forms were combined and together are still spoken as Basque,* in close to the same way as it was five or six thousand years ago. The original form was subject to gradual change as other languages are, but the invented language has remained the same throughout 5,200 + years. This last one must be the only language on earth that did not, or only barely, change with time. Probably because throughout this long period it has remained the preserve of priests and scholars.

The Magical Language

How old? We do not know when this language was invented. All we know is that it was fully developed and in use by 5,200 years ago to make up the names of the earliest deities (Osiris, Isis, Horus etc.) and the pharaohs. For the language to be practical, the meanings associated with the VCV's had to be carefully chosen, so that the encoding and decoding of the VCV's, making up the sentence, would be possible in the majority of cases. It was truly a language which was designed to be manipulated, the only one ever.

Organization of the VCV morphemes. The artificial language was meant to enrich the spoken language with carefully designed words and names. These words and names were basically sentences written in shorthand, which can be restored with the use of the VCV formula even many millennia later. The reorganization of the Saharan language, done so long ago, was so far-reaching that even today half of the Basque vocabulary is made up of the original words invented so long ago by the Egyptian scholars. The basis for the VCV structure were the 16 consonants, each flanked by two vowels. Starting with B the first VCV would be ABA which was subdivided into five syllable groups, ABA, EBA, IBA, OBA, UBA , each of which was composed of five syllables: ABA, ABE, ABI, ABO, ABU / EBA , EBE, EBI, EBO, EBU / IBA, etc., 25 in all. Each of the 16 consonants therefore was associated with 25 VCV syllables for a grand total of 400 syllables. In addition there was the double RR (pronounced as a rolling R), with 25 VCCV syllables, ARRA, ARRE, ARRI etc. making a total of 425 different roots. Most of these syllables were assigned groups of related words, others had only a single meaning (e.g. EBO for: 'to develop' or UTO for 'utopia') and a large number (104) was left free, possibly for future expansion of the language (e.g. EBU, IMO). A great deal of thought must have gone onto the composition of these word groups because even today it is not difficult to select from the choice available the correct word which was used in the make up of the hidden sentence. As is usual with invented words, some of these over time may have been dropped or forgotten through non use, which would have freed some of the VCV's for other words or non-use. For instance, one of these may well be the verb *ulatu*, which is still used in some Polynesian languages as *hulatu*, meaning 'to welcome.' Visitors to Hawaii are often met at the airport by *hula* girls dancing a welcome. It has been said that the system was never completed because there are still some 104 out of 425 VCV's without vocabulary designations. However, there may well be a linguistic need for these unused VCV's. See the VCV dictionary in the appendix.

A Complete Language

Every effort was made to include all possible meanings in the VCV's while still retaining a practical encoding and decoding system. When this language was combined with the naturally evolved Palaeolithic language it was ready to be used for discussing and teaching every possible subject and today the Basque language, in combination with the unmanipulated form, with some modernization, is entirely capable of being used for teaching all disciplines at university level.

Creating New Languages

After the decision was made by religious authorities in the Near East to confuse the Universal Language and to create individual languages and scripts for each large region, the linguists assigned to this task used the ancient Egyptian Magical Language to bring this about. The vowel-interlocking system as practiced by the Egyptians was not used for all languages created in the same manner. For some the strict early rules were only applied haphazardly. However, for languages like Sanskrit, Latin, Greek, English etc. the early Egyptian system was fully utilized. Hebrew and Yiddish often used more than three letters but the decoding process was still not difficult. Today the VCV encoding formula can be detected in all "Indo-European" and Semitic languages which testifies to the invented nature of these languages.

In this book I show how the ancient invented language was used by religious linguists to invent the "Indo-European" and "Semitic" languages, including Sanskrit, Greek, Latin, German, Hebrew, Yiddish etc. This was done with the use of different manipulations of the first letters of the VCV vocabulary, creating totally invented (non-genetic) language groups, not "families." In Genesis 11:1 the early form of this language is said to be spoken in the whole world. It may indeed be called the Universal language, the language of the first civilization on earth, because it can still be found as a substratum language of all the European languages, in the Near East, the Middle East, the Far East, as well as on all the Pacific Islands and even in arctic America. The earliest form is still spoken in unmanipulated, but time-altered form by the Dravidians of India and the Ainu of Japan. The Guanche language of the Canary Islands was one of these but it is no longer spoken. The linguistically enhanced form is still spoken as Euskera in the Basque country. In Genesis 11:7 we are told: "Come, let us confuse their language that they may no longer understand one another's speech." The clergies of Judaism, Christianity and Islam all considered this a holy command and spent an enormous, costly and long sustained effort to bring about this confusion. The formula used by these monk-linguists in many of the artificially constructed vocabularies is called the "vowel-interlocking formula" or "VCV formula." In most cases, the first 2, 3 or 4 letters of each Basque word were agglutinated into a new word. After this was done, some or many of the vowels and h's were removed according to a pre-determined plan to give the new words special characteristics. In Hebrew most, if not all, of the vowels were removed for writing, but not for speaking e.g. the name Talmud, was spelled 'lmd' but pronounced 'tal-mud,' from Basque *tala – mudapen*, watch out – alteration: "Watch out for alteration," which is the essence of an oral law. In Egyptian writing the vowels were also removed but in this case no Talmud was available to fill in the missing vowels and linguists had to consult the Coptic language and other scripts to recover the vowels. There still are many problems in transliteration and translation.

The First Steps

It is the task of the linguistic archaeologist to research languages existing before the invention of writing, before historical linguistics; to search for the very roots of the languages mankind speaks. The subject could also be called pre-historical linguistics. The study can identify the difference between natural and invented languages To make this process possible, other disciplines such as religion, mythology, archaeology and historical linguistics must be included in the study of archaeo-linguistics, while earlier research results and hypotheses in this field should be carefully re-examined.

As I have shown in the articles published in this book, many languages, including such early languages as Hebrew and Sanskrit, were created by formulaic manipulation of Basque vocabulary. However, the name Basque, or more accurately Bask because there is no Q in the language, did not exist at the time this language invention was done. The name Euskera is probably the proper and age-old name for the language. The research done by Dr. N. Lahovary and published in his book "Dravidian Origins and the West" shows conclusively that Basque and the old Dravidian languages of India are closely related. My own research into the Ainu language of Japan shows the same results, as documented in this book. The Ainu are thought to have been isolated in the Far East for at least 9,000 years, possibly as many as 13,000 years, yet they retain an early, non-agglutinated, form of the Saharan language. The original language must have been very old, possibly dating back some 40,000 or more years. These startling finds seem to indicate that the earliest form of this language was already spoken by the first modern people fanning out over the world from its place of origin in Africa, and was therefore spoken very early in Europe, Africa and Asia. The palaeolithic form of the Saharan-Basque language was likely the language spoken in the beautifully painted cathedral caves in southern France and northern Spain. The ancient religious scholars doing the inventing of new languages such as Sanskrit, used the magic language from Egypt. That many words in the Saharan-Basque vocabulary are artificially assembled is quite obvious from words like **alkar** (Dutch: 'elkaar'), meaning **mutual**. It comes from three VCV roots:

al. – .ka – ar.
ala – aka – are
alai – akatsbako – arreman
happy – perfect – relationship
"A perfectly happy relationship."

This is a very good definition of the meaning: 'mutual.' Applying the same system of analysis to other words, it becomes clear that thousands of Basque words have been similarly assembled using the VCV vowel-interlocking system, amounting to about half of all the words in Aulestia's dictionary.

THE MEANING OF THE NAME SAHARA

The Basque word *zahar* means old, and the name Sahara could therefore be interpreted as "the old country," but the Basque 'z' and the 's,' which is pronounced as 'sh,' are quite different sounds so *zahar* may not be the origin of the name Sahara. However, there appears to be another meaning embedded in **"Sahara."** It is analyzed as:

.sa-aha-ara
esa – aha – ara
esan – ahalguzti – aratz
to say/speak – Almighty – pure/refined
"The speech of the Almighty is refined."

Could this interpretation of the name mean that the original language had been refined or enhanced by early linguists? The logical and highly organized structure of the Basque language surely seems to support this possibility. The name used by the Basques for their own language is **"Euskera,"** analyzed as:

eu – us. – .ke – era
eu – usa – ake – era
euki – usaiako – akela – erabildura
to retain/preserve – usual/traditional – Great Goddess – usage/speech
"We preserve the traditional speech of the Great Goddess."

The most holy centre of the Great Goddess of the first civilization was located at the 2100 metre level in the Ahoggar mountains of south east Algeria and its beautiful art work may still be seen there on the rock walls. In order to bury the true meaning of the word "akela," the quite obvious '.ke' for 'ake' was changed by church linguists to '.ka,' so that now we have both Euskera and Euskara in the dictionary. De Basaldua (1925) called his native language "Eskera" and explained the meaning as *esk* (hand) and the ending *era* as form, wave, grace, beautiful, good, and he pulled these words together to mean **"way to move the hand; wave with grace"** which, he said, was also called 'ademan' in Spanish, meaning gesture (see p. 55). I find his interpretation rather difficult to accept because it appears to have little bearing on the language.

To this day the Tuareg tribe lives near the Hoggar Massif and has defended the area fiercely from the invading French foreign legion. Everyone thought that they were defending their own territory. However, the translation of their name tells a much more interesting story: **Tuareg:**

.tu – are – eg.

atu – are – ega

atutxa – arrerosle – egapetu

evergreen oak forest/paradise – redeemer – to protect

"We protect our Redeemer's Paradise."

It appears that this faithful tribe has been protecting the holy Hoggar region for possibly as many as ten thousand years. Their Tuareg language is still recognizable as a distant dialect of Basque. However, lately the severe desertification is driving even these indomitable people out of the area. What stories they would be able to tell if records had been kept! Still, the memory men among them must have many stories to tell that should be preserved before it is too late, but since they live in a Muslim country, that could be dangerous. This memory retention system is still being maintained as much as possible in Euskadi, the Basque country, and also among the Ainu people of Hokkaido in Japan.

STAGES OF DEVELOPMENT OF BASQUE

Many people have theorized about how language began, some suggesting that the first words used were imitations of spontaneous articulation of sounds in nature, such as animal cries, expressions of pain, happiness, fear etc. Others searched for the origin by studying the first utterings of small children. English possesses a large number of onomatopoeic words such as crack, bang, splash, splatter, bash, crash, thump, sneeze etc. It is certain that such onomatopoeia play a role in language formation but it is doubtful that such words are the origin or main source of the language. The word itself is of Greek origin and means:

onomatopoiia (onomatopoeia)

ono – oma – ato – opo – o.i – i.i – ia
ono – oma – ato – opo – oi – ihi – ia
onon – oma – atondu – opor – oinordetzia – ihite – ia
wonderful – grandma – to arrange – time off – inheritance – resemblance – almost/close
**"Our wonderful grandma arranged in her spare time
an inheritance of close resemblance."**

She probably had fun doing it. Basque contains more onomatopoeia than any other language but palaeolithic words such as *aitz* (rock, stone), *ur* (water), *euri* (rain), *lur* (earth, soil, floor), *elur* (snow) and *izotz* (ice) have no onomatopoeic origin.

The well known linguist Noam Chomsky reasoned that the structural facets of language, the ground rules of speech, had to be inborn. If that is the case, speech must be very old. Building on this reasoning, speculatively, I would say that the Saharan language may have gone through at least three main stages such as:

Stage 1) the basic, natural language evolved during the Palaeolithic, prior to ca 10,000 years B.P. It appears that the words in this language mostly named tangible items. No skillful word manipulation.

Stage 2) the evolution of clear vowel differentiation and the introduction of onomatopoeia, possibly about 12,000 B.P. It is this non-agglutinated phase of the language which was taken east and became the basis of the Ainu and Dravidian languages, still spoken today by some 160 million people. This vocabulary included many intangible items. Introduction of some invented vocabulary.

Stage 3) the skillful invention of morphemic (VCV) agglutination which resulted in the development of a greatly diversified vocabulary in which each one of the new words started with vowel-consonant-vowel (VCV). This process, which had been completed before 5,200 years B.P., likely in Upper Egypt. This is the totally invented magical language.

In the early stages the new words were created by making a description or comment pertaining to the thought to be expressed, and the morphemes were then carefully assembled to create words needed in science and technology. The earliest invented languages of the Near East, such as Hittite, Luvian, Palaic, Sumerian, Akkadian etc. were also constructed out of this invented vocabulary, starting possibly shortly before 4,000 years B.P. After Shakespeare's time the invention of new words has increased enormously to accommodate medici, biologists, geologists etc. and many of these new words and names do not follow the old rules. But the basic vocabulary is still part of every day spoken language.

It may not be possible to reconstruct Stage 1, but the existence of the Dravidian, Ainu and Guanche languages, with their well established relationship to Basque, may make it possible to reconstruct many of the words and much of the grammar of Stage 2. My work in linguistic archaeology up to now has mostly been based on Stage 3, because the built-in sentence in many of the agglutinated words, created with the VCV formula, can still be restored with my system of decoding. Research into the vocabulary and sentence structure of Stage 2, of necessity, will require a thorough knowledge of the Dravidian languages, such as Dr. N. Lahovary possessed, or a similar study of the Ainu language.

MAGIC IN NUMBERS AND LETTERS

Detailed study of the enormous stone monuments in Egypt have brought home the realization that sciences such as mathematics, astronomy and acoustics were highly developed and applied, long before the Greeks and Arabs had been heard of. We also know that magic played a big role in the thinking and functioning of these people, and that it tended to promote dedication to the task at hand and resulted in superior achievements. The Ogam research by Anthony Jackson, anthropologist at Edinburgh University, shows that prime numbers, numbers which cannot be divided by any whole number, were ascribed superior magical properties.

Another source of magical fascination for the priests was the mirror-like pattern in numbers e.g. 121, 87178, 1399931, most composed of odd-numbered digits. A special case is 'Pi' parsed here to make certain groups stand out more. Note in about 17 characters the combination **238-46-2-64-832** forms a typical sort of mirror-like characteristic:

3.14-15-926-**535**-89-793-**238-46-2-64-33-832**-795-02-88-41-9-71-69-**3993**-751-0-58-2-09-749-44-592-3-07-81-640-628-620-**8998**-6280 etc.

If you look around in there, you see numbers like 793 and 795, 751 and 749, 582 and 592 and the sequence at the end where 640 links to 620 with an overlapping link of 628 and 6280 with 8998 in between. It is not surprising that 'Pi' was a major source of magical fascination for the mathematicians of the pre-patriarchal civilization.

Another very important number in modern science and especially to the ancient Egyptians is natural E = 2.71**8281828**459... note the mirrored numbers **828-1-828**.

It is created by the series: $1/1! + 1/2! + 1/3! + 1/4!$ etc., where the exclamation mark means "factorial" (4! means 4 x 3 x 2 x 1).

It appears that the early scholars developed a "symbolic mathematical language" which was embedded in their monumental structures. The measurements of the great pyramid at Gizeh show many such mirror-like numbers according to Jim Branson in Boise, Idaho, who studies the acoustical characteristics of the spaces in the pyramid (his book as yet unpublished). This mathematical language magic was also used in the formation of Stage 3, the improved and enriched Saharan language we know today as Basque. The **mirror-like VCV pattern** became the basic structure of the new morphemes. These were used to construct the new vocabulary which has vowel interlocking as the main rule. Where vowel interlocking is interrupted, a break in the word is required which usually means that a new word begins.

VOWEL INTERLOCKING

Vowel interlocking may have been another form of magic with letters and, thanks to it, the hidden sentences in many words and names can be recovered. This system proved to be so successful that the scholars who made up the later Semitic and Indo-European languages, adopted the practice of abbreviating the word to the first three letters, of which the last vowel of the first VCV had to be the same as the first vowel of the following VCV:

$$VCV_1 - V_1CV_2 - V_2CV_3 - V_3CV_4 - V_4CV$$

In other words, the vowels on either side of the hyphens are the same. The Sanskrit language was made up almost entirely out of that half of the Saharan vocabulary which starts with VCV, while the scholars creating the Romance languages and English used the same system as a priority but sometimes felt obliged to use a CV word for the first morpheme. For the Semitic and Germanic languages the entire Saharan/Basque vocabulary was used.

BASQUE, AN AGGLUTINATED LANGUAGE

Webster's dictionary defines "agglutination" as: "Word formation in which the morphemes retain an independence of meaning and form, rather than fusing or blending with combining elements." This is a rather inadequate definition because not only whole morphemes, but also parts of morphemes, as small as one letter, retain independence of meaning and also whole words were being agglutinated and fused. In this writing, dots replace the letters which were removed. In the case of double vowels an 'h' is often omitted. The 'rr' morphemes are classed with the 'r' VCV's.

Combining complete words:

jokaleku (playing field)
joka – leku
hitting, striking – place, location
"Place of hitting (the ball)"

gurdibide (cart path)
gurdi – bide
Cart – path

Combining only VCVs:

sagu (mouse)
.sa – agu
isa – agu
isasluze – agudo
long tailed – quick
"Long tailed and quick."

ainguratu (to anchor)
a.i – in. – .gu – ura – atu
ahi – ine – egu – ura – atu
ahi – inertzia – eguzkisarrera – urandi – atxurbegi
I hope – inertia/tied down – sunset – ocean – hole in the anchor stone
"I hope to be tied down to the hole in the anchor stone when sun sets on the ocean."

bazko, (Easter)
.ba – az. – .ko
eba – aza – ako
ebanjelio – azalpen – akorduan euki
Gospel – manifestation – to remember
"Remember the manifestation (predicted in) the Gospel."

errukizko (merciful)
er. – .ru – uki – iz. – .ko
ere – eru – uki – iza – ako
erresumina – erruki – ukitu – izan – akorduan euki
charity – compassionate – to touch – to be – to remember
"He/she was remembered for touching, compassionate charity."

ezpatalari (swordsman)
ez. – .pa – ata – ala – ari
eze – epa – ata – ala – ari
ezereztu – epaitu – atalbanatu – alabeharrez – arimagalduko
to extirpate – to slash – to cut into pieces – fatally – merciless
"He extirpates by slashing and cutting into pieces, fatally and mercilessly."

izigarrikeria (atrocity)
izi – iga – ar. – .ri – ike – eri – i.a
izi – iga – ara – ari – ike – eri – iha
izi – igarrezin – arakintza – arrigarrizko – ikertu – erio – ihaurri
fright/horror – unpredictable – massacre – awful – to investigate – deaths – many
**"They investigated the many deaths and the unpredictable
horror of the awful massacre."**

laranja (orange)
.la – ara – an. – .ja
ala – ara – ano – oja
alaitu – aratz – ano – oian
to fill with joy – pure – juice – forest, trees
"Pure juice from the trees fills us with joy."

mendebaleko (of the west)
.me – en. – .de – eba – ale – eko
ume – ena – ade – eba – ale – eko
umel – ena – adelatu – ebakin – ale – ekoiztu
overripe – (superlative) most – to prepare – to produce – grain – to produce
"They prepare to produce a most prolific grain harvest."

Vitoria, (city)
ibi – ito – ori – ia
ibili – itoaldi – orrits – iaio
to be – to laugh a lot – celebration – cheerful
"There was a lot of laughter at the cheerful celebration."
(Two vowels together often means that an 'h' was omitted but not here.)

merezi (merit)
ome – ere – ezi
omendu – eredu – ezinobe
to honor – example – excellent
"Honor the excellent example."

Combining a VCCV with VCV's.

ospegabeko (unknown) (was: *otspegabeko*)
ots. – .pe – ega – abe – eko
otse – epe – ega – abe – eko
otseintza – epel – egarri – ebegikortasun – ekoiztu
subjection – timid – strong desire – hospitality – to acquire
"With timid subjection (he/she) had a strong desire to acquire hospitality."

ustekabezia (unforeseen)
uste – eka – abe – ezi – i.a
ustekeria – ekarri – aberekeria – ezinukatuzko – ihabali
prejudice – to bring/cause – brutality – ezinukatuzko – ihabali
"Prejudice can cause undeniably frightening brutality."

Euzkadi (the Basque Country)
eu – uzka – adi
eupada – uzkali – adierazgai
call – to overthrow the gov't – signal
"(Upon) the signal overthrow the government."

Bask *(the language)*
.ba-ask.
eba – aska
ebatzi – askatasun
to decide – freedom
"We decided to be free."

aritz (oak tree)
ari – itza
arrigarri – itzalesko
marvelous – majestic.
"Marvelous and majestic."

Combining a full word and VCVs:

larkeria (excess)
lar _ .ke – eri – i.a
lar _ oke – eri – iha
lar _ okerrez – erion – ihaurri
too much _ mistakenly – to spill – to scatter
"Too much was mistakenly spilled and scattered."

zabaltasun (openness, honesty)
zabal – al. – .ta – asu – un.
zabal – ale – eta – asu – une
zabal – alegeria – eta – asuri – une
sincere – rejoicing – abundance – new born lamb – place
"There was sincere rejoicing at the place with the abundance of newborn lambs."

zorigabeko (dismal)
zori – iga – abe – eko
zori – igarri – abereretsu – ekonomo
fate – to predict – brutal – administrator
"The fate of the brutal administrator was predicted."

Combining CV and VCV morphemes:

Bizkay, (Bay of Biscay)
bi- iz.-.ka-ai
bi – ize – eka – ai
bidegaitz – izentxar – ekaizpera – aipu
dangerous crossing – bad name – stormy – reputation
"It is a dangerous crossing and has a bad name because of its stormy reputation."

Zuberoa, (Basque province in France.)
zu-ube-ero-oa,
zue – ubel – erro – oartu
all of you – purple, royal – origin, descent – to perceive
"All of you are perceived to be of royal descent."

kaiku (wooden bowl for boiling milk)
ka – iku
kaldatu – ikusbera
to heat up – watchful
"Be watchful while heating."

Using a combination of CV, VCV and VCCV's such as in:

Gipuzkoa (Basque province in Spain.)
.gi-ipu-uz. _ ko-o.a
egi-ipu-uzka _ ko-oha,
egin – ipurterre – uzkali _ kontrako – oharkabe
to be – impatient – to overthrow ' enemy – spontaneously
"We are impatient to overthrow the enemy spontaneously."
(A break in the word is necessary because the vowel interlocking was broken.)

Pyrenees, (mountain range between France and Spain.)
pi – ire – ene – eske
pikaldi – irestzaile – enetan – eskerga
clearing the forest – destructive – always – enormously
"Clearing the forest (with fire) is always enormously destructive."

gorputz (body)
go – or. – .pu – utz.
go – ori – ipu – utzi
gogor – orriztatu – ipurtmami – utzi
ruthless – to cover with leaves – rump, corpse – to abandon
"The ruthless (killers) covered the corpse with leaves and abandoned it."

Recently created words lack the interlocking structure, such as *maribidetako and eskualdunak*, which have to be new words.

maribidetako (prostitute)
.ma – ari _ bide _ tako
emagalkeria – arriskudun _ -bide _ takoidun oinetakoak
prostitution – dangerous _ occupation _ high heeled shoes
"Prostitution is a dangerous occupation in high-heeled shoes."

eskualdunak (Basque speakers)
es. – .ku _ ald. _ una – ak.
esi – iku _ alde _ una -aku
esinguratu – ikurrin _ aldekide _ unagarri – akuilatu
to gather around – flag _ partisans _ downhearted – to motivate
"Partisans, gather around the flag. Motivate the downhearted."

Words with "ur" (water)

The re-organization of the language was consistently done in groups of related words. In the Basque language almost all words connected with water contain the root '*ur*' (water). Descriptive terms were then attached to designate the kind of water. A small sampling is given and compared here with the English equivalents, many of which appear strangely unconnected and artificial among themselves.

uraldi	flood	*alditxar* = misfortune
urandi	ocean	*andi* = enormous
uraz garbitu	to wash	*azal* = skin, *garbitu* = to wash
urazpil	washbasin	*azpil* = large dish
urbide	canal	*-bide* = route
uregazti	waterfowl	*gazti* = fowl
ureztaketa	irrigation	*eztasun* = scarcity, *-keta* = quantity
urgarri	water soluble	*-garri* = suffix which denotes cause
urgeldi	stagnant water	*geldi* = quiet, stagnant
urgora	high tide	*gora* = high
urjauzi	waterfall	*jauzi* = to leap, jump
urlamia	waternymph	*lamia* = gnome, troll
urlandare	waterplant	*landare* = plant
urlurrin	steam	*lurrin egin* = to vaporize
urmargo	water color	*margo* = color
urodi	irrigation canal	*odi* = pipe
urtatu	to soak	*-eztatu* = to cover with
urtzulo	waterhole	*txulo* = little hole
urzozo	water ouzel	*zozo* = blackbird
euri	rain	*e* = exclamation to draw attention

and many more. The only way to explain the reason for the English words in this list to be so very different and unconnected among themselves, is to show the way in which they were constructed with the use of the vowel-interlocking VCV formula, which can then be used to restore the hidden meaning in most of the words (see English etymological vocabulary).

Basque, A Highly Organized Language

Although the grammar of Basque is complicated, difficult to learn for an English speaker and obviously evolved over a long time, the vocabulary is so well organized, even regimented, that it cannot have evolved naturally over time into this condition and obviously has been arranged by scholars. As all the early invented languages such as Sumerian, Egyptian, Hebrew, Sanskrit etc. use its VCV system, the agglutination of the Saharan language must have been done first, more than five millennia ago. Some of these vowels may be omitted in the word invention process, but the consonant is always retained. One exception is the consonant 'h' which may or may not be shown in the dictionary or used in the invention process e.g. both *andi* and *handi* (large, enormous) are found in the dictionary, or *elberri* and *helberri* (newly arrived); the 'h' is often removed from words, even from whole dialects.

The Benedictine monks, who created all the west-European languages, were at first instructed in the word invention science by the people who worked on the Latin language in Monte Cassino which had been developed into the liturgical language of the Roman Catholic church. The basic rule of word invention was that the new word had to have no visible or sound relationship with the original Basque word. These highly educated and dedicated monks then fanned out over western Europe, established mission stations with scriptoria, created libraries and started the language invention process. For over 1000 years they employed non-Benedictine grammarians who spoke the Saharan/Basque language, probably originating from Liguria in the Alps and from Euskadi in the Pyrenees region. In the monks' writings it is often indicated that there are children in the monasteries; most of these belonged to the families of the grammarians. Also, young boys were given by their parents to the monastery residential school as child oblates, to be trained as deacons, monks and linguists, just like Alcuin had been. Several Benedictine monasteries to this day conduct boys' schools within the walls of their monasteries but the practice of accepting child oblates was abandoned long ago.

Mutilating a Beautiful Language

The monk-linguists used a large number of tricks to make the languages they created sound and look very different from spoken Basque. First the periphrastic word order of Basque was completely reversed, which created a fundamental difference and became the main characteristic of the Indo-European "family" of languages.

Samples borrowed from Aulestia (p. a30):

negation +auxiliary verb +complements +main verb

1   2   3   4   5
Ez naiz zurekin etorriko
I am will not come with you
2   5   1   4   3   3

1   2   3   4   5
Zu bezain ona naiz ni
I am as good as you
5   4   2   3   2   1

1 2 3 4 5 6 7 8
Ikusi duzun mutila Jon da
John is the boy that you have seen
7   8   6   5   4   3   2   1

1   2   3   4   5 6
Zu baino jakintsuagoa naiz ni
I am more intelligent than you.
6 5   4   3   2   1

For English, the pronounciation of the alphabet was changed from the usual Latin to the "English" sound, which instantly caused the words to be pronounced very differently. Relatively few vowels had been removed from the Latin agglutinations, but many more from the English ones, giving it a very different 'feel.' Most languages received newly invented "characteristic" letters, ô, ü, ø, ö, ñ, è, etc. and/or unusual combinations of letters such as 'eau' in French pronounced 'o,' or the Dutch 'ui' which is pronounced something like 'oi' but can only be said properly by a Dutchman. No doubt intended as a joke, Dutch also ended up with the embarrassing deep throat scrape, written as 'g' or 'ch' such as in Scheveningen, schaap, gaan, gooien, a sound which the monks probably borrowed from Hebrew and carelessly tossed into Dutch.

Thank goodness the Benedictines resisted these peculiar urges when they created English, which therefore became the simplest of all to learn and speak, and eventually became England's most successful export, in spite of its often ridiculous pronounciation of the word at hand. For some languages the monks assigned a sex to each word e.g. in French and German, which led to dumb cases such as the 'soldier on guard duty' who is female: "die Schildwache" in German and "la sentinelle" in French. Holland is the only country which rid itself in the 20th century of this incredible sex nuisance, retaining today only the neutral form 'het' e.g. "the horse" is not "de paard" but "het paard." Grammatical rules for each language were invented, some more appropriate and more easy to use than others, but only German ended up with endless and frustrating lists of "Ausnamen," exceptions to the poorly designed and ungainly grammatical rules. However, none of these languages was saddled with grammatical rules as complicated as the Basque grammar possesses, although Latin came close.

In English, the original verb was separated e.g. the 'tu' at the end of *zerbitu* (to serve) became 'tu zerbi' (b = v): to servi and 'to serve' in English, 'te dienen' in Dutch and 'zu dienen' in German. In English the original 'i' was maintained in the word 'service,' broken down into zerbi-ike, (*serbi-ikerlari*), serve-the visitor. English is full of such Benedictine tricks. Other examples which show that the 'tu' at the end of the Basque verbs became the 'to' before the English verb: *begitu* (to look), *apurtu* (to break, to destroy), *kisitu* (to whitewash), *neurriratu* (to regulate) etc.

COMPARING BASQUE WITH DRAVIDIAN

THE MAIN DRAVIDIAN LANGUAGES

About one quarter of India's population speaks Dravidian, a language family usually considered to have four branches:

Northwest:	Brahui, spoken in Baluchistan,
Northeast:	Kurukh and Malto in Bengal,
Central:	Telugu, Kui and Kolami-Parji,
South:	Tamil, Kannada, Tulu, Malayalam, Bagada, Toda, Kota, Kodagu.

There are four major languages, each having its own independent script and literature dating from pre-Christian times:

Telugu	(Te), the state language of Andhra Pradesh, spoken by some 60 million people.
Tamil	(Ta), the state language of Tamilnadu, spoken by about 45 million people.
Kannada	also called Kanarese (Ka), of the state of Karnataka with about 34 million speakers.
Malayalam	(Ma), the state language of Kerala, with some 25 million speakers.

The Dravidian language family was first described in 1816 by Francis Ellis, a British civil servant who recognized the relationship between the four literary languages as well as Tulu, Kodagu and Malto. In 1856 Robert Caldwell added several more languages, Kota, Toda, Gondi, Kui, Kurukh and Brahui. He then took the Sanskrit word *dravida*, supposedly meaning "Tamil," and used it to name the family (Merritt Ruhlen p136-141). We may presume that Dravidian was the language family of all of India before ca.1500 B.C. This was an early form of the language we today call Basque, but the Basque dictionary could still be used to translate many of the Dravidian names and words in this article. It is thought that the language was brought to India by a group of people emigrating from the Sahara at the time of the desertification, some 8,000 years ago. The Goddess religion may have been already long established in India. I suggest that the newcomers were white, well educated and aggressive, and their numbers may not have been high. The language they offered may have arrived at a time the people were in need of a more evolved language. How this language came to be accepted by the many tribes in India is a good question. The genes of the newcomers must have been absorbed by the dark-skinned population.

IN INDIA, BASQUE CAN BE DETECTED EVERYWHERE

We don't have to look far in India to recognize Basque-related names and words, such as:

Himalaya, ima – alaia, *imajina* (image, scenery) *alaia* (pleasing): "Pleasing scenery."
Harappa, the famous 5000 year-old ruined city in Pakistan; *harrapa* means "plundered" in Basque, from *harrapatu* (to plunder), which therefore can hardly be considered the true name of the city.
Goa, abbreviated from *goardia* (to stand guard), referring to the town's defenses.
Bihar, from bi – iha – ar, ibi – iha – arro, *ibildari* (nomadic) *iha'urri* (to scatter, to roam) *arro* (proud): "Proud roaming nomads."
Punjab, .pu – un. – .ja – ab., ipu – uni – ija – abe, *ipuinexko* (legendary*) unibertsal* (universal) *iaio* (cheerful) *abegion* (hospitality): "Our cheerful hospitality is legendary and universal."
Taxila / Taksila, .ta – ak. – .si – ila, ata – aka – asi – ila, *ataurre* (introduction) *akatsbako* (perfect) *asi* (to begin) *ilarteko* (lifetime): "Perfect introduction to begin a lifetime."

In the spoken language we find thousands of examples of words related to Basque, such as *kut* (in Malto) meaning "to burn," *kutu* (in Tamil) meaning "to be hot, to heat up," while *kutxer* (in Basque) means "frying pan" in which *xer* or *xerra* means "small steak" (in Basque the "x" is pronounced as "sh"). The Dravidian words *ole* (hearth, fireplace) and *ola* (inside) correspond exactly to Basque *ola* (cabin, hut). Being unable to read the different scripts in use by the Dravidian peoples, I took the easy way out and used the transliterations and Basque translations provided by Dr. N. Lahovary in *"Dravidian Origins and the West,"* published by Orient Longmans, Bombay, 1963. The page numbers in the following list refer to his book.

Page	Dravidian	English	Basque	English
164	ura	wife	*urruxa*	female
165	irru (Ta)	to bring forth	*errun*	to lay eggs
165	iru	to be	*iruditu*	to resemble
165	il	to be	*illi* (Berber)	to be
165	ul (Ta)	to exist	*ulertu*	to understand
165	aru	to give birth	*aur*	child
166	ali (Ma)	woman	*ala*	girl
166	ir (Brahui)	sister	*arre*	sister
167	kappu (Ka)	meat	*kaba*(l)	domestic animal
167	odal (Te)	body	*odol*	blood
167	biho	heart	*bihotz*	heart
167	pala	flesh	*opa*	offering
167	iracci (Ma)	meat	*aragi*	meat
168	suri (S.Dr)	to pour	*isuri*	to pour
168	ana (Ka)	breath	*asnasa*	respiration
168	naru (S.Dr)	odour	*narru*	skin
168	usir (Ka)	breath	*usna*	smell
168	u-suru	nose	*sur*	nose
169	sindu (Ka)	bad smell	*sund-da*	stink
169	kuku (Malto)	summit	*kukula*	summit, peak
170	buru (Te)	something round	*bular / burar*	breast
171	karata (Ka)	skull, coconut	*garaun*	brain
171	mula (Ma)	brain	*muin*	brain
171	kara	height	*garai*	high, prominent
171	bhala	forehead	*belar* (Zuber)	forehead
172	gadda	chin	*ganga*	mouth
172	ba (Ka)	mouth	*abo*	mouth
174	begu (Ka)	to spy	*behatu*	to observe
175	kan (Brahui)	to know	*ikan*	to look
175	aks (S.Dr)	sight	*ikus*	to see
175	vili	eye	*igi*	eye
175	mugu (Ka)	face	*musu*	face
175	muso (Malto)	nose	*musu*	face
175	muti (Ka)	face	*mutur*	snout
175	motu (Ta)	stupidity	mutur	snout
175	mukka-ra(Te)	nose-ring	*moko*	beak
176	musu (Ka)	to smell	*mustur*	snout
176	ba (Ka)	mouth	*abo*	mouth
177	appu (Ka)	to embrace	*apa*	kiss
178	alasu (Ta)	to rinse	*latsatu*	to wash
180	ele (Te)	song	*ele*	story
180	gol (Ka)	throat	*golo*	goitre
180	karai (Ta)	to cry out	*garrasi*	shrill cry
181	kar-utti (Ma)	neck	*garondo*	nape of the neck
182	kai (Tulu)	hand	uka	hand
183	kurukh (C.Dr.)	to seize	kargatu	to load
183	kadi (S.Dr.)	to steal	kaldar	thief, scoundrel
184	adi (S.Dr.)	foot	adar	foot of chair
184	anga (Tel)	stride	*anka*	foot
186	karu (Tu)	leg	*garra* (Navar)	leg
188	ola (Ka)	inside	*ola*	cabin, hut
189	bikku (S.Dr)	heart	*bihotz*	heart
189	alku (Ta)	vulva	*alu*	vulva
190	eru (Ka)	dung	*errai*	dung

Page	Dravidian	English	Basque	English
191	tottu (Ma)	nipple	*titi*	nipple
191	borra (Te)	potbelly	*zilbor*	navel
192	pal (Ka)	milk	*galatz*	milk
192	putti (S.Dr)	to be born	*puta*	womb
193	pukku (S.Dr)	vulva	*puta*	womb
195	tshika (Tulu)	small child	*txiki*	small
195	tkuri (S.Dr)	short	*korro*	short
195	tkittu (S.Dr)	small	*kuto*	small
196	iri (S.Dr)	sick	*eri*	sick
196	kira (Gond)	old man	*kira*	age
196	agura	old man	*agure*	old man
197	ala (Ta)	affliction	*aldia*	mental disorder
197	eriyu (Te)	to grieve	*auri*	lamentation
197	karai (Ta)	to cry out	*garrasi*	cry, scream
197	madi (Ta)	death	*amata*	to kill
197	mara (Ka)	death	*marrakari*	tearful
198	malagu (Ta)	to perish	*malgu*	soft, weak
199	adu (S.Dr)	age	*adin*	age
199	gasi (S.Dr)	hunger	*gose*	hunger
199	manku (S.Dr)	staggering	*mainku*	crippled, lame
199	ala (Ta)	afflicted	*alusu*	feeble, weak
199	alasu (Ka)	exhausted	*lazu*	weak man
200	elli (Te)	night	*ilun*	darkness
200	lamba (S.Dr)	to totter	*laban*	slippery, sliding
201	ema (Ta)	mother, female	*ama*	mother
201	amma (Ka)	female	*ama*	mother
201	pen (S.Dr)	woman	*pena*	sorrow, grief
201	ali	woman	*alaba*	daughter, native of...
201	al	male	*ar*	male
202	unmu (Ka)	birth	*ume*	child
202	maintu (Ta)	love	*maita*	love
202	maru-vu (Ta)	intimacy	*marruskatze*	fondling, pawing
202	appu (Ka)	to embrace	*apatz*	to kiss
203	manju (S.Dr)	amiable	*maina*	liking, pampering
203	iru (Ta)	come into existence	*iruditu*	to appear
203	uru (Ta)	to give birth	*aru* (Berber)	to be born
204	atta (Malto)	grandfather	*aita*	father
204	apa (S.Dr)	father	*ata*	father (child's)
204	ana (Ta)	brother	*anai*	brother
204	asa (Kui)	daughter	*aizpa*	sister
204	ari	she	*arreba*	sister
205	ila (Ta)	youth	*iloba*	niece
207	maran (Ta)	bravery	*mardul*	robust, strong
207	marru	enemy	*amarru*	cunning, shrewd
208	buti (Ka)	man servant	*botoi*	man servant
210	burade (S.Dr)	head	*buru*	head
210	bhuka	opening	*bukatu*	to end
210	kara	height	*garai*	high
210	gubbi (Ka)	hump	*gupi*	deformed spine
210	kerki (Tulu)	throat	*gurka*	throat
210	suri (S.Dr)	to pour	*isuri*	to pour
210	khala	thief	*kaldar*	thief
210	kiram (Ta)	old	*kira*	period of time
210	konku	curved	*makur*	roundness

Page	Dravidian	English	Basque	English
210	in (Brahui)	to say	*min*	tongue
210	pura (Malto)	belly	*para*	belly
358	ari	rock	*arri*	rock
359	kabi	cave, hollow	*kabia*	nest, hollow
360	kam	something round	*kamuts*	blunt
360	kuku	summit, peak	*kukula*	summit, peak
360	men (Ma)	mound, hillock	*mendi*	mountain
360	murru	wall, quarry	*murru*	wall
361	padu	village	*padur etxe*	lake dwelling
361	turu	hill, mound	*torre*	tower
361	mugul (Ka)	flower bud	*mugil*	flower bud
362	bar (Ka)	stream, to flow	*ibar*	river valley
362	ala (Te)	wave, surge	*olatu*	wave
362	garo (Kui)	deep hollow, dig	*goratu*	to raise, to carry up
362	tura-i	stream, pond	*iturri*	source of water
362	sala (Ka)	to enter	*salazar*	country house
363	kara (Ta)	to wash	*garastatu*	to sprinkle, to water
363	pani (Ta)	rain	*panin* (Zuber)	water

THE GENETIC RELATIONSHIP

A group of comparative linguists in the U.S.A. developed a system which they called the "lexico-statistical method" and attempted to put a percentage figure on the degree in which languages are related (M.Swadesh, Linguistics to-day, 1954). It is based on the percentage of resemblances between 200 words considered to be essential in a language:

1) the oldest names for parts of the body and its functions

2) pronouns and numerals

3) names for dwellings, children and families

4) domestic animals

The well-known Basque linguist A. Tovar followed this method to measure the degree of kinship of Basque with other languages of non-Indo-European origin. The closest relationship he found was with Berber (11%) followed by Circaskian/Kirrukaskan (7.5%), Coptic (6.5%), Arabic (3.25%). Then he asked Dr. Lahovary to try this method on Dravidian, with the astounding result of 50+%. This meant that, of all the languages tested so far, the Dravidian language was closest to Basque by far. However, the ease with which I assembled the long list of related Basque-Ainu words, makes it likely that Ainu could even be closer to early Basque than Dravidian. A person knowledgeable in the lexico-statistical method should test this possibility.

This method is of no use with invented languages such as Latin, Greek, Sanskrit, Hebrew, English, German etc. because all of these are made up almost 100% by formulaic manipulation and mutilation of the Universal/Basque language.

WHY THE RELATIONSHIP BETWEEN BASQUE AND DRAVIDIAN?

It may have been a calamity of unprecedented scale which drove large numbers of people from their homes in the once well-populated Sahara, starting about 9,000 B.C. Or it could have been over-population in North Africa resulting in voluntary migration east. Some of the Sahara tribes living along the Atlantic, Mediterranean and Indian ocean shores had developed excellent skills in boat building, sailing techniques and star navigation, which specialized knowledge was carefully guarded by the families involved. Those living on the Mediterranean and the Atlantic seaboard became later known to the Egyptians as the Sea Peoples. Other tribes in the interior had no relationship to salt water and were dependent upon the Sea Peoples for ocean transport when the time came to seek a new homeland. All of these people had the same universal language which I called Saharan, they adhered to the Goddess religion and had strong oral traditions. It is very likely that their Saharan language was the only highly developed language in the entire world at that time, the product of a marvelous oral educational tradition. History proved that they were well equipped for pioneering anywhere in the wide world. As Lahovary writes:

> *"One of the most common linguistic phenomena is the ease with which a new language can impose itself on vast masses, even if spoken only by a relatively small minority, should this minority have political power or the prestige of superior civilization"* (p.371).

To political power and civilization we might add the vibrant Goddess religion of the Neolithic. The present evidence of significant remnants of the Saharan language in distant parts of the world shows that their language took hold wherever they settled.

All of these people believed absolutely in re-incarnation, which meant that nobody died, that a person with all his/her knowledge, skills and experiences, would live on in a newborn when the body died. Risk taking was part of the joy of living, even if lives of productive people were frequently lost. Reincarnation would then restore the deceased person to active life to risk again. It was all part of living. As a result, these people were timeless and they totally believed that it was their duty to continue with the tasks and ideals of their previous lives. They had no idea of what we call history because they were history themselves. A son would always follow in the footsteps of his incarnation, whether farmer, ocean navigator, herdsman or fisherman, a system which created enormous stability in their civilization, and which was also at the root of the caste system. The women were responsible for the home-front, the men for the out-service which included long distance exploration, ocean travel and trading, whaling, fishing, herding etc.

Several writers have speculated about the origin of the Dravidian people and how they acquired their language and religion. Most of the Saharans were white-skinned, but in or near Ethiopia there lived a population of dark-skinned and black people (still there) who did not have negroid characteristics. The Dravidians may be distantly related to them, long ago. One theory is that white refugees from the Sahara then entered the land of the indigenous people of India and introduced their language and religion. However, it is likely that the ancient Goddess religion was already long before established in India. Sailing east some 5 or 6,000 years ago, the migrants had found Mesopotamia already fully occupied so they settled in the fertile Indus valley, where they built their villages which around 3,000 B.C. grew into major cities like Mohenjo-Daro and "Harappa." The Goddess religion was further developed into the characteristic and artistic religion of today. The Saharan language was mixed with the indigenous languages of the people and over time these evolved into a number of related languages. It is likely that present day Dravidian is closely related to palaeolithic Saharan-Basque.

It must be noted that the Basques and the Dravidians may have never been in physical contact with each other, living in widely separated areas, therefore the language they shared with the Dravidians must have been acquired from a common, central source. The Basques and Berbers have a special characteristic: Rh-negative blood. The Dravidians also have some of this blood peculiarity, more than any other tribe in Asia, about 4 % frequency. It has been proposed by Dr. Linton Herbert that all human beings were Rh. negative originally and that the Dravidians and the Berber/Basque/Irish tribes are the last hold-outs of this blood in the world. Only tribes which had the strength, or the isolation, to restrict inter-tribal mixing retained some of this blood type.

THE COMING OF MALE DOMINATION

Some 3,800 years ago the thriving land of the Indus civilization attracted a large land-migration of tall, white herdsmen, coming from the Near East or the Sahara. They brought with them a new religion which they had created by turning the Goddess religion inside out. Where the old society had been a gentle and matrilineally organized, yet egalitarian society, the newcomers were patriarchal warriors, extremely aggressive and dictatorial; they promoted writing and forbade the maintenance of the ancient oral traditions. A start was made with the creation of a new language, later called Samskrta (Sanskrit), new legends and traditions were invented to replace the ancient lore, and eventually the speaking of their Saharan language was forbidden. Under this new order the formerly highly respected and independent women became the property of fathers and husbands, to be given away, used, punished, mutilated or disposed of at will, never again to be without supervision of a man. They no longer had any say in the running of the tribe. For the resident dark-skinned Dravidians the choice was either the newcomers' way, slavery or go away. The Dravidian peoples chose not to submit and decided to leave the Indus valley. The newcomers, being herdsmen, had no knowledge of city management and had no desire to live in this manner, so the ancient cities were plundered and abandoned. Those Dravidians who stayed, mixed in with the new population and in time altered the character of the Caucasian herdsmen to create the distinctive race of people we see today in northern India. The majority of the Dravidians migrated south and entered the area of other tribes, which move created a domino effect of new and sometimes bloody conflicts, one of which, the Tamil fight for a part of Sri Lanka, is still making headlines in our newspapers today.

The Relationship Between Basque and Ainu

Introduction

The language of the Ainu bear-worshipers of the isle of Hokkaido in North-ern Japan has generally been considered a language-isolate, supposedly being unlike any other language on earth. A few researchers noticed a relation-ship with languages in south-east Asia, others saw similarity with the Ostiak and Uralic languages of northern Siberia. The Ainu look like Caucasian people, they have white skin, their hair is wavy and thick, their heads are round and a few have gray or bluish eyes. However, their blood types are more like the Mongolian people, possibly through many millennia of intermixing. The Ainu are a semi-nomadic hunting and fishing tribe but also practice simple planting methods, which knowledge may have been acquired from the newcomers. The invading people, under their Yamato government, called them the *Ezo*, the unwanted, and forced the Ainu in fierce fighting to retreat north to the island of Hokkaido. The name *Ezo* likely is an abbreviation of the Basque word *ezonartu* (disapproved of). The Japanese today still disapprove strongly of the manner in which the Ainu women tattoo their bodies and especially around the mouth.

Archaeology

Archaeologists have determined that the Ainu have been living on many of Japan's islands, from Okinawa to Sakhalin, for 9,000 years and very likely much longer (13,000 years has recently been suggested). Their Jomon pottery is found everywhere; it is highly characteristic and can be dated from 5,000 B.C. until just before the Christian era. It is very attractive and is distinguished by the fantasy of its shapes with elegant and imaginative cord decorations. Some of the most striking finds were the clearly anthropomorphic clay and stone figurines resembling pregnant females with mask-like faces and protuberant eyes; very similar to those found in many other parts of the world, especially in Europe and the Near East.

A number of stone circles have also been found, similar to those in Cornwall (England) and Senegal (North-West Africa). A few still have the slender upright stone in the centre, also found in the British Isles and elsewhere in Atlantic Europe and N.W. Africa. Around 300 B.C., Mongolian type people moved in from Korea and aggressively forced the Ainu north onto the large island of Hokkaido where an estimated 17,000 of them are still living. Some 10 dialects have been recognized, such as those of Sakhalin, Hokkaido and the Kurils, but several are at the point of being lost for ever. In Hokkaido young Ainu are now making an effort to restore their ancient language and traditions.

Religion

There are many intriguing resemblances between the religious customs of the Ainu and the Shinto Japanese. The Ainu called their God Kami while the Japanese called him Kamisama. The Aleut and Eskimo word *kammi* means "ancient thing" or "at the beginning," one of a great many correlations between Ainu and Inuktitut. (The Eskimo people call themselves the Inuit; note the similarity between the names Inuk and Ainu). Bear worship is still part of the Ainu religion and is described in detail by Joseph Campbell in "*Primitive Mythology*." This paleolithic bear-worship may date back as far as 200,000 years, to the early days of the Neanderthal people. It appears to have been practiced world-wide; wherever the bear was not found (mainly in Africa), its place was taken by similar panther-worship.

Bear worship was not tolerated in those areas later dominated by the major religions, therefore it was only possible for anthropologists to study the religion in the peripheral areas of northern Europe and Siberia. This gave rise to the idea that the Ainu must have moved eastward through Siberia, even though the nearest people of their type are found almost 5,000 miles away. But bear-worship has also been reported from Indonesia where languages similar to the Ainu language are still spoken. Could it be that the Ainu were part of the mass migration of "Caucasian" type Sea Peoples who fled the burning Sahara? The following Ainu – Basque language comparison seems to indicate that this may have been the case.

THE NAMES AND WORDS OF JAPAN

In books about Japan it is often remarked that many of the names of Japan's geographical features were taken over from the Ainu. For instance the many names beginning or ending with *ama* (Goddess) are all thought to be of Ainu origin. In 1994 the newly married prince and princess of Japan travelled to the cave of the Goddess Amaterasu to ask her blessings for their marriage. The name **Amaterasu** is almost certainly agglutinated from three Basque words:

ama-atera-asu
ama – atera – asturu
Goddess – to come out/to appear – blessings flow
"Blessings flow when the Goddess appears."

This name is made up of perfect Basque! Other well-known names were similarly assembled such as

Hokkaido
oka-aidu:
oka – aiduru
big meal – looking forward to
"Looking forward to a big meal."

Fujiyama
fa-uji-ama
fa – uju – ama
happy – cry of joy – Goddess
"A happy cry of joy for the Goddess."

is uttered by everyone who reaches the top of the holy mountain, just like is still being heard on many other mountains of the world (e.g. at Croag Patrick in Ireland, on the last Sunday of July). The Basques even have a word for this yodel cry for the Goddess, they call it the *irrintzi*.

The name **Amaterasu** is made up with the vowel-interlocking Ogam formula, which was surprising to me because in the Ainu language itself there is not a hint of this agglutinating formula. I then searched for more Japanese names and words which were assembled with the vowel-interlocking VCV formula and found several such as *Kamikaze* and *Samurai*. The surprise which came from this comparison was that those words which showed vowel-interlocking were usually associated with fighting and male domination. This appeared to be true all over the Pacific. Could this mean that there were two major migrations, the first one many millennia ago, possibly from Mesopotamia, which brought the peaceful people of the Goddess to the Pacific, centred on Formosa, now Taiwan, and a much later one, missionary based, bringing aggressive male domination and the language-distorting vowel-consonant-vowel (VCV) formula to these same areas?

None of the Ainu words were exactly the same as in Basque, but many were extremely close such as *ikoro* and *koro* (money), *kokor* and *gogor* (to scold), *tasum* and *eritasun* (illness), *iska* and *xiska* (to steal). A surprise was the Ainu word *nok* (testicle) which is much like the Basque word *noka* (familiarity with women). In English slang the same word is used in "to knock up" meaning "to cause a woman to become pregnant." In Indonesian *nok* means "unmarried young woman," while *dénok* means "slender, elegant woman." In Dutch slang the word is slightly altered to *neuk* (sexual intercourse). There is little doubt that the word goes way back to the Paleolithic. From the following comparisons it seems clear to me that the Ainu and Basque languages are genetically related. Comparing Ainu with Dravidian in a quick survey, I did not find an obvious relationship but this needs to be looked into much more deeply by someone who can speak Dravidian. Dravidian itself is obviously also related to Basque so there has to be a connection. Another language which appears to be related to Dravidian and Basque is Guanche, which used to be spoken in the Canary Islands. Three separate branches of the same tree?

The following words were taken from: "*An Ainu Dialect Dictionary*" edited by Shiro Hattori and (thank goodness) printed mostly in our Latin characters. This work provided a wealth of excellent material for my comparison. Don't forget that the Basque "s" is pronounced as a soft "sh" and that our sharp "sh" is written as "x" in Basque. (*The page column shows the word number/page number.)

Page*	AINU	ENGLISH	BASQUE	ENGLISH
2/5	*tontone*	to be bald	*tontordun*	crested, plumed
2/6	*kepsapa*	bald head	*kepireska*	heads or tails
6/38	*aspa*	to be deaf	*aspaldiko*	old, ancient
6/41	*papus*	lips	*papar*	breast
6/69	*taspare*	to sigh	*asparen*	to sigh
11/82	*aske*	hand	*esku*	hand
12/94	*poro monpeh*	thumb	*erpuru*	thumb
15/130	*nok*	testicle	*noka*	familiarity with women
15/131	*pok*	vulva	*puki*	vulva (slang)
16/133	*uka'un*	sexual intercourse	*eukan*	to possess, to have
16/134	*meno kupuri*	to menstruate	*kopor-kupuri*	goblet, quantity
17/136	*kema*	eg, foot	*kemen*	vigour, strength
17/137	*hera*	to limp	*herren*	cripple
18/149	*kiski*	hair	*kizkur*	curly, wavy hair
18/152	*kamihi*	surface of	*kamisoi*	nightgown, the skin
19/161	*tur*	dirt	*lur*	dirt
23/188	*hatcir*	to fall(down)	*atzeratu*	to fall (back)
24/194	*hotkuku*	to stoop	*kukutu*	to stoop
24/201	*mokor*	sleep	*makar*	sleep
28/1	*siko*	to be born	*zikoina*	stork
28/4	*hetuku*	to grow up	*gehitu*	to grow up

Page*	AINU	ENGLISH	BASQUE	ENGLISH
28/4	*sikup*	o grow up	*siku*	miserly
29/14	*sinki*	to get tired	*inkulin*	crying, whining
29/15	*yasumi*	to rest	*jaso*	to get better
29/16	*tasum*	illness	*eritasun*	illness
29/16	*araka*	illness	*arakatu*	to be examined
30/22	*ukikosmare*	to sprain	*ukitu*	to touch, to affect
31/34	*pirika*	to recover	*pirri*	shaky, jittery
31/36	*kusuri*	drug	*kutsu*	infection
31/38	*shuruku*	poison	*shurrut*	gulp, drink
34/2	*okkai*	man	*oka egin*	to eat too much
34/3	*meneko*	woman	*eme*	female
35/7	*sukukur*	young man	*sukor*	having a temper
			kuraia	strength
35/10	*poro aynu*	adult	*porrokatu*	tired
35/11	*onne kur*	old person	*onegi*	benign
			kurrinka	moaning
36/12	*ekasi*	old man	*ekarri*	to contribute, provide
36/13	*hutci*	old woman	*hutsikusle*	fault-finding
36/13	*ruhne mah*	old woman	*urrumakatu*	to sing a lullaby
36/16	*pon*	to be very young	*ponte*	baptismal font
39/12	*ona*	father	*onartzaile*	authority
40/16	*po*	child	*poz*	happiness
42/31	*uriwahnecin*	sibling	*aurride*	sibling
42/31	*irutar*	siblings	*rutara*	three different ways
42/35	*umatakikor*	to be sisters	*umatu*	to reproduce
44/52	*kok*	son-in-law	*kok*	bellyful
45/56	*aukorespa*	to be engaged	*aukeratu*	to choose, select
45/58	*usante*	to marry	*usantza*	tradition
45/59	*umurek*	married couple	*umotu*	to have children
47/68	*ekkur*	guest	*ekuru*	peaceful, peace of mind
47/73	*ipakasnokur*	teacher	*ikaserazi*	to teach
48/75	*kusunkur*	enemy	*kuskusean*	spying
50/1	*kotan*	village	*-kote*	multiplicity, many
50/2	*porokotan*	city	*porrokatu*	to destroy
50/3	*sinotusi*	open space	*sinotsu*	strange, unfamiliar
50/8	*oiakunkur*	out of doors	*oian*	forest
51/10	*ankahpaaki*	foreigner	*ankapetu*	to trample under foot
51/13	*uraiki*	to make war	*jarraiki*	to attack
51/17	*kotankoro*	tribal chief	*koroa*	crowned, glorified
52/18	*tono*	official	*tontor*	plumed, feathered
52/21	*u'ekari*	meeting	*ekarle*	bringer (of news)
52/21	*u'ekarpa*	meeting	*ekarpen*	contribution
52/23	*kotan orake*	to go to ruin	*oraka*	financial ruin
52/23	*kiru*	to die out	*kirru*	blond
52/23	*sikupu*	to perish	*siku*	shriveled up
53/32	*isocise*	jail	*isolamendu*	isolation
56/1	*itah*	language	*itano*	speaking in second person
57/12	*kayo*	to cry out	*kaio*	seagull
58/15	*ese*	to answer	*esetsi*	to argue
58/15	*itasa*	answer	*itaun*	question
58/18	*u'uste*	to pass along	*uste*	opinion
58/19	*sonko*	information	*esonde*	advice
58/21	*senpir*	backbiting	*senper*	suffering
58/22	*sinititak*	to joke	*sinoti*	crazy

Page*	AINU	ENGLISH	BASQUE	ENGLISH
58/23	*sunke*	falsehood	*suntsun*	foolish, idiotic
59/26	*esina*	to conceal	*esinguratu*	to surround, to block
59/27	*etekke*	confidential	*etekin*	profit, wages
59/28	*eramankorka*	to pretend	*eramankor*	tolerant, enduring
59/28	*ennuka*	to pretend	*enulkeria*	weakness, debility
60/40	*itokpa*	to mark	*itoka*	quickly
64/1	*ariki*	to come	*ariketa*	assignment, activity
64/2	*koman*	to go	*komandante*	commander
64/5	*eson asin*	to go away	*esonde*	advice
			asi	to start, to begin
65/11	*rutu*	to move aside	*urrundu*	to move away
65/12	*somaketa*	to approach	*somaketa*	attention, perception
65/14	*etaras*	to stop	*etapa*	stage, stretch
66/15	*kus*	to pass through	*kuskusean*	to peek, to snoop
68/33	*kaya*	sail	*kaiar*	very large seagull
70/2	*ko'ekari*	to encounter	*elkarikusi*	to see each other
70/3	*aske'uk*	to invite	*aske*	free, independent
70/5	*ekari arki*	to go out, to meet	*ekarri*	to bring, to provide
70/7	*umusa*	to bow	*kilimusi*	to bow
72/20	*omonnure*	to praise	*omendatu*	to praise
73/24	*kokor unpeki*	to scold	*gogor egin*	to scold
73/25	*ikohka*	punishment	*iko*	stone hammer
75/35	*ukonkep*	strength, contest	*ukondoka*	elbowing, forcing a way
75/35	*puni*	strength, contest	*puntzet*	sword
75/39	*inospa*	to pursue	*inozotu*	to be intimidated
76/40	*oskoni*	to overtake	*oskol*	armour
76/41	*akkari*	to outrun	*akarraldi*	to anger
76/46	*ikasuy*	to help, assist	*ikastun*	student
77/50	*kukocan*	to refuse	*uko egin*	to refuse
77/51	*ese*	to undertake	*esetsi*	to attack, to debate
80/1	*konte*	to give	*kontentatu*	to please
80/8	*uk*	to receive	*ukan*	to have
81/12	*ipuni*	to distribute	*ipuina*	to tell a story
81/13	*esikari*	to rob	*esi*	fence, enclosure
81/14	*iska*	to steal	*xiskatu*	to steal
83/29	*ikoro*	money	*koro*	money
87/15	*pita*	to untie, loosen	*pita*	fishing line
87/17	*tekkas*	glove	*teka*	pod, covering
88/25	*atusa*	naked	*atutxa*	better world
88/26	*hantasine*	barefoot	*hankagorri*	barefoot
96/38	*seku*	to suck	*sikui*	dry
97/46	*cikaripe*	to prepare	*sikatu*	to dry
97/52	*hu*	raw, unripe	*huruppa*	to swallow
158/21	*eraman*	to get used to	*eramanpen*	patience, tolerance
187/59	*peko*	ox	*menpeko*	controlled by

It is easy to find hundreds more like the ones above, all it takes is time, but I can see little reason for doing that. To me this comparison is quite convincing: the Ainu language is genetically related to the universal language, Saharan/Basque; the similarities are just too many to be accidental. Considering that the Ainu have probably been separated from the west for some 9,000 years, if not

13,000, it is not surprising that the language has drifted away from the neolithic language as it had developed in the Sahara. The fact that so many Ainu words are still clearly recognizable when compared to modern Basque words is nothing short of amazing and tells us that the ancient oral traditions had been faithfully maintained since they left the Sahara or Mesopotamia. The Ainu had no writing system but memorized their history and legends as *yukar*, which means that the poetry and epics were performed by professional memory men with elaborate display and ritual. The word "yukar" is interesting because the Basque equivalent is *eukar* (your resemblance) and *eukarista* (eucharist). In the west, the universal language was maintained by regular meetings, probably at the central shrine on Malta, where the *bertsolari* (professional memory men) of all the tribes and regions met to re-fresh and standardize their language and knowledge.

The Pacific sea peoples settled on hundreds of islands, they scattered over the entire endless Pacific, and it must be assumed that the single unifying educational exchange practiced in the Mediterranean was impossible to repeat. However, regional meeting-places must have been designated such as in the Marianas, Polynesia, Melanesia, Indonesia, New Zealand etc. but regular contact with the far-away Ainu could hardly have been maintained. Consequently the formerly universal language drifted and diversified into what we know today as the many languages of the Pacific islands, including those of the Kurils and Aleutians, however, early Basque is still recognizable in all of them as a substratum language..

Some of the Pacific languages, such as Japanese and Hawaiian, do not have the "r." It has been theorized that these languages have lost this letter over the centuries. Another suggestion was that the original "Caucasians" coming from Africa or Mesopotamia, some 9,000 + years ago, did not know this letter. However, it appears that the Ainu were by far the first to arrive in the Pacific and they have maintained the "r." The lost "r" theory may therefore well be correct. It is interesting to note that the name Ainu possibly comes from *ain'u*, an abbreviation of *ainbanatu* (to distribute evenly, to scatter all over). Another origin could be the Basque word *aienatu* (the disappeared, departed). These astute navigators of the Pacific must also have discovered the west coast of North America at a very early date. The island-chain of the Aleutians was a ready-made pathway to Alaska, which must have been reached as early as 12,000 B.C., before the east coast of North America was reached. A Caucasian skeleton was recently found in Oregon, U.S.A. and was called the Kennewick man. It has been dated to some 9,200 years old and it has been suggested that his skeletal characteristics closely resemble the Ainu. No doubt we will hear more about this possibility. It may have been about the same time that the Aleut/Eskimos started to spread east into Arctic Canada and Greenland, bringing along a pidgin-type, Ainu-related, Basque language to Labrador and Greenland, but I will discuss this with the Eskimo language.

Were the Ainu "Nomads of the Wind"?

There is an oral tradition that the Ainu sailed regularly to Alaska to obtain reindeer hides from the Aleuts established there, which they needed for their sails, exactly the same as was done by the Basques, the Irish and Scots who went to Arctic Norway for their reindeer-leather sails (the Mt. Komsa people). The Ainu must have been great long-distance sea-farers to keep up contact with their home-base which may have been in Mesopotamia. All over the Pacific this incredible sailing tradition waned fast when the social structure changed with the coming of European or Asiatic domination. Today the Ainu still sail the ocean but mostly on fishing trips. The complex navigational techniques, acquired over millennia had been the property of a few special families and were never general or popular wisdom. These techniques are now thought to be lost. The astonishing amount of astronomical knowledge which the members of such navigator families had to memorize was taught them at a very young age and was built up during a lifetime on the ocean. To these highly skilled and proud people, the Pacific was no hostile place, the ocean was their life and joy, and an indispensable part of their culture. Only in the Carolines the ancient spirit, some of the secret navigational techniques and much astronomical wisdom has been maintained to this day. All this is described in a wonderful book called: "*We, the Navigators*" by David Lewis.

The people who sailed the Pacific without the aid of modern instruments have recently been called the "Nomads of the Wind," a most appropriate title for these courageous and resourceful people. The Ainu appeared to have been the avant garde of the Pacific migration. Some disaster, such as an ice-age, must have forced these tribes to flee so far from home. Or was it the early desertification of the Sahara? It was then that the name "**Africa**" was coined:

af. – .ri – ika
afa – ari – ika
afa – arinari eman – ikara
happy – to escape – terror
"Happy to have escaped the terror."

At least one of these displaced tribes then sailed around Asia and started to populate the nearest Pacific islands such as Formosa (Taiwan), all of them speaking the same universal language.

While looking in more detail at the names in the Pacific, I found that many of the Pacific islands had names which could be translated with the Basque dictionary such as: **"Tahiti,"** from tahi-iti, *tahiu* (appearance) *iti* (ox): **"Resembles an ox"** the sharp pointed mountains indeed resemble ox horns. Or: **"Rapa Nui"** (Easter Island)

ra – apa _ nu – u.i
erra – apa _ enu – ui
erraldoi – aparta _ enuldu – uiol
giant – far, far away _ petrified – ocean
"Enormous giants, petrified in the ocean."

Or: **"Hawaii"**

ha'u-ahi:
ha'u (this one) *ahigarri* (exhausting)
this one – exhausting
"This one is exhausting (to reach)!"

Or: **"Papua,"** *apapua* (living in poverty); stone age people don't have many possessions, they don't pollute and they live as part of nature. One tantalizing hint comes from Peru where the patriarchal Incas established a complex civilization, complete with highly evolved Sumerian-type irrigation. The Inka was living god and the Basque word for "God" is *ainkoa*!

The Relationship between Basque and the Eskimo (Inuit) Language

Introduction

What I had noticed didn't appear to make sense; many names in use by the Eskimo people of Arctic Canada appeared to be related to Basque. The land north of the tree line is called Ungava, which in Basque would be Ungaba, Unagaba. Many Basque names are assembled from several words by agglutinating the first letters of these words. Unagaba sounded like it came from the first letters of two Basque words: una – gaba, *unagarri* (boring) *gaba* (night). Calling the long, dark, northern night a "boring night" made very good sense, but the apparent relationship with Basque just had to be accidental. The North American reindeer is called "cariboo," spelled karibu in Basque; from kari-bu, *kari* (reason, purpose, destination) *burdun* (roasting spit): "Destination roasting spit" again made good sense. The Indian people of the Arctic call themselves the Dene, meaning "all of us"; *denen* in Basque means "general, universal" while *denak* means "everybody" and is the same word as in Denmark. Having been alerted to the possibility of an unsuspected and unlikely link between Europe and the eternally frozen land of the Eskimos, I looked for a possible path the Eskimo language could have taken. Both the names Alaska and Canada looked promising; Alaska, alas-ka, from *alatz* (miracles) *-ka* (suffix denoting continuous action, unending), "Miracles unending" is exactly the reason why so many tourist ships cruise along the Alaska coast. Canada, spelled Kanada in Basque, clearly is assembled with the vowel-interlocking formula: .ka-ana-ada, *akabu* (ultimate, extreme end) *anaitu* (to get together) *ada* (noise of...), "At the far end we'll have a noisy-get-together" i.e., "On the other side we'll have a party." Makes good sense.

In the far northern village of Old Crow lives a native woman who writes a regular newspaper column about life in the far north. She is no Eskimo but her people have been living side-by-side with them for millennia. Her name is Edith Josie; the Basque word *josi* means "to sew" and that was exactly what she was doing when I first met her. She was embroidering a pair of beautiful mukluks for one of the cariboo hunters while I told her about the Canadian government's plans to build a forest-ranger station in her village. All these Basque connections in the Arctic could not be accidental. What was going on here?

How Did "Basque" Enter the Eskimo Inuktitut Language?

The following may sound far-fetched, but until I get better information, this is how I presume it happened. To answer the above question, I have to dig deep into the origin of the "Basque" language. The story started during the Ice Age, which had peaked 18,000 B.P. The melting of the massive glaciers covering the Alps had caused profound changes in air-circulation over North Africa. It is estimated that by 11,000 years B.P. the effect was starting to be felt by the people living in the central Sahara. By 10,000 years B.P. the increasingly dry conditions caused serious droughts, and starting about that time the tribes living in the affected areas had to escape to the shores of Africa, the higher elevation areas and the major river valleys like the Senegal, Niger and Nile.

Tribes which had traditionally lived along the ocean shores of the Sahara had long been involved in long distance ocean travel and had discovered many lands. They were also developing star navigation into a science and, while bringing this into practice, were well on their way to discover all the continents of the world, with the likely exception of Ant-Arctica. By the time the refugees from the central Sahara reached the coast, the Sea-Peoples living there were ready to ferry them to new homes on the north coast of the Mediterranean and to the fertile and beautiful lands around the Black Sea, especially the Danube, Dniepr and Volga river valleys and also the Caucasus region. The sailors living along the coasts of Arabia and Mesopotamia had scouted out the entire south and east coast of Asia and discovered Indonesia, Formosa (Taiwan) and the Japanese islands.

An estimated 9 to 13,000 years ago, following the path of the early explorers from the Near East, the tribe which became the Ainu of Japan sailed east. They probably sailed from somewhere around the Red Sea or Mesopotamia to settle on some of the beautiful and richly forested islands of Formosa and Japan. It was a risky migration with a long supply line, requiring a strong commitment of support from the people back home. There may have been a good reason for this particular group to migrate so far away. The Ainu had adhered to the extremely ancient religion of the bear worshippers, evidence of which has been found in the Alps as far back as 200,000 years. Changing times in Mesopotamia may have caused them to leave civilization behind to seek a country where they could practise their bear sacrifices without obstruction. Trade prospects may have had something to do with the support they received from, and gave to, the mercantile class back home. The Japanese islands, which were already sparsely populated, must have appealed to these intrepid pioneers. The newcomers, with their superior technical and linguistic skills taught their Saharan language, boat building, leather tanning, ocean navigation etc. to the native population with whom they appear to have been on generally good terms.

The long ocean voyages necessary to stay in touch with the homeland, as well as their long discovery trips in the Pacific, required an active boat-building and sail-making industry. Wood was no problem in Japan, the country was full of it in all sizes and qualities. The problem was skins for sails. These people were hunter gatherers and wove no cloth, so leather was the best alternative. Back home in the Sahara, this problem had been solved by the Basques who set up a large hunting camp in Arctic Norway near Mount Komsa in Finnmark around 10,000 B.P., where they annually killed large numbers of reindeer from the herds migrating through the area and then sent the skins to the oak forests of southern Sweden and Conamara in western Ireland for tanning with oak bark. This example was followed by the Ainu whose scouts had discovered the astonishing wildlife riches of Alaska, especially the large herds of cariboo migrating through Alaska and the Yukon, whose numbers were counted in the hundreds of thousands. Camps were established in the arctic tundra of Alaska and the hunt began. The skins were either tanned locally with the brains of the killed animals, or taken back to Japan and possibly Korea for bark-tanning. Thus equipped they explored far and wide and it is likely that the west coast of North America was discovered by Caucasian type people, the Ainu, long before the east coast was. It is well possible that the west coast of America was reached by the Ainu some 9 to 12,000 years ago.

THE ESKIMO RELIGION

The hunters in Alaska, who later became the Eskimos, do not appear to have established a religious centre similar to Mount Komsa in the Norwegian Arctic. The people involved in this hard work were mostly the native population of the Aleutian Islands, who did not share exactly the same religious traditions with the Ainu. Both the Ainu and the Eskimos practiced the ancient religion of the Goddess, who represented the life-generating and nurturing powers of the earth, in other words, the Goddess was nature as created and sustained by the living earth. To the Ainu black was the color of life, the rich black soil which sustained all living things and in itself was alive. Black was also the holy darkness of the sacred cave, regarded as the womb of the Goddess, the central point of their worship. However, the eternally frozen earth of the Arctic and the absence of caves was not representative of the Goddess and thus required an adaptation in belief. In the Arctic it was not the land, but the ocean which was vibrantly alive and which provided all the riches necessary to sustain life in the far north. To this day Eskimo elders still teach that the Goddess "Sedna" lives at the bottom of the Arctic Ocean, a Goddess who controls the movements of the seals, the Beluga whales, the arctic char swimming up the rivers to spawn, the drifting ice floes and the winter storms. In Alaska this Goddess is known as Nulirahak and in the Central Canadian Arctic as Nuliaguk. The Eskimo did not worship her exactly like the Ainu did, but they had great respect for her, trying to secure her cooperation and goodwill by persuasion and sometimes by threats.

Some Speculation

There is little doubt that some Ainu individuals had joined the hunters and that Ainu blood became mixed in during the long and dreary Arctic nights. Although living conditions were difficult, once the housing and travel problems had been solved, the population thrived because there was abundant food in the ocean. The skin boat technology developed by the Sea Peoples of North Africa, was adapted to arctic conditions by the Eskimos and has been maintained up to the present, both for the one-man kayak and for the large family boat, the umiak. As the population grew, the people became more confident of their ability to cope with the extremely uncooperative climate and the annually repeated extended periods of darkness, so the population spread ever farther eastward until they had populated the entire arctic coast of North America from Bering Strait to Labrador and Greenland, where they met sailors speaking Basque. To the surprise of the Basques they found they could communicate with the Eskimos in simple matters. The language had travelled clear around the earth, carried by population migration. No people on earth ever had to do more creative adapting to their environment than the Eskimos.

It must be clear by now that the language at the root of the Eskimo language cannot be Basque because these intrepid sailors were never active in the northern Pacific. Instead the relationship lies with the Saharan language from which Ainu, Basque, Dravidian and a host of other languages derive. The name Inuit, which many Eskimos prefer for themselves, may come from inu-it, *inular* (sunset, low-angle sun) *itsu* (blind), sun-reflection blindness, or "snow-blind." Their reputation of staunch independence and high self-esteem may have given the Eskimos their name "ezki-mo," from *ezkibel* (easily offended) *molde* (manner, behaviour), "They are easily offended" a name likely given to them by the Basques in Labrador.

A Basque Pidgin in Eastern Canada

For at least 500 years, the Basques have been fishing the Grand Banks of New Foundland for cod, while their whalers were actively harpooning off Labrador. Many early visitors had commented over the years that the Indians living south of the St Lawrence estuary and the Eskimos living to the north, used a Basque pidgin language to communicate with the visitors. The pidgin's existence was explained by the many years of contact with Basque fishermen and whalers. This could have been the case with the Indians, however, the Eskimos, as a general rule, kept their distance and avoided unnecessary contact. Yet they could also talk with the Basques.

A linguist from the University of Amsterdam, Peter Bakker, documented historical and linguistic evidence of the Basque elements he found in the pidgin and published this in the fall 1989 issue of "Anthropological Linguistics." His article was entitled "The Language of the Coast Tribes is Half Basque," which was an exaggeration because he gave only a handful of examples. When I met him I suggested to him that he could have found many more Basque-related words in the Eskimo language spoken all the way to Alaska, thousands of miles to the west, but he wouldn't hear of it. This left me no choice but to document the existence of Basque throughout the range of Inuktitut and to provide an explanation for this startling phenomenon.

To show that Basque vocabulary can also be recognized in the high Western Arctic, where no other races ever came, I examined two dictionaries for Basque-related words. I could not have found a more isolated and unaffected part in the north:

1) The "Kangiryuarmiut" dialect, spoken in Holman on Victoria Island; published 1983.
2) The "Siglit Inuvialuit" dialect spoken in Aklavik, Paulatuk and in Sachs Harbour on Banks Island; published in 1984.

Both dictionaries were written by Ronald Lowe of Laval University and were published by the Committee for Original Peoples Entitlement.

The Inuktitut Language

Linguists have been at a loss to explain the development of the language. The Eskimo people have a rather small population, totaling about 100,000 but these are scattered over an enormous area from Eastern Siberia to Greenland. The number and diversity of Eskimo dialects and sub-dialects surely points to groups living in isolation for millennia. Even dialects spoken in relatively close proximity, such as the two named above, show extreme differences. Ronald Lowe writes about one of them: "Siglitun seems to belong to no recognized family of Eskimo dialects and its loss would mean the permanent loss to the Eskimo language of those characteristics that are uniquely Sigliq." The speakers often have difficulty communicating with nearby tribes. Therefore it is surprising that some Eskimo words like amaruq (wolf) have survived almost unaltered through the millennia; in Basque the word *amarruki* means "cunningly." Another obvious one is aqittuq (weak), in Basque *akitu*(tired); also ipun (ear) and *ipuin* (story). There is a clear difference in pronunciation between *k* and *q*; the *q* is a uvular stop sound, pronounced like a *k* but much farther back in the throat. The *r* sounds like the French uvular *r*. The *g* is pronounced halfway between *h* and *g*. The *l* is more like the French *l*.

Eskimo – Basque Vocabulary Comparison

Eskimo	English	Basque	English
aliak	to please	*alaia*	pleasing
amaamak	mother	*ama*	mother
amaruq	wolf	*amarruki*	cunningly
aming	skin for kayak	*mintz*	skin
angi	tall	*andi*	tall
angiak	spirit of a murdered child	*angaila*	stretcher
angun	man	*ango*	native person
ania	brother	*anaia*	brother
aninga	her brother	*anaia*	brother
ano	dog harness	*ano*	dog feed
apumang	gunwhale	*apurkor*	fragile
aqittuq	tender, weak	*akitu*	tired
aqu	stern of the boat	*akulu*	to push, to prod
ataatak	grandfather, father	aita	father
atiq	name, namesake	*atikidura*	family tie
arautaq	snow beater	*arrau-taka*	oar-to hit, hit with the oar
aulajursiutuk	anemic	*aulaldi*	period of weakness
Inuit	Eskimo	*inu-itsu*	snowblind
ikumajaq	lamp	*ikusi*	to see
iloga	my friend	*ilagun*	friend
ipiutaq	chain to tie a boat down	*ipini*	to put on, to tie
ipun	ear	*ipuin*	story
isumairutivuq	mad	*isurikatu*	to spill blood

Eskimo	English	Basque	English
isurtuq	water	*isuri*	to flow
ituk	milk	*itukin*	outflow
kallupilluk	monster	*kalte*	to hurt, to harm
kangaq	ankle	*anka*	foot
kayak	kayak	*ekai-akitu*	work-tiring
kukiktuq	to steal	*kukuka*	to conceal
makitauti	support	*makila*	stick, cane
mamitsiarittuq	properly healed	*mamitu*	to coagulate
pallu	handle	*palu*	stick
piliutiva	play a game	*pilota*	handball
po	to blow	*poker*	to belch, to burp
tainiq	to name	*bataiatu*	to baptize
tamaryangayuk	retarded, stupid	*tamalez*	unfortunately
ublik	water coming to the surface	*ubil*	whirlpool
uluriahuktuq	feel a pain	*uluka*	wailing
umiak	family boat	*umeak*	children
unaguiqhituq	to rest	*unatu*	to get tired
uqaqtigiya	talked with him	*ukakor*	pessimistic talk

THE ESKIMO – AINU RELATIONSHIP IS NOT OBVIOUS

During the thousands of years that the Eskimo have lived in the Arctic, they have created a very special society in a most hostile environment. Their civilization and art are so unique that nothing on earth compares with it. It is therefore not surprising that it takes much more time to find Basque-related words in the Eskimo language than it took to do the same for the Ainu language. As the Sahara language was introduced to the people who later became Eskimos, those words which still resemble Basque, may have been brought to them by the Ainu people at a very early time, possibly as early as 9,000 years ago. To finish the above comparison job would be a good project for a linguistics student.

It had been a long way and taken many millennia but the Saharan language did circumvent the earth when the Inuit reached Greenland, where they met the Basque whalers and fishermen. Still it is surprising that there still were enough words left in common for the two groups to speak to each other.

COMPARING DRAVIDIAN
WITH GUANCHE

Guanche is the name of the language which was spoken by the native population of the Canary Islands until the Spaniards came and massacred a
large number of the inhabitants around 1500 A.D. Mr. Arysio Nunes dos Santos
discovered a relationship between Guanche and Dravidian, similar to what the
eminent linguist Dr. N. Lahovary had described between Basque and Dravidian
in his book: "Dravidian Origins and the West." What we are likely dealing with
in these languages is remnants of the original language spoken in the neolithic
Sahara. This happened at the time of the disastrous desertification of that part
of the world which had scattered the population to almost all ocean shores of
the earth. That original language is not the same, of course, as the Basque
spoken today, but a much earlier form of it, without the invented, formulaically
enhanced VCV vocabulary added in.

A few linguists have identified a large number of languages which also belong
to to this group: Numidian, Tuareg, Western Berber (Zenaga), Northern Berber
(Tamahac), Southern Berber (Tamazheq), Eastern Berber (Siwa, Awjila-Sokna,
Ghadames), Atlas (Shilha, Tamazight), Kabyle, Zenati (19 dialects) several of
them still spoken. To this neolithic group we must also add the large group of
Dravidian languages spoken in India by some 160 million people, the Ainu
language of Northern Japan with 18,000 speakers and Ancient Egyptian (extinct), including Coptic which is still spoken as a liturgical language. Even the
Polynesian languages seems to fit in this group.

Arysio Nunes collected as many Guanche words as he could find and then
compared them with Dravidian. Dravidian equivalents were obtained from "A
Dravidian Etymological Dictionary" by T. Burrows and M.B. Emeneau (Oxford 1984). Arysio added: "The reader should pay attention to the phonetic

correspondences only, disregarding the actual spelling, as a result of the Dravidian alphabet being different from the Roman one adopted for the Guanche language. I have to assume that he did his work well, because I have been unable to verify it. The condition for using his material is that his web address is given in full: http://www.atlan.org/articles/dravida/index.html

Guanche	Meaning	Dravidian	Meaning
achaman	heaven	ox-am-an	the upper expanse
achano	year	ajja-no	time division
achicaxna	people	acchi-sagina	lowly crowd
achimencey	king's relative	acchi-menka	king's relatives
achit	long live, hail	akchi, agi-t	hail
achimayek	mother, grandmother	acchi-mayi-ek	Great Mother of God
achoron	earth	achurun	marshy land
ahico	leather shirt	ayi-kov	breast cover
ahof	milk	ay-ubi	breast food
amulan	lard	am-ullu	liquid fat
ahoren	barley bread	av-ari	baked-barley
añepa	royal staff	anne-pal	royal staff
ara	goat	ar	goat
armenine	grasslands	aram-meyni	grazing field
banot	javelin	ihpa-not	sharp-javelin
beñasmen	crop, harvest feast	panna-as-men	ripe fruit crop
bucio	conch trumpet	pucci	spurt of sound
cancha	dog	kunchi	red dog
ere	pond	eri	pond
ganigo	pot, jar	kann-iku	water vessel
gofio	bread	guvi-u	parched sweet cake
goro	corral	gor-o	sheep pen
guan	man	gand	hero, male
guanamene	prophet, seer	kan-amani	father seer
guanar-teme	king of the nation	gan(d)-ak-tempe	king of the nation
guañac	country, nation	gan(d)-ak	land of the heroes
guanil	loose cattle	kan-iyal	loose cattle
guayca	leather legging	kay-ka	leg protection
guayota	the devil	kay-ota	the fiery lord
gujon	ship	kuccham	mast
hachichey	peas, beans	a-chik-kay	edible beans
haña	sheep herd	ana, kana	flock, herd
irichen	wheat, grain	arichi	rice, grain
magec	god (the sun)	mangeh	bull = Shiva
mencey	king	menkay	king
mocan	type of fruit	manka	mango
quevehi	your highness	cevvai	your highness
sigoñe	captain, chief	cek-kon	head leader
tabone	knife	tarpuni	knife, blade
tagoror	council,	takkor	worthy persons
tajaraste	name of dance	takcha-arasati	royal dance
tamazanona	barley mixed with ground meat	tam-acchana-anna	food made of ground grain and ground meat
tamaragua	good morning	itam-eruka	promising morning
tamarco	goatskin dress	atta-makar	goat skin
tano, taro	barley, grain	(t)aru	grain, food

Guanche	Meaning	Dravidian	Meaning
tenique	flexible mace	tanka, donik	mace
toya	fern	tai	tender edible sprouts
teme	king ?	tempe	chieftain
vacaguare	I prefer to die	vaka-k-ari	I choose to die
xerco	sandals	cherpu	sandals
xaco	mummy, corpse	chacchu	corpse

Guanche toponyms and theonyms (interpretation in Dravidian)

The Dravidian etymologies for these names are tentative and are offered as evidence of the explanatory power of that language.

Guanche	Etymology or Place	Dravidian	Etymology or Place
Acentejo	falling waters	a-cem-tiyu	place of water fall
Aguare	Paradise (valley)	akar-e	celestial heights
Añaze	Name of beach	aniy-acha	beautiful beach
Anaga	kingdom in Tenerife	an-aka	supreme
Arautapola	city of Taoro kingdom	Arayata-poly	Royal City
Atidamane	Name of great queen	atti-tamman	mother of the people
Benahoare	my land	(M)ena-(kh)are	my country
Bimbache	people from Hierro	Vin-bach	land of the brave
Canarias	Island of the dogs	cham-ari	island of Cham
Chenech, Chinech	name on Tenerife	che-nek	pure land
Echeyde (Teyde)	the luminous one	Ecch-eyd	white, fiery mountain
Gomera	one of the Canaries	Gomeda	fat cattle
Guachimara	royal princess	kaci-mara	golden beauty
Guanche	purified by fire	Cham-che	the golden heroes
Guan-Chenech	of chenek, Guanches	gan(d)-che-nek	pure land
Hero	Hierro, Ferro	Hiera	holy
Magec	the sun as god	Machek	dark sun = Vishnu
Maxorata	Fuerta Venture	Macchu-irata	golden abode
Tacaronte	Guanche realm	ita-koruntu	land of fat cattle
Tamaran	Gran Canaria	ita-maram	land of the braves
Taoro	kingdom of Tenerife	ita-oru	land of union
Tenerife	white mountain	tin-eriv	shiny mountain

A similar Guanche-Basque list could easily be made, e.g. achimencey (king's relative) relates to *atxikidura* (family relation), achaman (heaven) comes close to *akabu* (death, supreme), ara (goat) and Basque *aragi* (meat), kara (goat) and Basque *kara* (in heat), Arautapola (capital of the Taoro kingdom) and Basque *arautu* (to legislate) etc. It looks to me like Guanche is derived from the original, unmanipulated Saharan language, just like Basque, Berber, Tuareg and Ainu.

AFTER THOUGHT

Arysio Nunes dos Santos, the author of the above word comparisons, expresses amazement at the fact that Guanche and Dravidian, separated by such a huge gap in both time and space, still resemble each other so closely. He attributes this to the fact that both races were fairly well sheltered from alien contact and influence, the Dravidians down to the present, the Guanches down to the extinction of their culture at the end of the 15th century. He goes on to speak about the relationship to the Aryan languages, which is where he and I part ways. He is convinced that the Guanches were blond, blue-eyed people, just like the Aryans and that they came from Java or Sumatra in Indonesia. Having been in both these places, I can assure the reader that there are no blond, blue-eyed and tall tribes in Indonesia which even remotely resemble the blond people of Europe.

I find it very hard to believe that any of the original Guanches was blond and blue eyed. Virtually all blond people are Rh-positive. The Berbers from Morocco are Rh-negative and they have been sailing this part of the ocean for well over 12,000 years. The nearest blond people were the Shardana from Cyrenaica (Kirru-unai-ika) in eastern Libya and they concentrated their activities in the Black Sea, not the Atlantic ocean. There is no evidence of these two very different races mixing in the Canaries until the blond Spaniards arrived. It will take some convincing to make me believe that the original Guanches were blond. Until then I would say that they were dark-featured Berbers.

HIDDEN HISTORY IN BIBLICAL NAMES

INTRODUCTION

Where do the Biblical names come from? How were the letters assembled? Is it possible to find out what they mean? If so, will it give us a deeper insight into the origin of Christianity and Judaism or will it create more questions? The Christian faith is being debated and analyzed more than ever before and that is good because it feels like a fresh wind is blowing through the churches, so this may be the right time to ask these questions.

This study started with the Christian Ogam inscriptions, carved by early Irish missionaries on pre-Christian standing stones in Ireland and Scotland, on cave walls, spindles, knife handles etc. They were written in a form of shorthand in which one consonant often represented one full word, yet were arranged in such a way that the original meaning could be recovered. Most of the messages they wrote were evangelical such as: "Come to Christ, he will heal you and give you peace" This study eventually led to the names of the Bible which, to my great surprise, turned out to be written in exactly the same language and encoded with the same formula, the same as the more recent inscriptions carved by the Irish monks. In Genesis 11:1 we are told "Now the whole world had one language" and the challenge for me became to discover if this was factual and if so, what language this was. Would it be possible to show that this single language had indeed been spoken over the entire world? Are there any remnants alive?

Many Have Said it Before I Did

In 1825 the French Abbot Diharce de Bidassouet wrote in his "Histoire des Cantabres" that Basque was the original language spoken by the Creator. For that remark he has been ridiculed ever since. At about the same time the Basque priest Erroa maintained that Basque was the language spoken in the earthly paradise. For that his colleagues treated him as a harmless lunatic, however, Erroa was so convinced that he was right, that he appealed to the Bishop of Pamplona (Navarra) who referred the appeal to the Chapter of the Cathedral of Pamplona. This august body considered the matter seriously and, after several months of deliberations it solemnly gave judgment in Erroa's favour and publicly subscribed to his theory (Gallop p4).

Abbot Dominique Laetjuzan (1766-1818) had earlier concluded that Basque was the language of the Garden of Eden and wrote a book with the interesting title: "Essai de Quelques Notes sur la Langue de Basque par un Vicaire de Campagne sauvage d'origine." (Bayonne, 1808.) In it he showed that the names of the main characters in the Book of Genesis were all Basque in origin and had appropriate meanings. However, the church fathers in Rome were neither pleased with, nor supportive of, his findings and the abbot's research was forgotten.

Laetjuzan
.la – et. – .ju – .za – an.
ala – etsitu – uju – uza – ani
alabaina – etsitu – ujuju – usaindu – anitzetan
indeed – disillusioned – joyful – to suspect – as a rule
"Indeed I may be disillusioned or joyful, but as a rule I am suspicious."

Decoding the Names

In my Ogam research I had discovered that the first three letters, vowel-consonant-vowel, of each Basque word were used to agglutinate the inscription and that several vowels were subsequently removed according to a complicated system which allowed only specialists to decode the message. However, the consonant was never removed, unless it was an 'h.' As an example let us take **Mozes** which has three consonants to be separated as follows: **.mo – oze – es.** and immediately the letters oze' make sense in Basque, because they are the first letters of the word *ozen,* meaning 'penetrating voice.' Now the problem was to find out the two missing vowels, the first and the last. In both cases they had to be 'a' because no other vowels created words which matched with the penetrating voice:

Mozes
.mo – oze – es.
amo – oze – esa
amorrazio – ozen – esan
anger – penetrating voice – to express
"He expresses his anger in a penetrating voice."

The majority of Biblical names can be decoded by this method so let's take some simple names:

Genesis
.ge – ene – esi – is.
age – ene – esi – isa
ageri – ene – ezingehiagoko – izadi
revelation – my – supreme – creation
"Supreme revelation of creation."

Revelation
.re – ebe – ela – ati – on.
are – ebe – ela – ati – one
arrerosle – ebertar – ela – atxikimendu – oneste
redeemer – Hebrew – story – faithfulness – blessing
"Our Hebrew Redeemer's (Jesus's) story of faithfulness and blessing."

Sarah
.sa – ara – ah.
asa – ara – aha
asaba – arauzale – ahaidego
ancestor – lawful – kinship/tribe
"Lawful ancestor of the tribe."

Zion
.zi – on.
azi – one
azitoki – onetsi
place where I grew up – to bless
"Bless the place where I grew up."

Moab
.mo – ab.
umo – aba
umoretxar – abade
bad tempered – priest
"Bad tempered priest."

Bethlehem,
.be – et. – .h. – .le _ he – em.
abe – eto – oha – ale _ he – emo
abelaska – etorberri – ohartzaile – alegera _ heben – emoi
manger – newborn – observer/wise man – rejoicing/glorifying _ here – gift
"The newborn is in the manger. The wise men are here glorifying with gifts."

A slightly more complicated one because the 's' is pronounced as 'z.'

Israel
is. – .ra – el.
ize – era – eli
izendu – eraspen – elizlur
celebrated – devotion – holy land
"Devoted to our celebrated Holy Land."

Nod
.no – od.
no – odo
norberaganatu – odolbateko
to attract to oneself – of the same kinship
"He attracted to himself someone of the same kinship."

Euphrates
eu – uf. – .ra – ate – es.
eu – ufa – ara – ate – esi
eurizaparada – ufatu – arao – aterperatu – ezinjasanezko
downpour – wind – curse – let's get out of the rain – unbearable
"The downpour and the wind are a curse, let's get out of this unbearable rain."

None of these name translations are very controversial, but this changes fast when we decode some names given to **Gentiles**:

Gentile/Jentil
.je – en. – .ti – il.
aje – ene – eti – ila
ajenatu – enetan – etikoagaitz – ilartzaile
to drive away – always – unethical – murderers
"Always drive away the unethical murderer."

Milcom
.mi – il. – .ko – om.
omi – ila – ako – ome
Omia Saindu – ilarazi – akordiozko – omendatu
Hallow Mass – to sacrifice – traditional – to pay tribute
"At Hallow Mass he will be sacrificed to pay the traditional tribute."

Jezebel
je – eze – ebe – el.
jentil – ezetsiz – ebertar – eleizakoak
Gentile – disdainful – Hebrew – sacraments
"This Gentile is disdainful of the Hebrew sacraments."

Jero'boam
je – ero _ bo – am.
jentil – erostatu _ bortiztasun – ama
Gentile – to mourn _ cruelty – priestess
"Gentile who mourns the cruelty of the Priestess."

Tammuz
.ta – am. – .mu – uz.
ita – ama – amu – us
itaro – ama – amuros – uso
to await – Goddess – loving – dove/holy man
"The loving Goddess awaited the holy man."

The sexual role of the loving Goddess was played by the chief priestess at the May 1 Sacred Marriage celebration, the day when the girls of the tribe danced around the May Pole, the phallic symbol of the prince. Prince Tammuz knew that he was to be sacrificed after a specified time period, usually seven or eight years, in Scotland on November 1, to ensure the return of spring, prosperity and happiness to the peoples of the Goddess. During his seven and a half year tenure as "prince" he wore the purple robe, signifying the bridge between the people and the Deity, which accorded him enormous prestige and respect. His voluntary sacrifice, during which he proved his absolute faith in his deity, ended this reign and he went to his death with great dignity, knowing full well that he would be reincarnated soon thereafter in the body of a newborn. For three days his body was placed in a cave, representing the womb of the Goddess, after which a light phenomenon (in Basque: *printz*) was seen, the glorious light which heralded the release of his spirit, ready for reincarnation in a new body which could then take place as soon as a suitable child was available. A Prince of peace and happiness had been reborn from the womb of the Goddess.

The Christian Faith, Founded in the Egyptian Religion

The most startling information that comes from analyzing the names of the Old Testament is the prominent and fundamental role the ancient Goddess (Ashera, Isis) religion played in the formation of both Judaism and Christianity. It seems certain that Judaism was formed by inverting all important aspects of the Goddess religion into a totally negative image. The dressed-in-white priestesses of the earth Goddess became the black-coated male clergy of the sky god, tribalism became nationalism, the sex act was switched from beautiful to despicable etc. Even the word for woman, *andre*, was inverted to mean man, *andros* (Greek) which in Saharan/Basque really means "fond of woman" (*androzale*).

Ashera
ash. – era
ashola – -era
care – -ing
"Caring."

The Bible tells us about the pleasing memories of the Goddess religion and the pain the new Judaism brought:

> *All the women who dwelt in Pathros in the land of Egypt answered Jeremiah: "As for the word which you have spoken to us in the name of the Lord, we will not listen to you. But we will do everything that we have vowed, burn incense to the queen of heaven and pour out libations to her, as we did, both we and our fathers, our kings and our princes, in the cities of Judah and in the streets of Jerusalem; for then we had plenty of food and we prospered, and saw no evil. But since we left off burning incense to the queen of heaven and pouring out libations to her, we have lacked everything and have been consumed by the sword and by famine"*
>
> (Jer. 44:15-19)

During that time the Hebrew people had two religions which could not be reconciled because they were the exact opposite to each other. The holistic Ashera religion of the caring, loving Goddess of the earth became dualistic Judaism with the cruel and jealous, God of the sky. It was likely the Levites who enforced the conversion to male domination and every effort was made by them to blacken the reputation of the adherents to the earlier religion and to eliminate the memory of it as much as possible. However, as 2nd Kings, Jeremiah and other books document, the Queen of Heaven returned to Jerusalem many, many times (e.g. 2 Kings 17:9-10, 23: 4-15 etc).

> *And the people of Israel did against the Lord their God things that were not right. They built for themselves high places at all their towns, from watchtower to fortified city; They set up for themselves pillars and Asherim on every high hill and under every green tree; and there they burned incense on all the high places...*
>
> (2Kings 17:9-10)

The destruction of the ancient Ashera religion by the patriarchal tribes took many centuries and was pursued with brutal determination, some of it graphically documented in the Bible and expressed in the names:

armageddon
ar. – .ma – age – ed. – .do – on.
ara – ama – age – ede – edo – one
aragikor – ama – ageriko – ederrak hartu – edonongo – onezkero
lustful – Goddess – notorious – to be defeated – everywhere – right now
"The lustful and notorious Goddess must be defeated, everywhere and right now."

apocalypse
apo – oka – ali – ip. – .se
apo – oka – ali – ipu – usa
apokeria – okastagarri – alienazio – ipuinezko – usario
filthy deed – disgusting – killing of a person – legendary – tradition
"The killing of a person in the legendary tradition is a filthy and disgusting deed."

THE EGYPTIAN CONTRIBUTION

During many centuries before Christ's birth, the people of the Near East experienced enormous religious turmoil. For many years, within the ranks of the clergy of the Ashera religion, the value of the voluntary sacrifice of a special young man, including some pharaohs, had been hotly debated. This sacrament had been done away with in Egypt, probably as late as early in the 12th Dynasty, because they considered this tragedy to belong to a bygone age. By the time of the 18th Dynasty some pharaohs' names sound very Christian, e.g:

Ahmosis (18th Dynasty)
ah. – .mo – osi – is.
aha – amo – osi – ize
ahalguzti – amodio – osin – izenandiko
Almighty – love – very deep – celebrated
"The Almighty's very deep love is celebrated."

Tuthmosis (18th Dynasty)
.tu – ut. – h – .mo – osi – is.
atu – uto – oha – amo – osi – isa
atutxa – utopia – ohartasun – amodio – osintsu – izan
evergreen forest – utopia – thoughtfulness – love – very deep – to exist/live on
"In the evergreen forest of utopia his thoughtfulness and very deep love lives on."
The evergreen forest referred to was not in Egypt but on the Hoggar
Mountains in SE Algeria, the traditional home of the Great Goddess.
Some of the trees of that forest have managed to survive."

Siptah (19th Dynasty)
.si – ip. – .ta – ah.
si – ipi – ita – aha
sinestu – ipini – itxaro – ahalguzti
to believe – to place – trust – Almighty
"To believe is to place your trust in the Almighty."

Siamon (21st Dynasty)
.si – i.a – amo – on.
isi – iha – amo – one
isilki – ihardun – amodio – onesan
quietly – to take time – love – to praise
"Quietly take time to love and praise."

Amonirdis (22nd Dynasty)
amo – oni – ir. – .di – is.
amo – oni – ira – adi – iza
amodio – oniraun – iradoki – adiskidego – izaera
love – goodness – to inspire – friendship – character
"Love and goodness inspire friendship and character."

It is difficult to imagine how much more these names could resemble the later Christianity. In my mind, there is no doubt that the Egyptian religion, with its loving Goddess, was the forerunner of the Coptic Christian religion and, by extension, of Judeo-Christianity. The early Christians believed that the human sacrifice was inseparably tied to the Goddess. Well before the time of Christ, already in the 18th dynasty, some Egyptian believers changed the caring, passionate Goddess into a loving God, while at the same time doing away with the contentious Tammuz sacrifice. However, the bridge between the deity and the people had to be preserved. There appears to be little doubt that Christianity was the product of a renaissance within the Egyptian religion and so Early Christianity was born, called Gnosticism in North Africa. It is difficult to avoid the conclusion that the religion of the loving God is much older than Judaism, which later infiltrated Coptic/Gnostic Christianity to form our present Judeo-Christianity.

Gnostic
.g. – .no – os. – .ti – ik.
igo – ono – osa – ati – ika
igoarazi – onon – osatasun – atxikigarri – ikaskai
to lift up – exquisite – perfection – faithfulness – teachings
"Lift up to exquisite perfection our teachings in faithfulness."

But which of the two conflicting religions of the Hebrews, Judaism or the Gentiles, did Jesus belong to? The answer to that question is written in his name:

Jesus/Jezus Christ/Krist
je – ezus   kri – ist
jentil – ezustelkor   kriatzaile – istun
Gentile – incorruptible   God – speaker
"Incorruptible Gentile, God's speaker."

As the Bible tells us, Jesus was of the line of David. King David was the father of King Solomon who built the first temple in Jerusalem. The interesting thing about the line of David is that many continued to adhere to the Ashera religion. During the 370 years of the existence of the Solomonic temple, it was a Goddess temple for no less than 236 years, as Dr. Raphael Patai documents in "The Hebrew Goddess":

> ... *the worship of Ashera was introduced into the Jerusalem Temple by King Rehoboam, the son of Solomon in or about 928 B.C.E. Her statue was worshiped in the Temple for 35 years, until King Asa removed it in 893 B.C.E. It was restored to the Temple by King Joash in 825 B.C.E. and remained there for a full century, until King Hezekiah removed it in 725 B.C.E. After an absence of 27 years, however, Ashera was back again in the temple. This time it was King Manasseh who replaced her in 698 B.C.E. She remained in the Temple for 78 years until the great reformer King Joshiah removed her in 620 B.C.E. Upon Joshiah's death eleven years later (609 B.C.E.) she was again brought back into the Temple, where she remained until its destruction 23 years later in 586 B.C.E. Thus it appears that, of the 370 years during which the Solomonic Temple stood in Jerusalem, for no less than 236 years, (almost two-thirds of the time) the statue of Ashera was present in the Temple, and her worship was a part of the legitimate religion approved and led by the king, the court and the priesthood and opposed by only a few prophetic voices crying out against it at relatively long intervals.*
>
> (p. 50)

King David's line was a Gentile line and it is therefore not surprising that Jesus was no Judaist, even though he belonged to the Hebrew tribe. Instead he was a Gentile, as his name confirms. It is very likely that he had been destined to be the last voluntary Tammuz sacrifice of the Goddess in the Near East and that he fulfilled this role courageously. If so, Jesus was sacrificed in the cruel age-old way, and this act must have been preceded seven or eight years by the Sacred Marriage ceremony. The only person we know of who could have been his partner in this Marriage was Mary Magdalene. If so she must also have been the officiating priestess at the tomb/cave. The fact that she was called a prostitute would support this because all priestesses were called prostitutes by the Judaists. Indeed the Bible tells us that she was the first one to report that the body was gone. Like all the other Tammuz sacrifices, Jesus had confidently walked to his death, even though he knew exactly what was to happen to him. Jerusalem was known to be a place where this, to us so tragic, event had been practiced since time immemorial and Ezekiel 8:14 tells us that the women at the temple were weeping for Tammuz. No doubt they had been weeping for Jesus also.

The authorities of the time considered Jesus to be a dangerous revolutionary to say things like:

> *"There is neither Jew nor Greek, neither bond nor free, neither male nor female, you are all one in Jesus Christ."* (Galatians 3:28).

Only a Gentile would speak such words and then go voluntarily to his death, because death was part of life through reincarnation.

Jerusalem
je – eru – usa – ale – em.
je – eru – usa – ale – ema
jentil – errukigabe – usaio – alegia – emankortasun
Gentile – cruel – custom – fake – fertility
"Cruel Gentile custom (to achieve) fake fertility."

Jerusalem was one of several places where a young man voluntarily died to prove his absolute faith in the Goddess. The most dramatic of the Tammuz sacrificial deaths took place, not in the Mediterranean, but in the whirlpool of Corrivreckan, located 70 km west of Glasgow, Scotland, in the Holy Land of the Great Goddess, the *Donetu Alde* (Don-ald). It was the only such sacrificial place in NW Europe and this holy sacrament was attended by thousands of people coming from as far away as Norway, Denmark, the Baltic region, Scotland and Ireland, even Russia and the western Mediterranean. The island where they gathered, used to be called "Hinba" (see Adomnan) from *hinbasio* (invasion). This name referred to the flood of people who arrived like an invasion to attend the sacrifice and to watch the life struggle of the young man in the coracle, which was anchored at dead tide to an anchor stone thrown in the whirlpool, all observers standing and watching in total silence. From the high viewpoint Cruachan at the far north tip of the island everyone could observe the tragedy. The cable with which the boat was tied to the anchor stone was woven out of the long braids which young women had cut off for this purpose. It was a great honor to have your hair selected for this purpose, and to this day, many women in NW Europe carefully save their long braids as long as they live, even though the reason for this has long been forgotten. When the Benedictines arrived, the island's name was quickly changed from Hinba to Jura, from *juramendu* (cursed). They changed it from the most holy isle to "the Cursed Isle" and a very determined, and almost successful, effort was made by the church to eliminate all evidence and memories of this happening. To this day tourists visiting the nearby Isle of Iona are told that 60 kings, read princes, of Scotland, Ireland and Norway etc. are buried in the sandy graveyard by the restored monastery. Martin Martin, in his book *The Hebrides*, writes in 1695:

> *"They can boast that they are honored with the Sepulchres of eight Kings of Norway, who at this day, with forty eight Kings of Scotland, and four of Ireland lie entomb'd in the Isle of Iona; a Place fam'd for some peculiar Sanctity."*

It is likely that there are many, many more unreported princes graves. None of the stone grave markers are now visible, having all been destroyed and covered over by the monks, but the slab-stone coffins are probably still in the ground. When the Benedictine monks first came to Britain they had this sacrifice in the whirlpool on their minds, and they made up some names referring to it:

Albion
al.-.bi-on.
alu – ubi – ona
alukeria – ubil – onartezin
repulsive deed – whirlpool – unacceptable
"The repulsive deed in the whirlpool is unacceptable."

Subiaco
.su-ubi-ako
isu-ubi-ako
isurikatu – ubil – akorduan euki
to waste a life – whirlpool – to remember
"Remember the waste of life in the whirlpool."

"Subiaco" became their rallying cry when they first established their monasteries in Britain. It also became the name of their mother house in Italy. This brings us to the name of the Bible or **Biblos**, a name which refers to a whirlpool:

Biblos
.bi – ib. – .lo – os.
ubi – ibi – ilo – ose
ubil – ibilkeriak – ilordu – ozendu
whirlpool – immorality – death throes – make your voice resound
**"Make your voice resound against the immorality of
the death throes in the whirlpool."**

There were at least two whirlpools known where similar human sacrifices took place. The oldest one was in the First Cataract of the river Nile in Egypt, which tragedy was ended in the 12th dynasty when the Cataract was made navigable for large ships and the whirlpool was eliminated. The other one was in Corrivreckan (Charybdis), at the north tip of the Isle of Jura in Scotland. Both places of sacrifice were known in Israel and the name Biblos may refer to both of them. There may have been a third one in the Euphrates but nothing is known to me about this.

TRANSLATING A FEW NAMES OF GENESIS

To give the reader a taste of what may be expected from decoding the hidden sentences in Biblical names, I start at the beginning of Genesis, I will list the names according to the numbering in the Bible. The space gobbling system I used in the examples above will be altered, therefore I condense the translations like was done in my English vocabulary list.

2:11. Pishon, from *pixontzi* (chamberpot): "Chamberpot."

2:11. Havilah, .ha-abi-ila-ah, uha-abi-ila-ahu/au, *uhalde* (flood) *abiatu* (to begin) *ilarazi* (to kill) *aurrean erabili* (to harass): "The flood is beginning to kill and harass."

2:13. Gihon, .gi-iho-on., agi-iho-ona; *aginerakuste* (threat) *ihortziri* (thunder) *onago* (closer): "The thunder threatens to come closer."

2:13. Cush, .ku-ux., iku-uxu; *ikusbide* (scenery, countryside) *uxu* (cry of happiness): "A cry of happiness for the scenery."

2:14. Tigris, .ti-ig.-.ri-is., uti-ige-eri-iso; *utikan* (get away) *iges egin* (to escape) *erioaldi* (agony) *isola* (torrential rain): "Get away from here and escape from the agony of the torrential rain."

2:14. Assyria, as.-.si-iri-iha, ase-esi-iri-iha; *aserrez* (angrily) *esinguratu* (to surround) *iri* (city) *ihabali* (frightened): "They angrily surrounded the frightened city."

2:15. Euphrates, eu-uf.-.ra-ate-es., eu-ufa-ara-ate-ezi, *eurizapparada* (downpour) *ufatu* (blowing wind) *arao* (curse) *aterperatu* (let's get out of the rain) ezinjasanezko (unbearable): "The downpour and the wind are a curse, let's get out of this unbearable rain."

3:17. Adam, ada-am., ada-ama; *adarra sartu* (to deceive) *amarruki* (cunningly): "(He was) cunningly deceived."

3:20. Eva, eba, from *ebasle* (thief): "Thief." She stole the apple and, ever since, women have suffered for her misdeed.

3:24. Cherubim, che-eru-ubi-im., xe-eru-ubi-ima; *xedatu* (to dispose of) *errukigabe* (cruel) *ubil* (whirlpool) *imagina* (idol, prince of light): "The cruel disposal of the prince-of-light in the whirlpool." The moment of the resurrection of the drowned prince's spirit after three days was observed by the crowd as a glorious light shining from the cave, where the priestess was with the body (*printz* is Basque and means ray of light). A printz of light had been reborn.

4:1. Cain, from *kahin* (dowsing rod or divining rod): "Diviner." The word *kahin* has been lost from the Basque vocabulary, but it was retained in Berber and Arabic.

4:2. Abel, abe-el., ebe-ele; *abeldun* (cattleman) *eleienda* (legend): "The legend of the cattleman."

4:17. Enoch, eno-ok., eno-oka; *enoradun* (covered with warts) *okaztagarri* (disgustingly): "Disgustingly covered with warts."

4:18. Mehuja'el, .me-ehu-uja'el., ame-ehu-uja'ele; *amerikak egin* (to make a fortune) *ehunsaltzaile* (textile merchant) *uja* (shout of joy) *ele* (story): "Story of the textile merchant who shouted for joy when he made a fortune."

5:18. Methusha'el, .me-et.-.hu-usa-el., ame-ete-ehu-uxa-ele; *amerikak egin* (to make a fortune) *etekin* (profit) *ehunsatzaile* (textile merchant) *usain* (suspicion) *ele* (story): "The story of the textile merchant who made a fortune is suspicious."

The supply of Biblical and other religious names is almost endless and I am confident that the translation of many of them will give us some very interesting information.

VI

THE LATE BRONZE AGE

Turn The World Around
From Great Goddess to Jealous God

The Aftermath of the Holy War

The awesome strength in numbers and fighting ability shown by the united peoples of the Goddess in 1186 B.C. (see Linear–B chapter) had been devastating for the patriarchal tribes of the eastern Mediterranean. This was a particularly brutal holy war between the peoples of the Goddess and those eastern Mediterranean peoples which had accepted patriarchy. Only the military genius of Ramesses III had saved the Egyptians from being obliterated as well. The pharaoh had been prepared for the attack. As it was, one major tactical error, made by the command of the Sea Peoples at the end of their successful campaign, caused the collapse of the attack and allowed the survival of patriarchy. The Hittites were wiped out, never to rise again, the pirate states of the Achaians in Greece were devastated, the entire eastern Mediterranean seaboard was in smoking ruins and almost depopulated. Then the full might of the huge fleet from the islands of the Great Green Ocean bore down on Egypt. They sailed up the Nile river and were met by the pharaoh's soldiers who lined the river banks, armed with longbows, which the Sea Peoples did not have. All they had was swords and spears, none of them long enough to reach the soldiers on the shore, and the attackers, clustered on their ships, were massacred. Some units managed to land and fight, one of them being Odysseus' force as described by Homer in the Odyssey, but the attack was a total failure. The large sailing ships could not manoeuvre in the shallow river and ran aground. The oar-driven smaller ships of the Pharaoh made sure that no-one escaped. After being given a very difficult time, the surviving prisoners of war were given a chance to form mercenary units to fight the pharaoh's wars in the east. After seven years of faithful service they were given their ships back and were allowed to sail home. The battle for the Goddess was lost, never to be re-kindled. The wailing in England, Scotland, Norway, the Baltic, Euskadi etc. could be heard for many years after. A whole generation of young men, tens of thousands of them, had been lost in the fighting. The whole sad story is told on the walls of Ramesses III temple at Medinet Habu. Homer's 'Nestoi' in the "Odyssey" describes the home-coming of some of the survivors of the attacking army.

It must have taken at least two generations for the eastern tribes to recover somewhat from their devastating defeat and for the leaders to come together to assess what had happened. Revenge with force was out of the question, they could not get at the homelands of the Sea Peoples in the Great Green, because they lacked the ships and the skilled sailors. So they decided to organize a Council where all the leaders of the patriarchal tribes would come together to discuss strategy for the future. Where this took place we do not know yet, but it seems to me that this could well have taken place in the Anatolian province of Kizzuwadna. Archaeologists have found and explored an important religious town named Nerik where a library of clay tablets was said to have been found, but no one seems to know where these tablets ended up or who controls them.

Nerik
.ne – eri – ik.
ene – errime – ikaskintza
come to me – excellent – instruction/teachings
"Come to me for excellent teachings."

It may be that this was the training centre for the missionary groups. In order to put a name to this important meeting, let us call it the "Nerik Council," held possibly 1130 B.C. Its goal was to set a new course for the civilization of the world. The people of Nerik probably spoke the Luvian language and to this day are known as the Luvians or Levites.

At the Nerik Council it was decided that the great strength of the peoples of the Goddess lay in 1) their universal language, 2) their ancient, caring religion of the Goddess, 3) their naval control over all the seas and 4) their unity of purpose. It was well known that the peoples of the Great Goddess were peaceful and hospitable folk, but at the same time could generate enormous strength and unity when aroused. The use of force had therefore been ruled out by male domination from the beginning, to be replaced by diplomacy, underhandedness and superior magic, which included reading, writing and arithmetic.

The council members decided to tackle the most vulnerable part of the ancient religion. Dissatisfaction with the human sacrifice of one very special young man in each of a number of religious centres every eight years, was widespread and in some places had already been changed to be practiced symbolically i.e. either by replacement of Tammuz with a criminal or prisoner, or by an animal. The human sacrifice was still being practiced in Scotland, the only place in the Great Green ocean where this took place.

THE INVERTED RELIGION

If the patriarchal tribes were to succeed in their desire to defeat the Goddess, they would have to stop fighting among themselves and act united. This meant that the core religion of male domination had to be well organized, standardized and generally accepted. It is not known who had the original idea of turning literally all the attributes and aspects of the Goddess' faith inside out in their eventually successful quest to destroy the ancient Goddess religion but that is what was done. They then decided to accept this negative image of the ancient gylanic faith as the foundation of their own male-dominated religion. In doing so they changed the semi-democratic and holistic character of the old faith into dictatorship and dualism, which meant the introduction of confrontation, discord, selfishness and guilt into all aspects of life. The foundation was thus laid for the well organized woman-despising Proto-Judaic religion. The process which the ancient patriarchs set in motion is still with us today. Their main goal is expressed in the word **"armageddon,"** ar.-.ma-age-ed.-.do-on.:

ar. – .ma – age – ed. – .do – on.
ara – ama – age – ede – edo – one
aragikor – ama – ageriko – ederrak hartu – edonongo – onezkero
lustful – Goddess – notorious – defeated – everywhere – right now
**"The lustful and notorious Goddess must be defeated
everywhere and right now."** (2Kings 23:13-14)

With this goal in mind, the leadership of the new religion drew up a task list. It was decided to work towards:

Religion:

1) The entire world shall be under male control and shall have one supreme male deity.

2) The Ashera/Goddess religion and all evidence of its past must be destroyed everywhere and forgotten forever.

3) Eliminate the tribal system by disposing of the original male and female clergy, by totally destroying the holy sites of the Great Goddess, barrow tombs and the peoples' places of ancestor worship.

4) Alter the ancient belief in re-incarnation by teaching that life without end is

only for god. This god would sit in judgment at the end of life and decide the place of residence for the soul. This eliminated the need for huge barrow tombs of the ancestors, which had been the religious centre and pride of each tribe.

5) Create decadent names for anything to do with the ancient religion e.g. the meaning of the name Akela, which originally meant Great Goddess, became 'witch.' The male clergy of the Goddess, the Abade, were renamed druids.

Women:

1) No woman shall ever be without a man to supervise and direct her. At weddings she shall be formally transferred from her father to her new husband.

2) No woman shall ever function as clergy of the supreme god, and in addition shall never be placed in a position of decision making or teaching (1 Tim. 2: 11-14).

3) Reduce the sexuality and attractiveness of women by:

  a) genital mutilation,

  b) placing all women in subservient positions doing menial tasks at low pay.

  c) preventing women from receiving education.

4) Women must remain at home, faithful to their husbands and shall not talk to strangers.

Missionary efforts:

1) Missionary training schools shall be created to train highly educated teams which will then peacefully penetrate assigned areas where the Goddess still reigns. They are to convert the target people to the new patriarchal religion.

2) Teams of highly qualified linguists shall be attached to such missionary groups to manipulate the language of the people of the Goddess into a multiplicity of invented languages, so that peoples in different countries can no longer talk to each other.

3) The newly established clergy is to direct the organization of strong, disciplined nations, capable of fighting wars and to select, install and crown autocratic kings with subservient queens.

4) Replace all ancient legends and history of the people with a whole new vision of an aggressive male-dominated past, heralding an all-seeing, all-knowing, all-controlling male deity in the sky. All repositories anywhere of written pre-patriarchal knowledge must be burned or otherwise destroyed. Any new discoveries of pre-Judaic writing must be placed under strict control of the patriarchal authorities and hidden from the people until cleansed, altered or destroyed by approved clergy.

General:

1) Make sexuality into something very dirty and despicable and describe sexual festivities as abhorrent free-for-alls. The traditional male kilts are forbidden, because they allow a quick display of male sexual prowess. From then on men will wear long pants, and women long skirts.

2) Phase out the memorizing tradition by teaching bright boys to read and write and to rely on books and less on memory. All existing books are to be censored, cleansed and if necessary re-written, to guide the new society. Written knowledge must be encouraged. Memorized knowledge is far more stable because it is for life, which makes it impossible to manipulate for two or three generations. Dispose of the memory men and women.

3) Inscriptions and writings in unintelligible script shall be immediately destroyed, even if they have nothing to do with the Goddess religion. All pre-Judaic statues shall be defaced by cutting off the noses.

4) Introduce land ownership and divide the communally held lands and herds of the tribes by rewarding important warriors with large holdings.

Inventing New Languages

The decision to create a variety of new languages and scripts required highly educated scholars and schools in which to train them. Linguistics became the first academic subject to be taught in state institutions which later evolved into our universities, a tradition at least 5,200 years old. Confused remnants of the once great discipline of linguistics are still being taught in our universities today, but the ancient language invention science has been forgotten.

Adopt the Egyptian System of Word Agglutination

Inventing a new language when there is only one existing, may sound like an impossible task. A new and practical language did not come out of thin air or a dream. Fortunately for the Luvian priests, the ancient Saharan language was extremely logical and well-organized, it having been the product of much earlier linguists who had taken the first three letters, vowel-consonant-vowel, of groups of words and assigned each of such VCV's a number of mostly related meanings:

aba: priest, rectory, advantage, surpass, shade
abi: departure, speed, impulsive, begin, skillful

ibi: vagabond, nomadic, behave, impassible, to cross
ade: temple, gentle, adorn, courteous, prepare
ida: write, document, clerk, subject, title, underline, literature
odo: blood, martyr, rage, relative, angry, cruel, apathy
oha: bed, concubine, spontaneous, lookout, distracted

This structure allowed plenty of opportunity for manipulation. Any associated information could be attached or agglutinated to the first VCV syllable. Methods were slowly developed which could convert and mutilate the language in such a manner that the final product was not recognizable as a dialect of the Universal Language, but had its own invented rules of grammar and structure. The first step in this direction was the complete reversal of the periphrastic word order of Saharan.

The genius who invented this reversal of the ancient word order created the basics of the "family of Indo-European languages," something none of our modern linguists have been able to fathom, so far. The priests thus laid the foundation for a large number of invented languages which were so designed that they looked like they were genetically related but were only a formulaically related grouping.

That the established order was deliberately turned topsy-turvy is shown in the meaning of many important words, which were reversed such as in:

woman to man: *andre* (woman) which became *andros* (male) but in reality was an abbreviation of *androzale* (fond of woman).

black became white: the Universal word *u'it / u'itsu* (tar) was used to make the Dutch word "wit," English "white," German "weiss."

hot to cold: *kalda* (heat) became "kalt" in German, "cold" in English. (In Latin "caldus" still means "hot." Also consider English "scalding.")

cold to hot: *hotz* (cold) became "hot" in English, "heiss" in German.

friend to foe: the Bible tells us that a "host" is an enemy, armed might; this agrees with Basque *hostu/ohostu* (to rob, to pillage). Yet "host and hospitable" are now words for "friend" in English.

good to bad: the highly respected male clergy of the Goddess was called *abade* (priest). By removing the two outer vowels, our English word "bad" was created.

This game of word distortion and meaning reversal was carried on during the next millennia in all invented languages. A word such as *ashera*, from ash – era, *ashola-era* (care-ing) was used to create our English word "ash," because "ashera" was also the name of the trees planted beside the Goddess' altar and the Bible had ordered the tree to be burned. (Deut. 12:3 and 2 Kings 23:15; asherim is plural).

COLLISION BETWEEN TWO IDEOLOGIES

Archaeologist Dr. Marija Gimbutas in her book "The Civilization of the Goddess" (p.396) came to a somewhat different conclusion:

> *The Indo-European society was warlike, exogamic, patriarchal, patrilineal and patrilocal, with a strong clannic organization and social hierarchy which gave prominence to the warrior class. Their main gods were male and depicted as warriors. There is no possibility that this pattern of social organization could have developed out of the Old European matrilineal, matricentric and endogamic balanced society. Therefore the appearance of the Indo-Europeans in Europe represents a collision of two ideologies, not an evolution.*

I took this train of thought one step further by suggesting that **this collision between ideologies was the result of planned religious chicanery** and enforced by the clergy of all the male-dominated cults. I cannot agree with her that Indo-Europeans were involved because in my opinion there never have been Indo-Europeans, the I-E theory is a fallacy.

MAJOR CHANGES OCCURRED WHEN MALE DOMINATION ARRIVED

The early goddess religion had been a holistic one in which the men were either away shepherding, out on the ocean or hunting. Male and female had complemented each other in mutual respect and a well-balanced division of labour and responsibilities. The arrival of agriculture upset this ancient way of life. The men were now at home and demanded a say in the running of the community. Male domination meant that the former state of affairs was turned into dualistic confrontation between the sexes. Not only did the male demand the respect formerly accorded the woman, but also to dominate and use and dispose at will. The priests wanted to make sure that paternity was always known, and that never again would the children and the children's inheritance be handled through the female line. The result was that married life for many women often became hell on earth. The German word for wife, **"Frau"** expresses this mentality well; it was coined from:

f. – .rau

fa-arau

afa – arau

happy – discipline

"happy (under/with) discipline"

and the Prussians' insecurity made sure that this discipline was enforced. Here follow some more changes that were brought about by the reversal of the Goddess' attributes.

From:	To:
Female Deity or Goddess	Male Deity or God
Ashera means "caring disposition"	YHWH, means "frightening" (YHaWaliH, ihabali)
the Goddess was part of The All (the universe)	the God created The All (the universe)
Goddess immanent within every person	God is transcendent, distant
idols revered	idols forbidden
both female and male clergy	male clergy only
clergy dressed in white	clergy dressed in black
communal thinking: we, us, the tribe	selfish thinking: I, me, my son
individual responsibility, consensus sought	leadership gives orders, dictatorial
community rights	individual rights
all property and land communally owned	all property and land privately owned
artwork lavished on boats, religious objects	artwork lavished on personal jewelry, weapons
man born from woman	woman created from man's rib
encourages individuality within family limits	conformity demanded, independence punished
women adored, held in high esteem	women cannot be trusted, must always be under control of men
no slaves, all people free, women persons	slavery, males fully human, women non-persons
generally egalitarian	patriarchal, stratified, dictatorial society
martyrdom incomprehensible	martyrdom encouraged
writing for clergy only, memorizing required	memorizing discouraged, writing required
every child wanted and part of the family	only children whose paternity is known are wanted
unqualified welcome to all strangers	strangers are the enemy, keep away
respect for all that lives, mankind part of nature	all that lives created for man's use by god
large communal projects, people have little	ruling classes gather personal riches
universal language	many invented languages
the world lies open, no boundaries, hospitality	rigid boundaries, tight controls, strangers killed
one world, one people, one faith, one language	nationalism, many peoples, many languages, several male dominated religions
prophetic thinking part of faith, encouraged	prophetic thinking discouraged

doctrines approach the truth	doctrines are the truth
sexuality beautiful, uninhibited, celebrated	sexuality dirty, degrading, despised, hidden
first menstruation a blessing, to be celebrated	first menstruation a curse, to be quarantined
direct access to deity through prayer	path to deity via church hierarchy
genital mutilation unknown	male and female genital mutilation enforced
the drums of the Goddess	the trumpets of male domination
tattooing encouraged and done by the clergy	tattooing considered degrading, discouraged
animal sacrifices common, one voluntary human every eight years	animal sacrifices common among early Hebrews, no human
individual names had to be earned	individual names given at birth
life unending through re-incarnation	life ends in judgment day, choice: hell or heaven
death is part of living	death is the end of living
civilization based on caring and respect	civilization based on greed and shortsightedness

This Artificial World

The coming of patriarchy with its insistence on gathering riches, has removed us from living natural lives in a healthy world. First we were part of, and inseparable from creation, but now the new definition of the word **"creation"** tells us what it means:

.k.-.re-ati-on.;

.k. – .re – ati – on.
oke – ere – ati – one
okergabe – erregali – atikitzaile – onetsi
pristine – gift – faithful – to bless
"Pristine gift to the blessed faithful."

This hints that the world still existed in near pristine condition when patriarchy arrived. The trouble is that the "blessed faithful" turned greedy and soon started plundering everything in the sea, on the land and even from the air; it didn't take the faithful long to destroy nature's riches. In just one short century, since patriarchy finally arrived, North America has lost well over half of its agricultural topsoil, most of its forest wealth and all of its enormous fish resources. We have polluted much of the fresh water in our lakes and poisoned the air in many cities. North America was pristine before patriarchy arrived, not very long ago. Isn't it time that we started to pay attention to and learn from the holistic manner in which the world environment was managed before patriarchy? Which system was more civilized and which one gave us happier lives? If the will doesn't exist to stop the madness of "progress," nature will send some means to stop the population explosion, limit the greed and restore some balance between people and the natural world. There is no "nice" way to do it. Better learn from the past.

VII

THE FINAL SOLUTION

THE FINAL SOLUTION
HOLOCAUST WITHOUT EQUAL

INTRODUCTION

Much is known about the witch hunts of the 16th and 17th centuries. In some countries, a great deal of the original Inquisition documentation has survived in archives such as in the "Archivo Historico National" in Madrid, and these records have been used by a number of scholars from different countries to document the "witch" phenomenon. What emerged from their independent and unemotional assessments amounted to a terrible indictment of the politics of the church in Rome. Most of these researchers concluded that the brutal burnings had been a terrible mistake; but were they really a mistake? It was also clearly shown that among the members of the Inquisition there were some very responsible, honest and courageous people, who were, however, unable to control the excesses of some of their colleagues or of the local government officials, once the process was out of hand. My translations of some of the names, associated with this dreadful epidemic of burnings and hangings tell their own tragic stories.

WITCHCRAFT IS AN IMAGINARY OFFENCE

The church knew from the beginning that witchcraft did not exist. Its own staff said so. The social anthropologist Evans-Pritchard wrote in 1935:

> *"Witchcraft is an imaginary offense because it is impossible. A witch cannot do what he/she is supposed to do and has in fact no real existence. A sorcerer, on the other hand, may make magic to kill his neighbours. The magic will not kill them, but he can and no doubt, often does with that intention."*

One of the bright lights during the time of the witch craze, which had thrown a cloud of death and despair over the beautiful Basque countryside, was the Bishop of Pamplona, the influential Antonio Venegas de Figueroa. His investigations had led him to believe that the witch craze was almost entirely based on deceit and self-delusion, and he gave expression to this view in a letter to the Inquisition in March 1610. After interrogating various people the bishop established that there had been absolutely no mention or knowledge of witchcraft before the persecutions had commenced. Many of the inhabitants had gone to the witch burnings in France and brought back the knowledge from there. Before that time the people had known nothing about witch sects or aquelarres (witch gatherings) or evil arts (Henningsen p.127). The bishop had learned that uneducated and lonely people or people who deviated from the norm of their society, were the first to be supposed to be members of this secret confederation, where all the virtues of society were inverted.

What he probably did not know was that the very name of his own Basque language had a special hidden message built into it: **Euskera**

eu – us. – .ke – era
eu – usa – ake – era
euki – usaiako – akela – erabildura
to retain/preserve – usual/traditional – Great Goddess – usage/speech
"We preserve the traditional speech of the Great Goddess."

The name 'akela' at that time was officially translated as 'witch' but some of the people still knew that it was the old name for the Great Goddess of their ancestors. The secret meaning of Euskera was known in Rome and regarded as anathema by the R.C. church leaders. The spelling of the language name was ordered to be changed to Euskara, to hide the ake, a name change which was only reluctantly accepted by the people, but is now found in the dictionary together with the proper spelling.

Alonso de Salazar Frias, one of the Inquisition's own scholars, who was sent to report on the epidemic of witchcraft, wrote in 1612: "There were neither witches nor bewitched until they were talked and written about" (Henningson, p.ix). So why did the church unleash this most demonic of all holocausts? The church had kept de Salazar's, the bishop's and similar reports secret and it was not until three centuries later that several of Salazar's (purposely mislabeled) submissions to the Inquisition's leadership were re-discovered in Madrid by the American historian Henry Charles Lea, who used them in his monumental book "Inquisition of Spain" (p 211-237). The question now is: was there a reason for the church to continue the witch charade for so many years (throughout the 16th, 17th and part of the 18th century) when it knew very well that there never had been any witches or aquelarres? The word "aquelarre" comes from Basque akelarre, akela-arre, Akela (witch) arremankor (social): "The witches' social (gathering)." Our English word **"witch"** is taken straight from the Basque language; the first three letters of the verb *itxuraldatu* (to transform, to change shape) were used; *itx*, pronounced "itch" with a "w" stuck onto it to mask the Basque origin. Changing shape was something the "witches" themselves had admitted to during questioning and torture, to escape from the supervision of their husbands by squeezing through the keyhole of their front door.

But first I must make it clear that there is a great difference between "witch-craft," also called the traditional distrust between people, and the "witch-craze," also known as "demonical witchcraft" which is the product of "syncretism of the witch beliefs of the common people with those of the more specialized or educated classes" (Henningsen p.391). The last type was spread by the preaching of the fanatical Franciscan Zealots, telling fabricated, detailed witch stories from the pulpits. The existence of witches, as a group or coven, was therefore a fictitious product of the church's own propaganda.

The Roman Catholic clergy knew four classes of non-believers:

1. the **heretics**, who were Gnostic Christians from Ireland, Southern France and North Africa.
2. the **witches**, a class invented by the church itself to eliminate the last speakers of the Saharan language of the Goddess,
3. the **pagans**, who were polytheists (believing in many Gods), practicing animal sacrifices, like the Romans and Greeks had been, and the Vikings and Germans still were accused of, but were not,
4. the **heathens**, also called Gentiles, who were the people of the ancient monotheistic, gylanic society of the Goddess.

THE EXECUTION OF THE WITCHES

"Thou shalt not suffer a witch to live" Exodus 22:18.

In Spain the burning of heretics had been on the decline in the late 16th century and none had taken place since the auto-da-fe (act of faith) at Logroño in 1593. At that time, twenty-three cases had been prepared: six for Judaism, one for Mohammedanism, one for Lutheranism, one for bigamy, twelve for blasphemous or heretical utterances, and two for impersonating agents of the Inquisition. There were no witches around yet. The auto-da-fe's had attracted many people to witness the event, but nothing compared to what was to come. The people who had been executed in 1593 had been punished for offenses which mattered little to the local population. The auto-da-fe of 1610 was very different. Fifty three people were to be sentenced, but eleven of the group were covered with figures of devils and flames, because they were condemned to die for witchcraft. In reality there were only six left alive, the other five had "died" in prison and were represented by effigies carried on long poles. These eleven women were their own local people, and they were going to die for a non-existent offense. This was not justice, this was known to the people as a sacrifice.

The peoples' response to the happenings at Logroño had been astonishing to the church representatives. The scene was described by the inquisitorial commissioner at Vitoria, the treasurer Pedro Gamiz:

> *I can assure your Grace that never before have so many people been gathered together in this town. It is estimated that over thirty thousand souls have assembled here from France, Aragon, Navarra, Vizkaya and parts of Castilla. The reason for such enthusiasm was the publication of the announcement that the vile sect of the witches was to be revealed at this auto-de-fe.* (Henningson p.184).

But Pedro Gamiz did not realize what he had witnessed, or at least could not admit it. The attraction had been something totally different. The Tribunal sent another account of the auto-da-fe to the Inquisition's "La Suprema" on November 13, 1610:

> *The people observed the deepest silence during the entire ceremony and paid the greatest attention, and no untoward incidents of any kind occurred. The auto-de-fe has been to the great edification of the people. For all agree that never before have they experienced anything more solemn, more strange, and more authoritative.* (Henningson p.194).

What these Inquisition members had witnessed was the last of the human sacrifices of the Goddess religion in western Europe, at least that is how the local people had seen it. It is appropriate to compare this event with the human sacrifice of the Prince in the Scottish Hebrides (also of the early pharaohs in the First Cataract). Large crowds had, centuries before, travelled to the north half of the Isle of Hinba, (from *hinbasio* meaning invasion) when the northern Tammuz was sacrificed in the whirlpool of Corryvreckan, 70 km west of Glasgow. People from as far away as Norway, the Baltic states and even Russia had attended these sacrifices, once every eight years. No wonder the church in Rome quickly changed the name of the island from Hinba to Jura (from *juramendu* meaning cursed), when they gained the upper hand. Those observing the sacrifice had done so because speaking at such a holy sacrament would have jeopardized a quick reincarnation for the young man, called Tammuz in the Bible, into a newborn body. Therefore the entire sacrifice sacrament was conducted in absolute silence. It is likely that something very similar happened at Christ's crucifixion.

The Actors

The names of five church organizations come up regularly in the reports of the inquisitioners: 1) the Benedictines, by far the oldest order (582 AD), 2) the Franciscans (1209), 3) the Dominicans (1215), 4) the Inquisition (1231), and last 5) the Jesuits (1540). Originally they all had different functions to perform, as the translations of the names of the organizations show.

The Benedictines.

St. Benedict started his new order in 528 A.D. and gathered a large number of highly educated and dedicated Christian men around him. The name Benedict urges people to come and join him in the evangelization process:

Benedict, .be-ene-edi-ik.-.t.,

.be	abe	*abe*	cross
ene	ene	*ene*	come to me
edi	edi	*ediren*	to find
ik.	ika	*ikasgintza*	learning
.t.	ate	*ateratu*	to take along with you

"Come to me (under) the cross and find learning to take along with you."

The Benedictines had been the first monastic order created by the church of Rome. For 1000 years prior to the witch craze they had laboured, often under great duress, to bring Judeo-Christianity to western and central Europe. In the process they created new countries out of tribal regions and invented a new language for each such new country. They were pioneer scholars who worked towards a continental goal but were never very involved in the nitty-gritty business of eliminating out-of-the-way pockets of people who had either been missed in the overall evangelization effort, or of searching out people who insisted on maintaining their own ancient religion and language. Putting the finishing touches on the evangelization effort required a different type of training and mentality among the monks. Although the Benedictine name appears in some of the documents relating to the witch trials, this was only because of their historical and omnipresent role in bringing Judeo-Christianity to all of western Europe. Their main opposition had come from the local Priestess and her male clergy (abadeak) of the Goddess religion and to a lesser degree from the Gnostic Irish evangelists, but certainly not from the witches, who had not been invented yet. To their eternal credit, the Benedictines decided to have nothing to do with the witch-craze that festered and exploded all around them and would rather see the demise of their order than participate in something so very offensive to Christian teachings. The horrible task of carrying out the accusing, judging and killing was assigned to the Dominicans and Franciscans, who enthusiastically carried the torch.

The Franciscans

The Franciscan friars were a ragtag group of urban wandering lay preachers and looked their part as unkempt and threadbare evangelists. They appeared little different from the wild-eyed prophets who had roamed the countryside of France for many years. The fact that they expanded into a strong continent-wide organization must be attributed to leadership provided by some church officials who saw a use for their rather primitive mentality. Their evangelical zeal and simple education made them ideally suited for being brainwashed against the perceived threat posed by witchcraft and the terrible witch aquelarres which persisted in inverting all of the virtues of society. Again, their task is written in the name:

Franciscan, f.-.ra-an.-.ki-is.-.ka-an.,

.f.	fe	*fedehausketa*	heresy
.ra	era	*errausketa*	destruction
an.	ane	*anega*	measure
.ki	eki	*ekinaz*	persevering
is.	isi	*isil*	quiet
.ka	ika	*ikaskintza*	instruction
an.	ana	*anaitasun*	brotherhood

"Destruction of the heresy (requires) persevering measures and quiet instruction by the brotherhood."

It seems that St. Francis was given his name after the Order had been formed and the task had been assigned. History books tell us that Pope Innocent III gave St. Francis of Assisi approval in 1209 to create an Order whose goal was a life of preaching and penance. The analysis of the name of the Order tells a different story because the eradication of the heresy was its stated reason for being. The various popes named Innocent were far from being as innocent as their name would make us believe. The subsequent endorsement of the hated "Malleus Maleficarum," the witches' handbook, and its ruthless and devilish instructions made Innocent VIII possibly the most brutal and decadent of all popes.

There were three types of Franciscans:

1) the Zealots, insisting on observance of the primitive rule of total poverty. One of their reform groups became the Capuchins.
2) the Laxists who favoured many mitigations.
3) the Moderates, wanting a structure that permitted some form of communal possessions. Their friars' houses in Paris and Oxford became schools of theology.

It appears that the Franciscans participated in the witch trials in an initiating, supporting and facilitating function by gathering and manufacturing evidence such as for the Logroño witch tribunal (in Spain), for which they interrupted their preaching crusade to present a "dressed toad" and pots of "witches' salve" as evidence of witchcraft (Henningson p.345). They were deeply involved in spying out potential witches and reporting them to the authorities. The Franciscans were not beyond forcibly extracting false confessions such as done for instance by the monk Fray Juan de Ladron. He took part in the witch-hunt in Alava in the capacity of one of the Inquisition's special emissaries. Three women were reported by him after the priest at Larrea, Martin Lopez de Lazarraga, had tied them by the hands and neck, assisted by de Ladron, who then threatened to take the women to the Logroño showcase witch-trial if they did not confess. They did confess but later told de Salazar what happened. Lazarraga had been appointed inquisitorial commissioner and put into the head of one of the women the idea of accusing six uncooperative local priests of witchcraft. At Logroño many people were tortured into admitting anything the Franciscans told them to say. One of the women, Mariquita de Atauri, felt so terribly distressed after denouncing so many innocent people under torture that she drowned herself in the river near her house. The main culprit in extracting the confessions was identified again as the Franciscan Fray de Ladron (Henningson p.292). The still existing records tell of many such cases where the Franciscans were instrumental in extracting confessions and reporting all to the witch-tribunals, complete with samples of witches' regalia and concoctions. Their involvement in the witch burnings can only be called revolting.

The Dominicans

Dominic was a Castilian priest of aristocratic birth who was assigned the task of countering the wayward Catharist Christians. In years gone by, this task had been the responsibility of the **Order of Cistercian** monks since 1209 when Pope Innocent III had ordered them to preach a crusade against the Albigencians. They were called the "White Benedictines" because of their white habits. The Cistercians had split off from the Benedictine Order in 1098 A.D. but these highly educated and motivated monks had no stomach for getting involved in a murderous crusade against the Gnostic Christians, who had been of great help to the Benedictines in their initial evangelical work, centuries before. The translation of their name tells us that their assigned task was to educate the people, not to make war against them:

Cistercian, .ki-is.-.te-er.-.ki-ia-an.

.ki	eki	*ekinaldi*	perseverance
is.	isi	*isil*	quiet
.te	ite	*itegun*	work performed

er.	era	*erakutsi*	to educate
.ki	aki	*akigabe*	tireless
ia	ia	*iaio*	cheerful
an.	ana	*anaia*	brother

"With quiet perseverance the cheerful brothers tirelessly work to educate."

The Catharist clergy had a spiritual elite who were famous for their austerity and self-denial. To be able to argue religion with these highly educated Christians on an equal footing, Dominic decided that his evangelists had to be a clerical order from the beginning and needed specialized education. This was quite a change from the training the Cistercians had received to overcome the biblical arguments of the devoted Catharist theologians. From the beginning, the Dominicans therefore were a learned order and all efforts were aimed at furthering the needs of the pastoral mission. In 1215 Pope Innocent III gave provisional approval to Dominic to create an institute of preachers to convert the deeply devoted Gnostic Albigencians of southern France, the "heretics," to the "proper" form of Christianity. The church in Rome was on record as having created this special order of monks to preach against the Albigencians and to prepare for the entire infamous episode of the crusade against these austere Christians. The translation of the name "Dominican," however, appears to have no relationship to the Albigencians, because they had nothing to do with Hallowmass.

Dominican, do-omi-ini-ika-an.,

do	do	*dongakeria*	perversity
omi	omi	*Omia Saindu*	Hallowmass
ini	ini	*initz/ainitz*	many
ika	ika	*ikara*	horror
an.	ana	*anaitu*	to unite, to gather

"(During) the perversity of Hallowmass, many gather (to watch) in horror."

This name tells us that the Dominican Order was created to combat the Gentiles and the human sacrifice of the ancient Ashera religion, which took place at Hallow Mass (November 1). The only place in western Europe where this took place was at the north end of the island of Jura (*juramenu* means cursed) in Scotland. The fact that this name was given to the order at that time probably means that this ancient sacrifice continued to be practiced and that a major effort was needed to eliminate it. Dominic likely was given his name after the name for the Order had been decided. He may not even have known what it meant. When the Inquisition was established in 1231, the Dominicans were entrusted with its organization, the judging, convicting and the execution of heretics and witches. They created schools of theology at the Universities of

Paris, Bologne, Oxford and Cologne to train and brainwash a fanatic cadre of monks.

Especially in the mountainous regions, many people still adhered to their ancient Goddess religion, guided by their priestesses. The Inquisition and the Dominicans concentrated on the Alps of southern Germany, Switzerland, northern Italy and eastern France. This was the Ligurian region from which the Benedictines for many centuries had obtained their Basque speaking (Basque/Ligurian) grammarians who had been instrumental in creating the new languages of Europe. To detect and destroy the adherents to the Goddess religion, the use of torture had been officially authorized by Pope Innocent IV in 1252. The monks were to extract admissions of heresy, sorcery and witchcraft from the people, many of whom were the families of the grammarians, working for the Benedictines. The witch craze in the Alps and southern Germany killed more people than in any other region but next to nothing of the documentation has survived.

The friars took the initiative in collecting ancient lore connected with the peoples' belief in magic. When the time was right for the witch hunt to begin, all of this gathered hearsay and gossip was authoritatively assembled into the "Malleus Maleficarum," the witch hunter's handbook. The Dominicans trained and guided the judges of the Inquisition and wrote justifications why people should be so very cruelly put to death, in spite of the commandment: "Thou shalt not kill." They laid the entire blame for the existence of witches on the pre-Christian Goddess religion although the witches and their aquelarres had been a total fabrication of the church of Rome. But it was a fabrication which served a very specific purpose, which was the elimination of the last pockets of the adherents to the Goddess religion, the Gnostic heretics and of the ancient language of the Goddess which many still spoke; it was to be the final solution by "Christian" Europe. They succeeded everywhere except in Euskadi, where the Basque language is still spoken to this day.

The Inquisition

Pope Gregory IX instituted the papal Inquisition in 1231 for the apprehension and trial of heretics such as the Cathari and Waldenses. The medieval Inquisition functioned in northern Italy and southern France. In 1478 Pope Sixtus IV authorized the Spanish Inquisition to combat apostate former Jews and Muslims, and the heretic Alumbrados. This inquisition proved so severe that Pope Sixtus IV tried to interfere but the Spanish crown forced the pope to give up his efforts. In 1483 Sixtus IV authorized a grand-inquisitor for Castile, a few months later for Aragon, Valencia and Catalonia. The first inquisitor was de Torquemada. The name Inquisition means:

Inquisition, ink-isi-ishi-on.,

ink.	inke	*inkestatu*	to make an investigation
isi	izi	*izigarrikeria*	atrocity
ishi	ixi	*ixil*	calmly
on.	one	*onegitasun*	extreme patience

"Calmly and with extreme patience make an investigation of the atrocities."

The person responsible for organizing the Inquisition in Spain, the Dominican Tomas de Torquemada, is regarded as the epitome of the zealous witch hunter:

Tomas de Torquemada: .to-oma-as./ .de/ .to-or.-.ke-ema-ada,

.to	eto	*etorkizko*	tribal
oma	oma	*oma*	grandmother
as./	ase	*aserregorritu*	to become furious
.de/	ede	*ederrak hartu*	to be defeated
.to	ito	*itotzaile*	murderer
or.	ori	*ori*	that
.ke	ike	*ikertu*	to investigate, prosecute
ema	ema	*ematxar*	prostitute, witch
ada	ada	*adarra sartu*	to deceive

"The tribal grandmother makes me furious; that murderer must be defeated and the deceiving prostitute prosecuted."

This, of course, referred to the female head of the matrilineally organized tribe, or even the Priestess herself. The murder must refer to the voluntary death of a young man (Tammuz) who had participated in the Sacred Marriage with the Priestess on May 1, and then was sacrificed seven and a half years later on November 1 (Hallowmass) so others might live. In NW Europe this sacrifice took place in the whirlpool of Corrivrecken, in Egypt in the First Cataract of the Nile. The death of Tammuz is still being remembered in our churches on Good Friday, when many Christians in Europe and elsewhere wear black mourning clothes to church (Ezekiel 8:14). This most holy sacrament of the pre-Christian religion was an extremely ancient tradition, the memory of which the church in Rome was unable to extinguish and therefore decided to incorporate it into the church's calendar as Hallowe'en, thoroughly ridiculed and distorted.

The Malleus Maleficarum

The Dominican monks Heinrich Kramer and James Sprenger assembled many fairy tales and magic stories, nightmares, hearsay, confessions and accusations and put this all together as factual information in what became the handbook for the witch hunters, examiners, torturers and executioners, called the Malleus Maleficarum, a title which was translated as Hammer of Witches. It was published in 1487, but two years previously the authors had secured a bull from

Pope Innocent VIII, authorizing them to continue the witch hunt in the Alps which they had already instituted, against the opposition from clergy and secular authorities. They reprinted the bull of December 5, 1484 to make it appear that the whole book enjoyed papal sanction. Both names of the authors tell us about their fanaticism:

Heinrich Kramer, .he-in.-.ri-ik.-.h. / .k.-.ra-ame-er.,

.he	ihe	*ihesegin*	to escape, to run away
in.	ino	*inorenganatu*	to change shape
.ri	ori	*orritz*	feast
ik.	ika	*ikarragarri*	frightening
.h./	aho	*aho*	cave entrance
.k.	ake	*akela*	witch, Great Goddess
.ra	era	*erraustu*	to annihilate, to burn
ame	ame	*amestxar*	nightmare
er.	ero	*erotiko*	erotic

"(They) change shape to escape to the frightening feast at the cave entrance. Burn the witches with the erotic nightmares."

James Sprenger, ja-ame-es. / .s.-.p.-.re-en.-.ge-er.,

ja	ja	*jainkogabe*	godless, sinful
ame	ame	*ameslilura*	fantasy
es./	ese/	*esetsi*	to attack
.s.	ase	*aserrez*	angrily
.p.	epa	*epaipatu*	to sentence
.re	are	*aren*	her
en.	-ena	*-ena*	suffix to express future
ge	age	*ageriki*	publicly
er.	era	*erraustu*	to burn

"To attack that sinful fantasy, he angrily sentenced her to be burned publicly."

Anybody with a grudge or suspicion, very young children included, could accuse anyone of witchcraft and be listened to with attention; anyone who wanted someone else's property, or wife could accuse. Any old woman living alone, anyone with a disfigurement, with a physical or mental problem, in fact anybody was likely to be accused. Open hunting season was declared on women, especially herb gatherers, midwives, widows and spinsters. Women who had no man to supervise them were of course highly suspicious. It has been estimated by Dr. Marija Gimbutas, professor of archaeology at the University of California, that as many as 9 million people, overwhelmingly women, were burned or hanged during the witch-craze. For nearly 250 years the Witches' Hammer was the guidebook for the witch hunters, but again some of the inquisitioners had misgivings about this devilish book. In a letter dated November 27, 1538 de Salazar advised the inquisitioners not to believe everything they read in Malleus Maleficarum, even if the authors write about it as something they themselves have seen and investigated (Henningson p.347).

The Jesuits

 Special obedience to the pope was the hallmark of the Jesuits. Pope Paul III had approved the outline of the order's organization on Sept. 27, 1540. The order functioned quite differently from the other orders with its special flexibility, allowing them to get involved around the globe. The Jesuits were cosmopolitan Christian clerics, trained to function in the urbane world of the courts; many of them were distinguished classicists. They were the educators and confessors of the leading men of France and Spain and were highly respected. Many of them were of Basque birth, which made them ideally suited to communicate with the thousands of bewildered Basque speaking refugees who had fled the brutal French witch hunt and trials, ordered by King Henry IV of France. They had fled across the border to Spain because at least half of the women had been accused by witch-hunter de Lancre of being witches. The Jesuits do not appear to have had any part in the gory details of the witch-hunt, but instead they mediated, interviewed, observed, reported, translated, helped and advised where this was necessary and possible. It appears that their good services were mainly responsible for saving the lives of thousands of women and for the fact that the Basque language is still spoken today. The meaning of the name **Jesuit** has nothing to do with the witch-craze or any other confrontation. The name comes from: jesu-it.:

jesu	Jesus
itzeman	committed to

"Committed to Jesus."

The leader of the Jesuits was Ignatius de Loyola;

Ignatius Loyola,

ig.	iga	*igarobera*	tolerant
.na	ana	*anaia*	brother
ati	ati	*atxikigarri*	faithful
us.	uso	*uso*	holy man

"Tolerant brother, faithful holy man."

.lo	alo	*alogereko*	mercenary
oio	oio	*Oion*	village in Aleba
ola	ola	*ola*	cabin/hut

"Mercenary from a hut in Oion."

THE END OF THE HORRIBLE NIGHTMARE

Reading in this our modern age about this dreadful, blackest page in our European history, makes one think that the witch-craze must have been just a horrible nightmare; it couldn't have happened; but it did. Henningsen sums up some of the important points at the end of his book. The research he did was impressive but in no way was it the final word. Three of the conclusions which he, de Salazar, the Bishop of Pamplona and others reached are:

Firstly: the belief in witchcraft and in witches as a sectarian organization practicing inversion of Christianity, including pacts and fornication with the devil, was totally irrelevant to popular belief.

Secondly: that the application of hallucinatory witches' salves give the flying witch phenomenon a rational explanation, could not bear critical examination.

Thirdly: that the persecution of witches was often instigated by people who gained economic or social advantage from them. They saw in zealous Christian preachers, officials, judges, inquisitors and bishops excellent instruments through which to forward their personal and private interests.

What they did not emphasize was that the Roman Catholic church knew all along that witchcraft itself had not been the motivating factor in this holocaust. Instead it was the existence of out-of-the-way settlements of Basque speaking people, all over Europe, that had to be exterminated to put an end to the long, long history of language conversion and Basque/Ligurian elimination. It had been an expensive and draining effort and the church had to go on to bigger and better things. If it had not been for the good services of the Jesuits, thousands more innocent Basque women would have been killed mercilessly and the Basque language would no longer be spoken in Euskadi, the Basque country. The final solution, so carefully planned, had been cut short by the Jesuits. For that alone they deserve our respect and admiration. The Jesuits lived up to their name "Devoted to Jesus."

It would be marvelous to think that such a horror would never happen again, but it did a few years ago in Uganda, Rwanda and then in Bosnia and Kosovo. Likely it will happen again somewhere else.

—

VIII

WHERE DO WE GO FROM HERE?

CLASSIFYING THE WORLD'S LANGUAGES

A POSSIBLE NEW APPROACH

INTRODUCTION

Since the 18th century, attempts have been made to classify the world's languages into one comprehensive genetic system of families, shown as a tree with branches, sometimes called the Stammbaum model. This effort has been very frustrating for many linguists because organizing languages into such a system has been like playing a game of musical chairs. Major languages were shifted from one language family to another, whole families were bundled into super families on very shaky assumptions, others were split off and given their own family tree. Faulty reasoning and wishful thinking resulted in some of these assumptions being accepted as gospel and given credibility by contrived systems of phonological correspondence, created by an obsessive group of linguists known as the Neo-Grammarians. The best known example of this is the theory of the Indo-European "family" of languages which is based on the faulty reasoning that if the observed relationships between the languages are not accidental, they must be genetic. Most of the Neo-Grammarians' inventions have long ago been put into the dustbin, but what remains of them is taken as evidence that modern linguistics, in some important sense, is still to be considered as a science.

In a desperate attempt to make some sense out of the profusion of languages and observed relationships, linguists have been searching for the "Mother Tongue," also called "Proto-World." This initiative is now considered a most controversial contrivance in linguistic circles. Many linguists shy away from attempting to re-construct the ancestral language, calling such attempts speculative and sensational. The much quoted Dr. Vitaly Shevoroshkin (University of Michigan) is a great supporter of the "Mother Tongue" theory and he assumes that "most words are stable and change very little… words such as body parts have been with us from the beginning." This assumption could have been correct except for one small problem: during the past 5 to 6,000 years some of the major religions have put linguists to work, subjecting the early language to acrostic manipulation and mutilation. Hundreds, if not thousands, of these fabricated words are shown in this book. Their efforts have resulted in a very large number of invented languages which at first sight have no relationship to the original language, but upon detailed examination can be shown to have originated from the ancient neolithic language. If it hadn't been for the drastic and prolonged efforts of the ancient grammarians, a few genetic trees of languages would likely have done the job, but such was not our luck.

Through the years, there have been a few courageous doubters among the linguists such as M. E. Landsberg (Columbia Univ. S.C.) who wrote:

> *"Indeed, courses in historical linguistics at Universities all over the world, in spite of much perplexing evidence to the contrary, mostly still persist in adhering to strict Indo-European theories."*

Those who did not follow the Indo-European gospel and sounded the alarm bells risked their immaculate academic reputations by indulging in what was called "translinguistic investigations," resulting in being censored by the dogma-ridden majority which still rules the discipline. Students are forbidden to study the possible academic fallacy behind the Indo-European theory, and those who did look into it were stonewalled, isolated and ridiculed. Doubting the Indo-European theory became "taboo" and even resulted in a quick forced exit from the profession. One professor to whom I explained my findings commented: "You are excavating recesses into which an academic with the instincts of a gentleman, would never venture." Is it a surprise that this subject of invented linguistics is so totally unexplored?

A New Classification is Needed

First we must distinguish between:

   1) naturally evolved or unmanipulated languages. It is these that are candidates for being organized in the Stammbaum model. Within this group we can recognize many divisions e.g. the gradual development of clear vowel differentiation, the addition of onomatopoeia etc.

2) invented languages, also called products of intelligent design. None of these fit the Stammbaum model. All highly developed languages capable of being used to teach at university level fall into this category. The first of this type of language was created during the Neolithic in north Africa, possibly in Upper Egypt and I have called it "Invented – Level 1."

INVENTED LEVEL I, THE MAGICAL LANGUAGE

Based on the existence of ancient and still beautiful works which show the complexity of religious thinking, amazing stone structures and scientific knowledge, it is now quite obvious that North Africa and especially Egypt, was the location of the first true civilization on earth, guided by 1) a holy respect for the wondrous reproductive and nursing capabilities of the human female, 2) a fully evolved language, 3) a democratically organized and highly disciplined system of tribal groups, 4) a strong oral literary tradition, and 5) a number of sciences such as astronomy, mathematics, architecture, engineering, medicine, agriculture, irrigation, leather tanning, boat building and star navigation.

The language had to evolve along with these developments. However, the people involved in science, the priesthood, did everything in their own very special way. A language was developed by them which was based on a vocabulary in which each word started with vowel-consonant-vowel. These VCV's were then agglutinated into words, out of which several unnecessary vowels were removed. Carefully selected meanings were then assigned to each VCV in such a manner that almost all non-technical thoughts could be expressed with it. The agglutination was only allowed to happen if the adjoining vowels were the same, called vowel-interlocking. These two special characteristics, carefully selected meanings and vowel-interlocking, made it possible to encode new words and names which could also be decoded and the hidden sentence restored. I give hundreds of examples of decoding in this book. For much more detail see the VCV list in Appendix 1.

The result was that a very special language was created which survived the test of time and throughout all ages has remained the preserve of the successive priesthoods. In the Auraicept, a Benedictine monk called it: Forfeda, meaning: "That infernal fabrication." He obviously resented the fact that he had to use a product which was invented so long ago that the world was still ruled by a Goddess. The astonishing thing is that this invented language was married to the paleolithic and early neolithic language spoken by the many tribes in the Sahara and today is still spoken by 800,000 people as Euskera in almost unaltered form.

This language creation effort took place at the same time that the burning Sahara emptied of people, who brought their religion, their natural language and traditions along with them. They settled all over Europe, western Asia and the Near East. When the new patriarchal religion of the sky gods was invented, several new names were given to the old language still spoken by the emigrants, such as: Elamite (Mesopotamia), Canaanite (Palestine), Minoan (Crete), Hatti (Anatolia), Ligurian (Italy), Pictish (Scotland), Cruithin (Ireland), Cythian (Black Sea), Basque (Pyrenees), Guanche (Canary islands), Ainu (Japan), Dravidian (India), possibly even Polynesian (Oceania). All of these languages changed and evolved but those that are still spoken today, such as Ainu, Berber and Dravidian, can easily be recognized as belonging to the truly genetic group of Saharan languages. Of all these isolated languages it appears that the Basque language is still the closest, by far, to the original Saharan language. The survival of this 5,200+ year old language in its original condition is something that is hard to believe.

Second Level Invented Languages

As a result of the creation of the new Proto-Judaic religion, which could have taken place in the cult town of Nerik, in the Hittite province of Kizzuwadna, a whole new world order was being proposed. The decision was made to destroy the ancient language of the Goddess, its oral tradition and its tribal system, by any means possible. This decision was repeated much later in Genesis 11:7 "Let us confuse their language so they may no longer understand each other's speech." The religious powers began with creating new languages for the Near East: Sumerian, Akkadian, Old Egyptian, Lycian, Luwian, Palaic, Lydian and Hittite, creating each with its own script, all with the use of the old Magical Language of the Egyptians, because they could not think of any other system that was better.

Third Level Invented Languages

Proto-Judaism was a missionary type religion. Over many centuries, the religious centre in Kizzuwadna sent out groups of highly educated missionaries to various parts of the world with orders to introduce male domination, a new religion, create a new language and an original script. This effort resulted in: Sanskrit (India), Ge'ez (Ethiopia), Greek (Greece), Latin (Tuscani), Iberian (Spain), Hebrew (Israel), Ugaritic (Syria), Tocharian (China), Japanese (Japan), and possibly Yiddish and Gothic– related languages in Russia. Could the teams of linguists creating these languages have been the so-called twelve tribes of Israel?

FOURTH LEVEL INVENTED LANGUAGES

Several of these languages spawned their own when: Hebrew scholars created the Semitic languages e.g. Arabic, Phoenician, Syriac, Aramaic. Sanskrit scholars created a host of Northern Indian languages: Maldivian, Sinhalese, Vedda, Kalasha, Kashmiri, Nepali, Bengali etc. Ge'ez spawned Tigre, Amharic, Tigrinia, Harari etc. Latin spawned Spanish, Portugese and Catalan, French and Provencal, Italian and Rumanian.

FIFTH LEVEL INVENTED LANGUAGES

The Benedictine monks, working in scriptoria on the east coast of England and using the already well established Latin language, developed the basic structure of the Germanic group of languages such as: English, German, Dutch, Friesian, Norwegian, Danish, Swedish etc. Benedictine monks working from the Pannonhalma scriptorium in Hungary created Hungarian, which special invention technique was taken north to create Estonian, Finnish and Lappish.

With linguistic help from the Pannonhalma monks, the Eastern Orthodox monks, working from the scriptoria attached to the monasteries in Kiev and Novgorod, created the Slavic group of languages such as Russian, Ukrainian, Serbian etc. Polish was likely developed in the Benedictine scriptorium at Tyniec.

All these languages have the Saharan/Basque language as their substratum. The above is preliminary and needs more work. It appears that the Sino-Tibetan, Amerind, Austric, Australian and Khoisian language groups were not involved in this effort to distort and make over, so these may fit the Stammbaum model.

APPENDIX I

VCV DICTIONARY
(ABBREVIATED)

Simplified
Vowel–Consonant–Vowel
(VCV) Dictionary

It was invented by ancient Egyptian scholars before the first pharaoh was named, and has been used ever since in the agglutination of names and words for many languages. The primary organization of this Magical Language is according to the 16 consonants. Each one of the consonants then was subdivided into 25 VCV's. for a total of 400 VCV's. Double R was regarded as another consonant, adding 25 more VCV's, for a total of 425, of which 104 were reserved for non-use or future expansion of the VCV dictionary.

Every grammarian apparently had made up at least one set of cards for himself, one card each for the 321 VCV's which had meanings associated. Each card showed one VCV in large letters, with the assigned meanings written under it in small letters. These cards were then laid out on large tables with the interlocking vowels forming pairs of cards. This provided the grammarians not only with an enormous number of vocabulary possibilities but also creative entertainment. If a specific word needed to be assembled, a definition or related comment was written and the applicable word cards arranged and shifted until the vowel-interlocking rule was satisfied. New words would often be accidentally invented which had not yet been called for. In this manner a very large vocabulary was invented creating many words with similar meanings, but only the best were accepted. The result was that English obtained a great many words which became the foundation of the well over one million which now make up our language. English now needs a "Thesaurus" to keep them all available and ready for use. It is the only language in the world with such a problem.

B

ABA. priest, rectory, occasion, chance, opportunity, slingshot, advantage, surpass, rower, almost, branch, shade, sound.
ABE. support, cross, receive, hospitable, animal, manger, stable, cattle, race, fertile, elegant, wealth, rich, brutality, patriotic, choir, concert, to sing.
ABI. nest, home, speed, hurry, departure, impulsive, start, walk, talent, to begin, skillful.
ABO. voice, approve of, lawyer, to proclaim, to shout out.
ABU. opinion, agree, to express an opinion, thought.

EBA. cut, slice, harvest, remnant, evaluation, evangelist, gospel, fraud, plunder, hide-out, thief, to decide.
EBE. Hebrew, patriarchy, wild boar.
EBI. N.A.
EBO. to develop, evolution.
EBU. N.A.

IBA. river, lowland, confluence, shore, ferry, valley.
IBE. to place, to put on, to introduce, act of putting on, to start.
IBI. to ford, to cross, to walk, trip, route, roadmap, to run, vagabond, nomadic, impassible, to behave, to act, to recede, to wade, to be, to go.
IBO. N.A.
IBU. N.A.

OBA. better, naturally, improvement.
OBE. preferable, to improve, well-meaning, obedience, to sin, guilty, blame.
OBI. tomb, cemetery, to bury.
OBO. oboe.
OBU. N.A.

UBA. cormorant.
UBE. purple, royal, livid, bruise, cistern.
UBI. canal, aqueduct, bruise, cistern, whirlpool.
UBO. N.A.
UBU. N.A.

D

ADA. noise, to mend, patch, horn, branching, to tease, to gore, firewood, deceive, long hair, ramification, trumpet sound, being swallowed.

ADE. temple, rude, gentle, adorn, courteous, to prepare.

ADI. watch out, announce, interpret, advice, meaning, suggestive, sign, symbol, logical, care-less, dumb, intelligent, judgment, friendly, to explain, understanding, be careful, significant.

ADO. courage, bravery, stimulate, agree, worship.

ADU. slobber, luck, to be charmed.

EDA. to drink, thirst, drunk, glass, poison, potable.

EDE. to take from, poison, beautiful, esteem, to be pleased, exaggerate, to be defeated, mislead, history.

EDI. to find.

EDO. or, anytime, common, anywhere, to suck.

EDU. to have, to keep, powerful, possession, snow.

IDA. to write, subject of writing, document, clerk.

IDE. companion, idea, invent, to open, same, to adjust, to compare, ideology, homogeneity.

IDI. ox, crib, to open, wisent, bison.

IDO. mud, torrential rain, idol, dry, unfeeling, discovery.

IDU. to have, to appear, to imitate, to distrust, resemblance, apparently.

ODA. N.A.

ODE. cloud, horizon.

ODI. pipe, round opening.

ODO. blood, relative, martyr, rage, impulsive, nervous, apathy, cowardice, cruel, angry, butchery.

ODU. N.A.

UDA. summer, spring, autumn, dog days, pear.

UDE. summerhouse.

UDI. sometimes used instead of *uti* (*utikan* = go away, get out).

UDO. N.A.

UDU. N.A.

F

AFA. happy, pleasing, supper, mealtime.
AFE. N.A.
AFI. N.A.
AFO. N.A.
AFU. N.A.

EFA. N.A.
EFE. N.A.
EFI. N.A.
EFO. N.A.
EFU. N.A.

IFA. north, north wind.
IFE. hell, damned, infernal.
IFI. sometimes used instead of *ibi* (*ibili* = to go, to be).
IFO. N.A.
IFU. N.A.

OFA. N.A.
OFE. N.A.
OFI. official, craftsman, job, living, specialist.
OFO. N.A.
OFU. N.A.

UFA. panting, scornful, to blow, to stink.
UFE. N.A.
UFI. N.A.
UFO. N.A.
UFU. N.A.

G

AGA. long pole/stick, abundance, hitting, to lash, to whip.

AGE. agency, rod, notorious, symbol, sign, to declare, document, public, revelation, obvious, sample, discovery, to appear, honest, view.

AGI. may be, I wish, I hope, tooth, yew tree, dentist, powerful, to order, to promise, obedient, threat, reprimand, chief, legacy, blame.

AGO. mouth, edge, be!, dry, sterile, hard, drought, yawn, scarcity, to dry, to be exhausted.

AGU. quick, active, good-bye, old man, worship, to greet, farewell.

EGA. wing, to fly, to evaporate, edge, escape, protection, thirsty, anxiety, aircraft, shelter, to favour.

EGE. N.A.

EGI. to do, truth, likely, true, to verify, to be(come), you do, author, to create, to bet, possible, duty, mandatory, to make (something), to undo, bargain, action, to convince, false.

EGO. south, resident, attitude, adequate, to fit, opportunity, to concern, to arrange, to stay, home, to boil, raw, sunburn, to throw, to nurse, rest, to vomit, to expel.

EGU. day, noon, dawn, eternal, never, daily, life, modern, good morning, wage, punishment, strolling, cut wood, woody, to beat, sunlight, east wind, to burn, sunset.

IGA. fruit, to rise, sunday, dress up, wilted, to wither, sign, prophet, to guess, to travel, to pass by, bearable, tolerant, to notice, last year, dead, unpredictable.

IGE. frog, to plaster, mason, to swim, to float, escape, to evade.

IGI. harvest, sickle.

IGO. to rise, to lift up, to raise, to climb, sender, to anoint, to rub.

IGU. despite, to wait, expectation, tolerance, scraper, sun, east.

OGA. wealth, property.

OGE. bed, 20, 30.

OGI. bread, crust, sandwich, baker, weasel, to thresh, maid, easy going.

OGO. N.A.

OGU. to pronounce, to say out loud.

UGA. abundant, fruitful, to abound, bountiful, bountiful, breast, stepchild, parent.

UGE. belt, dirty, swimmer, to rust, muddy.

UGI. N.A.

UGO. N.A.

UGU. N.A.

H

AHA. I hope, perhaps, anger, argument, power, helpless, trial, capable, attempt, possible, almighty, shame, bold, shy, mouthful, to forget, injury, ram, yawn, dirt, duck, to bark.
AHAI incest, relative, clan, affinity, anger, to argue, power.
AHE. disease of the mouth.
AHI. porridge, fatigue, custard, to end, sister, inexhaustible. (*ai* = I hope, strong desire, lament, addiction)
AHO. mouth, crater, cave entrance, tasteful, eloquent, flavor, bite, vocal, bad breath, tooth, to give advice, indiscrete, to stutter, to pronounce, to bridle, to mention, spoken language, chaf, to exaggerate, to yawn, to kneel down, to deceive, astonished, to utter.
AHU. weak, depression, female goat, palm of the hand, by the handful, goatherd, goat meat, concave, cheek. (*au* = this one, *auek* = these ones) Many more *au*'s in dictionary.

EHA. used as *ea or eja*, the emphasis of an indirect question.
EHE. bleach, ee = calling someone's attention..
EHI. hunting, game animal, net. (*-ei* = dry, they say, certainly, to grind, to them)
EHO. to grind, milling, to digest, molar, grave digger, burial.
EHU. 100, century, to weave, textile merchant, centipede. For *eu* see dictionary.

IHA. almost, jovial, expertise, dry, wallow, answer, frightened, argue, spend time, carnival, to scatter, to discuss, weak. (*ia* = almost, cheerful, hardly)
IHE. escape, inevitable, shelter, unavoidable.
IHI. rushes, dew, to hunt, hunting blind, to cover.
IHO. thunder, iodine.
IHU. thunder, dwarf elder forest.

OHA. bed, concubine, warning, comment, thoughtful, spontaneous, distracted, attention, look- out, counselor, to perceive, innocent.
OHE. bed, brood, time in bed, mistress, canopy.
OHI. custom, usual, to adjust, savage, stampede, suffering, timid, usual, to get used to, flower (archaic), forest, cloth, sailboat. Many with *oi*, see dictionary.
OHO. thief, accomplice, hideout, chalkboard, lumber, scaffold, honorable, famous, to kick, to praise.
OHU. N.A.

UHA. belt, pebble, coast, flood, deluge, to fasten, water tower, riverbed, turbidity, island, to turn yellow, floodgate, lettuce.
UHE. gray, naughty, turbid, malicious, confusion, naughty.
UHI. wave, ripple, undulate, break water.
UHO. flood, deluge, ravine, torrential.
UHU. cry of happiness, to hoot.

J

AJA. ha-ha-ha, laughter.
AJE. to deteriorate, defective, upset. Also *aie*: suspicion, conjecture, to drive away.
AJI. N.A.
AJO. care, concern, interest, negligent, to take care, heedless, worry.
AJU. field of heather.

EJA. or **EA**, emphasizes an indirect question.
EJE. N.A.
EJI. N.A.
EJO. N.A.
EJU. N.A.

IJA. N.A. , *ia*: almost, hardly
IJE. N.A.
IJI. gypsy, gypsy language.
IJO. N.A.
IJU. N.A.

OJA. or OIA: forest, wood, weaver, textile, to knit.
OJE. N.A.
OJI. N.A.
OJO. N.A.
OJU. N.A. or oiu screaming.

UJA. N.A. (*uha* = archipelago)
UJE. N.A. but occasionally used in place of *uhe* = turbid, malicious)
UJI. N.A.
UJO. N.A.
UJU. shout of joy, to yell.

K

AKA. the end, death, ultimate, to argue, notched, defective, chip, fault, perfect, superior, to end a life.

AKE. Great Goddess of our ancestors, priestess, witch, sheep tick, male goat, coffee, pointed beard, male pig.

AKI. fatigue, tiring, excuse, aged, tireless.

AKO. agreement, accordion, memory, traditional, to remember.

AKU. to incite, to spur on, to stimulate, to rent, to lease, acoustics.

EKA. substance, solstice, storm, to be used to, bringer, transport, contribution, to bring, habit.

EKE. N.A.

EKI. sun, eastern, perseverance, initiative, attempt, as much as possible, militant, activist.

EKO. to produce, fertile, fruitful, administrator.

EKU. equator, worried, peace of mind.

IKA. familiar, fright, terror, enormous, timid, to terrorize, teachings, example, to learn, student, class, coal, fig trees, horror, to come, to cause.

IKE. slope, to explore, research, scrutiny, examine, to visit.

IKI. N.A.

IKO. that, swelling, mason's hammer, lump.

IKU. stable, touch, to mention, flag, motto, curious, watchful, visible, gift, scenic, curiosity, to look, good-bye, inspection, spectator, to visit, to wash, bucket, hostility, admirable.

OKA. overfull, nausea, satiety, to vomit, belly full, plum, occasional, disgust, despise, plentiful.

OKE. meat, twisted, mistakenly, bad, perverted, injury, error, astray, wrong, corrupt, oblique, winding.

OKI. satiety, woodpecker, frightened, baker, to become bored, complete, total.

OKO. stable, chin, pasture.

OKU. fertile field.

UKA. hand, sock, boxer, forearm, pummel, elbow, to have, possession, wrist, to deny.

UKE. N.A.

UKI. to touch, intangible, contact, mention, to refer to, tangential.

UKO. refusal, denial, elbow, negative.

UKU. stable, to go bad, falsify, to rot, smelly.

L

ALA. in that way, even-so, as, so-so, daughter, indeed, however, fate, casual, amen, fatally, I swear to, happy, similar, sudden, wire fence, outcry, widow, to cause pain, miracle, feeding, widow, to fill with joy, destiny, necessary.

ALE. fruit, button, to be happy, grain, fake, certainly, rejoicing, fable, parable, simulation, trial, effort, carefully, grain abundance, total, barn, threshing, to attempt, make effort, to try.

ALI. to destroy someone, to destroy a personality, possible, capable, pliers, to kill a person.

ALO. wage, hire, salary, to rent, wine storage, field, farmer, to engage, mercenary, marine algae.

ALU. stupid, vulva, feeble, repulsive action.

ELA. story, word, novel, talkative, swallow, elastic.

ELE. story, news, to talk, sacristan, sacraments, church, marriage banns, sacred, gossip, cattle, flattering, nonsense, to deceive, adulation.

ELI. food, to feed, church, canon-law, pious, council, holy ground, oblation, procession.

ELO. thorn, spiny, thistle.

ELU. snow, slushy mud, avalanche, edelweiss, snowball, reindeer, to freeze.

ILA. dead, month, hair, fur, pea, in a row, to murder, moon, lunatic, tombstone, lifetime, white ash, to destroy, to weaken.

ILE. hair, fur, to comb, to cut hair, to turn gray, silky, teasing, joking, menstruation, barber, burning wood, toupee, balding, grave yard, funeral, complaint, mourner, everlasting, immortal.

ILI. burning wood, firewood, stir up, half burned wood, to revive, firebrand, preacher, fiery, to revive.

ILO. nephew, niece, grandson, to bury, agony, grave, corpse.

ILU. darkness, shady, sad, confused, sunset, dim, mournful, to dye, to get angry. worry, vague, obscure, evening.

OLA. factory, foundry, cabin, plank, octopus, sledge, like this, canopy, wave, just like this.

OLE. last rites, poet, poem, summons, to call upon.

OLI. anoint, oil, vendor, olive oil, holy.

OLO. oats, to feed oats to, oatmeal.

OLU. N.A.

ULA. to receive, to welcome (was lost from Basque, but still used in related languages).

ULE. hair, example, intelligible, understanding.

ULI. fly, coward

ULO. N.A.

ULU. wail, howl, bark, cry.

M

AMA. mother, priestess, Goddess, 11, 12, 15, two weeks, end, many, to destroy, grand-mother, rope, to fasten, to lace, cunning, decade, to turn off, to quench, spoiled child, endless.

AME. oakum, burlap, make your fortune, dream, unreal, nightmare, delirium, fancy, whim, idealize, fantasy.

AMI. stork, ravine, to throw off, cause to fall, tumbling, falling down, waterfall, administrator, amnesty.

AMO. love, kind, affectionate, grand-mother, clan-mother, mistress, gallantry, to yield, to oblige, strict, tolerant, fury, molest, annoy, wrath, refund, blunt.

AMU. fishhook, line, affectionate, tender, distrust, bait.

EMA. female, vagina, menstruation, prostitute, to calm, lust, result, generous, lady, to give, to hit, receipt, emission, performance, fruitful, to abduct, wife, single, to get married, to produce, to teach.

EME. female, smooth, soft, shy, here, to enlarge, native, 19, peaceful.

EMI. N.A.

EMO. present, to give, prolific, future, to transmit.

EMU. N.A.

IMA. statue, image, sculptor, magnet, wicker, wattle, idol.

IME. N.A.

IMI. unit of measure, gesture, imitation, reproduction, exemplary, repeat, to serve, to put on, act of offering.

IMO. N.A.

IMU. to pinch.

OMA. grandma, house of Oma.

OME. honor, fame, rumor, tribute, famous, according to.

OMI. All Saints' Day, Hallowe'en, Hallowmass, rarely: prophesy.

OMO. N.A.

OMU. N.A.

UMA. child, pregnant, procreation, fertile, birth, mature, ripening, humanist.

UME. child, young, offspring, give birth, litter, fetus, prolific, childish, overripe, nursery, womb, apple core, to adopt, orphan.

UMI. humble, humility

UMO. ripe, mature, sensibly, uterous, humor, wit, mood, funny, bad tempered, prudent.

UMU. N.A.

N

ANA. brother, congregation, religious order, civil war, anarchy, anatomy, to unite, to gather, to cllect. (*aña* = wet nurse)
ANE. grain measure, (*añe* = to curse, to swear).
ANI. animal, many, often, multiple, increase.
ANO. food supply, portion, wine, anonymous, abnormal,
ANU. fainting, fall back in fear.

ENA. to swallow, that, -superlative.
ENE. my, exclamation (pain, surprise), property, in me, to me, to attract to me, come to me, when, my dear, before, always, since.
ENI. to me.
ENO. wart, covered with warts, afflicted.
ENU. useless, inertia, weakness.

INA. hail, to swallow, to agitate, to shake, to open, to trim, pruning.
INE. inertia, passiveness, neutrality, do-nothing, downtrodden.
INI. N.A. rarely *ainitz* = many

INO. ever, never, time to time, sometimes, in any manner, somehow, somewhere, absolutely not, dew, no-one, any place, alienated, vacant, naive, stupid, to be cowed.
INU. to nurse, sunset, evening, twilight, ant, heath, prickly, tingle, inspiring, thunder, stupid.

ONA. here, closer, prosperity, unacceptable, welcome, approval, admit.
ONE. too good, kind, benefit, to enjoy, extreme patience, doing good, these, thus, like this, the best, to recover, exemplary, piety, advantageous, improve, to come here, to accept, to praise, decent, tolerant, honesty, blessing, charity, right now, reconciliation.
ONI. real estate, success, safe and sound, funnel, consent, useful, luck, acceptable.
ONO. exquisite, very good, wonderful.
ONU. profit, earning, useless, beneficial, good faith, perfect, very nice.

UNA. boredom, annoying, dull, cowherd, fatigue.
UNE. moment, place, spot, instant, short distance.
UNI. wet nurse, funnel, general, university, universal.
UNO. N.A.
UNU. N.A.

P

APA. kiss, sit down, to cook, elegant, ornament, to make up, bathroom, to organize, luxury, priest, humble, shelving, dinner guest, ravine, meek, poverty, foam, special, hoof, spongy.
APE. whim, fancy, priest, bishop, tendency, priest's dress.
API. may be, accidental, April.
APO. toad, tadpole, to bet, apostle, filthy deed, insult, lodger, hoofed.
APU. breadcrumb, little bit, fragile, frugal, to shred, to destroy, to crush, to break.

EPA. decision, trial, court, judge, to cut, sentence.
EPE. term, postpone, due, indefinite, to defer, to warm, timid, to decrease, cool, give time, to expire, credit, indecisive, prolong, bottom, glowworm, kinglet, short of time, weak.
EPI. epic.
EPO. dwarf, to grow small.
EPU. juniper, fragrant wood.

IPA. north, polar, N.W., nordic, northern.
IPE. buttocks, rump.
IPI. placeable, patch, to place, put on, installer, plantation of wicker.
IPO. dwarf, little chap.
IPU. story, legend, imaginary, narrative, moral, upside down, adulating, bottom, rump, anal, yoke pad, gospel, impatient, legendary.

OPA desire, offering, sacrifice, gift, rich, abundant, to wish for, to give.
OPE opera, operate, surgeon, to offer.
OPI bun, roll, flatten out, baker, opium.
OPO vacation, time off, to do nothing, lazily, go against, opposition, wooden pouch.
OPU N.A.

UPA. barrel, cooper, to advance *(hupatu)*.
UPE. wine cellar, store in vats, cask.
UPI. N.A.
UPO. stave of a barrel.
UPU. N.A.

aR

ARA. there, proportion, according to, to adapt, to conform, agreement, apt, adequate, meat, lustful, scraped, carnivorous, butcher, to assimilate, sexual, farther, curious, massacre, spider, plum, echo, prong, towards here, thorny, curse, exorcise, interval, immediate, mediator, closet, duck, corrupt, pure, job, employ, worried, refine.

ARAU. discipline, proportion, legally, violator, regulation, code of laws, there.

ARRA. repetition, handful, scar, refine metals, gentle, split, to get drunk, fish, hell, reflection, curse, happiness, shouting, boastful, to complain, careful, eagle, arrogant, weep, disorderly, plunder, greed, hastily, capture, rare, to drag, rat, evening, oar, egg, row, yawn, race, breed, reason, absurd, arbitrary, stone, infrequent, heartbreak.

ARRAU. oar, caviar, egg, yolk, to lay eggs, to row, to yawn, pancake, omelet, egg seller.

ARE. even so, sand, more, to grow, rake, those, like that, his/her, approach, enemy hostility, recent, cover with sand.

ARRE. sister, sociable, please, prayer, to beg, impatient, welcome, redeemer, care, turbid, quarry, relationship, complaint, equipment, kind, from then on, beggar, lamenting.

ARI. mission, thread, to him/her, wire, active, until, exercise, to wind, soul, ruthless, light, hasten, escape, race, thoughtless, pertinent, oak grove.

ARRI. rock, stone, surprise, marvelous, amazing, awful, quarry, throwing stones, pebble, landmark, to risk, danger, fantastic, to pave.

ARO. weather, season, epoch, all, carpenter, blacksmith, forge.

ARRO. proud, riverbed, quarry, softening, excavation, vain, boastful, rose, rosary, yawn, stranger, innkeeper, exile.

ARU. toward, farther, movement, to wander.

ARRU. chasm, vulgar, simply, commonly.

eR

ERA. manner, appearance, opportunity, cause, to decide, sentence, entirely, reform, polite, use, profit, to move, available, nonsense, exercise, effective, promote, influence, trouble, builder, murder, milk, scatter, active, method, sample, education, explain, to spend, patience, to suffer, sticky, attack, devotion, fulfillment, murmur, according to, convenient, ring (on finger), agitation, to carry, agression.

ERRA. radical, bowels, rail, speaker, daughter-in-law, sunlight, radiant, giant, palm, rower, to say, to tell, to confess, gossip, to wander, sting, to sweep, destructive, to burn, to cremate, negligence, easy.

ERE. too, as well, example, statue, ideal, to sow, to scatter, laurel wreath, wasteland, desert, wilderness, hymn, occasion, side, indulging.

ERRE. to burn, to bake, to smoke, reaction, realistic, irritable, root, to reform, proverb, gift, burnable, princess, throne, regal, law, king, region, prayer, kingdom, stream, south wind, stream, care, to claim, corrosive, cure, to remedy, blacksmith's shop, tool, tugboat, charity, growl, cripple, refund, to surrender, row, limp, renter, royal road, tolling bells, slowly, to reserve, respect, result, to retire, argument, touchy, simple, suspicious, welcome.

ERI. sickness, finger, vigil, noxious, death, recovery, agony, fatal, to have an opinion, unanimous, to compare, common, to think, to call, to spill, to flow.

ERRI. village, town, public, region, to slacken, shore road, to argue, fight, raffle, native, shyme, strong, skillful, rite, common people, castor oil.

ERO. redeemer, redemption, crazy, every, carrier, to suffer, to tolerate, patience, transport, insane, to decline, ruin, risky, to fall, to die, slide, to cause, to buy and sell, merchandise, bribe, to redeem, comfort, mourning, store, basket, erotic.

ERRO. root, origin, cause, crow, egg laying, crack, basic, romantic, narrative, pilgrim, to beg, twig, dispute, clothes, yawn, mill, robust, to settle,to take root, secure.

ERU. N.A.

ERRU. mistake, blame, guilt, innocence, wheel, to forgive, sadly, pity, mercy, cruel, compassionate, egg producing, to beg, abundant, to accuse.

iR

IRA. profession, profitable, to earn, to grow up, lucrative, victorious, paying, to mix, to make, suggestion, bargeman, migratory, to spend time, to suffer, past, durable, constant, safe conduct, profit, warning, to announce, filter, offense, to injure, to leave, shot, schoolday, education, teacher, school, boiling, fervor, enraging, passion, reading, print, to stick, ghost, exciting, to wake up, to upset, to plow, revolt, to endure, perishable, patient, firmness, to ignite.
IRRA. radiating, to spread.

IRE. your, opener, to open, to dig, hole, crack, to devour, destructive, to swallow, to absorb, to ruin.
IRRE. N.A.

IRI. town, city, to open, civic, to pulverize, wasteful, to squander, achievement, to acquire, to arrive, to get, to judge, opinion, agreement, moderator, unanimous.
IRRI. malignant smile, mockery, laughable, funny, jovial, ridicule, to scoff, ambition, anxious, to whynney, risk, to slide, skate, sled, to yearn for, sarcastic, desire.

IRO. reproach, toilet, manure pile, outhouse, garbage dump, irony, culvert.
IRRO. N.A.

IRU. 3, three sided, image, picture, to seem, to resemble, symbol, conceivable, worship idols, to simulate, false belief, to represent, to appear, trimester, trio, weaver, to reverse, clover, one third, 60, 70, 300, fraud, trick, deceit, cheat, crook.
IRRU. N.A.

oR

ORA. dog, filling, present, now, modern, yet, right now, to catch, to grab always, update.
ORRA. there, up to that point, surprise, anger, eye of a needle, comb, to touch, sewing, to strip, to rob, to despoil.

ORE. putty, dough, deer, mole (on skin), beauty mark, balance, aerialist, hour, o'clock, to watch, dentist.
ORRE. juniper, because of that, that one, thus, as much as, like that.

ORI. that, yellow, gold colored, except, pale, to paint, freckle.
ORRI. leaf, sheet, to that one, foliage, banquet, feast, full of leaves, covered with leaves.

ORO. all, every, also, in addition, totality, similar, to unify, to monopolize, to buy up, to hoard, Creator, monument, memory, to remind, universal, moss, ambitious.
ORRO. roaring, mooing, to shout, to scream.

ORU. lower part of ground, building site, lot, place of oats.
ORRU. N.A.

uR

URA. he, she, that one, him, her, his, watery, bank of the river, to flood, ocean, watered wine, to float, washbasin, sugar water.
URRA. hazelnut, scratching, to touch, to move, closer, to claw, rupture, step by step, footstep, track, to tear, to violate, break a law, lettuce.

URE. waterfowl, boiled water, water carrier, nobility, dropsy, warm water, runny nose, irrigation ditch, riverbank, flood, aquatic, water, to launch, beach resort, by the sea, to dilute, honey water.
URRE. gold, glitter, jewelry, to tarnish, next, to get closer, approach, silver.

URI. city, communal forest, low tide, butter, grease, urban.
URRI. scarce, rare, defective, poor, miserable, to decrease, lack of, to be merciful, pitiful, reduction, repentant, aroma, scent, stink, freely, gratis, female animal, grove of hazel trees.

URO. irrigation canal, brick casing, water pipe, marsh hen, cistern, reservoir, cold water.
URRO. hazel tree, grove of hazels.

URU. flower, to dip in flower.
URRU. to scorn, to reject, to despise, cooing of dove, sing a lullaby, far, distant, to leave, to move away, nostalgia.

S

ASA. ancestor, to go away, to reject, shocking, agitation, excitement, revolt, to disturb, scared, alarm, to get angry, to annoy, enraged.

ASE. to be full, abundant, stuffed, greedy, to insure, craving, to anger, to irritate, to get tired, feed.

ASI. to begin, to start, initial, elementary, to bite, first fruit, origin.

ASO. N.A.

ASU. nettle, new-born lamb.

ESA. to say, expression, witty, wise, phrase, speaker, gossip, weaving back and forth, to relate, meaning, lecture, moral of the story.

ESE. to hang, to suspend, to and fro, to sit, chair, to attack, battle, to object, to argue, to debate, essence.

ESI. fence, siege, blockade, to surround, to gather, round-up.

ESO. advice.

ESU. N.A.

ISA. blow with a broom, long-tailed, short-tailed, broom, furze, gorse, tail.

ISE. joke, make fun of, derisive, to ridicule, act of satirizing.

ISI. quiet, secret door, in low voice, bastard, reserved, to scheme, secret, in a whisper, to hide, to pause.

ISO. whoa!, torrential rain, isolation.

ISU. fine, to flow, to run, flowing ditch, canal, liquid, to shed, to spill, outlet, to inspire.

OSA. to get well, uncle, unfinished, therapy, composition, incurable, component, health, doctor, healer, sick, integrity, perfection, hospital, to unify.

OSE. N.A.

OSI. pit, abyss, very deep.

OSO. total, global, entire, sincere, simple, very, thorough, absolutely, perfectly, integrity.

OSU. N.A.

USA. dove, usage, usual, get used to, sense of smell, suspicion, to guess, to stink, to smell, aroma, custom, habit, to use, holy man, to suspect.

USE. to sneeze.

USI. to sneeze.

USO. dove, man of peace.

USU. often, frequently, habitual.

T

ATA. door, drummer, lintel, main entrance, exterior, fragment, simple, to divide, whole, member, integral part, evergreen forest, advantage, benefit, introduction, to smash.
ATE. gate, outside, porch, knock at the door, beggar, to take out, to leave, to get, abrupt, remark, result, protection, refuge, clear, calm, shelter, door to door, to stretch, continually.
ATI. usually spelled **ATXI**: loyal to, faithful, to retain, to seize, to attach, to catch, to pinch.
ATO. tow, tugboat, to drag, to arrange, to prepare, to embellish, to solve, come!, shirt.
ATU. also spelled **ATXU**, tuna, stony place, to dig, to hoe, evergreen oak forest (= a better world, hereafter).

ETA. and, abundance, era, stage.
ETE. perhaps, profit, wages, benefit, to break, to cut, to become tired, to interrupt, to break, continuously, to switch, to break in, fragile, breaking point.
ETI. ethics, etiquette, formality, to label, to interrupt.
ETO. come! newcomer, origin, nature, caste, lineage, immigrant, original, inborn, docile, accommodating, arrival, welcome, eloquence, to adapt to, to agree, inspiration.
ETU. bramble patch, (rarely: *etsitu* = to despair, to be resigned to)

ITA. harvest with sickle, leak, drip, manger, to ask, interrogation, to question; **ITXA**: hope, trust, to await, have faith in
ITE. oxen's stable, work performed by one team of oxen.
ITI. ox.; also **ITXI**: to close, to plug, to abandon, to denounce, to stop, to cloister, shut in, to permit, to allow, faithfulness.
ITO. to drown, to smother, to disgrace, to shame, to worry, anxiety, quickly, leak, drip, pigpen, filthy place, mud hole, anguish, impure, murderer. Also **ITXO.** waiting.
ITU. also spelled **ITXU.** leakage, agreement, testament, covenant, treaty, sad, melancholic, to agree, to be advised, spring, fountain, source, frontal, origin, senseless.

OTA. gorse, stubble, crumb, basket, lobster, prawn, mouthful, bite, wild mountains.
OTE. perhaps, furze field, may be.
OTI. grasshopper.
OTO. prayer, request, please, to beg, devout, rogation, mealtime, oratory, meal, chapel.
OTXO. wolf.
OTU. to occur to, meal.

UTA. N.A.
UTE. N.A.
UTI. go away! get out! (also written as *udikan*); **UTZI**: omission, merely.
UTO. utopia, idealistic.
UTU. N.A. (rarely used for *utsune*= empty space).

X

AXA. N.A.
AXE. N.A.
AXI. N.A.
AXO. care, concern, interest, worry, negligent, carefree, grave.
AXU. shoelace, young/newborn lamb.

EXA. N.A.
EXE. example, to sit.
EXI. N.A.
EXO. exorcism, exotic, cast out, eliminate, discharge.
EXU. N.A.

IXA. pruning, to wake up.
IXE. N.A.
IXI. be quiet, calm.
IXO. quiet!, to light.
IXU. N.A.

OXA. N.A.
OXE. N.A.
OXI. oxide, oxygen.
OXO. N.A.
OXU. N.A.

UXA. to shoo away, beating for game.
UXE. N.A.
UXI. N.A.
UXO. N.A.
UXU. Yodel cry of happiness.

Z

AZA. cabbage, bark of tree, skin, water surface, shallow, make-up, explanation, to scar, to appear, to warn, to discover, crust, to show, manifest, to cover, difficult to explain, proposal, insincere, to peel, noise, planting season, sheaf, furrow, to dare.

AZE. starter, to speed up, fox, shrewd, cunning, to burrow.

AZI. to grow up, seed, big, acidity, livestock, wealth, birthplace.

AZO. open-air market, market day, merchant, cabbage, to cause, to happen, to bring about.

AZU. sugar, candy, to sweeten, boneless, bony, skeleton, carcass, bone deposit.

EZA. lack, shortness, negative, cancellation, to erase, signal, judgment, one who knows, knowledge, reason, evident, to introduce, to guess, to recognize, ugly, to silence, to omit, founder, distinctive, discussion, careless.

EZE. damp, green, nothing, humidity, omission, instability, somehow, any kind, that, anything, to destroy, needy, poor, useful, to omit, to deny, disdain, fragile, unknown, except, not only, negative response, to extirpate, anonymous.

EZI. to tame, to domesticate, to train, educate, savage, except, without, invisible, educator, can't, impossible, destiny, fate, impatient, excellent, supreme, grudge, ill-will, unbearable, inability, undeniable, precarious, nickname.

EZO. inexperienced, unaccustomed to, dishonor, to reject, unwell, wrong time, incomplete.

EZU. period of poverty, bone, skeleton, coincidence, spontaneity, by chance, unexpectedly, incorruptible, skinny.

IZA. nature, creation, character, to be, to exist, reality, past, entity, in fact, except, it will be, co-exist, procedure, star, celebrity, moderation, to twinkle, island, identity, inborn.

IZE. aunt, name, fame, anonymous, to designate, specifically, to register, to discredit, nickname, signature, bad name, sweat, to burn.

IZI. frightening, horror, enormity, to scare, atrocity.

IZO. salmon, pregnant, ice, frost, glacial, icicle, iceberg, to freeze.

IZU. panic, fright, to terrify, fearful, tremendous, very, daring, shocked, spooked, to terrorize, curl, epidemic, to infect.

OZA. cold, insolent, arrogant.

OZE. oceanic, sharp, penetrating voice, to resound, out loud.

OZI. bramble bush.

OZO. N.A.

OZU. N.A.

UZA. N.A.

UZE. N.A.

UZI. N.A.

UZO. N.A.

UZU. N.A.

Appendix II

State Names in the U.S.A.
translated

The Meaning of State Names
in the U.S.A.

Most of the names of the states of the U.S.A. are made up in a form of shorthand, written in the Basque language. The people who made up these names were likely Basque-speaking Roman Catholic priests. In assembling these names they quite consistently used the vowel-interlocking VCV formula. But how did they manage to get their name inventions accepted by the local and federal governments? Was the power of the R.C. church in America that great?

Below my translation of each state name I record the origin of the name as taught to school children in the U.S.A, if available to me. The children are told that many of the 50 states have names that are derived from the native peoples who lived in that area and from the explorers that discovered and settled the area. However, my research does not support this. Only the name Dakota may have been taken from the local tribe. The priest-linguists who made up these names knew how to hide sentences which contain information very different from the obvious meaning of the name, such as Virginia and Maryland.

It has been suggested many times that the name 'America' has nothing to do with Amerigo Vespucci. Instead it comes from the Basque verb '*amerikak egin*' which means "to make a fortune." Many have come over the centuries to do just that.

ALABAMA

ala – aba – ama
alaitu – abagadune – amaika
to fill with joy – opportunity – many
"The many opportunities fill (us) with joy."

Tradition: Thought to mean "tribal town" in Creek Indian language.

ALASKA

alas – ka
alatz – kalifikaezin
miracle – indescribable
"Indescribable miracles."

Tradition 1: Thought to be based on Aleut word "alaxsxaq" meaning "object to which the action of the sea is directed."

Tradition 2: An Aleut word for mainland.

ARIZONA

ari – izo – ona
arrigarrizko – izotzaize – ona
awful – icy wind – here
"An awfully icy wind here."
or:
arriskatu – izotz egin – ona
to risk – to freeze – here
"One risks freezing here."

Tradition 1: Thought to be the Spanish interpretation of "arizuma" meaning "silver bearing"

Tradition 2: Papago, place of the small spring.

ARKANSAS

ar. – .ka – an. – .sa – as.
ara – aka – ana – asa – ase
arrailagarri – akabu – anaiguda – asaldagarri – aserretu
heartbreaking – death – civil war – shocking – to anger."
"The heartbreaking deaths in the shocking civil war anger me."

Tradition: An Indian tribal name, pronounced Arkansaw. The 's' was added by the French to make it plural.

CALIFORNIA.

.ka – ali _ bo – or. – .ni – ia
oka – ali _ bo – ori – inji – iha
okaztagarri – alienatu _ borrokari – oribizi – injineru mea – ihabali
disgusting – to kill a person _ quarrelling – gold miner – frightening
"The disgusting killing of a person by the quarrelling gold miners is frightening."

Tradition 1: Thought to be named by the Spanish after Califia, a mythical paradise in a Spanish romance written by Montalvo in 1510.

Tradition 2: An invented name for an imaginary island. The explorer Enrico Cortes is said to have transferred the name to the Baha peninsula.

(The name California appears on some old, pre-gold mining, maps usually indicating Baha California, however, all these maps were redrafted for publication and the name is likely to have been extended north or inserted on these redrawn maps after the gold rush started in 1849.)

CAROLINA

Named in honour of England's King Charles I.

COLORADO

kolora – ado
kolora gailu – adoratu
color – to adore
"I adore the colors."

Tradition: Thought to have been taken from Spanish word "Colorado" for "color red" and was applied to Colorado river.

CONNECTICUT.

.ko – on. – .ne – ek. – .ti – iku – ut.
ako – ono – one – eka – ati – iku – uto
akorduan euki – onon – onespen – ekarkortasun – atxikitasun – ikustatu – utopia
remember – wonderful – blessings – productivity – tenacity – to visit – utopia
**"Remember the wonderful blessings of productivity and
tenacity when you visit our utopia."**

Tradition 1: Name is thought to be based on Mohican and Algonquin Indian words for "place beside the river."

Tradition 2: Algonquian meaning "long river."

DAKOTA

Tradition 1: Land of the famous Sioux or Dacotah Indians.

Tradition 2: Tribal name meaning "alliance of friends."

DELAWARE

de – ela – are
deadar egin – ela – arrerosle
to publicize/spread – word – Redeemer
"Spread the word of the Redeemer."

Tradition: Thought to have been named after Thomas West, Lord de la Warr, (1577-1618) an early governor.

FLORIDA

Tradition: Named on Easter Day 1513 by Ponce de Leon for Pacua Florida, Flowery Easter. Thought to be the correct interpretation.

GEORGIA

Named for King George II of England.

Correct.

HAWAII.

Ha'u – ahi
hau – ahigarri
this one – exhausting
"This one is exhausting (to reach)."

Tradition 1: may be based on Hawaiian word for homeland "Owhyhee."

Tradition 2: meaning "place of the gods."

IDAHO

ida – aho
idazpen – ahoberokeria
description – exaggeration
"An exaggerated description."

Tradition 1: Guessed to be from native "E Dah Hoe" supposedly meaning "gem of the mountains."

Tradition 2: An Apache name of uncertain meaning.

ILLINOIS

il. – .li – ino – is.
ila – ali – ino – isi
ilarteko – alik – inora – isil
a lifetime – possible –place – quiet
"This quiet place possibly (will do) for a lifetime."

Tradition 1: Algonquin Indian word for "warriors."

Tradition 2: Algonquian meaning men and warriors.

INDIANA.

indi – ana
indi- – anaia
prefix: from America – brother
"Our American brothers."

Tradition 1: "Land of the Indians."

Tradition 2: Latinized name in honor of Indian tribes.

IOWA

iho – oha
ihortziri – ohartu
thunder storm – to warn
"Be warned about the thunder storms."

Tradition: Guessed to come from Kiowa tribe"

KANSAS

.ka – an. – .sa – as.
aka – ana – asa – ase
akabu – anaiguda – asaldagarri – aserretu
death – civil war – shocking – to anger
"The deaths in the shocking civil war anger me."

Tradition 1: from Sioux Indian "south wind people."

Tradition 2: based in the name of an Indian tribe.

KENTUCKY

.ke – en. – .tu – uk. – .ki
ike – ena – atu – uko – oki
ikertu – ena – atutxa – uko egin – okitu
to explore – that – stony place – to refuse/reject – completely
"I explored that stony place and rejected it completely."

Tradition 1: from Iroquois Indian word "Ken-tah-ten meaning land of tomorrow."

Tradition 2: Iroquois meaning meadow land.

LOUISIANA

Named after King Louis XIV (1638-1715) of France.
Sold to U.S.A. in 1803 for $15 million.

MAINE

.ma – ine
ama – ine
amarruki – inertzia
cunningly – neutral
"Cunningly neutral."

Which may refer to its refusal to take sides in the Civil War.

Tradition 1: The name is assumed to be a reference to the state region being a mainland, different from its many surrounding islands."

Tradition 2: from mainland; changed by the French to correspond to a French province.

MARYLAND

.ma – ari – ila – and.
ama – ari – ila – andi
amaika – ariztegi –ilaundu – andi
many – oak groves – to reduce to ash – tall
"The many tall oak groves are reduced to ash."

Suggestion 1: Named to honor Henrietta Maria, wife of England's King Charles I.

Suggestion 2: Named by the supporters of the Catholic Lord Baltimore for the Virgin Mary.

MASSACHUSETTS

.ma – as. – .sa – atxu – use – et. – t. – .s.
ma – azo – osa – atxu ' se – eta – ata – azo
manadatu – -azo – osatze – atxurkatu ' segatu – -eta – atalkatu – -azo
task – to bring about – unification/statehood ' to till the soil – abundance – to subdivide – to cause / to do
"Our task is to bring about statehood, tilling of the soil, harvesting the abundance and to do subdivision.

Tradition 1: named after a local Indian tribe whose name means "a large hill place."

Tradition 2: Algonquian word meaning "at the big hills"

Boston (city)
.bo – os. – .to – on.
abo – oso – oto – one
abots – oso – otoi – onezkoak
voice – simple – prayer – reconciliation
"(They) voiced a simple prayer of reconciliation."

MICHIGAN

.mi – ixi – iga – an.
mi – itxi – iga – ano
militar – itxi – igarrezin – ano
military – to leave – unpredictable – food supply
"The military had to leave because of the unpredictable food supply."

Tradition 1: named after local Indian word "meieigama" meaning "great water" referring to the Great Lakes."

Tradition 2: Algonquian word meaning "forest clearing."

MINNESOTA

mi – in. – .ne – eso – ota
mi – ino – one – exo – ota
miragarritsy – inora – oneik – exotiko – otalurmendiak
marvelous – anywhere – these – exotic – wild hills/mountains
"It is marvelous anywhere in these exotic wild hills."

Tradition 1: Sioux Indian word for "sky-tinted water."

Tradition 2: Sioux word meaning "cloudy water."

MISSISSIPPI

.mi – is. – .si – is. – .si – ip. – .pi
ami – isi – izi – iso – osi – ipu – upi
amilka – isilgarri – izi – isola – osi – ipuinezko – ubil
to fall down – unspeakable – horror – torrential rain – very deep – legendary – whirlpool
**"To my unspeakable horror he fell into the very deep torrential rain
(swollen river) like into the legendary whirlpool."**

Tradition: from Chippewa Indian words "mici zibi" meaning "great river."

The last 'p' in the name is a letter switch from 'p' to 'b,' not uncommon.

MISSOURI

.mi – is. – .so – uri
ami – isi – iso – uri
amiltze – isilpetu – isola – urri
to fall down – to hide from – torrential rain – miserable
"Hide from this miserable torrential rain which keeps falling down."

Tradition 1: named after Missouri Indian tribe whose name means "town of the large canoes."

Tradition 2: Algonquian word meaning "muddy river."

MONTANA

.mo – on. – .ta – ana
amo – ono – ota – ana
amodiotu – onon – otalurmendiak – anabitarte
to love – wonderful – wild mountains – among the pastures
"I loved it among those pastures in the wonderful wild mountains."

Tradition: from Spanish word for "mountainous."

NEBRASKA

.ne – eb. – .ra – as. – ka
one – eba – ara – asi – ika
oneratu – ebanjelari – arraitasun – asi – ikasbide
to come here – evangelist – happily – to begin – teachings
"Happily the evangelist comes here to begin his teachings."

Tradition 1: based on Oto Indian word that means "flat water," referring to the Platte river.

Tradition 2: Sioux word meaning "flat water."

NEVADA

ne – eba – ada
nehon – ebaki – adarki
nowhere – to cut – firewood
"Nowhere is firewood to be cut."

Tradition: Spanish for "snowy," a reference to the Sierra Nevada mountains.

NEW HAMPSHIRE

Tradition: Named by an early settler, John Mason, who came from Hampshire county in England.

NEW JERSEY

Tradition: Named by Sir George Carteret after his home island in the Channel.

NEW MEXICO (original name is Mexica).

.me – ek. – .si – ika
eme – eka – asi – ika
emeki – ekarri – asierako – ikasbide
gently – to bring/introduce – elementary – teachings
"Gently we introduce elementary teachings."

Tradition 1: Supposedly named by Spaniards for lands north of the Rio Grande.

Tradition 2: Named in the hope that the area would prove as rich in resources as Mexico.

NEW YORK.

Both the former name, New Amsterdam, and the present name, New York, are taken from cities in Europe. York in N.E. England had an important Benedictine presence which the meaning of the name probably refers to.

.jo – or. – .k.
ajo – ora – aku
ajola izan – orain – akuilatze
to care – always – stimulating
"Always caring and stimulating."

Tradition: the state was named after the Duke of York, the brother of Charles II.

OHIO

ohi – iho
ohitu – ihortziri
to get used to – thunder storm
"Get used to the thunder storms."

Tradition 1: from Iroquois Indian word for "good river"

Tradition 2: Iroquoian name meaning "beautiful river."

OKLAHOMA

ok. – .la – aho – oma
oki – ila – aho – oma
okitu – ilarteko – aholkaketu – oma
entire – lifetime – to give advice – grandma
"Her entire lifetime grandma was giving advice."

Tradition: based on Choctaw Indian word for "red man."

OREGON

ore – ego – on.
ore – ego ono
orrenbeste – egokiera – onon
so many – opportunity – wonderful
"So many wonderful opportunities."

Tradition: Unknown origin. Possibly from a misreading of the Wisconsin River shown on a 1715 map as "Ouaicon-sint." (?)

PENNSYLVANIA

Named in honor of Admiral William Penn, father of the state's founder, William Penn. Latin 'sylvan' means woodland (Penn's woodland). Pena/pen is Basque word for suffering.

RHODE ISLAND

.r. – .ho – ode
ari – iho – ode
arrigarrizko – ihortziri – odei
awful – thunder – clouds
"Awful thunder clouds."

Tradition 1: named in honour of Greek Island of Rhodos,

Tradition 2: named by the Dutch explorer Adriaen Block: "Roode Eylandt" (red island) because of its red clay."

TENNESSEE

.te – en. – .ne – es. – .se – ee
ate – eno – one – eza – ase – ee
aterpetu – enoradun – onetsi – ezagule – asetu – ee
to protect – afflicted – to bless – one who knows – to nourish – call for attention
"The blessed one who knows will nourish and protect the afflicted; so pay attention."

Tradition 1: Supposedly after Cherokee Indian villages called "tanasi."

Tradition 2: Anglicized spelling of a Cherokee river name.

TEXAS

.te – ek. – .sa – as.
ate – eka – asa – ase
aterbetu – ekaitz – asaldagarri – ase
to seek shelter – storm – frightening – abundant/many
"Seek shelter from the many frightening storms."

Tradition 1: From an Indian tribal name.

Tradition 2: Thought to be a misunderstanding of a native American greeting meaning "good friends."

UTAH

uta – ah.
utza – aha
utzarazi – ahaideria
to leave behind – kinship
"(They) left their kinship behind."

Tradition: Said to come from the Ute Indians whose name means "people of the mountains.

VERMONT

.be – er. – .mo – on. – .t.
obe – ere – emo – one – eto
obetu – eremu – emon esker – onespen – etorki
to improve – wilderness – give thanks – blessings – nature
"We improve the wilderness and give thanks for nature's blessings."

Tradition: based on "verts monts," French for "green mountains."

VIRGINIA

.bi – ir. – .gi – ini – ia
ubi – ire – egi – inji – ia
ubidehe – ireki – egin – injineru – iaoitasun
canal bed – to dig – to accomplish – engineer – expertise
"The digging of the canal bed was accomplished by the engineer's expertise."

This is a very firm translation but I had never heard of an early canal in that area. A search in the library came up with not one, but two very early, large canals: 1) the Chesapeake and Delaware canal, 22 km, completed 1829. And 2) The Chesapeakee and Ohio canal, 297 km. Between Washington D.C. and Cumberland in Western Maryland, 1828.

Tradition: guessed to be named for England's "Virgin Queen," Elizabeth I.

WASHINGTON (This is a personal name brought over from England).

ash. – ing. – .to – on.
axo – ingi – ito – one
axolagabetsu – ingira – ito – on esan
carefree – disposition – to laugh a lot – to speak well of
"Well spoken of person with a carefree disposition who laughs a lot."

Seattle (city),
.se – at. – .t. – .le
ese – ata – ate – ele
asezinez – atano – ateratu – eleztatu
greedily/eagerly – evergreen forest – to get out/log – to talk about
"They eagerly talk about logging the evergreen forest."

WISCONSIN

is. – .ko – on. – .si – in.
iso – oko – oni – isi – inu
isola – okolu – onik – isilpetu – inusturi
torrential rain – stable – safe and sound – to hide – thunder
"(During) the torrential rain we hid from the thunder, safe and sound, in a stable."

Tradition 1: from Chippewa word "Ouisconsin," meaning "grassy place."

Tradition 2: An Algonquian word meaning "long river."

WYOMING ('w' is meaningless)

io – omi – ing.
iortziri – omia – inguratu
thunder – all around – to draw near.
"The thunder is drawing near from all around."

Tradition: from Algonquin or Delaware Indian word meaning "large prairie" or "broad plains."

LITERATURE CITED

Aulestia, Gorka. *"Basque – English Dictionary."* Reno: University of Nevada Press, 1989.

Aulestia, Gorka. *"Improvisational Poetry from the Basque Country,"* University of Nevada Press, 1995.

Auraicept na n'Ecez, see **Calder**, George.

Basaldua, Florencio Canut de. *"Prehistoria E Historia de la Civilizacion Indigena de Amerika I De Su Destruccion por los Barbaros del Este,"* Buenos Aires, 1925.

Basaldua, Florencio Canut de. *"Prehistoria E Historia de la Civilizacion Indigena de Amerika, I De Su Destruccion por los Barbaros del Este,"* Toulouse, Imprimerie Régionale, 59 rue Bayard, 1931.

Bergin, O. *"The native Irish Grammarian,"* p.207. Proceedings of the British Academy 24, 205-235. (1938)

Boland, Charles M. *"They All Discovered America."* New York: Pocket Books Inc. 1963.

Calder, George. *"Auraicept na n'Eces."* Edinburgh: John Grant, 1917.

Carney, J. *"The Invention of the Ogom Cipher."* Eriu 26, 53-65; 1975.

Cavalli-Sforza, L.L. *"Genes, Peoples and Languages."* Scientific American, November 1991.

Christiansson, Hans & Povl Simonsen. *"Stone Age finds from Spitsbergen,"* Acta Borealia B. Humaniora No. 11. Tromso/Oslo/Bergen, Universitetsforlaget, 24pp, 11 figs.

Cox, Richard A.V. *"The language of the Ogam Inscriptions of Scotland."* Department of Celtic, University of Aberdeen, Scotland 1999.

Diharce de Bidassouet. *"Histoire des Cantabres."* Pau, 1825.

Diop, Cheikh Anta. *"Civilization or Barbarism"* , Lawrence Hill Books, Brooklyn, 1991.

Fell, Barry. *"America B.C."* New York: Quadrangle / The New York Times Book Co., 1977.

Fester, R. *"Sprache der Eiszeit,"* Die Archetypen der Vox Humana. Berlin 1962; 255 pp.

Friedrich, Johannes. *"Extinct Languages,"* Barnes and Noble Books, 1993.

Frymer-Kensky, Tikva. *"In the Wake of the Goddesses,"* Fawcett Columbine, New York, 1992.

Gimbutas, Marija. *"The Language of the Goddess."* San Francisco: Harper, 1991.

Gimbutas, Marija. *"The World of Old Europe."* Harper SanFrancisco 1991.

Gimbutas, Marija. *"The Goddesses and Gods of Old Europe."* Univ.of California Press, Berkeley, 1992.

Goppold, Andreas. "Neuronal Resonance Fields, Aoidoi, and Sign Processes." 7th International Congress of the IASS-AIS, University of Ulm, Germany, 2000.

Guiter, Henri: *"La Langue des Pictes,"* in Boletin de la Real Sociedad Vascongada de los Amigos del Pais, XXIV (San Sebastian, 1968) 281-322.

Guiter, Henri: *"La Pensée Picte"* in Bulletin de l'association Guillaume Budé, XXIX (Paris 1970), 259-271.

Gurney, O.R., *"The Hittites,"* Penguin Books Inc., Baltimore 11, Md. 1962.

Henningsen, Gustav: *"The Witches Advocate."* University of Nevada Press, Reno 1980.

Jackson, Anthony. *"The Symbol Stones of Scotland."* The Orkney Press, 1984.

Jackson, Anthony. *"Pictish Symbol Stones?"* Monograph #3, Edinburgh: The Association for Scottish Ethnography, 1993.

Johnson, George *"Computers crack language puzzle,"* The Globe and Mail, January 6, 1996 p.D8.

Jones, Prudence and Nigel Pennick. "A History of Pagan Europe," Publ: Routledge, 1995.

Kramer, Heinrich and James Spencer. The Malleus Maleficarum. New York: Dover Publications, 1971.

Krutwig, Frederico. *"Garaldea"*, Editorial Txertoa, San Sebastian, 1978.

Lahetjuzan, Dominique. *"Essai de Quelques Notes sur la Language Basque par un Vicaire de Campagne sauvage d'origine."* Bayonne, 1808.

Lancre, Pierre de. *"Tableau de l'Inconstance des Mauvais Anges et Demons."* Paris, 1613.

Lancre, Pierre de. *"L'Incredulite et Mescreance du Sortilege."* Paris, 1622.

Lahovary, N. *"Dravidian Origins and the West."* Bombay : Orient Longmans, 1963.

Lea, Henry Charles. *"A history of the Inquisition of the Middle Ages,"* New York 1888, 3 volumes, reprinted New York 1955.

Löpelmann, Martin. *"Etymologisches Wörterbuch der Baskischen Sprache."* Berlin: Walter de Gruyter, 1968.

Macalister, R.A.S. *Corpus Inscriptionum Insularum Celticarum.* Dublin: Stationary Office, Vol. 1: 1945, Vol. 2: 1949.

Muck, Otto. *"Cheops et la Grande Pyramide."* Payot, Paris, 1978. Translated from German.

McManus, Damien. *"A Guide to Ogam."* Maynooth Monographs #4. Maynooth, Ireland: An Sagert, 1991.

O'Boyle, Sean. *"Ogam, The Poet's Secret."* Dublin, Dalton 1980.

O'Meara, John J. *"The Voyage of St. Brendan."* 1976.

van Oostrom, Frits. *"Omstreeks 1100,"* Chapter 1 of *Nederlandse Literatuur,* ed. M.A.Schenkeveld-van der Dussen. Groningen: Martinus Nijhof, 1993.

Padel, Oliver J. *"Inscriptions of Pictland"*; M.Litt. University of Edinburgh, 1972.

Patai, Raphael. *"The Hebrew Goddess,"* Wayne State University Press, Detroit, 1990.

Parkinson, Richard. *"Cracking Codes, the Rosetta Stone and Decipherment."* University of California Press, Berkeley, 1999.

Pyle, Robert L. *"All That Remains."* Charleston, WV: Cannon Graphics, Inc., 1991.

Quinn, Bob. *"Atlantean, Ireland's North African and Maritime Heritage."* Quartet Books, New York, 1986.

Quirke, Stephen. *"Who were the Pharaohs?"* Dover Publications, Inc. Mineola, New York.

Renfrew, Colin. Pages 1-32 *"The Human Inheritance"* edited by Bryan Sykes, Oxford University Press, 1999.

Ringe, Don. Pages 45-74 of *"The Human Inheritance"* edited by Bryan Sykes, Oxford University Press, 1999.

Ruhlen, Merritt. *"A Guide to the World's Languages,"* Vol. 1, Classification. Stanford Univ. Press, 1991.

Saks, Edgar V. *"Esto-Europa"* Studies in Ur-European History, Part II. Montreal/ Lund 1966. Distributed by: Verlag Voitleja, Postfach 28, Heidelberg 2, Germany.

Sandars, N.K., *"The Sea Peoples,"* Warriors of the Ancient Mediterranean. Thames and Hudson 1987.

Sanders, Willy. Text of *"Der Leidener Willeram,"* München: Wilhelm Fink Verlag, 1971.

Sanders, Willy. *"Der Leidener Willeram."* München: Wilhelm Fink Verlag, 1974.

Scaliger, J.J. Quoted from Ladislav Zgusta, *"Manual of Lexicography,"* The Hague: Mouton, 1971, page 15.

Shipley-Ducket, Eleanor. *"Alcuin, Friend of Charlemagne."* New York: The Macmillan Co., 1951.

Sturluson, Snorri, *"Heimskringla, History of the Kings of Norway,"* translated by Lee M. Hollander. Published by the University of Texas Press, Austin.

Sykes, Brian. Editor of "The Human Inheritance, Genes Language and Evolution," Oxford University Press 1999.

de Vooys, C.G.N. *"Geschiedenis van de Nederlandse Taal."* Groningen: Tjeenk Willink, 1975.

Wagner, Heinrich. *"Common problems concerning the early languages of the British Isles and the Iberian Peninsula,"* Universidad de Salamanca, 1976.

Wagner, Heinrich. *"Near Eastern and African Connections with the Celtic World."* Chapter in "The Celtic Consciousness," edited by Robert O'Driscoll. Publ. George Braziller, New York, 1982.

Whittall, James P. *"Precolumbian Parallels between Mediterranean and New England Archaeology."* *Occasional Publications of the Epigraphic Society,* Vol 3, No 52, 1975.

Wickham-Jones, C.R.: *"Scotland's First Settlers,"* Publ: B.T. Batsford Ltd, Historic Scotland, 1997.

Wittgenstein, L. *"Tractatus Logico-philosophicus."* London: Routledge and Kegan, 1922.

INDEX

ISBN 1-55212668-4

Printed in Great Britain
by Amazon

12287739R00325